THE WAR YEARS

1939–1945

DIARIES AND LETTERS

Principal Books by Harold Nicolson

THE WAR YEARS, 1939–1945
(VOLUME II OF DIARIES AND LETTERS)   *1967*

DIARIES AND LETTERS, 1930–1939   *1966*

MONARCHY   *1962*

THE AGE OF REASON   *1960*

JOURNEY TO JAVA   *1957*

SAINTE-BEUVE   *1957*

GOOD BEHAVIOUR   *1955*

KING GEORGE V: HIS LIFE AND REIGN   *1952*

BENJAMIN CONSTANT   *1949*

THE ENGLISH SENSE OF HUMOUR   *1947*

THE CONGRESS OF VIENNA   *1946*

ANOTHER WORLD THAN THIS   *1945*
(*editor, with V. Sackville-West*)

THE DESIRE TO PLEASE   *1943*

WHY BRITAIN IS AT WAR   *1939*

DIPLOMACY   *1939*

HELEN'S TOWER   *1937*

DWIGHT MORROW   *1935*

CURZON: THE LAST PHASE   *1934*

PEACEMAKING   *1933*

PUBLIC FACES   *1932*

PEOPLE AND THINGS   *1931*

LORD CARNOCK   *1930*

THE DEVELOPMENT OF ENGLISH BIOGRAPHY   *1928*

SOME PEOPLE   *1927, 1944, 1959*

SWINBURNE   *1926*

BRYON: THE LAST JOURNEY   *1924*

TENNYSON   *1923*

SWEET WATERS   *1921*

PAUL VERLAINE   *1921*

HAROLD NICOLSON

THE WAR YEARS

1939-1945

VOLUME II OF

DIARIES AND
LETTERS

EDITED BY

NIGEL NICOLSON

ATHENEUM *NEW YORK*

1967

Dedicated to

BENEDICT NICOLSON

by his father and brother

Contents

CONTENTS

CONTENTS

CONTENTS

Illustrations

HAROLD NICOLSON

Sir Harold Nicolson was born in Teheran in 1886. After his graduation from Balliol College, Oxford, he entered the British Foreign Service and from 1909 to 1929 held diplomatic posts in Madrid, Istanbul, Teheran and Berlin. From 1935 to 1945 he was a Member of Parliament. During his active career he wrote 35 books of history, biography and fiction. Some of his chief works are *Tennyson* (1923), *Some People* (1927), *Lord Carnock* (1930), *Public Faces* (1932), *Peacemaking* (1933), *Dwight Morrow* (1935), *The Congress of Vienna* (1946), *King George V: His Life and Reign* (1952), *Journey to Java* (1957) and *Monarchy* (1962). He contributed to British, American and European journals all his life. His most famous series of articles, "Marginal Comment," ran in the *Spectator* from 1938 to 1952.

NIGEL NICOLSON

Nigel Nicolson was born in 1917 and, like his father, was educated at Balliol College, Oxford. As a member of the Grenadier Guards he served in Africa and Italy during World War II, and later wrote the official war history of his regiment. He became a founder-director of the British publishing firm Weidenfeld & Nicolson in 1946. Six years later he was elected Conservative Member of Parliament for Bournemouth and in 1960 became Chairman of the British United Nations Association, which post he still holds. Mr. Nicolson's books include *People and Parliament* (1958), *Lord of the Isles* (1960), and *Great Houses of Britain* (1965).

Introduction by Nigel Nicolson

A diary', Harold Nicolson came to consider, having kept his own for twelve years, 'should be written for one's great-grandson. The purely private diary becomes too self-centred and morbid. One should have a remote, but not too remote, audience.'[1] Thus, although he affirmed towards the end of his life that the flywheel which kept his diary turning over day after day was nothing more than the force of habit, he also had one eye cocked on a morsel of posterity. His diary was the only one of his possessions which V. Sackville-West was instructed to take with her should she be forced to flee Kent by the threat of a German invasion.[2] At a certain moment during the war he considered publishing his 1939 diary as a cautionary tale, and only abandoned the idea when he found that it would mean omitting the most interesting parts through fear of political scandal. Now I, two generations earlier than he had intended, but with the advantages, which my grandson would not have enjoyed, that I lived through those same days, many of them in my father's company, and that I understood the workings of his mind as well as any son can, have edited a version which he has been able to read and approve, and which has lost almost nothing of the original by discretion.

From the first page of this volume to the last, Britain was at war; from the first to the last but one, Harold Nicolson was a Member of Parliament. He saw the war from the middle distance, close enough to be exposed to some of its dangers when the battle reached out over Sissinghurst and London, but remote enough to have the leisure, knowledge and perspective to worry about our fluctuating strategy and the nature of the peace which would follow victory. A diarist can have second, third and fourth thoughts, but he cannot, except by mutilation, obliterate the first. Much of what he writes one day will be revealed as nonsense by the events of the next. This applies particularly in

[1] p. 199.   [2] p. 88.

15

wartime. But Harold Nicolson never worried that his great-grandson would think his forecasts, his moments of ill-founded exhilaration or despair, foolish in retrospect. He never hedged about his prophecies with escape-clauses. 'This is what I think will happen,' he would write. 'Russia will make a separate peace with Germany. Hitler will attack Turkey. Britain will be invaded.' He knew that future readers, should there be any, would find false prophecy not merely pardonable, but the diary's most interesting part, like a parlour-game when everyone knows the answers except the victim.

He tried to satisfy the curiosity of his great-grandchild by filling the gaps left by contemporary journalism and official records such as *Hansard*. Accounts of private conversations form the major part of the diary. At the same time, he would describe the look and feel, the sound and smell, of London under fire; the precise circumstances in which he came to hear the most dramatic news; the gestures with which Churchill accompanied his greatest phrases, and how his manner changed when he left the Chamber for the smoking-room. Thus the complete diary is already selective in accordance with his preconceived idea of what a diary should be, but in its entirety it would probably make dull reading. 'How the past slides like a great mass of vegetable matter down the sluice!' he sighed, in one of those phrases that he spun so effortlessly from his typewriter. James Pope-Hennessy, after reading a few pages at Sissinghurst, exclaimed that he found it 'unbelievable that a man who in ordinary life is gay and amusing should become so pompous and dull when he comes to write his diary'.[1] Harold Nicolson himself once commented on it, 'The day-to-day impressions of a greengrocer in Streatham would really be more interesting.'[2]

I do not believe that the reader of this volume will share these opinions. The diary has been pared by editing of all its repetitions and staleness. As in the first volume, barely one-twentieth part of the whole is here reproduced, and the meat has again been sauced by extracts from his letters to V. Sackville-West and, in the later pages, to his sons. His diary-style did not, however, vary greatly from the style of his letters. In both there are set descriptive pieces, verbatim records of conversations and passages of reflection. In both there is a deliberate variation of speed (as of a stream flowing through a spinney, now with the inner strength of elastic, now running fast over pebbles); in both flashes of wit and quotations from half-a-dozen European literatures;

[1] p. 335.   [2] p. 147.

in both the sudden bathos with which he would puncture his fundamental seriousness. The reader will easily imagine the pleasure which
his letters gave to the recipients at Heliopolis, Cassino or Sissinghurst.
'I take them away to my tent', I wrote to him from Italy, 'and for
fifteen minutes I hear your unmistakable voice.' By chance these
last three words were also used by V. Sackville-West in writing to him.
We all sensed it. His style was as immediately identifiable with his
personality as his conversation.

II

Harold Nicolson sat in Parliament as the National Labour Member for
West Leicester, the seat which he won in 1935 by a majority of only 87.
For just over a year, from May 1940 till July 1941, he was a junior member of Winston Churchill's Government, as Parliamentary Secretary to
the Ministry of Information. His loss of that office, not because he was
found incompetent but because it was needed for a Labour Member
in the Party share-out of offices in the Coalition Government, caused
him acute distress. Whatever excuses there were, however genuine
the commiserations of his friends and colleagues, he felt that if he had
been a tougher and more ambitious person, he would not have been
left stranded on the back-benches for the remainder of the war. He
attributed his imagined failure in politics to his lack of forcefulness. He
was 'dispensable' because he was not 'formidable'. It is true that his
name does not appear at all in the six volumes of Churchill's history
of the war, and only once in Anthony Eden's three volumes (referring
to an incident before the war started), but he was not a negligible personality in Parliament. 'You never realise that you are a national figure',
Robert Bernays once said to him, and then added with that frankness and stutter which endeared him so greatly to Harold Nicolson,
'of the s-s-s-s-second d-d-d-d-d-degree.'[1] His influence was considerable because he had had the experience of twenty years in
diplomacy and had used those years to study the historical roots of
diplomatic practice and the policies of the countries to which he was
accredited, and to form a circle of friends abroad which was far wider
than almost any other Member of Parliament could then claim. Moreover, he loved the House of Commons, where he found 'that combination of genial surroundings with useful activity, which is the basis of
all human happiness'. He treated the House with respect, and was

[1] p. 402

H.N.D.   17   B

treated by it with respect. He spoke but seldom, and then shortly and well. He spoke only on subjects, usually Foreign Affairs, of which he had direct knowledge. He never advertised himself at Question-time. In the smoking-room he took pains to know the unimportant Members, and never toadied the famous. He was very much liked.

Why, then, was he never offered another post by Churchill, not even in the Caretaker Government of 1945? It may have been for quite different reasons than he supposed. He was not by nature an administrator; he was not a fit person to run a Department in wartime. He was known to dislike the Conservative policies which the Caretaker Government was formed to espouse. The junior Minister's job at the Ministry of Information under Duff Cooper had suited him perfectly. There he was concerned with the policy of news-presentation, with questions of morale, with the exposition of British war-aims and relations with foreign Governments in London. He did not have to organise anything. He was by nature an observer, a marginal commentator. He would be more useful as a freelance and informed critic on the back-benches than as a war-leader on the front bench. Churchill's choice of compensation for his loss of office seems to confirm this view: Harold Nicolson was made a Governor of the B.B.C.

The B.B.C. Board did not play an important part in his life, although it took up much of his time. There was constant uncertainty about the division of responsibility between the Board, the Director-General and the Minister of Information. Within the Board, too, there was never any real agreement on its functions and the standards of broadcasting which it should apply. Harold Nicolson had a firm ally on the Board in Lady Violet Bonham Carter, and the letter which he wrote to her on 28th August, 1943, is an outburst of despair that could be taken as a summing-up of his whole outlook on life. It was an affirmation of faith, but implicitly a confession of his limitations. He had no real sympathy with popular broadcasting. 'A dreadful programme' meant a programme to which he had no desire to listen himself. He felt as lost in these surroundings as he did in the working-men's clubs of Leicester.

His most important wartime activity was in reconciling British opinion to the Free French. His role was comparable to that of only one other back-bench Member of Parliament, Sir Edward Spears. Harold Nicolson spoke French almost perfectly, but not as well as V. Sackville-West, for whom it was her mother's tongue. He went three times to France during these years, in October 1939, in March 1940 and in March 1945, and once to the French territories in North Africa in April–May 1944. On each of these occasions he spoke to audiences which applauded him more vociferously than any audience ever did in England. He knew their minds, loved their country and their culture, and because he could identify himself so completely with their despair and resurgence, he became the best of interpreters of France to England, and of England to France. What an Ambassador he would have made in Paris after its liberation! But in London his usefulness was scarcely less. Among those who followed de Gaulle to England and later to North Africa were many of his personal friends: men like Massigli, Palewski, St Denis, Pléven; women like Eve Curie. Not all of them stood by de Gaulle, and Harold Nicolson himself was at first put off by his arrogance and attitude of disdain. In the end he came to acknowledge de Gaulle's outstanding gifts as a leader, admiring him perhaps all the more for the mettle which he lacked himself. In the House of Commons, and in his articles and other speeches, he spoke up consistently for the rights and honour of France, accusing Churchill to his face of 'administering any snub [to the Free French] which ingenuity can devise and ill-manners perpetrate'.[1] 'The French, of course', he wrote to his sons afterwards, 'were delighted.' And then, transforming Churchill's famous sneer: 'Well, I bear many crosses, and the *Croix de la Libération* is not the least desirable.'

But it is above all as a patriot that Harold Nicolson emerges from these pages. He was surprised at discovering the depth of his feeling for England, just as he was by the sudden awareness of his affection for London when it lay blackened and bedraggled. The reader of the first few pages of this volume might imagine that he was about to follow in the footsteps of an ageing defeatist whose spirits would only revive four years later when victory seemed certain. In 1939, when France was intact and her leaders firm, Harold Nicolson gave way to a despair which never afflicted him when Britain's cause seemed hopeless. Then his diary and letters mirrored the exaltation of the whole people, and historians may well look upon them as among the finest personal expressions of courage and determination to have survived from those times. 'We are in a bad way', he wrote on 3rd May, 1940, after the Norwegian disaster. 'We shall win!' As the way became worse, his spirits rose higher. On 12th June he wrote to V. Sackville-West, 'I am *embattled*. I did not know that I possessed such combative instincts.

[1] p. 373, note 1.

19

Why is it that I should feel so *gay*?' On 31st July he wrote to her, 'I have always loved England. But now I am in love with England. What a people! What a chance! The whole of Europe humiliated except us. And the chance that by our stubbornness we shall give victory to the world.' Seven months later, defeat had been avoided, but there was still no answer to the question how we were to win. 'If only we could show people some glimmer of light at the end of the tunnel', he wrote in his diary on 2nd March, 1941, 'we could count upon their enduring any ordeal. But the danger is that there is no light beyond the light of faith. I have that light. I know in the marrow of my bones that we shall win in the end.' These words are now weakened by our knowledge of how we did win. At the time they were defiant, almost absurdly defiant. How did it come about that a man like Harold Nicolson, an intellectual who in the summer of 1940 was aged 53, who loathed violence and foresaw that his life, and perhaps his family, would be shattered by this war, should suddenly have discovered his courage and infected others with it? Why did someone 'with an almost morbid dislike of emotion' (V. Sackville-West's phrase) begin suddenly to shout aloud with patriotism and joy? How did a man so untypical of his race come to identify himself so passionately with it?

The first reason was Winston Churchill. In this edition I have retained in full almost every mention of him in the original diary and letters except where they overlapped, and this makes him rightly the central figure of the book. Harold Nicolson's friendship with him, though of very long standing, was not an intimate one. He had been a follower of Anthony Eden more than of Churchill before the war. He was hurt by Churchill's dismissal of him from the Ministry of Information, and it is quite clear from many entries that he was alarmed by him, distraught by any imagined or actual rebuke from Downing Street, and eagerly grateful for the slightest word of praise. He admired Churchill more than he had admired any other man, even Lloyd George, even Roosevelt. 'What a speech!' he wrote to his wife after one of Churchill's broadcasts. 'One could feel after that as if the whole world might fall. . . . Thank God for him.'[1] He saw in him all the qualities, infinitely magnified, to which he aspired himself—tenderness, humour, a sense of language, a sense of fitness, great-heartedness, pertinacity, courage, and the capacity to love, hate and forgive. Everyone felt this at times, but Harold Nicolson felt it always. It was easy

[1] p. 102.

20

to admire Churchill in the summers of 1940 or 1944. What was difficult was to retain complete faith in him after Crete, Singapore or Anzio. One of the surprises of this volume may be the degree to which Lobby criticism of Churchill continued almost until the end. Harold Nicolson swatted such mutterers like flies.

The second reason was his deep-rooted conviction that Hitler represented evil. This was said in a thousand speeches, but few felt it as he did. He knew the Germans, having served in the British Embassy in Berlin for three years, and he knew many of Hitler's victims, now dead or exiles in London. He had been a leading opponent of appeasement in the House of Commons before the war. He went back over the details of the story when he wrote *Why Britain is at War* for Penguins in October 1939, and the concentrated effort of writing that book in three weeks left a deeper mark upon him than on the majority of its readers. But he was incapable of hating his enemies collectively. When the *Graf Spee* was about to emerge from Montevideo harbour, he wrote, 'I hate it all. . . . I loathe the idea of these brave men steaming out in cold blood either to our destruction or to their destruction. . . . It is no more than blood-sports. . . . Definitely I hope she escapes.'[1] Eighteen months later, when Churchill announced to the House the sinking of the *Bismarck*, he was probably the only Member not to cheer.[2] Hitler was the enemy, not the Germans; Mussolini, not the Italians. When both lay dead, he wrote to his son without pity, 'So that was Mussolini and Hitler within two days. Not a bad bag as bags go.'[3]

Thirdly, he was thrilled by the conduct of the war. He had never served in the Forces himself, having been exempted by the Foreign Office during the First World War, and had little knowledge of defence matters except as an extension of Foreign Affairs. But he followed the campaigns and speculated on strategy with the mounting excitement of a strongly partisan supporter of a football team. Even as a junior Minister he was rarely informed of strategic plans. So when the dam burst at Alamein, the Allies landed in North Africa, Tunis fell, Italy capitulated, Rome was captured or Normandy was invaded, the news came to him with the same dramatic suddenness as it did to the great mass of British citizens, and he was astonished and exultant. He could not understand the mentality of those who affected little interest in the progress of the war outside their immediate zone of responsibility. To him it was as unintelligent as indifference to politics. As his experience and knowledge grew, his guesses improved. The short

[1] p. 51. [2] p. 169. [3] p. 434.

titles which, after 1941, he attached to each year on 1st January were summaries of what in fact occurred: '1942—A year, I hope, of recovery'; '1943—I should like to feel that this is the year of victory, but I don't'; '1944—Perhaps the beginning of the end'; '1945—A year, I trust, of victory.'

III

The fourth reason why Harold Nicolson was so profoundly moved and stimulated by the war was the impact it made upon his family and friends. His immediate family survived all dangers except a road accident in Italy which broke two vertebrae in Ben's back. But he lost a favourite nephew, Peter Nicolson, and many friends, like Christopher Hobhouse, John Macnamara and Robert Bernays. The almost constant risks to which his sons were exposed abroad, and V. Sackville-West at Sissinghurst, further deepened his love for them. As in many other families, the war discovered hitherto unrevealed traits in the characters of those whom he knew best. It was a test of his upbringing of his children, and of the mutual trust and sympathy established during the previous thirty years between himself and his wife. The habit which they had all formed of writing frequently to each other now bore fruit in the skein of letters which knit them together while they were apart. They expressed in writing what they found difficult to express in speech—their emotional response to each other's affection and to the unfamiliar situations in which they all found themselves involved.

Sissinghurst, twelve miles south of Maidstone, was in the part of England where civilians saw most of the war at first hand. The Battle of Britain was fought above their heads. It lay in the direct path of the V.1s and V.2s. It was the area which would almost certainly bear the first shock of a German invasion, and an assembly area for the Allied invasion of Normandy. Night after night the bombers streamed overhead to attack London, or, in the opposite direction, the cities of Germany and France. The farm, castle and garden were spattered with the débris of the air-battles. Bombs and parachutists fell in the neighbouring fields. On one occasion a German bomber, crashing in flames, missed the Elizabethan tower by only a few yards.[1] In London, Harold Nicolson was more directly exposed to the bombardment. Twice his flat in the Temple was badly damaged, and for many months

[1] p. 346.

during the worst period of the Blitz, he slept in the sturdy block of London University, which had been taken over by the Ministry of Information.

Harold Nicolson and V. Sackville-West were far more worried about each other's safety than their own. Both were physically courageous. He endured without a qualm, but she with agony, his dangerous flight to Sweden in November 1943.[1] He lost more nights' sleep from the snoring of his companions when he was on fire-guard at the Palace of Westminster than from fear or the clatter of the bombardment. V. Sackville-West, who only came up to London two or three times during the entire course of the war, was more distressed by the invasion of her woods by British tanks on exercise than by the probable invasion of Kent by the enemy. But there is no doubt that the strain of the war told on her mentally more than it did on him. At about the time of Virginia Woolf's death in March 1941, he was worried by the depression which he sensed in her and which she only half denied.[2] But this was a passing phase. She was busy with the Women's Land Army, with writing *Grand Canyon*, *The Eagle and the Dove* and her poem *The Garden*, and trying somehow to keep the garden at Sissinghurst going when labour was almost unobtainable. The war brought out her profound patriotism, which was centred, like Harold Nicolson's, upon the titanic figure of Winston Churchill, and evoked her romantic attitude to war and history, as if she were reliving the days of the Armada. She had no sympathy for the enemy. 'Those filthy Germans!' she wrote when she heard that Knole had been damaged. 'Let us level every town in Germany to the ground! I shan't care.'[3] She found some consolation, which Harold Nicolson never did, in religion. When they wrote to one another, 'I pray for you six times a day', she meant it literally; he didn't. When she said that she would kill herself if he were killed, she intended it seriously. And there is no doubt of their joint determination to swallow the lethal pill (referred to in their correspondence as 'the bare bodkin'[4]) which he obtained as a precaution against either of them falling into German hands.

To me, who considered that I knew most of their thoughts and moods, it came as a surprise to find that they both believed that the world which they knew and loved would be irreparably broken by the war. They saw in it the end of *les douceurs de la vie*, represented by Sissinghurst and King's Bench Walk. They thought that their past

[1] p. 325. [2] pp. 156 ff. [3] p. 350. [4] pp. 90, 93, 97.

life of literature, Bloomsbury, 'the purchase of books and pictures and the unthinking enjoyment of food and wine',[1] a large garden and sufficient servants, was now 'an obsolete tradition'. They feared the permanence of the new vulgarity which the war had introduced. 'I have always been on the side of the under-dog', wrote Harold Nicolson, 'but I have also believed in the principle of aristocracy. I have hated the rich, but I have loved learning, scholarship, intelligence and the humanities. Suddenly I am faced with the fact that all these lovely things are supposed to be "class privileges".'[2] 'We shall have to walk and live a Woolworth life hereafter.... I hate the destruction of elegance.'[3] She went further than he did. The exaggerated conservatism of her nature led her to protest even against the running of a local bus-service between two neighbouring villages: 'Why people have this passion for moving about passes my understanding ... I hate democracy. I hate *la populace*. I wish education had never been introduced. I don't like tyranny, but I like an intelligent oligarchy. I wish *la populace* had never been encouraged to emerge from its rightful place.'[4] On the Beveridge Report she poured equal scorn,[5] while Harold Nicolson strongly supported it. All this was due to her belief, expressed in such very different ways in *The Edwardians* and *The Land*, that the fine rhythm of English life was due to its graduated functions, each person to his place, each person to his traditional job, and that any attempt to spread the benefits of 'the new world' to 'the masses' (she would expel each of these terms with alarming contempt), would end in the loss of all refinement. And yet, whenever she could, she threw open the garden at Sissinghurst to the public. 'How much I prefer strangers to my friends!'[6] she wrote in an unguarded moment, and it became increasingly true. It was because one could escape from strangers: one had no obligation to sustain a conversation with them once its momentum was lost. How shy she was! How sensitive, and how passionate! How noble! How wise! How wrong!

The third volume of these diaries and letters will show that their fears about the future were ill-founded. They continued to live after the war the same life as they had lived before it. Sissinghurst recovered rapidly, and although Harold Nicolson never regained a seat in Parliament, his industry, intelligence and enjoyment of people remained unabated until V. Sackville-West's death in 1962. A dozen more books lay ahead of each of them. Looking back on the Second German

[1] p. 170.   [2] p. 57   [3] p. 170.   [4] p. 433.   [5] pp. 264-5.   [6] pp. 472.

War, they would see it, like the first, as a major incident which left them the same people as they were before. But during those six years they had found in themselves reserves of strength which neither had known to exist.

Sissinghurst Castle,
May 1967   *Kent*

ACKNOWLEDGMENT: the Editor is greatly indebted to Sir Alan Lascelles, Sir John Wheeler-Bennett, Kenneth Rose, Benedict Nicolson and Atheneum (New York) for correcting the proofs of this volume. He is also grateful to Lady Diana Cooper for permission to quote the letter from Duff Cooper on pages 403-404.

1939

The second day of war – H.N.'s early fears of defeat – grievances of the American correspondents in London – evacuation of children – Russia declares war on Poland – Lloyd George's defeatism – Churchill outshines Chamberlain – the Eden Group plan pressure on the Government – H.N. writes 'Why Britain is at War' – a visit to the Maginot Line – interviews with Reynaud and Daladier – Russia invades Finland – the Battle of the River Plate – C. E. M. Joad at Sissinghurst

After hearing Neville Chamberlain's statement to the House of Commons that Britain was at war with Germany, Harold Nicolson went down to Sissinghurst on the evening of 3rd September. He returned there each weekend, and during the week stayed in his chambers at 4 King's Bench Walk, Inner Temple. As Member of Parliament for West Leicester, his first wartime activities included the Chairmanship of the back-bench Air Raid Precautions Committee and membership of Duff Cooper's Committee on German Refugees. But more of his time was occupied by journalism (his book-reviews for the 'Daily Telegraph' and his weekly article 'Marginal Comment' for the 'Spectator') and by writing in less than three weeks a 50,000-word Penguin Special 'Why Britain is at War', which was published on 7th November and soon sold over 100,000 copies. V. Sackville-West remained at Sissinghurst, where she joined the Kent Committee of the Women's Land Army, on which she continued to serve throughout the war. Both their sons were soon in uniform—Ben as a private in an anti-aircraft battery outside Rochester, and Nigel as an officer-cadet at Sandhurst.

These first entries in Harold Nicolson's war-diary reflect the nation's growing despondency, passing defeatism and uncertainty about its war-aims. Hitler conquered Poland in less than a month (Warsaw, which held out longest, surrendered on 27th September), and the Russians, who invaded Poland from the opposite direction on 17th September, partitioned the country with Germany. The war in the West was carried on mainly at sea by German U-Boats. Not a single move was made by Britain and France to relieve pressure on the Poles. Even bombing of industrial targets in Germany was forbidden for fear of German reprisals on France. On land, 106 French Divisions in the Maginot Line faced only 23 German Divisions while the Polish campaign lasted, but General Gamelin, the Allied Commander-in-Chief, said privately that no major offensive could be launched before at least two years. Criticism mounted in Parliament, and the group of M.P.s, including Harold Nicolson, who still called themselves 'the Eden Group', though Anthony Eden was now a member of the Government and could take no part in it, remained convinced that the British war effort would stiffen only if Winston Churchill, now First Lord of the Admiralty, succeeded Chamberlain as Prime Minister.

29

4th September, 1939

I get up early. It is a perfect day and I bathe in the peace of the lake. Two things impress themselves on me. 1. Time. It seems three weeks since yesterday morning and it is difficult to get one's days of the week in chronological order. Everybody after this will be convinced of the relativity of time. 2. Nature. Even as when someone dies, one is amazed that the poplars should still be standing quite unaware of one's own disaster, so when I walked down to the lake to bathe, I could scarcely believe that the swans were being sincere in their indifference to the Second German War.

Up to London. The posters carry the words 'British Liner Torpedoed'. It is the *Athenia* out from Liverpool to Canada or the United States which was torpedoed off the Hebrides.[1] Many Americans must have been drowned. How insane the Germans are to do this at the very moment when Roosevelt has put out his neutrality proclamation. It is a bad proclamation from our point of view. He says that nothing on earth will induce the Americans to send forces to Europe. But he also says that no man can remain neutral in mind and that he knows where the right lies.

5th September, 1939

The evening broadcast says that the Germans claim to have captured a Polish town only 56 miles from Warsaw. It looks as if the Polish resistance was nothing at all. We had foreseen that, but it is distressing to get no real news.

I was glad to attend Jessica's wedding,[2] since it made me feel that there was something outside this present horror. But in fact I am in a mood of deep depression. I do not really see how we can win this war, yet if we lose it, we lose everything. It may be that I am old[3] and sad and defeatist. But one thing I do know and it comforts me. I would rather go down fighting and suffering than creep out after a month or two at the cost of losing our pride. That may be the only thing left to us.

[1] The 13,500-ton *Athenia*, carrying 1,400 passengers, was torpedoed by a German U-boat in the Atlantic at 9 p.m. on 3rd September. 112 lives were lost, including 28 Americans.
[2] Jessica St Aubyn, H.N.'s niece, was married to Patrick Koppel at Sissinghurst parish church earlier that day.
[3] He was 52.

I wake up on a lovely morning and lie there thinking how foul it is that this late summer dawn should be bruised by fear and horror. I am thinking these uplifting thoughts when Vita flings open the door and announces, 'There is an air-raid.' It is such a lovely morning that we do not take the air-raid too seriously and remain outside in the sunshine looking at the Alpine plants. Then off I go to catch the train. We are stopped by air-raid wardens in Sissinghurst and Staplehurst but I tell them that I am going to London to execute my functions as a Member of Parliament. They are much impressed by this information and pass me on.

I go down to the House and find that it has risen. In the smoking-room I find Bob Boothby talking to Arnold Wilson.[1] The latter is putting it about that Germany will mop up Poland and that we must then make peace. He is a dangerous, well-meaning but slightly insane person. Not that his view is incorrect. I feel perfectly certain that Germany will mop up the Poles in a week or so. She may also seize the Rumanian oil-fields, solidify her agreement with Russia, and then offer us the most favourable terms of peace. It will then be that our ordeal (and when I say 'our', I mean the Eden Group) will arrive. If we insist upon the continuance of battle, we may condemn many young men to death. If we urge acceptance, we are ending the British Empire. The appeasers will gamble upon the defection of Russia and Italy and good terms with Germany. Again one comes back to the point that Chamberlain did not want this war, and is continually thinking of getting out of it. He may be right. But he has not behaved with sufficient honesty and moral courage to carry the country with him.

How odd one's feelings are at this moment! I hate this war and dread its consequences. I know that whatever happens it will destroy everything I care for. Thus there is a little timid selfish side of myself that tempts me by still murmurings to hope that we shall reach a form of appeasement after the Germans have conquered Poland. Yet the

[1] Lt.-Col. Sir Arnold Wilson, Conservative M.P. for Hitchin, 1933–40. He had the reputation of a pro-Fascist, and in his books *Thoughts and Talks* (1938) and *More Thoughts and Talks* (1939) he expressed admiration for Hitler and Mussolini. But in 1940 he volunteered as a rear-gunner and was killed in action on 31st May, 1940.

real thing in me loathes and detests any such capitulation. If Anthony[1] had said, 'We will consider peace', I should have been wretchedly relieved. As he said, 'We shall fight to the end', I am stimulated and happy. Yet I dread what I know to be the consequences. This means, I suppose, that we all want leadership, and that Anthony's lead encourages us to endure what we well know will be terrible ordeals and to rejoice in the endurance. It was the best speech that I have ever heard Anthony make.

H.N. TO V.S-W.   *14th September, 1939*
                                              4 King's Bench Walk, E.C.4

The House sits till Friday and I shall therefore come down that evening. The Opposition are getting somewhat restive, especially about the Ministry of Information. The latter has been staffed by duds at the top and all the good people are in the most subordinate positions. The rage and fury of the newspapermen passes all bounds. John Gunther[2] for instance, told me that he had asked one of the censors for the text of our leaflet which we dropped over Germany. The request was refused. He asked why. The answer was, 'We are not allowed to disclose information which might be of value to the enemy.' When Gunther pointed out that two million of these leaflets had been dropped over Germany, the man blinked and said, 'Yes, something must be wrong there.'

Victor Cazalet[3] had the leading American correspondents to dinner to meet Anthony Eden and Duff Cooper. I came in afterwards. It was a valuable meeting. They poured out all their grievances and Anthony was obviously horrified by the stories they told. He will, I'm sure, do something about it. Anthony hinted that he thought I ought to do something. I said that I should like to be an Admiral as I enjoy the sea, and if I am deprived of the *Mar*,[4] I may as well have a battleship and a squadron. But I was careful to tell him that I was not good at actual navigation myself. Anthony was in perfect form. The Prime Minister is very cordial to him and all is well.

[1] Anthony Eden, Secretary of State for Dominion Affairs since 3rd September, had been broadcasting to the nation that evening.
[2] The American writer, then a war-correspondent in London.
[3] Conservative M.P. for Chippenham since 1924.
[4] The small yawl which H.N. had purchased in 1938, and in which he sailed during the summer of 1939. She was laid up in the Hamble River and was later damaged by a bomb.

Harold Nicolson at his typewriter at Sissinghurst

Benedict and (left) Nigel Nicolson
at the outbreak of war

The South Cottage and tower at Sissinghurst
—Vita Sackville-West in the doorway

DIARY   *14th September, 1939*

The House is mainly concerned with the evacuation of children. It
seems that where children have been evacuated along with their school-
teachers everything has gone well. But when the mothers have come,
there has been trouble. Many of the children are verminous and have
disgusting habits. This horrifies the cottagers upon whom they have
been billeted. Moreover, the mothers refuse to help, grumble dreadfully, and are pathetically homesick and bored. Many of them have
drifted back to London. Much ill feeling has been caused. But the
interesting thing is that this feeling is not between the rich and the
poor but between the urban and the rural poor. This is a perplexing
social event. One thing that they say is that these children were
evacuated at the end of the holidays and were therefore more verminous and undisciplined than if they had been taken in the middle
of the term. But the effect will be to demonstrate to people how
deplorable is the standard of life and civilization among the urban
proletariat.

DIARY   *15th September, 1939*

To see Vansittart[1] at the Foreign Office. He does not think that we
should make a violent war at present or provoke Italy. We are too
weak for the moment. Nor is he absolutely certain that Germany will
after all make a peace proposal when she has conquered Poland. They
are so delighted by their Blitzkrieg (and it seems that they have almost
reached Brest Litovsk[2] and have surrounded Warsaw) that they may
try a Blitzkrieg over here and invade France via Holland, Switzerland
and Italy. I do not derive the impression that he thinks we shall win
this war.

DIARY   *16th September, 1939*

Wake up early and have a bad gloom. I try to think of something
which is not painful, and all I can manage to think of are the telephone
numbers of my friends. It is always the worst time, this early awaken-
ing. I get a letter from John Sparrow,[3] who has joined up as a private
in the Oxford and Bucks Light Infantry. His idea is (a) that although a

[1] Sir Robert Vansittart was Chief Diplomatic Adviser to the Foreign Secretary,
1938–41.
[2] The Germans captured Brest Litovsk on the 16th, and joined up there on the 18th
with the leading Russian troops.
[3] Fellow, later Warden, of All Souls College, Oxford.

Fellow of All Souls, he is not a good military man and that it is better to obey orders than have to give them; (b) that it is less painful if one breaks entirely with one's previous life. He is not too unhappy. I daresay he is right about all this. My appalling depression may be due to the fact that I am living my former life with all the conditions altered. Rob Bernays[1] told me yesterday that all the front-bench people keep exclaiming, 'I wish I were twenty. I cannot bear this responsibility.' What they really mean is, 'I wish I did not know how bad things are!' The whole world is either paralysed or against us. These are the darkest hours we have ever endured.

DIARY   17th September, 1939

Write my *Spectator* article. At 11 am. (a bad hour) Vita comes to tell me that Russia has invaded Poland and is striking towards Vilna. We are so dumbfounded by this news that there is a wave of despair over Sissinghurst. I do not think that the Russians will go beyond her old frontier or will wish to declare war on us. But of course it is a terrific blow and makes our victory even more uncertain.

Let me review the situation. It may be that within a few days we shall have Germany, Russia and Japan against us. It may be that Rumania will be subjugated and that the Greeks and Yugoslavs will succumb to Germany. The Baltic and the Scandinavian states will be too frightened to do anything. Holland, Belgium and Switzerland will have to capitulate. Thus the Axis will rule Europe, the Mediterranean and the Far East. Faced by such a combine, France may make her terms. Hitler is then in the position of Napoleon after Austerlitz, with the important difference that whereas we were then in command of the seas, our command of the seas is not now absolute. It is not so much a question of us encircling and blockading Germany; it is a question of them encircling and blockading us. Japan might threaten our position in Australia and the Far East. Russia might threaten us in India. Italy might raise the Arab world. In a few days our whole position might collapse. Nothing could be more black.

And yet and yet, I still believe that if we have the will-power, we might win through. The Germans, who are diffident by nature, can scarcely believe in this fairy-tale. A single reverse and they will be overcome with nervous trepidation. Our position is one of grave danger. A generous offer of an immediate truce with the prospect

[1] Liberal National M.P. for Bristol North since 1936, and Parliamentary Secretary to the Ministry of Transport, 1939-40.

of an eventual conference might tempt us sorely. But we shall not have a generous offer. What will happen? I suppose that there will be a German ultimatum and a Coalition Cabinet. Chamberlain must go. Churchill may be our Clemenceau or our Gambetta. To bed very miserable and alarmed.

DIARY   *20th September, 1939*

Go round with Bob Boothby, Eleanor Rathbone[1] and Wilfrid Roberts[2] to see Lloyd George[3] at Thames House. The old lion sits there in his room at the top of the building with a wonderful view of the river down to St Paul's. He begins by discussing the general situation. He says that he is frankly terrified and does not see how we can possibly win the war. He contends that we should insist immediately upon a secret session of Parliament in which we should force the Government to tell us exactly how they estimate the prospects of victory. If our chances are 50/50, then it might be worthwhile organising the whole resources of the country for a desperate struggle. But if the chances are really against us, then we should certainly make peace at the earliest opportunity, possibly with Roosevelt's assistance. He indulges in a fierce onslaught on the stupidity and lack of vigour of the present Government. He contends that to have guaranteed Poland and Rumania without a previous agreement with Russia was an act of incredible folly and one which was due to the essential weakness of Chamberlain's character.

The House is in one of its worst moods. The Prime Minister rises to make his weekly statement. He reads it out from a manuscript and is obviously tired and depressed. The effect is most discouraging and Members drop off to sleep. From my seat in the Gallery I can see at least ten Members slumbering. The Prime Minister has no gift for inspiring anybody, and he might have been the Secretary of a firm of undertakers reading the minutes of the last meeting. His speech is followed by an appeal by Archie Sinclair[4] for a secret session. Bob Boothby in a vigorous speech supports this request and advances the theory that the Russian occupation of Polish territory is ultimately to

[1] Independent M.P. for the Combined English Universities, where she had defeated H.N. in the Election of 1931.
[2] Liberal M.P. for North Cumberland, 1935–50.
[3] David Lloyd George was then aged 76.
[4] Leader of the Parliamentary Liberal Party, 1935–45. Secretary of State for Air, 1940–45. Later Lord Thurso.

our advantage. When he got up to speak, David Margesson[1] turned round to him with a gesture of anger and exclaimed, 'You would!' Altogether, tempers are becoming somewhat frayed.

The House rises early and I dine with Rob Bernays, Sibyl Colefax, Guy Burgess[2] and Ronald Cartland[3] at the Savoy Grill. Cartland is extremely pessimistic about our prospects. He says that we are frightfully short of ammunition in every branch, that we have, in fact, no Army, Navy or Air Force and that we should make peace at once. He would like to see Margesson and Chamberlain hung upon lamp-posts. He also feels that Burgin[4] and Hore-Belisha[5] should be shot. He is particularly indignant at Winston Churchill having been silenced and blanketed at the Admiralty. The original idea (and Lloyd George told me the same) was that Winston should be a member of the War Cabinet without portfolio. Margesson insisted that he would be dangerous in such a position and that he must be 'nobbled' by having a department which would occupy all his time.

I must say that if an old warrior like Lloyd George and a young warrior like Ronald Cartland both feel equally defeatist, the general feeling in the country must be pretty bad.

DIARY   *24th September, 1939*

The effect of the blackout, the evacuation and the general dislocation has been bad for morale. The whole stage was set for an intensive and early attack by Germany which would have aroused our stubbornness. The Government had not foreseen a situation in which boredom and bewilderment would be the main elements. They concentrated upon coping with panic and have been faced with an anticlimax. They have not sufficient imagination to cope with that. We have all the apparatus of war conditions without war conditions. The result is general disillusion and grumbling, from which soil defeatism may grow.

[1] Government Chief Whip, 1931–40. Secretary of State for War, 1940–42.
[2] Guy Burgess had resigned from the B.B.C. in December 1938 and joined Section Nine of the Secret Service, where he was mainly concerned with propaganda and underground resistance to Hitler on the Continent. He defected to Russia with Donald Maclean in 1951.
[3] Conservative M.P. for King's Norton, 1935–40. One of Chamberlain's most pugnacious back-bench opponents. He was killed during the retreat to Dunkirk in May 1940.
[4] Leslie Burgin, M.P., Minister of Supply, 1939–40.
[5] Leslie Hore-Belisha, Secretary of State for War, 1937–40.

DIARY   *25th September, 1939*

Allen Lane[1] comes to see me, and it is agreed that I do a Penguin Special for him on why Britain is at war.

DIARY   *26th September, 1939*

The Prime Minister gets up to make his statement. He is dressed in deep mourning relieved only by a white handkerchief and a large gold watch-chain. One feels the confidence and spirits of the House dropping inch by inch. When he sits down there is scarcely any applause. During the whole speech Winston Churchill had sat hunched beside him looking like the Chinese god of plenty suffering from acute indigestion. He just sits there, lowering, hunched and circular, and then he gets up. He is greeted by a loud cheer from all the benches and he starts to tell us about the Naval position. I notice that *Hansard* does not reproduce his opening phrases. He began by saying how strange an experience it was for him after a quarter of a century to find himself once more in the same room in front of the same maps, fighting the same enemy and dealing with the same problems. His face then creases into an enormous grin and he adds, glancing down at the Prime Minister, 'I have no conception how this curious change in my fortunes occurred.' The whole House roared with laughter and Chamberlain had not the decency even to raise a sickly smile. He just looked sulky.

The effect of Winston's speech was infinitely greater than could be derived from any reading of the text. His delivery was really amazing and he sounded every note from deep preoccupation to flippancy, from resolution to sheer boyishness. One could feel the spirits of the House rising with every word. It was quite obvious afterwards that the Prime Minister's inadequacy and lack of inspiration had been demonstrated even to his warmest supporters. In those twenty minutes Churchill brought himself nearer the post of Prime Minister than he has ever been before. In the Lobbies afterwards even Chamberlainites were saying, 'We have now found our leader.' Old Parliamentary hands confessed that never in their experience had they seen a single speech so change the temper of the House.

Dine at the Beefsteak. Dufferin[2] is there. He tells me that Winston, in drafting his speech, had put in a passage as follows: 'Our destroyers

---

[1] (Sir) Allen Lane, Chairman and Managing Director of Penguin Books Ltd.
[2] The fourth Marquess of Dufferin and Ava, Parliamentary Under-Secretary of State for the Colonies, 1937–40.

then engaged that particular submarine, and all that thereafter was seen of the vessel was a large spot of oil and a door which floated up to the surface bearing my initials painted on it in white paint.' I think he was wise to suppress this particular quip.

DIARY   27th September, 1939

Lunch with Sibyl Colefax. The others there are H. G. Wells, G. M. Young,[1] Victor Cazalet and Jan Masaryk. The Duke and Duchess of Windsor appear, although I had imagined that he was over in France. He is going there shortly.[2] He is dressed in khaki with all his decorations, and looks grotesquely young. H. G. Wells, who is a republican with a warm sympathy for the Duke of Windsor, does not bow to him but treats him with great friendliness. I have seldom seen the Duke in such cheerful spirits, and it was rather touching to witness their delight at being back in England. There was no false note. Walking away with H. G. Wells, I said to him, 'You admit that that man has got charm?' 'Glamour', he said. 'Charm', I said. 'Oh very well', he said, 'have it your own way.' Go back to King's Bench Walk and go on with my Penguin Special.

DIARY   3rd October, 1939

We have an [Eden] Group dinner at the Carlton. Waldorf Astor[3] attends. He feels that it is essential that the Prime Minister should be removed and that Winston Churchill should take his place. The question is how and when. We discuss this matter in all its bearings. I suggest that in any case the Prime Minister will have to deal with this peace offer[4] and that thereafter, when the war really begins, there will be such an outburst of public indignation that a Coalition Government will have to be formed. It is evident that none of the Opposition leaders will enter a Cabinet which contains Chamberlain, Simon and Hoare, and that therefore the removal of these three will take place almost automatically. Duff Cooper and [Leo] Amery, while agreeing with this argument, contend that we have no time to lose. The armament situation is really very bad and it is feared that our army in

[1] The historian, 1882–1959.
[2] He was assigned to the British Military Mission at the French General Headquarters at Vincennes.
[3] The second Viscount Astor.
[4] On 28th September a joint German–Russian statement called for an end to the fighting, now that Poland had ceased to exist.

France is not sufficiently equipped. It is absolutely essential that Burgin be dismissed from the Ministry of Supply and a really formidable figure be put in charge. The tragedy is that we have so few formidable figures.

I go on with Duff Cooper to the Carlton Grill, where Diana [Cooper] has a supper party in honour of Burckhardt, the former League of Nations High Commissioner in Danzig. In view of the fact that Hitler has twice referred to him in his speeches as '*ein Mann von Format*' and 'a most tactful person', I had somehow imagined him to be another Horace Wilson.[1] Not at all. He is rather a dapper, smart, fresh-coloured Swiss aristocrat speaking the most beautiful French. I sit next to him and find him most intelligent and amusing. He talks a great deal about Hitler. He says that Hitler is the most profoundly feminine man that he has ever met, and that there are moments when he becomes almost effeminate. He imitates the movements of his white flabby hands. He says that Hitler has a dual personality, the first being that of the rather gentle artist, and the second that of the homicidal maniac. He is convinced that Hitler has no complete confidence in himself and that his actions are really governed by somnambulist certainty. He says that the main energy in Hitler is an energy of hatred, and that he has never met any human being capable of generating so terrific a condensation of envy, vituperation and malice. Yet now and then there is a pathetic side to him. For instance, he once heard Hitler say, 'It is a great sorrow to me that I have never met an Englishman who speaks German well enough for me to feel at ease with him.' It was evident to Burckhardt that he was fascinated, 'as so many Germans are fascinated', by the problem of our easy-going self-assurance.

DIARY   *12th October, 1939*

Walk away from the Foreign Office with Rab Butler.[2] He asks me what I would like the Prime Minister to say this afternoon in reply to Hitler's peace offer. I say that I should like a speech saying quite shortly that we are only too anxious to make peace but that we must have a guarantee before entering a conference. That guarantee would be the withdrawal of German troops from Prague and Warsaw. He laughs and says, 'I am afraid that that sounds rather like appeasement.

[1] See p. 51, note 4.
[2] He was Under-Secretary of State for Foreign Affairs, 1938–41, and spokesman on Foreign Affairs in the House of Commons while Lord Halifax was Foreign Secretary.

The Prime Minister is much more bellicose than that.' He is a curious man. I have a suspicion that he does not really agree with the appeasement policy and has all along been on our side. He has seen in some paper that I was writing this Penguin Special and he asked me if he could see the proofs. I said, 'There is a great deal in the book which will annoy the Government terribly.' He answered, 'It won't annoy me!'

DIARY   25th October, 1939

Dine with the Eden Group. Hore-Belisha is our guest. He says that if the Germans do not attack us within the next fortnight, they will probably wait till March. He is extremely confident, and although he is preparing for a three-years war he does not think it will last anything like as long as that. There is in fact a general feeling in Ministerial circles that the war will peter out before the spring. I cannot get anyone to give me any serious grounds for such optimism.

On 28th October Harold Nicolson flew to Paris with a party of eight other back-bench M.P.s,[1] led by Sir Edward Spears, Chairman of the Anglo-French Parliamentary Committee. The purpose of the visit was to exchange views with French politicians and to gain first-hand knowledge of the Maginot Line. They visited the sector of the line at its northern extremity near the French frontier with Luxembourg, where at this stage of the war there was no hostile activity except the occasional exchange of counter-battery fire and patrols across no-man's land. The British visitors were much impressed by the professionalism and high morale of the Maginot defenders and by the confidence of the French political leaders, which at this period exceeded that of the British themselves.

DIARY   29th October, 1939
                                                        Paris

We are called at 6.30 am. and are driven to the Gare de l'Est. It pours with rain the whole morning and the valleys of the Marne, Meuse and Moselle are completely flooded. 'The elements', Delbos[2] says to me, 'are fighting on our side.' Eventually we arrive at Nancy. We enter

---

[1] The others were Leo Amery, Hugh Dalton, James de Rothschild, Philip Noel-Baker, David Grenfell, Sir John Wardlaw-Milne, Sir Robert Bird and General Spears.

[2] Yvon Delbos, a former French Minister of Foreign Affairs and Minister of Education.

a convoy of five military cars and are driven to the French Head-quarters, where the Chief of Staff explains exactly how the present line runs. We then drive on through the rain.

After passing Thionville we begin to realise that we are entering the zone of the Armies, since the ordinary road signs are supplemented by huge white and red boards bearing the words 'Section A', 'Section B', marked with arrows. On we go in our five cars until suddenly a platoon of soldiers rush out and remove a barbed wire barricade across the road. We then suddenly draw up in front of a sharp hill under a wood containing a great gateway with an iron grille. Above the arch-way is an inscription in stone running as follows: *'Ligne Maginot. Ouvrage de Soetrich.'* Underneath it run the words, *'Ils ne passeront pas.'* We are met at the gateway by General Cousse who commands the local group of armies, and by General Condé who is in command of that sector of the Maginot Line. There is a very smart guard of honour. We enter under the arch and see that the outer hallway is packed with cages of pigeons and, I regret to say, mice.[1] That is for gas. We enter the tunnel and walk about fifty yards to a point where we are faced by a lift-shaft just like that in the underground. We enter the lift and go down about 300 feet. When we get out of the lift we are faced with a tunnel brilliantly lit and reminding me of the Mersey Tunnel. In front of the lift is drawn up a long train or tramway similar to those tramways which conduct one round exhibitions. Our particular tram-way is decorated with French and British flags. We all take our seats and the tram starts off, clanging a bell the whole time. To me the distance seems as if we had travelled from Gordon Square to the Temple. The atmosphere is very like that of a tube-station and there is a sort of hum in the air of motors pumping through ventilation.

We are first taken into the control chambers of this particular *ouvrage*. It consists of three large rooms separated from each other but each containing a hatchway by which each section can communicate with the others. The walls of these chambers are papered by a top line of elaborate photographs depicting the area facing this *ouvrage*, and underneath this row another row of diagrammatic plans giving the range of each single tree or hedge. There are about thirty men and four officers in this basement, sitting round tables on which are spread other diagrams. The General explained to us the system of fire-control which, of course, I did not understand. He then said to us, 'Now supposing that you were in the observation post and you saw German

[1] H.N.'s regret was due not to sympathy, but to his life-long horror of mice.

tanks advancing on any particular point of this area, what would you do?' We said we did not quite understand that question. 'Well, now, put your finger upon one particular field in this photograph (as it might be the field that leads to Frittenden) and tell me that you see tanks coming from that area.' I put my finger upon a distant field on one of the photographs. In a second, each one of the three basement rooms hummed into activity. All the young men there (and I should add that they were dressed in white overalls like in a hospital) immediately rushed to a particular job. Some of them clamped earphones to their heads, others rushed with dividers to their maps, and in a second a great buzz of telephonic conversation began. Two or three of them held pieces of white chalk in their hands and stood by the telephone operators. The latter flicked words at them, at which they rushed to the blackboards on the wall which were divided up into squares and began writing on these blackboards numbers such as 235, 410, 789. The officers watched these figures accumulating and when they had reached a certain point they turned a dial in the wall which rang a bell, and when that bell had rung they all suddenly relaxed and took off their earphones. 'That,' the General said to us, 'means that full firing has been directed on the point you marked.'[1]

We were then taken round the kitchens, canteens and dormitories of the men living in the lower basement. What was so extraordinary was that they did not look like soldiers at all, but had the white faces of troglodytes and the nervous white hands of scientists. We then entered the lift again and went upwards out of this great basement which seemed to me like the B.B.C. buried in a mountain. We were taken to a casement in the flank of the hill lit by brilliant electric light. It was exactly like a gun-emplacement in a battleship. All we could see was the backs of enormous guns, mortars and machine-guns embodied in the outer wall. They said to us, 'Would you like to see the Germans?' We said, 'Yes, we would.' The Commandant then pressed a button and there was a gentle hum. Gradually one of the guns began to swing backwards, and as it did so, it disclosed a long aperture about two feet high by ten feet wide through which we suddenly saw wet daylight. They turned out the blaze of lights. We could see a line of high ground about the distance of Staplehurst from Sissinghurst.[2] 'Voilà les Boches',

[1] In imagination, of course. It does not seem to have struck the Delegation as strange that, even for the purposes of demonstration, the French refused to fire on their enemies.
[2] Five miles.

the General said to us. We were allowed to look for a few minutes, then they quickly shut the thing up again. We again entered the lift and went up to the top storey. We were to be shown the '75s. We were first taken up into the topmost observation chamber which actually shows above the surface of the hill, little more than the height of a wine-glass. By some mechanical method this observation is exaggerated, like a camera-obscura, and we can see the whole front from that area. Only two men are kept at this topmost point. It is they who communicate with the great battery inside. We then went down steps to the battery itself. It was exactly like some enormous telescope in an observatory. Again they said to us, 'Put your finger on one point of the map which you wish to bombard'. We did so. At this the turret immediately filled with some twenty men each one of whom rushed to a particular point. Switches were turned and a loud hum echoed in the air. The telescope, which until this moment had looked no more than a ventilation shaft, shifted suddenly, began to rise in the air directly upwards and at a certain point the ceiling above it swung away and exposed the damp afternoon sky above it. The great shaft of the gun rose like a lift into the air and then stopped suddenly. 'Fire!' remarked (he did not shout) the Commanding Officer, and at that the shell-casings began to revolve accompanied by an intermittent click. Although the shells were packed all round us they did not actually put them into the cases, but we knew that each click represented a shell. There was a click every second and it went on for eighty seconds. The Commandant explained to us that that represented a deluge of fire such as no tank or infantry could possibly withstand. When it was over the gun hummed again, descended into its recess and the cupola was closed.

We got back to Nancy at 9 o'clock where we had a large banquet with the Prefect and the local military.

DIARY   *31st October, 1939*

We reach Paris at 12.30 and are driven off at once, without being allowed to wash, to the Ministry of Finance. Paul Reynaud[1] is there to meet us. He is very anxious to hear what we think of the Maginot Line and is frankly delighted by our enthusiasm. I have a good talk with him and am enormously encouraged. He keeps on repeating, 'We've got them already, and they know it!' He realises that we shall

[1] Reynaud was French Minister of Finance, and was to succeed Daladier as Prime Minister on 21st March, 1940.

have great disasters and moments of defeat, but he seems to have no doubt whatsoever that, Russia or no Russia, we shall be victorious. 'It is absolutely inevitable,' he says, 'and you know that I would not say so to you who have shared my doubts in the past unless I really believed it. I should say to you, "We have to face great perils." I don't say that now. I say, "We have to prepare for inevitable victory", and when I say that, I say it after having estimated all our dangers, all our capacities, and being a pessimist at heart.'

We then go on to see Daladier.[1] The whole place hums like a General Headquarters and in every ante-room there are officers waiting with portfolios under their arms. We are conducted into Daladier's room where he sits at an enormous Directoire writing-table with masses of papers in front of him and a bowl for his pipes and tobacco. We start the proceedings by a few set speeches which go very well and then we sit down. Daladier starts to talk. He is not an attractive man. He looks like a drunken peasant. His face must once have had sharp outlines but now it is blurred by the puffiness of drink. He looks extremely exhausted and has the eyes of a man who has had a bad night. He has a weak, sly smile. The conversation is perfectly easy and we ask him what he thinks the Germans are going to do. He replies: 'I have no idea at all. I hope they will attack the Maginot Line, but I don't think they will be so foolish. I think they may direct against you in England in the next few days an absolutely overwhelming air-attack. I think they may try to encircle the Maginot Line by driving through Holland and Switzerland. I think they may remain where they are and hope that their propaganda will dislocate us during the coming winter. I don't know which of these alternatives they will adopt.' I think that he was moved by our visit and by the really excellent little speech which Spears made. He was tremendously friendly to us and said that if any one of us ever wanted to see him again, he would cut any engagement to do so.

We filed out into the ante-room, and there we find an old man in a wheeled chair dressed in full uniform with the Star of the Legion of Honour on his chest. Spears rushes up to him and greets him warmly. It is Franchet d'Espérey.[2] He says to us, 'Well, gentlemen, you see a ghost revisiting the scenes of his past.'

---

[1] Edouard Daladier was not only Prime Minister, but Foreign and Defence Minister as well.
[2] Commander of the Fifth Army at the Battle of the Marne, 1914. He was later made a Marshal of France. In 1939 he was 83 years old.

We then go on to a Reception given by the President of the Chamber,[1] where we are offered a large buffet with champagne. I have a talk with Giraudoux[2] and certain members of the French Foreign Office. I also have a talk with Léon Blum[3], and all of these conversations convince me that we are much too defeatist in London and that these people are absolutely certain of victory. They think that we shall suffer very much from the air and that this time it will be we and not they who are invaded. They are convinced that if we can stick it for six months, the whole German edifice will collapse.

Hitler had already made his firm decision to attack in the West through Holland and Belgium. The date of the offensive was set for 12th November, postponed for three days on 7th November, and again postponed, almost week to week, on fourteen separate occasions during the winter for various political and military reasons. The closing months of 1939 imposed on the British the strain of inactivity. There was still no fighting on land. The first British Army casualty of the war did not occur till 9th December (a corporal shot on patrol). At sea the magnetic mine was mastered, and the 'Graf Spee' was scuttled off the River Plate on 17th December after a dramatic engagement with British cruisers.

The only large-scale military event was the invasion of Finland by Russia on 30th November, following the rejection of Soviet demands for slices of Finnish territory. As Harold Nicolson recorded in his diary, the Finns were expected to capitulate 'in a day or two'. To everyone's astonishment, they flung back the Russian troops at every point except Petsamo in the far north, and held them pinned down by the Mannerheim Line a score of miles from their starting-point near Leningrad in the south.

DIARY   2nd November, 1939

The Prime Minister makes his weekly statement. It is as dull as ditchwater. I admit that there was little for him to tell us, but he need not have done it in so glum and gloomy a form. I hear that Halifax[4] said recently, 'I wish the P.M. would give up these weekly statements. It is as if one were in East Africa and received the *Times Weekly Edition* at regular intervals.' It is certainly very bad. Attlee and Archie [Sinclair] are little better. I am ashamed, as there are Dominion representatives

[1] Edouard Herriot.
[2] Jean Giraudoux, the playwright, recently appointed Minister of Information.
[3] Prime Minister of France, 1936–38.
[4] Lord Halifax was Foreign Secretary, 1938–40.

recently arrived who are crowded in the Gallery. They had come expecting to find the Mother of Parliaments armed like Britannia. They merely saw an old lady dozing over her knitting, while her husband read the evening paper aloud.

DIARY   *24th November, 1939*

Round to Horace Rumbold's[1] house. Steed[2] is there. He has been seeing Villard,[3] the American correspondent, who has been in Germany. They had filled Villard with panic. It seems that they are going to lie low during the winter, shake us with their magnetic mine, and then on 1st May launch a terrific offensive by air and sea. Italy and Spain may join in, and we shall be brought to our knees by 16th July. They are producing aeroplanes and submarines on the Ford system. They are confident that they will crush us completely. Horace Rumbold listens to all this with a glassy stare and his mouth half-open. When Steed has finished, he drops his eyeglass suddenly. 'Bilge', he says.

DIARY   *25th November, 1939*

How curious are the moods through which one passes! I sit here in my room at Sissinghurst thinking back on the days since 3rd September. The acute depression and misery of the first weeks has passed. I have accepted the fact that we are at war, and I suppose I am physically relieved by the fact that there are not likely to be any raids during the winter upon London and that the Germans have not made a dash through Holland. Yet the fact that this war is costing us six million pounds a day and that I am not really certain that we shall win it, fills me with acute sadness at times. We all keep up a brave face and refuse to admit that defeat is possible. But my heart aches with apprehension.

Then Victor Cazalet rings up to say that Ben has got his stripe and is now a Bombardier.[4] We are absurdly pleased by this. A windy night with a scudding moon. I think of the people at sea and all those devils in Germany and Rome plotting, plotting, plotting our destruction in the spring.

---

[1] Sir Horace Rumbold, British Ambassador in Berlin, 1928–33.
[2] Wickham Steed, formerly Foreign Editor, and later Editor, of *The Times*.
[3] Oswald G. Villard, Editor and owner of the *New York Nation*. He was 67 in 1939.
[4] Victor Cazalet, M.P., was Commanding Officer of the anti-aircraft battery in which Benedict Nicolson was then serving at Rochester.

DIARY   *30th November, 1939*

The Russians send an ultimatum to Finland and start bombing Helsinki and Vyborg. The Prime Minister makes a statement. The Labour Party are enraged with Russia and even little Gallacher,[1] who makes a plucky intervention on behalf of the U.S.S.R., is none too happy. There are cries of 'Shame!' from all the benches. I was amused at Question time to watch a discussion between the Whips as to whom they should put up from the back-benches to answer Dalton. I saw them pointing at me, at which David Margesson shook his head in fierce negation. He never forgives nor forgets.

DIARY   *3rd December, 1939*

The news is encouraging. We have sunk another submarine and the Finns seem to be putting up quite a good show. They will collapse in a day or two, and all they need to do is to demonstrate a few hours' heroism. They are doing that.

After the news there is a B.B.C. scrap-book for 1910. It is rather moving for Vita and me, since it brings in *The Speckled Band*,[2] which was the play at which we met for the first time. There is also a record of Florence Nightingale. Very squeaky and interrupted it is, but still recognisable. She says the last words as if she were signing her signature on a cheque. 'Florence' (pause) 'Nightingale' (defiantly). All this comes out at us from the past. From the distant past. Princess Louise is dead.[3] My God! How the past slides like a great mass of vegetable matter down the sluice.

DIARY   *7th December, 1939*

Lunch with Sibyl Colefax. Dickie Mountbatten is there on leave.[4] He looks so well and is so keen that it is like a breath of sea air. He feels that the Navy do not get enough publicity. The Air Force seem to bag the whole thing. For instance, the other day a merchant ship was arriving in the Firth from the Argentine. As they came in, a Messerschmitt swooped down upon them and raked the bridge with machinegun fire. The navigating lieutenant was killed, and the old captain was wounded by thirty bullets. He picked himself up and said to the

[1] William Gallacher, Communist M.P. for Western Fife since 1935.
[2] A play based on one of Conan Doyle's Sherlock Holmes stories.
[3] Princess Louise, Duchess of Argyll, daughter of Queen Victoria.
[4] Lord Louis Mountbatten, then in command of H.M.S. *Kelly* and of the Fifth Destroyer Flotilla.

signaller, 'Is Lieutenant Jones dead?' 'Yes, sir.' 'Then bring me a chair.' He sat down and steered the ship in. Finally he signalled, 'stop engines'. He remained sitting, and then they found that he was dead. Dickie feels that that story ought to have been written up, but I gather that they won't do so, since it might show the Germans how effective is machine-gun fire on the bridges of merchant vessels.

DIARY   9th December, 1939

It starts fine, and then as usual turns into driving rain. Never have I known so phenomenally wet a winter. The historians will probably record these constant days of rain as a main factor in the strategic development of the war. I see it as sodden chestnut leaves, bursting streams and a brown and turgid lake.

The Finns seem to be holding out for the moment, but that does not mean much. What I fear is that the Germans and the Russians will feel that this winter pause will damage their prestige, and that (even unwillingly) they will be forced to provide conquests at the expense of the Scandinavian and Balkan powers. The sum of these will expose us to grave strategical disadvantages when the real war begins. Meanwhile Russia has repudiated any designs on Bessarabia, and Alba[1] has announced that Spain will never become an area for German action. I do not believe all this. I believe that it looks as if we were going to be beaten, and all the vultures and all the crows will gather to peck at our corpse.

Read Cyril Connolly's new paper *Horizon*. The editorial note says that in this war we are not inspired by 'pity or hope' as in the Spanish war. No pity. No hope. Glum. Glum. Glum. All this business about our having lost what we used to describe as 'patriotism' must be thought out carefully. The old national theory has been cut horizontally by class distinctions. We used to cut it like a cake in perpendicular wedges. Now it is cut sideways. This is a difficult alteration.

V.S-W. TO H.N.   12th December, 1939
                                                                                                   Sissinghurst

The Lion pond is being drained. I have got what I hope will be a really lovely scheme for it: all white flowers, with some clumps of very pale pink. White clematis, white lavender, white Agapanthus, white double primroses, white anemones, white camellias, white

[1] The Duke of Alba, Spanish Ambassador in London, 1939-45.

lilies including *giganteum* in one corner, and the pale peach-coloured *Primula pulverulenta*.

H.N. TO V.S-W.   *13th December, 1939*
                                          4 King's Bench Walk, E.C.4

You don't know what pleasure your letters are to me. After I have ploughed through an endless mass of cadging letters, I come upon yours and it is like a puff of summer air. I love your idea about the Lion pond. Only of course it gets no sun. You know that. You are a horticulturalist. It is impudence on my part to remind you that the Lion pond gets almost no sun. Just a beam at dawn is all it gets. We have the Japanese anemones which do well. We know that the blue Agapanthus flowers, so why not the white? But what about the clematis, the camellia, the lily, and the *giganteum* ditto? But you know. Only it is such a good idea that I want it to succeed. I like the *Campanula pyramidalis* there, don't you? Of course there is not much room. Then we have the *Clematis montana* above. Yes, it is certainly a good idea. Darling, how these things take one away from the sorrow of this war.

I find people in a mood of depression. I have always expected the worst and feel that my best role is to go about with a bright face. But people now see that their hopes of a row between Russia and Germany are illusory, that each is out to loot, and they are beginning to fear lest Italy may join in the scramble. I shall write a *Spectator* article on that subject this week.

I met Axel Munthe[1] at luncheon yesterday. He is very gaga and blind. Everything seems to have oozed from him except that secretion of oil with which he flatters. God how he flatters one! I do *not* like it.

My Penguin is selling like hot cakes.

V.S-W. TO H.N.   *14th December, 1939*

You wrote me such a nice letter about my silly letters to you. I always feel that they are so 'Our Village' compared with the interesting things you do. But when you say they bring you a puff of summer, I feel consoled. As a matter of fact, I don't think it is a bad thing for you (or any of us) to switch away from the horrors of Europe to things of calm and beauty for three minutes a day.

Of course I realised the Lion pond was in the shade, and I chose the

[1] By origin a Swedish physician, he lived in Italy and achieved great popularity with his book *The Story of San Michele*. In 1939 he was 82, and he died in 1949.

things accordingly. Primulas and the Giant Himalayan lily simply revel in a north aspect. I have been rather extravagant, I fear, on the principle of 'Let us plant and be merry, for next autumn we may all be ruined.' After all, if I spend £20 on plants now, they will go on increasing in beauty for years, and we may never be able to afford it again.

I can't help feeling sentimentally glad that the *Bremen* escaped.[1] I know it is a pity, but I should mind feeling that that beautiful ship had gone down.

DIARY   *14th December, 1939*

The *Graf Spee* put out and was engaged by three of our little boats who drove her back into port.[2] 6 in. versus 10 in. A fine performance. It cheers us all up.

Talk to Paul Evans.[3] He agrees that yesterday's sitting[4] was a great blow to the Party machine. They must have realised the underlying force of the opposition on our side. The effect of the Secret Session was not to divulge secrets which could not have been divulged in public. It was to show the Whips what their supporters really felt. The tremendous reception given on our benches to Archie Sinclair's speech must in itself have shown the Whips how precarious is their hold on their own Party. This marks a stage in the end of this administration. They will try to placate us by appointing Amery[5] Minister of Economics. But our implacability remains. We have got them.

Let me be quite clear in my own mind about this. I comb my conscience with a fine comb and do not find any traces of resentment. Yet I am sure that we shall not win this war with Chamberlain at the head and with people like Simon, Hoare, Hore-Belisha and Burgin in key positions. I do not want a Coalition Government at this stage, since we must keep our second wind for the moment when true disaster occurs. Let Chamberlain remain. But let him know, and his satellites know, that he remains on sufferance and under the very sharpest observation. He must know that now.

[1] The great German liner (in which H.N. and V.S-W. had sailed to and from America in 1933) had reached Hamburg from the Soviet port of Murmansk.
[2] The *Graf Spee* had in fact been raiding the South Atlantic since the outbreak of war. She only took refuge in Montevideo after the action on 13th December. The *Spee* had 11 in. guns; the British cruisers 8 in. and 6 in.
[3] Paul Emrys-Evans, Conservative M.P. for South Derbyshire.
[4] The first of the Secret Sessions of the House of Commons.
[5] L. S. Amery became Secretary of State for India and Burma in 1940.

DIARY   *17th December, 1939*

After dinner we listen to the news. It is dramatic. The *Graf Spee* must either be interned or leave Montevideo by 9.30. The news is at 9. At about 9.10 they put in a stop-press message to the effect that the *Graf Spee* is weighing anchor and has landed some 250 of her crew at Montevideo. As I type these words she may be steaming to destruction (for out there, it is 6.30 and still light). She may creep through territorial waters until darkness comes and then make a dash. She may assault her waiting enemies. She may sink some of our ships.[1] But I hate it all. I wish she had consented to be interned. I loathe the idea of these brave men steaming out in cold blood either to our destruction or to their destruction. Few things have convinced me so much of the idiocy of modern warfare. It is no more than blood-sports. The bull is being driven out to face the bull-fighters. But the bull is as noble an animal as the bull-fighter. I have in mind, on the one hand, the picture left by Rauschning's book[2] of this perverted sadist planning the rape of nations, and on the other hand the officers and crew of the *Graf Spee*, obeying his orders, yet doomed either to murder or to be murdered. Definitely I hope she escapes. Even a dramatic and heroic episode such as this blurs our feelings. We simply do not want either side to win in this combat. There will be no sense of triumph or defeat whatever happens to the *Spee*. Merely a dull sense of the ineptitude of the human mind.

DIARY   *18th December, 1939*

Have a long talk with Rab Butler. He tells me that my book[3] is a work of art and perfectly correct. He thinks that I am right about Chamberlain and Horace Wilson[4] in so far as diplomacy is concerned, but that

[1] He did not foresee what actually happened. Hitler ordered the *Graf Spee's* commander, Captain Langsdorff, to refuse internment in Montevideo, and to fight his way out, scuttling the ship as a last resort. Langsdorff transferred 700 of his crew to a German merchant ship in the harbour and sailed out to sea at 6.15. At 8.45 she blew herself up within sight of the waiting British cruisers. Two days later Captain Langsdorff shot himself.

[2] Hermann Rauschning's *Hitler Speaks*, which had just been published. Rauschning was by that time a refugee in England.

[3] *Why Britain is at War.*

[4] Sir Horace Wilson was Permanent Head of the Civil Service, 1939–42, and chief Industrial Adviser to the Government, 1930–39. But he was also unofficially chief adviser to Neville Chamberlain on foreign affairs, 1937–40, and had a room in 10 Downing Street while Chamberlain was Prime Minister.

Horace is really a very gifted man nonetheless. He says that his influence over Chamberlain is something extraordinary and that the latter simply cannot move without him. He says that Chamberlain is tough without being strong.

DIARY   *31st December, 1939*

Cyril Joad[1] expounds pacifism after dinner. His line is that the ordinary person in England would be less unhappy after a Nazi victory than if he or she lost their sons, lovers or husbands. He thinks only of the greatest unhappiness of the greatest number, and accuses me of national and spiritual pride. It is a pleasure talking to him. He stirs up the mind. He is extremely imaginative about physical pain, and the picture of young men being gored by bayonets is so terrible to him that he would prefer sacrificing liberty to prevent it happening.

I do not stay to watch the New Year in or the Old Year out. I write this diary at 11.45 and shall not wait. The old year is foul and the new year terrifying. I think, as I go to bed, of Nigel and Ben, Ben and Nigel. How stupid life is. Not evil, only stupid. What shall I have to record this time next year?

---

[1] The author and philosopher. He was an old friend of H.N., with whom he had been associated during the days of the New Party in 1931. He was a leading pacifist at the beginning of the Second World War as he was in the First.

1940

A long talk with Eden – 'the war will destroy all the things we care for' – disquiet in the Eden Group about the British war-effort – the 'Altmark' incident – H.N.'s lecture-tour of France – Hitler invades Norway and Denmark – 'I have seldom seen Churchill to less advantage' – Duff Cooper on American opinion – the morality of bombing German towns – interview with Halifax – Lloyd George considered as Prime Minister – the great House of Commons debate of 7th-8th May – Chamberlain falls and Churchill becomes Prime Minister – German invasion of Holland, Belgium and France – H.N. joins Churchill's Government – Sedan and Dunkirk – morale in Leicester – proposal to evacuate Kent – Italy enters the war – Churchill's great speeches – the fall of France – 'practically certain the Americans will enter the war in November' – the naval action at Oran – H.N. drafts Cabinet paper on war aims – the threat of a German invasion – H.N.'s confidence – the Battle of Britain – trouble in the Ministry of Information – beginning of the Blitz on London – public morale under bombing – the Dakar incident – discussion with Huxley at the Zoo – Churchill on reprisal raids – reported peace-offer from Hitler to Pétain – H.N.'s admiration for Churchill – Roosevelt re-elected – death of Neville Chamberlain – Churchill at Ditchley – 8th Army offensive in desert – H.N.'s talk with General Alexander

*As a speaker, writer and member of many Committees, Harold Nicolson
was very active in what Churchill later called 'these months of pretended
war', but his activity, like that of everyone else, was a whirring in a
vacuum. All were awaiting Hitler's next move. Scarcely one proposal
for an Allied initiative survived the discussion stage. Aid to the Finns
was still under debate when at last the Russians broke through the
Mannerheim Line in mid-March and Finland capitulated. The 'Altmark' incident on 16th February was the bright spot in a winter of exceptional cold and gloom. At home Hore-Belisha's replacement at the War
Office by Oliver Stanley was more popular in Parliament than with the
general public, and Chamberlain's leadership was accepted on sufferance
until great events should reveal its inadequacy.*

DIARY   *1st January, 1940*

A pleasant dinner with Cyril Joad and Vita. We listen to Lord Haw
Haw[1] afterwards. Joad does not think that he will have any effect on
his young pacifists. It is upon the middle, uncertain people that he will
have an effect, the untrained mind. He simply must be answered.
Joad teases me for being self-depreciative. He says that I lack the
competitive instinct and that I never throw the whole of myself into
what I believe. He is, in a way, right about this. But what does it
come from? Do I lack courage? But in the House I have been brave
enough. It cannot be fear of responsibility or hard work, since I
enjoy both. It is, I suppose, a profound disbelief in myself coupled
with a rather self-indulgent and frivolous preference for remaining an
observer.

DIARY   *6th January, 1940*

We dine with Victor Cazalet, who has Eddy[2] and the Anthony Eden
family staying with him. Anthony is in good form. I can see that he
still loathes the Prime Minister, whom he regards as obstinate, opinion-

---

[1] William Joyce, the Anglo-American who broadcast anti-British propaganda from
Germany, was so named from the superciliousness of his voice. He was found
guilty of treason and executed after the war.
[2] Edward Sackville West, the author and musical critic, and V.S-W.'s first-cousin.

ated, rather mean and completely ignorant of the main issues involved. He also dislikes Sam Hoare,[1] whom he calls 'Aunt Tabitha'. He feels that Kingsley Wood[2] is a help since he is truthful. He believes that the manner of Hore-Belisha's dismissal will have shaken the P.M.'s position.

He repeats at length the story of his own resignation. It boils down to this. He said to the P.M., 'If you check Italy in Spain you will check Germany in Austria.' The P.M. simply could not understand that formula. The final Grandi interview, which led to his resignation, was a farce.[3] Grandi said things that were not true, and the P.M. nodded his head in acquiescence throughout. He is certain that it was Horace Wilson who secured his dismissal.

Anthony is very much in favour of my Penguin, and has bought many copies. He says that I have not stated the Rhineland thing correctly. Hitler's aim was (1) to get the Rhineland; (2) to split France and us over it. Gamelin wanted to resist, but Flandin[4] was not with him. We wished to keep out of it. If Flandin had said, 'We attack', then we could not have kept aloof. But as he said, 'We shall apply economic sanctions', we were able to say, 'We cannot follow you.' He contends therefore that though Hitler got the Rhineland, he did not succeed in separating France from us, and that although he scored a great strategical triumph he did not score a diplomatic triumph.

DIARY   *7th January, 1940*

I am amused by the effect of Hore-Belisha's dismissal. We in the House would assume that it was due to the fact that having told so many lies he had sacrificed the confidence of the country. But not at all. It seems that the country regard him as a second Haldane and a moderniser of the Army. The line is that he has been ousted by an intrigue of the Army chiefs, and there is a general uproar about being ruled by dictators in brass hats. The Germans could make great capital out of all this consternation, were it not that Belisha is a Jew. Yet the general effect will be (a) among the unknowing that Belisha has been sacked

[1] Sir Samuel Hoare was then Lord Privy Seal, with a seat in the War Cabinet.
[2] Secretary of State for Air, 1938–40.
[3] This interview took place at Downing Street on 18th February, 1938. In his notes of the conversation with the Italian Ambassador and Chamberlain (printed in *Facing the Dictators*, p. 582), Eden recorded: 'The Prime Minister sat there nodding his head approvingly, while Grandi detailed one grievance after another. The more N.C. nodded, the more outrageous became Grandi's account.'
[4] Pierre Etienne Flandin, who was French Foreign Minister in 1936.

because he supported the private against the officer; (b) among the *cognoscenti* that he has been ousted because he told lies, but that Chamberlain has managed the thing clumsily; (c) a vague suspicion that the Press are really anti-Chamberlain and are exaggerating this incident in order to attack him. My own feeling is that this is less a pro-Belisha than an anti-Chamberlain outburst.[1]

DIARY   *13th January, 1940*

There is a letter from St John Ervine[2] in the *Spectator* attacking me bitterly for the article I wrote for the 5th January issue. I had told a story about a private being turned out of a restaurant by 'a major in a minor regiment'. It is interesting to observe that what arouses Ervine's rage is not the ills of the poor private, but my reference to 'a minor regiment'. This is another indication of the great and angry tide which is rising against the governing classes. I have always been on the side of the under-dog, but I have also believed in the principle of aristocracy. I have hated the rich but I have loved learning, scholarship, intelligence and the humanities. Suddenly I am faced with the fact that all these lovely things are supposed to be 'class privileges'. The snobbishness of the British people (that factor upon which the aristocratic principle relied and often exploited) has suddenly turned to venom. When I find that my whole class is being assailed, I feel part of them, a feeling that I have never had before. Thus this afternoon, as we walked through the frozen woods together, Vita said, 'It is not as if we were fighting to preserve the things we care for. This war, whatever happens, will destroy them.' We imagine that we are fighting for liberty and our standards of civilization. But is it perfectly certain that by these phrases we do not mean the cultured life which we lead? I know that such a life, as lived by Vita and myself, is 'good' in the philosophical sense. We are humane, charitable, just and not vulgar. By God, we are not vulgar! Yet is it any more than an elegant arabesque upon the corridors of history?

---

[1] What H.N. could not then know was that relations between the Minister of War and General Gort, the Commander-in-Chief of the British Expeditionary Force in France, had degenerated to the point of complete loss of mutual confidence. Their dispute was about strategy, and had nothing to do with Hore-Belisha's democratic reforms within the Army.

[2] The dramatist and novelist.

DIARY   *17th January, 1940*

An Eden Group dinner at the Carlton. Amery, Cranborne, Spears, Harold Macmillan and others. Bower[1] is there. He is very frank and informative. He says that we have got the submarine menace taped, and although there will be occasional losses, it is no longer a major menace. We have also been able to discover the nature of the magnetic mine and devise adequate counter-measures. But the bombers are prohibited by the Cabinet from bombing, and although they have been two or three times over Wilhelmshaven and seen below them a huge battleship in course of construction, plus endless submarines, they have been prohibited from dropping a single bomb. The Group agrees that this is a very serious situation, and it is disclosed that there is still a group in the War Cabinet working for appeasement and at present in negotiation via Brüning[2] to make peace with the German General Staff on condition that they eliminate Hitler. We discuss the means by which this intrigue can be countered. Shall we organise an attack upon Horace Wilson in the Press? Should we start a House of Commons campaign and distribute questions among our Group in such a way as will indicate to the House that there is a concerted movement? Here again we hesitate, for we do not wish to give the impression of disunity. Cranborne[3] then suggests that a very small committee should be created of very respectable Conservatives like Wardlaw-Milne upon which we should be represented by Amery and who would exercise pressure on the Cabinet. We all agree that such pressure would only be possible if it could be indicated that in the event of reluctance on the part of the Government, we should tell them quite frankly that we will go to the leaders of the Opposition and promise them that if they insist on a Secret Session we shall go to the point not only of supporting them at that session but of voting against the Government if necessary. I really feel that our Group is in a very strong position and can exercise what may prove to be a determinant influence.

---

[1] Commander Robert Bower, Conservative M.P. for Cleveland, 1931–45. He was then working in the Air Ministry department dealing with Coastal Command.

[2] Heinrich Brüning, German Chancellor, 1930–32. He was then in the United States.

[3] Later Fifth Marquess of Salisbury. He had resigned with Eden in 1938.

DIARY   *20th January, 1940*

We listen to Winston Churchill on the wireless after dinner. He is a little too rhetorical, and I do not think that his speech will really have gone down with the masses. He is too belligerent for this pacifist age, and although once anger comes to steel our sloppiness, his voice will be welcome to them, at the moment it reminds them of heroism which they do not really feel.

Get a letter from Walter Lippmann.[1] He says that the American people want us to win but wish to keep out. Thus there is a conflict in their desires, and they want to be assured that they *ought* to keep out. It is this gap between one desire and the other desire which offers so wide a fissure for German propaganda.

DIARY   *3rd February, 1940*

There is snow everywhere. The little paths cut through it are strewn with ashes. All very ugly and sad. On my table is a bowl of *Iris reticulata*. Those gay and fragile flowers remind me of the life that existed before 3rd September. It is as if some apoplectic dimly remembered the days before he had his stroke.

DIARY   *20th February, 1940*

The Prime Minister makes a statement about Finland which is very loudly applauded. Also one about Norway and the *Altmark*.[2] Winston, when he comes in, is loudly cheered. I talk to Roger Keyes who was in the Admiralty while it was all going on. He says that our flotilla commander was assured by the Norwegians that there were no prisoners aboard the *Altmark*. He was shaken by this and telegraphed home. Winston replied, 'Well, find out from the Captain of the *Altmark* what he has done with his prisoners.' It was clear that the Norwegians would not cooperate and the final decision had to be made. Winston rang up Halifax and said, 'I propose to violate Norwegian neutrality.' The message was sent and they waited anxiously in the Admiralty for the result. What a result! A fine show. Winston, when he walks out of the House, catches my eye. He gives one portentous wink.

---

[1] The distinguished American writer on international affairs.
[2] This German merchant-ship with 300 British prisoners aboard took refuge in Norwegian territorial waters and was intercepted by H.M.S. *Cossack*.

DIARY   *29th February, 1940*

I go to see Vansittart. He is very worried by the return of Joseph Kennedy, the American Ambassador. He says that Kennedy has been spreading it abroad in the U.S.A. that we shall certainly be beaten and he will use his influence here to press for a negotiated peace. In this he will have the assistance of the old appeasers, of Maisky,[1] and of the left-wing pacifists.

Between 6th and 18th March Harold Nicolson was in France, lecturing on British war aims for the Ministry of Information in Chalon-sur-Saône, Grenoble, Lyons, Besançon and Paris. He was recovering from a prolonged attack of influenza, and the French trains were as slow, cold and crowded as the British. His lectures, all of which he delivered in French, were a great success.

H.N. TO V.S-W. (*translation from French*)   *8th March, 1940*
                                                              Chalon-sur-Saône

It appears that all letters written from the Army zone must be in French. So here you are. The officers of the local Franco-British Association gave me an excellent dinner. Then to the Town Hall for my speech. A very receptive audience. I find it almost impossible to make a speech from a prepared text, and having started by trying to read it, I threw it aside and launched into a speech in French which was, I'm sure, full of grammatical errors, but even so was much better than my prepared speech. They all clapped, particularly at the mention 'of Winston's name. Afterwards I was given champagne, and at last am back in my room.

H.N. TO V.S-W. (*translation from French*)   *10th March, 1940*
                                                              Grenoble

It amuses me so much to write to you in French. But one problem worries me. While admitting that this will help the French censorship, what about the British censorship? I don't know the answer.

My throat hurt a good deal last night after my ghastly journey from Chalon, and I passed a night haunted by voices which spoke to me from the cupboard, the curtains and the looking-glass above the mantelpiece and spun me absurd yarns. But I had no fever, and I woke up this morning light-headed but calm. The bells of Grenoble emit a soft, lazy sound which quietens the nerves. Then the sun rose

[1] Soviet Ambassador in London, 1932–43.

—not a silent sun like ours, but a talkative sun. I opened the window and gulped it in. It was worth more than all the gargling in the world.

I worked all the morning and lunched with the British Vice-Consul and his wife, who is French. Nice, modest people. Back to the hotel, and slept till 4. Then to the University. The guests of honour are shown into the ante-room: the Préfet, the Mayor, the Chancellor of the University, the local military commander with his aides, the senior professor. We talk. I secretly suck a throat-lozenge. At 5 we enter the hall. It is absolutely packed, and people are standing in the gangways.

I am introduced by the senior tutor in literature. I ascend the tribune. I make my speech, or rather I give my talk, which lasts fifty minutes. Again I abandon my prepared text, and talk just as if I were speaking in English. The audience listen with evident attention. At the end there is applause. The people in the front rows clap and murmur discreetly, 'Well done'. Suddenly, from the gallery where the students are seated, comes a second wave of applause accompanied by the stamping of feet. Everyone takes it up. It becomes a demonstration. I say a few words of thanks. And then the young people in the gallery rise to their feet and begin to shout. It becomes an ovation. I was much moved.[1]

They talked about you at the meeting. Professor Blancagard said that you were one of the most admired poets in England. That gave me great pleasure and produced in me a wave of vague nostalgia. I leave for Lyons tomorrow.

DIARY   14th March, 1940
                                                                        Paris

Finland appears to have surrendered completely,[2] and loses one-tenth of her territory and her strategic independence. I go to see Georges Mandel[3] at the Colonial Ministry. I find him seated at a desk on which the papers are piled as if they had just been spilled out of a suitcase. He asks me about the effect of the Finnish collapse upon British opinion. I say that I cannot tell from the newspapers and must wait till I get

[1] In his diary that night, H.N. added: 'The mountains hang like black curtains against the stars. I look at myself in the mirror. An old buffer. Yet I made a speech tonight which made people stand up and shout.' After the war he was made an Honorary Doctor of the University of Grenoble.

[2] On 12th March the Russo-Finnish war ended with Finland's acceptance of Russia's harsh terms of peace.

[3] The extremely able French Minister for the Colonies.

back to the Lobbies. He says the effect on France will be tremendous. 'You see,' he says, 'our Governments decided on war as the only alternative to admitting German domination. Yet when one decides on war one also decides to sacrifice many lives, to run many risks and to endure many defeats. We are at present trying to conduct a war of appeasement, which means that Hitler may win.' He asks me what they think of the French Government in England.[1] He is also very anxious to know about our coming men. What of Eden? Is he a strong man? What about Herbert Morrison? '*Il nous faut des hommes!*' he says.

Dine with Bob Boothby at Maxim's. He has been in Switzerland, and has in fact set foot in Germany, having placed one foot over the frontier at Basel. He had met many Germans and many Swiss. He says that the Swiss think that we *can* win but that we won't. Unless we seize Narvik and Baku[2] we shall not win. Never has Hitler had such a hold upon his own people. His conduct since the war has been admirable, his speeches moderate and his general drive superb. But the Germans are very frightened that we may bomb the Ruhr, and they are also afraid that they may run out of petrol and iron-ore. They think it will take them years to get the Russian machine working. The atrocities in Poland are unbelievable. They are killing all the young men, driving the old into the fields and sterilising the women. A German Colonel who had been dining with Bob's Swiss friend broke down in the middle of dinner and cried. His nerves had been shattered by what he had seen in Poland.

DIARY   *16th March, 1940*
                                                                 Paris

Try to write my *Spectator* article, but I am interrupted all the time. Mario Pansa[3] comes. He says that Sumner Welles[4] was horrified by his reception in Berlin. Their confidence in their coming victory was

---

[1] The defeat of Finland brought about the fall of Daladier's Government on 21st March. He was succeeded as Prime Minister by Paul Reynaud, but retained his office as Minister of Defence.

[2] Narvik in northern Norway, in order to interrupt supplies of Swedish iron-ore to Germany; and Baku on the Caspian, to deprive Russia and Germany of oil.

[3] One of H.N.'s oldest Italian friends. He was then Counsellor at the Italian Embassy in Brussels.

[4] The American Under-Secretary of State, who arrived in Berlin on 1st March on a mission from President Roosevelt, to see if the war could be stopped before the slaughter began.

unbounded and their manner was arrogant and brutal. He also tells me that the German invasion of Holland in November and March was prevented by Mussolini and Roosevelt.[1] The former said that if the Germans did anything so suicidal he would part company; the latter said that it would practically mean war with the United States. The moderates were therefore strengthened in Germany.

Lunch at the British Embassy. Malcolm MacDonald[2] is there, as he is over for a conference with Georges Mandel. Go a short walk with him afterwards. He is none too happy about the way things are going. Louis Gillet[3] comes to see me. He is horrified by the lack of energy and drive in the [French] Cabinet. He says that there are two central points at which this war can be won—Narvik and Baku—and that we are mad to dawdle on, waiting for Hitler to accumulate his advantages one by one. We cannot go on conducting this war in kid gloves.

DIARY   *19th March, 1940*
                                                              London

Have a terrific time dictating accumulated correspondence. John Sparrow looks in. He is about to get a commission and hopes for the Coldstream Guards. Lunch with Ronnie Tree and Dick Law.[4] We try to persuade Dick not to make too violent a speech this afternoon. The House is very crowded. Chamberlain makes a good debating speech, putting the whole blame for the Finnish collapse on the Scandinavian powers,[5] and claiming that we had 'answered' all Finland's demands and had done all we could. Dick Law makes his speech. He says that the P.M.'s arguments are all very fine, but we have seen again and again a Minister stand up 'at that box' and explain the reasons for failure: people who have made so many mistakes should not remain in power. Harold Macmillan also makes a fine attacking speech, pointing out the discrepancy between what we sent to Finland

---

[1] The postponement of the German offensive in November had been due to quite different reasons. The Army was not ready and the weather was very bad. Mussolini had no influence on Hitler's plans at this stage, and was not even told of the projected offensive. Hitler had no intention of attacking France in March, for he was busy planning his campaign against Norway.
[2] Secretary of State for the Colonies, 1938–40.
[3] The elderly and scholarly French Academician.
[4] Conservative M.P. for S.W. Hull, 1931–45.
[5] Norway and Sweden had refused to allow British troops to pass through their territory to the aid of Finland.

and what she actually received. Chamberlain, who had sat through the whole debate, replies vigorously. He is a remarkable man: there is no doubt about that. There is also no doubt that he wants to win the war. He gave the impression of great obstinacy and has enhanced his reputation. One thing that strikes drama is that he announces that at that very moment we are attacking the German air-bases at Sylt.

DIARY   25th March, 1940

After luncheon I walk to Sissinghurst Place and drive with Lindsay and Bunny Drummond to Fisher's Gate.[1] We call in at Withyham and visit the Sackville Chapel. I choose the little plot of ground where my urn will repose.[2] I tell Bunny where it is. I feel in a strange way rather invigorated by this grim expedition. Then on to Buck's.[3] Billy is there, and Harry and Kitty,[4] and a young Coldstreamer of the name of Christopher Soames. Buck does not think that Chamberlain will get the Opposition leaders to join his Cabinet. He feels with me that this would be a mistake. On the one hand, they are needed to keep their own left wing in order, and on the other, we must keep up our sleeves some alternative Coalition for the moment when real disaster comes. It would be just like Chamberlain with his total lack of vision to get them in now when it is not really necessary. We are gay for once and happy, and it cheers me up.

DIARY   27th March, 1940

For once things seem to be going well, which always preludes a major disaster. Yet three things are now apparent. (1) The Germans dare not attack the Maginot Line. (2) We have won the war at sea. (3) In the air our pilots are superior to the German pilots. If only we can convey the possibility of our victory to the neutrals they will pluck up heart. At present they seem convinced that the Germans must win.

---

[1] Lord De la Warr's house near Withyham, Sussex.
[2] The Sackvilles had been buried in the crypt of Withyham church since the sixteenth century, and V.S-W.'s ashes were placed there in 1962. But H.N. later changed his mind on the grounds that he was not himself a Sackville, and requested that his ashes be placed in the churchyard at Sissinghurst.
[3] Lord De la Warr, who was then President of the Board of Education.
[4] Lord De la Warr's three children.

Vita Sackville-West in her writing room in the tower at Sissinghurst

Sissinghurst Tower and the South Cottage with the moat in the foreground

2nd April, 1940

Dine with Kenneth Clark.[1] Willie Maugham,[2] Mrs Winston Churchill and Leslie Howard[3] are there. We have an agreeable dinner and talk mostly about films. Leslie Howard is doing a big propaganda film and is very keen about it. We discuss the position of those English people who have remained in the United States. The film-stars claim that they have been asked to remain there since they are more useful in Hollywood, but we all regret bitterly that people like Aldous Huxley, Auden and Isherwood should have absented themselves. They want me to write a *Spectator* article attacking them. That is all very well but it would lose me the friendship of three people whom I much admire. I come back with Leslie Howard and he continues to talk excitedly about his new film. He seems to enter into such things with the zest of a schoolboy, and that is part of his charm.

3rd April, 1940

A Group dinner at the Carlton. Anthony Eden is there. He begins talking about the Dominions and is rather worried about the situation in Australia. There is a strong isolationist group there and he is frightened about what may happen at their Elections. He said that Sumner Welles returned from Germany much impressed by their power and confidence, and that Mussolini was also convinced by Hitler at the Brenner meeting[4] that Germany is certain to win. On the other hand, all the news the Cabinet receives from Germany goes to show that they are in a state of anxious depression and that the war of inaction is telling on their nerves more than on ours. He thinks that Hitler is almost certain to attack in the West owing to this loss of morale among the German people. He says that it will be his supreme throw and that he will choose his weather carefully.

At that stage of the dinner we get over the telephone the final text of the Government reshuffle. Kingsley Wood has become Lord President. He is succeeded at the Air Ministry by Sam Hoare. Hudson is made Minister of Shipping, and Churchill is made Chairman of the Committee for coordinating the fighting services. Buck De la Warr becomes First Commissioner of Works and Ramsbotham Minister of

[1] Then Director of the Film Division of the Ministry of Information.
[2] Somerset Maugham, the novelist, then aged 66.
The actor and film-star. He was killed in 1943 when his aircraft was shot down.
[4] On 18th March. At this meeting Mussolini confirmed his intention to enter the war on Hitler's side when the right moment came.

Education. Ned Grigg goes to the War Office. Harold Macmillan remarks, 'Tweedledum, having been informed by his doctor that his health cannot stand the strain of his present office, is succeeded by Tweedledee, who has also been informed by his doctor that his present duties impose too great a strain upon his health.' Anthony Eden is very discreet about it all, but he much relishes our criticism of Sam Hoare's appointment. I am glad myself, since the changes are so bad that they will render inevitable a complete reconstruction within a certain period. Anthony feels that the whole thing is due to Chamberlain's refusal to part with Sam Hoare. The general opinion is that the Chamberlain Cabinet will not now last for more than three months.

DIARY   5th April, 1940

I lunch at the Beefsteak. Harold Macmillan tells us Peter Fleming's[1] *mot* about the Cabinet reshuffle: 'I do not understand why they bothered to exchange Ministries; surely it would have been simpler to exchange names?'

It is curious to think back upon my moods since 3rd September. I recognise the first stage of acute depression, due, I suppose, to the fear of an immediate Blitzkrieg and to hatred of war. Then came the second stage, trying to sort my ideas in order. And now there comes a third stage when I feel that we *can* win the war but that we may fail to do so. My attitude to the future is one of acute interest rather than acute dismay. But my anger has increased. I want to win. My God! I am prepared to sacrifice my whole happiness for victory. I feel resolute and well. I shall have my chance. I feel that in my odd, fiddling, marginal way I am helping. The *Spectator* articles have their effect. I feel combatant.

DIARY   8th April, 1940

Come up in the early train with Walter Elliot,[2] Rob Bernays, Raymond Mortimer and Paul Hyslop,[3] all of whom have been staying with Victor Cazalet. We do not, for once, discuss politics, but we do discuss why I should hate T. E. Lawrence so much. After all, he was a friend of mine and our personal relations were never strained. I say that I feel for him that distaste that I feel for Sir James Barrie and John Galsworthy, namely that he acquired a legend without deserving it: he

[1] The author and traveller. Later in April he was to take part in the British campaign in Norway.
[2] Minister of Health, 1938–40.   [3] The architect.

was fundamentally fraudulent. Walter Elliot asks if I really think that the Arab campaign was fraudulent. I say No, but everything that came after. The *Pillars of Wisdom* and that inane translation of Homer. He says that I must be jealous of a man of action who achieved more than I did and a man of letters who attempted more than I did. That may be true. But I am not a jealous person and I feel that there must be some other explanation of my antipathy.

We have decided to lay mines in Norwegian territorial waters.[1] This will create a rage. We did it at dawn today and already two German ships have been sunk.

Two tremendous months followed. April was the month of the Norwegian campaign: May the month of Hitler's attack in the West. As the consequence of the first campaign, and almost coincident with the opening of the second, Neville Chamberlain fell and Winston Churchill became Prime Minister. Harold Nicolson was a spectator of these great events from the middle distance. As a prominent back-bench critic of the Government, he was well-placed to record the rumours and shifting attitudes of the Lobbies, but his information about the course of military operations was inevitably second- or third-hand, and even the succession of Churchill came to him as a surprise. It is not Churchill or Halifax who is mentioned most frequently in the diary as the future leader of the Coalition Government, but, strangely, Lloyd George. The fact that many of Harold Nicolson's closest friends were now members of the Government paradoxically dried up his sources of information. Political discretion and military security dropped a curtain between him and them. Nevertheless, the diary is of importance for its very errors of fact and judgement. Events which now appear to us so clear emerge as dim shapes looming through a fog. The diary for the critical four days 7th–10th May is reproduced unabbreviated, except for one short passage on 9th May dealing with the personal troubles of a non-political friend.

Hitler's motives for invading Denmark and Norway were three. He had information, not unfounded, that the Allies were preparing to occupy Norway in order to deny Germany the Swedish ore shipped through Narvik. Secondly, he needed bases on the west coast of Scandinavia in

---

[1] The mining of Norwegian waters in order to impede the flow of Swedish iron-ore to Germany through Narvik had been suggested by Churchill as early as 29th September. The French and British Cabinets had postponed a decision until now, for fear of German retaliation against Norway and the effect upon neutral and world opinion.

order to pursue his naval and air offensive against Britain. Thirdly, he wished to protect the Baltic coast of Germany from any Allied outflanking movement through Norway and Sweden. He had begun to plan the invasion early in December simultaneously with the offensive in the West. On 2nd April he decided that the Scandinavian campaign should precede the attack on France by a month. It was brilliantly successful. Denmark was overrun in a few hours, Copenhagen being occupied by a single German battalion in face of only token resistance. The Norwegian ports of Narvik, Trondheim and Bergen were seized on 9th April from the sea, and Oslo was captured by a force landed from the air on the 10th. While the traitor Quisling set up a pro-Nazi Government in Oslo, King Haakon fled with his Cabinet to the northern mountains, rallied the remnants of the Norwegian Army and appealed for Allied help.

Britain and France responded immediately by two successful naval actions on 10th and 13th April on the approaches to Narvik, and by despatching three small military forces to Namsos, Andalsnes (north and south of Trondheim) and Harstad outside the Narvik fjord. All these military operations failed. The advance on Narvik, the main objective, was held up by deep snow and the reluctance of the British military commander to take advantage of the naval victory to force a landing at the port itself. At Trondheim, the proposal for a direct assault on the town was abandoned on naval advice, and the two military pincers from Namsos and Andalsnes were each turned back by energetic German counter-attacks. The British command of the sea-approaches was outweighed by German superiority in the air and on land. The Allied forces on each side of Trondheim were slowly beaten back to their starting points without ever having linked up, and were evacuated to Britain on 2nd and 3rd May. In this first clash of the war between the German and Allied Armies, the Allies were routed.

The political consequences in Britain were serious. The accumulated discontent with Chamberlain's leadership exploded in the House of Commons debates on 7th and 8th May. On the 10th, Hitler opened his offensive in the West, but Chamberlain's fate had already been decided. Churchill had carried great responsibility for the Norwegian disaster, and, as he wrote in his Memoirs, 'it was a marvel that I survived'. He came to power as the direct consequence of one of the greatest failures of his career.

DIARY   *9th April, 1940*

Miss Niggeman[1] arrives to say that there are posters up to the effect that Germany has invaded Denmark and Norway. The 1 pm. wireless indicates that Oslo, Bergen and Narvik have been captured.

Lunch at the Beefsteak. Walter Elliot there and Ned Grigg.[2] The news about Scandinavia is still very vague, but Ned Grigg assures me that there is no chance of Narvik having been occupied.[3] It must be a misreading for Larvik.[4] I go down to the House. The Prime Minister. who is looking very haggard, makes a statement. It is rather well done and he admits quite frankly that the Fleet is out and that we do not know exactly what is happening. He discredits the rumour that Narvik has been occupied. I go round to see Mummy[5] on her eightieth birthday.

The House is extremely calm and the general line is that Hitler has made a terrible mistake. I feel myself that I wish that we could sometimes commit mistakes of such magnitude.

DIARY   *10th April, 1940*

The news is bad. It seems that the Germans really have occupied Narvik, have completely overrun Denmark and have occupied Oslo and Trondheim. Look in at the House for a minute. See Jim Thomas.[6] He says that Winston and Anthony Eden were very happy at 7 o'clock last night, but that the Foreign Office are in the depths of gloom. The latter are terrified that the Norwegian Government are going to make an immediate peace. Meanwhile a vague running battle is now passing up and down the Norwegian coast, and we have already lost two destroyers while the Germans have lost two cruisers.[7] The whole issue is still uncertain and vague.

---

[1] H.N.'s secretary from 1938 till 1965.
[2] Financial Secretary to the War Office since 3rd April.
[3] Narvik was seized at 8 a.m. that morning by ten German destroyers and two battalions.
[4] In southern Norway, at the entrance to Oslo Fjord.
[5] Lady Carnock.
[6] Conservative M.P. for Hereford since 1931, and Parliamentary Private Secretary to Anthony Eden.
[7] This was true: the German cruisers *Hipper* and *Scharnhorst* had been damaged, and the *Koenigsberg* and *Karlsruhe* sunk. The British losses so far were the destroyers *Glowworm* and *Gurkha*.

DIARY   *11th April, 1940*

This great battle by air, sea and land shows me what a child I am about strategic matters. To me it would have seemed an almost impossible operation of war for the Germans to maintain detachments in Norwegian ports without having complete command of the sea. I should imagine that the German General Staff were also of that opinion and had been overruled by Hitler. Thus if he succeeds, he will be thought the greatest military genius since Napoleon, but if he fails, his prestige will be tremendously damaged. Stockholm reports that we are bombarding the German ships in Oslo and have reoccupied Narvik and Bergen.[1]

To the House. It is packed. Winston comes in. He is not looking well and sits there hunched as usual with his papers in his hand. When he rises to speak it is obvious that he is very tired. He starts off by giving an imitation of himself making a speech, and he indulges in vague oratory coupled with tired gibes. I have seldom seen him to less advantage. The majority of the House were expecting tales of victory and triumph, and when he tells them that the news of our reoccupation of Bergen, Trondheim and Oslo is untrue, a cold wave of disappointment passes through the House. He hesitates, gets his notes in the wrong order, puts on the wrong pair of spectacles, fumbles for the right pair, keeps on saying 'Sweden' when he means 'Denmark', and one way and another makes a lamentable performance. He gives no real explanation of how the Germans managed to slip through to Narvik. We have sunk some eight German transports and two cruisers have been damaged. He claims that this has 'crippled' the German Navy. He says that the Faroe Islands have been seized and that Iceland will be protected. His references to the Norwegian Army and Navy are vague in the extreme. One has the impression that he is playing for time and expects that at any moment some dramatic news will be brought to him. It is a feeble, tired speech and it leaves the House in a mood of grave anxiety.

DIARY   *12th April, 1940*

I go up to Leicester. Have some sandwiches with Bertie,[2] and then to the Corn Exchange where I make a speech. It is packed and the

---

[1] This false report was put out deliberately by the Germans in order to create further dismay among the Allies when it proved untrue.

[2] W. B. Jarvis, Chairman of the West Leicester Conservative Association.

audience are receptive. They seem to be far less depressed than in London. It may be that they do not understand what has happened. I feel (1) that Hitler may now convince his people and the neutrals that sea-power is of little real use in narrow seas. This means that the Italians will not care a hoot about us, and already their newspapers are working up an anti-British feeling. Thus Hitler's internal and external prestige will be enormously enhanced and we shall gain nothing. (2) The whisper will spread here that if the Germans can invade Norway with impunity, they may also be able to invade Scotland. Confidence in the Navy will be shaken. Great depression may set in.

DIARY   *14th April, 1940*

I arrive late for breakfast, and ask Mrs Staples[1] for the news. She says, 'We have sunk seven German destroyers at Narvik.' I can scarcely believe it. Then the newspapers come. It is true. At noon yesterday the *Warspite* and a flotilla, including the *Cossack*, entered Narvik fjord. They silenced the shore-guns and sank four destroyers. Three others bolted up a fjord behind Narvik town but were pursued and sunk. Our own ships suffered little.[2]

The news in the evening is dramatic. Our hold upon Narvik fjord now seems to be complete and I suppose that troops will be landed at any minute. The Norwegians appear to have recovered from the initial blow and to be mobilising as far as is possible for them now that all their control centres have been occupied. And above all we are laying mines outside German ports in the Baltic. I have a feeling that Hitler (being totally ignorant of sea-warfare) has made a grave mess of this Scandinavian bluster. He relied too confidently, it would seem at present, upon his mastery of the air. His naval losses have been most damaging to his prestige. But he is still landing troops at Oslo. I feel that the land-slide has begun and that we may at any moment be faced by an attack on Holland and Belgium, coupled with an Italian occupation of the Balearics and Corsica.

I am fascinated by this crucial stage, since it really boils down to the incessant problem whether mastery of the sea is more important than mastery of the air. The early stages of the Scandinavian campaign seem to have shown that the air was the more important. The later stages have suggested that sea-power in the end prevails. It is too early

[1] The Nicolsons' cook from 1925 to 1967.
[2] In fact eight enemy destroyers were sunk without the loss of a single British ship.

to decide which of these two theories is correct. But it may prove that Narvik is one of the decisive battles of history.

DIARY   *16th April, 1940*

There is a general feeling of apprehension regarding Italy's intentions. It is feared that at any moment she may seize the Adriatic seaboard while the Germans advance into Yugoslavia from the north. There will be a great feeling in this country that the seizure of Yugoslavia does not concern us and that whatever we do we must keep out of war with Italy. That is a depressing thought.

DIARY   *17th April, 1940*

I find people like Stephen King-Hall and Bob Boothby terribly gloomy. In fact, King-Hall thinks that we may lose the war. The reaction after our first hopes of the Norwegian expedition is bitter, and the fear that Italy, Germany and Russia are about to make a con-certed pounce on the Balkans fills us with dismay. As I have always been expecting Italy to come in, I am less depressed. There is a rumour that the *Scharnhorst* is aground in a damaged condition.[1] If this is true, then Hitler's Norwegian adventure has cost him about half his fleet. But he does not care a hoot about that. We are landing, I gather, at Namsos. But there is no concerted plan, the Norwegian generals are all defeatist and I fear we shall not make a good show. The Germans have already cut Norway in half by occupying the railway from Trondheim to the Swedish border.

I go on to the Eden Group dinner at the Carlton where they are entertaining Duff Cooper.[2] His account of the propaganda-conscious-ness of the United States is terrifying. He thinks the Germans have really persuaded them that black is white. It is of course the mothers of America who dictate the tone, which is one of smug escapism.

DIARY   *23rd April, 1940*

I attend the Watching Committee[3] in Arlington Street. Lord Salisbury tells us that he had been to see Winston Churchill and had asked him

[1] It was not true then, but on 8th June the *Scharnhorst* was so severely damaged by British torpedoes that she was out of action for several months.

[2] Duff Cooper had recently completed a lecture-tour of the United States. In *Old Men Forget* (1953) he summed up his impressions of the tour as follows: 'It was to be hoped that the British would win, but it was to be hoped still more that no American boy's life would be thrown away fighting for the British Empire.'

[3] A new group of Peers and members of the House of Commons, including the majority of the Eden Group, meeting under the chairmanship of Lord Salisbury.

quite frankly whether he believed he could carry on concurrently the job of First Lord and Co-ordinator of Defence. Winston told him that he is feeling in perfect health, that he would die if the Admiralty were taken away from him, and that the Press had much exaggerated his role as Co-ordinator of Defence, which was little more than Chairman of a Committee of the fighting services. He had no right to initiate suggestions or make decisions. He did hint, however, that he would rather welcome it if we could induce the Prime Minister to appoint a Deputy First Lord of Cabinet rank to take the routine business off his shoulders. Salisbury gave him the names of our Committee and he purred like a pleased cat.

We then discuss the question of bombing German towns. The French have always asked us not to do this since they are frightened of reprisals and the natural timidity of the Government rather welcomes this excuse. On the other hand, the impression is being increasingly conveyed that although if one shepherd is killed in the Shetlands we raid Sylt, yet we allow the whole civil population of Norway to be decimated without taking any action against Germany. We don't seem to mind endangering the lives of Norwegians and Danes by bombing Stavanger or Aalborg, but we allow the German factories in the Ruhr to continue at full pressure.

DIARY   *29th April, 1940*

The Watching Committee have an interview with Halifax. We have three main themes. (1) Lack of initiative, which Halifax counters by saying that we are necessarily on the defensive. (2) Why do we not bomb German towns? Halifax, who seems tired and distressed, does not really reply to our arguments. He merely says that the Government must abide by the advice of the service departments. (3) Our lack of effort as illustrated by the Budget, and our lack of courage against such neutrals as Italy and Portugal who are not being really neutral. Halifax says he has sent a stinker to Salazar.[1] But it is not a successful interview as Halifax is tired and grim.

Spears told me that the French local mission had told him that our Norway expeditionary force was in a state of indescribable chaos, and that Brigadier Morgan[2] and two battalions had been lost somewhere in the rocks. We may have to evacuate. That will be a shock to public

[1] Dr Antonio Salazar, Prime Minister of Portugal since 1932.
[2] Brigadier Morgan was in command of the southern pincer at Andalsnes. He had already lost some 700 men, and was retreating to his base.

opinion. I find that people at last realise that we are up against a very rapid enemy and one which possesses equipment more modern than our own. I always expected this and am not perturbed. But the others are glum, glum, glum.

DIARY   *30th April, 1940*

Roger Keyes accosts me in the Lobby. He is in despair. He says that if only we had struck quickly with the Navy all would have been well.[1] He says that the Admiralty Board refused to take naval risks since they were frightened by the possible attitude of Italy. He says that we have been outmanœuvred and beaten because we were too afraid. He says that Winston's drive and initiative have been undermined by the legend of his recklessness. Today he cannot dare to do the things he could have dared in 1915.

The news begins to creep through that the Germans have occupied Stören.[2] That means that we are done. I talk to Arnold Wilson who is heroic. I talk to Harold Macmillan who has heard that we shall begin to evacuate Norway this evening. I go to Arlington Street for the Watching Committee and find a glum crowd. The general impression is that we may lose the war. The tanks position is appalling and we hear facts about that.[3] We part in gloom. Black Week in the Boer War can hardly have been more depressing. They think that this will mean the fall of Chamberlain and Lloyd George as Prime Minister. The Whips are putting it about that it is all the fault of Winston who has made another forlorn failure. That is hell. I spoke to some Labour members tonight. They said that we should only win this war under a Labour Government. I think they are right.

DIARY   *1st May, 1940*

I have a talk with Buck De la Warr and Stephen King-Hall in the former's room at the House of Lords. Buck seems to think that if Norway is lost, the P.M. will have to resign. I say that what will happen is that Reynaud will resign and the P.M. will stay put. The tapers and tadpoles are putting it around that the whole Norwegian

[1] Admiral Sir Roger Keyes M.P. had sought command of the naval assault on Trondheim, but the operation was cancelled on 18th April.

[2] A railway junction 30 miles south of Trondheim.

[3] The British Expeditionary Force in France had only one Army Tank Brigade, comprising 17 light tanks and 100 infantry tanks. Only 23 of the latter carried even the 2-pounder gun: the rest machine-guns only. See Churchill, *The Gathering Storm*, p. 441.

episode is due to Winston. There is a theory going round that Lloyd George may head a Coalition Cabinet. What worries people is that everybody asks, 'But whom could you put in Chamberlain's place?'

DIARY   *3rd May, 1940*

People are saying that Lloyd George should come in. They are saying that Margesson destroyed the Conservative Party since he put obedience above ability. We are evacuating Namsos as well [as Andalsnes]. We are in a bad way. We shall win!

DIARY   *4th May, 1940*

I find that there is a grave suspicion of the Prime Minister. His speech about the Norwegian expedition has created disquiet. The House knows very well that it was a major defeat. But the P.M. said that 'the balance of advantage rested with us' and that 'Germany has not attained her objective'. They know that this is simply not true. If Chamberlain believed it himself, then he was stupid. If he did not believe it, then he was trying to deceive. In either case he loses confidence. People are so distressed by the whole thing that they are talking of Lloyd George as a possible P.M. Eden is out of it. Churchill is undermined by the Conservative caucus. Halifax is believed (and with justice) to be a tired man. We always say that our advantage over the German leadership principle is that we can always find another leader. Now we cannot.

DIARY   *5th May, 1940*

I read Dylan Thomas' *Portrait of the Artist as a Young Dog*.[1] I am slightly disgusted by all the urine and copulation which occurs. I have a feeling that these people do not believe that they can write powerfully unless they drag in the latrines. And yet it is quite clear that this young Thomas is a writer of great merit.

The lovely day sinks to sunset among the flowering trees. The Italian news is bad. It seems incredible to us that Italy should really come in. If she does, it must mean that Mussolini is convinced of our early defeat. That is what fills me with such depression. Not Italy as an enemy, but Italy convinced as an intelligent and most admirably informed nation that Germany is going to win this war.

[1] Just published. Dylan Thomas was then 26.

DIARY   *7th May, 1940*

Finish my review[1] and then go round for an E.N.S.A.[2] meeting. It is evident from the first reports that we have received that the soldiers prefer lectures having some relation to the war to lectures devoted to perfectly irrelevant subjects such as 'Climbing the Himalayas'.

Lunch with Cyril Joad. He is rather pathetic. He minds dreadfully being out of things, and yet as a pacifist and one of the leaders of the Pleace Pledge Union, he can scarcely eat his words. But he has written to the Ministry of Information offering his services. I think I cheered him up, since he has no feeling of false pride in admitting to me that he cannot stand pacifism any longer.

Down to the House for the Norwegian debate. I have a talk with Clem Davies[3] about possible alternative Cabinets. He makes the point that we all forget the constitutional position, which is extremely difficult. If there is not to be a Coalition, the King would have to send for Attlee and it would be extremely difficult for him to send for Lloyd George.

The House is crowded, and when Chamberlain comes in, he is greeted with shouts of 'Missed the bus!'[4] He makes a very feeble speech and is only applauded by the Yes-men. He makes some reference to the complacency of the country, at which the whole House cheers vociferously and ironically, inducing him to make a little, rather feminine, gesture of irritation. Attlee makes a feeble speech and Archie Sinclair a good one. When Archie sits down, many people stand up and the Speaker calls on Page Croft.[5] There is a loud moan from the Labour Party at this, and they practically rise in a body and leave the House. He is followed by Wedgwood[6] who makes a speech which contains everything that he ought not to have said. He gives the impression of being a little off his head. At one moment he suggests that the British Navy have gone to Alexandria since they are frightened of being bombed.

A few minutes afterwards Roger Keyes comes in, dressed in full uniform with six rows of medals. I scribble him a note telling him

[1] H.N. was still writing a weekly book-review for the *Daily Telegraph*.
[2] A War Office Committee dealing with education in the Forces.
[3] Clement Davies, Liberal M.P. for Montgomeryshire, and leader of the Liberal Party, 1945–56.
[4] In a speech on 4th April, referring to the lack of offensive operations by Hitler, Chamberlain said, 'One thing is certain: he missed the bus.'
[5] Conservative M.P. for Bournemouth, 1918–40.
[6] J. C. Wedgwood, Labour M.P. for Newcastle-under-Lyme, 1906–42.

what Wedgwood has just said, and he immediately rises and goes to the Speaker's chair. When Wedgwood sits down, Keyes gets up and begins his speech by referring to Wedgwood's remark and calling it a damned insult. The Speaker does not call him to order for his un-parliamentary language, and the whole House roars with laughter, especially Lloyd George who rocks backwards and forwards in boyish delight with his mouth wide open. Keyes then returns to his manu-script and makes an absolutely devastating attack upon the naval conduct of the Narvik episode and the Naval General Staff. The House listens in breathless silence when he tells us how the Naval General Staff had assured him that a naval action at Trondheim was easy but unnecessary owing to the success of the military. There is a great gasp of astonishment. It is by far the most dramatic speech I have ever heard, and when Keyes sits down there is thunderous applause.

Thereafter the weakness of the Margesson system is displayed by the fact that none of the Yes-men are of any value whatsoever, whereas all the more able Conservatives have been driven into the ranks of the rebels. A further terrific attack is delivered by Amery, who ends up by quoting from Cromwell, 'In the name of God, go!'

I go out into the Lobby where I met Camrose[1] and take him off for a drink. Although a firm supporter of Chamberlain, I can see that he has been much shaken and he admits that if we have to leave Narvik, Chamberlain will fall. The general impression left by the debate is that we are unprepared to meet the appalling attack which we know is about to be delivered against us. The atmosphere is something more than anxiety: it is one of actual fear, but it is a very resolute fear and not hysteria or cowardice in the least. In fact I have seldom admired the spirit of the House so much as I did today.

I have some people to dine in the Strangers' Dining-room, namely Sibyl Colefax, Baffy Dugdale, Violet Bonham Carter and Hugh Walpole. Oliver Stanley winds up with an able but ineffective speech. There is no doubt that the Government is very rocky and anything may happen tomorrow.

DIARY   *8th May, 1940*

Watching Committee at 21 Arlington Street.[2] Lord Salisbury begins by criticising the Prime Minister's attempt to bolster up his Cabinet

[1] The first Lord Camrose, proprietor and Editor-in-Chief of the *Daily Telegraph*.
[2] Lord Salisbury's house.

by announcing that extra powers have been given to Churchill.[1] It is impossible for the head of one Service department to arbitrate in disputes affecting two other departments, and in any case no human being could stand running the Admiralty and a Defence job such as this. He feels that what we have to do is to restore shaken confidence both at home and abroad, and that no ordinary reshuffle will do this. Lloyd[2] says that he knows that Labour will not enter any Government which contains Chamberlain, Simon and Hoare. The present agitation is not due solely to Norway, but to very widespread anxiety about supply and labour conditions. It was really no alternative to create a strong War Cabinet under Chamberlain, since the efficacy of the Government depended upon the character of the Prime Minister and the Prime Minister's character had not proved sufficient.

Nigel comes back from France.[3] He had been over to the Base Camp with a draft and enjoyed himself immensely. He lunches with me at the Travellers and walks down with me to the House.

The second day's debate is opened by Herbert Morrison who makes a very damaging attack. Chamberlain intervenes at the end to say that the situation is grave and that the attack which Morrison has made upon the Government 'and upon me in particular' makes it graver still. This really horrifies the House, since it shows that he always takes the personal point of view. He goes on to say that he accepts the challenge of a Division,[4] since it will show who is with him and who is against him. 'I have,' he says with a leer of triumph, 'friends in this House.'

Until that moment the House had not really foreseen that the Opposition were to press for a Division. I think that it was a mistake that they should do so, since it will create a bad impression in the country and leave such bitterness behind. Lord Salisbury had begged us this morning not to vote against the Government if a Division came, but we find on reaching the House that so many unexpected people

[1] Since 1st May, Churchill had been made responsible for giving 'guidance and directions to the Chiefs of Staff Committee' in addition to acting as the Prime Minister's deputy chairman on the Military Coordination Committee. 'I was to have immense responsibilities,' he later wrote, 'without effective power in my own hands to discharge them.'

[2] Lord Lloyd, formerly High Commissioner for Egypt and the Sudan, and soon to be appointed Secretary of State for the Colonies.

[3] He was now a 2nd Lieutenant in the Grenadier Guards.

[4] The Division was technically on the Motion for the Adjournment, but in fact it became a vote of censure on the Government's conduct of the war.

such as the Service Members and Lady Astor are determined to vote against the Government that we have no alternative. We hope to get as many as thirty people to join us.

At 6 we go upstairs to a Committee Room and join with Clem Davies' Committee in discussing action. We agree that we must vote against the Government. At 7 Dunglass[1] comes to Paul Evans and Gunston,[2] indicating to them that if we will agree to vote for the Government, the Prime Minister will see us tomorrow and that we will find him ready to meet our demands. When asked what that means, he indicates (although without committing the Prime Minister) that in order to save himself, Chamberlain is prepared to sacrifice Hoare and Simon. We say things have gone too far. Meanwhile in the debate both Duff Cooper and Lloyd George have made devastating speeches.

I dine with Rob Hudson and Sir Patrick Hannon, and go in to hear Alexander's winding-up speech. He is followed by Winston. He has an almost impossible task. On the one hand he has to defend the Services; on the other, he has to be loyal to the Prime Minister. One felt that it would be impossible to do this after the debate without losing some of his own prestige, but he manages with extraordinary force of personality to do both these things with absolute loyalty and apparent sincerity, while demonstrating by his brilliance that he really has nothing to do with this confused and timid gang.

Up to the last moment the House had behaved with moderation, and one had the sense that there really was a united will to win the war. During the last twenty minutes, however, passions rose, and when the Division came there was great tensity in the air. Some 44 of us, including many of the young Service Members, vote against the Government and some 30 abstain.[3] This leaves the Government with a majority of only 81 instead of a possible 213, and the figures are greeted with a terrific demonstration during which Joss Wedgwood starts singing *Rule Britannia*, which is drowned in shouts of 'Go, go, go, go!' Margesson signals to his henchmen to rise and cheer the Prime Minister as he leaves, and he walks out looking pale and angry.

[1] Later Sir Alec Douglas-Home. He had been Parliamentary Private Secretary to Chamberlain since 1937.

[2] Sir Derrick Gunston, Conservative M.P. for Thornbury since 1924, P.P.S. to Chamberlain, 1931–36, and since earlier in 1940, P.P.S. to Sir Edward Grigg.

[3] The division-lists showed that 41 supporters of the Government voted in the Opposition lobby, and about 60 Conservatives abstained. See A. J. P. Taylor, *English History 1914–1945* (Oxford, 1965), p. 473, note 1.

I go round to Ronnie Tree's house where there are Buck De la Warr and Rob Hudson. They both agree that the Prime Minister can scarcely survive.

DIARY   *9th May, 1940*

At 9.30 in the morning we have a meeting of the Watching Committee. Lord Salisbury is very moderate and distressed. We give him our impressions and Amery makes it quite clear that the Prime Minister cannot really survive for more than a week or two. The sooner he goes the better. We therefore agree to the following formula:

1. That a Coalition Government is essential.
2. That Labour will not enter such a Coalition if Chamberlain, Hoare and Simon remain; and that therefore
3. They must go.

There is some suggestion that in order to mitigate this blow, Chamberlain should be asked as a patriotic duty to become Chancellor of the Exchequer. Salisbury agrees to convey all this immediately to Lord Halifax.

Down to the House, which meets at 11. Clem Davies has put down a motion regretting the Whitsun Recess, but it is not well supported and he withdraws it. It is all rather an anti-climax after yesterday. We have a National Labour meeting at noon. Even Elton agrees that the Prime Minister must go, but Lord Amulree and Sir Ernest Bennett are in a minority in thinking that Chamberlain is always right and must be supported whatever he decides. We pass no resolution at all.

I walk across to the Club with Stephen King-Hall and we meet Tom Martin.[1] He tells us that the Whips are already putting it about that the whole business was a snap vote cunningly engineered by Duff Cooper and Amery, and that all good Party men must rally round the Prime Minister. At the Travellers I meet Tommy Lascelles,[2] to whom I impart all the information I have and who tells me that, contrary to Press rumour, Chamberlain has not asked to see the King.[3]

Lunch at the Beefsteak, and find that all are unanimous in feeling

[1] Political Correspondent of the *Daily Telegraph.*
[2] Sir Alan Lascelles, Assistant Private Secretary to the King, 1935–43.
[3] That afternoon, 9th May, Chamberlain saw Churchill, Halifax and Margesson at Downing Street, and it became evident that Churchill was the only possible choice as Prime Minister of a Coalition Government, since Halifax himself declined the office because he was not a Member of the House of Commons. Late the following afternoon, Chamberlain advised the King to send for Churchill, who agreed to form a Government.

that Chamberlain must go. Admiral Hall[1] tells me that the whole Navy are absolutely insistent upon it and that it is even worse in the Army. Walk down to the House with Barrington-Ward[2] who has come completely round and agrees with me (a) that the Germans may attack at any moment; (b) that we cannot have a prolonged Cabinet crisis; (c) that Chamberlain ought therefore to resign within the next few hours.

We have a meeting of the rebels under Amery's chairmanship in Committee Room 8. Amery says that the Whips are being very active, and that Chamberlain has given vast promises of conciliation to those Tories who were not contented but who voted with the Government. We realise that it would be quite impossible in the state of public and Press opinion for him to make a reshuffle by putting in Yes-men in important places, but we recognise that there is a danger that Margesson will organise an Iron Guard and fight a rearguard action. This will delay matters. We decide therefore that we shall support 'any Prime Minister who enjoys the confidence of the country and is able to form an all-Party Government'. We decide not to publish this for the moment.[3]

Go down to Brighton to see Richard Rumbold[4] who has got into another mess.

DIARY   *10th May, 1940*

It is a beautiful morning, and I reflect how, if it had not been for the war, I should be going off on the boat this morning.[5] I drive to the station,[6] and on the way I see posters, 'Holland and Belgium invaded'. In the train coming up there are two Dutchmen, one of whom was in the Legation when I was in Berlin. He is hurrying back to Holland to fight. He says there is no doubt that they will fight to the last man, but that they are worried about their Quislings.

The news is still rather vague when I get to London, although there is a report that Lyons has been bombed. This looks as if they were about to invade Switzerland. Nigel rings up to tell me that he has been confined to Wellington Barracks, since they fear parachute

[1] Sir Reginald Hall, Director of Naval Intelligence throughout the First World War.
[2] Assistant Editor, later Editor, of *The Times*.
[3] The decision was nevertheless published in the morning newspapers.
[4] The author of *My Father's Son*, etc. He was a very close friend of H.N.
[5] H.N. had been planning another lecture-tour of France for the Ministry of Information, due to start that very day.
[6] At Brighton.

descents and leave has been stopped. I receive a cable from the *Montreal Standard* asking me to describe the scene in the House, and I write 1,500 words which are cabled back.

While I am doing this, a telegram arrives summoning me to a meeting at Lord Salisbury's. I reach it late. There is not much definite information, but it seems that the Germans have landed parachute troops on Dutch aerodromes and have heavily bombed Brussels and several French towns. It seems almost inevitable that Italy will come in, although Kennedy, the American Ambassador, told Lord Salisbury this morning that he had received definite information by telephone from Phillips in Rome that they were not going to do so.[1] I rather distrust this information. The meeting breaks up fairly early, and I go down to the Club with Dick Law.

We are joined by Paul [Emrys] Evans, who, after leaving the meeting, had bumped into Brendan Bracken who had told him that in view of the military crisis, the political crisis had been postponed, and that Hoare was insisting on remaining at the Air Ministry.[2] He telephones this information to Salisbury, who says that we must maintain our point of view, namely that Winston should be made Prime Minister during the course of the day. I am still at the Travellers when the wireless news comes through that the invasion of Holland and Belgium is complete, and that both countries have mobilised and appealed for our assistance. Alec Dunglass comes in and we tell him that our Group will never allow Chamberlain to get away from the reconstruction owing to this invasion. He says that the reconstruction has already been decided upon, but that the actual danger of the moment really makes it impossible for the Government to fall. The situation is really one of *videant Consules*, and that we must have a triumvirate of Chamberlain, Churchill and Halifax to carry us over these first anxious hours. Sam Hoare, for instance, must be at his desk night and day for the next 36 hours, and it would be quite impossible to replace him by another Minister. There is some sense in this, and it is hoped that the Labour and Liberal Oppositions will agree. At that moment the wireless announces a statement on the part of the Labour Party,

[1] Ciano, in his diary for that day, wrote: 'It appears that they [the American, French and British Ambassadors] are expecting our intervention at any moment. I try to calm them down and partially succeed.'

[2] Sir Samuel Hoare's autobiography, *Nine Troubled Years* (1954), includes this sentence: 'Chamberlain's first inclination was to withhold his resignation until the French battle was finished.' But he says nothing about his own inclinations at that moment.

which is really quite helpful, in that they call for national unity and imply that the political controversy is suspended for the moment.

I go to the Beefsteak where I find Barrington-Ward, Ned Grigg and others. Grigg says that the War Office have little more news than what has been on the tape. There is a rumour that we have managed to get the Rotterdam aerodrome and a statement that no information regarding the movements of British or French troops will be issued. There is a general feeling of relief that the thing has now come to a head and that we shall know the worst within ten days. Grigg thinks that the only thing they know for certain is that the German losses in aeroplanes over Belgium and Holland have been terrific, but that French towns including Orleans have been very heavily damaged.

I go back to King's Bench Walk and on the way I see posters saying, 'Brussels bombed, Paris bombed, Lyons bombed, Swiss railways bombed'. We are all most anxious regarding the position of our Army on the Belgian frontier, since we dread it being caught in the open. What makes it worse in a way is that it is a beautiful spring day with the bluebells and primroses in flower everywhere.

Salisbury's Committee are pressing for the House to be called on Sunday or Monday [12th or 13th May] for the purpose of giving whatever Government is established (even if it be a Chamberlain triumvirate) the necessary vote of confidence to carry on.[1]

I go down to Sissinghurst. Met by Vita and Gwen.[2] It is all looking too beautiful to be believed, but a sort of film has obtruded itself between my appreciation of nature and my terror of real life. It is like a tooth-ache. We dine alone together chatting about indifferent things. Just before nine, we turn on the wireless and it begins to buzz as the juice comes through and then we hear the bells.[3] Then the pips sound 9.0, and the announcer begins: 'This is the Home Service. Here is the Right Honourable Neville Chamberlain M.P., who will make a statement.' I am puzzled by this for a moment, and then realise that he has resigned.

He begins by saying that recent events in Parliament and elsewhere have shown that the country wants a Coalition Government. He has since understood that the only obstacle to such a Coalition is himself. Therefore he has tendered his resignation, and Churchill is Prime Minister. For the moment, acting Ministers will carry on. He will

[1] Up to this point H.N. had dictated the day's diary in London. He finished it that night at Sissinghurst on his own typewriter.
[2] Mrs St Aubyn, H.N.'s sister.   [3] The B.B.C.'s identification signal.

agree to serve under Churchill. He ends with a fierce denunciation of the Germans for invading Holland and Belgium. It is a magnificent statement, and all the hatred that I have felt for Chamberlain subsides as if a piece of bread were dropped into a glass of champagne.

Then we have other news thick and fast. The Germans have dropped parachute troops on Dutch and Belgian aerodromes. They have appealed for our help and we are moving onwards. At one moment the Dutch Foreign Minister (who has flown today from Amsterdam) intervenes with a short and admirable discourse. After-wards we hear for a moment Lord Haw Haw telling us that we really started the whole thing. Never have I heard a more dramatic broad-cast. It is like something in a play. The Swiss will mobilise tomorrow morning.

This is the final fight. I go to bed and shall, I hope, sleep. We shall be attacked from the air tonight in all probability. We have already announced that we shall bomb German towns since they have bombed French towns. At Sissinghurst the gas-proof room which had been created in the library and since dismantled is re-established. Bombs dropped in Chilham[1] today.

The new War Cabinet—with Churchill as his own Minister of Defence, Eden at the War Office and Chamberlain as Lord President of the Council—was formed immediately, and the minor appointments followed during the next few days. Harold Nicolson was one of the last to be offered a Government post. Churchill asked him to go as Parliamentary Secretary to the Ministry of Information, of which Duff Cooper had just become Minister. He accepted without hesitation. In such a position he might have been expected to acquire more information than most people about the battle in Northern Europe. But he was still rather remote from the centre. The Ministry was only one of many filters for the news, and it was not, except obliquely, a department of Press censorship. Harold Nicolson was chiefly concerned with questions of morale at home. He broadcast frequently. He was made responsible for coordinating the advice given to the public about the possibility of invasion, and he re-wrote the Government's pamphlet on the subject. Sissinghurst lay close to the probable invasion coast, and he faced in his own life the problems on which he was trying to advise the public as a whole. What he did not pass on was the decision to which he and V. Sackville-West quickly came, that they would commit suicide rather than fall into German hands.

[1] A village near Canterbury, 20 miles from Sissinghurst.

They supplied themselves with lethal pills, referred to in the letters as 'the bare bodkin'.

The German armoured attack through the Ardennes reached the Channel coast on 20th May, cutting off the B.E.F. from the main French armies to the south. The Belgian Army capitulated a week later. The evacuation from Dunkirk began on 27th May and ended on 3rd June. On the 5th the Germans attacked the new French line on the Somme and entered Paris on the 14th. On 17th June the French sued for an armistice. These are the essential dates in a familiar story.

In Harold Nicolson's diary it is presented as daily slices of concentrated meat. He had no time to elaborate the news as he received it, and it was often wrong. The following extracts have therefore been chosen more for the light they throw on his personal reactions at the time than for the narrative of events, and for the same reason I have added to the diary a larger proportion than usual of his correspondence with V. Sackville-West. For them, as for everybody, these six weeks were a test of their courage and of the ties which bound them.

DIARY   *13th May, 1940*

When Chamberlain enters the House, he gets a terrific reception, and when Churchill comes in the applause is less. Winston sits there between Chamberlain and Attlee,[1] and it is odd to see the Labour Ministers sitting on the Government Bench.[2] Winston makes a very short statement, but to the point.[3] Percy Harris replies for the Liberals and makes an absurd anti-climax. 'The Lord President of the Council', he says, referring to Chamberlain, 'has set a great example . . .' at this there are cheers from every quarter of the House '. . . for constant attendance on the front bench.' Everybody laughs a great deal. Then Lloyd George gets up and makes a moving speech telling Winston how fond he is of him. Winston cries slightly and mops his eyes.

Harold Macmillan told me that Brendan Bracken[4] had given him a vivid description of Cabinet-making. He sat up till three in the morning with David Margesson going through lists. Winston was not in the least interested once the major posts had been filled, and kept on

---

[1] Now Lord Privy Seal, and, in effect, Deputy Prime Minister.
[2] Such as Arthur Greenwood, Minister without Portfolio; A. V. Alexander, First Lord of the Admiralty; and Ernest Bevin, Minister of Labour.
[3] This was the 'blood, sweat and tears' speech.
[4] Parliamentary Private Secretary to the Prime Minister. Later Minister of Information.

trying to interrupt them by discussing the nature of war and the changing rules of strategy. Meanwhile they would come back to their list, and Brendan would say, 'Well what about So-and-So?' Margesson would reply, 'Strike him out. He's no good at all.' 'Why then,' Brendan would ask, 'did you appoint him?' 'Oh well', Margesson said, 'he was useful at the time.' Macmillan had asked Brendan what was Winston's mood. 'Profound anxiety,' he replied.

The wireless announces quite gaily in the evening that the Queen of Holland has arrived in London and was met at the station by the King.[1]

DIARY   *17th May, 1940*

I fear that it looks as if the Germans have broken the French line at Mezières and Sedan. This is very serious. These surely are the saddest moments of my life, and I don't know how I could cope with it all were it not for Vita's serene and loving sympathy.

At 12.40 the telephone rings, and Mac[2] in an awed voice says, 'The Prime Minister's Private Secretary'. I lift the receiver and wait without hearing anything. Then after about two minutes' silence, a voice says, 'Mr. Nicolson?' I say, 'Yes'. 'Please hold on. The Prime Minister wishes to speak to you.' Another long pause and then Winston's voice: 'Harold, I think it would be very nice if you joined the Government and helped Duff at the Ministry of Information.' 'There is nothing that I should like better.' 'Well, fall in tomorrow. The list will be out tonight. That all right?' 'Very much all right.' 'O.K.', says Winston, and rings off.

Come up from Sissinghurst. Ring up Duff Cooper who welcomes me warmly.

H.N. TO V.S-W.   *19th May, 1940*
                                Ministry of Information, London University Building

It is funny being back in an office. I feel surrounded by friends here and that makes it all very pleasant indeed. Our War Room is perfectly thrilling. It is kept going night and day, and there are maps with pins and different coloured bits of wool. The chiefs meet in conference twice a day at 10.30 and 5.30, and the Press Conference is at 12.30. I have to attend all these, and in addition I shall be given specific branches of the work to take over. I have a nice sunny little room, and

[1] Queen Wilhelmina had come to England to beg in person for British air support for her Army. Two days later the Dutch capitulated.
[2] Miss Macmillan, the secretary at Sissinghurst.

if bombing starts, I shall sleep here. They say that the shelter under our tower is proof even against a direct hit.

DIARY   *20th May, 1940*

Go round to the Ministry early. We discuss the dreadful problem of wireless while an attack is on. If we remain on the air we definitely assist enemy bombers, but they are frightened that if we go off the air, the Germans will use our wave-length to issue false messages which will much alarm the public. A clever impersonator might imitate Winston's voice sufficiently well and give instructions that all troops are to lay down their arms. Duff will take this problem up in the Cabinet.

The Germans, so far as we can make out, are at Albert[1] and pretty close to our communications. They are massing for further terrific attacks and we cannot hope to get many reserves.

DIARY   *21st May, 1940*

The situation is terribly obscure. It is just like an immense cavalry invasion such as the Russians used to practise in the Napoleonic wars. But it is not yet clear whether these little highly mechanised units are being mopped up or whether the main forces are advancing. Meanwhile, of course, terrific panic is being spread in France. The telephone connections with Paris have been temporarily severed, but some lines are working. The general impression is that the first panic is drawing to a close and that the French are recovering their nerve. Walter Monckton[2] said, 'I was at the Foreign Office this morning and heard someone laugh, quite loud, a sound which I have not heard there for a week.'

V.S–W. TO H.N.   *22nd May, 1940*
                                                               Sissinghurst

How ghastly it all is. How thankful I am to think of your dugout. I dread the possibility of Nigel being sent out to France. But what's the good of going on like this? Supposing Kent is evacuated, and I have to go? To think that we should come to this! And the eventual outcome—victory, or defeat? Anyhow you and I have always seen

[1] Between Cambrai and Amiens. On the previous day the Germans had captured not only Albert, but Amiens and Abbeville as well.
[2] Sir Walter Monckton was then Director-General of the Press Bureau at the Ministry of Information.

the possibility of defeat since the beginning of the war and even before that. Darling ... the dots represent all the things I can't say.

H.N. TO V.S-W.   *22nd May, 1940*
                                              Ministry of Information

Of course we hope to pinch out the German bulge and throw them back from the Channel. They are not there in strength and we have already retaken Arras.[1] I don't know whether the Government have prepared any scheme for evacuation, but you should think it out and begin to prepare something. You will have to get the Buick in a fit state to start with a full petrol-tank. You should put inside it some food for 24 hours, and pack in the back your jewels and my diaries. You will want clothes and anything else very precious, but the rest will have to be left behind. After all, that's what the French did in 1915 and we have got to do it ourselves. I should imagine that the best thing you can do is to make for Devonshire. This all sounds very alarming, but it would be foolish to pretend that the danger is inconceivable.

V.S-W. TO H.N.   *23rd May, 1940*
                                                      Sissinghurst

The only nice thing that comes out of the war is that we now have a guard on top of the tower. In a steel helmet and rifle he looks most picturesque in the moonlight over the parapet. Ozzy[2] is in command of the local squad of Volunteer Defence.[3] They have got 32 from Sissinghurst village. Not bad.

V.S-W. TO H.N.   *24th May, 1940*

Ozzy came here yesterday with the officer in charge of all the searchlights in this district. He wanted to inspect the country from the top of the tower. He was very frank. It is not only parachutes that they are afraid of, but troop-carrying 'planes landing on our fields. If this happens, our tower-guard rushes downstairs, informs Ozzy who telephones, and shock-troops arrive. They have pickets all over the

[1] Arras was not 'retaken', since it had not yet been captured by the Germans. On the 21st there had been a limited counter-attack by British troops west of Arras, which was partially successful in delaying the German advance.
[2] A. O. R. Beale, the tenant-farmer of Sissinghurst Castle farm.
[3] The Local Defence Volunteers, later rechristened the Home Guard, which was formed by Anthony Eden on 14th May.

district. The young officer was obviously longing for German 'planes to choose Sissinghurst or Bettenham to land on. I wasn't so sure that I shared his longing. Nor was Ozzy. 'My wheat . . .,' he remarked ruefully.

DIARY   24th May, 1940

Up to Leicester where there is a huge dinner of the 1936 Club. I get an excellent reception and find that their morale is very good. It is not mere complacency, since I give them a test question to vote on, namely, 'Should the Derby be put off?' They voted some 88 per cent in favour of postponement. I notice the rather dangerous anti-French feeling and the belief that the French Army has lost its morale.

DIARY   25th May, 1940

Go down to the War Office to discuss with Ned Grigg the question of civilian morale in case of invasion. He feels pretty certain that the Germans will attempt to make an attack on London, and he says that the possibility of evacuating the Channel and East Coast towns is now being considered. He indicates on the map the area which they are thinking of evacuating, and although it does not include Sissinghurst, it is only some twelve miles off. This makes me feel rather glum inside.

The Germans occupy Boulogne and Calais.[1] Our communications are almost completely severed, and it is possible that the B.E.F. may be cut off. There is a belief, however, that Weygand[2] will be able to re-establish his own line within two weeks. We may have to ask the French to send some Divisions across here to help us.

H.N. TO V.S-W.   26th May, 1940
                                          4 King's Bench Walk, E.C.4

What a grim interlude in our lives! The Government may decide to evacuate Kent and Sussex of all civilians. If, as I hope, they give orders instead of advice, then those orders will either be 'Go' or 'Stay'. If the former, then you know what to do. If the latter, we are faced with a great predicament. I don't think that even if the Germans occupied Sissinghurst they would harm you, in spite of the horrified

[1] This news was premature. Boulogne was captured on the 25th, but Calais not until the 26th.
[2] General Weygand had succeeded General Gamelin as Commander-in-Chief on 19th May.

dislike which they feel for me. But to be quite sure that you are not put to any humiliation, I think you really ought to have a 'bare bodkin' handy so that you can take your quietus when necessary. I shall have one also. I am not in the least afraid of such sudden and honourable death. What I dread is being tortured and humiliated. But how can we find a bodkin which will give us our quietus quickly and which is easily portable? I shall ask my doctor friends.

My dearest, I felt so close to you yesterday. We never need to put it all in words. If I believe in anything surviving, I believe in a love like ours surviving: it is all so completely unmaterial in every way.

V.S-W. TO H.N.   *27th May, 1940*
                                                   Sissinghurst

I could not trust myself to say much to you yesterday, but I expect you know what I felt. Every time we meet now, it must be in both our minds that we may possibly never meet again; but it must also be in both our minds (as you said) that we have known what few people know: a great happiness and a great unalterable love.

I am sending your diaries to Eric,[1] also my Will.

H.N. TO V.S-W.   *27th May, 1940*
                                                   Ministry of Information

I am afraid that the news this afternoon is very bad indeed, and that we must expect the Germans to surround a large proportion of our Army and to occupy the whole area of Belgium and Northern France.[2] We must also face the possibility that the French may make a separate peace, especially if Italy joins in the conflict. I warn you of this so that you will prepare your mind for the bad news when it comes and be ready to summon all the courage that is in you. I think you had better keep this to yourself for the moment.

V.S-W. TO H.N.   *28th May, 1940*
                                                   Sissinghurst

God help us, I have just heard about the Belgians! Well, we must wait. In the meantime, how deeply I agree with you about love and also about the bodkin. I promise you never to do anything rash or impetuous with the latter, but I should like to have it by me. So see

---

[1] Eric Nicolson, later 3rd Lord Carnock, H.N.'s elder brother. He lived at Burrator, on the edge of Dartmoor.

[2] This was the day of the capitulation of the Belgian Army.

Pierre Lansel[1] as soon as you can, for both our sakes, and get it for yourself and also post me a little parcel. There must be something quick and painless and portable. Oh my dear, my dearest, that we should come to this! Anyhow, we have had our lives, or at any rate more than half of them,[2] so let us never repine. I won't write more. I know you are busy, and it is not necessary for me to say more than that I have loved you more than anyone or anything in all my life.

DIARY   *29th May, 1940*

We are creating a Corunna Line along the beaches around Dunkirk and hope to evacuate a few of our troops. The Navy is superb. I find a passionate letter from the French Ambassador saying that our Press is putting all the blame on the French Army. I take this to Walter Monckton's Committee and we hope to improve the situation. I then belatedly try to dictate correspondence. The work is as urgent and cumulative as during the Paris Peace Conference. But then we were happy in those days and not in a state of fear.

H.N. TO V.S-W.   *31st May, 1940*
                                                    4 King's Bench Walk, E.C.4

Our Army has fought the most magnificent battle in Flanders. They have created what they call the 'Corunna Line' and are holding it. We never hoped to rescue more than 20,000, and we have already saved 80,000[3] and hope to do more. Moreover we are now able to supply them with some food and ammunition. It is a magnificent feat once you admit the initial misery of the thing. It is perhaps fortunate that the B.E.F. is so good at retreating, since that is what it mostly has to do. But I am not sneering. They have done more than just rescue themselves. They have killed two dangerous legends: (1) that no army could stand up to German mechanised attack; (2) that complicated naval operations such as embarking troops under fire could not be undertaken in the face of air superiority.

My darling, how *infectious* courage is. I am rendered far stronger in heart and confidence by such bravery.

---

[1] H.N.'s doctor.   [2] At this date V.S-W. was 48 and H.N. 53.
[3] By midnight on the 30th, 126,600 men had been evacuated from Dunkirk or its neighbouring beaches.

DIARY   *1st June, 1940*

We have now evacuated 220,000 men,[1] which is amazing when I recall
how we feared that we should lose 80 per cent. But there are few
grounds for enthusiasm really, except moral grounds. We have lost
all our equipment. The French have lost 80 per cent of their forces
and feel that we deserted them. Gort[2] says that he offered to take more
French off, but that they were too dead-beat to move and that all
those who could be galvanised into marching a few miles further
were in fact rescued. This may be true, but the French with their
tendency to attribute blame to others will be certain to say that we
thought only of rescuing the B.E.F. and let them down.[3]

I escape at 6.15 to Sissinghurst. Our train is $1\frac{1}{2}$ hours late, because
trains are pouring up and down the line transporting remnants of the
B.E.F. We pass twelve trains packed with tired, dirty but cheering
troops. I only see one man who is shell-shocked, and he sits staring in
front of him with drooping eyelids, as if drugged. The others might
have been returning from a two-days' route march.

V.S-W. TO H.N.   *3rd June, 1940*
                                                               Sissinghurst

Last night was one of the most beautiful nights I ever remember. I
was out late by myself getting some of Ozzy's sheep back into the
field from which they had escaped. One lamb got *égaré* into another
field, and I pursued it through the long wet grass, led by its bleatings,
and the faint glimmer of its little body. The rim of the sky was still
pink with sunset. Venus hung alone and enormous. The silhouette
of the sentry appeared above the parapet of the tower.

H.N. TO V.S-W.   *4th June, 1940*
                                                               4 King's Bench Walk, E.C.4

I was terribly rushed yesterday as I had to get out a Memo for the
Cabinet about invasion. We do not know whether to warn people
now, or to wait till it becomes likely. It is 80 per cent probable that the
enemy will attack France first and only go for us afterwards. Yet we

---

[1] On this day 64,000 men were landed from Dunkirk at southern British ports.
[2] Lord Gort, Commander-in-Chief of the B.E.F., had landed in England on the
previous day and reported to the Cabinet. H.N. had been given the gist of this
report.
[3] The final total of evacuations from Dunkirk was 370,000, of which approximately
110,000 were Frenchmen.

must be prepared for the invasion when it comes and the public must be told what to do. We have got a long list of instructions, but do not like to issue them without Cabinet orders. As Duff was over in Paris, I had to do this all myself.

My dearest Viti, I suppose it is some comfort to feel that it will either be all over in August or else we shall have won. Hitler will not be able to go on into next year. The whole thing is, 'Shall we be able to stand it?' I think we shall. And if we win, then truly it will be a triumph of human character over the machine.

But actually I do not believe that invasion will come, especially if the French are able to put up some show of resistance on the Somme. How I long for the spirit of Verdun to revive! It may—you know what the French are. I feel so deeply grateful for having hard work to do in these days. And now comes Italy.[1] My dearest, what a mean skulking thing to do. The French have offered them practically all that they want in Tunis etc, but they want more and more. They are like the people who rob corpses on the battlefield—I forget what these people are called. The Greeks had a name for it.[2]

Bless you. Courage and hope. This afternoon Winston made the finest speech that I have ever heard.[3] The House was deeply moved.

V.S-W. TO H.N. *5th June, 1940*
Sissinghurst

I wish I had heard Winston making that magnificent speech! Even repeated by the announcer it sent shivers (not of fear) down my spine. I think that one of the reasons why one is stirred by his Elizabethan phrases is that one feels the whole massive backing of power and resolve behind them, like a great fortress: they are never words for words' sake.

How strange it is to have no knowledge of what is about to befall us. In ordinary times one seldom thinks how odd it is to have no knowledge of what may happen even within the next hour, but now the consciousness of this ignorance becomes acute. I see the future only in terms of colour: scarlet and black. But as you say, courage and hope. And there is always the bare bodkin.

---

[1] Mussolini did not actually declare war until 10th June, but it was already obvious that he was preparing to do so.
[2] Necrosylia.　　[3] The 'We shall fight on the beaches . . .' speech.

H.N. TO V.S-W. *6th June, 1940*
4 King's Bench Walk, E.C.4

I dread the result of this battle.[1] The French are outnumbered both in men and material, and not too good in heart. If they can only hold the Huns this time, then we are all right. And even if they lose Paris, it is not the end in so far as France is concerned. I feel so much in the spirit of Winston's great speech that I could face a world of enemies.

There is a growing feeling against what is called 'the old gang'. Our reports say that the men who have come back from the front feel that Kingsley Wood and Inskip let them down and must go. Chamberlain would have to go too. How odd the world is. Yesterday in the Ministry I observed Lord Salisbury in a top hat and frock-coat coming down the stairs. I said, 'What are you doing here?' 'Trying to save the Conservative Party.' I did not press him, but I suppose that he feels that Duff and Winston are the hopes of the Party and that Anthony is too weak. But I gather that Anthony is doing well in the War Office.

DIARY *10th June, 1940*

I give my draft of the Invasion pamphlet to the Director-General, who takes it down to the meeting of the Home Defence Ministers. The War Office, to my mind, do not seem to have faced the problem that the Germans will treat as saboteurs any civilians who obstruct them. If we encourage sabotage, a tremendous responsibility will rest upon our heads and only the Cabinet can decide.

The Duty Room Committee is about as gloomy a meeting as we have had. The German mechanised Divisions have crossed the Seine at two places and have managed to throw pontoon bridges over the river. All the other bridges have been destroyed. The petrol dump at Rouen has been set on fire. We have begun to evacuate Le Havre, and the Division that we had there is apparently being brought back to England.[2] It seems inevitable that Paris will fall shortly. Meanwhile we have evacuated Narvik.[3] The Cabinet decided that no news of this should be given to the public, but as the evacuation is front-page news

[1] The German attack on the Somme. The attack had opened at dawn on 5th June, between Amiens and the sea. Soon the offensive spread to the whole 400-mile front. But against 143 German Divisions the French could deploy only 65.

[2] The evacuation of Le Havre was completed in the early morning of 13th June. 2,200 British troops were brought back to England, and another 8,800 carried round by the Navy to Cherbourg to continue the fight.

[3] Narvik was abandoned to the enemy on 8th June.

in the New York newspapers, we send Walter Monckton down to the Cabinet to persuade them that if we withhold the news any longer, all confidence in our communiqués will be destroyed. Italian intervention seems a matter of hours.

We all feel in a strange way exhilarated by this day of disaster.

H.N. TO V.S-W.   *12th June, 1940*
                                                         4 King's Bench Walk, E.C.4

I saw André Maurois this morning. He had left Paris yesterday. He said that never in his life had he experienced such agony as he did when he saw Paris basking under a lovely summer day and realised that he might never see it again. I do feel so deeply for the French. Paris to them is what our countryside is to us. If we were to feel that the lanes of Devonshire, the rocks of Cornwall and our own unflaunting England were all concentrated in one spot and likely to be wiped out, we should feel all the pain of all the world. What makes me gnash my teeth is that Hitler said he would be in Paris by 15th June, and I think he will meet that date, thereby increasing his mystic legend.

I had to go this morning to represent Duff on the War Cabinet Committee of Home Defence. What is so odd is that there were all those Cabinet Ministers and they were completely unguarded. We all stood in Whitehall afterwards and chatted amicably. And not one policeman or detective was there. I rather like that in the British manner, but I don't think it wise.

What a joy it is for me to be so busy at this moment and in so central a position. I really feel that I can do some good, and I am *embattled*. I did not know that I possessed such combative instincts. Darling, why is it that I should feel so *gay*? Is it, as you said, that I am pleased at discovering in myself forces of manliness which I did not suspect? I feel such contempt for the cowards. And such joy that you and I should so naturally and without effort find ourselves on the side of the brave.

DIARY   *15th June, 1940*

I have been too rushed this historic week to write my diary in any detail. The events crowd thick and fast and each one seems worse than the other. Yet a curious psychological effect is produced. Fear and sorrow seem to give way to anger and pride. It may be because I know that I shall kill myself and Vita will kill herself if the worst comes. Thus there comes a point where Hitler will cease to trouble either of us, and meanwhile by every means in our power we will continue to worry him.

Then there is another state of mind which I notice. I am able almost entirely to dismiss from my thoughts any consideration of the future. I do not even have such pangs about the past as I had when the situation was less catastrophic. My reason tells me that it will now be almost impossible to beat the Germans, and that the probability is that France will surrender and that we shall be bombed and invaded. I am quite lucidly aware that in three weeks from now Sissinghurst may be a waste and Vita and I both dead. Yet these probabilities do not fill me with despair. I seem to be impervious both to pleasure and pain. For the moment we are all anaesthetised.

DIARY   *17th June, 1940*

The Reynaud Cabinet has resigned and Pétain has formed a new Ministry including Darlan. The Germans have broken through as far as Dijon, and the French are apparently evacuating the Maginot Line and destroying the works. Camrose telephones me in some agitation. He is very much afraid that if the Germans get hold of the French fleet, we shall have no chance at all. I try to cheer the old boy up, but find it difficult to adduce arguments other than blind confidence and blind determination not to give way.

At 12.30 I go to Sammy Hood's[1] room and find that he has been listening to Pétain on the wireless. The important phrase is, '*Il faut cesser la lutte*'. This is most inconvenient to us, especially if the French Navy is also surrendered. Lunch with Robert Vansittart at the Carlton Grill. He also feels that everything turns on what happens to the French Fleet. If they manage to join us, then we are all right. If they scuttle themselves, there is a chance. But if they fall into the hands of our enemies, then we shall indeed be in a dangerous and even desperate position.[2]

H.N. TO V.S-W.   *19th June, 1940*
                                                4 King's Bench Walk, E.C.4

I think it practically certain that the Americans will enter the war in November, and if we can last till then, all is well. Anyhow, as a

---

[1] Viscount Hood, Private Secretary to Duff Cooper.

[2] The Armistice agreement stipulated that the French Fleet should be demobilised and the ships laid up in their home ports for the duration. But several units escaped to British ports.

precaution, I have got the bare bodkin. I shall bring down your half on Sunday. It all looks very simple.

How I wish Winston would not talk on the wireless unless he is feeling in good form. He hates the microphone, and when we bullied him into speaking last night, he just sulked and read his House of Commons speech over again.[1] Now, as delivered in the House of Commons, that speech was magnificent, especially the concluding sentences. But it sounded ghastly on the wireless. All the great vigour he put into it seemed to evaporate.

I saw Louis Spears for a moment just back from France. He said that the confusion was almost unbelievable. Our offer to unite with France fell very flat.[2] I was pleased to feel that I was going to be a French citizen and am sorry it did not come off.

DIARY   *21st June, 1940*
Today the French delegates were received by Hitler in the dining-coach at Compiègne in which the Armistice of 1918 was signed. Hitler gave them an allocution scolding them for having been so wicked as to win the last war.[3] Poor people, my heart bleeds for them.

A note of elation permeates the diary after the fall of France, but it becomes at times almost telegraphic in its concentrated brevity, since Harold Nicolson was busier than at any other period of his life, working at the Ministry of Information throughout the week with only an occasional night at Sissinghurst. The Ministry soon became the target for criticism by a Press resentful at being fed the news which officials thought fit to print, and by a public who disliked the idea of having their morale investigated and analysed. Duff Cooper made matters no easier by his ill-concealed disdain for journalists. In addition, it was a new Ministry, staffed for the most part not by regular civil-servants who would have been prepared to accept orders, but by brilliant amateurs from the Universities and the intellectual world of London. 'The presence of so many able, undisciplined men in one Ministry', wrote Duff Cooper in his autobiography,[4] 'was bound to lead to a great deal of internal friction....

---

[1] The 'finest hour' speech.
[2] This proposal, originated by Vansittart, de Gaulle and Jean Monnet, was for a single Government and common citizenship between the two countries.
[3] In fact, Hitler did not speak a word to the French delegates. He left the railway-car immediately after the preamble to the Armistice terms had been read out.
[4] *Old Men Forget.* Hart-Davis. 1953.

I was never happy there. . . . With other departments I was continually squabbling, especially with the Foreign Office and the three Service departments.' But while Duff Cooper was unhappy, Harold Nicolson was not. He was his Minister's lightning-conductor. Since British relations with defeated France was the dominant topic of these weeks and France was the country which he knew best after his own, he was a key person in the right job. Many of Harold Nicolson's own friends were among those people, British and exiled, who stormed the Ministry with offers of their services and ideas for influencing British and neutral opinion. A great deal of his time was spent in such interviews, and in attending Standing Committees at the Ministry several times a day. He drafted the Cabinet statement on British war aims, advocating a Federal structure for postwar Europe and increasingly Socialist measures at home. His Parliamentary work was slight—a few questions to answer but no major debate.

Week by week, as the Diary shows, a German invasion of Britain was expected. It is curious that so little thought was given, at least in the Ministry of Information, to the difficulties which the Germans faced in improvising so colossal an operation. The Germans had made scarcely any plans before the fall of France. Hitler expected Britain's surrender as a natural consequence of it. 'I can see no reason why this war must go on', he declared to the Reichstag on 19th July, but the British reply was unequivocal defiance. Orders were given by Hitler to prepare for a landing by forty divisions on a 200-mile front between Ramsgate and Lyme Bay, but tactical disagreements between the German Army and Navy, the essential condition that air superiority must first be won over Britain's southern coast and the organisation of invasion transports, made it impossible for Hitler to contemplate a landing before mid-September. The frequent invasion scares in Britain were due to nothing more than nerves and German propaganda. In July probing attacks by the Luftwaffe on British Channel shipping began, but the Battle of Britain proper did not start until August, and there was as yet no bombing of London.

DIARY   *29th June, 1940*

Guy Burgess comes to see me, and I tell him that there is no chance now of his being sent to Moscow. Jean Monnet[1] comes to see me. He says that there is no chance of France in her present stunned and wounded condition accepting any Government, National Committee or indi-

[1] Head of the Anglo-French Coordinating Mission in London until the fall of France, and author of the postwar *Plan Monnet* for the economic integration of Europe.

vidual established under our protection. Pétain and Weygand are still great names in France, and the French people are mitigating their humiliation by saying it was all our fault and that we deserted them. Monnet thinks that a really national movement may some day emerge in the French Colonies, but that meanwhile we should avoid anything which might look as if we were using any body of Frenchmen in our own interests. I agree with him absolutely. I beg Spears[1] not to encourage de Gaulle too much. The difficulty is that Duff himself is very Gaullois.

DIARY   *30th June, 1940*

Have a long talk with Eve Curie[2] who is determined to remain here while she can. The French Government are becoming definitely hostile, and are turning all their propaganda against us not only in France but in the United States. The French sailors in our harbours are worried about their families and such help as we hope to get from the French colonies is melting away. In fact it is clear that throughout Europe people imagine that we stand little chance in the great invasion, and they are all, including Rumania and to some extent Turkey, coming to terms with Germany.

DIARY   *3rd July, 1940*

Have a talk with Jenkins,[3] Attlee's P.P.S. Attlee is worried about the B.B.C. retaining its class voice and personnel and would like to see a far greater infiltration of working-class speakers. He also feels that we should put before the country a definite pronouncement on Government policy for the future. The Germans are fighting a revolutionary war for very definite objectives. We are fighting a conservative war and our objectives are purely negative. We must put forward a positive and revolutionary aim admitting that the old order has collapsed and asking people to fight for the new order.

---

[1] General Spears, who had been Churchill's personal liaison officer with the French Government, had brought de Gaulle to London on 17th June, and was now head of the British Mission at de Gaulle's Headquarters.

[2] The biographer of her mother, Marie Curie, the famous French physicist.

[3] Arthur Jenkins, Labour M.P. for Pontypool, 1935–46, and Parliamentary Private Secretary to Clement Attlee, 1940–45.

DIARY   *4th July, 1940*

The news about the French Fleet was not released till 3 in the morning and therefore missed most of the morning papers. This is very bad publicity, and we shall of course be blamed. The fact is that Winston never thinks for a moment about the publicity side. Duff tells me that the *Dunkerque* has apparently been sunk and that the *Strasbourg* has escaped and that a very serious battle is in progress.[1] We may find ourselves actually at war with France, which would almost break my heart. The House is at first saddened by this odious attack but is fortified by Winston's speech. The grand finale ends in an ovation, with Winston sitting there with the tears pouring down his cheeks.

H.N. TO V.S-W.   *10th July, 1940*
                                                          4 King's Bench Walk, E.C.4

I told the Queen today[2] that I got home-sick, and she said, 'But that is right. That is personal patriotism. That is what keeps us going. I should die if I had to leave.' She also told me that she is being instructed every morning how to fire a revolver. I expressed surprise. 'Yes', she said, 'I shall not go down like the others.' I cannot tell you how superb she was. I anticipated her charm. What astonished me is how the King is changed. He is now like his brother. He was so gay and she so calm. They did me all the good in the world. How I wish you had been there. Gort was simple and modest. And those two resolute and sensible. *We shall win*. I know that. I have no doubts at all.

Meanwhile Hitler seems to be funking the great attack upon England. All our reports from abroad (I see the Foreign Office telegrams) show that he is not now quite so sure. I do not see how he can abandon this great project. If we can stick it, we really shall have won the war. What a fight it is! What a chance for us! Our action against the French Fleet has made a tremendous effect throughout the world. I am as stiff as can be.

[1] Churchill was determined to prevent important units of the French Fleet at Oran from falling under German control. The British Admiral was instructed to present the French with an ultimatum to come over to Britain's side, sail to neutral ports or scuttle their ships. When the French in Oran refused, the British sank the battle-ship *Bretagne* and the battle-cruiser *Dunkerque*. The battle-cruiser *Strasbourg* escaped to Toulon.

[2] H.N. lunched that day with Mrs Arthur James to meet the King and Queen. The other guests included Lord Gort, Sir Alexander Cadogan (Permanent Under Secretary of State for Foreign Affairs, 1938-46) and the Duchess of Devonshire.

H.N. TO V.S-W.   *11th July, 1940*
Ministry of Information

I had about eleven people to see me today. I wish I were a Cabinet Minister and could keep them off by a barrage of private secretaries. All this means that I do not see Duff enough. We take taxis together and devise all sorts of dodges. But the result is that he is seeing the Alpha Plus people all day and I am seeing the Beta Plus people whom he throws on to me. But that is the right system. I am there to take things off him and to collect Parliamentary opinion.

The German bombings of some of our ports are already pretty bad. God knows what they will be when they start full out. But our morale is perfect. I am cocky about this war. Cocky. I really and truly believe that Hitler is at the end of his success. They expect an invasion this week-end. That is Hitler's last horoscope date. After that the stars are against him. I feel like a doctor watching a dangerous case of illness. But I like being a doctor. I am so busy that my beloved diary is becoming no more than an engagement book.

DIARY   *12th July, 1940*

At the Policy Committee I bring up my draft of War Aims. I say that we are about to be faced by a dual problem, one international and the other national. The international problem is this. Hitler may call a European Economic Conference, announce the economic consolidation of Europe, and say, 'Here is a vast purchasing organisation. The Americans wish to sell us their consolidated stocks. What prevents the suppliers from sending their stuff to the consumers? The British blockade. Great Britain is thus imposing famine and pestilence on Europe, and ruin upon the two Americas.' The national problem is this. When bombing begins on a large scale, people will ask, 'What are we fighting for? Would we not be better off with peace plus Hitler?' In order to combat the first, we must have Free Trade and pooled resources. In order to combat the second we must have Socialism. I suggest that I should draft in leaflet form a manifesto promising the world free trade and our own country equality of opportunity. They agree. But it will be difficult to get Duff to put it to the War Cabinet. Will it not be felt that we had better leave this sleeping tiger to sleep in its own way?

DIARY   *13th July, 1940*

The Germans have been trying to convince us that they will invade us tonight. There is a goodish gibbous moon and fine weather. I go to bed without apprehension.

Ben has bought a Picasso portrait of a woman entirely composed of grey cubes. It was very expensive. It is a determined portrait and it says what it thinks. But I do not like these affirmations in art. I like art to be a relief and not a challenge. But Ben, who is far more expert than I am, regrets this sentimental approach. I am sure he is right.

H.N. TO V.S-W.   *14th July, 1940*
                                                        Ministry of Information

I do so hate saying goodbye to you on Sunday afternoons. It is like going to Persia. I do love you so deeply. It is like the Grand Canyon: as if the surface of my life were up on top in the hotel, and the real depths deep down in rose-coloured layers. Not a romantic analogy— but, oh my dear, I do love you so.

Tray[1] was so happy with us. We must ask him again. He loves coming. I dined with him and Roger Senhouse[2] at the Reform and we listened afterwards to Winston. I clapped when it was over. But really he has got guts, that man. Imagine the effect of his speech in the Empire and the U.S.A. I felt a great army of men and women of resolution watching for the fight. And I felt that all the silly people were but black-beetles scurrying into holes. What a speech! One could feel after that as if the whole world might fall.

> *Si fractus illabatur orbis,*
> *Impavidum ferient ruinae.*[3]

Thank God for him. And for you. Winston's best phrase was, 'We shall show mercy, but we shall not ask for it.'

DIARY   *16th July, 1940*

I have a long talk with Duff Cooper about my leaflet on War Aims. He quite agrees that we may be faced at any moment by a German peace move, and that a purely negative attitude is not sufficient. He also agrees that nothing will prove an alternative to Hitler's total programme except a pledge of federalism abroad and Socialism at home. He fears, however, that this is too much of an apple of discord

---

[1] Raymond Mortimer.   [2] The publisher and translator, a very old friend of H.N.
[3] Horace, *Odes*, III iii. 'If the whole world were to crack and collapse about him,
                    Its ruins would find him unafraid.'

to throw into a Coalition Cabinet. 'You see', he says, 'I am myself more Conservative than you are.' He asks me to draft a Memorandum for the Cabinet putting the thing as tactfully as I can.

DIARY   *18th July, 1940*

Lunch at the Rumanian Legation. Arthur Henderson[1] is there and Brendan Bracken. The Labour people say that they hope Winston will carry on after the war in order to inaugurate the New World. Brendan says that the moment the war is over, Winston will want to retire. He says that Winston is convinced that he has had all the fun he wants out of politics, and that when this is over he wants to paint pictures and write books.[2] He adds that in the twenty years he has known Winston, he has never seen him as fit as he is today, and his responsibilities seem to have given him a new lease of life. He adds that he is very determined not to become a legendary figure and has the theory that the Prime Minister is nothing more than Chairman of the Cabinet. We discuss the question of a General Election, in view of the fact that the House is not in the least representative of the country. Were there such an Election, we might well get rid of some of our diehard Tories.

DIARY   *20th July, 1940*

I think that Hitler will probably invade us within the next few days. He has 6,000 aeroplanes ready for the job.[3] How strange it all is! We know that we are faced with a terrific invasion. We half-know that the odds are heavily against us. Yet there is a sort of exhilaration in the air. If Hitler were to postpone invasion and fiddle about in Africa and the Mediterranean, our morale might weaken. But we are really proud to be the people who will not give way. The reaction to Hitler's speech yesterday[4] is a good reaction. Yet I know well that we shall be exposed to horrible punishment. It is so strange that in this moment of anxiety there is no hatred of Hitler or the Germans. Opinion slides off into oblique animosities such as criticism of the Old

[1] Labour M.P. for Kingswinford since 1935. He had been serving on the General Staff since 1939, and was to become Under Secretary of State for War in 1942.
[2] Anthony Eden (*The Reckoning*, p. 145) confirms this: 'Winston reiterated that he was now an old man [in September, 1940, when he was 65] and that he would not make Lloyd George's mistake of carrying on after the war.'
[3] He had, in fact, only 2,670 fighters and bombers deployed in the West.
[4] To the Reichstag, to whom he hinted that he was willing to discuss peace-terms with Britain.

Gang and rage that the L.D.V.[1] are not better equipped. All this is dangerous, since it is in essence a form of escapism and appeasement. We are really frightened of Hitler, and avoid the dynamic resistance to him which is uniform hatred. 130 years ago all this hatred was concentrated against Bonaparte. We flinch today from central enmity. If we are invaded we may become angry.

DIARY   *22nd July, 1940*

Philip Lothian[2] telephones wildly from Washington in the evening begging Halifax not to say anything in his broadcast tonight which might close the door to peace. Lothian claims that he knows the German peace-terms and that they are most satisfactory. I am glad to say that Halifax pays no attention to this and makes an extremely bad broadcast but one which is perfectly firm as far as it goes.

H.N. TO V.S-W.   *31st July, 1940*
4 King's Bench Walk, E.C.4

We had a Secret Session today. Mm. Hush. All that I can say is that Winston surpassed even himself. The situation is obscure. It may be that Hitler will first bomb us with gas and then try to land. At the same time, Italy and Japan will hit us as hard as they can. It will be a dreadful month. On the other hand, Hitler may feel that he cannot bring off a successful invasion and may seek to gain new, easy but sterile conquests in Africa and Asia. Were it not for this little island under a great leader, he would accomplish his desires. We may fail. But supposing we do not fail? That was their finest hour. I have always loved England. But now I am in love with England. What a people! What a chance! The whole of Europe humiliated except us. And the chance that we shall by our stubbornness give victory to the world.

DIARY   *3rd August, 1940*

I am feeling very depressed by the attacks upon the Ministry of Information. What worries me is that the whole Press, plus certain pro-Munich Conservatives, have planned and banded together to pull Duff Cooper down. Since the M. of I. should be an offensive instrument, its value to our war-effort will be diminished by this constant

[1] Local Defence Volunteers.
[2] Lord Lothian had been British Ambassador to the United States since 1939.

sniping from the rear. I well know that much of the Press campaign is selfish, conceited and unfair. But there does remain a grain of truth at the bottom of it. The Ministry is ill-organised and mistakes are made. A Ministry of this character cannot really be conducted efficiently if the majority of the Press are out to sabotage it. And it may be true that if our propaganda is to be as effective as that of the enemy, we must have at the top people who will not only command the assent of the Press, but who will be caddish and ignorant enough to tell dynamic lies. At present the Ministry is too decent, educated and intellectual to imitate Goebbels. It cannot live by intelligence alone. We need crooks. Why I hate Hitler so much is that he has coined a new currency of fraudulence which he imposes by force. I am prepared to see the old world of privilege disappear. But as it goes, it will carry with it the old standards of honour.

DIARY   *11th August, 1940*

A lovely clear morning but rather cold. I bathe nonetheless. A great heron flaps away from the lake. The cottage garden is ablaze with yellow and orange and red. A real triumph of gardening. Viti, who is so wise and calm, asks the unspoken question which is in all our minds, 'How can we possibly win?'

It does seem as if we shall shortly be assailed from all angles. The Italians will drive into Somaliland, Kenya and the Sudan as well as Egypt. The Japanese will attack us in the Far East. And Germany, while threatening us at home, may send armies to Spain, Portugal, Morocco and Dakar. Then will come the heavy bombing here and great peace propaganda both here and in the United States. It will be represented that Churchill in his sullen obstinacy is imposing tremendous suffering upon the world, and that if only we would recognise the fact that Hitler has now consolidated Europe, peace and prosperity would return. We shall become the most hated race on earth.

And then gradually the Fifth Column here will get to work. There will be the extreme left taking its orders from Moscow. There will be the extreme right, angry at the humiliation by Churchill of the Conservative Party, and feeling in their blindness that anything is better than the triumph of the Reds. There will be the lower middle-classes who will be frightened of the bombs, and will say, 'Anything better than this. What does Aden or Malta matter to us?' And then there will be the pacifists and the Oxford Group people who will say that material defeat means nothing and that we can find in moral rearmament that strength that is greater than the riches of this world. I can see a man like Lloyd George or possibly Beaverbrook coming out as the prophet of all this, and a situation arising analogous to that which arose in France. Fortunately the whole toughness and strength of this country seems to have passed into organised Labour. They are superb.

I place my trust in the mechanical nature of the Nazi system. If we can, even in a little thing, dislocate that machine, then the inherent self-distrust of the Germans will begin to operate. Just as here people are comforted by the feeling that it is all too bad to be true, so in Germany they are disconcerted by the reflection that it is all too good to be true. If we can last out this winter, prove that they cannot reduce us by bombs or blockade, get the U.S.A. to furnish us with real war-standard production and take some offensive against Italy, then by the autumn, when starvation really spreads in Germany, they may be ready to make a possible peace.

Meanwhile I fear that the invasion threat has created in the last few weeks something like panic in Service circles. The Army were so appalled by the internal collapse of France that they forced the Cabinet to take panic measures over here. The ill-planned and quite heartless internment of all aliens was part of this ten-day panic. Another part were the prosecutions for 'spreading alarm and despondency'. And a third part were our instructions to mount an offensive campaign against rumour and to consider a tightening of the censorship. When invasion did not come, all these three have been modified and the full brunt of public indignation has fallen upon the Ministry of Information and Duff Cooper in particular. It is not a very bright page in our rough island story.

I have come to the conclusion that my character is like a drawing of a very excellent character, only it is unfortunately slightly out of drawing.

On 13th August Goering issued orders to the Luftwaffe for the start of the air offensive against Britain. It was not immediately apparent that the war had entered a new phase, since attacks on coastal towns and shipping had intensified throughout July and early August, and it seemed at first that these raids were merely an extension inland of the earlier raids. Harold Nicolson had not yet heard a shot fired in anger, but during August and September he and V. Sackville-West were spectators from their own garden of a great part of the Battle of Britain, since its centre was the Weald of Kent and Sissinghurst lay near to the centre of the

Weald. It also lay directly on the centre-line of the intended advance of the German armies from the coast to London, now that Admiral Raeder had persuaded Hitler that the landings must be confined to the stretch of coast between Folkestone and Bognor.

Hitler's decision to attempt the invasion depended primarily on the issue of the air battle, but even if he had won it, the Channel crossing in face of overwhelming British naval superiority would have made it extremely risky, and on land the British Army was already more powerful than that which the Allies faced in Normandy four years later. Goering's error was to scale down his attacks on the south-eastern airfields and control-centres at the very moment when the R.A.F. was beginning to find the strain intolerable, and gradually to switch to day and night bombing of London, by which he hoped to break civilian morale. These attacks began in earnest on 7th September, and from then until 3rd November London was raided every night. The Germans made their supreme fighter effort on 15th September, when the R.A.F. maintained their 2 to 1 average by bringing down 56 German 'planes for the loss of 26 of their own. Two days later Hitler postponed the invasion 'indefinitely'.

H.N. TO V.S-W. *13th August, 1940*
Ministry of Information

I had a long talk with Duff yesterday. He thinks that invasion will come since he does not see how Hitler can get out of it. But if it does not come within the next two weeks, it will probably be too late. He must have perfect weather for the attempt. Meanwhile we do not understand why he is wasting so many machines off our coasts. He has lost 200 for certain in the last three days, and although he can replace the machines he cannot replace the 200 pilots. Anyhow the thing is hotting up and I am glad of it.

DIARY *15th August, 1940*

Go to see a Leslie Henson show. The theatre is packed and everybody is in high spirits about our air triumphs. In fact the superiority shown by our men is a miracle. Duff told me today that the only explanation is the lack of German training. There can be no question of German courage or efficiency. Their machines (though inferior) are not a real explanation. Therefore it must be that in their desire to save petrol they do not give their men sufficient training. Our triumph today was superb.

DIARY   *18th August, 1940*
                                                     Sissinghurst

A lovely day. I bathe in the morning and find a widower sitting by the lake fishing sadly. Ben comes over to luncheon. While we are sitting outside, the air-raid siren sounds. We remain where we are. Then comes the sound of aeroplanes and, looking up, we see thin streamers from the exhausts of the German 'planes. Another wave follows, and we see it clearly—twenty little silver fish in arrow formation. There is no sound of firing, but while we are at luncheon we hear 'planes quite close and go out to see. There is a rattle of machine-gun fire and we see two Spitfires attacking a Heinkel. The latter sways off, obviously wounded. We then go on with our luncheon. Ben talks to us about Roger Fry and Virginia.[1] He had written to the latter saying that Fry was too detached from life, and she had written a tart letter in reply.

DIARY   *19th August, 1940*

Frank Pick,[2] our new Director-General, attends the Duty Room Committee. He throws his weight about. He first rages at our delay in releasing the story of Thursday's air battles. We say it is the fault of the Air Ministry. He asks why the Air Ministry should object. We say that it is because if we inform the Germans of the success or failure of their raids while the latter are still in progress we shall be giving them valuable information. Pick says that he doesn't care a hoot for the Air Ministry. He then criticises us for holding up the Somaliland news[3] until tomorrow, when the Prime Minister is to make a statement in the House. He says, 'To hell with the Prime Minister.' We all look very shocked. I think his ideas are right, but his manner is really terrible. Sly and violent he looks, but I daresay that the former is due merely to shyness.

DIARY   *20th August, 1940*

Winston makes his speech in the House. He deals admirably with Somaliland and the blockade. He is not too boastful. He says, in referring to the R.A.F., 'never in the history of human conflict has

[1] Virginia Woolf's biography of Roger Fry, the art critic, had just been published.
[2] Frank Pick, who was 62, had been a distinguished Managing Director of the London Underground and Chairman of the Council of Art and Industry. He resigned from the Ministry in December 1940 and died in November 1941.
[3] On 15th August the British garrison withdrew from British Somaliland under pressure from a greatly superior Italian force.

so much been owed by so many to so few'. It was a moderate and well-balanced speech. He did not try to arouse enthusiasm but only to give guidance. He made a curious reference to Russia's possible attack on Germany and spoke about our 'being mixed up with the United States', ending in a fine peroration about Anglo-American cooperation rolling on like the Mississippi.

DIARY   *26th August, 1940*

A lovely morning. They raided London yesterday, and we raided Berlin. I work at my broadcast talk. At noon I hear aeroplanes and shortly afterwards the wail of the siren. People are becoming quite used to these interruptions. I find one practises a sort of suspension of the imagination. I do not think that that drone in the sky means death to many people at any moment. It seems so incredible as I sit here at my window, looking out on the fuchsias and the zinneas with yellow butterflies playing round each other, that in a few seconds above the trees I may see other butterflies circling in the air intent on murdering each other. One lives in the present. The past is too sad a recollection and the future too sad a despair.

I go up to London. After dinner I walk back to the Temple. It is a strange experience. London is as dark as the stage at Vicenza after all the lights have been put out. Vague gleamings of architecture. It is warm and the stars straddle the sky like grains of rice. Then the searchlights come on, each terminating in a swab of cotton-wool which is its own mist area. Suburban guns thump and boom. In the centre there are no guns, only a drone of aeroplanes, which may be enemy or not. A few lonely footsteps hurry along the Strand. A little nervous man catches up with me and starts a conversation. I embarrass him by asking him to have a cigarette and pausing lengthily while I light it. His hand trembles. Mine does not.

When I get into my rooms, I turn the lights off and sit at the window. There is still a drone of 'planes, and from time to time a dull thump in the distance. I turn on my lights and write this, but I hear more 'planes coming and must darken everything and listen in the night. I have no sense of fear whatsoever. Is this fatalism or what? It is very beautiful. I wait and listen. There are more drones and then the searchlights switch out and the all-clear goes. I shut my shutters, turn on my lights and finish this. The clocks of London strike midnight. I go to bed.

DIARY   *28th August, 1940*

Christopher Hobhouse's widow comes.[1] She tells me that he left her on Monday evening at 4.30 in their little bungalow at Hayling Island. He went down to the Fort [at Portsmouth] and half-an-hour later there was a bombing attack and Christopher and three fellow-officers were blown to pieces. They would not let her even attend the funeral since there was so little left. Poor girl. She is to have a baby in March and wants me to be godfather. She is left without a bean. I feel so sad about it.

DIARY   *2nd September, 1940*
                                                        Sissinghurst

There is a tremendous raid in the morning and the whole upper air buzzes and zooms with the noise of aeroplanes. There are many fights over our sunlit fields. We go up to see Gwen at Horserace[2] and suggest improvements in her garden. Raids continue the whole time. It is evident that the Germans are sending more fighters to protect their bombers, and our losses are therefore in higher proportion.[3]

In the evening Vita and I discuss the high-spots in our life. The moment when I entered a tobacconist's shop in Smyrna, the moment when we took Ebury Street, our early days at Long Barn, the night that Nigel was born, the night at Kermanshah, and so on. Vita says that our mistake was that we remained Edwardian for too long, and that if in 1916 we had got in touch with Bloomsbury, we should have profited more than we did by carrying on with Mrs George Keppel, Mrs Ronald Greville and the Edwardian relics. We are amused to confess that we had never even heard of Bloomsbury in 1916. But we agree that we have had the best of both the plutocratic and the Bohemian worlds, and that we have had a lovely life.

V.S-W. TO H.N.   *4th September, 1940*
                                                        Sissinghurst

Whenever the siren goes, I wonder where you are: in the Ministry, in the streets, in King's Bench Walk, in a theatre? It is bloody. Mean-

[1] Christopher Hobhouse was the author of *Fox* and several other highly successful books. For a time he had shared King's Bench Walk with H.N., who was one of his closest friends.

[2] Mrs St Aubyn, H.N.'s sister, was now living at this little house, half a mile from Sissinghurst.

[3] During this fortnight (24th August–6th September) Fighter Command lost a quarter of its pilots and 466 Hurricanes and Spitfires.

while we have found machine-gun bullets, one in the lake-field and one came through the roof of the garden shed. So, you see, I am right to tell you to keep indoors when they fight just overhead. They are nasty pointed things.

We had a fine pyrotechnical display after dinner last night, when a German got caught in our searchlights and fired tracer-bullets. Blood-red they streamed down the sky. The rest of the night was quiet here.

DIARY   *7th September, 1940*

At Tonbridge, where we change trains, there are two German prisoners. Tiny little boys of 16 they are, handcuffed together and guarded by three soldiers with fixed bayonets. They shuffle along sadly, one being without his boots, shuffling in thick grey socks. One of them just looks broken down and saturnine; the other has a superior half-smile on his face, as if thinking, 'My Führer will pay them out for this.' The people on the platform are extraordinarily decent. They just glance at them and then turn their heads away, not wishing to stare.

The sirens yell and we get into our train for Staplehurst. At Sissinghurst, we have tea and watch the Germans coming over in wave after wave. There is some fighting above our heads and we hear one or two aeroplanes zoom downwards. They flash like silver gnats above us in the air. The all-clear sounds at 6, but there is another warning at 8 which actually lasts till 5.30 am., but I go to sleep.[1]

DIARY   *12th September, 1940*

The damage done last night was less terrible than on the former four nights. The barrage put up by our A.A. guns has cheered people enormously, although people in the East End are still frightened and angry.

I lunch at the Savoy with Erika Mann.[2] She is a fine woman. Knickerbocker[3] dashes up to me aflame with rage. He says he has the best story in the world and the censors are holding it up. It is the story about the time-bomb outside St Paul's Cathedral which may go off

---

[1] This was the first main daylight attack on London. As it coincided with the massing of invasion barges in the French Channel ports, and the moon and tide conditions were right, the British Chiefs of Staff concluded that invasion was imminent and the warning code-word 'Cromwell' was issued by Home Forces at 8 pm. that night.
[2] The daughter of Thomas Mann, the German novelist, and wife of W. H. Auden.
[3] The American journalist, H. C. Knickerbocker.

at any moment and destroy the great work of Sir Christopher Wren. 'Cannot the American people be brought in to share my anxiety?' Also why is he not allowed to mention the destruction of Bond Street and the Burlington Arcade, so dear to many Americans? I leave Erika and hurry back to put this right. Cyril Radcliffe[1] is most helpful. The reason why the story about St Paul's was held up is because no time-bombs may be mentioned. The reason why Bond Street is held up is that Knickerbocker had written, 'That street, comparable to Fifth Avenue and the Rue de la Paix'. The censor held that the mention of those two streets might indicate to the enemy further desirable objectives! Anyhow Cyril gets the whole message cleared.

Michel St Denis[2] comes to see me. All the French émigrés are at loggerheads. All of them come to see me and say how ghastly everyone else is. Dine with Guy Burgess at the Reform and have the best-cooked grouse that I have ever eaten. The bombardment begins again at 9.15. I have to walk back to the Ministry through a deserted London. I have no tin hat and do not enjoy it. When things get very hot, I crouch in a doorway. In one of them I find a prostitute. 'I have been drinking', she says: 'I am frightened. Please take care of me.' Poor little trull.

DIARY   *13th September, 1940*

There is a great concentration of shipping and barges in France, and it is evident that the Cabinet expect invasion at any moment. A raid starts at about 11 am. I go upstairs and go on with my work. At about 12.15 I meet Walter Monckton in the passage. He whispers, 'They have just dive-bombed Buckingham Palace, and hit it three times. The King's safe.'[3] The raid continues till about 2.30. There are delayed-action bombs in St James's Park and the whole park-side of the Foreign Office has been evacuated. I cannot find any trains at all running down to Kent and I have to give up going home. Another raid begins about 3.45. Bombs are dropping close to us in Howland Street and without warning. We go down to the dug-out. I then go up to the sixth floor and look over London. There is a triumphant double-rainbow circling

[1] The barrister. Later the first Viscount Radcliffe. He had been in the Ministry of Information since the outbreak of war, and was to become its Director-General, 1941–45.

[2] Dramatist, actor and producer. Head of the French section of the B.B.C. 1940–44.

[3] Two bombs fell in the quadrangle of Buckingham Palace, 30 yards from the room where the King was talking to his Private Secretary. The same attack wrecked the Chapel at the Palace. The King was badly shaken.

the City and basing itself upon St Paul's which shines in the evening sun. At 9.15 the sirens start to yell again. It is a wonderful night with a full moon. When I get back to the M. of I., I start typing this, and as I do so, the guns boom.

DIARY   *15th September, 1940*[1]
                                                                   Sissinghurst

A slack morning with the usual raid going on overhead. After luncheon there is a terrific dog-fight above us. Two 'planes come down near Sissinghurst village and one crashes in flames at Frittenden. We see a parachute descending slowly with the man below it wriggling as if on a pendulum. They take four German prisoners. The station at Staplehurst has been laid flat by a Spitfire which crashed upon its roof. A Spitfire comes down in Victor Cazalet's park, only a hundred yards from Swift's.[2] In the evening we have the news. They say we have brought down 185 of the enemy against 30 of ours.[3] They have again bombed Buckingham Palace. We are told that Goering is directing this campaign.[4] If so, he must be a stupider man than I thought. There is another raid at night. Poor Vita worries about my going up to-morrow. As Priestley[5] said tonight, London is in effect in the front line. Thank God they have got the delayed bomb out from under St Paul's.

During the remaining months of 1940 the bombardment of London was intensified. The German survivors of the air-fights which V. Sackville-West watched from her garden went on to bomb Harold Nicolson in London—or so she imagined, for her days and nights were filled with anxiety for him. He reacted with a physical courage which surprised him. When the Blitz grew really bad, he slept in his office at the Ministry of Information, a huge concrete tower which stood up to at least six direct hits, and walked back each morning through the littered streets to break-fast at King's Bench Walk. The diary became fuller as his evenings became emptier. London social life was almost dead, and he needed some distraction from the perpetual bombing. An average of 200 German

[1] In January 1947, H.N. pencilled a marginal note against this date: 'This was the day we won the Battle of Britain'.
[2] A mile from Sissinghurst.
[3] The actual numbers were 56 German and 26 British.
[4] This was correct: he had taken over direct command on 7th September.
[5] J. B. Priestley's wireless talks at this period of the war were as popular as those of Churchill himself.

bombers came over London every night for 57 nights in succession. 'At this time', wrote Winston Churchill, 'we saw no end but the demolition of the whole Metropolis.' Goering switched the weight of his attacks to provincial cities (the worst, and one of the first, was directed against Coventry on 14th November) when Londoners had taken almost more than they could stand. It was only in the next year that an adequate defence against night-bombing was found in radar-controlled anti-aircraft guns and night-fighters.

Harold Nicolson was closely informed about the material and psychological effects of the bombardment, for he was representing his Ministry on the Cabinet's Civil Defence Committee. At the same time he was much concerned with the propaganda aspects of events abroad—de Gaulle's failure at Dakar, the relations between the Axis powers and Vichy France, Mussolini's invasion of Greece, American reactions to the attack on London and our retaliatory bombing of Berlin, the mounting losses of British shipping in the Atlantic, and (a bonus to the British at the end of the year) Wavell's offensive against the Italian desert Army. He was even busier than during the Battle of Britain. He spent most week-ends and even Christmas Day in the Ministry. He constantly attended the House of Commons and spoke at meetings in all parts of the country. In the last week of December he began a fortnight's tour of the Ministry's Regional Centres.

DIARY   17th September, 1940

Down to the House. I have a question to answer. Chamberlain is there for the first time after his operation.[1] He has aged much: his nose looks larger and his head and face smaller. Winston warns us that the bombing will get worse and that the Germans may seek to land 500,000 men in this country.[2] I must say that he does not try to cheer us up with vain promises.

Have a talk with Clem Davies and Euan Wallace[3] afterwards. Everybody is worried about the feeling in the East End, where there is much bitterness. It is said that even the King and Queen were booed the other day when they visited the destroyed areas. Clem says that if only the Germans had had the sense not to bomb west of London

[1] In August Neville Chamberlain had undergone an operation for cancer. It did not restore his health, and he resigned his office at the end of September.

[2] This speech was made in Secret Session.

[3] Conservative M.P. for Hornsey since 1924. Formerly Minister of Transport, and now Senior Regional Commissioner for Civil Defence in London.

Bridge there might have been a revolution in this country. As it is, they have smashed about Bond Street and Park Lane and readjusted the balance.

The only thing I really mind myself is walking back from the Club after dinner under bombardment. I know that it is unwise to do so, and our motto should be 'Where I dine, I sleep.' Tonight I try a new experiment and dine at the White Tower in Percy Street. At 8.10 the siren howls and I walk back to the Ministry. By the time I enter the forecourt the guns have started booming. I therefore find myself back in my room at 8.30 with no books or wireless and my work locked away. I type this as something to do.

At the back of everybody's mind is this question: 'Hitler has done great material and moral damage in London by employing only a few 'planes on nightly raids. He can, if he wants, send 'planes across London for the whole twenty-four hours. Shall we be able to stand it?'

DIARY   *18th September, 1940*

To the Civil Defence Committee of the Cabinet. The Home Secretary[1] tells us that during the last two nights the Germans have dropped land-mines by parachute. These engines of destruction carry a lateral drive of 500 yards. We have recovered one and taken it down to Portsmouth to be examined. Miss Horsbrugh[2] tells us that evacuation and relief are being improved. The East End people now refuse to be sent to the West End, especially anywhere near Buckingham Palace. There are still 32 unexploded bombs on the Southern Railway. Bevin[3] presses for communal feeding, an issue of some *ersatz* helmets and more ingenuity on the part of works-managers to avoid wastage of working hours.

As I write this (8.10 pm.) the first gun booms out for the bombardment which I know will continue all night.

DIARY   *19th September, 1940*

We all refuse to face the fact that unless we can invent an antidote to night-bombing, London will suffer very severely and the spirit of our people may be broken. Already the Communists are getting people in

[1] Sir John Anderson, later Viscount Waverley.
[2] Parliamentary Secretary to the Ministry of Health, 1939–45.
[3] Ernest Bevin had been Minister of Labour since Churchill formed his Coalition Government in May.

shelters to sign a peace-petition to Churchill. One cannot expect the population of a great city to sit up all night in shelters week after week without losing their spirit. The only solution I can see at present are reprisals, which we are both unable and unwilling to exert. If we are saved, we shall be saved by our optimism. Few people really believe that this ordeal can be continued for ever. They hope that 'something may turn up'. And, by God, so it may. I think we shall win through owing to our unswerving pride.

I get sleepy and go back to my room. I turn out the lights and listen to the bombardment. It is continuous, and the back of the museum opposite[1] flashes with lights the whole time. There are scudding low clouds, but above them the insistent drone of the German 'planes and the occasional crump of a bomb. Night after night, night after night, the bombardment of London continues. It is like the Conciergerie, since every morning one is pleased to see one's friends appearing again. I am nerveless, and yet I am conscious that when I hear a motor in the empty streets I tauten myself lest it be a bomb screaming towards me. Underneath, the fibres of one's nerve-resistance must be sapped. There is a lull now. The guns die down towards the horizon like a thunder-storm passing to the south. But they will come back again in fifteen minutes. We are conscious all the time that this is a moment in history. But it is very like falling down a mountain. One is aware of death and fate, but thinks mainly of catching hold of some jutting piece of rock. I have a sense of strain and unhappiness; but none of fear.

One feels so proud.

DIARY   *20th September, 1940*

I dine at the Travellers with Gladwyn Jebb.[2] We talk about propa-ganda in Germany, with which he is much concerned. He does not care for our Mr Pick. It seems that the latter was asked to luncheon by Winston Churchill. He announced that he would never countenance any form of propaganda which was not in accordance with the strict truth and his own conscience. Winston replied, 'I am indeed flattered and proud to find myself at luncheon with so exceptional a man.' This left Pick guessing.

We have a pleasant quiet dinner and my affection for Gladwyn warms my soul. In the middle of it there is a bomb which sets the

[1] The British Museum.
[2] He was then Private Secretary to the Permanent Under-Secretary of State at the Foreign Office, and a close friend of H.N.

Club swaying slightly as if in an earthquake. At 8.45 Gladwyn and I
start off in his car and in pitch darkness return to our respective offices.
The guns are flashing over the northern heights, but no bombs fall as
we creep through the empty streets.

DIARY   *22nd September, 1940*
                                                              Sissinghurst

We dine with the Drummonds.[1] There is, as always, that sense of
mahogany and silver and peaches and port-wine and good manners.
All the virtues of aristocracy hang about those two crippled and aged
people, and none of the vulgarity of wealth. We listen to the news while
distant bombardments thump and crunch over the hills and plains of
Kent. Priestley gives a broadcast about the abolition of privilege,
while I look at their albums of 1903 and the Delhi Durbar and the
Viceroy's train. Priestley speaks of the old order which is dead and of
the new order which is to arise from its ashes. These two old people
listen without flinching. I find their dignity and distinction and patriotism deeply moving. I glance at the pictures of the howdahs and
panoply of the past and hear the voice of Priestley and the sound of
the guns. We go out into the autumn night and see the searchlights
swinging their shafts across the sky. There are clear stars and a moon
struggling in eastern clouds. I write this before going to bed. A
butterfly with white outstretched legs and dark closed wings has
settled upon the black cloth of the screen across my window. Beyond
it I can hear the drone of an aeroplane. Tomorrow I return to London
and the bombardment which goes on and on and on.

DIARY   *24th September, 1940*

I detect in myself a certain area of claustrophobia. I do not mind being
blown up. What I dread is being buried under huge piles of masonry
and hearing the water drip slowly, smelling the gas creeping towards
me and hearing the faint cries of colleagues condemned to a slow and
ungainly death. Always as I write this diary the guns boom. One
writes that phrase, yet it means nothing. There is the distant drum-
fire of the outer batteries. There is the nearer crum-crum of the
Regent's Park guns. Then there is the drone of aeroplanes and the
sharp impertinent notes of some nearer batteries. FF-oopb! they
shout. And then in the middle distance there is the rocket sound of the
heavy guns in Hyde Park. One gets to love them, these angry London

[1] Major-General Laurence Drummond (1861–1946). He lived at Sissinghurst Place.

117

guns. And when they drop into silence, one hears above them, irritating and undeterred, the dentist's drill of the German aeroplanes, seeming always overhead, appearing always to circle round and round, ready always to drop three bombs, flaming, and then ... crump, crump, crump, somewhere. Is it Bond Street, or Lincoln's Inn Fields? Are Victorian or Georgian buildings slipping down under the crunch of that distant noise? I feel no fear nor anger. Hum and boom. Always I write my nightly diary to that accompaniment.

DIARY   *25th September, 1940*

It was a bad night. As I leave the office to walk to King's Bench Walk, I see two bandaged people being put into an ambulance. There is a cold bright sun and a cloudless sky with the barrage-balloons shining silver and small. But in the lower sky hangs a pall of smoke and there is a smell of burning in the air. I walk through Lincoln's Inn and am stopped by firemen. Water and soot and burnt paper everywhere. The Hall of the Middle Temple has a bomb through the roof and all the stained glass has been blown out into Lamb Court where it lies smashed and twisted. A block of Chambers is down in Elm Court and another in Crown Office Row.

Mrs Groves[1] had tried to spend the night in the tube, but when she got there she found the whole place full up with 'foreigners'. 'Greeks, they were, sir, by the look of them, and they made themselves comfortable with mattresses and suchlike. I never did hold with foreigners. My father was an Indian Mutiny veteran and always warned me against them since I was a child.' She also tells me that St Clement's Dane has been hit 'something frightful'. 'Is the steeple down?' I ask. 'I didn't notice that, sir. I never look up.'

Back to the Ministry. We get the news about de Gaulle. The whole thing has failed utterly and we are withdrawing our forces.[2] Many casualties have been caused on both sides. It is about as bad a show as it could be. It will ruin de Gaulle's prestige and will affect Winston's. The

[1] H.N.'s housekeeper in King's Bench Walk.
[2] This was the abortive raid on Dakar. A large Anglo-French force, headed by de Gaulle in person, appeared off Dakar in West Africa on 23rd September with the object of winning over the French garrison to the Gaullist cause. The plan had leaked, and Vichy reinforced Dakar before de Gaulle arrived. His ultimatum was rejected, and a three-day battle between the Anglo-French fleet and the Vichy ships and shore-batteries in Dakar resulted in a War Cabinet decision, with the concurrence of the local commanders, to abandon the expedition as too costly and likely to involve Britain in war with France.

effect on France and America will be deplorable. I am deeply depressed. Why is it that we are never successful? This is worse than Norway. What we need is a neat little triumph somewhere.

I do not feel that I am pulling my weight in the Ministry, and that makes me feel that I have mighty little weight to pull. I lack authority in this place, which is not due to any lack of unwillingness in others, but to my own lack of strength and drive. I am too acquiescent.

DIARY *29th September, 1940*
Sissinghurst

I read *Vanity Fair* and write an article for the *Round Table*. The bits of *Vanity Fair* which I can recognise as trailing on into my own life are now dead. Vita and I discuss how human vanity, expressed in the nineteenth century by snobbishness, will express itself in the twentieth. It was not that they liked peers and baronets as such, but that they wanted to prove that they were connected with the governing class. The urge to be identified with the élite will always be an urge in active men. But where are they to find the élite? In Russia and Germany today a whole class of 'party members' and children of party members must be growing up, as selective as any Debrett. The old aristocracy may be derided, as after the Wars of the Roses, but even as then the Cecils and others emerged, so some new class will emerge now. They will grapple privileges for their children. It is impossible, in fact, to achieve equality of opportunity. The only thing to do is to go to bed and not bother about such things. Therefore I go to bed. But I shall always be fascinated by this problem.

V.S-W. TO H.N. *8th October, 1940*
Sissinghurst

Lord! we have had a lot of raids this morning. They began at 8.30 and are still going on at 11. There was a most lovely sight: ten white machines climbed absolutely sheer, leaving perfectly regular white streaks of smoke like furrows in a cloudless blue sky, while a machine lower down looped smoke like gigantic spectacles before shooting up to join its friends. We saw one catch fire and fall. 'That's one less to go after Hadji',[1] I thought.

---

[1] She called him Hadji throughout her life.

DIARY   *8th October, 1940*

Go round to see Julian Huxley[1] at the Zoo. He is in an awkward position since he is responsible for seeing that his animals do not escape. He assures me that the carnivores are perfectly safe, although a zebra got out the other day when its cage was bombed and bolted as far as Camden Town. While we are at supper a fierce raid begins and the house shakes. We go on discussing war aims. He feels that the future of the world depends upon the organisation of economic resources and the control by the U.S.A. and ourselves of raw materials. The raid gets very bad, and at 8.30 he offers to drive me back. It is a heavenly moonlit night, and the searchlights are swaying against a soft mackerel sky and a great calm moon. The shells light up their match-flares in the sky. A great star-shell creeps slowly down over the city under a neat parachute. We hear loud explosions all round as he drives me bravely back to the Ministry.

DIARY   *15th October, 1940*

Last night was the worst that we have had since 7th September. There is a meeting of the War Cabinet's Civil Defence Committee with Herbert Morrison[2] in the chair. We are told that the only two railway stations still able to handle the morning mail are Paddington and King's Cross. All the rest are out of action. The Germans have been sending fighter-bombers in groups of three which have flown comparatively low. People are not at all happy about our ability to cope with this new form of warfare and we are rather grim. Morrison says, 'Well, let's all indulge in wishful thinking.' In the East End they are saying that the diminution of our barrage defence is because we have run out of shells.

I go down to the Chamber where I listen to Duff Cooper answering some questions. There is some anxiety in the lobbies since people feel that the public, having got over the shock of the first bombardments, are now worried about this second phase. In particular they are frightened by the magnetic mine[3] which the Germans drop and which does such terrific damage. One was dropped in St James's Park yesterday and damaged both St James's Palace and the Foreign Office simultaneously.

[1] The scientist and author. He was Secretary of the Zoological Society, 1935-42.
[2] Herbert Morrison had succeeded Sir John Anderson as Home Secretary at the beginning of October and remained in that office till the end of the war.
[3] It was not magnetic, but a naval mine dropped by parachute.

I go back to the Ministry and then to the Beefsteak, which has been badly shaken. I find Harold Macmillan sadly contemplating the ruisn of Leicester Square. He tells me that he had been in the Carlton Club last night when the bomb fell. He had been having a glass of sherry before dinner with David Margesson. They heard the bomb screaming down and ducked instinctively. There was a loud crash, the main lights went out and the whole place was filled with the smell of cordite and the dust of rubble. The side-lights on the tables remained alight, glimmering murkily in the thick fog which settled down on every-thing, plastering their hair and eye-brows with thick dust. They saw through the fog the figure of Quintin Hogg escorting old Hailsham[1] from the ruins, like Aeneas and Anchises. There were some 120 people in the Club at the time and nobody was hurt. An astonishing escape.

DIARY   *17th October, 1940*

King's Bench Walk is still all right and Mrs Groves is there, as deter-mined as usual to pretend that all is unchanged. I used to be irritated by the Cockney love of the familiar, feeling that it closed their minds to new experiments, but now their obstinate clinging to the rock of our tradition fills me with pride.

I go to the smoking-room with Harry Crookshank[2] and Charles Waterhouse.[3] Winston is at the next table. He sits there sipping a glass of port and welcoming anyone who comes in. 'How are you?' he calls gaily to the most obscure Member. It is not a pose. It is just that for a few moments he likes to get away from being Prime Minister and feel himself back in the smoking-room. His very presence gives us all gaiety and courage. People gather round his table completely unawed. They ask him questions. Robert Cary[4] makes a long disserta-tion about how the public demand the unrestricted bombardment of Germany as reprisals for the raids on London. Winston takes a long sip at his port gazing over the glass at Cary. 'My dear sir', he says, 'this is a military and not a civilian war. You and others may desire to kill women and children. We desire (and have succeeded in our desire) to destroy German military objectives. I quite appreciate your point.

---

[1] The first Viscount Hailsham (1872–1950). Lord Chancellor, 1928–29 and 1935–38. Quintin Hogg was his son.
[2] Financial Secretary to the Treasury, 1939–43.
[3] Conservative M.P. for South Leicester since 1924.
[4] Conservative M.P. for Eccles since 1935.

But my motto is "Business before Pleasure".[1] We all drift out of the room thinking, 'That was a man!'

DIARY   *22nd October, 1940*

There is a Press Conference for Lord Lothian.[2] He sits there quite placidly under the glare of arc-lamps and the barrage of questions. He manages the thing with consummate ease. He says that in the early stages America had felt that this was merely a European war. They had rather despised us for our muddle in Norway. Then came the collapse of France and the sudden realisation that the British Fleet was their first line of defence. In July they were really terrified that we would go the same way as France. Then came Dunkirk, the triumph of the R.A.F., the abandonment of invasion and the Pact with Japan.[3] Those four things swung American opinion over in six weeks. They were still averse to any European commitments, but they had come to understand that our interests and the strategic points of the Commonwealth were essential to themselves. It was a fine talk and it went well. Our Press were delighted. Then refreshments. I creep out to a hotel in Russell Square. It is hell. A great ugly room filled with Belgian refugees and a gloomy set dinner which is uneatable. I creep back in the dark fog with stars and shells glimmering overhead.

H.N. TO V.S-W.   *23rd October, 1940*
                                                        Ministry of Information

We have had an easier time lately, and as I write this, there is not the usual sound of guns crashing. Hitler is preparing some Mediterranean coup. He has already been plotting something with Laval and will be seeing Franco shortly. All very unpleasant, but not nearly as disturbing as the invasion of England. How history repeats itself! First the great battles of Jena and Austerlitz. Then the threatened invasion of England and the camp at Boulogne. Then the Peninsular War. And then, let us hope, Moscow, Leipzig and Waterloo.

[1] But Churchill wrote in *Their Finest Hour*, describing this period of the Blitz: 'The abandonment by the Germans of all pretence of confining the air war to military objectives had raised this question of retaliation. I was for it, but I encountered many conscientious scruples.'
[2] British Ambassador in Washington. He died seven weeks later.
[3] The Tripartite Pact between Germany, Italy and Japan was signed in Berlin on 27th September.

DIARY   *26th October, 1940*

My train from Leicester is much delayed by air-raids and I get to the office very late. I am shown the latest telegrams. They make the blood run cold. A telegram from Sam Hoare[1] to the Prime Minister evidently based on very reliable information, which I suspect to be the French Ambassador and therefore quite authentic. The Germans have offered Pétain peace on condition that (1) he 'restores' Alsace-Lorraine to Germany; (2) he gives Italy the Department of Alpes Maritimes; (3) he allows Germany to remain in possession of the Channel ports plus a corridor down to Spain for the duration of hostilities; (4) half Tunis and Algeria is ceded to Italy; (5) Morocco is given to Spain; (6) the French colonies in Africa are administered by a joint German-Italian and French Commission; (7) all French bases and aerodromes in Africa and the Mediterranean are placed at the disposal of Germany and Italy; (8) France 'safeguards' the flank of Italy's attack on Egypt, Syria and Algeria; (9) the French Fleet in the Mediterranean is placed at the disposal of our enemies. If the French do not accept these terms, Hitler will 'starve' France. If they do accept, then their prisoners will be released and they will be given food.[2]

These terms have filled us with anger and alarm. We have already taken certain steps. The King has telegraphed direct to Pétain begging him not to accept such iniquitous terms. We have sent a similar message to Weygand. And above all Roosevelt has sent a message to Pétain which should make him sit up. He tells him quite frankly that if he commits this enormity, he will destroy the respect which America has felt for France for 150 years and will make it quite impossible for America to send any relief to France.[3] Poor old Pétain may resign. Weygand may come over to us. But Laval and Baudouin[4] will be there to obey the German orders. What will the French people say?

[1] Then British Ambassador in Madrid.
[2] This meeting between Hitler and Marshal Pétain had taken place at Montoire, near Tours, on 24th October. The full text of the agreement has not yet been published, but it is doubtful whether any ultimatum was given to Pétain or such details were entered into as H.N. records. But it was bad enough. Pétain assented to Hitler's statement that 'the Axis Powers and France have an identical interest in seeing the defeat of England accomplished as soon as possible'.
[3] The President's message to Pétain emphasised that if the French Fleet were allowed to fall into German hands, such action would constitute a flagrant breach of faith with the United States Government.
[4] Paul Baudouin was Minister of Foreign Affairs in Pétain's Government. On 28th October he was succeeded by Pierre Laval.

I fear so much that we shall now have a peace offer from Hitler which will be difficult to explain away to our people. I talk to Charles Peake[1] before going to bed. He shares my anxiety about the French situation. Halifax is down at Chequers to be with Winston. Charles shows me a pathetic little draft of peace-terms drawn up by Halifax. It is all about God.

DIARY   *28th October, 1940*

Motor up to London with Sam.[2] At 3 am. this morning the Italians addressed an ultimatum to Greece. Metaxas refused and war will ensue.[3] It is rumoured that Athens was bombed at dawn. Lunch with Guy Burgess and Isaiah Berlin,[4] who is just back from Washington. There is such a sense of suspense in the air that ordinary work seems hopeless.

DIARY   *29th October, 1940*

I have a talk with Charles Peake about the German peace terms to France. Unless we are quick and clever, Laval will give the French people one teaspoonful of the terms at a time. Our business is to tell them at once what they are in for, including the Alpes Maritimes to Italy and Indo-China to Japan. We go to see Duff. 'This', I say, 'is the supreme moment for a calculated indiscretion.' He takes it at once, and says he will bring it up in the Cabinet in half-an-hour's time. He does so. We are authorised to arrange a leakage, provided that it does not compromise the French Ambassador in Madrid. We there-fore get Reuter to put it out in different terms, and as if it came from Stockholm and Zurich. It gets on the tape by 6 pm. A good piece of work.

Dine with Diana [Cooper] at the Dorchester. I tell them of the German terms to France which are by now on the tape. They do not believe it. They say it is 'a German balloon'. I go back in a taxi which I find providentially. It is a calm star-lit night with guns flashing in the distance.

[1] Head of the News Department in the Foreign Office and Chief Press Adviser to the Ministry of Information.
[2] Francis St Aubyn, H.N.'s brother-in-law. He was to succeed to the peerage of St Levan on 10th November, 1940.
[3] Mussolini attacked Greece through Albania without the consent or even knowledge of Hitler, whom he met at Florence that same day.
[4] The Fellow of All Souls and New College.

DIARY   *5th November, 1940*

The Prime Minister makes a statement after Question-time. He is rather grim. He brings home to the House as never before the gravity of our shipping losses and the danger of our position in the Eastern Mediterranean. It has a good effect. By putting the grim side foremost he impresses us with his ability to face the worst. He rubs the palms of his hands with five fingers extended up and down the front of his coat, searching for the right phrase, indicating cautious selection, conveying almost medicinal poise. If Chamberlain had spoken glum words such as these the impression would have been one of despair and lack of confidence. Churchill can say them and we all feel, 'Thank God that we have a man like that!' I have never admired him more. Thereafter he slouches into the smoking-room and reads the *Evening News* intently, as if it were the only source of information available to him.

DIARY   *6th November, 1940*

I pause outside the tube-station and buy a wet copy of the *Daily Express*. 'Roosevelt leading', it says. I get to K.B.W. in time for the 8 am. news and the first words are, 'Roosevelt is in'. Our later news tells us that he is not only in, but in by a huge majority and that he has also got a Congress to back him.[1]

Now this is odd. I try to be absolutely frank with myself and with my diary. Yet my delight at Roosevelt's victory shows me that underneath I had been anxious about Willkie. I should have said, if asked, that it did not really matter to us if Willkie won, since he was also pledged to our assistance.[2] True it is that there would have been some confusion caused by the change of administration. On the other hand we should, with Willkie's help, have had Big Business solid on our side. Yet my heart leapt like a young salmon when I heard that Roosevelt had won so triumphantly, which showed me that underneath I had been longing for his victory. In the last week, the Germans, the Italians and occupied France have made it clear that they would regard the defeat of Roosevelt as a triumph for themselves. It would mean that the U.S.A. felt our eventual victory to be impossible. Thus

---

[1] President Roosevelt was elected for his third term with a majority of five million votes. He carried 38 States and Wendell Willkie 10.

[2] In the course of his campaign, Willkie had said: 'All of us believe in giving aid to the heroic British people. We must make available to them the products of our industry.'

the moral effect of his sweeping the board will be very great. It is the best thing that has happened to us since the outbreak of war. I thank God!

H.N. TO V.S-W.   *8th November, 1940*
                                                      Ministry of Information

I was busy last night after I got back from dining at the Etoile, since Halifax had taken kindly to my paper on war aims and wanted me to make some further emendations. So I sat drafting away as if I were back in the Foreign Office twenty years ago. Then I got to bed and curled up on my rubber mattresses and went fast asleep. *Splaaassh! Craash! Tinkle! Tinkle!* Oh, I was no longer in my bed but on the floor. Charles Peake burst in. 'Are you all right, Harold?' 'Yes', I said. 'We've had another direct hit: a bad one this time.' Well, up I got, and into my trousers I got, and into my British-warm[1] I got. The passage outside was filled with a red fog which was just dust. There were air-raid wardens rushing about in steel helmets. And would you believe it? We really had been struck on the boko by the Luftwaffe. Not a single soul was hurt. I went round the shelters on a tour of inspection. I brought one or two of the paler people up to my room and gave them sherry which Miss Niggeman had thoughtfully provided. And then I went to sleep again and did not wake up till my alarm clock went off at 7.30. A bomb had hit us just on the shoulder. It had broken through one floor and exploded on the floor below. It had done in the University library.[2] Our windows on the courtyard side had been twisted out into shreds. The courtyard is full of masonry. But not a single soul even scratched. It was all great fun and I enjoyed it. This is not a pose. I was exhilarated. I am odd about that. I have no nerves about this sort of thing. Mentally I am like the people who stick daggers into their flesh.

I think we have managed to avoid losing this war. But when I think how on earth we are going to win it, my imagination quails.

I go to Manchester tomorrow.

DIARY   *10th November, 1940*

There are three things that I have discovered about Manchester. (1) That they are far more frightened of air-raids than we are in London,

[1] An Army-type of short overcoat which was very popular during the war.
[2] The Ministry of Information was housed in Senate House, Malet Street, part of London University.

and one finds oneself adopting an old veteran attitude towards their nervousness. (2) That there is a shortage of matches. (3) That there is no Benedictine. Hitler's blockade is beginning to grip the provinces.

Neville Chamberlain died last night.[1]

DIARY   *13th November, 1940*

The House is meeting in what is called 'the Annexe', but which is really Church House.[2] I bump into Brendan Bracken who says, 'Wonderful about Italy, isn't it?' I imagine he is referring to their Greek reverses and say, 'Yes'. But I have a feeling that there is something more, and when I get to the Ministry, I ask if there is any Italian news. They say, 'You have seen the communiqué?' I had not. It seems that we have sunk half the Italian Fleet at Taranto.[3] Really the Greeks cannot now say that we have failed to help them.

James has won the Hawthornden Prize.[4] I am overjoyed.

DIARY   *20th November, 1940*

We go to the Prime Minister's room to be told about the King's Speech. We hang about in the corridor while the Chiefs of Staff creep out after a conference. Then we all troop in and there are glasses of sherry about. The P.M. reads the speech ('It is cuthtomary to thand up when the Kingth thpeech is read'), and then we have a sort of party. I see out of the corner of my eye that Winston is edging in my direction and I am embarrassed. He slouches up. 'I see you have been speaking in Scotland?' 'Yes.' 'Was it a good meeting?' And so on. He seems better in health than he has ever seemed. That pale and globular look about his cheeks has gone. He is more solid about the face and thinner. But there is something odd about his eyes. The lids are not in the least weary, nor are there any pouches or black lines. But the eyes themselves are glaucous, vigilant, angry, combative, visionary and tragic. In a way they are the eyes of a man who is much preoccupied and is unable to rivet his attention on minor things (such as me). But in another sense they are the eyes of a man faced by an ordeal or

[1] At Highfield Park, near Reading. He was 71.
[2] As a precaution against a sudden daylight attack on the House of Commons.
[3] On 11th November three Italian battleships, including the new *Littorio*, were sunk by British torpedo-carrying aircraft from the *Illustrious*. Taranto was the main naval base in the heel of Italy.
[4] James Pope-Hennessy was awarded this major literary prize for his first book *London Fabric* (Batsford, 1939).

tragedy, and combining vision, truculence, resolution and great unhappiness.

H.N. TO V.S-W.   *20th November, 1940*
                                                Ministry of Information

My day began with the Civil Defence Committee of the Cabinet, at which we had Herbert Morrison's report on the visit to Coventry.[1] What amused me was Morrison's almost sobbing reference to the King's visit. He spoke about the King as Goebbels might have spoken about Hitler. I admit that the King does his job well. But why should Morrison speak as if he were a phenomenon? How odd these Labour people are! I prefer Ellen Wilkinson's[2] realism. She said to me, 'You deal in ideas, and one can never see how an idea works out. I deal in water-closets, and one can always see whether it works or not.' I do so like that little spitfire. She and Florence Horsbrugh are really the only two first-class women in the House. I should like to see both of them made Cabinet Ministers.

DIARY   *22nd November, 1940*

I go up to Leicester with Ronald Tree[3] as it has been badly bombed. Not many casualties and the people seem amused more than anything else. Ronnie says that I must come on with him to Ditchley.[4] Ditchley is being used as one of the alternative places to which Winston goes for the week-end. It is quite a business. First come two detectives who scour the house from garret to cellar; then arrive valet and maid with much luggage; then thirty-five soldiers plus officers turn up to guard the great man through the night; then two stenographers with masses of papers; then Professor Lindemann,[5] Brendan Bracken and the Private Secretary on duty; and finally Winston and Clemmie [Churchill].

Winston arranges his Sundays with complete regularity. He remains in bed till luncheon, working and dictating all the time and drinking quantities of Malvern water. After luncheon he works till 4.30 when he has a little walk and then tea. Then work again till 6.30 when he

[1] The raid on Coventry on 14th November was carried out by nearly 500 German aircraft which dropped 600 tons of high-explosive and thousands of incendiary bombs. 400 people were killed.
[2] Parliamentary Secretary to the Ministry of Home Security, 1940–45.
[3] Conservative M.P. for Harborough, 1933–45. P.P.S. to Duff Cooper in 1940.
[4] His house near Oxford.
[5] Later Lord Cherwell. Scientific adviser to the Prime Minister.

goes to bed with a hot-water bottle and is called at 8. Then a jovial dinner and bed.

Ronnie says that Winston is convinced that the Germans will strive by every means to smash us before the spring. 'We are in for a very terrible ordeal.' After that we shall have a very strained summer and then supremacy in 1942. Meanwhile the Italian collapse in Greece is of great value to us. We may attack the Dodecanese shortly.

He says that someone complimented Winston upon his obituary oration on Neville Chamberlain. 'No', said Winston, 'that was not an insuperable task, since I admired many of Neville's great qualities. But I pray to God in his infinite mercy that I shall not have to deliver a similar oration on Baldwin. That indeed would be difficult to do.'

Then we get to Ditchley. The great mass of the house is dark and windowless, and then a chink in the door opens and we enter suddenly into the warmth of central heating, the blaze of lights and the amazing beauty of the hall. Nancy Tree is there and her sister and Rob Bernays, Leonora and young Michael Tree who has just had an operation. Dick Law comes later and there are airmen from the neighbouring aerodrome for dinner. The beauty of the house is beyond words. Nancy has been over with her canteens to Coventry.

H.N. TO V.S-W.   *26th November, 1940*

We had a quiet night last night since the fog hung damp over the aerodromes of Artois and Picardy. But at 3 am. I was rung up from New York by the United Press asking me whether it was true that Lord Lothian had asked the President for two battleships. 'I'm not awake!' I yelled across three thousand miles. 'But I thought you were secretary to the Ministry of Information?' Oh hell! What a world and what a whirligig! I kept my head. I was polite—so polite, so cold, so sleepy.

The Greeks have landed a detachment north of Santi Quaranta to blow up the bridges. A suicide squad I expect it was. But it has put the fear of God into the Italians. The odd thing is that the Italian Air Force has not appeared at all for two days. I expect the Greeks will take a knock at any moment. But they have won a fine victory and dislocated the plans of the Axis at a vital moment.[1] How proud I should feel if I were Greek!

[1] The first Italian assault on Greece had been repelled by Greek counter-attacks which had captured Koritza in Albania on the 22nd. By the end of the year the Italians had been forced thirty miles behind the Albanian frontier along the whole front.

DIARY   *3rd December, 1940*

I tell Halifax that our paper on war aims must, when passed, be shown to us at least a week before publication. We shall have to prepare for its reception. I also tell him that it does not include enough about home reconstruction. We must say that we accept Socialism. He does not seem to think that the thing will in the last resort ever see light and that depresses me.

Most of the conversation afterwards circles round Jo Kennedy[1] and his treachery to us and Roosevelt. The general idea is that he will do harm for the moment but not in the end. How right I was in warning people against him. I was the first to do so.

DIARY   *5th December, 1940*

There is a wave of defeatism. Were I not so busy and happy, I should notice it. What is so curious is that people do not believe the Taranto victory[2] and the Greek success is partly dismissed as another Finland and Norway and partly rejected as implying that the Greeks can turn the Italians out of Albania whereas the Italians turned us out of Somaliland.

DIARY   *12th December, 1940*

Lunch with Guy Burgess at the Garrick. On my return, Geoffrey Neville[3] rushes up to me and says that we have captured 20,000 prisoners at Sidi Barrani.[4] A major victory. Ronnie Tree comes in and says that Lothian is dead. It is a blow over the heart. I say good-bye to Pick who is leaving us, somewhat embittered. Walter Monckton is to succeed him.

Charles Peake has been dining with Anthony Eden and has the latest news about Africa. We have mopped up Sidi Barrani and taken much booty. The Italian tanks are retreating towards Sollum[5] with our Navy bombarding them all the time. We are in hot pursuit. Our armoured Division is lost in the desert and Anthony fears that they will catch the Italians at Sollum and that a bottle-neck will ensue in which our columns will be shelled by our own ships. It is a great victory all the same. Anthony says, 'I was thinking of the capture of

[1] American Ambassador in London, 1937–41.
[2] Photographs of the sunken Italian battleships had been published, but their outlines below water had shown up very badly when reproduced on newsprint.
[3] The spokesman for the War Office at the Ministry of Information.
[4] Wavell launched his attack on the Italians in the Western Desert on 9th December. By the 15th all enemy troops had been driven from Egypt.
[5] On the Egyptian–Libyan border.

Sidi Barrani. Then I began to think of the capture of Sollum. Now I am beginning to think of the conquest of Libya.' This sounds bombastic, but the Italian defeat is very like a rout. The Italian general whom we captured admitted that he knew that 'something was up, although we expected nothing like this'. It is a fine show.

DIARY   20th December, 1940

Go down to Nether Wallop[1] to lecture to the Air Force about the German character. I do not feel that the young men really like it. They are all fascists at heart and rather like the Germans. I am taken into the operations room afterwards where I watch girls moving sinister disks over a great map. It all seems very efficient. I go to bed as soon as I can and am later joined by a scientist who snores and snores.

DIARY   23rd December, 1940

Back in time to hear Winston's message to the Italian people. I had been bothered during the afternoon by people who urged me to stop him emphasising Italian links with America. I refused to intervene in any way, saying that I had confidence in Churchill's conception of great events. Then I listened with some trepidation. As a message to Italy, and to the Italians here and in the U.S.A., it was magnificent. But even as a message to our own people it shows that he was not a war-monger but a heroic pacifist. He read out his letter to Mussolini of May last. It was tremendous. He read out Mussolini's reply. It was the creep of an assassin. Afterwards some of the American correspondents tell me that they think it is the best thing that Winston has ever done.

DIARY   25th December, 1940

The gloomiest Christmas Day that I have yet spent. I get up early and have little work to do. Finish reading the memoranda on local organisations with which I have been supplied. Have a talk with Hall about the reorganisation of our propaganda among minor nationalities in war U.S.A. Lunch alone at Antoine's and read a book of Pitt's war speeches. Hear the King on the wireless. Pick Raymond [Mortimer] up at the Ritz Bar where I meet Puffin Asquith[2] and Terence Rattigan.[3] After that I have a nice dinner with Raymond at Prunier. I then go

[1] An R.A.F. station on the Hampshire–Wiltshire border.
[2] Anthony Asquith, the film director.
[3] Author of French without Tears (1936) and other plays. He was then 29.

back to the Ministry, where there is a party downstairs followed by a film.

Poor old London is beginning to look very drab. Paris is so young and gay that she could stand a little battering. But London is a charwoman among capitals, and when her teeth begin to fall out she looks ill indeed.

H.N. TO V.S-W.   *31st December, 1940*
                                          In the train from Bristol to Cardiff

I have found a new pleasure in life—travelling with a Private Secretary. One just walks about in a fur coat and things get done. Moreover, he keeps the purse and gives mean little tips such as I should never dare to give. But it is at him the porters scowl, not me. I just walk away and gaze at the show-cases in the hall.

I lunched with the Regional Commissioner yesterday to meet Alexander, the C.-in-C. of Southern Command.[1] He is believed to be a great soldier. He thinks the Battle of England has already begun— Coventry, Southampton, Bristol, the City. They will burn and destroy them one by one. 'Archie Wavell', he says, 'mops up 40,000 Libyans and we claim a victory. In two hours the Germans destroy 500 years of our history.' I do think we are going through a hellish time.

[1] General, later Field-Marshal, Alexander had commanded the First Corps of the B.E.F. and supervised the final stages of the evacuation from Dunkirk. He was to remain G.O.C. of Southern Command until 1942, when he was sent as G.O.C. to Burma.

1941

H.N.'s tour of England and Scotland – lunches with de Gaulle – 'we shall win in the end' – Wendell Willkie – H.N. in trouble with Churchill – the Axis invade the Balkans – H.N. invited to lead the National Labour Party – discussions with the Free French – British troops in Greece – Duff Cooper's treatment of journalists – meeting with Maisky – suicide of Virginia Woolf – H.N. to V.S-W. on their marriage – Germany attacks in Libya and Greece – the battles of Greece and Crete – Chamber of the House of Commons destroyed – H.N. lunches with Churchill – the Rudolf Hess incident – sinking of the 'Bismarck' – Hitler attacks Russia – British propaganda in the United States – H.N. is dismissed from the Ministry of Information and made a Governor of the B.B.C. – his sense of failure – Stephen Spender on democracy – H.N. patrols the River Thames with A. P. Herbert – Dylan Thomas – John G. Winant – an evening in Cambridge – Lease-Lend – Harold Macmillan on Beaverbrook – new British offensive in Libya – Bevan on intellectuals in war – Pearl Harbour – H.N. talks with de Gaulle – loss of the 'Prince of Wales' – 'it has been a sad and horrible year'

Having beaten the German fighters and survived the German bombers, Britain hung on in the hope that somehow or other, at some time or other, the German economy would collapse and America or Russia would enter the war on our side. We had no allies outside the Commonwealth except Greece. Vichy France was almost a declared enemy, and de Gaulle had few gains to show in the French territories overseas except in Equatorial Africa. The threat of invasion was still a very real one to the British, for it was not then known that in the previous October Hitler had told his Army that they could release formations from the Channel coast 'for employment on other fronts', and that since then his mind had been preoccupied with 'Barbarossa', the invasion of Russia which was timed to start on 15th May.

We were fighting a defensive battle in the Atlantic against German surface and underwater raiders, and an offensive battle on land against the Italians in north-east Africa. The latter was highly successful. Wavell's desert troops captured Bardia on 5th January, Tobruk on the 22nd and Benghazi on 6th February, and pressed on to El Agheila on the border of Tripolitania, having advanced 500 miles in two months and wiped out ten Italian divisions for the loss of 438 British soldiers killed. Simultaneously the Sudan was cleared of Italian troops, Italian Somaliland overrun, British Somaliland regained and Eritrea invaded. In Abyssinia a patriot uprising was stimulated and fed by British officers and arms.

These successes released troops for use elsewhere. The greatest danger was in the Balkans. Rumania had become a German satellite and Hitler massed an Army on her border with Bulgaria, which he expected to collapse with equal ease. She did so on 28th February, and the Germans now stood within striking distance of Salonika. Britain reacted strongly. Since the outbreak of the Graeco-Italian war, we had given Greece the support of a few R.A.F. squadrons. Now we offered her troops. Eden flew out to Cairo and Athens in mid-February to discuss the details. Our purpose was not merely to honour our pre-war pledge of aid to Greece, but to persuade Yugoslavia and Turkey that if only the three countries would act in combination with Britain, the German occupation of the southern Balkans and the Turkish Straits could be successfully resisted.

The manoeuvre would also have its effect on Russia, who regarded German domination of south-east Europe with misgivings as great as our own. A further advantage was that an advance southwards by the Yugoslavs into Albania would trap the Italian Army facing Greece. The issue turned on the attitude of the Yugoslav and Turkish Governments. Would the former be frightened, like Bulgaria, into signing the Axis Pact? Would the latter prefer neutrality to a defensive war?

During the first two months of 1941 Harold Nicolson learned little of these higher strategic objectives. The general design was concealed by the surrounding darkness. The Ministry of Information, which to outsiders sounded like a central control panel, was in fact the interpreter more than the transmitter of news. He was particularly busy with questions of civilian morale, now that the provincial cities were bearing the brunt of the German air attacks, and with British relations with neutral and defeated countries. In early January he continued his tour of the Ministry's centres outside London. It was in his own constituency of Leicester that he received from his secretary the news that his rooms in the Temple had been badly shaken by a bomb.

ELVIRA NIGGEMAN[1] TO H.N.   *2nd January, 1941*
                                              Ministry of Information

I am sorry to tell you that there was either a land-mine or a heavy bomb on the Temple last night, and the windows and window-frames of No. 4 have gone, and some of the panelling is completely destroyed. I will get some stuff to patch over the windows, because you couldn't sit there at all as it is.

I walked up to St Paul's, where things are still smouldering, and then back along Holborn and Guildford Street to the Ministry, and all along there were little groups of people talking quietly but quite determinedly about revenge. There is no doubt that the feeling is growing that similar treatment of the Germans is the only thing they will understand. I also went to a News film and saw the film of London's fire, and when the commentator spoke about doing the same to Germany, there was decided applause in a subdued way— since West End audiences do not shout like suburban ones. When I stood on the steps of St Paul's on Monday, while the fires were still raging, at one moment I caught that subdued muttering, in the way they do the crowds in *Oedipus Rex*, only it didn't grow louder, and I have never seen a crowd so determined and grave and thoughtful.

[1] H.N.'s private secretary from 1938 to 1965.

I have lived at fever pitch, which the intense cold does not cool. We are fighting devils, and I don't see why we shouldn't fight like devils in order to let them see what it is like. They always get out of everything.

H.N. TO V.S-W.   *7th January, 1941*
                                                   Queen's Hotel, Leeds

We had a ghastly drive here, or rather the country through which we drove [from Manchester] is hell. Great rolling moors under a grey sky, not unhedged or unvintaged enough to be magnificent, but like soiled grey counterpanes. Then in between and all along the valleys dark mills belching smoke. God how I wish man had never invented the machine! I sympathise with the Nottingham frame-breakers. They saw the light.

I dined with Billy Harlech,[1] the Regional Commissioner. He had been spending the day with the Queen visiting Sheffield. He says that when the car stops, the Queen nips out into the snow and goes straight into the middle of the crowd and starts talking to them. For a moment or two they just gaze and gape in astonishment. But then they all start talking at once. 'Hi! Your Majesty! Look here!' She has that quality of making everybody feel that they and they alone are being spoken to. It is, I think, because she has very large eyes which she opens very wide and turns straight upon one. Billy Harlech says that these visits do incalculable good.

DIARY   *11th January 1941*

Go by train to Glasgow. They are all alive and vivid, and I feel that the M. of I. can leave Scotland to look after itself. The clean sense of the Scottish makes me feel sick at heart with the muddy timidity of the English. Even Alan Hodge,[2] who comes from Liverpool, catches the atmosphere. 'Are Scottish people really nicer and more alive than English people, or is it only a first impression?' He is very bright in the head, that boy.

As we have nothing to do in the afternoon, we motor out to Loch

---

[1] Lord Harlech, the North-Eastern Regional Commissioner for Civil Defence. He had been Secretary-of-State for the Colonies, 1936–38, and later in 1941 was to become U.K. High Commissioner in South Africa.

[2] He was Assistant Private Secretary to the Minister of Information, 1941–45, and accompanied H.N. throughout this tour. In 1951 he became Joint Editor (with Peter Quennell) of *History Today*.

Lomond. We have a lovely day and it is very beautiful. Then I start writing my report for Duff and take the night train down from Glasgow.

V.S-W. TO H.N.   *11th January, 1941*
                                                                    Sissinghurst

I like Jack Macnamara,[1] and do ask him to lunch next Sunday. But warn him that he may not get much to eat. We are in real difficulties down here. I don't think I have eaten meat more than twice this week, and we have depended almost entirely on eggs and vegetables. It is not only that the meat ration is reduced, but there simply isn't any meat to be had. The arrival of a leg of mutton causes a commotion in the village; everybody talks about it and wonders how it will be divided. One cannot even get cheese. I suppose it will improve, and after all, as Lord Woolton[2] remarked, 'Which would you rather have, meat or Bardia?', a brilliant phrase which put everybody back in a good temper. One or two days I have honestly been hungry; not very, but hungry enough to notice.[3]

DIARY   *20th January, 1941*

I lunch with General de Gaulle at the Savoy. Attlee and Dalton are there. De Gaulle looks less unattractive with his hat off, since it shows his young hair and the tired and not wholly benevolent look in his eyes. He has the taut manner of a man who is becoming stout and is conscious that only the exercise of continuous muscle-power can keep his figure in shape. I do not like him. He accuses my Ministry of being 'Pétainiste'. '*Mais non*', I say, '*Monsieur le Général.*' '*Enfin, Pétainisant.*' '*Nous travaillons*', I said, '*pour la France entière.*' '*La France entière*', he shouted, '*c'est la France Libre. C'est moi!*' Well, well. I admit he has made a great Boulangiste gesture. But the spectre of General Boulanger passes across my mind. He begins to abuse Pétain, saying that once again he has sold himself to Laval, saying that Weygand showed cowardice when bombed at the front. Osusky[4] says that French opinion imagines that de Gaulle and Pétain are at heart as one. '*C'est une erreur*', he says sharply. I am not encouraged.

[1] Colonel John Macnamara, Conservative M.P. for Chelmsford since 1935. He was then in command of a battalion of the London Irish Rifles.
[2] Minister of Food, 1940–43.
[3] This letter may give the false impression that England was living on a siege-diet. In fact, shortages of the kind described were local and temporary.
[4] Czech Ambassador in Paris before the fall of France.

To change the subject I say that I have received a letter from occupied France which I was surprised had passed the censor. De Gaulle says that he had received a long letter of the most Gaulliste nature, the writer of which had written on the top, 'I am sure the censor will stop this'. Underneath in violet ink was written, '*La censure approuve totalement*'. We discuss Darlan. He says that Darlan loves his ships as a race-horse owner loves his horses. It does not matter to him whether he races at Longchamps or on Epsom Downs. What matters is that it should be a great race and that he should win it. '*Mais il manque d'estomac.*' Had he been a strong man, he would either have fought his fleet with us against the Italians or fought with the Germans against us. As it was, he was preserving his race-horses and they would become old, old, old.

I turn on Roosevelt's inaugural address from Washington. I am still young enough to be amazed at hearing a voice from Washington as if it were in my own room. It is a good speech. He recalls the great blows which America has struck for liberty. He reminds them that Washington created the American idea, that Lincoln saved it from disintegration, and that now they must save it from a menace from outside. 'We do not retreat,' he concludes. 'We are not content to stand still.' I enjoyed that part very much indeed.

We discuss the infinite complexity of arranging the reception of Halifax, who should arrive tomorrow at Baltimore in the *King George V*.[1] How I wish I were with him, except that I could simply not bear to leave London or England in these days. One's patriotism, which has been a vague family feeling, is now a flame in the night. I may have felt arrogant about the British Empire in past years; today I feel quite humbly proud of the British people.

DIARY   *22nd January, 1941*

Winston refuses to make a statement on war aims. The reason given in Cabinet is that precise aims would be compromising, whereas vague principles would disappoint. Thus all those days of work have led to nothing.[2] Winston replies to the debate on man-power. He is in

[1] Lord Halifax had been appointed Ambassador in Washington, and was succeeded as Foreign Secretary by Anthony Eden. Churchill, with a typically imaginative gesture, had sent Halifax to America in our newest battleship, *King George V*.

[2] The statement on war aims, which advocated a European Federation and increased Socialism at home, had been drafted by H.N. in collaboration with Halifax. His disappointment at its rejection was natural, since it was his greatest single contribution to British policy during his period at the Ministry of Information.

terrific form. Authoritative, reasonable, conciliatory and amusing. In the course of his speech he uses the phrase, *primus inter pares*. The Labour people cry out, 'Translate!' Winston, without a moment's hesitation, goes on, 'Certainly I shall translate'—then he pauses and turns to his right—'for the benefit of any Old Etonians who may be present.'

Back and work hard. James Pope-Hennessy comes to dine at Boulestin. I love his sharp and gentle mind.

DIARY *23rd January, 1941*

We have taken Tobruk. I go down to Cambridge. I go to see Sir Will Spens, Master of Corpus and Regional Commissioner. He feels that it would be dangerous to be complacent about the public morale. He feels that the people lack imagination and are not aware of the terrific ordeals which lie ahead. He admits that they have shown some sense of proportion about the Libyan victories, but he is not sure that they realise how gigantic the German knock-out blow will be when it comes.

I go round to Trinity, and there to my surprise I find Gerry Wellesley[1] and Anthony Powell.[2] I sit next to the Vice-Master. The lights in hall are shaded but the portraits are still lit up and the undergraduates in their grey flannel bags are still there. Afterwards we adjourn for port and coffee to the Combination Room. I sit next to George Trevelyan, the Master.[3] I look round upon the mahogany and silver, upon the Madeira and the port, upon the old butler with his stately efficiency. 'It is much the same', I say to him. 'Civilisation', he replies, 'is always recognisable.' I then walk back with Gerry to the hotel. It is a joy for me to be with this dear old friend again.

DIARY *26th January, 1941*
Sissinghurst

Sibyl[4] comes to stay. As usual she is full of gossip. She minds so much the complete destruction of London social life. Poor Sibyl, in the evenings she goes back to her house[5] which is so cold since all the

---

[1] The architect, and a serving soldier. He was to become the seventh Duke of Wellington in 1943.
[2] The author, then aged 35.
[3] The great historian. He was Master of Trinity from 1940 till 1951.
[4] Lady Colefax, the literary and political hostess, and a very old friend of the Nicolsons.
[5] At 19 Lord North Street, Westminster.

windows have been broken. And then at 9 she creeps round to her shelter under the Institute for the Blind and goes to sleep on her palliasse. But all this leaves her perfectly serene. We who have withstood the siege of London will emerge as Lucknow veterans and have annual dinners.

We have not yet taken Derna but we have invaded Italian Somaliland. In every direction the Italians must feel that their Empire is crashing round their heads. Eritrea has been badly pierced, and we are within striking distance of Massawa. But all this is mere chicken-feed. We know that the Great Attack is impending. We know that in a week or two, in a day or two, we may be exposed to the most terrible ordeal that we have ever endured. The Germans have refrained from attacking us much during the last ten days since they do not wish to waste aeroplanes and petrol on bad weather. But when the climate improves they may descend upon us with force such as they have never employed before. Most of our towns will be destroyed.

I sit here in my familiar brown room with my books and pictures round me, and once again the thought comes to me that I may never see them again. They may well land their parachute and airborne troops behind Sissinghurst and the battle may take place over our bodies. Well, if they try, let them try. We shall win in the end.

DIARY   *31st January, 1941*

Lunch with Sibyl [Colefax]. I discuss with Hugh Dalton[1] whether our children will tell their children that we members of Churchill's Government 'were giants in those days'. We are not so sure that anyone will ever say that Kingsley Wood was a giant. Winston, of course, will emerge as a terrific figure, and perhaps Portal.[2]

DIARY   *1st February, 1941*

Wendell Willkie[3] is over here. He is astonished by our attitude. For instance, he was driving through Trafalgar Square yesterday when the sirens sounded. He thought it was merely a midday trial. But when

---

[1] Minister of Economic Warfare, 1940–42.

[2] Chief of the Air Staff, 1940–45. It is curious in this connection that neither H.N.'s diaries nor letters make a single mention of Air Chief Marshal Dowding, C.-in-C. Fighter Command and chief architect of our victory in the Battle of Britain.

[3] Republican candidate in the recent American Presidential Election. Roosevelt had sent over his defeated rival with a special note of introduction to Churchill.

told that it was a real raid (as many as 25 aeroplanes came over), he was startled at the fact that the traffic continued as usual and above all that people continued to feed the pigeons under Nelson's column. I must say, the indifference of the London public to daylight raids has to be seen to be believed. While those dear old ladies were feeding their pigeons, A.A. guns were booming overhead.

DIARY   *4th February, 1941*

I go to the Dorchester where Rebecca West is giving a dinner for Wendell Willkie. The others are Lady Rhondda,[1] Sibyl [Colefax], Kingsley Martin, Wilson Harris,[2] Julian Huxley, L. B. Namier, Lord Horder,[3] Priestley and others. I sit next to Willkie. He is not tired but he is evidently bored. He turns his charm on but drums with his fingers. We go up to his room and then he settles down to be interviewed. He has had a busy day. He has flown to Dublin to see De Valera and is flying tonight to America. He says that his two major impressions are: (1) Cohesion in the country. He is amazed that Big Business are as determined on victory as anybody. They know that it means their ruin, but even Montagu Norman[4] had said to him, 'Ruin? Go to hell. We must win.' (2) Leadership. He quite saw that in normal times Winston might be a 'lousy' Prime Minister, but that today not only was he superb in himself, but the Labour people all recognised his superiority. I could see that what had struck him most was the patriotism of the capitalists.

We asked him about his interview with De Valera. He was very frank. De Valera had produced a map showing how the English still threatened his country by their monstrous occupation of Northern Ireland. Willkie had said that all this did not matter now, but what about the bases?[5] Ireland was definitely proving a disadvantage to the cause of freedom, and American opinion would not be with her. Dev was startled by this and tried to dodge and edge away by accusing the British Government of stupidity. Willkie said, 'But we all know about

[1] Editor and Chairman of *Time and Tide*.   [2] Editor of the *Spectator* since 1932.
[3] Physician to the King.   [4] Governor of the Bank of England, 1920–44.
[5] Eire had declared her neutrality in this war, even though the British Government had not yet recognised her existence as a sovereign State. The Southern Irish ports were denied to Britain in conformity with this 'neutrality', and the range of our destroyer escorts was thereby reduced. At this very moment highly secret negotiations were in progress between the British and American Governments to organise joint ocean convoys in the Atlantic, and this measure partly offset the disadvantage of our exclusion from the Irish ports.

that. That doesn't count anyway. You want Britain to win?' De Valera assented to this. 'And yet you are making it more difficult for her?' So in the end that fine and obstinate Spaniard was obliged to say that he was afraid that if he leased the bases, Dublin might be bombed. Willkie (having been at Coventry and Birmingham) did not conceal his contempt. 'American opinion', he repeated, 'will not be with you.' Dev writhed. Lady Rhondda asks him whether we have made any mistakes with our propaganda. He replies, 'Not a foot or a toe placed wrong.' I am delighted by that. A very attractive man.

DIARY   6th February, 1941

To the Civil Defence Committee. We begin by discussing the new invasion leaflet. Herbert Morrison says, 'These points should have been settled months ago; they should have been settled before the war.' For instance, nobody is quite clear whether the public should be asked to store food or not. I gather that they do not expect invasion before 25th February. The area east of Ashford will be evacuated. I tremble for my poor Vita.

In the House there is a supplementary estimate for the tidy little sum of sixteen thousand million pounds. We have to sit there all the time expecting our subject to come up. Finally Philip Noel-Baker opens the debate and concentrates on the German wireless. Every speaker pays a great tribute to the improvements effected since Duff took over and the debate is a howling success. This is a great encouragement to us.

The Germans are definitely infiltrating into Bulgaria, and the Turks are showing cold feet. The pressure on Vichy continues. The Germans are saying, 'Pétain may have to be removed from those evil counsellors who now surround him.' Darlan has gone back to Paris. The situation is rather disturbing.

H.N. TO V.S-W.   11th February, 1941

Oh dear, I have got into trouble.

Five months ago I gave a talk about war aims to a private meeting of the Fabian Society. I said nothing that I did not know was approved by the Cabinet at that date. There were no Press present. The Fabian Society did, however, publish the talk in their Year Book and eventually that reached America. My address was lifted by the New York *Nation* and reproduced as an article. That article reached England and a long extract from it was published on 3rd February by the *Manchester Guardian*. It came to Winston's notice. He absolutely blew up, and sent a stinking note to Duff asking by what right I was writing about war aims when he himself had deprecated any mention of them. I wrote a minute explaining what had happened, and Duff will of course back me up. But the P.M. is too busy to go into the rights and wrongs of little things and will feel that I have spoken out of my turn.

I do have such bad luck about this sort of thing. The reason is that although a humble member of the Government, I have news-value abroad. I must say, I was rather shattered when I read the P.M.'s minute. I met him in the smoking-room today and I observed that he was not as genial as usual. I hope it does not mean that I shall lose my job.[1]

H.N. TO W. B. JARVIS[2]   *11th February, 1941*
You will wonder what this Balkan drive means and you may be interested to have my views on the subject.

In the first place, it is not in the least unexpected, and in fact our Minister in Bucharest was given authority to break off relations two months ago. Being a stout fellow he said he would prefer to stay on and act as a channel of communication as long as possible.

We have little doubt that the original Axis plan was for Italy to make a drive against Cairo from the west and Khartoum from the east. At the right moment Germany would drive through the Balkans. The almost complete collapse of the Italian strategy has altered the situation and the German failure with their dive-bombers at Malta has also made them think again. They are thus driven back upon using overwhelming land-power since they cannot prove effective against us either by air or sea. We must expect them to occupy Bulgaria within the next few weeks and possibly also to drive on to Salonika. It may be, however, that they will make a dash for Constantinople and the Dardanelles on the assumption that both Russia and Turkey are too frightened to take any action.

The universal feeling is that unless Germany can knock us out within the next three months she has lost the war. On the excellent principle that we must expect the worst, we are all saying and thinking that

[1] Shortly afterwards, Duff Cooper received from Churchill a note saying, 'Please thank Mr Nicolson for his explanation.' H.N. drew comfort from the word 'thank'.
[2] Chairman of the West Leicester Conservative Association.

invasion of this country is inevitable. It seems absolutely impossible that they should succeed in this, although they will expose us to very great trials and their submarine activity may bring us very close to food-shortage.

On the other hand they are now forced to hold on to the whole of Europe which is seething with discontent and the morale of their troops is none too good. One has the impression of a very hard core which will be difficult to crack, and inside a state of putrid corruption. I had a long talk with Benes[1] today, who is one of the best-informed people in Europe. He confirms absolutely the above view. He feels that Russia will, in the end, be obliged in her own interests to intervene on our side, and that if we can only withstand the appalling blitz which is coming to us, we shall have won the war.

DIARY   *14th February, 1941*

Dear London! So vast and unexpectant, so ugly and so strong! You have been bruised and battered and all your clothes are tattered and in disarray. Yet we, who never knew that we loved you (who regarded you, in fact, like some old family servant, ministering to our comforts and amenities, and yet slightly incongruous and absurd), have suddenly felt the twinge of some fibre of identity, respect and love. We know what is coming to you. And our eyes slip along your old untidy limbs, knowing that the leg may be gone tomorrow, and that tomorrow the arm may be severed. Yet through all this regret and dread pierces a slim clean note of pride. 'London can take it.' I believe that what will win us this war is the immense central dynamo of British pride. The Germans have only assertiveness to put against it. That is transitory. Our pride is permanent, obscure and dark. It has the nature of infinity.

But I wish all the same that I had not annoyed Winston. I feel in disgrace with fortune and men's eyes. And then I think about Vita, and the rest of the sonnet is completed.[2]

---

[1] Edouard Benes, President of the Czechoslovak Republic, 1935–38. In July 1940, he was recognised by the Allied Governments in London as leader of his people in exile. In May 1945 he returned to his liberated country as President, and died in September 1948 after the Communist *coup*.
[2] Shakespeare's sonnet xxix.

H.N. TO V.S-W.   *18th February, 1941*
                                          Ministry of Information
I had the dreaded meeting of the National Labour Party.[1] Malcolm[2] was in the chair. He told us exactly what had happened about his being sent off to Canada. He had said to Winston, 'But you are condemning me to exile. All the lights will be on in Ottawa and I shall yearn for the dark of London.' He refused to go. He said that he would much rather join up. Winston was evidently touched by this attitude and asked him not to decide till next day. After sleeping it over, 'I saw', said Malcolm, 'that if Winston asked me to go to Timbuctoo, I should have to accept.' All this sounds awful bunk when one writes it down afterwards, but if you had been there and heard Malcolm speak so simply and frankly, you would have known that the whole thing was true, and that it reflects great credit both on the P.M. and on Malcolm.

Then the leadership question came up. They wanted me to be leader. But I knew that they did not want it very much. So I said, 'But it is absurd that a Party which began under the leadership of Ramsay MacDonald should end under the leadership of the Parliamentary Secretary to the Ministry of Information. I have neither false pride nor false modesty. But you, as sensible people, will agree that such a solution would make both the Party and myself seem ridiculous.' They agreed, and thus we have left the leadership in suspense and only pray that there will be no Press publicity. How silly and out of proportion it all is!

V.S-W. TO H.N.   *18th February, 1941*
                                    Monk's House, Rodmell, Sussex
Virginia[3] has gone to talk to the servants, and I sit alone in her friendly room with its incredible muddle of objects, so crowded that I am terrified of knocking something over. I've already broken a chair. Leonard has departed for the market, laden with baskets of apples and

[1] It should be remembered that H.N., although supported by the Conservatives in West Leicester, sat in Parliament as a member of the National Labour Party. The Party had, however, almost ceased to function as an independent group since the outbreak of war.
[2] Malcolm MacDonald, the leader of National Labour, was Minister of Health in Churchill's Government. He now became U.K. High Commissioner in Canada and remained there till early in 1946.
[3] This was V.S-W.'s last meeting with Virginia Woolf, who killed herself a month later.

carrots. They *are* nice. Leonard has now got a cat, which means that the rooms are further crowded by tin dishes on the floor.

DIARY   *26th February, 1941*

I walk back under the cold stars with some shells bursting around them. I am rather fussed about this diary. It is not intimate enough to give a personal picture. The really important things that I know I cannot record.[1] And this gives a picture of someone on the edge of things who is so certain that he knows what is really happening that he does not dare say so. The day-to-day impressions of a greengrocer in Streatham would really be more interesting. I must try henceforward to be more intimate and more illuminating. It is half that I feel that if I survive, this diary will be for me a record from which I can fill in remembered details. And half that I find some relief in putting down on paper the momentary spurts and gushes of this cataract of history.

DIARY   *27th February, 1941*

I attend the Anglo-French Parliamentary Association's lunch for de Gaulle and Muselier.[2] I sit bang opposite to de Gaulle and have much talk with him. I dislike him less than I did at first. He has tired, ruminating but not unkindly eyes. He has curiously effeminate hands (not feminine hands, but effeminate, without arteries or muscle). He abuses the newspaper *France*[3], which he says is not '*avec moi*'. He is off to Africa soon.

During March events led up to the almost simultaneous German attacks in the western desert and on Yugoslavia and Greece. The first was delivered by General Rommel on the British El Agheila position on 2nd April; the second from the central Balkans four days later.

The British strategy had been to hold the Tripolitanian frontier with light forces based on Benghazi as a far-flung screen for the movement of our troops to Greece, which began on 5th March; and to continue our

---

[1] He was not consistent about this. For example, the last line of the entry on 2nd March speaks of 'important events' to come, without specifying what. It was clearly Cabinet information about the sending of British troops to Greece. This news was not made public until a month later, but H.N. records the build-up in Greek ports by frequent references to it in his diary during March.

[2] In the previous month, Admiral Muselier, de Gaulle's Naval Commander, had been accused of betraying the plan to attack Dakar. Forged evidence was produced, and he was flung into jail. He was released when the forgery was exposed.

[3] Published by the Ministry of Information.

political efforts to form a southern Balkan bloc composed of Yugoslavia, Greece and Turkey. This strategy failed for three reasons. First, Wavell had miscalculated the speed at which Rommel (who had only begun to land his Afrika Korps at Tripoli at the end of February) could assemble a dangerous striking force at the end of his long lines of communication. When he attacked, the sparse British defences at El Agheila were quickly swept aside, and Benghazi itself was lost on 6th April. Secondly, the Turks politely opted for neutrality in spite of Eden's efforts in Ankara, declaring that they would fight hard if directly attacked, but that they were not looking for trouble. Thirdly, and most serious, the Yugoslav Government, urged by Prince Paul, adhered to the Axis Pact on 25th March. Two days later, a coup d'état in Belgrade forced the Prince's abdication, but British jubilation was premature. The new Government, with young King Peter as its figurehead, showed increasing hesitation to join the Allies. Hitler, however, did not hesitate. Enraged by the Belgrade coup, he gave orders for an improvised invasion of Yugoslavia, timed to coincide with his planned attack on northern Greece. Belgrade was obliterated from the air on 6th–8th April, with the loss of 17,000 lives.

DIARY   1st March, 1941

The Bulgarian Ministers went to Vienna yesterday and signed a pact adhering to the Axis. At the same time German mechanized forces thundered into Sofia. This is bad for Yugoslavia and Greece and will have a depressing effect here. People do not care so much about how many square miles we occupy in Eritrea so long as Germany is creeping ever closer to our jugular arteries. We know that in a few weeks we shall be exposed to a terrific ordeal.

We have a row in the Duty Room with General Tripp, who represents the Admiralty, on the subject of the Castelorizzo communiqué.[1] We point out that our objectives were to occupy the island, and that as we were turned out by troops brought in from Rhodes, we failed to carry our objectives. Why, therefore, should they pretend that we had succeeded? We are the Department charged with Government publicity and our policy is to tell the truth. If other Departments without our consent put out untrue statements, our work becomes impossible. I am angry about all this.

[1] The island of Castelorizzo, which lies between Rhodes and Cyprus, had been captured by British Commandos on 25th February. Our naval forces then withdrew, and the Italians, under cover of heavy air attacks, reoccupied the island.

DIARY   *2nd March, 1941*

Viti asks me how we are going to win this war. Hitler will shortly have the whole of Europe under his control, and how are we going to turn him out? It will require all our strength to resist the appalling attack by air and submarine which is shortly coming to us. We shall be shattered and starved. Yet how are we to tell our people how we can win? The only hope is that America and Russia will come in on our side. I think that we can resist the worst. But we shall be so exhausted by that resistance that Hitler may offer us an honourable peace which will be difficult to reject. I have an uneasy feeling that when things get very bad there may be a movement in this country to attribute the whole disaster to 'the war-mongers' and to replace Churchill by Sam Hoare or some appeaser. That will be the end of England. If only we could show people some glimmer of light at the end of the tunnel, we could count upon their enduring any ordeal. But the danger is that there is no light beyond the light of faith. I have that light. I know in the marrow of my bones that we shall win in the end. But I get depressed when I realise how difficult it is to convey that faith to the public, since it is not based, as far as I can see, on reason or calculation.

We are expecting important events in the next week.

DIARY   *4th March, 1941*

I dine with Louis Spears in his upstairs room at the Ritz. Mary Spears is there, also Ned Grigg and Monsieur and Madame Dejean.[1] The latter has been in Morocco and brings back disturbing news. The Germans are gradually infiltrating into Morocco, and unless we do something within the next few months, he fears that they will have it in their power as they have Rumania and Bulgaria. It was a great mistake on our part not to have pushed on to Tripoli after our Benghazi victories, since a common frontier would have had a stimulating effect upon the African French. In fact, he thinks that the main object of the German Balkan drive was to prevent Wavell from seizing Tripoli. He thinks we are ill-informed and optimistic about the French Empire. We seem to imagine that Pétain is determined to stick to the Armistice and not to surrender one inch beyond it; that Weygand is really our friend and is determined to defend the Empire against the Germans;

[1] Maurice Dejean had been diplomatic Chef de Cabinet to Reynaud at the time of the collapse of France. He rallied to de Gaulle, and was to be put in charge of Foreign Affairs in de Gaulle's National Committee formed in September 1941.

and that Darlan is in fact a fine fellow who would never dream of using the Fleet against his former allies. This is an illusion. Pétain is really passing into a state of senile coma. Darlan is ambitious and has now got control of all the key positions. He feels that he may save something for France by bargaining with Germany about the Fleet, but he would be quite capable (if the Germans were prepared to pay a sufficient price) to sell the Fleet to them. He thinks that our line of propaganda should be to destroy the Pétain legend. That is a disturbing suggestion from so intelligent and well-informed a man.

He tells us the full story of Hélène de Portes.[1] He admits that it is '*inénarrable et inavouable*'. But, after all, he was there and he knew. He said that she really believed that Reynaud would become the dictator of France and she the power behind the throne. She was passionately anti-British, since she felt that our democratic ideas would prevent this strange pattern of state governance. The extent of her influence and interference cannot be exaggerated. It was not so much that she dictated policy but that she surrounded Reynaud with fifth-columnists and spies. For instance, he and Roland de Margerie had managed at a crucial moment to convince Reynaud that he should send the Fleet, and what remained of the Army and material, to North Africa. All the plans were made. But it was Madame de Portes who made him change his mind and accept Baudouin as Foreign Minister.

We discuss how it came about that this frousy soiled woman with the dirty fur tippet managed to sway the destiny of a great nation. He said that it was because Reynaud had an inferiority complex about his small stature and that she made him feel tall and grand and powerful. 'Had Reynaud been three inches taller, the history of the world might have been changed.' He and Spears talk together about the final *débandade*. Those hurried rushes through the night from château to château, only to find that there was but one telephone in the butler's pantry and that France could not communicate with its Prime Minister. Madame de Portes was always there and keeping away from Reynaud anybody whom she felt might spur him to resistance. '*C'est moi*', she used to scream, '*qui suis la maîtresse ici!*' And my God she was right. Then the final scene in the two-seater car. Reynaud was driving. The luggage was piled behind. He was always a bad driver and he crashed into a tree. A suit-case hit Madame de Portes on the back of the neck and killed her instantly. Reynaud was hit by the steering-wheel and

[1] La Comtesse de Portes was the woman, of undoubted intelligence and determination, behind Paul Reynaud. She was killed in a motor-accident in June 1940.

rendered unconscious. When he recovered in hospital, they broke the news to him that Madame de Portes was dead. *'Elle était la France'*, he said. Dejean thought he really felt it. *La fausse Marianne.*

DIARY   *6th March, 1941*

Duty Room. General Tripp reads out the Admiralty communiqué about the raid on the Lofoten Islands.[1] It is a fine story, but so badly worded that the whole point is missed. It states that one of our main objectives was to destroy stocks of cod-liver oil because of its vitamin properties. We say that we shall not issue the communiqué unless that is taken out. Tripp just grins and giggles. He is becoming past a joke.[2]

A funereal luncheon at the Piccadilly Hotel as a farewell to Malcolm MacDonald. There is a gathering of National Labour supporters and at the back of it all a feeling that Nat.Lab. has been a sad flop. I sit next to Lady Something who tells me of the really great trouble she has been having with Molly, her head parlour-maid; the odd-man has also been a nuisance.

In the Duty Room afterwards we are glad to learn that the Admiralty have cut out the bit about cod-liver oil from the communiqué. What we are to do with the ten quislings captured is a great problem. The Germans say, 'Only a country which has sunk so low as England could have attempted such a Don Quixote action.' Their ten ships were sunk even lower.

DIARY   *7th March, 1941*

The Cabinet met twice. I gather that at their first meeting the feeling was that we should let Greece down. This would have had a terrible effect both here and throughout the world. At the second meeting it seems that more adventurous counsels were advanced. Yet we know that any landing on the Greek mainland would be a forlorn hope. Ought we to risk that forlorn hope? One of our main preoccupations is the dropping of aerial mines in the Suez Canal. That is causing very serious inconvenience. In fact we are all a trifle gloomy tonight. Dine at the Greek restaurant.[3] I may never be brave enough to set foot there again.

[1] A highly successful raid by British Commandos on the Lofoten Islands in northern Norway. Much shipping was destroyed and 200 German prisoners taken.
[2] Nevertheless, Lieut.-General W. H. L. Tripp (1881–1959) remained Naval Adviser to the Ministry of Information until the end of the war.
[3] The White Tower, in Percy Street.

H.N. TO V.S-W. *10th March, 1941*
Ministry of Information

I lunched with some of de Gaulle's people. There was a little man opposite to me, and I said brightly to him, 'Have you met a man called Dejean who is just back from Morocco?' 'I am Dejean', he answered. I blushed to the roots of my hair, which is now a longish distance across, and up, my face. But truly I am hopeless about recognising people.

H.N. TO V.S-W. *17th March, 1941*
Ministry of Information

I lunched with James [Pope-Hennessy] and he took me to see the devastation round St Paul's. It is unbelievable. A great space as wide as Trafalgar Square laid low. I feel that at any cost we should retain it as a memorial to London's civilians. They deserve it, and it gives a magnificent vista of St Paul's such as Wren would have given his soul to achieve. It is as if St Paul's stood where the National Gallery now stands. To get that permanently cleared is worth 40 million pounds in site-value and should be done.

Our landing in Greece (although we all feel it may end in disaster) has had a magical effect upon the Yugoslavs. I do not think the effect will last. But it was a fine thing to do, and it is now quite clear that it was the only thing to do. We may be turned out by the Germans, but they will have a nasty time.

DIARY *20th March, 1941*

At Duty Room we raise the question of the suppression of the news that we have landed in Greece. We point out that such suppression does harm to public confidence. Nonetheless, Wavell and Eden insist upon our maintaining silence. The Press as usual are behaving admirably on the whole front.

Dine with Violet Bonham Carter. Bongie[1] appears dressed as a warden in skiing clothes. They have both behaved heroically. Mrs Gilbert Russell and Mark [Bonham Carter] are there. Ben and Bubbles and Cressida[2] come in afterwards. An agreeable evening.

[1] Sir Maurice Bonham Carter, who had married Lady Violet in 1915.
[2] Cressida Bonham Carter, the elder daughter of Sir Maurice and Lady Violet, had married Jasper Ridley ('Bubbles') in 1939. He was killed in Italy in 1943, and was regarded by all his contemporaries as one of the most brilliant men of his generation.

What puzzles us is the hesitancy of the Germans. Is it possible that they are really contemplating an attack on Russia and the seizure of the oil-wells?

DIARY   *21st March, 1941*

Luncheon for the editors. I sit between Cudlipp[1] and Frank Owen.[2] They are very agreeable. What a funny man Duff is! He keeps on referring to me in the course of his remarks. 'Don't you think so, Harold?' 'You know more about this than I do, Harold. Don't you agree?' Whereas in the Ministry he never asks my opinion at all.

Anyhow he talks excellently. He begins by warning them that the great thing is not to antagonise the United States; that the bases agreement[3] would be signed on Tuesday and that people would not like it since it implies a surrender of a portion of our sovereignty. When we offered the bases against the destroyers we imagined, in Winston's words, that we were exchanging 'a bunch of flowers for a sugar cake'. But not at all. The Americans have done a hard business deal.

Duff says that the Lease and Lend Bill[4] is probably the decisive fact of the war, and he is sure that America will be in the war before long. He then talks about the despatch of troops to Greece, and explains that in order to do so, we had to abandon the far more attractive and remunerative objective of seizing Tripoli. We have sent some 80,000 men, only 20,000 of whom have by now arrived. He thinks we shall have a hard knock but they agree that there was no other course to take. The Yugoslavs are going over to the Axis. This will have a bad effect on Turkey.

I have a quiet talk with Duff afterwards. He agrees to recommend Violet Bonham Carter as one of the B.B.C. Governors.

---

[1] Percy Cudlipp, Editor of the *Daily Herald* since 1940.
[2] Editor of the *Evening Standard*, 1938–41.
[3] An agreement with the United States to make available to the American Navy bases in the Western Atlantic and the United Kingdom in order to facilitate joint Atlantic convoys.
[4] It had become law on 11th March. By it the United States enabled Great Britain to purchase American goods without cash payment.

H.N. TO V.S-W.   *27th March, 1941*
Ministry of Information

The news is good today. In the morning two things happened. (1) I
read a telegram from Belgrade saying that Subotic[1] was sending
information to his Government regarding our attitude. (2) An hour
later I learned that the Yugoslav Government had been arrested by
Simovic.[2] (3) An hour later I had to lunch with Subotic. You admit
that this was an awkward concatenation.

When I arrived I found my old friend Tilea[3] as the first arrival. He
whispered to me, 'Be careful, they are not pleased.' I said nothing.
Then in pranced the Turkish Ambassador and seized a glass of sherry.
'Je bois', he said, *'à la santé de Sa Majesté le Roi Pierre II et à l'alliance
Balkanique.'* The Subotics put on a blue face.

The Yugoslavs may try to gain time by saying that their foreign
policy is unaltered. But in fact they have come in on our side and
God help the Italians in Albania. The Germans will probably invade
the northern parts, but their Balkan expedition becomes very perilous.
It is a fine show and I give Ronnie Campbell[4] full marks. But in the
final examination let us remember that we owe this to the Greeks.
Their resistance made it impossible for the Yugoslav Army to capitulate
to the Axis. I feel sorry for Prince Paul. He sacrificed all his affections
and all his principles in the hope of saving his country, and now the
rumour is that he has been shot.[5] I have tried to get our Press to treat
him gently.

Then this evening late news came in that we had taken Keren.[6] It
may not be true. But if it is true, it means that we have got the whole
Italian Empire with the exception of Tripoli. If they have the Yugoslavs on their backs now, they are done. I truly believe that if this
Yugoslav thing is as real as we imagine, we have won the war. Of
course the Germans may now invade Yugoslavia and Greece. It will
take them a great effort, and it means that during these vital months

[1] The Yugoslav Minister in London.
[2] In the early hours of this day, General Simovic staged the *coup d'état* in Belgrade
which ousted Prince Paul and replaced him by a pro-Allies Government under
King Peter.
[3] V. V. Tilea, previously Rumanian Minister in London, and since July 1940 leader
of the Free Rumanian Movement.
[4] Sir Ronald Campbell, British Minister in Belgrade, 1939–41.
[5] This was incorrect. He was allowed to leave with his family for Greece.
[6] The main Italian stronghold in Eritrea. It fell that day, and the whole of Eritrea
was in our hands by 8th April.

of 1941 (when all their efforts should be concentrated on defeating us) they will be diverted to side-shows. What a triumph! Truly it is all over. I think you should hoist the flag on Sunday.

DIARY   *29th March, 1941*

Rab Butler agrees with me that as the Germans have come up against a difficult problem in their invasion of this country and in their invasion of the Balkans, they may strike suddenly at Russia. Everybody else regards this idea as fantastic, but I am not so sure.

DIARY   *31st March, 1941*

Go to see the Russian Ambassador, Maisky. He sits there in his ugly Victorian study like a little gnome in an arm-chair, twiddling his thumbs, twinkling his eyes and giving the impression that his feet do not reach the floor. He says that he takes an objective view of all this. We shall not be beaten. Our Navy is the finest in the world and perhaps our Air Force also. But what about our Army? Is it good for anything but a colonial war? Shall we be able to resist the Germans in Greece or even in Cyrenaica? We cannot afford another Norway. And how on earth do we imagine that we shall ever defeat the Germans? Italy we may knock out. But Germany never. I reply that I rely on my instinct and my knowledge of the German character. They will assuredly crash before we do. He says that this may be so: 'Time will show', he says, grinning mischievously. He thinks that the Labour people here are not strong enough. They do not force the Government to come to terms with Russia. 'The Labour people are as bad as Chamberlain.' I ask him whether he sees any prospect of a Yugoslav–Greek–Turkish alliance. He says that Turkey is too cautious. I ask him whether he has any fear that Russia will be attacked. He says, 'Germany is too cautious.'

DIARY   *1st April, 1941*

In the smoking-room Winston sits down and has his glass of Bristol Milk and is prepared to answer questions. Members cluster round him rather ingratiatingly. 'How well you are looking, Prime Minister.' He does in fact look better than I have seen him look for years. All that puffy effect has gone and his face is almost lean, with the under-lip pouting defiance all the time. He says: 'Yes, I am well. I am in fine trim. More than I was this time last year. We are doing well. We have a real Army now. We have tanks—good tanks. We have guns.

In the air our position is not merely absolutely, but relatively, stronger.' He talks of the battle of the Ionian Sea[1] or whatever it will be called. He says that the Italians displayed poor seamanship and violated 'those elementary rules of strategy which are familiar to every Dartmouth cadet'. He speaks very bitterly of Darlan. 'I should like to break that man. Expressing gratitude to Germany, which has humbled his country in the dust.' He tells me to get out the *Voelkischer Beobachter* statement that Germany's war aim is to reduce this country 'to degradation and poverty', and to placard it throughout the country. 'It should be on every wall', he says. I go back to the Ministry and repeat this to Duff and Walter Monckton.

At this moment, when Hitler was about to attack Yugoslavia and Greece and Rommel launched his desert offensive, Harold Nicolson was worried by V. Sackville-West's state of physical and mental health under the strain of war. In fact his fears were exaggerated, but she suffered a severe shock in the suicide of her most intimate friend, Virginia Woolf. Her letter breaking the news to him crossed with his own letter expressing his concern about her state of mind.

H.N. TO V.S-W.   *31st March, 1941*
                                                 Ministry of Information

It is always a gloomy moment for me when I unpack the *panier* which we packed together. I take out the flowers sadly and think of you picking them and putting the paper round them. But today it was worse, as I feel such a failure as a help to you. I do not know what it is, but I never seem to be able to help you when you are in trouble. I loathe your being unhappy more than I loathe anything. But I just moon about feeling wretched myself, and when I look back on my life, I see that the only times I have been really unhappy are when you have been unhappy too.

I wonder whether you would have been happier if married to a more determined and less sensitive man. On the one hand you would have hated any sense of control or management, and other men might not have understood your desire for independence. I have always respected that, and you have often mistaken it for aloofness on my part. What bothers me is whether I have given way too much to

[1] The Battle of Cape Matapan on 28th March, when Admiral Cunningham sank three Italian heavy cruisers and two destroyers without loss to himself. The battle gave Britain naval mastery of the Eastern Mediterranean at this critical time.

your eccentricities. Some outside person might imagine that I should have made more of my life if I had had someone like Diana De la Warr to share my career. There are moments when I think you reproach yourself for not having been more interested in my pursuits and for not having pushed against my diffidence. I never feel that myself. I have always felt that the struggle in the market-place was for me to fight alone, and that you were there as something wholly different.

But what has always worried me is your dual personality. The one tender, wise and with such a sense of responsibility. And the other rather cruel and extravagant. The former has been what I have always clung to as the essential you, but the latter has always alarmed me and I have tried to dismiss it from my mind—or, rather, I have always accepted it as the inevitable counterpart of your remarkable personality. I have felt that this side of you was beyond my understanding, and when you have got into a real mess because of it, you have been angry with me for not coping with the more violent side in yourself.

I do not think that you have ever quite realised how deeply unhappy your eccentric side has often rendered me. When I am unhappy I shut up like an oyster. I love you so much, darling. I hold my head in my hands worrying about you. I was nearly killed by a taxi today. I only missed an accident by a hair's breadth. And my first thought was, 'If I had really been taken to hospital in a mess, then Viti would have been shaken out of her muzzy moods.' I love you so much.

V.S-W. TO H.N.   *31st March, 1941*
Sissinghurst

I have just had the most awful shock: Virginia has killed herself. It is not in the papers, but I got letters from Leonard[Woolf] and also from Vanessa [Bell][1] telling me. It was last Friday. Leonard came home to find a note saying that she was going to commit suicide, and they think she has drowned herself, as he found her stick floating on the river. He says she had not been well for the last few weeks and was terrified of going mad again. He says, 'It was, I suppose, the strain of the war and finishing her book, and she could not rest or eat.'

I simply can't take it in. That lovely mind, that lovely spirit. And she seemed so well when I last saw her, and I had a jokey letter from her only a couple of weeks ago. She must have been quite out of her

[1] Virginia Woolf's elder sister, the painter. She married Clive Bell, the art critic, in 1907 and died in 1961.

mind or she would never have brought such sorrow and horror on Leonard. Vanessa had seen him and says he was amazingly self-controlled and calm, but insisted on being left alone.

V.S-W. TO H.N.   *2nd April, 1941*
                                                              Sissinghurst

Your letter made almost unbearable reading, partly because I had expected it to be about Virginia and was genuinely surprised. I cannot bear you to be unhappy, especially about me. But, darling, honestly there is no need for you to be. I have a very happy nature really, and only get into moods of despair occasionally. It is silly and selfish of me to say I mind the war, when so many people are suffering from it so infinitely more, but one does mind watching the downfall of all the things one cared about, and then I am perpetually haunted by the terror that something might happen to you (really haunted to a morbid degree) and I suppose that that does constitute a strain. You see, I love you so. I suppose I pray for your safety six times a day.

I don't quite see what you mean by my eccentricity. I can't see that I am eccentric in the least, unless liking to live here is eccentric, but lots of people have been recluses by nature (which I suppose I am), and not being in sympathy with the modern world, one's natural avoidance deepens. It is a form of escapism.

You have always been more sweet to me than I could describe, and I *quite* certainly don't wish that I had married anybody else! Your coming down here yesterday touched me so deeply. We are funny people, though, you and I: it was Virginia's death that brought you, and yet we never mentioned it.

Your story about the taxi makes my blood run cold. If anything happened to you, I should never get over it. In fact, I don't think I should go on living.

H.N. TO V.S-W.   *3rd April, 1941*
                                                              Ministry of Information

I got a nice long letter from you today and you seem less wretched. Of course I came down because of Virginia. But I saw no reason to mention the thing. There was nothing that could be said. I just wanted to be with you. I hate it so. It is horrible to see her picture in the papers. My heart absolutely aches with sympathy for Leonard.

V.S-W. TO H.N.   *8th April, 1941*

I went to see Vanessa [Bell] yesterday at Charleston. She could not have been nicer and told me all about it. Rather to my dismay, she said that Leonard wanted to see me. So I went to Monk's House. He was having his tea—just one tea-cup on the table where they always had tea. The house was full of his flowers, and all Virginia's things lying about as usual. He said, 'Let us go somewhere more comfortable', and took me up to her sitting-room. There was her needle-work on a chair and all her coloured wools hanging over a sort of little towel-horse which she had had made for them. Her thimble on the table. Her scribbling block with her writing on it. The window from which one can see the river.

I said, 'Leonard, I do not like your being here alone like this'. He turned those piercing blue eyes on me and said, 'It is the only thing to do.' I saw then that he was right. But it must take some courage.

He talked about the whole thing perfectly calmly and in great detail, shirking nothing. Some phrases bit. He said, 'When we couldn't find her anywhere, I went up to a derelict house which she was fond of in the Downs, called Mad Misery, but she wasn't there.' I remember her telling me about Mad Misery and saying that she would take me there one day. They have been dragging the river, but are now giving up the search. As the river is tidal, she has probably been carried out to sea. I hope so. I hope they will never find her.

She could swim. I knew this because of a story she once told me about Rupert Brooke at Cambridge, when they were both very young, and he took off all his clothes and plunged naked into a moonlit pool, and she thought she must do likewise; so she did, although very shy, and they swam about together. But it appears that when she went to drown herself, she was wearing big gum-boots (which she seldom did because she hated them), and if those had filled with water, they would have dragged her down. Also she may have weighted her pockets with stones. The river is banked up with stones. The only thing that puzzles them is that they never found her hat floating. But Vanessa thinks it had an elastic to keep it on, so went down with her.

In the month of April the Germans threw the British out of Greece and Cyrenaica, and in May they won Crete. The Allied successes in East Africa and Iraq, and the sinking of the 'Bismarck', were poor consolations for two disastrous months. Morale at home, weakened by renewed air-raids on London and provincial cities, showed signs of strain.

The Greek débâcle was due to the quick collapse of Yugoslavia, which capitulated on 17th April. The left flank of the Allied line in northern Greece was thereby exposed to a German outflanking movement through the Monastir gap, and the Greek army in Albania and Eastern Macedonia was surrounded. This left the Commonwealth force of four Divisions to face almost alone a German army of fifteen, including four armoured Divisions. They retreated slowly towards Athens, but the decision to evacuate the country was made in principle on 21st April to save Greece from needless devastation. The last men got clear of southern Greek ports on the 29th. Of the 53,000 British and Commonwealth troops landed in Greece, 41,000 were taken off by the Navy, most of them to Crete.

The German airborne assault on Crete began on 20th May, and although the Navy prevented a single enemy soldier landing on the island from the sea, German air superiority gradually overcame resistance, and a further evacuation began on 27th May. 16,500 men returned safely to Egypt, but 13,000 others were killed, wounded or taken prisoner. The Germans, too, suffered severely. Their victory had been so costly that the Airborne Division, the only one they had, was never able to go into action again.

It fell to Harold Nicolson during Duff Cooper's illness to direct much of the Ministry of Information's policy during this unhappy period. The Ministry was in trouble. The Service Departments claimed the right to issue their own communiqués, and the B.B.C. was also largely free from control by the Ministry which existed for no other purpose than to coordinate British information policy. It was therefore constantly held to blame for other people's errors of judgement. Harold Nicolson handled this difficult situation skilfully in the House of Commons, but he was depressed by the unfairness of much of the criticism directed against his Department, and by the lack of full support from the Prime Minister, to whom information policy was of small interest or importance. The treatment of the Rudolf Hess incident is one example of this. Harold Nicolson was also worried by personal financial troubles. He gave up smoking for 34 days in an effort to economise.

DIARY   *4th April, 1941*

The Libyan news is worse than I had supposed. I see a newspaper outside the Underground bearing the ominous headline, 'British troops evacuate Benghazi'. At the Executive Board we have a serious inquest upon the handling of the Libyan news. The optimistic com-

muniqués put out from Cairo during the last three days had not prepared the public for the dreadful shock of the Benghazi evacuation.
It will have a very bad effect everywhere. People will feel, 'We can
beat the Wops, but the Huns are irresistible'. The only way to meet
this would be by stark and full information. But we have very meagre
information and Cairo has dressed those slight *pudenda* in the most
foolish and unnecessary frills such as 'A mere propaganda victory',
'Our light covering forces', or 'General Wavell can be counted on to
choose his own battleground'. The fact is that we have been taken by
surprise and badly beaten, and that there is little to stop the Germans
from getting to Sollum. The only thing that might assuage public
opinion is to tell them that this has happened because we sent our army
to Greece. But we are not allowed to say that. We do two things.
We send an urgent telegram to Anthony Eden asking him to let us
publish the facts about our landing in Greece. And we decide that the
War Office must send out to Cairo somebody who has some idea of
public feeling here and will stop them putting out these idiotic communiqués.

After dinner I find a taxi under the wet April moon. Poor old
battered London slides past me as I drive to the Ministry. I think of
our armies in Greece and Libya and Abyssinia under the same slim
moon. I think of the bodies of Virginia and Robert Byron[1] tossing in
the sea. War assuredly is the ugliest of all things. I think of old
women panting under a mass of cement and brick—panting in terror
and death.

> 'More brain, oh Lord, more brain: else we shall mar
> Utterly that fair garden we might win.'[2]

DIARY   *9th April, 1941*

I go down to the House to hear Winston make his statement [on the
invasion of Greece]. It had been devised as a motion congratulating
the fighting Services on their victories, and I remember a few days
ago how Winston promised that he would say to us, 'Fly your flags
in celebration.' These victories are now dust and ashes.

The P.M. comes in at 11.56 and is greeted with cheers. He sits
between Greenwood and Attlee, scowls at the notes in his hand, pulls

---

[1] The author and traveller. He was drowned in 1941, perhaps in the Bay of Biscay,
when his ship was torpedoed on its way to Alexandria. But the date and exact
circumstances of this event have never been established.

[2] Meredith. *Modern Love.*

out a gold pencil and scribbles an addition to the last sheet. He then gets up to speak in a grim and obstinate voice. He throws out news incidentally. We have taken Massawa.[1] The Germans entered Salonika at 4 am. this morning. At this news there is a silent wince of pain throughout the House. He discloses that the U.S.A. have given us their revenue cutters. His peroration implies that we are done without American help. He indulges in a few flights of oratory. There is a little joke about the boa-constrictor, and a little joke about the revenue cutters having previously been used for prohibition. But he evidently feels that even graver news is ahead of us. The House is sad and glum.

DIARY   *13th April, 1941*

It looks as if the Germans have isolated our force at Tobruk, and got round them to Bardia. This is most disturbing, since, as far as I can gather, all our forces are at Tobruk, and if they isolate that, then they have nothing in front of them.[2] In the Balkans the news is better. The Yugoslavs seem to be snipping some of the fingers of the German advance. They are rallying and counter-attacking. But Libya is the main preoccupation and Libya is bad indeed. We cannot trust Egypt, and Iraq has already gone.[3] Turkey will not stand up to a bad strategic position, and we may lose Egypt and all that this implies.

From the propaganda point of view, all that the country really wants is some assurance of how victory is to be achieved. They are bored by talks about the righteousness of our cause and our eventual triumph. What they want are facts indicating how we are to beat the Germans. I have no idea at all how we are to give them those facts. Fundamentally (although they are unaware of the fact) the British public have lost confidence in the power of the sea. Norway was a nasty knock, but Libya was a nastier knock. 'How', they ask, 'was Germany able to land four divisions in Libya?' There are many explanations of this feat but none of them really disposes of the question, 'But if they can land four divisions in Libya, what prevents them obtaining mastery of Africa and Asia?' I see no ostensible answer to

[1] The chief port of Eritrea, which surrendered, with 10,000 Italian prisoners, on 8th April.

[2] This was fortunately not true. The troops cut off in Tobruk were only the 9th Australian Division and one other Australian brigade group.

[3] Only temporarily: in March 1941 Raschid Ali, who was working with the Germans, became Prime Minister of Iraq, but on 18th April a British brigade landed without opposition at Basra, the main Iraqui port on the Persian Gulf.

that terrible question. At the back of my mind there always hums and buzzes Darlan's reply to someone who suggested that we might win in the end. He asked his interlocutor what justified that assumption. He spoke of our naval supremacy. Darlan replied, '*Mais ça—c'est de la folie pure.*' The events of the Balkans and Libya may confirm that theory. I have no doubt that we shall win in the end. But we shall have to learn the new technique, the secret of mobile warfare, and only when we have learnt it (as we shall learn it) will the efficacy of our sea-power be brought to bear. Meanwhile, as in last July, I wake up with terror in the dawn.

DIARY   *16th April, 1941*

Dine with Sibyl [Colefax] at the Dorchester. I get away as early as I can, but have to walk the whole way back to the Ministry. There is a hot blitz on. To the south, round about Westminster, there is a gale of fire, as red as an Egyptian dawn. To the north there is another fire which I subsequently see at closer quarters. The stump of the spire of Langham Place church is outlined against pink smoke. I walk on under the guns and flares and the droning of the 'planes. I fall over a brick and break my glasses. I limp into the Ministry to be told that we have sunk a large convoy between Sicily and Tripoli. This is the news we wanted.

After typing this I go to bed. I get off to sleep all right, but the blitz gets worse and worse, and the night shrieks and jabbers like an African jungle. I have never heard such a variety of sounds—the whistle of the descending bombs, the crash of anti-aircraft, the dull thud of walls collapsing, the sharp taps of incendiaries falling all around. The British Museum opposite my window turns rose-red in the light of a fire in the University. Every now and then it turns sharp white when a magnesium flare descends. Then rose-red again. It goes on all night and I sleep fitfully.[1]

DIARY   *21st April, 1941*

We are evacuating from Greece. The Americans will take this badly and there is a wave of defeatism sweeping that continent. Lindbergh has been proclaiming that we are in a desperate position. I confess that my mind goes back to my last talk with Maisky when he said, 'You cannot stand another Norway.' Another Norway is now upon us,

[1] In the raids on London on 16th and 17th April, over 2,300 people were killed and more than 3,000 seriously injured.

and the news from Spain is equally bad.[1] Hitler is evidently determined to turn us out of the Mediterranean.

DIARY   7th May, 1941

A Civil Defence Committee at the Cabinet Offices. Herbert Morrison is worried about the effect of the provincial raids on morale. He keeps on underlining the fact that the people cannot stand this intensive bombing indefinitely and that sooner or later the morale of other towns will go, even as Plymouth's has gone.

To the House. Lloyd George makes a speech. Very gloomy and realistic he is, pointing a forefinger constantly and speaking about 'dark chasms'. His main theme is that the public must be told the truth. Of course in one way it was a damaging speech, since he made it abundantly clear that we were in danger of being starved and defeated. But from another point of view my pride swelled to think that nowhere else except in our own beloved House of Commons could such a speech have been made and received with calm and even with welcome. When he criticised the Prime Minister he gazed across at him with a firm aggressive chin of combat and opposition, but his little eyes twinkled with admiration and (I am not in the least exaggerating) with love. It was a good day for Parliament.

After lunch I return to the House. Winston is speaking as I enter. He holds the House from the very first moment. He stands there in his black conventional suit with the huge watch-chain. He is very amusing. He is very frank. At moments I have a nasty feeling that he is being a trifle too optimistic. He is very strong, for instance, about Egypt and our position in the Mediterranean. He attacks Hore-Belisha mercilessly. The vote of confidence is given 447 to 3. Pretty good. As Winston goes out of the Chamber towards the Members' Lobby, there is a spontaneous burst of cheering which is taken up outside. He looks pleased.

I then go to the annual meeting of the London Region of the League of Nations Union. I am being divested of my Presidency and it goes to Violet Bonham Carter who makes a fine speech. Very clear and logical. Then I call in for a few minutes at a film I wanted to see. Then have a late dinner with Peter Quennell at Olivelli's and return to the Ministry to work a bit.

I am happy about the House today. Members are a bit defeatist. But

[1] Hitler planned to capture Gibraltar during the summer, with the active participation of Spain.

Winston cheers them up. Yesterday it was rather like a hen-coop of wet hens: today they all strutted about like bantams.

DIARY   *8th May, 1941*

The cold is incredible. It is like February. The barrage-balloons have returned to an irritating inflexibility with their noses pointing north-east and their little fins trailing behind.

This is the eighth day of my renunciation of smoking. It gets more difficult instead of less difficult. But I do observe that it is a thought which suggests a pang rather than a pang which suggests a thought. Thus an aching tooth twitches into consciousness and says, 'I have tooth-ache.' But this nicotine hunger is only stimulated by some outside occurrence such as the sight of someone else smoking or an advertisement for Craven A. Then the pang lights up. Apart from that it is a vague feeling of something missing, as if one had had no breakfast.

I go to the House for questions. They want us to divulge the whole story of our sinkings in the Atlantic. As a matter of fact, we have only lost some 3 per cent of American supplies. But the Germans imagine that they have sunk some 40 per cent. Far be it from us to tell them. I reply accordingly.

Home Planning Committee. We discuss the possible decline of morale. It is true that nobody actually speaks of the possibility of defeat or surrender but this silence is a bad sign of repression. I fear that people will jump at any escape which makes cowardice appear respectable, and that the Oxford Group with their 'moral rearmament' may be the channel of sublimation. We must be very careful about all that. Morale is good—but it is rather like the Emperor's clothes.

DIARY   *14th May, 1941*

Defence Committee. There is the usual complaint that the newspapers will insist upon publishing defence details. The present grumble is that they say that half the House of Commons remains intact.[1] Walter Elliot is very keen that the House should now sit in St Stephen's Chapel. That, after all, is the historic place.[2] But the Prime Minister,

[1] The House of Commons was bombed on the night of 10th May, and the Chamber was completely gutted.
[2] St Stephen's Chapel, part of the Palace of Westminster, was where the Commons sat from 1547 to 1834. After the bombing, the Commons sat in the Chamber of the House of Lords.

when I suggest it to him, says, 'Too narrow. It would not do at all. We must have the Royal Gallery.'

I lunch with the Prime Minister and Mrs Churchill in the flat which has been constructed for them in the Office of Works. It is not very large, but it is well done and comfortable. Winston has brought some of his pictures in and the general effect is very gay. Winston sits there beaming, with his ugly watch-chain and his ugly ring. I try to get directives from him about Hess,[1] but he will go no further than to say that we must not make a hero of him. We have white wine and port and brandy and hors d'oeuvre and mutton. All rather sparse. Winston had been seeing the film *Comrade X*[2] and simply loved it. I told him that Maisky had tried to get it suppressed. He was overjoyed that it had not been. He is in a good purring mood. We discussed whether it would be a good thing to give bombed towns some decoration on the analogy of the French practice in the last war when they gave the Legion of Honour to Rheims and other towns. Winston snorted loudly, 'Legion of Honour? They have the ribbon today and the enamel cross. But where is the honour? Gone! Gone!'—and then a wide despairing gesture—'GONE!'

DIARY   *16th May, 1941*

I go to see the ruins of the old Chamber. It is impossible to get through the Members' Lobby which is a mass of twisted girders. So I went up by the staircase to the Ladies' Gallery and then suddenly, when I turned the corridor, there was the open air and a sort of Tintern Abbey gaping before me. The little Ministers' rooms to right and left of the Speaker's Lobby were still intact, but from there onwards there was absolutely nothing. No sign of anything but *murs calcinés* and twisted girders.

Duff is in a depressed mood. He had managed yesterday to persuade the P.M. that we must put out some directive about our attitude towards Rudolf Hess. Then Winston says, 'We must think this over. Come back at midnight and we shall discuss it again.' But when he

[1] Rudolf Hess, Hitler's Deputy Führer, flew alone to Scotland on 11th May to make contact with the Duke of Hamilton, whom he had known very slightly before the war. His purpose was to persuade the British that Germany was certain to win the war, and that Britain could have peace with Hitler in exchange for the previous German colonies. He was slightly insane, and his mission was quite unauthorised by Hitler.

[2] A film about a fictional Russian spy.

gets back he finds Max Beaverbrook[1] there, and Max persuades Winston not to make any statement at all. Now this is bad, since the belief will get around that we are hiding something and we shall be blamed in this Ministry. The real fact is that we cannot get maximum propaganda value out of this incident both at home and abroad. I feel a terrible lack of central authority in all this. Then today Max has a luncheon for the editors and lobby correspondents. He tells them that Hess had come over to explain to the Duke of Hamilton that we are beaten and had better give way. This is not going to help matters.

DIARY   *21st May, 1941*

I answer questions in the House, and then I meet Anthony Eden in Beaverbrook's room. The theme of our discussion is greater information and help for American correspondents, but the underlying theme is our publicity generally. We say that we shall be unable to carry on unless we are given greater powers over the Service Departments. Beaverbrook is on our side and so is Anthony. They end by drawing up a recommendation to the Cabinet which gives us much of what we want. Walter [Monckton] and I go away delighted.

It is not clear what is happening in Crete.[2] Winston regards it as rather a crucial battle. 'Neither side', he says, 'can escape.' But the Germans are landing troops all the time by air and we seem unable to land troops by sea. Meanwhile we ought to be in Baghdad at any moment,[3] and Aosta plus five generals have surrendered.[4]

DIARY   *22nd May, 1941*

Before midnight I am picked up by Kenneth Clark and we go to the B.B.C. where we are met by Ed Murrow.[5] Jane [Clark] comes with us. As usual she looks as smart and neat as a new pin. It is rather a curious experience. K. and I sit opposite each other and have earphones. Then we hear that we are linked up to New York and Kenneth starts doing

[1] Lord Beaverbrook had been Minister of Aircraft Production till 1st May, when he was appointed Minister of State with a seat in the War Cabinet.
[2] The New Zealanders had lost the airfield at Maleme, and the German troop-carriers continued to land there throughout the day.
[3] Baghdad was not in fact captured by British forces till 30th May, when Raschid Ali fled to Persia and the whole of Iraq came into British hands.
[4] The Duke of Aosta surrendered with the remnants of the Italian East African Army, and died as a prisoner of war at Nairobi in 1942.
[5] Then European Director of the Columbia Broadcasting System.

his piece. He is opening the exhibition of British war artists in the Museum of Modern Art in New York. While he talks I listen on my earphones and can hear Kenneth talking opposite me, and a fraction of a second later, Kenneth saying the same thing from New York. The distance of 6,000 miles does not exactly give a time pause but merely a faint duplication of what I hear him say in London. I then do the same, and then we both listen to Halifax.

DIARY   *27th May, 1941*

Winston gives the House the latest news. He says that the situation in Crete is none too good. He goes on to talk about the position in Libya and Iraq. To my great satisfaction he announces our naval losses in the Cretan campaign. And then he passes on to the battle of the Denmark Straits.[1] He does it beautifully. He builds up the whole picture from the moment when we heard that the *Bismarck* and the *Prinz Eugen* were driving westwards against our convoys to the moment when we came into contact with them and the *Hood* was sunk. After paying a tribute to the loss of these men, he passed on to the further pursuit. The *Prinz Eugen* had disappeared, but the *Bismarck* was followed closely and bombed. This bombing slowed down her escape, which by then was evidently directed towards some French port. Further arrangements were made to intercept her, but then the weather changed and visibility diminished, and by a sudden change of course the *Bismarck* managed to elude our vigilance. The whole House felt at that moment that Winston was about to break to us that the ship had escaped. There was a hush of despair. At dawn next morning (Winston continued) we again resumed contact. He told us how the Fleet Air Arm then fired torpedoes at the ship, destroying her steering gear and forcing her to go round and round in immense circles in the ocean. From all sides our fleet approached to destroy her. Such is the innate sporting feeling of the House that we all began to feel sorry for the *Bismarck*. The P.M. went on to say that our ships had established contact; that they had begun to fire; that their shells had not made any effect; and that the only hope was to fire torpedoes. 'That process', he said, 'is in action as I speak.' He then went on to speak about conscription in Northern Ireland and left the House with a sense of *coitus interruptus*. Hugh O'Neill rose to protest about his Ulster statement, and then Griffiths in his pompous way

[1] The pursuit of the *Bismarck*, the most powerful battleship afloat, began on 21st May. She sank the *Hood* on the 24th. The rest of the story is outlined above.

arose. 'Mr Speaker, I ask for your guidance. . . .' As he said this, I saw one of the secretaries in the official gallery make a violent sign with a small folded sheet to Brendan Bracken. He took the missive and passed it on to Winston. The latter rose at once and interrupted Griffiths. 'I crave your indulgence, Mr Speaker', he said, 'I have just received news that the *Bismarck* has been sunk.' Wild cheers, in which I do not join.

Poor old Horace Rumbold is dead.[1] I loved that man.

DIARY   *29th May, 1941*

Here is an instance of how one suffers from bad reporting. On Tuesday I deputised for Duff at the Advertisers' luncheon. I did not give a hand-out to the Press, since I am always afraid that the P.M. may read what one says and make a fuss. Then today when I entered Church House,[2] I bumped into him. There was a moment of silence as we climbed the stairs together, and then he said, 'I thee that you have thaid that I am about to propothe peathe terms.' I said, 'But what on earth made you think that?' He said, 'I read it in the newspapers. I read that you had said that if Hitler proposed peace, nobody would believe him, but that if I proposed peace, everyone would believe me.' 'That,' I said with some heat, 'is a false rendering of what I said.' 'I believe you', he said. 'I was only getting a rise out of you.'

That is all very well. But somewhere he may be left with the feeling that I say indiscreet things. What I had really said was this: 'The German propaganda method is based upon seizing immediate advantages with complete disregard of the truth or of their credit. Our method is the slower and more long-term method of establishing confidence. At the moment, the Goebbels method is the more successful. In the end ours will prove decisive. For the moment will come when Hitler will sell his soul to be believed. He will wish to make a compromise peace in order to save himself from disaster. But nobody will believe him. Whereas if Winston Churchill made an offer to the world, 90 per cent of the world would know that this was sincere.' I do not really believe that Winston thought that I had said anything silly. But my word, how he scrutinises one's speeches.

[1] H.N.'s Ambassador in Berlin, 1928–33.
[2] The Commons were again meeting in Church House, while the House of Lords was being prepared for them.

DIARY   *4th June, 1941*

I am rather amused, and slightly shocked, by my attitude towards my finances. I have always cherished the fantasy that I do not care about money. I made a great show of being completely independent of my wife's income. Well, now it has all crashed, and I am reduced, it seems, to £400 a year without the possibility of earning more.[1] I realise that this residue would seem to the working classes a good £8 a week. To me it appears an utter impossibility. Meanwhile I have written to Ben asking for a loan of £500.

This shows how in this dynamic age people who adjust themselves to modifications of the static are caught out. Thus I, realising dimly that the old Edwardian world of bath-salts and ortolans[2] was doomed to disappearance, trained myself from the age of 22 to despise (and thereby not to desire) that shape of civilisation which I foresaw would not last. It meant nothing whatsoever to me that Derby House and Stafford House and Chatsworth should become shabby and then dead. I achieved a different and no less self-indulgent form of elegance which seemed to me likely to survive my own lifetime. It consisted of comparatively modest establishments in the country and in London, and a gay combination of the Café Royal, Bloomsbury, rooms in the Temple, the Travellers Club, the garden at Sissinghurst, foreign travel, the purchase of books and pictures and the unthinking enjoyment of food and wine. That all seemed to us very bohemian and far more modern and self-denying than Polesden Lacey or Londonderry House. And now this tide of self-sacrifice is lapping at our own feet. We shall have to walk and live a Woolworth life hereafter. I feel so poor. I hate the destruction of elegance. The drabness of Berlin or Moscow will creep into my lovely London streets.[3]

We have taken Mosul.[4] But the public are in a trough of depression over Crete and acclaim victories slightly, feeling that we shall probably be turned out again. The B.E.F. is being called 'Back Every Fortnight'.

---

[1] His salary as a Junior Minister was £1,500, and Income Tax was 10/- in the pound. But V.S-W.'s income was added to his for the purpose of assessing surtax. He had been obliged to give up all his journalistic work.

[2] A small bird, considered a delicacy.

[3] This picture of his impoverishment is endearing but fantastic. He had no financial responsibility at all for Sissinghurst, and his style of living never varied then, nor after the war, from what he here describes as modest.

[4] The last German base in Iraq.

Big Ben stopped today because a workman left his hammer inside it. William II died.[1] The newspapers devote little space to it. If Hitler dies in 1962, will there be equal indifference?

H.N. TO V.S-W. *5th June, 1941*
Ministry of Information

Duff has returned.[2] He does not look too well. I took him to a film of the 1938 Nuremberg Party Rally. I do not think it cheered him up very much. It has all come so damned true. All those Hitler Jugend were the men who came down in shoals upon Crete. That battle has, I fear, dealt a very severe blow to our morale. People say, 'If we had 30,000 men there, plus Navy, plus guns and tanks, how on earth could the Germans take it from the air?' I must say that this 200-mile jump is terrifying. No wonder people say that if they can take Crete from 200 miles away, what will happen to Great Britain? Our General Staff will have to think it out all over again.

The Labour Party appear to want to get my job for a Labour man and are making rather a drive against me. Meanwhile the Ministry is still blowing up from internal combustion. Duff has sent a paper to the Cabinet in which he demands certain conditions and threatens to resign if they are not granted. He is quite right. We cannot go on being the football of every Ministry.

DIARY *10th June, 1941*

Duff tells us that the P.M. is under the impression that the anxiety which exists is purely a House of Commons anxiety and is not shared by the country as a whole. We all say that this is not true, and that the country is deeply anxious and shocked.

The Middle East have no sense of publicity. The Admiralty is even worse. We complain that there are no photographs of the sinking of the *Bismarck*. Tripp says that the official photographer was in the *Suffolk* and that the *Suffolk* was too far away. We say, 'But why didn't one of our reconnaissance machines fly over the ship and take photographs?' He replies: 'Well you see, you *must* see, well upon my word, well after all, an Englishman would not like to take snapshots of a fine vessel sinking.' Is he right? I felt abashed when he said it. I think he is right. It reminds me of Arthur Balfour when Brockdorff-

---

[1] At Doorn in Holland, at the age of 82.
[2] After a month's illness, which he spent at his house in Bognor.

Rantzau refused to stand when he was handed the Treaty.[1] 'Did he remain seated?' said someone to Balfour afterwards. 'I did not notice. I do not stare at a gentleman in distress.'

DIARY   17th June, 1941

We are puzzled why, in this lovely weather, the Germans have not seriously attacked us by air. It may be that they are massing on the eastern front as part of their intimidation of Russia. It may be that their whole Air Force will be used for a mass attack on our front in Egypt. It may also be that they are equipping their machines with some new device, like wire-cutters.[2] In any case it bodes ill.

DIARY   18th June, 1941

We have a short meeting of the Planning Committee and decide to raise the question what is to be said if Russia goes to war with Germany. I think that very unlikely indeed, but if it happens then we must be prepared to regard Russia as an ally. Are we to play the Red Flag on Sundays and so on? I raise the matter in a minute to the Policy Committee.

The news at the Duty Room is none too good. Our offensive at Sollum has been beaten back with heavy losses and we have to withdraw.[3] What distresses us is that the Middle East have put this out in a silly way: 'Our troops, having accomplished their purpose, withdrew slowly to their base.' That sort of thing. It simply will not do. We protest loudly against it.

Dine with Camrose at the Dorchester. He says that he thinks that Chamberlain was done for the day he appointed Sam Hoare Secretary of State for Air. Trenchard,[4] who is there, is a fine fellow with a great admiration for Portal but a sublime contempt for everyone else. He admires Winston but regrets that there is nobody to control him. He thinks the Cabinet such little men. And in truth, when we discuss it,

[1] Count Ulrich von Brockdorff-Rantzau, German Foreign Minister, 1918–19, was the chief German representative at the presentation of the Treaty of Versailles. Balfour was British Foreign Secretary at the same period.

[2] For cutting the steel cables of the balloon-barrages.

[3] This was Operation Battleaxe, a British counter-attack designed to drive Rommel west of Tobruk. It started on 15th June. The Guards Brigade took Fort Capuzzo facing Sollum, but we were outflanked by the German armour and withdrew to our original positions on the 17th.

[4] Marshal of the Royal Air Force Lord Trenchard had been Chief of the Air Staff, 1918–29, and Commissioner of the Metropolitan Police, 1931–35.

there emerge the great figures of the past—Curzon, Balfour, Carson, Birkenhead, Smuts, Kitchener. None of them would have been so frightened of Winston as the whole Cabinet are today.

Harold Nicolson considered a German attack on Russia 'very unlikely indeed', but it had been planned by Hitler since July 1940, and during the early months of 1941 he had been moving his Divisions eastwards from the Channel coast. The offensive had been set for 15th May, but the Balkan operations delayed it by five weeks and the attack opened on 22nd June. In spite of warnings from Britain and the United States, Stalin refused to believe in the imminence of Hitler's betrayal of their non-aggression pact, and although the Russian Army was mobilised, it was caught tactically unprepared and a large part of the Soviet Air Force was destroyed on the ground on the opening day. Within three weeks the German armoured Divisions had penetrated 450 miles into Russian territory and had captured Smolensk. Few experts, including the British General Staff, thought that the Russians could possibly hold out for more than a few weeks. Britain's attitude was immediately declared by Churchill as one of full support for the Soviet Union. 'Russia's danger', he said, 'is our danger', and although he took back not one word of what he had often said about Russian communism, he promised to help in any way he could. But how? A landing in force on the coast of France was out of the question, though Stalin began to demand it from the outset. British air-attacks on Germany and German bases in France were stepped up, but did little to relieve the pressure on the Eastern front. Supplies of war-materials from Britain through the northern Russian ports were promised, but were not to become effective for many months. The chief gesture was a political one: a pact signed between Britain and Russia by which they agreed to prosecute the war together and not to make peace separately.

The German attack on Russia led to a relaxation of pressure on Britain. The air-bombardment of England diminished perceptibly, and in the Middle East there was a pause on both sides while each gathered its strength for a desert offensive in the autumn. General Wavell, who had by then lost the Prime Minister's confidence, was replaced as Commander-in-Chief by General Auchinleck.

Meanwhile the crisis in the Ministry of Information developed into a struggle for power between Duff Cooper and other Cabinet Ministers for control of national propaganda and publicity. The 'Miniwar' or 'the Battle of Bloomsbury' was decided by a compromise about which nobody was happy. For a few more weeks the Ministry struggled on, bearing the responsibility for the publication and interpretation of news, but without the proper powers to exercise it. A change of Ministers appeared imminent. On 18th July the blow fell. Duff Cooper was sent to Singapore as the Prime Minister's representative, and Harold Nicolson was asked to give up the Parliamentary Secretaryship in favour of a Labour Member, being offered a Governorship of the B.B.C. in consolation. Duff Cooper wrote in his Memoirs, 'I left the Ministry of Information with a sigh of relief.' The same cannot be said of Harold Nicolson. He was deeply shocked and saddened. He was wounded by the curtness of the Prime Minister's letter. He felt that he had been sacked. This was not so. He was merely a victim of the general unpopularity of his Ministry, and of the Labour Party's search for positions of authority.

DIARY   *22nd June, 1941*

A marvellous morning, with the smell of roses and hay and syringa in the air. We have breakfast outside. Vita arrives to say that the 7 o'clock news announced that Germany has invaded Russia. Goebbels has declared that Hitler's patience was exhausted and that the frontier has been crossed in Poland and Rumania.

Most people in England will be delighted. I am not so optimistic. It will have a bad effect on America, where many influential people do not like to see themselves as the allies of Bolshevism. It will have a bad effect on Conservative and Catholic opinion here. And if, as is likely, Hitler defeats Russia in three weeks, then the road to the oil is open, as also the road to Persia and India.

Bunny and Lindsay [Drummond] come over, and then V. and I are left alone in the amazing beauty of this garden. At 9 Winston broadcasts. He says that he is on the side of the Russians who defend their homes. He does not conceal that Russia may be beaten quickly, but having indicated to us the approaching collapse of India and China, and, in fact, of Europe, Asia and Africa, he somehow leaves us with the impression that we are quite certain to win this war. A masterpiece. Vita and I go out afterwards to make a little hay in the orchard. It is very hot tonight. Every flower pulsates with scent. Most people will be feeling happy tonight at the thought that we have got a new ally. I am not so sure. Not that I have the slightest objection to Russian communism. But I feel that they are so incompetent and selfish that they will be bowled over at a touch.

DIARY   *24th June, 1941*

Walk to the Beefsteak with Ned Grigg.[1] He says that 80 per cent of
the War Office experts think that Russia will be knocked out in ten
days. They are not at all pleased by this new war, which will give
great triumphs to Hitler and leave him free to fling his whole force
against us.

DIARY   *25th June, 1941*

I dine alone with Rob Bernays.[2] He curses me for lacking in self-
assertiveness. He is too polite to say so, but he thinks that I have been a
softy in this job. He feels that all would be well if I had less desire to
please and more desire to dominate. I confess that it has often puzzled
me why a person of my ability, knowledge, experience, industry and
integrity should not somehow make a certain effect. I am not exaggerating. I do not say that I score more than 62 marks in any of the
above qualities; but I do claim that I score 62 in each. Why the aggregate of such scoring should make so little impression on my contemporaries, I simply do not understand. I suppose it is because
people say, 'Oh Harold! Well, he won't make trouble whatever
happens.'

Pondering these sad things, and upon the imminent collapse of
Russia, I walk back from Rob's flat in the late twilight. The balloons
are flung across the sky in thousands. The flag flops lazily (though it is
well after sunset) over Buckingham Palace. As I pass the gates, out
comes the Chancellor, Lord Simon. I thank him for having given us
the House of Lords.[3] He has been dining well with the King and
Queen. His speech is slow and thick. But how suave he is! How suave!
Off he goes in a taxi to the Dorchester with a comradely wave of the
hand.

DIARY   *26th June, 1941*

Nigel drives me down to Sissinghurst in a car he has hired. He has
managed to get to the Shiants[4] for one night at the cost of four nights

[1] Edward Grigg, later Lord Altrincham, Parliamentary Under-Secretary of State for
War, 1940–42.
[2] Robert Bernays, Liberal National M.P. for Bristol North since 1931, and Parliamentary Secretary to the Ministry of Transport, 1939–40. He was one of H.N.'s
closest friends in Parliament. He was killed when his aeroplane crashed in the
Adriatic in January 1945.
[3] For the meetings of the House of Commons. Lord Simon (previously Sir John
Simon) was Lord Chancellor, 1940–45.
[4] The uninhabited islands which he had purchased in the Outer Hebrides.

travelling. He arrived in a pouring deluge, but when the fishing-boat had gone, the sky cleared and all night he was there alone on his island with nothing but flowers, sheep, seals, porpoises and birds. He said that his chest (which is stout enough) almost burst with happiness. Is not that the spirit and the tone in which to go to death?[1]

DIARY   *30th June, 1941*

On arrival at the Ministry I find some feeling of gloom about the Russian situation. Molotov has given Cripps[2] the impression that the Russians had been taken so much by surprise (since they had expected to be asked for their money before their lives), that many losses were sustained at the beginning. The War Office have taken this up in order to put across 'a grave situation'. I cannot but feel that the W.O. view is coloured by political prejudice and by the fact that Stalin murdered most of his senior officers. Looking at it as an amateur, it does seem to me that the Germans have pierced the Stalin Line in the Minsk area but that they are held in other places. They have not got the roads which they had in France. I am not in the least in despair. Moscow has been taken before.

At the Planning Executive we discuss the scheme for home morale in the event of a Russian collapse.

DIARY   *2nd July, 1941*

The Press publish Wavell's resignation, or rather his transference to India in place of Auchinleck, and Oliver Lyttelton's appointment as Minister of State in the Middle East. Duff had seen the editors last night in order to explain it to them, but had not told the staff here. Thus, although all was understood at the top level, it was very bad at the middle levels. Grave public apprehension will be caused by the *dégommage* of Wavell, and we have not handled it properly. The P.M. simply does not understand that one cannot land the public with shocks.

As I go through Whitehall I see that the sand-bags and corrugated iron around King Charles' statue are being removed. In fact the statue itself is exposed and is being fitted with a wooden cradle under the horse. When I repass some hours later, I see the horse and statue

---

[1] The 3rd Battalion Grenadier Guards, in which he was then a subaltern, formed part of a force concentrated at Glasgow for the invasion of the Canary Islands. They were then at a few days' notice to sail, but the operation was cancelled at the last moment.

[2] Sir Stafford Cripps was British Ambassador in Moscow, 1940–42.

off the pedestal and facing quite truculently towards the National Gallery upon the pavement. What a relief, after three hundred years, to face the other way! Then off the statue will go to some cave at Malvern.

DIARY   *8th July, 1941*

I drive down to White's Club with Duff and beg him to treat the P.R.O.s[1] this afternoon with all gentleness. They are a touchy lot. There are 21 of them, and we meet after luncheon in the Chancellor's Hall. Duff glowers at them as if they were coolies in some Cingalese copper-mine. He then tells them an angry story about how he had been brought up from Bognor on false pretences. He then scowls at them and says that this is all he has to say. He then stalks out of the room. We are left ashamed and wretched and do not know which way to look. I cannot make out what happens to Duff on such occasions. He seems to lose all power over himself. I think it is a sort of shyness.[2]

DIARY   *10th July, 1941*

I go down to the House for questions. The most serious issue is Walter's indiscretion about 'pitchforks and tanks'.[3] Mander has a question down asking whether ordinary civil service rules apply to

[1] The public-relations officers of the different Ministries were meeting to discuss with Duff Cooper how the information services could be better coordinated.

[2] In fairness to Duff Cooper, it should be added that he was still suffering from the effects of his illness.

[3] Walter Monckton, then Director-General of the Ministry of Information, had said publicly that the Cabinet's compromise solution to the problem of coordinating the information services had left the Ministry 'with a pitchfork to deal with a tank'. As an example of H.N.'s style at the dispatch-box, this is the *Hansard* report of his replies:

    Mr Mander: Is it not one of the rules that Civil Servants are not allowed to criticise their Department, and therefore was it in order for one of the chief officials of the Hon. Gentleman's Department to criticise the Government, and say that the Department had been given a pitchfork to deal with a tank?

    Mr Nicolson: The British Civil Service is an organism and not a machine. It owes its vitality to the fact that even its most rigid rules are sometimes violated.

    Mr Mander: Does the Hon. Gentleman agree that the particular statement was not a proper one to be made by an official of his Department?

    Mr Nicolson: In the circumstances, I think the statement was of public value.

    Mr Mander: Is it to be understood that in future officials of the Department may make statements of that kind without any restraint?

    Mr Nicolson: A very exceptional official in very exceptional circumstances.

our Ministry. I manage to get out of it with the full support of the House. When I told him that I rather approved of the statement, there are loud cheers and the whole episode ends in laughter.

DIARY   *18th July, 1941*

We have a meeting with Gerald Campbell[1] to discuss what propaganda we are to put out to America in the event of a complete German victory over Russia. The fear is that Hitler may get Russia to make some form of separate peace: that he will then proclaim that he is master of Europe and completely invincible: that he may then start a great peace drive, representing himself as the crusader against Bolshevism and offering us the most flattering terms: and that then he will represent to America that we are refusing an honourable peace. We agree that the best thing to do is to forestall this by warning America of the peace offensive: by assuring them that Britain will not let America down or betray our joint cause: and by doing all we can to substitute the yellow for the red bogey.

When I get back to the Ministry after lunch, I get a message from the Prime Minister's Private Secretary to say that he wants to see me at No. 10 at 5.30. I discuss this with Duff. He says that he is to be made Chancellor of the Duchy of Lancaster and to go to Singapore to coordinate. The P.M. had just mentioned me, and said that the Labour Party wanted a Labour man in my job. Duff thinks that if I am offered something as good, I should accept it, but if something worse, I should refuse and go back to my writing. A later message comes that the interview is cancelled and that I shall receive a communication 'in another form'.

At 5.55 it arrives in the shape of a black box from Downing Street. I get Sammy Hood to open it for me, and I find inside the letter which is attached to this.[2] I think it might have been more politely worded.

[1] Sir Gerald Campbell, Director-General of the British Information Services in New York, 1941–42.
[2] This was the Prime Minister's letter:
18th July, 1941   *10 Downing Street*
My dear Harold Nicolson,
   The changes at the Ministry of Information lead me to ask you to place your Office as Parliamentary Secretary at my disposal.
   I should be very much obliged if you would give your services to the public as a member of the Board of Governors of the B.B.C., where I am sure you could make a most effective contribution. This would not entail the vacation of your seat in the House of Commons, nor the renouncement of your salary as a Member.

Could I afford it, I should not accept a Governorship of the B.B.C. But both Duff and Walter [Monckton] urge me to accept. I realise that this means the end of any political ambitions which I may ever have cherished. I am hurt and sad and sorry. The P.M.'s Secretary telephones to say that he wants a reply at once, and could I send it by taxi. Well, I send it.

DIARY   *19th July, 1941*

I wake up feeling that something horrible has happened, and then remember that I have been sacked from the Government. Go to the Ministry and start clearing out some of my private possessions. Then attend the Duty Room, probably for the last time. I meet Gerald Campbell in the passage. 'I hear', he says, 'that you have been thurtled?'[1] Everybody expresses dismay at my going.[2] I have a final drink in the Press Bar with Osbert Lancaster, and then lunch at the Travellers with Robin Maugham. He is as charming as he could be.

But I mind more than I thought I should mind. It is mainly, I suppose, a sense of failure. I quite see that if the Labour leaders have been pressing to have my post, there is good cause why they should have it. But if I had more power and drive, I should have been offered Rab Butler's job at the Foreign Office,[3] which I should dearly have loved. As it is, I come back to the bench below the gangway having had my chance and failed to profit by it. Ever since I have been in the House I have been looked on as a might-be. Now I shall be a might-have-been. Always up till now I have been buoyed up by the hope of writing some good book or achieving a position of influence in politics. I now know that I shall never write a book better than I have written already, and that my political career is at an end. I shall merely get

---

I propose to issue a certificate under the House of Commons Disqualification (Temporary Provisions) Act, 1941.

Yours sincerely,

Winston Churchill

[1] H.N. was replaced as Parliamentary Secretary by Ernest Thurtle, Labour M.P. for Shoreditch, who retained the office till the end of the war. Duff Cooper was succeeded as Minister by Brendan Bracken.

[2] Duff Cooper wrote to him: 'I think you have received very shabby treatment, and I find that everybody shares that view.'

[3] R. A. Butler, Under-Secretary of State for Foreign Affairs since 1938, was now appointed Minister of Education, and was succeeded at the Foreign Office by Richard Law.

balder and fatter and more deaf as the years go by. This is an irritating thing. Success should come late in life in order to compensate for the loss of youth; I had youth and success together, and now I have old age and failure.[1] Apart from all this, I mind leaving the Ministry where I did good work and had friends.

This space indicates the end of my ambitions in life. *Omnium consensu capax imperii nisi imperasset.*[2]

H.N. TO V.S-W.
                                                        21st July, 1941
                                                4 King's Bench Walk, E.C.4

Well, the worst is over. I have said goodbye, and here I am back in K.B.W. It was none too pleasant. I went in to see Duff. He was in good form, being pleased to be going on a mission to the Far East. Really people were most awfully sorry that I was going. They can't quite make out why. While I was in the middle of it, my successor Mr Thurtle arrived. He was rather embarrassed, but I told him about everything and took him round to see Walter Monckton. I lunched with Osbert Lancaster. It was good of him to ask me, as I was feeling rather unwanted.

After luncheon, I went down the street with nothing to do. I went to a dull film, and then I came on here. I have too heavy a heart to write more. God bless you, my dearest. So long as you are there nothing really matters.

For a few months after his fall from office, Harold Nicolson's diary became scrappy and dispirited, as if a sparking-plug had been removed. His disappointment was not eased by the remark of his successor, Mr Thurtle, that B.B.C. Governors have no war-time function. This was later denied by Brendan Bracken in Parliament, but it was true that the responsibilities of the Board were slender compared to those of the Ministry, and had it not been for the friendship and close support given to him by Violet Bonham Carter, he would have found his new job scarcely worth while. He was, of course, still a Member of Parliament, and his access to confidential information was little less than before. He was able to resume his weekly articles for the 'Spectator', but as a B.B.C. Governor he was

---

[1] H.N. was then 54.
[2] Tacitus on the Emperor Galba. 'Had he never been placed in authority, nobody would ever have doubted his capacity for it.'

not permitted to broadcast. Once a week he did his duty as a fire-guard in the Palace of Westminster, and was able to spend more time at Sissinghurst, where V. Sackville-West was finishing her new novel 'Grand Canyon'.

In early August Churchill met President Roosevelt in Placentia Bay, Newfoundland, where they drew up the Joint Declaration on war aims, later known as the Atlantic Charter, which virtually committed the United States to see the destruction of the Nazis and the disarming of the aggressors. In the same month British forces occupied Persia, in agreement with the Russians, in order to expel German agents from the country and safeguard a warm-water route through the Persian Gulf for supplies to Russia.

The German invasion of the Soviet Union, which had started so well, ran into such serious trouble in the late autumn that the myth of the invincibility of the German Army was at last broken. Hitler made great gains in the Ukraine, penetrating as far as Rostov on the Don, but he was held up outside Leningrad, and his main attack on Moscow was thrown back at its very gates. On 6th December, the day before Pearl Harbour, General Zhukov counter-attacked with 100 fresh divisions, the existence of which the Germans had not even suspected. They were ill-supplied with winter clothing, taken aback by the determination of the Russian troops to fight on even when surrounded, and harassed by partisans in the rear. The Russian Air Force and arms-production staged an equally astonishing recovery. It was only the iron will of Hitler which prevented the complete disintegration of his armies in the snow.

In North Africa the British under General Auchinleck launched their long prepared attack on 18th November. The aim of Operation 'Crusader' was to drive Rommel out of Libya and to encourage the French in Tunisia, Algeria and Morocco to form a common front with the Allies along the whole south coast of the Mediterranean. The opening nine-day battle, fought mostly by the armour of each side around Sidi Rezegh, led to the relief of Tobruk and the orderly retreat of the German and Italian forces. Seldom had a major battle fluctuated so violently, and the diary reflects the anxiety which it caused at home.

DIARY   25th July, 1941

After fire-watching all night in the House of Commons, I get up at 5 am. and walk down to the Temple. It is a beautiful morning. The river is swollen high and heaves slightly under a pink satin skin. The balloons are going up slowly all over London—at first clumsy tadpoles, and then, as they reach the upper air, little minnows flashing silver in the sun.

I dictate letters and then go up to Leicester. Rain lashes against the hot windows and the cornfields lean over into inconvenient shapes. I have a women's meeting first. They concentrate upon the troubles of the housewife. Eggs are torn from the hens and sent to places from which they are sent to other places at which they are packed into crates labelled 'new laid' and then placed in railway-trucks labelled 'immediate' and kept in sidings for three hot weeks. Lord Woolton is not liked. Was it not he (the Napoleon of the multiple store[1]) who said that they should all make plum jam? Where are the plums? Lord Woolton does not know.

Dine with Bertie [Jarvis] and go on to a party of the Leicester Home Guard. The officers are playing billiards. They are very polite to each other. 'Bad luck', they say, when an obvious shot is missed.

DIARY   27th July, 1941

Buck De la Warr comes to see me. He has been offered the Governorship of Bermuda. He had looked it up in the Encyclopaedia. 'Do you realise, Harold', he said, 'that it is no larger than Bexhill?' I replied that Gibraltar also was no larger than Bexhill. He speaks about his political ambitions. If only I had something of Buck's self-confidence! But I am a wee, sleek, cowering beastie. Anyhow, we talk about the future of National Labour. We agree that our function is over and that now all Nationalists are Labour and all Labour people Nationalist. The obvious thing is to close down. But the difficulty is that many of us were elected as National Labour. In my own case it may well be that I should not have got in under any other label. If I change my label, I am acting dishonestly. It is a grave moral problem.

DIARY   28th July, 1941

There was a raid on London last night, the first for eleven weeks. I work at the editing of my 1939 Diary, which I am thinking of publishing.[2] The worst of it is that I shall have to cut out so much for reasons of security and discretion.

[1] Lord Woolton, Minister of Food since 1940, had previously been Chairman and Managing Director of Lewis's Ltd.
[2] He revised his diary for that year and offered it to Constable for publication, who accepted it. Lord Cranborne then rightly advised him that publication was premature, and he abandoned the idea.

There is a rude article about me in *Truth* saying that I have 'the mincing manner of a French *salon*', that I lack virility and should retire from public life and bury myself in books. All rather true, I suppose. But I happen to enjoy public life. I could never be merely an observer.

DIARY   *29th July, 1941*

I walk away from the St James' with Momchiloff, the Bulgarian ex-Minister. He is the best informed of all London diplomatists. I say that I do not understand why Hitler attacked Russia. He said that he did so (a) to dislocate opinion in occupied Europe and the Americas: (b) to save his Army from dry-rot: (c) to knock out the eastern menace while he was preparing to deal with us: (d) to encourage Japan: (e) to get the oil in Iran and the Caucasus.

'But', I explain, 'Monsieur le Ministre' (since I am careful about such things, having derived pleasure from being called the same thing by Dejean yesterday—fallen Ministers like to be called unfallen), 'they have sacrificed immense amounts of oil ...' ('In second gear', he interpolates; 'the roads of Russia entail second gear and that means more oil') '... while depriving themselves of their main oil-supplies at Ploesti and Baku.' 'Yes', he says, 'but they counted on the destruction of the Russian Air Force and early anti-Soviet revolutions in the Ukraine and the Caucasus'. 'Then they have made a mistake?' I ask. 'Not yet', he answers. At that moment Kenneth Clark comes up and the Minister flits away.

At the House today Winston makes a long and careful speech about production. It does not go very well. There is a sense of criticism in the air. I have a talk with Brendan Bracken. He seems to be sacking everybody at the Ministry.

DIARY   *13th August, 1941*

I discuss at great length with Violet Bonham Carter our duties and functions as Governors of the B.B.C. She refuses to be treated merely as a figure-head, and I think that between us we shall be able to take on a good deal of work.

Dine with Camrose at the Dorchester. A. V. Alexander[1] and Oliver Stanley[2] are there, and the guest of honour is Dorothy Thompson.[3]

[1] First Lord of the Admiralty, 1940–45.
[2] Secretary of State for War, 1940, and for Colonies, 1942–45.
[3] The distinguished American journalist, then aged 47.

183

Alexander is extremely pleased by the naval situation and tells us that the sinkings for the last four weeks have not been really serious. He is a vigorous and interesting person. I can see that he is very worried about the situation in the Far East. We are to have an announcement tomorrow about the Churchill–Roosevelt meeting.[1] Alexander warns Camrose that it is not likely to be very exciting.

Dorothy Thompson talks a great deal about the difficulty of welding American opinion together up to the point where they will be prepared to enter the war on our side. She says that we must always remember that America is composed of many millions of people who left Europe because they hated it, and that there are many millions of Italians and Germans whose hearts go out to their mother-countries. Although these emotions pull America apart, they feel at the same time a strong longing to remain together. What we don't fully understand in this country is the actual dread of the American soul at being split. There is always the fear that they will cease to be a nation, and this is the fear which Roosevelt understands so perfectly and which he guides with such genius.

DIARY   17th August, 1941

Do my *Spectator* article. In the afternoon we go on pleaching the limes. It rains dreadfully and we are anxious about the harvest.

It seems that the southern Russian armies have been cut off and that the Germans will drive them beyond the Dnieper. Meanwhile Roosevelt has put out a most optimistic statement as a result of his meeting with Churchill. The eight points[2] themselves have fallen very flat, but they are good all the same.

In the afternoon Stephen Spender and his wife come over. He believes that ordinary men or women do not want either fascism or socialism, but that they do want 'democracy', if only we can infuse real meaning into that word. He agrees with me that after the war there will be a reaction against all government control and yearning to go back to laissez-faire. He says that the ordinary man in England does not feel that this is his war, but feels that it is Mr Churchill's war. He compares the feeling with that in Spain during the Civil War, when every peasant was raised above himself by faith and excitement and hope. In a curious way the entry of Russia has heartened even the most anti-Bolshevik. 'Now at last', they say, 'we are fighting

[1] The meeting in Newfoundland had ended on the previous day.
[2] Of the Atlantic Charter.

with people who really believe in something. They may be wrong. But they believe.'

DIARY   *9th September, 1941*

The House meets. The Prime Minister makes a long and optimistic review. He stands there very stout and black, smoothing his palms down across his frame—beginning by patting his chest, then smoothing his stomach and ending down at the groin. He does not attempt any flight of oratory but he quotes Kipling's lines about the mine-sweepers, and is so moved by them that he chokes and cannot continue. His speech has a good effect, and the slight anti-Churchill tide which had begun to be noticeable was checked.

H.N. TO V.S-W.   *11th September, 1941*
                                                  4 King's Bench Walk, E.C.4

I did not tell you about my boating trip.[1] I picked my way down Westminster steps rather gingerly and climbed across a patrol-boat to the *Water Gipsy.* It is a long torpedo-shaped motor-boat with three cabins and an engine-room. There was only A. P. Herbert on board and Ed the engine-man. We cast off and went under the dark bridges. Our job was to inspect the several posts down the river which are on the look-out for parachute mines. Herbert knows the river blindfold and hits off each post with miraculous ease. 'Post Number 31!' he shouts. 'O.K., sir', comes the answer. 'Anything to report?' and then off we chug to another dim post among the docks and wharves. It was quite warm and there was a moon driving behind scudding clouds. The sides of the river loomed dark against the luminous waters. The Tower of London glimmered white and Greenwich also. One could not see how damaged it all was since the cranes all seemed to be intact and stood out from the wharves against the night. The black-out was complete and there was not a light to be seen anywhere. Herbert was in his best mood. He talked of the London River which he knows better than most men, and of Old Wapping stairs, and how well Dickens understood the river and its tides. When we got to Woolwich we tied up to a barge and had some coffee and fish-cakes. Then back again through the dark sides of the great river.

He tried to land me at the Temple steps, but it was too dark to see safely. Thus I landed at Westminster Bridge and walked home,

---

[1] With A. P. Herbert down the Thames at night. He was M.P. for Oxford University and a Petty Officer in the Naval Auxiliary Patrol.

reaching the Temple at 4 am. "Alt', shouted a voice. 'Oo goes there?' 'Friend', I answered—and why not? 'Advance friend, and be recognised.' I advanced cautiously towards the torch and saw the nose of a rifle aiming at me. I got out my pass. 'Thank you, sir,' he said, and the rifle was lowered.

DIARY   *12th September, 1941*

Dylan Thomas[1] comes to see me. He wants a job on the B.B.C. He is a fat little man, puffy and pinkish, dressed in very dirty trousers and a loud check coat. I tell him that if he is to be employed by the B.B.C., he must promise not to get drunk. I give him £1, as he is clearly at his wits" end for money. He does not look as if he had been cradled into poetry by wrong.[2] He looks as if he will be washed out of poetry by whisky.

DIARY   *6th October, 1941*

I meet Malcolm MacDonald at the Travellers. He had been lunching with the Prime Minister and says that he has not appeared so fit for twenty years. He attributes this rejuvenation to the fact that he loves being Prime Minister and a historic figure. He then talks about Ireland. He contends that he was right to give up the Irish bases. Had we kept them, we might be at war with Eire today and American help would be more distant than it is. Besides, if we get through the war without breaking Irish neutrality, we shall have a grievance against Eire instead of Eire having her dull, unending grievance against us. I love talking to him. He is so simple and modest. He told me that the only happy people he had met were the British people, since we had been released from fear and released from the sense of property.

Dine with Sibyl [Colefax] in Lord North Street. The American Ambassador,[3] R. A. Butler, the Master of the Rolls,[4] and the Kenneth Clarks. Winant is one of the most charming men that I have ever met. He has emphatic eyes and an unemphatic voice. Rab says that he was dining the other night with Winston, Eden and Beaverbrook, and that Winston spoke with deep sympathy of Baldwin. Winston has no

[1] The poet.

[2]   Most wretched men
    Are cradled into poetry by wrong:
    They learn in suffering what they teach in song.
          Shelley. *Julian and Maddalo.*

[3] John G. Winant, American Ambassador in London since 6th February.
[4] Lord Greene.

capacity of meanness, and that it why we love him so. A great soul in a great crisis.

They bother me to write a book about the British Empire. I am tempted. Winant adds his persuasion. It was a lovely dinner, and we walked away in the mist with the moon, and felt so pleased to be in London in October 1941.

DIARY   *9th October, 1941*

There is deep gloom about the Russian news. It looks as if Moscow might be taken and the Russian armies divided. Hitler will then declare that the Russian war is over and turn to the south-east. There will be great resentment in this country that we did not strike while the iron was hot, and Winston will be blamed. I have complete confidence, however, that everything strategic will be done: it is in administration and tactics that we are so weak.

To the B.B.C. Board. Thurtle made a statement in the House to the effect that the Governors were not concerned with the war-effort of the B.B.C. and were only concerned with culture and entertainment. The Chairman had protested against this to Brendan Bracken, who said that Thurtle would not be allowed in future to answer questions about the B.B.C. We are not content with this, and point out that if what Thurtle said was really B.B.C. policy, then we were not worth collectively £7,000 a year of Government money.

DIARY   *10th October, 1941*

Vita comes up in the morning, the first time she has been in London for two years. I have always tried to explain to her that the destruction of London is very bad in the places where it is bad, but not very bad in the places where it is not very bad. That sounds a dull way of putting it. She now agrees that it is absolutely right. She cannot conceive why St Paul's is still standing, or why our dear Temple should have been banged so badly about the head.

We go down to Evesham, I to inspect the B.B.C.'s monitoring service which is established there, and Vita to visit the garden at Hidcote.[1] The latter is devised on the right scheme of vistas running through small intimate gardens. I am much impressed by a quincunx of hornbeam trees (not hedges) round a grass plot. There is also a

[1] The famous Gloucestershire garden (now the property of the National Trust) created by the American, Laurence Johnston. It is often supposed that the design of Sissinghurst was based upon it, but this was H.N.'s first visit there.

marvellous huge lawn enclosed by yew, with elms upon a stage in the background. Vita meets me at the station with a huge sack of lilac and many cuttings from Laurie's garden. When we get home, we put our loot from Hidcote into pails and have a lovely dinner.

DIARY   *16th October, 1941*

Down to Cambridge. I drop my luggage at Trinity and read Rohan Butler's book on the foundations of National Socialism. Our meeting takes place in the Guildhall and is crowded. Admiral Muselier speaks, then Tissier,[1] then I. We get a fine reception, and it is clear that in Cambridge at least there is a strong pro-French feeling.

It is a wonderful evening, and the Master and Mrs Trevelyan take me for a walk down the limes and on to the Fellows' Garden beyond. George Trevelyan tells me that Gladstone told his father that they should always be grateful for living in the great age of Liberalism. 'Other generations, my dear Trevelyan, will be less fortunate.' But who could have conceived that any generation would suffer as we have done? As I walked from the Guildhall to Trinity, the newsboys had chalked up on their display-cards, 'Russians admit break-through near Moscow'. The sun is so soft on the limes that it seems incredible that that horror should be going on in the eastern snow.

Dine in hall. We have Madeira afterwards in the Combination Room. It is a most agreeable evening, which does me spiritual and intellectual good.

DIARY   *22nd October, 1941*

I go to see Maisky at the Soviet Embassy. He says that the situation is rather better at the moment, but they feel that the Germans are gathering their muscles for a further pounce on Moscow.[2] He puts the German casualties as somewhere in the region of three million. He is worried at our inability to help. We have sent 36 aeroplanes and pilots. What is that? In July Stalin wrote to Churchill asking for a diversion in France. In September he wrote again saying that if we did not draw off some of the German divisions, Russia would be in a bad way. He begged us to give him 25 to 30 divisions either at Murmansk or in the Caucasus. We had refused. We were now recon-

---

[1] Colonel Tissier, a member of de Gaulle's personal military staff.
[2] At that moment the Germans were within 30 miles of Moscow, and were making a supreme effort to capture it. However, the rain was making movement very difficult and the first snow had already fallen on 6th October.

sidering our refusal. He said that Eden was the best of the lot and really understood that our fate was tied up with that of the U.S.S.R. Beaverbrook also took that point of view. Winston, though sympathetic and possessing no reactionary prejudices, was dominated by the idea that the war would last six or seven years. Maisky did not honestly believe that either the Russians, the British or the conquered peoples would last out that period. We ought to take risks now. Of the Chiefs of the General Staff he found Dill[1] by far the most open to suggestion. Portal was grim and silent. Pound[2] was against doing anything at all, and had no conception that political or civilian considerations entered into it.

I went away feeling sad, and liking Maisky more than ever.

Brendan [Bracken] said such a funny thing to me today: 'I wish you were my Under Secretary! What fun we should have!'

DIARY   *28th October, 1941*

Roosevelt last night made an address in which he pledged the U.S.A. to bring supplies to British ports in their own bottoms and escorted by their own Navy. This is a tremendous advance. He said, 'We know who fired the first shot!' A great date. A very great date. Probably the turning-point of the war. I walk the streets in silent elation. What a master he has been! I am cheered when I think of the aged and bewildered Mussolini (for whom I have a growing sympathy) and the neurotic genius of Berchtesgaden—and then of dear Winston and that consummate politician of Hyde Park.

On to Grosvenor House for a party given by Hamish Hamilton[3] for John Gunther.[4] The whole of the Press, Ministry and B.B.C. are there. Gunther tells me that isolationism is dropping slowly like a pierced blimp.

DIARY   *17th November, 1941*

I go round to Pratts and find Harold Macmillan[5] there. He talks about Beaverbrook. He thinks him half mad and half genius. He says that

---

[1] Field-Marshal Sir John Dill, Chief of the Imperial General Staff, 1940–41.

[2] Admiral of the Fleet Sir Dudley Pound, First Sea Lord and Chief of Naval Staff, 1939–43.

[3] The publisher.

[4] The American journalist and author, who had just returned to London as a war-correspondent.

[5] He was Parliamentary Secertary to the Ministry of Supply, 1940–42, and Lord Beaverbrook had been his Minister since June 1941.

he thinks only of his present work, and that all his old fortune, news-papers and women are completely forgotten. But he also says that Beaverbrook gives no man his complete confidence. Thus, although there is great enthusiasm among the staff, and a feeling that they are important and useful, there is also a sort of uneasiness at not knowing what is really happening.

DIARY   *19th November, 1941*

We have moving speeches congratulating the Speaker[1] on his golden wedding. The old boy nearly breaks down. Afterwards, in Committee Room 14, there is a mass meeting to present him with a really beautiful piece of 1705 gold plate. I envy him it. Mrs Fitzroy is there, and Lloyd George makes a very suitable speech. He looks like a lion standing there. His accent is far more Welsh when he is being conciliatory than when he is being combative.

I have been worried all day about the lack of news of the Libyan offensive.[2] The Italians put out something about heavy bombardment. Then in the afternoon Middle East put out a short communiqué to the effect that 'in spite of heavy rains' our 'aggressive' operations have continued. Nothing definite, but the suggestion is that bad weather has spoiled the surprise and that it may all fail. Meanwhile the Germans have got Kerch and are pressing on to the Caucasus.

New Army changes. Alan Brooke[3] becomes C.I.G.S. Paget[4] becomes C.-in-C. Home, and Montgomery gets the South Eastern Command.[5] Jack Macnamara tells me that Montgomery thinks that it will fall to him one day to drive the politicians out of England.

DIARY   *20th November, 1941*

The papers and even the B.B.C. take a very optimistic view of our Libyan offensive. This distresses me, since if things go wrong (as they

[1] Captain E. A. Fitzroy. He had been Speaker of the House of Commons since 1928.
[2] 'Crusader', the British attack across the Egyptian frontier towards Tobruk, had opened in pouring rain early the previous morning. Up to this point all had gone well. Complete tactical surprise had been achieved, and our armour was making ground fast towards Sidi Rezegh.
[3] He had been C.-in-C. Home Forces since 1940, and was to remain C.I.G.S. until 1946.
[4] General Sir Bernard Paget had been C.-in-C. South Eastern Command since early in 1941, and Chief of General Staff, Home Forces, in 1940.
[5] General Montgomery had commanded the 3rd Division in the B.E.F., and the 5th and 12th Corps in England since the fall of France.

well may) public opinion will have a bad shock. Winston in the House today, while warning us against premature exultation and making it clear that the real fighting has not yet begun, makes the error of proclaiming that this is the first time we have met the Germans on equal terms.[1] I dread these forecasts. Moreover, in his Order of the Day to the troops, he said that the battle might prove the equal of Blenheim or Waterloo. The 1 o'clock news announces progress in almost hysterical terms. At the B.B.C. Board I bring up the question of the Libyan bulletins, and we damp them down.

I go down to the House to fire-watch. Sleep badly on my pallet. It is stuffy and itchy. The other occupants of my dormitory are Wright, the waiter, and a man who stokes the boilers.

DIARY   26th November, 1941

I walk back in the dark with Derrick Gunston.[2] He is not happy at all about the Libyan battle, and the most he can say is that there is no reason 'even now' why we should not win it.[3] 'What a humiliation it will be', he says, 'if our main effort is beaten in what for the Germans is a mere side-show compared to Moscow.'

We may be faced with a very black week. Moscow may fall. Japan may come in against us. France may join the Axis. We may be beaten in Libya. I fear that all this will react very badly on Winston's prestige. I regret bitterly that he boasted so much at first.

DIARY   1st December, 1941

I dine with Eric Allden[4] to meet Burckhardt,[5] whom Hitler described as '*Ein Mann von Format*', which he assuredly is. I am careful not to ask him embarrassing questions, since it is not fair on the neutrals to tempt them to disclose information. He does, however, let drop certain things: that the food in Germany is not as good as in London but better than in France and even than in Switzerland: that we have done great damage to Cologne and Hamburg, which is a pity, since

[1] In fact, on land and sea and in the air, we had a considerable superiority.
[2] Joint Under-Secretary of State for War since 1940.
[3] On this day, after very heavy tank battles, the New Zealanders had recaptured Sidi Rezegh and made contact with the garrison of Tobruk, which had made a sortie to meet them. But on the 25th General Cunningham, C.-in-C. 8th Army, was relieved of his command by General Auchinleck.
[4] Of the Foreign Relations Department of the British Red Cross.
[5] Dr Carl Burckhardt, a Swiss, who had been League of Nations High Commissioner at Danzig at the time of the German attack on Poland.

they were pro-British centres: that he was in Vichy when the news of the sinking of the *Bismarck* came in, and that the people in the café stood on chairs and cheered: that Pétain had said to him, '*Si seulement les Anglais pouvaient voir le fond de ma pensée.*' He says that the Italians are wholly pitiable. He says that the only thing he regrets in life is that Hitler should have praised him.

It seems that after two days of grave danger the Libyan battle is going better, but Rommel has got some of his tanks to the east of us. I notice that when we get on both sides of an enemy, that enemy is described as 'surrounded', but when the enemy get on both sides of us, we are told that we have driven 'a wedge' between his two armies.

DIARY   *4th December, 1941*

The Libyan news is really very bad. Rommel is massing for an attack on Tobruk, and I hear a rumour that his tanks are far superior to ours. The rat has not merely escaped the trap but is chewing it to pieces.[1]

Ben and Nigel both appear, the former very slim and smart in his uniform. I feel so proud of them, but I hide it, since it would drive them mad.

The House divides on the man-power Bill after a thunderous speech by Ernest Bevin. 42 Labour Members vote for an amendment recommending the nationalisation of coal and transport. I am in favour of this, and would have liked to vote with them, but it is essential to maintain the Government's prestige in these sad times. Had Libya been a victory I might have joined the rebels. There are rumours that Attlee may resign, since he told his Party meeting that if a substantial number voted against the Government, he would find his own position impossible.

In the evening I find the rebels still drinking in the smoking-room. Aneurin Bevan[2] says an interesting thing. He says that we intellectuals are in a difficult position. Our tastes attract us to the past, our reason to the future. Hitherto we have been able to appease this conflict since our tastes were still able to find their outlets, whereas our reason could

---

[1] This view was unnecessarily pessimistic. Rommel's attempts to rescue his forces trapped in Bardia failed, and the British corridor to Tobruk was clear and secure. The Commander of the 13th Corps telegraphed to Auchinleck, 'Tobruk is as relieved as I am.'

[2] He had been Labour M.P. for Ebbw Vale since 1929, and was now aged 44.

indulge in the picture of the shape of things to come. Now, however, the future is becoming very imminent and we are faced with the fact that our tastes can no longer be indulged. Gone are ease and income and travel and elegance. There is a tendency therefore for the weaker souls to escape into mysticism. Their reason tells them that the future is right, but it is agony for them to lose the past. This is what has happened to Aldous Huxley and Joad. I pray to God that it will not happen to me. 'I don't think it will, Harold', says Aneurin, 'your intellectual courage is great.'

I had a few minutes with Anthony Eden this afternoon. He asked me how I liked my B.B.C. job. I say I wish it were more of a job. He says, 'I thought you would feel that.'

On Sunday 7th December the Japanese attacked the American fleet in Pearl Harbour and sank four of their finest battleships. 'A mad decision', Churchill later called it; but he also reflected, 'So we had won the war after all. Hitler's fate was sealed. It was merely a question of the proper application of overwhelming power.' He crossed the Atlantic for the second time in five months to confer with his new ally. They agreed on their strategic objective—that Germany was the main enemy and must be knocked out first, and that the initial step must be a landing in north-west Africa during 1942. The invasion of the mainland of Europe could come a year later. Churchill's chief worry was that Roosevelt might continue to regard the United States as neutral in the European war while he prosecuted the war against Japan, but it had been dispelled by Hitler himself who declared war on America on 11th December. On the sitting-room wall at Sissinghurst a map of the whole world was substituted for the map of Europe and the Near East.

The new war began badly for Britain with the loss of the 'Prince of Wales' and 'Repulse' by Japanese aerial torpedoes on 10th December. Hong Kong was captured on Christmas Day, and the Japanese began their advance through Malaya towards Singapore. In face of these disasters the British public almost lost interest in Auchinleck's continued advance towards Libya and in the grave situation of the German armies before Moscow and Leningrad, let alone the decisive fact that America had entered the war on our side. Six months before, Hitler had had no more than a semi-impotent Britain to deal with: now he was faced by the Grand Alliance.

DIARY   *7th December, 1941*

After dinner we listen to the 9 o'clock news. The Japanese have bombed Pearl Harbour. I do not believe it. We then turn on the German and the French news and get a little more information. Roosevelt has ordered the mobilisation of the American forces and instructed the Navy to carry out their sealed orders.

I am dumbfounded by this news. After all, Roosevelt was still in negotiation with Kurusu,[1] and had dispatched a personal letter to the Mikado. While these negotiations are still in progress, the Japanese deliver a terrific air-attack 7,000 miles away from Japan. I seek for explanations. (a) It may be untrue. (b) The extremists in Japan may have feared that the Emperor would respond to Roosevelt's overtures and sought to force his hand. (c) They may have counted so much on this surprise attack that they hoped to sink the American Fleet at a single blow. We have not heard a word as yet about the effect of the bombardment. (d) Hitler may have wished to frighten the Americans into neutrality and divert all her equipment to the Pacific coast.[2] Yet whichever of these explanations is the correct one, the whole action seems as insane as Hitler's attack on Russia. I remain amazed.

The effect in Germany will be bad. They will not say, 'We have a new ally.' They will say (or rather they will think in the recesses of their anxious souls), 'We have outraged the most formidable enemy in the world.' Their sense of destiny will begin to hover again as a sense of doom.

DIARY   *8th December, 1941*

The House has been specially summoned. Winston enters the Chamber with bowed shoulders and an expression of grim determination on his face. The House had expected jubilation at the entry of America into the war and are a trifle disconcerted. He makes a dull matter-of-fact speech. He has a great sense of occasion. The mistake he makes is to read out his message to the Siamese Prime Minister. The Siamese are bound to capitulate, and it was a mistake to expect them to do anything else.

---

[1] Saburo Kurusu, the special Japanese envoy to the United States.
[2] Of these explanation (b) came nearest to the truth. Hitler was taken completely by surprise by the news of Pearl Harbour.

9th December, 1941

Lunch with de Gaulle at the Connaught Hotel. I cannot make out whether I really like him. His arrogance and fascism annoy me. But there is something like a fine retriever dog about his eyes. He challenges me on my defence of Weygand. He says that he was a bad strategic ally. He asks what I meant by saying that the French in England should 'compose their differences'. What he wanted me to say was that I had meant that they should all join de Gaulle. I am not prepared to say that as yet. I say that I was cross at having one Frenchman telling me that de Gaulle was surrounded by Jews and Freemasons, and another that he was surrounded by Jesuits and *cagoulards*. He does not like this at all, and his A.D.C. blushes. But it was not a bad thing to say.

De Gaulle says that he thinks that the Germans will have to abandon all further campaigns in Russia and will fail to take Moscow. What, therefore, will they do now? It must be something quick and large. They cannot keep all those divisions unoccupied. It will therefore be the battle of the Mediterranean, and we must expect the whole force of Germany to be flung against the Dardanelles and the Straits of Gibraltar.

I walk away with Van Kleffens.[1] He thinks the Americans were really caught napping and have suffered serious losses. But he also agrees that the political factor is in the end more important than the military factor. He thinks that we shall all suffer much from Japanese intervention for some six months. But after that it will prove an advantage rather than a disaster. The Japs in their idiocy have sent 'planes over San Francisco. As if one could frighten the American people!

10th December, 1941

An unhappy day. I begin by glancing at Gerald Berners' new novel *Far from the Madding War*, and am horrified to feel that Mr Lolypop Jenkins must be a portrait of myself.[2] Ben sees no resemblance, but I do. Then a Viennese actress comes to see me and wants a job, but what can I get for her? She stinks the room out with her exotic scent. Then I go to see Sir Kenneth Goadby.[3] He finds me tired. I have only taken off one pound in three weeks. I walk away from him, and

[1] Minister of Foreign Affairs for the Netherlands, 1939–46.
[2] Lord Berners, who heard of H.N.'s distress, denied this absolutely.
[3] H.N.'s doctor.

as I cross into Oxford Circus, I see a poster, '*Prince of Wales* and *Repulse* sunk'. The whole circus revolves in the air and I lose my breath. I feel sick. To the Beefsteak as quick as I can, where I have a glass of sherry to revive me. When disaster comes, we always flock to the Beefsteak to comfort each other.

The House is of course much distressed by the Far East news. We still do not know the extent of the losses of the Americans at Pearl Harbour, but we do know that many of their ships are unable to put to sea, and that their seaplane base was messed up. They will probably also lose Guam, Midway and Wake islands and eventually the Philippines. But all this pales before the fact that by the sinking of our two large ships Japan has got command of the China seas and can transport large armies to Malaya where they have already seized the northern aerodrome. Both Rangoon and Singapore will be menaced. Added to this situation of immediate danger is the depressing feeling that sea-power is at the mercy of air-power.

DIARY   *11th December, 1941*

The House is depressed. I have a feeling that our nerves are not as good as they were in July 1940, and that we are tired of defeat. We still face the central issue with courage and faith, but in minor matters we are becoming touchy and irritable.

Germany and Italy have declared war on the United States. The B.B.C. gives us extracts from Hitler's and Mussolini's speeches in the Reichstag and the Palazzo Venezia respectively. An admirable performance. But the main factor of this declaration (which should have filled us with the springing hope and aroused tumults of exultation) is ignored. We take it flatly. The loss of the *Prince of Wales* has numbed our nerves.

H.N. TO V.S-W.   *11th December, 1941*
                                                    4 King's Bench Walk, E.C.4

Winston this morning was very grim and said we must expect 'heavy punishment'. I like him best when he makes that sort of speech. I am full of faith. We simply can't be beaten with America in. But how strange it is that this great event should be recorded and welcomed here without any jubilation. We should have gone mad with joy if it had happened a year ago.

I bet de Gaulle that Germany would declare war on the United

States. He said, *'Jamais de la vie.'* I said, 'But will you take my bet?'
He said, 'No, since you may be right.'

Not an American flag flying in the whole of London. How odd
we are!

DIARY   *16th December, 1941*

Harry Strauss[1] attacks me on the grounds that the B.B.C. is almost
wholly left-wing. The Conservative view is never presented. It is
difficult to tell him that most of the right-wing people make bad
broadcasters. Let them find their own Priestley.

I dine with Juliet Duff. The guests are Moura Budberg and André
Labarthe.[2] The latter tells us that people who escape from France
come and see him, since it is his voice which they know and love on
the wireless. He is a passionate and brilliant man, and I cannot help
feeling that he represents France far better than de Gaulle. He is so
happy at the success of his review.[3] It is difficult for people like me
(who really love France passionately) to know what to do. The split
between de Gaulle and the intellectuals is very wide. The Carlton
Gardens[4] people are antipathetic to me. Yet de Gaulle is the great
name.

H.N. TO V.S-W.   *17th December, 1941*

Labarthe told us thrilling stories about the people who escape from
France. He also spoke about the courage of the people left over there.
Maurice Chevalier,[5] for instance, fills music-halls in Paris and the
Germans cannot catch him out. He has one song which he sings without words—just makes faces and gestures expressive of his loathing
of the Germans, but as he does not mention them or speak a word,
the *Commandatur* can do nothing. When he leaves the stage, he crosses
his arms and pats his sleeve, saying, *'Bravo les copains!'* The hall roars
with applause. Do you see the point? *'Les copains au-delà de la Manche.'*[6]

I like those stories. He said that a young Breton boy who came to

[1] Later Lord Conesford. Conservative M.P. for Norwich, 1935-45.
[2] He had broken with de Gaulle, but continued to give France great service in London
by his broadcasts and editorship of *La France Libre.*
[3] *La France Libre*, on which he was assisted by Baroness Budberg.
[4] De Gaulle's London Headquarters.
[5] The French stage and film actor, who was then aged 53.
[6] V.S-W. replied: 'It took me a long time to see the joke, but at last I got it.' It
turns on the word '*manche*', which means both 'sleeve' and 'Channel'. 'Bravo the
boys across the Channel!'

see him told him how our airmen's graves are heaped with flowers. *'Et je vous assure, Monsieur, ce ne sont pas des fleurs artificielles!'* How moving that sort of thing is!

DIARY   17th December, 1941

The House is very depressed about Malaya and fears that Singapore may fall. The Tories are angry with Winston, and are in fact in a bad mood. All the good Tories are either in office or serving in the forces, and the dregs stink. I am rather heckled about the B.B.C. If only people would take in the *Radio Times* and mark what they want to listen to, then there would be far less irritation. What happens is that they just turn the switch and get something which is not intended for them at all. As if I were to pick up the first book I found at St Pancras book-stall and then fume against the L.M.S. for not having given me a book I liked.

We have the American Ambassador afterwards to meet the Anglo-American Parliamentary Committee. Winant is very shy, twists his hands and makes a series of coy platitudes. Yet somehow the superb character of the man pierces through his ungainly charm and one realises he is a real if inarticulate force.

DIARY   19th December, 1941

Go up to Leicester. I find them all rather depressed. The sinking of the *Prince of Wales* has made an impression out of all proportion. They ignore the Russian victories, the Libyan advance and the entry of America. They are faced with the fact that two of our greatest battle-ships have been sunk within a few minutes by the monkey men, and that we and the Americans have between us lost command of the Pacific. I try to cheer them up.

DIARY   25th December, 1941

Vita gives me books and an alarm-clock to wake me up. But it stops at once. I sit indoors all day feeling rotten. We have surrendered in Hong Kong, and the enemy have surrendered at Benghazi. Hong Kong will be a blow to our pride. It also looks as if the Americans will be turned out of the Philippines.

DIARY   28th December, 1941

Feeling much better. I do a *Spectator* article on keeping diaries, in which I lay down the rule that one should write one's diary for one's great-grandson. I think that is a correct rule. The purely private diary becomes too self-centred and morbid. One should have a remote, but not too remote, audience.

The Russians continue to nibble at the German lines. In Libya we are 'mopping up', but it is not clear what has really happened. The public seem to have lost all interest in Libya.

DIARY   *31st December, 1941*

Read Rebecca West's book about Yugoslavia.[1] Feed the famished swans. We stay up late listening to the wireless and hearing Maisky, Wellington Koo[2] and John Winant exchanging polite messages. Then there is a Scottish service, in the middle of which Big Ben strikes and 1941 is finished. Not a year on which I shall look back with any pleasure. I shall say no more about it than that. It has been a sad and horrible year.

---

[1] *Black Lamb and Grey Falcon.*   [2] Chinese Ambassador in London, 1941–46.

1942

National Labour meeting – de Gaulle on Darlan – Vote of Confidence in Churchill – the loss of Singapore – Churchill's remarks on Army morale – the 'Scharnhorst' escapes up-Channel – Churchill's pledge to Austria – David Low – Maisky on Singapore surrender – H.N.'s lectures in Dublin – his interview with De Valera – accused of defeatism, and his personal statement to the House – 'our whole Eastern Empire has gone' – Trygve Lie – Harry Hopkins – Churchill's domination of the House – troubles among the Free French – Ed Murrow on anti-British feeling in America – 'victory by the spring of 1944 at the latest' – murmurs against Churchill's conduct of the war – Vote of Censure defeated – H.N. writes 'The Desire to Please' – retreat to El Alamein – H.N. worried about his eyes – reception for de Gaulle – the Germans at Stalingrad – debate on Old Age Pensions – Lord Ismay on Churchill – the Beveridge Report – the problem of Sir Stafford Cripps – H.N. to V.S-W. on 'the perfect family' – the diary of a complete day, 8th October – Field-Marshal Smuts – the battle of El Alamein – H.N. lunches with Churchill – landings in North Africa – Ben and Nigel go overseas – the Darlan episode – extermination of the Polish Jews – the Free French and Darlan – V.S-W. writes 'The Garden'

'A year, I hope, of recovery'[1]

The first two months saw a succession of disasters. Japan gained almost all her strategic objectives in the Far East; Singapore was lost; Rommel threw the British out of Cyrenaica; the sinkings in the Atlantic neared their climax; there were severe political strains on our relations with Russia, Australia and the Free French; and Churchill's leadership was challenged at home. The impact of these events on Harold Nicolson was as great as on any of his countrymen, yet he retained his profound confidence in Churchill's genius and in ultimate victory. But he had begun to wonder whether the young generation, on whom that victory depended, had in them the resolution to achieve it. The word 'cowardice' enters the diary for the first time.

The Allied objectives in 1942 were to regain naval supremacy in the Far East, to place American arms-production on a war footing, to follow up Auchinleck's initial victories in the desert by an invasion of Tripolitania, and, later in the year, to land an Anglo-American force in North Africa and deny the whole southern Mediterranean to the enemy. The Russian campaign, which absorbed the bulk of the German armies, gave the Allies a breathing-space in which to mature their own plans.

The first set-back was Rommel's reconquest of almost all the ground that had been gained since November. In early January the 8th Army had pushed on as far as El Agheila on the border of Tripolitania, and Auchinleck intended to renew his offensive in February. He considered it almost inconceivable that Rommel could mount an offensive of his own after so long and costly a retreat. But with inferior forces the Afrika Korps pushed back the British Divisions by an attack launched on 21st January, recaptured Benghazi on the 29th and continued as far as Gazala and Tobruk, where Rommel halted temporarily in preparation for his new onslaught in May. It was a major and humiliating defeat for British arms, but its consequences were even worse than the House of Commons supposed, for Churchill had naturally never told them of the strategic plan to advance as far as Tripoli and beyond. The loss of three major battleships and the 'Ark Royal' in the Mediterranean was also concealed from them. Rommel could now receive his supplies almost unimpeded.

[1] The subtitle which H.N. typed on 1st January.

*In the Far East, Allied defeats were even graver. The Japanese drove
back the British forces down the length of Malaya, until on 31st January
we held nothing more than the island of Singapore at its tip. This fortress
was considered an essential bastion to our position in the Far East. Under
strong pressure from Australia, it was heavily reinforced. Nevertheless,
it was invaded on 8th February and yielded on the 15th, with the surrender
of 60,000 men. Churchill called it 'the worst disaster and largest capitulation in British history'.*

*It profoundly shook his leadership, but not his confidence. In a three-
day debate, from 27th to 29th January, he had regained his mastery of
the House of Commons, calling for a vote of confidence which was granted to him by 464 votes to 1. Singapore fell after this, but an even
greater shock to British morale came on 12th February with the escape
of the two German battle-cruisers, 'Scharnhorst' and 'Gneisenau', up-
Channel in face of British air-attacks. Changes in the Cabinet were
demanded and conceded. Sir Stafford Cripps, who at that period was
regarded by many as the only possible alternative to Churchill, was
brought back from Moscow and made Leader of the House of Commons;
Oliver Lyttelton returned from Cairo as Minister of Production; and
Beaverbrook, Kingsley Wood and Greenwood were retired from the War
Cabinet.*

DIARY   *1st January, 1942*

Mr Auren, of a Stockholm newspaper, comes to see me. He asks how
I explain the British love of self-criticism. I say it is partly pride and
partly love of fresh air. He says it does our propaganda harm abroad.
I say it is worth it from our point of view, since it keeps our public
opinion healthy. We should die if we were not able to abuse our
institutions and public men. Moreover, it is good long-term policy
even from the propaganda point of view. He says that all Swedes
know they will come in in the end. I do not suggest to him that 'the
end' means the moment when it is quite clear which side is going to
win.

DIARY   *2nd January, 1942*

Dine at Brooks' with Jim Lees-Milne,[1] James Pope-Hennessy and Guy
Burgess. We discuss everything, but mainly the question of success.
James says, 'It is ridiculous of you, Harold, not to realise that it does
not matter your having been a failure at the Ministry of Information,

[1] The historian of architecture, and a life-long friend of H.N.

since you have written such good books.' This annoys me, since I was not a failure at the M. of I., merely politically inconvenient. I say that I would rather be able to send 100 tons of grain to Greece than write an immortal work. This impresses them, as they agree. What does even the *Symposium* matter compared to the death by hunger of 200 Greeks a day?[1]

DIARY   *14th January, 1942*

Meeting of the National Labour Executive. Kenneth Lindsay[2] says that we must concentrate on a long-term policy—the relations between the State and the individual and the State and industry. Frank Markham[3] says that, on the contrary, we must concentrate on winning the war. In order to do this, we must get rid of Churchill, who will never win the war. Others say that Winston is not an organiser and is no judge of men. His faith in Beaverbrook is lamentable. The latter thinks only of the sensational and the dramatic: for instance, he did produce a lot of tanks, but only at the expense of their own spare-parts, and the result was that most of our tanks in Libya went out of action. Kenneth Lindsay says that Shinwell is the only man in the House prepared to make a stand against Winston, and Cripps is the only possible alternative Prime Minister. Stephen King-Hall says that the mistake is for Winston to be both Prime Minister and Minister of Defence, and that he neglects production in one capacity and confuses strategy in the other. They all feel that he must be brought down, and yet they all agree (a) that there is no apparent successor, and (b) that his fall would give an immense moral shock to the country.

I am disgusted by all this, since they are only thinking in political and departmental terms, and have no conception of the effort of will involved. Winston is the embodiment of the nation's will.

DIARY   *15th January, 1942*

Eddy Winterton[4] says that Winston, when he returns,[5] will meet a very different House from the one he left. The feeling is that our continued defeats in Malaya show a grave underestimation of the

[1] H.N. had been talking to the Greek Prime Minister, Emmanuel Tsouderos, on the previous day, and had been horrified by his account of conditions in Athens.
[2] National Labour M.P. for Kilmarnock Burghs, 1933–45.
[3] National M.P. for S. Nottingham, 1935–45.
[4] Conservative M.P. for Horsham since 1904. Chancellor of the Duchy of Lancaster, 1937–39, and member of the Cabinet, 1938. Paymaster General, 1939.
[5] From the United States, where he had been since 22nd December.

position and that our comparative successes in Libya will not compensate for this. Go up to Lloyd George's room. Sylvester[1] comes in. He says that Ll.G.'s defeatism is largely that he feels out of it, and that once he could be induced to join the Cabinet, he would become a fighting tiger again. It seems that Stafford Cripps is leaving Moscow, and there is much speculation whether he will enter the War Cabinet.

I have a bad night in Committee Room 9.[2] There are two stokers in the room who spit and snore all the time, and I hear Big Ben booming hour after hour, while the paraffin lamp makes little round circles through its eye-holes on the ceiling.

DIARY   20th January, 1942

I arrive at the House a bit late and do not hear the reception given to Winston at his entry.[3] Some say that it was most enthusiastic; others say that it had about it a note of reserve. I ask Randolph Churchill[4] how it struck him. He said, 'Nothing like the reception Chamberlain got when he returned from Munich.' He tells me that Rommel is getting reinforcements, but only half what is sent ever reach him. He does not think that Germany will try to seize Malta, since that would be too arduous a task for the advantage to be gained. He thinks that they may well attack Turkey. Oil is now essential to them.

DIARY   21st January, 1942

I lunch with Camrose to meet de Gaulle, Trenchard, the Master of the Rolls and Lawson.[5] De Gaulle speaks English now in quite an effective way. He is very human for once, and speaks frankly. He says that France will never regain her soul unless she fights in the end on our side. He does not think that Darlan or anyone else would dare to use the French Fleet except in defence. I say, 'But if they convoy troops to Libya in return for food?' '*Ça*', he said, '*serait différent.*' Anyhow, it is the first time that I have ever got on with him. He is shy and authoritative, like Kitchener. He has strange hands, like those of a *lycéen*.[6]

[1] A. J. Sylvester, Principal Private Secretary to Lloyd George.
[2] The room in the House of Commons set aside as a dormitory for fire-watchers.
[3] Churchill had flown back from Bermuda on 15th January.
[4] He was Conservative M.P. for Preston, 1940–45. He was then on leave from the Middle East, where he was serving on Auchinleck's General Staff.
[5] General F. Lawson, later Lord Burnham, then Managing Director of the *Daily Telegraph*.
[6] A schoolboy.

DIARY   *23rd January, 1942*

At breakfast I am joined by Ben and Philip Toynbee.[1] I enjoy it very much indeed. Ben is always one of the most charming companions in the world.

I give Sibyl [Colefax] luncheon at Boulestin, and she bothers me hard to write a book on 'How we got our Empire'. She has been got at by Winant, who foresees a strain on Anglo–American relations and some difficulty owing to the fact that America has no idea at all of our imperial mission. I do not think I have the necessary afflatus to write such a book. There is India, for instance, about which I know nothing and regarding which I have a feeling that we are wrong. I could not write an 'apologetic book', and am certain that I had better not write the book at all. The worst book I ever wrote was *Dwight Morrow*,[2] which in a way was a command performance. I shall have no more command performances. The thing cannot be done.

DIARY   *26th January, 1942*

To Grosvenor House, where we have a hush meeting of the B.B.C. Board. We decide to retire Ogilvie,[3] and put Graves[4] and Foot[5] as joint Directors-General in his place. I am sure this is right, as Ogilvie is too noble a character for rough war-work. Yet I mind deeply in a way. This clever, high-minded man being pushed aside. I hate it. But I agree.

I am very worried about Libya. It looks as if we might be in for a major defeat. Why is it that we can never win any battle at all? The effect on Australia will be bad. 'Why take our men, when we are in danger here, and then muddle it all?'

DIARY   *27th January, 1942*

Down to the House. Winston speaks for an hour and a half and justifies his demand for a vote of confidence. One can actually feel the wind of opposition dropping sentence by sentence, and by the time he finishes it is clear that there is really no opposition at all—only a certain uneasiness. He says that we shall have even worse news to face in the Far

[1] The author and literary critic. He was then aged 24, and both Ben and he had commissions in the Intelligence Corps.
[2] The biography of the American statesman, which H.N. had written at the request of Mrs Morrow and J. P. Morgan & Co. in 1935.
[3] Sir Frederick Ogilvie, Director-General of the B.B.C., 1938–42.
[4] Sir Cecil Graves, who had been on the staff of the B.B.C. since 1926.
[5] Robert Foot, General Manager of the Gas, Light & Coke Co. since 1929.

East and that the Libyan battle is going none too well.[1] When he feels that he has the whole House with him, he finds it difficult to conceal his enjoyment of his speech, and that, in fact, is part of his amazing charm. He thrusts both his hands deep into his trouser pockets, and turns his tummy now to the right, now to the left, in evident enjoyment of his mastery of the position.

Herbert Williams[2] and Henderson Stewart[3] attack the Government. But the House is not with them. Winston has won in the very first round, and the future rounds will be dull and sad. My God, my love and admiration of Winston surge round me like a tide!

DIARY   28th January, 1942

Wardlaw-Milne[4] makes an impressive speech attacking the Government over Malaya. But the whole thing seems to me unreal since our misfortune is due entirely to the collapse of the American Navy. It is difficult for Winston to say this, and indeed he slid over the point neatly in his speech yesterday. But it is really absurd to expect our people at Singapore to have taken measures of defence on the assumption that the command of the sea would pass suddenly to the Japanese. And even if they had, we could not have provided sufficient to meet such a disaster.

Shinwell makes a vicious speech. Randolph Churchill intervenes to defend his father. He attacks most cruelly those who had abused him, and says that Winterton 'clowned himself out of office within a few days'. He is amusing and brave. Bob Boothby says to me, 'I am enjoying this very much, but I hope it does not go on for long.' I have a dreadful feeling that Randolph may go too far. I see his little wife squirming in the Gallery, and Winston himself looks embarrassed and shy. But I am not so sure that it has done Randolph harm.

DIARY   29th January, 1942

Third day of the Vote of Confidence debate. Winston winds up. He is very genial and self-confident. He does not gird at his critics. He compliments them on the excellence of their speeches. When he

[1] Rommel's attack on the 21st had led to a rapid British retreat from El Agheila, and Benghazi was to fall two days later.
[2] Sir Herbert Williams, Conservative M.P. since 1924 for Reading and S. Croydon.
[3] James Henderson Stewart, Liberal National M.P. for East Fife since 1933.
[4] Sir John Wardlaw-Milne, Conservative M.P. for Kidderminster, 1922–45, and Chairman of the Conservative Foreign Affairs Committee, 1939–45.

reaches his peroration he ceases to be genial and becomes emphatic. He crouches over the box and strikes it. 'It only remains for us to act. I offer no apologies. I offer no excuses. I make no promises. In no way have I mitigated the sense of danger and impending misfortunes that hang over us. But at the same time I avow my confidence, never stronger than at this moment, that we shall bring this conflict to an end in a manner agreeable to the interests of our country and the future of the world. I have finished.' (Then that downward sweep of the two arms, with the palms open to receive the stigmata.) 'Let every man act now in accordance with what he thinks is his duty in harmony with his heart and conscience.' Loud cheers, and we all file out into the thin and stifling lobby.

It takes a long time to count the votes, and finally they are recorded as 464 to 1.[1] Huge cheers. Winston gets up and we rise and cheer him. He turns round and bows a little shyly. Then he joins Mrs Winston, and arm-in-arm and beaming, they push through the crowds in Central Lobby.

There was a scene earlier in the day between Winston and Southby.[2] Yesterday, during Randolph's rather unfortunate speech, Southby had interrupted and hinted that Randolph was not a fighting soldier ('The Honourable and Gallant Member—I call him that because of the uniform he wears'). The Speaker shut him up, and in the corridor afterwards he went up to Winston and said that had he been allowed to finish, he would have congratulated Randolph on his rapid promotion. Winston shook his fist in his face. 'Do not speak to me', he shouted. 'You called my son a coward. You are my enemy. Do not speak to me.'

As I pass the tape I find it ticking imperturbably. It tells us that the Germans claim to have entered Benghazi, and that the Japs claim to be only eighteen miles from Singapore. Grave disasters indeed. At the same time we have released the news of the sinking of the Barham.[3] A black day for a vote of confidence.

---

[1] The three Independent Labour Party Members, two of whom acted as tellers in the Division, voted against the Government.

[2] Commander Sir Archibald Southby, Conservative M.P. for Epsom, 1928–47. In his speech he had also attacked Churchill for sending our naval forces to the Far East without sufficient air support.

[3] The battleship Barham had been torpedoed in the Mediterranean in December with the loss of 500 lives. But the news of the sinking of the Queen Elizabeth and Valiant in Alexandria harbour on 18th December had still not been released.

H.N. TO V.S-W.
3rd February, 1942
4 King's Bench Walk, E.C.4

George Peel[1] told me an interesting story at the Beefsteak today. When he was a boy, in 1888, he went out to Florence. The Duomo had been renovated and there was a great crowd in the piazza to see the west front unveiled. He watched it from the crowd, and while he was waiting, a carriage drew up just in front of him. In it was Queen Victoria and her lady-in-waiting. He noticed that the Queen fumbled in her corsage and took out a locket which she held up to the Cathedral at the moment of unveiling. He was puzzled by this odd behaviour in a Protestant woman, and meeting the lady-in-waiting some days afterwards, he asked her what it meant. She said, 'Oh, it was a miniature of the Prince Consort. She always holds it up so that he can see something interesting or beautiful.'

DIARY
4th February, 1942

The news is really very bad indeed. We are out of Malaya and hanging on by our eyelids to Singapore. Rommel is dashing on in Libya and has driven us out of Derna. As the Germans seem at the same time to be stabilising the Russian position, they may shortly attack the Middle East from the Turkish end. We never really allow ourselves to think how long this war will last, but I see no chance of the tide really turning till 1944, and what will have happened by then?

DIARY
11th February, 1942

We have a Secret Session on shipping. Our whole strategical effort is hampered by lack of tonnage and the situation is none too good. But I must not disclose even to my diary what happens in a Secret Session.

The House is not in a gay mood. Nancy Astor dashes up and says that I must join with her in forcing Winston to appoint a Minister of Defence and not waste all his time on strategy. Otherwise, she says, he is bound to fall. I admit that no other Administration could have survived such a series of disasters. People can understand Singapore,[2] as it was due to Pearl Harbour and the loss of Indo-China. But Libya (which is going even worse than we feared) is not understood, and there will be anxious criticism if Tobruk falls. A whisper is going

[1] The Hon. A. G. V. Peel (1868–1956), second son of the first Viscount Peel.
[2] The Japanese attack on Singapore began on 8th February.

around that our troops do not fight well. It is true that an Indian Division panicked in Malaya, but it is a little disturbing that the Australians there should have had so few casualties.

DIARY   *12th February, 1942*

What has saddened me is not merely the bad news from Singapore and Libya, but a conversation with Violet [Bonham Carter]. She had been to see Winston yesterday, and for the first time in their long friendship she had found him depressed. He was querulous about criticism, unhappy at Cripps not consenting to take office,[1] worried by the absence of alternative Ministers whom he could invite to join the Government. But underneath it all was a dreadful fear, she felt, that our soldiers are not as good fighters as their fathers were. 'In 1915', said Winston, 'our men fought on even when they had only one shell left and were under a fierce barrage. Now they cannot resist dive-bombers. We have so many men in Singapore, so many men— they should have done better.' It is the same, of course, in Libya. Our men cannot stand up to punishment. And yet they are the same men as man the merchant ships and who won the Battle of Britain. There is something deeply wrong with the whole morale of our Army.

DIARY   *15th February, 1942*

In the evening Winston Churchill speaks. He tells us that Singapore has fallen. He is grim and not gay. Unfortunately he appeals for national unity and not criticism, in a manner which recalls Neville Chamberlain. Moreover, although he is not rhetorical, he cannot speak in perfectly simple terms and cannot avoid the cadences of a phrase. I do not think his speech will have done good, and I feel deeply depressed and anxious.

DIARY   *16th February, 1942*

I find that people are more distressed about the escape of the *Scharnhorst* and *Gneisenau* than they are even by the loss of Singapore. They cannot bear the thought that the Germans sailed past our front door. Winston will have to face a bad situation in the House tomorrow. There will have to be a serious Government reconstruction. But what striking figures (other than Cripps) can Winston bring in? People

[1] Churchill had asked him to become Minister of Supply, but Cripps refused if he could not simultaneously join the War Cabinet.

are even suggesting that Wavell should be brought back[1] to become Minister of Defence.

I fear a slump in public opinion which will deprive Winston of his legend. His broadcast last night was not liked. The country is too nervous and irritable to be fobbed off with fine phrases. Yet what else could he have said?

H.N. TO V.S-W. *17th February, 1942*
4 King's Bench Walk, E.C.4

Winston made his statement this afternoon. It started all right, but when people asked questions, he became irritable and rather reckless. He spoke about 'anger and panic' which infuriated people and will, I fear, be broadcast throughout the world by our enemies. The pity of it is that he had a good case, and if only he had kept his head and produced his promises in the right order,[2] all would have gone well. He was not at his best.

I had an interview with Anthony [Eden], and he is really doing a great deal for Greece. I came away encouraged and happy.

DIARY *18th February, 1942*

I ran into the Archduke Robert[3] who was celebrating a speech made today by Churchill when accepting a Canteen given to him by the Free Austrians. In his speech he definitely pledged himself to the restoration of Austrian independence. Now this shows the difficulty of one-man leadership. For months, for years even, we have been longing to give such a lead in our broadcasts to Austria. But Winston, who never likes propaganda in any form, was just sulky and silent, with the result that we got no further at all. Now, merely because he has to say a few words of polite thanks, he says the very words which would have been invaluable to us two years ago.

DIARY *23rd February, 1942*

Cabinet changes announced. Margesson is sacked from the War Office, and his place taken by P. J. Grigg. Greenwood is also retired

---

[1] From the Far East, where he had been Supreme Commander of the Allied Forces since 29th December, 1941. Thus he had been ultimately responsible for the defence of Singapore.

[2] For instance, announcing the court of enquiry into the escape of the two German battle-cruisers.

[3] The second son of the Emperor Karl of Austria-Hungary.

from the councils of the Empire. Cripps becomes Lord Privy Seal and Leader of the House. Cranborne goes to the Colonial Office, and Wolmer becomes Minister of Economic Warfare having been out of office since Baldwin sacked him in 1924.[1] All very odd. The proletariat seem delighted, although it is a snub for the Labour people and the reinstatement of the upper class. I am sorry for Margesson. Only four days ago he introduced the Army Estimates with ability and confidence. He has for so many years been a power in the House, and now his political career is dashed, for no apparent reason except, I suppose, that Cripps insisted upon him and Greenwood going.

DIARY   *24th February, 1942*

Ralph Rayner[2] makes a speech in which he accuses the B.B.C. of issuing soft-soap bulletins. I interrupt him to say that they put out what they get. This is the first time I have raised my voice in the House since I was sacked.

Running through many of the speeches in the debate was the implication that our Army has not fought well. How comes it that we were turned out of Malaya by only two Japanese divisions? How comes it that our casualties were so few and our surrenders so great? This is the most disturbing of all thoughts.

In the evening I go to Pratts where I find Harold Macmillan and others. We discuss this issue frankly. The left-wing people say that you must create a 'revolutionary army' and that our 'class army' can never fight. The right-wing say that we should go back to our old system of regimental discipline. Macmillan says that we have not the time or scope to create a revolutionary army and that we must go back to discipline. We are between two stools, he says.

Walking down Whitehall this afternoon with Rob Bernays we passed David Low.[3] He has shaved his beard and looks like a New Zealander instead of an Australian. I greeted him and he returned my greeting. 'Who is your friend?' asked Rob. 'He is an interesting man', I said, 'since the future historian of the decline and fall of the British Empire will give him a front-rank seat in the gallery of our

---

[1] The third Earl of Selborne, Viscount Wolmer, who was Parliamentary Secretary to the Board of Trade, 1922–24. He was Director of Cement, Ministry of Works, 1940–42.

[2] Brigadier Ralph Rayner, Conservative M.P. for Totnes since 1935.

[3] The cartoonist, who was born in New Zealand in 1891, and first worked in Sydney before coming to London in 1919.

disintegrators. It is Low—the man who by inventing Colonel Blimp
sapped discipline.' 'And auth-th-th-th-tho-rity', stuttered Rob.

DIARY   *25th February, 1942*

I have a talk with young de Chair,[1] who is back wounded from the
Middle East. He said that the men fought well in Greece and Crete
and Libya. There is no decline in toughness. It is the officers and the
Generals who lack, not courage, but the intelligence to depart from
the text-books.

The debate on the war situation goes on all afternoon and Cripps
winds up drily, meticulously, helpfully, but without inspiration. He
may be the future Prime Minister, but he has not the shine or muscle
of Winston.

DIARY   *27th February, 1942*

I do a talk on Winston for the Empire programme. I cannot bear the
thought that this heroic figure should now be sniped at by tiny little
men. I fell asleep for one moment last night and dreamt of pain and
anxiety, and then suddenly I felt Vita's hands upon my shoulders.
'Is it you?' I asked. 'No', the wraith answered, 'I am Defeat.' I woke
unhappily and remained awake.

This Singapore surrender has been a terrific blow to all of us. It is not
merely the immediate dangers which threaten in the Indian Ocean
and the menace to our communications with the Middle East. It is
the dread that we are only half-hearted in fighting the whole-hearted.
It is even more than that. We intellectuals must feel that in all these
years we have derided the principles of force upon which our Empire is
built. We undermined confidence in our own formula. The intellectuals of 1780 did the same.

*On 8th March the Japanese occupied Rangoon, and began rapidly to
take over the rest of Burma, from which the British retreated into north-
east India. By the end of the month the Japanese held Siam, Malaya,
Hong Kong and nearly the whole of the Dutch East Indies. Their
successes caused consternation in Australia and India. The Australians
openly appealed for help to the United States. The Indian Congress
demanded immediate independence, thinking it less likely that the
Japanese would invade their country if it were not part of the British*

[1] Somerset de Chair, M.P. for S.-W. Norfolk, 1935-45. Author of *The Golden Carpet.*

Empire, and Sir Stafford Cripps' mission to Delhi at the end of March failed to persuade Congress that it was in their own best interests that independence should be delayed until the end of the war. The Japanese advance was, however, halted at the Battle of the Coral Sea (8th May) and the Battle of Midway (4th June), by which the U.S. Navy regained command of the western Pacific.

In Russia, Hitler intended to capture Leningrad and break through the southern front to the Caucasus, leaving the Moscow front relatively quiet. Leningrad held, but the Germans made deep advances towards Stalingrad and the lower Don. Stalin sent Molotov to London and Washington in May to plead for a Second Front in western Europe, but Churchill firmly replied that this would not be possible till 1943. The only help which we could give immediately was through our Arctic convoys of war-material to Russia, and by bombing German cities. The first mass-raids from the British Isles were made on Lübeck and Cologne at the end of May.

Churchill badly needed a victory to strengthen his own position at home, and to match the determined fighting of the Russian Army and American Navy. Instead, he was faced by the further retreat of the 8th Army in Cyrenaica, culminating on 20th June in the fall of Tobruk, where 33,000 British troops capitulated to a numerically inferior force. General Ritchie was replaced in command of 8th Army by General Auchinleck himself, but the retreat continued to the El Alamein line, and both Alexandria and Malta were in extreme jeopardy.

The news that Tobruk had fallen reached Churchill while he was on his second visit to Washington. He returned home to face a vote of No Confidence in the House of Commons on 1st and 2nd July. Although he won by 476 votes to 25 with 40 deliberate abstentions, his authority was severely weakened.

Harold Nicolson's diary indicates that of all these events it was the Japanese menace, the retreat from Libya and the decline of Churchill's prestige that caused him greatest concern. The Russian campaign, the Battle of the Atlantic, the bombing offensive and the Arctic convoys are mentioned only incidentally. His main personal contribution during these months was a visit to Dublin, but a few chance remarks led to him being accused publicly of defeatism, a charge to which he replied by a personal statement in the House of Commons. In his intervals of leisure, he put in a few hours a week at a light-engineering factory in London, and began to write 'The Desire to Please', the story of his ancestor, Hamilton Rowan, and the United Irishmen.

DIARY   *13th March, 1942*

Go to see Maisky. He seems pleased with the military situation and says that the Russians have new armies for the spring offensive. He says that they have now taken the measure of the Germans and will not be taken by surprise. The supplies are coming in fairly well, and he praises Beaverbrook for having tried so hard to keep his promises. But he asks me what has happened to the British Army. Why did they surrender so easily at Singapore? It is really a disgrace. He thinks it is due to the senior officers, and that we do not promote young men quick enough. He tells me that De Valera is very narrow indeed, and, to his mind, rather stupid.

Come back and find James [Pope-Hennessy] who is in one of his delightful moods. Then pack for Eire.

H.N. TO V.S-W.   *16th March, 1942*
                                           Farmhill, Dundrum, Co. Dublin

I flew to Dublin from Manchester. The 'plane smelled of sick and all the windows were covered with butter-muslin so that one could not look out. A faint bumping in the distance told me that we were moving along the ground, and an hour and ten minutes later another series of soft bumps told me that we had reached Dublin. In between I just read.

The High Commissioner[1] drove me out here, where he lives. It is about six miles from Dublin, a country house of small dimensions, with trees and cows and fields. Crocuses among the rock-work and some daffodils showing their long buds.

This morning I drove with him to the Wicklow mountains. Rain and sunshine over moors and streams gushing. We drove to the famous Powerscourt waterfall which I remember so well from childhood. The grass all around is springy and green from the spray. Then we went to the house where we lunched. A great ostentatious eighteenth-century mansion with a most elaborate Italian garden and a superb view of the Wicklow mountains. Powerscourt[2], whom I remember as a young guardee forty years ago, took me into the

---

[1] J. L. Maffey, later Lord Rugby. He was Permanent Under-Secretary of State for the Colonies, 1933–37, and had been U.K. Representative to Eire since 1939. The Irish did not like or use the term 'High Commissioner'.

[2] The 8th Viscount Powerscourt (1880–1947), a Protestant and Liberal Unionist. He had succeeded his father in 1904.

garden. We leant upon a gilt balustrade, looking down over the fountains to the great pool between the statues. He said, 'Here I am marooned—the last of the Irish aristccracy, with nobody to speak to.' I remembered when the place was the centre of social life in Ireland and two brass bands played upon the terrace and the great marquee seemed to provide innumerable ices for little boys. My granny[1] would not let me have more than one ice. She was a firm woman.

I gave a lecture in Dublin in the evening. It went well. There was one man afterwards who made an impassioned speech saying that there was only one thing that should be subject to Government censorship, and that began with the letters 'c.o.n.' I imagined, of course, that he was attacking the cruelty of Great Britain and all the wrongs that we were still doing to Ireland. I looked down my nose. I merely said, when, panting with passion, he had resumed his seat, that I did not wish to comment on controversial matters. It was only when I was walking away with one of the Professors that I was told that what he had meant was 'contraceptives'.

DIARY   *16th March, 1942*
                                                              Dublin

Binchy,[2] who was Irish Minister in Berlin when I was there, comes to see me. He says that a visiting Englishman is apt to be taken in by blarney and to imagine that the feelings of this country towards us are really friendly. Not in the least: at the bottom of almost every Irish heart is a little bag of bile, and although their hatred of us may die down at moments, it is there, even as our protestantism and puritanism are there subconsciously. He says that at the beginning of the war no Irishman really supposed that Eire would be able to maintain her neutrality. The fact that this neutrality has been respected is not accorded unto us for righteousness: most of it is attributed to the genius of De Valera, who has thereby gained enormous prestige and many new adherents. Those who refuse to admit Dev's part in it attribute it to a Merciful Providence who is recompensing Ireland for all her past sorrows. 'Neutrality' has thus taken on an almost religious flavour; it has become a question of honour; and it is something which Ireland is not ashamed of, but tremendously proud. The Irish

[1] Catherine Rowan Hamilton, who died in 1919 in her 99th year.
[2] Daniel A. Binchy, Professor of Jurisprudence in University College, Dublin, and Minister of the Irish Free State in Germany, 1929–32.

were 'relieved' by the American occupation of Ulster[1] and only a few of them have the sense to see that it will go far to explode the American legend about Ireland. 'You see', says Binchy, 'the Americans will find us out.'

To the University for the Inaugural Session of the Law Society. Professor Ryan is in the chair, and after the presentation of the year's medals, the Auditor (T. D. E. Williams) reads his paper on 'The End of an Era?' The hall is so crowded that every gangway is blocked. The Auditor's address is a covert attack on England and is designed to show that she has fallen from her high estate and reaped the penalty for many sins. I have to follow, and the audience receives me kindly. I was stimulated by the danger of it all and made a good speech. There is much applause at the end, with that carrying-through movement, the effect of a following wave of appreciation, which one sees in a good drive at golf. Then the Attorney General[2] speaks, and then Professor McGilligan.[3] The latter goes very far. He says that among Ireland's greatest woes is the present Government. He suggests that neutrality is not worthy of Irish ideals, and that he hopes Ireland will in the end find herself on the same side as 'our ancient enemy and our present dear friend and neighbour'. This is met with stony silence, but at least without protest.

DIARY   17th March, 1942
                                                                              Dublin

St Patrick's Day. John Betjeman[4] rings up to say that my speech went very well. I am, however, worried by the Irish Times and the Independent. They put in all my admissions about the danger of our position, and leave out all about my patriotism and desire to win. If this garbled account of what I said gets to London, I shall be in trouble.[5]

[1] The advance party of three American divisions arrived in Northern Ireland at the end of January 1942.
[2] The Hon. K. O'H. Haugh, Attorney General of Eire, 1940–42.
[3] Patrick McGilligan, Minister of External Affairs, 1927–32, and Professor of International and Constitutional Law, University College, Dublin.
[4] The author and poet. He was then U.K. Press Attaché in Dublin.
[5] When he had risen to speak in the Irish debate, H.N. first replied to Williams' attack on Britain by the following unprepared remarks: 'Imperialism is dead, and, I devoutly hope, buried. If you were to picture the British lion as a rampant beast, red in tooth and claw, seeking whom it might devour, then you would get a completely false and distorted picture of our war aims. It would be much wiser to think of the British lion as an elderly, replete, self-satisfied, moth-eaten animal,

DIARY   *18th March, 1942*
                                                              Dublin

I go to see De Valera in his office. In his waiting-room there is a statue of Lincoln and a copy of the American Declaration of Independence. His own room is ill-designed, with cold, high windows and two enormous plaques on the wall—of Griffiths, I suppose, and Michael Collins. There is a thick hibernian carpet and a clock that strikes the quarter-hours with a loud noise. On his desk he has a telephone box which buzzes occasionally and to which he talks in Gaelic.

He is not what I expected. I expected a thin sallow man with huge round black spectacles, a thin mouth, great lines from nose to lip-corner, and lank black Spanish hair.[1] But he is not thin, and pale rather than sallow, not a bit haggard, benevolent cold eyes behind steel-framed glasses, hair that is soft and almost brown, no great lines in his face anywhere. An unhealthy look about the gills, and faint indications of white puffiness. A firm gentle voice with a soft Irish accent. An admirable smile, not showing teeth, but lighting up the eyes and face very quickly, like an electric light bulb that doesn't fit and flashes on and off. Yet not an insincere smile. A happy smile.

His conversation is uninteresting. He talks rather in a monologue. He asks me about things at home and sympathises much with Churchill's difficulty in having to cheer up the country and yet not give us bright and optimistic forecasts. 'I know that difficulty—I know it all too well.' He talks about the 'partition', but in a stereotype way and I do not feel much fire behind that. He regrets the presence of the American troops [in Northern Ireland], 'since they won't understand our people as well as the Tommy does'. He speaks affectionately about France, and fears that the Germans will beat Russia this spring. He thinks that if we in Britain were beaten, America would not carry

---

whose tail in the last twenty years has been so frequently twisted that few hairs remain, but an animal which at this moment is alert and angry. We have suffered severe defeats and will have further disasters to meet in the future, but while these defeats and disasters have certainly diminished our conceit and destroyed our self-complacency, they have increased our pride.' He then turned to his prepared speech and spoke of British patriotism. The Irish newspapers headlined, '*Britain, a moth-eaten lion*'.

[1] Eamon De Valera was born in New York in 1882 of a Spanish father and an Irish mother. He had been head of the Irish Government and Minister of External Affairs since December 1937.

on an Atlantic war but would compromise with Germany and Japan. He is indignant with Churchill for not supplying Ireland with arms. I say that it is due to our shortages. He taps thick whitish fingers on the table. 'No, it is something more than that.' I fear he is right about this. He then touches on the Press. I tell him that he only gets the disagreeable cuttings, and that on the whole our Press is good about Ireland. I tell him that before I became a Governor of the B.B.C., I was under the impression that the papers were on the whole friendly to that institution. But now that I see files of press-cuttings, I have the impression that every paper devotes column after column to unfair attacks on the B.B.C. He is amused by this, and the faint flash of his smile lights up his porridge-coloured face.

He is a very simple man, like all great men. He does not look like a strong man, nor are there any signs in his face of suffering and endurance. Rather he reminds me of Lothian in his last years. Deep spiritual certainty underneath it all, giving to his features a mark of repose.

DIARY   *20th March, 1942*
                                                                    London

On the front page of the *Daily Telegraph*, I see a paragraph headed, 'Mr Harold Nicolson'. I read that Liddall,[1] the Member for Lincoln, has tabled a motion asking that I be 'dismissed' from the B.B.C. for having made a 'generally defeatist' speech in Ireland. This means that the *Independent* article has been republished over here. I do not know Liddall, but he was a fierce supporter of Chamberlain at the time of Munich, and has probably got a long grudge against me. All my pleasure and triumph at my Irish visit is suddenly damped, and I feel deeply depressed. This sort of thing can never really be explained away.

DIARY   *26th March, 1942*

I make a personal statement about the motion put down by Liddall. I start well enough, but I go on too long and make the mistake of abusing Liddall.[2] I see the Speaker shaking his head, and I stop as

[1] Walter (later Sir Walter) Liddall, a business-man and a prominent Conservative in Lincolnshire local politics. He was Member for Lincoln, 1931–45.
[2] H.N. complained that Liddall had based his motion on reports in Irish newspapers, which he should have known to be biased. Liddall withdrew his motion, as 'the Hon. Member has said he has been misquoted'.

quick as I can. The House is with me and against Liddall. Now it is all over and I have cleared my reputation.

I then broadcast a talk on modern English literature to Sweden.

Winston makes a speech to the Conservative Association in which he describes Singapore as the worst disaster the British Army has ever suffered. He is also gloomy about the Battle of the Atlantic. In fact we are going through a very bad period, and even the Russians do not seem to be doing too well.

DIARY   *30th March, 1942*

The wireless booms out the Indian agreement. 'Under Article Six it is provided that the States and Provinces . . .' I feel so enraged that the Cabinet did not listen to Leo Amery a year ago and did not give India Dominion status then. Now we have done it under threats from the Japanese.[1] Our whole Eastern Empire has gone. Australia has as good as gone. Poor little England. But I should not have minded all this so much if we had fought well.

Start work on my Search of the Past, vol. II. I think I shall call it *The Other Side*.[2]

DIARY   *10th April, 1942*

Lunch with Kingsley Martin.[3] He thinks that unless we have Socialism immediately, we shall lose the war. He is worried by the bad morale of the Army. This Singapore business goes round and round in the head like some horrible obsession. Meanwhile the Americans have surrendered at Bataan,[4] but after a resistance so magnificent that they put us to shame.

DIARY   *14th April, 1942*

I lunch with the Norwegian Government. I sit next to Dr Lie.[5] He is very bitter at our not doing anything, and almost writhes his fat body in irritation at our incapacity for attack. Roger Keyes is there, and

---

[1] The British proposal was to give India her independence after the war.
[2] In fact he called it *The Desire to Please*. The first volume had been *Helen's Tower* (Constable, 1937).
[3] Editor of the *New Statesman and Nation* since 1931.
[4] The surrender of General Wainwright in the Bataan Peninsula on 9th April brought to an end the long and gallant defence of the Philippines.
[5] Trygve Lie, Norwegian Foreign Minister, and Secretary General of the United Nations, 1946–53.

tells us how we could have taken Trondheim[1] easily at the time of the first invasion, and how we funked it. He is rather bitter against Winston, who, he feels, has lost all his courage and all his capacity for taking risks. He is of course nervous and disgruntled, but I fear that there may be something in what he says.

DIARY   15th April, 1942

We are addressed by Harry Hopkins[2] in the large Committee Room. He is very astute and makes a good impression. The implication of what he said was that we should be mad to get rid of Winston, since he is the only man who really understands Roosevelt. It was cleverly done. He talks of Anglo-American relations and says that there are many people in the U.S.A. who say that we are yellow and can't fight. It is true that we have been beaten in everything we do. Somebody asks him whether America can advise us on the sort of propaganda we ought to conduct. He gets out of it well. He says, 'Well, we are the worst propagandists in the world and you are the next worst. Why not consult someone better?'

DIARY   22nd April, 1942

Oliver Lyttelton[3] and Casey[4] address a large meeting of Members. Lyttelton says that when he arrived [in the Middle East], he found Wavell depressed at being dismissed after eight campaigns. He brought him a personal message from Winston: 'Do not worry. The war is certain to follow you however far away you get.' He says that Rommel is rather a false legend in this country. He is a tough fighter and a good tactician, but his strategy is poor. He ought never to have bunched so many of his forces in the Tobruk area without having assured his defence in depth. He says that the Libyan front is very much touch and go.[5] There are only a few bases from which to operate, and once you get beyond them the transport problem begins to tell against you. It is true that the German tanks were more formidable than ours, but it is still uncertain whether our scheme of cruisers

[1] In Central Norway. Keyes had offered to lead the assault himself. See pp. 76-7.
[2] Roosevelt's personal representative, then in London for talks on the Second Front.
[3] Previously Minister of State in the Middle East, and a member of the War Cabinet.
[4] R. G. Casey, later Lord Casey, who succeeded Lyttelton in the Middle East on 18th March. He was formerly Australian Minister in Washington.
[5] At this period there was a lull in the fighting, before the renewal of Rommel's advance in May. Auchinleck was also preparing for an offensive, but public attention was concentrated on Malta, which was being pounded to pieces from the air.

[light tanks] was not better than their battleships. He seems optimistic about our being able to defend the [Egyptian] frontier. He talks about Syria and Iraq and refers to the unlikely possibility of a German offensive there. He says the Turks will fight. He makes a very good impression. It is curious how these addresses to all-Party meetings in committee rooms can make or mar a man's standing. P. J. Grigg made a very bad impression. Nothing could be better than the impression Oliver made.

Dine early with Buck [De la Warr] and Malcolm MacDonald. We discuss the future of National Labour. Buck feels that it is so unreal that it had better die. Malcolm feels that we should keep the machine ticking over silently, and, that in the end new political parties will be formed. 'Independent' today means opposition to Winston, and all three of us regard this as impossible and unpatriotic.

Malcolm had been lunching today with Winston. He said that the latter has no illusions at all about the decline in his popularity. 'I am like a bomber pilot', he said. 'I go out night after night, and I know that one night I shall not return.' Malcolm is in fact rather appalled by the slump in Winston's popularity. A year ago he would have put his stock at 108, and today, in his opinion, it is as low as 65. He admits that a success will enable it to recover. But the old enthusiasm is dead for ever. How foul is public life and popular ingratitude!

DIARY   *23rd April, 1942*

Secret Session in the House. I am not allowed, even in my diary, to give all the details of what passed, but I can at least give the outline. Cripps, on his return from India, was received with a cheer stronger than that accorded to Winston. The latter when he rose (and after all the strangers had been spied and harried from the House) adopted his stolid, obstinate, ploughman manner. He tells of Singapore, where the conduct of our large army 'does not seem to have been in harmony with the past or present spirit of our forces'. He tells us of the Naval position in the Indian Ocean, and how the ships came to be lost.[1] He tells us of the Middle East and what happened at Alexandria.[2] He tells us of our present dangers and prospects and dwells at length upon the heavy sinkings which we are sustaining in the eastern Atlantic. It is a

[1] The *Prince of Wales* and the *Repulse*.
[2] The *Queen Elizabeth* and *Valiant* were sunk by Italian one-man torpedoes in Alexandria harbour on 18th December.

ong and utterly remorseless catalogue of disaster and misfortune. And as he tells us one thing after another, gradually the feeling rises in the packed House. 'No man', Members begin to feel in their hearts, 'no man but he could tell us of such disaster and increase rather than diminish confidence.' He has the psychological force of a supreme specialist who tells one that there are signs of tuberculosis, that one may become very ill, but that cure is certain. And as this feeling rises, there rises with it a feeling of shame at having doubted him. He ends without rhetoric, but with a statement about our aircraft production which is encouraging. The House gives him a great ovation and the debate thereafter peters out.

I go to the St George's Day pageant organised by the *Daily Express* at the Albert Hall. Winston is there in the royal box. He gives the V-sign to an audience which does not greet him with any tumultuous applause.

H.N. TO V.S-W. *29th April, 1942*
4 King's Bench Walk, E.C.4

I lunched with Victor Cazalet to meet Muselier.[1] Victor cannot see a pie without wishing to have his finger in it. I wish I could get a clear map of Victor's soul. I think you would find much swamp and little firm ground, and round the edges there would be a vague area labelled *terra incognita*. But really he does rush in where angels fear to tread, and I have the feeling that his rushes are merely the roaming of a cow seeking fresh grass and getting into the flower-garden. Anyhow, Muselier told his whole sad story. He was dressed in civilian clothes and seemed ill and miserable. He ate nothing, but kept on reading us the telegrams exchanged with de Gaulle over St Pierre and Miquelon. There is no doubt that he has been abominably treated.

H.N. TO V.S-W. *31st April, 1942*
4 King's Bench Walk, E.C.4

I lunched with André Labarthe. He was more brilliant than ever, and I find it difficult to disagree with him. He says, 'You admit that de Gaulle is untruthful, treacherous and unbalanced. Yet you persist in

---

[1] Admiral Muselier, who had seized the west-Atlantic islands of St Pierre and Miquelon on behalf of the Free French, quarrelled with de Gaulle on his return and was dismissed from his command of the Free French Navy. The British Government attempted to save the Admiral, but de Gaulle insisted that this was a matter entirely for the Free French to decide.

regarding him as representative of France. *Main non, mais non—la France c'est autre chose.*' It is indeed a difficult problem. I should like to admire de Gaulle, but I cannot do so.

DIARY   *31st April, 1942*

There are all sorts of rumours flying about. Italy is on the verge of cracking up. Germany is putting out peace-feelers. Mussolini is to have an urgent meeting with Hitler in Munich.[1] I discount all these, but feel that there is certainly great tension in Italy. If Germany wins the spring offensive, then the war may last for long. But if she loses, then we may get peace this year.

Jim [Lees-Milne] and James [Pope-Hennessy] are very bitter about our attack on Lübeck. They say that, in return, all our centres of art and culture will be bombed.[2] I also am rather shocked by it.

DIARY   *3rd May, 1942*

The wind changes to the South during the night and we wake to find a warm and cloudless morning. The tulips flush to colour under our very eyes. I work hard. Then Viti and I go and water the garden, and walk down to the orchard where we water the heifers. It is very beautiful. There is a slight haze, almost of summer, hanging over the Weald. Viti and I know how close we feel to each other on evenings such as this.

The news from Burma is bad. We have lost Mandalay and may lose some of our army. The Indian Congress has issued a manifesto which urges non-violence and is very anti-British. Our magnitude and renown is slipping from us. In the wireless postscript Stafford Cripps makes a speech which is uncompromisingly and radically Socialist. There will be no more rich, he says, and no more class distinctions. This will much annoy the Conservatives and was not wholly in harmony with the party truce. It will, I hope, be a far better world, but how drab things will become.

---

[1] The meeting had taken place at Salzburg on 29th April. Ciano wrote in his diary that night: 'Hitler talks, talks, talks, talks. Mussolini suffers.' The conference had no important results.
[2] The Germans did retaliate with the 'Baedeker raids' on historic cities like Exeter, Bath, Norwich, and York.

DIARY   *11th May, 1942*

I have a long talk with Ed Murrow, who has just returned after three months in the United States. He says that the anti-British feeling is intense. I ask him why. He says partly the hard-core of anglophobes (Irish, Italians, Germans and isolationists); partly the frustration produced by war without early victory; partly our bad behaviour at Singapore; and partly the tendency common to all countries at war to blame their allies for doing nothing. He feels moreover that we have sent the wrong type of person over there. Halifax is not popular with the people, although he has gained the esteem and confidence of the Administration. The problem is largely one of proper boasting. Why did we not boost Dobbie[1] and Malta, as the Americans created the Bataan-MacArthur legend? I tell him that it is profoundly repugnant for us to boast, and he replies that this is taken by the Americans to be either feebleness or arrogance. It is in fact a major element in the *superbia Britannorum*.

DIARY   *19th May, 1942*

Debate on the Adjournment. Attlee opens with a long and rambling statement which is so dull and so badly delivered that the House can scarcely refrain from yawning. The only interesting thing about it was the fact that the Deputy Prime Minister, at such a crisis in our history, *could* make a dull speech. But Attlee succeeded where lesser men would have failed.

DIARY   *20th May, 1942*

The House is in a bad mood and the debate consists of one long stab and dig at Winston. The difficulty is that serious people do not like getting up to defend Winston on strategical grounds. The critics always know some small detail which sounds damaging and which can only be answered by disclosing information of value to the enemy. Hore-Belisha makes a particularly damaging attack. Cripps winds up well and strongly, but I fear that Winston's position in the House (in spite of his triumph in the secret session) is not a strong one. This fills me with dismay.

---

[1] Lieutenant-General Sir William Dobbie, Governor of Malta, 1940–42. The long strain had at last worn him down, and he was succeeded as Governor by Lord Gort at the end of April.

DIARY   *3rd June, 1942*

I cannot quite understand the present optimism among serious people. The Russians have lost three armies at Kharkov. We have not done too well in Libya. The shipping position is horrible. Japan is about to cause the collapse of China. Our relations with America are pretty strained. But the wave of despair which is gathering head in Germany cannot be due only to the 1,000-bomber attacks which we are now delivering. It must be a growing sense that they cannot gain a decisive victory, and that after all the responsibility they have taken (to put it at its mildest) there is no alternative to defeat.

I was told today a story by Tilea which amused me. Three years ago he was outlining to Rob Hudson[1] all the dangers which were likely to happen to us. 'Yes', said Rob, 'you are probably correct and these things may well happen. But you forget that God is English.'

DIARY   *5th June, 1942*

I dine at All Souls, where there are only three Fellows present. We have coffee afterwards in the quad, and the sun sinks gently over St Mary's and the Bodleian. I gaze with love at those dear buildings, wondering whether they will be assailed by one of the Baedeker raids, and whether I shall ever see them again. We walk to Balliol, where I deliver an address on Franco-British relations. I am amused that de Gaulle has sent down two officers and one of his Foreign Department to spy upon me. I have a large audience and the speech goes well. There is a reception afterwards, and I return in the lovely warm night to the Randolph. Dear Oxford.

DIARY   *9th June, 1942*

At the Club I have an appointment with Muselier. He wants to be reinstated in some way. He says that if the British Government continue without modification of the Churchill–de Gaulle agreement to allow this fascist system to assume the functions of a French Government, then we are heading straight for civil war in France. He hints that he, Comert, Labarthe and Cambon are in fact a de Gaulle opposition. He thinks they have the support of intellectuals like Maritain, Bernanos and others, and that they will keep quiet 'for a while longer'. It is difficult to disentangle fact from fiction in the Free French movement. There is no doubt that de Gaulle's movements are treacherous and wrong. But are the others much better?

[1] R. S. Hudson (later Lord Hudson), Minister of Agriculture, 1940–45.

There is a slight lull in the fighting. The Germans are attacking Sebastopol and may be about to launch an offensive against Leningrad. In Libya they have for the ninth time attacked Bir Hacheim without result, and the Croix de Lorraine still floats above the hill.[1]

DIARY   11th June, 1942

B.B.C. Board. We discuss whether the clergy should use the microphone to preach forgiveness of our enemies. I say I prefer that to the clergy who seek to pretend that the bombing of Cologne was a Christian act. I wish the clergy would keep their mouths shut about the war. It is none of their business.

DIARY   17th June, 1942

Down to the House, where Dick Denman[2] and I have got a 'prayer' asking for the cancellation of the Order compelling young children to work on the land. We see Tom Williams[3] who begs us to withdraw it. He says that we have simply got to get in this year's harvest (which is enormous) as quickly as possible in order to start on next year's. Our shipping is very bad. Losses are terrible, and much more is wanted for the Second Front. Labour is very short. We have to prepare a hundred aerodromes for the Americans, a million of whom are about to arrive. We agree to withdraw if they will give us an assurance (a) that the kids will not be made to work for seven hours, but only four; (b) that parents' consent will be obtained.

DIARY   21st June, 1942

Midsummer day and a windless sun. After lunch I weed the lime-border, and then Tilea comes to tea. The 6 o'clock news tells us that the enemy claim that Tobruk has surrendered 'with 25,000 men and many generals'.[4] The news crashes on us in the lovely evening like a thunderstorm. I do some work on Chapter IV[5], but I have not the heart to continue.

I often wonder whether my grandson, reading this diary after many

[1] The stubborn defence of Bir Hacheim, the southern anchor of Ritchie's Gazala line, gained great honour for the Free French. It fell on 11th June.
[2] National Labour M.P. for Central Leeds, 1931–45.
[3] Parliamentary Secretary to the Ministry of Agriculture, 1940–45.
[4] The actual number taken prisoner at Tobruk was 33,000. Rommel began his attack at 6.30 in the morning of the 20th and by 6 pm. reached the water-front. The fortress surrendered at 7.45 am. on the 21st.
[5] Of *The Desire to Please*.

years, will not be irritated by my constant record 'lunch here, dined there', and will not ask himself what I really felt about the future on this midsummer day of 1942.

I think we shall prevent the Germans getting to the Suez Canal. I think that the Russians may lose the Caucasus and that Germany may attack Turkey. I think it possible that Russia may make a separate peace. In that event the whole might of Germany will be turned against us and we may be invaded. On the other hand I do not think that Hitler can afford to lose so many men as he did last year. I think we may anticipate him by invading Europe before the autumn. I think we shall have to pass through a very dangerous crisis in the shipping position, but that by the end of next year this will have improved. I believe that within a few months we shall have gained air superiority with all that it implies. I believe that it is unlikely that we shall be beaten this year, and that by 1943 our superiority will begin to assert itself. I believe that Japan may knock out China and attack India after the monsoon. I believe that the Germans, if they have scored no decisive result by the end of this year, will become discouraged. I believe that we shall have victory and peace by the spring of 1944 at the latest.

And what of home affairs? I believe that we shall have great disorders in Europe and possibly some sort of revolution here. We may even have republicanism and a certain amount of persecution of the governing class. But that will die down and we shall find some middle position between the extremes of the pendulum—a modified Socialism, rather dependent upon America, rather impoverished, rather weak. But still existent, and with our independence and our honour maintained. That is what I think.

DIARY   22nd June, 1942

Another lovely day, and I bathe before breakfast. I have not slept well, as I kept on waking up with the word 'Tobruk' echoing in my ears, and rolling from side to side with gigantic apprehensions. I do most of Chapter IV, but I am a little discouraged by the book. Hamilton Rowan is simply not interesting enough. I weed the lime-border, and after dinner, under a sickle moon (which hangs over Tobruk), Viti and I slash weeds by the lake. Great thistles fall to our slashing.

The *Chicago Sun* rings up to ask me whether I think the fall of Tobruk will lead to a major political crisis. I think it may, but I do not say so. If there were any alternative to Winston, he might be severely shaken by this event.

DIARY   *23rd June, 1942*

There is a sullen anxious feeling in the House. Wardlaw-Milne says he will put down a vote of No Confidence in the supreme direction of the war, i.e. in Winston. The general feeling is that in any case we must wait till he gets back.[1]

Victor Cazalet comes to me. He says, 'Let's have a word . . .' We sit on a retired bench. 'What do you feel?' he asks. I say, 'Well, Victor, there is one thing about which I am certain—we must all get together.' 'I am glad to hear you say that, Harold.' 'Yes, we have kept silence too long. We must now speak out with courage and together.' 'That is exactly my view.' 'You see,' I continue, 'you see, Victor, none of us who know what Winston did in 1939 and 1940 have really spoken out. We must now close the ranks to defend him.' Victor's jaw drops. 'You are pulling my leg again!' he says and walks away.

DIARY   *24th June, 1942*

The House is settling down after yesterday. Wardlaw-Milne, having announced that he will table a motion of No-Confidence, finds that he can get few to lend their names and is left high and dry, like a cod stranded among shrimps.

I go to Vincent Square and do munitions work. I am put in overalls, set to a bench and stand for three hours filing a thing into another thing.[2]

DIARY   *25th June, 1942*

How the public would stand the loss of Malta I cannot conceive.

The feeling is that we have in all respects thought in terms of the last war and have never realised the speed of this. The Germans and the Japanese have always been a march ahead of us. There is also a feeling that our production has been hampered by old-fashioned ideas.[3] The Navy clung too long to their big battleships. Even the Air Force

---

[1] Churchill had been in Washington since 17th June.

[2] Members of Parliament had been encouraged to undertake a little war-production in addition to their fire-watching duties at Westminster.

[3] But it should be remembered that one of Churchill's main objects in going to Washington was to acquaint the President with the progress made in Britain on the production of the atomic bomb.

has been opposed to the dive-bomber, since they know that it would have to be put under Army control. Beaverbrook was hypnotised by the mass-production of tanks and did not pause to think whether they were the right sort of tanks.

Anyhow a fresh armoured Division has just reached Egypt.[1] May it not be like the Divisions which reached Singapore just in time to surrender!

DIARY   *1st July, 1942*

To the House for the first day of the debate on the Vote of Censure. Wardlaw-Milne is an imposing man with a calm manner which gives the impression of solidity. He is in fact rather an ass, and the position he has acquired as one of the leaders of the back-benches has caused his head to swell badly. He begins well enough, but then suddenly suggests that the Duke of Gloucester should be made Commander-in-Chief. A wave of panic-embarrassment passes over the House. For a full minute the buzz goes round, 'But the man must be an ass.' Milne pulls himself together and recaptures the attention of the House, but his idictic suggestion has shaken the validity of his position and his influence is shattered.

Roger Keyes seconds. He is a very dull speaker, and most people troop out to luncheon. Keyes denies that the P.M. ever interfered with Service chiefs. In fact he complains that he never overrides their advice. They are all for caution, and the result was that when we might have won the battle of the Mediterranean, we hesitated and fumbled, and now it was too late.

Winterton rises to speak, and the P.M. strolls out deliberately with bowed shoulders. Bob Boothby makes an admirable speech supporting the Government, but I notice that in *The Times* it is not even mentioned. The debate goes on till after midnight.

DIARY   *2nd July, 1942*

The second day of the Vote of Censure Debate. Aneurin Bevan opens with a brilliant offensive, pointing his finger in accusation, twisting and bowing. Then comes Walter Elliot and then Hore-Belisha.

Winston sits there with a look of sullen foreboding, his face from time to time flickering into a smile. He rises stockily, his hands in his trouser pockets. He makes a long statement which really amounts to

[1] The 8th Armoured Division was about to disembark.

the fact that we had more men and more tanks and more guns than Rommel, and that he cannot understand why we were so badly beaten. He gives no indication of how the battle of Egypt is likely to go.[1] In the end, after one hour and thirty minutes, he is quite fresh and gay. He gets his vote of confidence by 476 to 25, plus a great ovation afterwards. But the impression left is one of dissatisfaction and anxiety, and I do not think it will end there. The only thing he could do is to bring back Wavell as C.I.G.S. I feel deeply sorry for him. Every weapon he uses smashes in his hands.

I hurry off to a B.B.C. Board. Violet [Bonham Carter] is very worried about the tank position. Jo Grimond,[2] who is in the tanks, says that they all knew the machines we had in 1940 were no good at all and that we were outclassed by the enemy.

Dine with Sibyl [Colefax]. Rothermere is there, very anti-Winston.

DIARY   4th July, 1942

The Germans have not yet broken through our positions at El Ameyn,[3] and this may give us time to bring up reinforcements.

For the first time an American squadron joined us on a raid on occupied France. This is the beginning of a great air offensive that will go on and on.

DIARY   5th July, 1942

The fifth day of the battle of El Aleyman.[4] We still hold out. 600 Germans surrender because they could stand it no longer. It may be that they are running short of water. The whole thing trembles in the balance, but every day is a day saved.

DIARY   6th July, 1942

I finish Chapter v. The battle of El Alemayn still hangs fire.

[1] On the day before the debate opened, the 8th Army occupied the El Alamein positions, sixty miles from Alexandria, and on 1st July Rommel began his attempt to break through.

[2] Jo Grimond, the future leader of the Liberal Party, was then aged 28.

[3] This is the first mention of El Alamein in the diary. He spells the name differently on four successive days.

[4] This was not, of course, the historic battle of El Alamein, which was fought in October. It was Auchinleck's first determined defence of the line. Rommel's troops exhausted themselves by their attempts to break through to Alexandria, and on 4th July he halted in order to regroup and build up his supplies.

DIARY   *7th July, 1942*

I lunch with Brendan Bracken and Walter [Elliot]. They are worried about the American Press, which heaps ridicule upon us for our failure at Tobruk, whereas our papers never said a word about Pearl Harbour. We have just got to be patient.

They are all very reserved about the El Alamayn situation, though they admit that it should be settled one way or another within the next forty-eight hours. Either Rommel or we are on the eve of a big victory.

During the summer and early autumn the Germans continued their offensive in southern Russia, striking with one Army Group for the Maikop and Baku oil-fields in the broad wedge of country enclosed by the Black Sea, the Caspian and the Caucasus; and with another Army Group for the crossing of the Volga at Stalingrad. Both were halted on the lip of success. Maikop was captured on 9th August, but Baku and Stalingrad eluded them. Hitler had now reached the limit of his conquests, and from November onwards went over to the defensive.

It was the same story in the Middle East. Rommel made two further attacks on the Alamein position, once between 15th and 20th July and again between 31st August and 5th September (the battle of Alam Halfa). Both failed. But although Auchinleck had successfully stabilised the line, Churchill had lost confidence in his ability to mount a counter-offensive and relieved him of his command on 8th August. Alexander was made Commander-in-Chief of the Middle East and Montgomery of the 8th Army.

That the turning-point of the war had been reached at its mid-point was not of course immediately recognised. During these same months Churchill took the lead in coordinating future strategy with his two major allies. In July, General Marshall and Harry Hopkins came to Britain from the United States to make the final decision that there would be no major invasion of France during 1942, but, instead, an Anglo-American force would occupy French North Africa in November, with the object of striking at Rommel's rear and gaining control of the Mediterranean sea-routes for a future invasion of southern Europe. In mid-August Churchill flew to Moscow via Cairo and Tehran to communicate these decisions to Stalin. While he was away, on 19th August, the Canadians carried out their costly cross-Channel raid on Dieppe.

The Japanese advance in the Pacific was simultaneously halted. By landing in the Solomon Islands on 7th August, the Americans began their

*long counter-offensive to regain all that they had lost since Pearl
Harbour.*

*Harold Nicolson continued his weekly 'Marginal Comment' for the
'Spectator', and finished 'The Desire to Please' in under six months from
the date of its inception, writing a chapter every two days during the
Parliamentary recess in early August. The B.B.C. Board also occupied
much of his time. The long entry in his diary for 8th October illustrates
in detail how he filled the majority of his days, and redresses any possible
impression that he had lapsed into the role of a mere observer of events.*

DIARY   8th July, 1942

A Scottish debate in the House. I like these family affairs. What a
good Parliamentarian was lost in me! I am too busy with other
interests to give to the House that passion for trivialities, that constant
assertion of an individual point of view, which leads to power. I feel
sometimes that my failure is due entirely to myself. I have had every
opportunity and have missed them. But I am a happy, honest, loving
man, and I don't care—not one hoot. When I think of the boys I don't
care about success. When I think of Vita I do not care even about
death. Few men have achieved that certainty of love.

I go to my munitions factory. I am worse than ever. I file a thing
too short and another thing too long. My belt jumps off the other
thing five times. I have discovered a trick by which I can adjust my
belt and avoid the incessant kindly reproach of my instructor. But I
go away at 9 covered in oil and frustration.

H.N. TO V.S-W.   9th July, 1942
                                                            4 King's Bench Walk, E.C.4

I did not disclose to you how worried I was about my eyes. I had a
dread lest some creeping illness was seeping up from the recesses of the
brain and destroying the opticles. I have no idea what the opticles
are, but I am sure they are something overwhelmingly optical. Anyhow, I at last plucked up courage and went to see Mr Juler.[1] My feet
crept up Harley Street (past the comforting door of Sir Kenneth
Goadby[2]) and to the battered and blitzed and far less accustomed door
of Mr Juler. He was a deft man and wasted no time. He sat me down
and turned several searchlights on me. He did not suggest that I

[1] F. A. Juler, Surgeon Occulist to H.M.'s Household and Consulting Surgeon to
Moorfields Eye Hospital.
[2] H.N.'s doctor.

should put Belladonna in my eyes, which was a thing I feared. It means that for two days one havers about seeing men as trees walking. 'Look up', Mr Juler said. The Virgin's prayer was not in it. 'Look down', he said, and never have human eyes displayed such powers of abasement. 'Look right', he said, and in a flash my eyes assumed the gyratory movements of Napoleon's at Austerlitz. 'Look left', he said, and in a twist I ogled in the direction of the Independent Labour Party. After all this he pronounced that there was no disease. So then I went out of the operation chamber back to the consultant chamber and was sat in a Venetian arm-chair. 'Can you read this?' he said, giving me an extract from Charles Dickens printed in the type of the *Magazin du Louvre*. I couldn't. He depressed a button and on the wall opposite letters appeared: 'A B K L N X'. I said I could read that sort of thing.

He said that all I needed was a tightening-up of my lenses and that there was *no disease*. He said my eyes would get better in five years. He said it was time of life. Well I never! Never have I felt my life at such a time. But truly, Vita, I feel younger now than I felt in 1932.[1]

DIARY   *15th July, 1942*

The Germans are at the gates of Voronezh and Rostov. If the Russians collapse, they and their friends here will say that it was due to Churchill's refusal of a Second Front. I very much fear that Churchill's own position will not survive a Russian defeat. Meanwhile the lull continues at El Alamein.

Our Anglo-French Parliamentary Committee receive General de Gaulle. He makes a most effective speech and does not shirk anything. He says that if *la France Combattante* is to be anything more than a detachment of the British Army, they simply must exercise political power. He is received, to my surprise, more warmly than I have ever seen anyone received. The room is crowded and there are loud cheers ending in the singing of the *Marseillaise*. Afterwards there is a small reception and a *vin d'honneur*. De Gaulle is rightly very pleased with himself.

DIARY   *22nd July, 1942*

Have a late supper with Victor [Cazalet[and Sibyl [Colefax], and find there Desmond Morton[2] and an American called Michie. We discuss

---

[1] H.N. was aged 55. He had worn spectacles since he was a boy, but his eyes gave him no serious trouble throughout his life.
[2] He was personal assistant to the Prime Minister, 1940–46.

Beaverbook's campaign for a Second Front. He says that he would do it even if we had to land 100,000 men without arms. I do not see the possibility of any such thing, regarded as an operation of war. The Government are in a difficult position. If they create a Second Front as a forlorn hope, we shall have another Dunkirk. If they do not do so, they will be accused of letting down the Russians. But if they explain why they cannot do so, people will feel that there is no chance of our beginning to fight this war before 1945. They cannot say that our Second Front will be in the Middle East and the Mediterranean, because Italy is the weak spot.[1]

Meanwhile the Germans are closing round Rostov and the Russians may be cut off from their oil-supplies and their morale much weakened. They are putting up a good fight at Voronezh, but we do not know (nobody knows) what reserves Timoshenko disposes of.[2] The Russians tell us nothing at all. The battle in Libya has flared up again, and Auchinleck has started a major push.[3] People say that if we do not win this battle, we shall never win another.

DIARY   26th July, 1942

Go on with my book.[4] The Germans have almost taken Rostov and are pushing on to Stalingrad. They are digging in at El Alamein. I work and weed.

DIARY   29th July, 1942

Debate on Old Age Pensions. It is a bad show. The dissident Labour feel that it is a useful occasion on which to belabour the Government without raising the general question of the war. They do so. Official Labour, in the persons of Arthur Greenwood and Pethick-Lawrence,[5] agree that if the Government promise to implement the Beveridge

[1] The Americans were then pressing for the landing of six British Divisions in the Cherbourg peninsula, but Churchill persuaded them to abandon this plan.

[2] Marshal of the Soviet Union S. K. Timoshenko, Commander of the Soviet armies on the south-west and southern fronts.

[3] The aim of this attack was to split Rommel's forces into two, and then roll up the northern part of his army. The initial attack made rapid headway, but the 8th Army lost over 100 tanks to the German counter-attack, and withdrew to their starting-line at El Alamein on the 27th.

[4] *The Desire to Please.*

[5] F. W. Pethick-Lawrence, Financial Secretary to the Treasury, 1929–31, and Secretary of State for India, 1945–47.

Report[1] when it comes, then they will not challenge a Division. That leads to a fierce altercation between Shinwell and Bevin, and a Division at which the Labour rebels register as high a vote as 63. That is serious. I do not feel that the proceedings were really very sincere. But at the back of it is the Second Front agitation and the feeling which is increasingly voiced that if Russia is beaten without action on our part, the present Government will fall. I do not blame the Labour people. They were staging a revolt upon a popular issue in which the Government case is weak to all appearances. But I am unhappy that the House should succumb to these separatist movements (even in a good cause) at the very moment when all is going so ill. It will hit Winston badly. It will disturb the country. Walk back depressed, noting for the first time the white pork-pie hats of many American sailors in the streets.

DIARY   *30th July, 1942*

Go with Violet [Bonham Carter] to see Dick Law at the Foreign Office. We express anxiety (1) about our pro-Horthy and appeasement propaganda to Hungary; (2) about our not being allowed to make more use of Winston's statement about Austria[2]; (3) about foreign Governments asking for free time on the B.B.C. He says that since the Hungarian troops have started fighting in Russia, we have modified our tone and are far more aggressive. Secondly, that Anthony Eden regretted Winston's speech about Austria gaining her independence and playing 'an honoured part' in the new Europe. People would ask 'What part?—*Anschluss*, a southern German federation, or a Danubian federation?' We could not answer any of these questions.

Dine with Sibyl [Colefax]. Go away early and fire-watch. There are two alerts during the night, and I dress and patrol with my little torch. In and out of the Prince's Chamber and the Royal Gallery I go, and into the dark House of Lords. I am tired and sit on the Woolsack with my tin hat on and my torch giving the sole illumination while the guns thunder outside.

---

[1] Sir William Beveridge's plan for universal social security was to be published on 1st December, 1942. Churchill decided to delay implementing its recommendations until after the war.
[2] See page 212.

DIARY   *3rd August, 1942*

The Germans are pushing south in the Caucasus. They may reach the Caspian. Meanwhile in Egypt they are accumulating strength faster than we can ever do. We are in a bad way indeed.

DIARY   *7th August, 1942*

I dine at Pratts and find Pug Ismay[1] next to me. He is in a confidential mood. He says that he cannot help minding constant criticism. He has been working sixteen hours a day for eight years. He loves it. But he does find that stupid criticism (such as that of *The Times*) hurts him more than it did ten years ago. He talks about the Libyan position. He says that he had hoped that Auchinleck would break through. 'He has failed to break the tough crust', he says, 'but I still think that he may do it. If he does, we can motor to Benghazi. But how wonderful the Germans are!'

He talks about Winston. He calls him 'a child of nature'. He says that when things are going well, he is good; when things are going badly, he is superb; but when things are going half-well, he is 'hell on earth'. He says that Winston has the deepest veneration for the House of Commons. One day Pug found him in distress at having to prepare a speech. He said to him, 'But why don't you tell them to go to hell?' Winston turned round on him in a flash and said, 'You should not say those things: I am the servant of the House.'

Pug is very bitter about those who make Second Front capital for themselves. He fears that a weaker man than Winston might surrender to the popular clamour. He is furious with responsible people who do not understand that we cannot have unity of command with Russia, since the Soviets tell us nothing—nothing at all. He then goes off wearily to work for another four hours and I go to bed.

DIARY   *18th August, 1942*

A perfect summer's day. I bathe. I write the epilogue. I finish clipping the hedge. After tea, at 7 pm., I finish my book. I call it *The Desire to Please*.[2]

We are told by the wireless that Claude Auchinleck has been succeeded by Alexander and that Montgomery is to have the 8th Army.

[1] General Ismay, Chief of Staff to the Prime Minister, 1940–46.
[2] It was published by Constable in May 1943.

DIARY   *19th August, 1942*

Another lovely day. As I walked down to the lake, I heard the guns bruising towards the south. We are making a big raid on Dieppe.

In the afternoon, as V. and I are clipping the holly hedge, a telegram comes from Eric saying that Peter was killed in action yesterday.[1] Poor Eric.

DIARY   *28th August, 1942*

Nigel appears in the morning, having travelled down from Scotland with the Duke of Kent's coffin.[2]

I go to see William Beveridge. We[3] had put to him a memorandum urging (a) that the medical services should be completely taken over by the State. He evidently doesn't think much of this. (b) That there should be an increase in old age pensions, on the theory that people should be bribed to retire from industry and thus leave more employment for young people. He takes exactly the opposite view. He feels that people should be encouraged to remain in industry as long as their health lasts. At present one person in twelve is over 65. By 1961 one in six will be old. Therefore we must provide for them. He hopes to create a contributory scheme which in the end will enable all old people to have a really life-giving benefit. He thinks that this self-supporting scheme will become practicable 'in my own life-time'. He foresees also a comprehensive family allowance giving people 7/6 a week for 'large families'. But when does a family become large? And if the allowance begins only for the third child, will that child not come to have a different status in the family from the others, and lose that atmosphere of sacrifice-gratitude which is the best parent-child relationship? He is optimistic about grappling with the unemployment problem after the war, and looks forward to a simplified all-in system of insurance. I come away more cheerful and encouraged than I have been for weeks.

H.N. TO V.S-W.   *6th September, 1942*
                                    St Michael's Mount, Marazion, Cornwall

In the train I went through the typescript of *The Desire to Please*. It is a dull book, but not ill-written. I am not sorry to have done it.

[1] Peter Nicolson, son of Eric, H.N.'s elder brother.
[2] The Duke of Kent, youngest brother of the King, had been killed on 25th August in an aeroplane crash in Scotland.
[3] The National Labour group.

I passed through Plymouth and on through Cornish fields. Then we swung down to the sea and the Mount appeared, looking very proud of itself. At Penzance there was Sam[1] and many people from the Ministry of Information and the Press. We drove to Marazion and walked across the causeway.[2] Then up the steep grass path between hydrangeas, fuchsias and pink lilies like hemerocallys. Great granite rocks above us among the pines and ilexes, and the blue sea below.

Gwen was terribly excited. I think she feels that I understand better than others in what a curious way this house is linked with Shanganagh and Clandeboye[3] and her intense childhood complex. I mean, I understand how she feels about plugs that pull upwards in w.c.s and rows of fire-buckets with crowns upon them and the sense of many servants cleaning plate in the background. The little sitting-room which she has chosen for herself has white and gold bookshelves like at Clandeboye. I understand her feeling.

Living here is like being on a boat. I am writing this in my cabin, and soon I shall go on deck. Their lives are governed by tides, by winds, by waves, by boats. We went into Penzance for the march-past of the Free French. Gwen was at her best, shy and yet polite. But it rained and rained and the wind howled. Then we came back here to receive the guests. The boat-fuss reached *Titanic* proportions, but in the end some 100 French sailors, fishermen, Generals and others were transported safely to shore and filed through the rooms. They were mostly Bretons, and God how homesick they were! Then we went back to Penzance and there was a man who made a speech in Cornish which the Bretons were supposed to understand, but I made out only three words—Marazion, St Levan and St Aubyn. I made a speech and was curiously nervous beforehand, since I was frightened of letting Gwen down.

H.N. TO V.S-W.   *9th September, 1942*
                                                4 King's Bench Walk, E.C.4

Winston was splendid yesterday. He reduced the art of understatement to a virtuosity such as I have never seen equalled. People were meaning

---

[1] Lord St Levan, who had succeeded to the peerage and to St Michael's Mount in 1940. In 1916 he had married Gwen, H.N.'s younger sister.
[2] St Michael's Mount is linked to the mainland by a stone causeway which is covered by the sea at high tide.
[3] In Northern Ireland.

to speak about the changes in command in Egypt,[1] about the Dieppe raid, about the Second Front. But he took the wind so completely out of their sails that they tore up their notes and remained seated. The debate therefore collapsed. This would have been all right if Cripps had not profited by the occasion to give the House a rather sharp talking-to and to accuse them of preferring their luncheon to their duties. This has enraged everybody, and will, I fear, do the House much damage in the country. It was unfair of Cripps and unwise, unless he is aspiring to some form of dictatorship. I dashed off to the B.B.C. to discuss with them the problem of how it was to be put over on the 6 o'clock news. We decided that there was nothing for it but to report exactly what happened. But the true record of what happened will give millions of people an untrue impression of what really happened.

DIARY   *9th September, 1942*

Guy Burgess has heard from his friends who are in close touch with Cripps that the latter is so discontented with the conduct of the war that he proposes to resign.[2] He has already sounded *The Times*, and possibly Kemsley's papers, to see if they will give him Press support. Guy and I agreed that Cripps' attitude was probably wholly disinterested and sincere. He really believes that Winston is incapable of dealing with the home-front and that his handling of the minor problems of production and strategy is fumbling and imprecise. We agreed also that Cripps would find the atmosphere of Downing Street (with its late hours, casual talk, cigar smoke and endless whisky) most unpalatable, while Winston never regards with affection a man of such inhuman austerity as Cripps, and cannot work easily with people unless his sentiment as well as his respect is aroused. We also agreed that Cripps, who in his way is a man of great innocence and narrow vision, might be quite seriously unaware that his resignation would shake Winston very severely, that around him would gather all the elements of opposition, and that in the end he would create an 'alternative Government' and take Winston's place. At the same time we felt

---

[1] The replacement of Auchinleck by Alexander and Montgomery. This was the speech in which the Prime Minister gave the House an account of his journey to see Stalin in Moscow.

[2] Cripps told Churchill on the latter's return from Moscow that he wanted a War Planning Directorate instead of the Chiefs of Staff Committee. Churchill called this a 'disembodied Brains Trust'.

that there was a hope that if Winston would show real consideration to Cripps and give him a vital part in the direction of the war, then something might be done to avert this disaster.

I suggested to Guy that we should visit Violet [Bonham Carter] and tell her the whole story. She is the only outside person I know who is on terms of intimate friendship with Winston and also has the confidence of Stafford and Lady Cripps. We told her the story. She said that she was in an awkward position as Lady Cripps had taken her into her confidence and told her much the same. She could not betray this confidence, much as she agreed with our point of view. We arranged therefore that Violet would see Cripps or his wife, and ask whether she might say a word to Winston—a word of warning. Failing this, I should see Brendan Bracken.

DIARY   *10th September, 1942*

Violet tells me that she saw Lady Cripps this morning. Stafford had written a letter to the P.M. saying that he saw he was not being accorded 'full confidence'. He contends that Winston really runs the war by himself, that the War Cabinet has only met once during the last week, that he never sees Winston alone and that he is sacrificing his whole future merely for a shadow. He will, however, take a week's holiday and will not come to his decision until that is over.

DIARY   *11th September, 1942*

I lunch with Walter Elliot. I ask him what I should do about the Cripps incident. His view is (a) that the P.M. probably knows all about it. (b) That if he doesn't, it shows an insensitiveness on his part and an obstinate conceit which would not be remedied by anything I did. It would be like some outsider interfering in a marriage that is going wrong. (c) Winston might think it impertinent and obtrusive on my part. I think he is right.[1]

---

[1] Churchill goes fully into this incident in *The Hinge of Fate*, pp. 497–503. Cripps put his resignation in writing on 21st September. Churchill persuaded him to suspend action until after the North African operation had taken place. In November Cripps became Minister of Aircraft Production, and left the War Cabinet.

H.N. TO V.S-W.   *24th September, 1942*
House of Commons

Ben said to me today, 'How happy I have been these days!'[1] I said, 'But you have done nothing.' He said, 'But I am always happy when I am at home with Mummy and you.'

Now truly that is a compliment (fresh with all his great sincerity) which I cherish more than any other. It is really an achievement on our part to have created an atmosphere which is more congenial to a fastidious young man like Ben than all the glitter of the Gargoyle. It gives me pleasure that he should have said this so spontaneously, since I know that it was true. Of course one can modify it by saying that he is sedentary by nature and likes his files and bcoks. But the fact does remain that poor old Sissinghurst (which offers no entertainment) does offer something which his sensitive and exacting criticism enjoys.

It is you, my darling, who have made this atmosphere (a) by great integrity; (b) by hating rows; (c) by a sense of real values. I do not think that, except for Winston, I *admire* anyone as much as I admire you.

I remember your saying (years ago) that you had never established a complete relationship with anyone. I don't think you ever could—since yours is a vertical and not a horizontal nature, and two-thirds of you will always be submerged. But you have established, with your sons and me, a relationship of absolute trust and complete love. I don't think that these things would be so fundamental to the four of us were it not that each one of the four is a private person underneath.

I have often wondered what makes the perfect family. I think it is just our compound of intimacy and aloofness. Each of us has a room of his own. Each of us knows that there is a common-room where we meet on the basis of perfect understanding.

If Ben were killed or drowned, I should always remember that remark. And I should know that from the difficult web of human relationship (now a spider's web, now a mass of steel hawsers) we—thanks to you only—have made a pattern which is taut where tautness is wanted, and elastic where we need to expand on our own.

(I can go on with my letter, since I am in the library with a green lamp.) I am thinking about the garden. We can't hope to make it

[1] He was then on embarkation-leave, but did not leave England till 26th October.

243

look very nice except for May, June and July.[1] There is no hope of us being able to make an August or autumn garden. But I think we can struggle along to make it the framework of the perfect garden. I think we should concentrate on increasing what does well. More elaboration of our own stock. Now, all annuals and even biennials involve more work than we, with our present resources, can perform. Cut them out. Away with antirrhinums. But we can legislate for 1946, grow seeds and take cuttings. More forsythia, more magnolia, more kerrya, more fuchsia—all the things that entail comparatively slight trouble and mean beauty in 1946.

DIARY   *29th September, 1942*

Aneurin Bevan stands me a drink. He bewails the Government and says that we shall lose the war if Churchill stays. This is all very difficult to answer. I agree that very serious strategic and supply mistakes have been made, but this is inevitable. I still see Winston as the God of War.

DIARY   *5th October, 1942*

Speak at the [Oxford] Union about Hitler's and Goering's speeches, the theme being that Germany is now talking of defence rather than offence. They are still held outside Stalingrad and have made but poor progress in the Caucasus. The future of the war lies in the Mediterranean.

DIARY   *8th October, 1942*[2]

Reading Thraliana[3] has shown me how apt all diarists are to mention only the striking or the unusual, and to leave out all record of their ordinary doings. As I shall probably leave this diary to Balliol, it may interest some student of 2042 A.D. to have at least one full day with all its events. As today was a typical and not exceptional day, and as I happen to have an hour free, I shall give that record.

I woke up at 7.30 to the sound of Mrs Groves[4] putting her key into

[1] The garden at Sissinghurst, which by 1962 employed six full-time gardeners, was kept going in wartime by a young man exempted from war-service on medical grounds, and a land-girl. V.S-W. herself did a very great deal of the rough work, as well as looking after the greenhouse and planting. H.N. confined his work to a single border, the lime-walk.

[2] This entry in the diary is printed unabridged.

[3] *Anecdotes of the late Samuel Johnson* (1786) by Mrs Thrale.

[4] The housekeeper at 4 King's Bench Walk.

the lock and opening the shutters in the sitting-room. At 10 minutes to 8 I got up, put on my dressing-gown, turned on the wireless and began to read the papers. First the *News Chronicle*, then the *Daily Telegraph* and then *The Times*. There was little news. Stalingrad still holds out. The Germans have advanced a little towards Grozny.[1] We are driving the Japanese away from Port Moresby in New Guinea. The Germans accuse one of our commandos during a raid on Sark of having tied up some German prisoners. They are retaliating by tying up all our prisoners captured at Dieppe.

I then had a cold bath (fuel economy) and at 8.30 I had my breakfast. Tea, toast, scrambled eggs from Sissinghurst, and plum jam. Ben joins me yawning after a late night. I read my letters. A furious letter from Viti about one of the local doctors who diagnosed Fay Copper's[2] illness as rheumatic fever when it was in fact tetanus. Poor girl, she suffered dreadfully, screamed all night, and was taken in an ambulance to Pembury Hospital. She is not expected to live. A letter from Bessborough[3] enclosing official letters exchanged between him and Cassin[4] laying down the future relations between the Institut Français and the *Conseil National* of General de Gaulle at 4 Carlton Gardens. A letter from Palewski[5] enclosing papers about Valin,[6] proving that he is not really a fascist. Many letters from constituents in which they ask for 'a fair deal', but in which they are really asking me to exert influence to give them privileged treatment in regard to leave or pay. Ben's tropical uniform arrives from Thresher and Glenny. He shows it to me with much pride. I handle it, wondering to what perils it will carry him.

At 9.30 Miss Niggeman[7] comes, and I dictate letters to her. I then read the memoranda and notes which have reached me from the B.B.C., and also the Corporation's budget estimate which is to be discussed at today's Board meeting.

---

[1] The Germans never managed to capture the Grozny oil-fields in the northern foothills of the Caucasus, because Hitler withdrew troops from that front to assist the Stalingrad offensive.

[2] The daughter of Jack Copper, the chauffeur at Sissinghurst. She survived.

[3] The 9th Earl of Bessborough, Governor General of Canada, 1931-35.

[4] Professor René Cassin, de Gaulle's diplomatic negotiator, and in charge of Justice and Public Education in the Free French National Committee.

[5] Gaston Palewski, de Gaulle's *Directeur du Cabinet*.

[6] Charles Valin, who had come over from occupied France as one of the leaders of the French Resistance.

[7] H.N.'s private secretary from 1938 to 1965.

At 10.45 I walk to the Underground station. I walk past the ruins of Crown Office Row, and cut across the grass on which there is a balloon barrage post with a circle of brick paving in the lawn. I take a ticket costing 1d to Westminster. The subway connecting this station with the House, which was closed when war broke out, has now been reopened. It is, however, more closely guarded and barricaded than in peace-time.

I enter the House and go to my place in The Chamber. It is Question time. There are questions about the massacre of British airmen in India, about the conditions under which Gandhi is interned,[1] about Italian internees in the Isle of Man, about sugar-beet and about immunization against diphtheria. After Questions, Herbert Williams complains to the Speaker that he is showing favouritism in selecting those who will catch his eye. He says he only selects Party nominees. The Speaker replies with calm and acumen, and the House applauds. It is an agreeable interlude. [Herbert] Morrison makes a statement regarding the passage of people from Eire to Ulster, and indicates that the security precautions are being increased. Then [Leo] Amery[2] introduces the India Bill. I only hear his opening sentences, as I am called out to meet a Colonel Etherton[3] who once, it seems, was rescued by my father in Russia.

Monsieur Roy, of de Gaulle's *Cabinet Civil*, is in the lobby to see me. As I am rushed, I get a lift in his car, driven by a French woman-driver. He says that de Gaulle wishes to enter into closer contact with me: he would like to have regular meetings. Knowing that de Gaulle and the Prime Minister have just had a terrible row over Syria and Madagascar[4] and are not for the moment on speaking terms, I say, 'But I trust that the General is under no misapprehension. I have no influence at all with Mr Churchill, nor would it be possible for me to act in any way without the knowledge of the Foreign Office.' He says, 'But surely it would be possible for you to establish close contact with Palewski, the *Chef du Cabinet*, and advise generally?' 'As for that', I say, 'Palewski is an old friend of mine, and I am always delighted to see him.'

[1] He was arrested with Pandit Nehru and other leaders of the Congress Party for fomenting riots and sabotage in India.
[2] Secretary of State for India and Burma, 1940-45.
[3] Colonel P. T. Etherton, Consul General in Chinese Turkestan, 1918-24.
[4] Madagascar had been seized by the British in May without the prior knowledge of de Gaulle, but he was allowed to appoint his own Governor General of the island in November.

I then reach the B.B.C. It is 1 pm. I go up by the stairs (since, owing to fuel economy, we are discouraged from using the lift below the third floor) and enter the Chairman's[1] room. Mallon[2] arrives, then Mann[3] and then Violet Bonham Carter. We start eating our sandwich lunch. We have ham sandwiches, tomato sandwiches, a plum tart, whisky, port and coffee.

I ask what attitude we propose to take towards the Beveridge Report. It is to be out on November 7th or so. It will be a document of the very greatest importance and will raise highly controversial issues. It will also be of use for propaganda abroad, since it shows what sort of social service we are contemplating. But all the Friendly Societies, and probably the City and the T.U.C., will be against it. Violet is in favour of giving it the greatest publicity possible. Mann is against it. Mallon is evidently suspicious that Beveridge wishes to advertise himself. The Chairman is evidently opposed to it from the Tory point of view.

I then read out to my colleagues the script of the talk which I propose to give on Monday regarding B.B.C. policy towards free speech. It is generally approved.

We leave the luncheon room and go into the Board Room, where we find the two Director-Generals[4] and Miss Fuller. We start on our agenda. We discuss the Archbishop of Canterbury's[5] intervention in social, economic and political matters, and express the hope that this will not encourage our own religious division to exceed their strictly religious functions. Dr √elch,[6] the head of our Religious Department, was at one time a pacifist and is a fervent adherent of Archbishop Temple.

We then discuss the reporting on the wireless of Parliamentary debates. It has been suggested that we could make these reports 'more attractive', if instead of just giving a bald statement of who said what, we gave an eye-witness account of the general atmosphere. In order to judge between the two methods, we had played to us two records— one showing direct narration, and the other introducing commentary and description. The former, to my mind, was good enough. The

---

[1] Sir Allan Powell.
[2] J. J. Mallon, a Governor of the B.B.C., 1937–39 and 1941–46.
[3] Arthur Mann, Editor of the *Yorkshire Post*, 1919–39; Governor of B.B.C., 1941–46.
[4] Sir Cecil Graves and Robert Foot.
[5] William Temple, Archbishop of Canterbury, 1942–44.
[6] J. W. Welch, Director of Religious Broadcasting, 1939–47.

latter begins, 'Under the blaze of four hundred lights, the House of Commons today discussed fuel economy.' I argued that the moment you got comment or colour, you were bound to cause offence. Violet argued that the House of Commons is the worst House we have had for a century, and that they ought to be exposed to criticism. Why should they be protected? But the other members of the Board agreed with me that although we might have occasional eye-witness impressions, the usual reports of debates should be wholly factual and objective.

We then discuss letters of complaint from Hore-Belisha saying he has been unfairly treated by the B.B.C. Ryan, the news-editor, puts up a very feeble case. We have deliberately ignored Belisha, who, as an ex-Minister of War, has some right to be quoted. We actually, in one bulletin, quoted what he had said but omitted his name and merely referred to him as 'another Member'. Ryan tried to argue that there was no space or time to mention every speech. I pointed out that it was just as quick to say 'Mr Hore-Belisha' as to say 'another Member'.

We then discuss the £200 a year given to G. M. Young[1] to watch the English of our bulletins. We agree that his caustic comment is worth this small sum and that it should be continued for another year. We then pass on to a row between the Chairman and Dr Iremonger,[2] who is furious because we asked him to alter a passage in a review of a biography of Canon Dick Sheppard,[3] in which he spoke of his 'great work for the Peace Pledge Union'. He is resigning in wrath from our Religious Advisory Committee and we let him go.

Tea, cake and biscuits are then brought in, and we discuss Sunday postscripts and whether Brendan Bracken has the right to dictate to us whom we should have and whom we should not have. It is then 4.25, and I have to dash back to the House for a Division on the India Bill.

I find a taxi by good fortune and arrive to find Attlee winding up. He has a tiff with Cove,[4] whom he accuses of having got his ideas and inspiration from 'a little pamphlet. . . .' Cove shouts out, 'It's a lie!' He is called to order and withdraws. We then have a Division, 360–17, and I find another taxi and return to the B.B.C., reaching it at 5.30. The Board by then has passed the estimates and is discussing getting

[1] The historian.
[2] Dean of Lichfield since 1939. Director of Religious Broadcasting, 1933–39.
[3] Of St Martin-in-the-Fields. Dean of Canterbury, 1929–31. He died in 1937.
[4] W. G. Cove, Labour M.P. for Aberavon since 1929.

Toscanini[1] over in the spring to give a series of concerts. We then discuss the calling-up of our ninety-five men under 30. If we lose these men, we shall be very gravely hampered. Foot has to see the Kennet Committee and plead on their behalf. The Cabinet have given us its blessing.

The Board then adjourns, and I go for a moment into the Chairman's room for a whisky-and-soda. It is by then 6.45. It is too late to return to K.B.W., but I walk away with Mallon and find a bus to the Haymarket. He is going to the Reform, and I to the Travellers. He says that Lloyd George,[2] after visiting the South Wales coal-fields, came back appalled by the lack of spirit in the men. The excuse is that they come from a generation poisoned by the dole and unemployment. Mallon says that this is rubbish. They are the brothers of our fighting men who also had dole and poverty. We discuss whether in fact there has been a decay of spirit in our country: is it something biological, or is it true, as the determinists say, that when an élite loses its self-confidence and ambition, there always arises an external and an internal proletariat to fill the vacuum until a new élite emerges? It is getting dark and we part gloomily in Pall Mall.

On entering the Travellers I find Roger Senhouse.[3] He talks to me about the difficulty of getting paper for a best-seller he has discovered. We are joined by Buck De la Warr. They talk to each other about old Etonian friends, and I am bored and go upstairs to dine. I have soup, vol-au-vent of chicken and cream rice. I talk to Roderick Jones,[4] who says how like Vita Ben is, how great a success Enid[5] has had with her play, how worried he is about his son Timothy[6] who is about to be called up. I have some coffee, and Gladwyn Jebb joins me. He says that the row between Winston and de Gaulle is 'very serious', that relations have practically been sundered, and that things are 'likely to get worse'.

---

[1] Arturo Toscanini, the celebrated Italian conductor, then aged 75. He broke with Mussolini, and was conductor of the N.B.C. Symphony Orchestra, New York, 1937–53. He died in 1957.

[2] Gwilym Lloyd George (later Viscount Tenby), Minister of Fuel and Power, 1942–45.

[3] The publisher and translator, and an old friend of H.N.

[4] Sir Roderick Jones, Chairman and Managing Director of Reuters, 1919–31.

[5] Enid Bagnold (Lady Jones), the novelist and playwright. The play referred to was her first, *Lottie Dundass*.

[6] Timothy Jones obtained a commission in the Grenadier Guards, and lost a leg in action during the Italian Campaign in 1944.

I then leave and go down to the House for fire-watching. I go to the post and am given my steel helmet, lamp and whistle. I then go to the room on the Lord Chancellor's corridor where the truckle beds are. I find Victor Raikes[1] there. He tells me about those parts of the debate today which I missed. He said that by far the best speech was that made by Oliver Stanley. I then read in the library, arranging to meet Raikes in the canteen at 9.45. I do so. We discuss how sad it is that the British public are wholly unaware of the true state of Russia, and imagine that it is some workers' Utopia. Anyone who makes even the slightest remark about the treatment of absenteeism in Russia or the standard of housing and living is branded as 'an enemy of the Soviet'.

I then (10.20 pm.) go upstairs and lay me on my truckle bed. I have army blankets which are none too clean. I do not undress. There are three other people in the room with me. I have the remains of my cold, and cough badly. I do not sleep. I hear eleven strike, and then one, and then four, five, six, seven. I then get up, fold my blankets, deliver up my lamp and whistle, and walk out into a lovely sunrise.

DIARY   13th October, 1942

Winston makes a statement about the chaining of the prisoners. He has evidently realised that the House and country feel that he has made a mistake in ordering reprisals, and he announces that he has applied to the Swiss Government asking them to use their good offices. He deprecates any further discussion, and when Cunningham-Reid[2] gets up to ask a supplementary, he is howled down. Winston has been with the Fleet and has wisely taken Cripps with him. The latter has returned bubbling with pleasure and renewed confidence. I do not think we shall hear any more about resignation for the moment.

Dine with Tilea. The other man there is the head of the Polish F.O., Jan Wizelaki. They are both much impressed by the altered tone of Hitler's speeches. It is evident to their minds that the Germans now realise they cannot win and are concentrating on the thought that they cannot lose. If our campaign in Africa comes off, then we shall win the war by next winter. If not, then it may go on till 1943. I call this most optimistic. Wizelaki calculates (having spent months on working

---

[1] Conservative M.P. for South-East Essex, 1931–45, and for two divisions of Liverpool, 1945–57.
[2] Captain A. S. Cunningham-Reid, Independent M.P. for St Marylebone, 1940–45. Author of *Besides Churchill—Who?*

out the figures with the military staff) that the Russian casualties (i.e. irreplaceable) must be between 6,500,000 and 7,500,000, and the German, on any computation, more than they lost in the whole of the last war.

DIARY   *14th October, 1942*

We repeal an Act of 1536 under which Welsh is not allowed to be spoken in courts in Wales. Herbert Morrison makes an amusing speech, but flatters the Welsh Members unduly. 'I would rather be blown up', Lady Astor says to me, 'than suck up.' I believe this to be true, and it is one of her good points.

In the evening I get Jack Macnamara to meet John Sparrow. Jack feels that there is a great wastage of man-power in the Air Force and that it should be combed out. He had lunched today with Winston at Downing Street *en famille*. He had been horrified by Winston's indiscretion in front of the servants. He spoke of everything. In the end Winston agreed with Jack's view about the Air Force. Jack feels that Winston does not usually like soldiers. He was rather shocked by (a) his indiscretion; (b) his egoistic and dictatorial manner; and (c) the immense amount of port and brandy he consumed.

DIARY   *21st October, 1942*

Duff Cooper tells me some of his experiences as head of the Cabinet Security Committee. Most of the indiscretions are due solely to an inability to make conversation or write letters. Young men having no power of invention fall back in despair upon talking shop. There have been grave cases lately: two staff-majors have been cashiered and one imprisoned for indiscretion. He told me of a letter from a young Air Force officer to his girl-friend. 'The ops', he wrote, 'which I told you about on my last leave, have been put off because some idiot of a man wrote and gave the exact date. I cannot understand how people can be so careless after all the warnings we have had. This particular op has been put off till October 22nd.'

We have a meeting in the Royal Gallery addressed by Smuts.[1] It is a tremendous setting and Smuts is introduced by Lloyd George and thanked by Winston. He looks bronzed and vigorous and speaks for 55 minutes. He utters every commonplace that we have all been trying to avoid for years. In the end we sing *For he's a jolly good fellow*, and it

[1] Field-Marshal Smuts, then aged 72, had been Prime Minister of South Africa since 1939.

is quite a friendly occasion. But no speech, except one of Winston's best, could have risen to so great an expectation.

DIARY   *22nd October, 1942*

Charles Peake tells me that after long negotiation they had at last succeeded in reaching an agreement about Syria with de Gaulle's Commissary of Foreign Affairs, Dejean. The documents were finished by Saturday, and on Monday they read in the papers that Dejean had been dismissed and Pleven put in his place. 'The General', says Charles, 'has no conception of the most rudimentary basis of negotiation. I am in despair. I do not think his quarrel with the P.M. will ever be patched up, and it seems to me that de Gaulle has outlived his usefulness.'

DIARY   *23rd October, 1942*

I dine at Pratts. The Duke of Norfolk[1] and Harold Macmillan there. The Duke says that by 1944 we shall be 90 per cent self-supporting if we want to be. Harold says that the British people are now supremely prosperous and happy. Were it not for the bombing, they would be perfectly content. But that they dread the future. If the present system can give them security and employment, they will support it: but if we fail to do so, we shall be swept away, politely but firmly. He regards extreme Socialism as inevitable, with the Conservatives standing, not so much for property, as for private lives. He is confident and interesting.

DIARY   *24th October, 1942*

A new offensive has started at El Alamein.

Between the 4th and 22nd November, 1942, the face of the war changed its entire expression. On the 4th, Montgomery won the battle of El Alamein. On the 8th, American and British forces landed in French North Africa. On the 22nd, the Russians closed the pincers behind the German 6th Army in Stalingrad.

At the time it was scarcely recognised in Britain that of these three tremendous events the last was the most significant. The Russian defence of Stalingrad had aroused as much astonishment as admiration, and after three Russian Army Groups had appeared out of nowhere to break through the German lines north and south of the city on 19th November, the fact that they encircled Paulus' 22 Divisions three days later was not even mentioned in Harold Nicolson's diary. Nor was Manstein's vast

[1] He was Joint Parliamentary Secretary to the Ministry of Agriculture, 1941–45.

counter-attack to relieve Stalingrad, which reached within thirty miles of the city before it was abandoned on 22nd December. Nor was the withdrawal in mid-December of the entire German Army Group in the Caucasus, for fear that it too would be trapped. Stalingrad did not fall until the end of January 1943, but its fate had been clear for months before, and the whole German army in Russia began moving slowly backwards to its starting-point.

Events in the Mediterranean overshadowed those in Russia. The battle of El Alamein, which began at 10 pm. on 23rd October, was a twelve-day slogging match in which all arms were simultaneously engaged. The German position could not be outflanked, and Montgomery relied on his superiority in men and weapons to wear down German and Italian resistance by ceaseless hammering at different parts of the line. He had over 1,000 tanks, of which nearly half were of the improved American design, against Rommel's 530. When the break came on 4th November there was no stopping the British armoured Divisions. The now familiar check-points—Mersa Matruh, Tobruk, Benghazi, El Agheila—were captured on the run. Rommel had lost 59,000 men, killed, wounded and prisoners, at Alamein, and managed to extricate the remainder only by a headlong retreat in defiance of Hitler's direct order. On 13th December the 8th Army crossed the border into Tripolitania, and by Christmas Day stood at Sirte.

At dawn on 8th November the Allied forces under General Eisenhower landed at Casablanca in Morocco, and at Algiers and Oran in Algeria. Three days later all three places had surrendered after little more than token resistance by the Vichy French, and the British 1st Army hurried overland into Tunisia, hoping to seize Tunis and Bizerta before the Germans reacted. We were too late. Hitler began to land troops at Tunisian airfields on 9th November, and the British, having advanced to within twelve miles of Tunis, were driven back to their winter-line at Medjez-el-Bab. The link-up between the 1st Army advancing east and the 8th Army advancing west was delayed until the following April.

The politics of French North Africa were thrown into turmoil by the Allied invasion. The American intention had been to put General Giraud in control of all the liberated French territories, but he failed to gain their expected adherence. It was Admiral Darlan, Britain's old critic and a leading advocate of Vichy collaboration with Hitler, who became the central figure, since he happened to be in Algiers visiting his sick son at the time of the invasion. At first his inclination was to resist, but when Hitler occupied the whole of southern France on 11th November, Darlan *considered himself free to turn his coat, and the French forces throughout Algeria and Morocco (but not immediately in Tunisia) obeyed his orders to cease fire. Eisenhower, with the approval of President Roosevelt, and (as a short-term measure) of Churchill, established Darlan as political head of French North Africa, while Giraud was made Commander-in-Chief of the French troops. The deal with the traitor Darlan aroused a storm of protest in Britain, even when it was explained by Roosevelt that this was but a 'temporary expedient' to save both Allies and French unnecessary bloodshed. Harold Nicolson called it 'this disgraceful and most profitable episode'. It certainly brought immediate results. The whole of French West Africa, with Dakar, came over on 23rd November, and the French fleet at Toulon scuttled itself to avoid falling into German hands. At a Secret Session of Parliament on 10th December, Churchill persuaded the House that Eisenhower had had no real alternative. The assassination of Darlan by a young French royalist on Christmas Eve relieved the Allies of a political embarrassment. Darlan's main work had been done. Giraud succeeded him, but the problem of Giraud's relationship with de Gaulle remained, since the latter had been excluded from all prior knowledge of the Allied operation, owing to American hostility towards him and the fear that the plans might leak, and de Gaulle staked his claim to the leadership of all Free Frenchmen wherever they might be.*

Both Harold Nicolson's sons left England for service overseas. Ben went to Cairo via Lagos on 26th October as an air-photograph interpreter in the Intelligence Corps: and Nigel sailed three weeks later in a 1st Army convoy for Algiers. As Intelligence Officer to the 3rd Battalion of the Grenadier Guards, he reached the Tunisian front line at Medjez-el-Bab on 10th December, and was almost immediately in action against the Germans. Every Sunday without fail Harold Nicolson wrote them a joint letter from Sissinghurst, sending the original to Ben and the carbon-copy to Nigel. The first letter was dated 25th October, 1942; the last, 4th June, 1945. Each was some 3,000 words long. They were based on his diaries, but infinitely elaborated and drastically censored. In the extracts that follow ('H.N. TO B.N. & N.N.') episodes have been lifted from these weekly letters and attributed to the date on which they occurred, in order to avoid confusing the sequence of events. During these two-and-a-half years Harold Nicolson was therefore making three distinct records of his life—in his diary, in his daily letters to V. Sackville-West, and in his letters to his sons. All of them, and the replies to them, have been preserved.

DIARY   *25th October, 1942*

Ben and I walk round to the Temple Underground, carrying his big fibre suit-case and his funny little handbag. We have to wait some time for the train, but eventually it lumbers through the tunnel. We sit beside each other for the short journey between the Temple and Charing Cross. I cannot speak. When the train stops, I get up and go. 'Goodbye, Benzie.' 'Goodbye, Daddy.' I close the carriage doors behind me. I stand there waiting for the train to go out. It jerks away, taking Ben to Paddington and then to Bristol and then to Avonmouth and then to Lagos and then to Cairo. My eyes are blinded with tears.

H.N. TO B.N.[1]   *25th October, 1942*
                                                    Sissinghurst

I have no news, since I saw you three hours and forty-four minutes ago. It was really horrible shuffling out on to the platform and hearing the train-door grate as it closed. It was *l'adieu suprème des mouchoirs*, and I feel as if I had been knocked down by a bus. But none of us really has cause for self-pity. We have had love and understanding and interesting work in which we have all done well. Nothing can take that from us, and although my heart aches at this moment, yet I know that there is no need for unhappiness, which always comes from frustration or false relationships or muddled personal affections.

This problem of displacement has never been really well expressed. It seems unaccountable to me that I should still be using the same cardboard box of cigarettes which I used at the Club last night and which I bought when you bought a fountain-pen. The box will go to salvage in a few hours, and the pen will go to hazards whence no tears can win it. It seems unaccountable to me that the present should so suddenly (at 8.13 am. on a Sunday) become the past, that the familiarity of King's Bench Walk should be succeeded by the un-familiarity of a cabin,[2] and that the voices you know should be merged with the voices that you do not know. It is a theme that never ceases to perplex me.

Bless you, my darling Ben, and may God preserve you from suffering or fear.

---

[1] The first three letters in this series were addressed to Ben only, as Nigel had not yet left England.
[2] Ben went by sea to Lagos, and thence flew across Central Africa to Khartoum.

DIARY   *1st November, 1942*

I go a long walk with Hugh Molson[1] in the pouring rain. He urges me to join the Conservative Party. I say that I cannot forgive them for Baldwin, Chamberlain and the Liddall's[2] of this world. Nor can I conceive myself being associated with the 1922 Committee. What I regret is that I did not start as a Liberal, which is my spiritual home, and that I was put off by their attitude on Free Trade. The National Labour Party has proved a grave disadvantage to me. In fact I have ruined my political career by not knowing enough about politics at the start.

DIARY   *2nd November, 1942*

Palewski tells me that Winston sent a message to de Gaulle congratulating him on the prowess of the Fighting French in Egypt.[3] Their Brigade has suffered terrible casualties. But the battle, though slow and hard, goes well. He says that de Gaulle's nervous state is due to the fact that his military genius is left unused, that he is 'pregnant with victory' and that he chafes at the idea that he could win the war in a few months and is not taken into our confidence.[4]

DIARY   *4th November, 1942*

I turn on the wireless at 11.40 pm. There is a piano-recital. It stops a few minutes before midnight and the announcer says, 'I advise listeners not to switch off, as at midnight we are giving the best news we have heard for years.' Then it comes. It is Alexander's communiqué. The Germans are in full retreat in Egypt, we have so far captured over 9,000 prisoners and are pursuing 'their disordered columns'. It is a great victory. How far shall we be able to exploit it? We have halved their tank force and knocked out their air force. Anything is possible now. I stretch my arms lazily as one does after an anxious night, for the menace to Alexandria is now removed and that is by no means the end of the story.[5]

[1] Conservative M.P. for the High Peak division of Derbyshire since 1939. He became Minister of Works, 1957–59, and was created Lord Molson in 1961.

[2] See pp. 220–1.

[3] The Free French Brigade stood on the left of the British line at the battle of El Alamein, which was then approaching its climax.

[4] Palewski's remark was thus reported in H.N.'s letter to V.S-W. that day: 'De Gaulle's udders are bursting with the milk of victory, but Winston won't allow him to be milked.'

[5] H.N. already knew the secret (which he did not confide to his diary) of the Allied armadas approaching North Africa.

V.S–W. TO H.N.   *5th November, 1942*
                                                    Sissinghurst

I was so thrilled by the news that I couldn't resist ringing you up. You sounded excited too. I envy you lunching with Winston tomorrow. Oh dear, I do hope we don't now have some awful reverse. I wish I could understand why Rommel wasn't there.[1]

DIARY   *6th November, 1942*

At 1.15 I stroll across to Downing Street where I am to lunch. As I have time at my disposal, I shall record what happened in full detail.

I turned into Downing Street where there is a barrier with barbed wire and police. I waved my blue pass and was not interrupted. The War Cabinet were breaking up when I got there. Portal swung past in his R.A.F. car. As I reached the door, Dudley Pound[2] came out. 'Any news?' I asked him. 'Good all along the line', he said. He took me by the arm. 'At last we are catching up with all the mess you fellows made at Geneva.' I enter No. 10. Attlee is there and waves. Eden is hurrying along the passage: 'Well, Harold, this *is* something like.' I go downstairs to the basement where the Churchills are living, since the upper floors have been knocked about.[3] They made it very pretty with chintz and flowers and good furniture and excellent French pictures— not only the moderns, but Ingres and David.

I find Lady Kitty Lambton[4] and Lady Furness[5] and Clemmie Churchill. We are given sherry. Eddy Marsh[6] comes in, and then the Private Secretary, Martin,[7] a neat alert young man: I should say Winchester, New College and Treasury. He tells us not to wait for Winston, as he is late. We go into luncheon: sea-kale, jugged hare and cherry tart. Not well done. In a few minutes Winston comes in.

---

[1] He was there. On the day after the battle began, he flew back from a sanatorium in Austria where he was receiving treatment for an infected liver, and took command at Alamein on the evening of the 25th.

[2] The First Sea Lord. He had been with H.N. at the Peace Conference in 1919.

[3] A bomb had fallen fifty yards from No. 10 on 14th October, 1940.

[4] The widow of Major-General Sir William Lambton (d. 1936), and formerly Lady Katherine de Vere Somerset, daughter of the 10th Duke of St Albans.

[5] Thelma, Lady Furness, who first introduced the Prince of Wales to Mrs Simpson.

[6] Sir Edward Marsh, the author and connoisseur, Private Secretary to Winston Churchill, 1917–22 and 1924–29.

[7] John (now Sir John) Martin, Principal Private Secretary to Winston Churchill, 1941–45. His background was Edinburgh Academy, Corpus Christi College, Oxford, and the Dominions Office.

He is dressed in his romper suit of Air Force blue and he carries a letter in his hand. He kisses Kitty Lambton. 'Good to have you here, Kitty. You must tell me about France.' He is introduced to Lady Furness. 'Good morning, Eddy.' 'Good morning, Harold.' He half bows and smiles, accenting the first syllable of 'morning'. He gives the letter to Clemmie. It is a long letter from the King written in his own hand-writing, and saying how much he and the Queen have been thinking of Winston these glorious days. Winston is evidently pleased. 'Every word', he mutters, 'in his own hand.'[1]

Kitty Lambton and Lady Furness have just escaped from the South of France. Lady Kitty has clearly known Winston from childhood and treats him with gay familiarity which is only slightly overdone. Lady Furness has been brought by Lady Kitty and is nervous. I sit between her and Mrs Winston. Winston talks to Lady Kitty and I talk hard to Lady Furness, as she is frightened of the gigantic figure on her right, and Winston is bad at putting people at their ease. Nor does Clemmie Churchill help much. Winston stops talking to Lady Kitty and gazes round the table with his curious eyes. They are glaucous and look dead. When he gazes at people like that, there is no light either of interest or intelligence in his eyes. There is a faint expression of surprise, as if he were asking, 'What the hell is this man doing here?' There is a faint expression of angered indignation, as if he were saying, 'What damned cheek coming to luncheon here!' There is a mask of boredom and another mask or film of obstinacy, as if he were saying, 'These people bore me and I shall refuse to be polite.' And with it all, there are films of stubbornness, perhaps even a film of deep inner thought. It is very disconcerting. Then suddenly he will cease thinking of something else, and the film will part and the sun comes out. His eyes then pucker with amusement or flash with anger. At moments they have a tragic look. Yet these passing moods and phases do not flash across each other: they move slowly and opaquely like newts in a rather dim glass tank.

Lady Kitty chaffs him. She says that *Malbrouk s'en va-t-en guerre* refers, not to his well-known ancestor, but to some Saracen of the name of Ma'barak who attacked the Crusaders. She tells him that he owed nothing to the Churchill blood but it is the Jeromes[2] who have

---

[1] The letter is reproduced in Sir John Wheeler-Bennett's *King George VI, His Life and Reign* (Macmillan, 1958), p. 553.

[2] Winston Churchill's mother was Jennie Jerome, daughter of Leonard Jerome of New York.

brought in genius, as to Shane Leslie[1] and Clare Sheridan.[2] 'I am proud', he says, 'very proud of my American blood, but do not impute Shane to me.'

He turns to me and thanks me for my article on his oratory.[3] I say I hope that I was right in saying that he was not a born orator. 'You are perfectly right', he mumbles. 'Not born in the very least—just hard, hard work.' He then talks to us about the battle. He begins with the first two battles of Alamein. 'I refuse', he says, 'to call it El Alamein. Like those asses who talk about Le Havre. *Havre* the place is to any decent man.[4] Now this third battle must not be called Alamein. It must be called "The Battle of Egypt". Harold, see to that at once. Tell your people henceforward to call it the Battle of Egypt.' He tells us at length how he decided to remove Auchinleck and how he broke the news to him. 'It was a terrible thing to have to do. He took it like a gentleman. But it was a terrible thing. It is difficult to remove a bad General at the height of a campaign: it is atrocious to remove a good General. We must use Auchinleck again. We cannot afford to lose such a man from the fighting line.' He admits that he wanted Gott[5] for the 8th Army. 'I saw that Army. It was a broken, baffled Army, a miserable Army. I felt for them with all my heart. I made my decision. I telegraphed to the Cabinet. I then took off all my clothes and rolled in the surf. Never have I had such bathing. And when I got back to Cairo, I heard at the Embassy that night that Gott was dead. I sent for Montgomery. I gather that there was some confusion and difficulty between him and Auchinleck. But by then the die was cast, and I, after all, was having my row with Jo [Stalin].'

He speaks of the battle. He thinks that the enemy is done. He thinks Rommel was right to abandon the Italians.[6] 'That was the correct military decision, but it makes excellent propaganda for us.' He warms to the subject. 'The enemy', he says, 'were stuck to the Alamein position like limpets to a rock. We cut them out'—at that he makes a gesture

---

[1] The author. His mother was Leonie Jerome, sister of Jennie.

[2] The sculptor, painter and author. She was the daughter of Clara, the eldest of the Jerome sisters.

[3] A recent 'Marginal Comment' in the *Spectator*.

[4] In telling me this story after the war, H.N. said that Churchill pronounced the word *Havre* to rhyme with 'Carver'.

[5] Lt.-Gen. E. H. E. Gott, who was shot down over the desert on 7th August.

[6] The records show this to have been rather unfair on Rommel. He escaped westwards with 25,000 Italians and only 10,000 Germans. Many other thousands of Italians had in any case already surrendered earlier in the battle.

of someone cutting a limpet off a rock with a knife—'we detached them utterly. And what happens to a limpet when it loses its rock? It dies a miserable death. Thirst comes to it—aching, inescapable thirst. I should not like our armies to be suffering what the Afrika Korps will suffer in these days.' He does not think that Rommel can make much of a stand before Halfaya, or even there. 'The next days will show. There is more jam to come. Much more jam. And in places where some of you least expect.'[1]

Brendan Bracken then comes in and Winston tells him to arrange for all the bells in England to be tolled on Sunday.[2] Some hesitation is expressed by all of us. 'Not at all,' says Winston, 'not at all. We are not celebrating final victory. The war will still be long. When we have beaten Germany, it will take us two more years to beat Japan. Nor is that a bad thing. It will keep America and ourselves together while we are making peace in Europe. If I am still alive, I shall fling all we have into the Pacific.'

Lady Kitty interrupts him to complain about the B.B.C. With a grin he waves her on to me. 'Here, Kitty, is the B.B.C. in person. Fling your darts.' But all she says is that we are wrong to talk of an increase in juvenile delinquency and venereal disease. It gives a bad impression abroad. Winston contradicts her. 'Not in the least. We speak for ourselves. We are not dependent on what others say.' I ask her whether it is not a fact that after the French collapse, the B.B.C. was the only hope of France. 'Of course', she says. 'Your people have done well', says Winston. 'Very well indeed.'

At that moment Mary Churchill[3] comes in in A.T.S. uniform. She flings her arms round Winston's neck and hugs him. 'Daddy,' she says, 'think of it. I have 48 hours leave and shall come to Chequers.' He beams at her.

We then go. He comes up with us to the ground floor and opens the door of the Cabinet Room. He stands there with the Corinthian columns showing inside. 'There is more news to come soon', he says. 'More jam. Remember that.' And he goes in smiling grimly.

---

[1] This was, of course, a reference to the invasion of North Africa two days later.
[2] The bells were rung, not on Sunday 8th November, but on Sunday 15th, when success in North Africa had been assured.
[3] Churchill's youngest daughter. She married Christopher Soames in 1947.

H.N. TO V.S-W.   *9th November, 1942*
                                                    4 King's Bench Walk, E.C.4

My first intimation that the American invasion of North Africa was imminent came from Fred Kuh, the United Press correspondent, whom I met at the Soviet Embassy. I never imagined, however, that it would be on so large or far-flung a scale. I got up yesterday morning and turned on the wireless. When I heard that they had landed at Algiers, I held my breath. That means, eventually, Tunis, and brings us within eighty miles of Sicily and closes the Western Mediterranean. The Italians must be in a grave state of alarm. Nor can they be feeling very pleased with their allies. The Germans just left them *plantés* and took all their cars with them. Six Italian Divisions (the whole Italian Army in fact) have been cut off and will have to surrender. There has been no such military disaster since Sedan. Moreover I gather that Rommel has almost no tanks left,[1] and it is doubtful whether he will be able to get even these through the Halfaya Pass.

I was worried about de Gaulle's reaction, since he had not been told of the North African landings. I hear that his first emotion was that he was '*profondément mortifié*'. But then his mood changed. He received a message from Winston asking him to luncheon. He emerged from Downing Street wreathed in smiles, and then agreed to give a broadcast welcoming Giraud.

But what a brilliant bit of timing and strategy it all is! I envy Winston at the Guildhall. I envy him in the House. But how he has deserved it all! I wonder what Victor Cazalet feels now about 'the supreme direction of the war'.

H.N. TO V.S-W.   *10th November, 1942*
                                                    4 King's Bench Walk, E.C.4

I am just back from Wellington College. I went down there last night and dined with the Master. Giles[2] was there. He is so charming and so good-looking. Everybody there seems to love him deeply. He is beginning to show real ability, and not just brilliance.

It was strange to be back at school. The sight of the two towers above the pine-trees brought a wave of depression followed by a wave of exhilaration. My old sadness that hung like mist among the bracken suddenly settled down on me again: and then I realised that it was

---

[1] He had about sixty left after the battle.
[2] Giles St Aubyn, H.N.'s nephew, then aged 17. He became an historian and a housemaster at Eton.

over and could never return, and my heart sang hymns at heaven's gate. I must have been *very* unhappy there for the mood to return to me after forty years.

DIARY   *11th November, 1942*

Walter [Elliot] and Rob [Bernays] and I walk down to the House. We are as gay as schoolboys. Winston is received with prolonged cheers. He embarks on a long description of the stages by which the present plan was prepared. He then passes to the Battle of Egypt. He tells us that the bells will ring. He says we have lost 13,600 men, and the enemy have lost 59,000, of which 34,000 were Germans and 25,000 Italians. This surprises me. We were told that at least six Italian Divisions had been cut off. And he concludes by saying that great things will happen in the next few days.

In the evening comes the news that under Darlan's orders the whole of French North Africa has capitulated. This is amazing. But we are still quite uncertain (a) what has happened to Rommel; (b) what the French fleet is doing; (c) what Darlan's position really is; (d) what Pétain and Weygand are doing.

DIARY   *14th November, 1942*

I get two letters from Nigel. In the first he had said, 'When you get a letter enclosing photographs, you will know that I am off'. In the second he enclosed photographs.

H.N. TO B.N. & N.N.   *16th November, 1942*
                                                            Sissinghurst

We celebrated the second anniversary of the founding of *La France Libre* by a grand dinner at Claridges. André Labarthe acted as host. He made a tense and nervous little speech about '*les amis éternels*'. Brendan Bracken made a rollicking, schoolboy speech about nothing at all. He is a shrewd, nice, kind-hearted man, but he is so determined not to be highbrow and to retain the common touch that he adopts a tone of hearty frivolity which is below the level of his very real intelligence. Duff Cooper made a speech of a very different order. Speaking with real emotion, he said how much those Englishmen who believed in France had suffered during all these years; how difficult it was to account for Vichy; how our faith in France had been saved by a few brave men; and how we still felt that France was the home of 'wisdom, wit and glory'.

But behind it all, of course, was the shadow of the Darlan episode. Assuming as I do that this letter will be read by Ribbentrop, I forbear to say exactly what I feel about this incredible diplomatic error. I do not see how one can maintain one's credit if one announces to the world that one has employed a trickster in order to trick his followers, and that one will discard him once it is clear that the trick has come off. My old group of the Munich days (which has disintegrated somewhat, owing to the high responsibilities which devolved upon its leading members) was again united by this regrettable action. And we were glad to find that our indignation was very fully shared by our leaders.

DIARY   *19th November, 1942*

I find that a reaction has set in after our victories. People are beginning to say (a) that we should not have rung the bells; (b) that our shipping losses in the Mediterranean are appalling; (c) that we ought to have gone straight to Tunis and not to Algiers; (d) that the Germans are building up a powerful force at Bizerta and will occupy Gabes and Sfax; (e) that Rommel has extricated most of his army and will turn and smite us at Agheila. I have no patience with such pessimism.

DIARY   *25th November, 1942*

I dine with Camrose. Winant is there. He talks very frankly about the Darlan episode. He said that Eisenhower had supposed that the French forces and civilians would obey Giraud. That was the American trump card. To their horror they found that the French would not do so. Darlan was there almost by chance (what does that mean?[1]) and they realised that he could deliver the goods. It means the saving of infinite time and 50,000 American lives. What did the mother in Ohio know about de Gaulle? What did she know about Darlan? All she felt was that it would be terrible if her boy died fighting the French. It was worth it. I say that it is difficult to explain to our people. Winant is such a splendid fellow that one is convinced by his advocacy of ill.

DIARY   *26th November, 1942*

Anthony [Eden] is heckled about Darlan and de Gaulle. He is very skilful. He manages to imply that he does not agree with the action of

[1] For a summary of the whole Darlan episode see the introductory note to this section, p. 253-4.

Eisenhower in giving Darlan authority, but that he begs the House to be discreet. I agree with this view. I regard it as horrible that Eisenhower should have promoted Darlan, and I do not want us to abandon de Gaulle. But we had best keep silence over this disgraceful and most profitable episode.

Dine at the Travellers with Godfrey Nicholson.[1] He is comforting about Nigel in the sense that he says that it is insane to worry about circumstances which one cannot even know of, far less control.

DIARY   *27th November, 1942*
Oxford

I go to Wadham, where Maurice Bowra[2] and I listen to the 10.45 European news. It seems that the whole French fleet was scuttled and many of the captains went down with their ships.[3] Thus Hitler has been cheated of his hope of getting the French Navy, and the whole repute of France has been enhanced. I am overjoyed.

DIARY   *2nd December, 1942*

The Lobbies are buzzing with comment on the Beveridge Report.[4] The 1922 Committee were addressed by Beveridge and gave him a cordial reception. The Tory line seems to be to welcome the Report in principle, and then to whittle it away by detailed criticism. They will say that it is all very splendid and Utopian, but we can only begin to know whether we can afford it once we have some idea what our foreign trade will be like after the war. They also suggest that in many ways it is an incentive to idleness, that some people are better off under the present arrangements, and that in fact it is the old Poor Law immensely magnified.

V.S-W. TO H.N.   *3rd December, 1942*
Sissinghurst

Our letters about the Beveridge Report crossed. I fear I am an instinctive Tory. I sincerely hope that it gets whittled away like an artichoke. I am all for educating the people into being less awful, less limited, less silly, and for spending lots of money on (1) extended education; (2)

[1] Conservative M.P. for Farnham since 1937-66.
[2] Sir Maurice Bowra, Warden of Wadham College, Oxford, since 1938; Vice-Chancellor of Oxford University, 1951-54.
[3] 73 naval ships were sunk in Toulon harbour as the Germans approached.
[4] The Report had been published the previous day.

better-paid teachers, but *not* for giving them everything for nothing, which they don't appreciate anyhow. Health, yes. Education, yes. Old age pensions, yes, I suppose so, in default of euthanasia which I should prefer, as also for the mental deficients. But not this form of charity which will make people fold their arms and feel that they need have no enterprise since everything will be provided for them. It is surely a psychological error.

V.S–W. TO H.N.   *8th December, 1942*
                                                 Sissinghurst

I am trying to write my gardening poem.[1] It is much more difficult than *The Land*, because the inherent dignity of agriculture is lacking, and seed-boxes are not so romantic as tilth. But I struggle on, and anyhow it is silly to think that anything in life matters very much, isn't it?

H.N. TO V.S–W.   *9th December, 1942*
                                                 4 King's Bench Walk, E.C.4

Why do you say 'it is silly to think that anything in life matters much'? I think everything in life matters terribly. I feel that this war is a test of our character and I rejoice that all those I love have come through it enhanced and not diminished. I want to live through this war with my courage unabated, my faith firmer, my energy increased, and my hopes and beliefs lit by a sun that has never lit them before. I have much pride in my own people and much faith in the future. I really do believe that we in England have set an example to the world. I think that we may solve the social and economic problems of the twentieth century with as much wisdom and tolerance as when we solved the political problems of the nineteenth. Surely this is worth while? Surely your dignity and calm and uncomplainingness and courage are an example to all who see you? Not worth while! Why, everything is ten times more worth while now than ever before!

V.S–W. TO H.N.   *10th December, 1942*
                                                 Sissinghurst

When I said that it is silly to think that anything in life mattered much, I suppose I meant one's personal life. Of course I think with you that

[1] V.S–W. had begun work on the first draft of *The Garden*, a companion poem to *The Land*, published in 1927. *The Garden* was not published till 1946, when it was awarded the Heinemann Prize.

the war and after-the-war matter. But, darling, you are a goose to talk about my 'uncomplainingness and courage', because (a) I have nothing to complain of, and (b) my courage is a very poor thing. I am sure it would go phutt if put to the test. My calm is merely my cabbagey nature. Luckily for you, you have never seen the more tempestuous side of my nature. You have only seen an occasional bubble rising to the surface, which has startled you and made you realise vaguely that I feel passionately, and am vindictive and uncontrollable when my emotions are aroused, but as you do not like that sort of bubble, you have always wisely looked the other way. The emotions I give you are deep and strong. You are about the only person in whose love I trust. I know that we will love each other till we die.

By the way, you said we ought to ask de Gaulle to luncheon. Shall we give a joint luncheon party? You ask the guests, and I will go shares with you. Shall we?

DIARY   9th December, 1942

We have a Committee meeting at which several representative Jews tell us of the extermination of their fellows by the Nazis. They have ringed off the Warsaw ghetto and transported two-thirds of the inhabitants in cattle-trucks to die in Russia.[1] It is a horrible thing to feel that we are so saturated with horrors, that this Black Hole on a gigantic scale scarcely concerns us. They put lime and chloride in the cattle-trucks and bury the corpses next morning. They are particularly vindictive against children. I have a sense that my fellow-Members feel not so much 'What can we do to such people?' as 'What can we do *with* such people after the war?'

DIARY   10th December, 1942

Secret Session on North Africa and Darlan. It is opened by Winston who speaks for an hour, and I have never heard him more forceful, informative or convincing. He refers to Pétain (whose name he pronounces as 'Peatayne') as 'that antique defeatist'. He convinces us (a) that we were never consulted about the Darlan move; (b) that when it

[1] By the late autumn of 1940 the German S.S. had rounded up some 400,000 Jews and sealed them off from the rest of Warsaw by a high wall. They were dreadfully overcrowded and kept short of food. By the spring of 1943 only 60,000 survived. Some had died of starvation; others were transported to extermination camps and gassed.

happened, he himself realised at once what trouble would be caused, and warned Roosevelt accordingly; (c) that it is purely temporary. I cannot say more than that.

I get in and make (if I may say so) a good speech. Afterwards I had a drink with Anthony [Eden] in the smoking-room. He says that Eisenhower is quite aware that Darlan wishes to suppress the de Gaullists and that he will have nothing of it. Béthouart,[1] for instance, is being given a good command. He says that the Americans are really like children regarding the whole situation and that it never dawned on them that steps should be taken to control the frontier into Spanish Morocco. But I'm sure that we shan't be exposed to similar situations in the future.

I am cheered by the debate. I see that it illustrates the difficulty of all Secret Sessions. Winston could not have convinced us as he did unless he had been able to quote telegrams and documents which it would have been quite impossible to quote in public. But some public statement can and must be made.

H.N. TO B.N. & N.N.   *12th December, 1942*
                                                       Sissinghurst

I am not really worried about you two. I do not suppose that many fathers are as devoted to their sons as I am, but I am a fatalist about such things. I worry much less than I used to when Ben was scrubbing floors at Chatham and I would think about how miserable he must be. It would be no relief to me to feel that you were safe again in Scotland, and I have a vicarious excitement in imagining the adventures which you must be experiencing. That is what one is always told about old men—how they sit sipping sherry in their Pall Mall clubs and relishing the ardours of the younger generation. But it is not that. I know you will pass through many hours of agony and fear. But I also know that it has been a dead weight on my life never to have known the dangers of the last war and never to have discovered whether I am a hero or a coward.

---

[1] General Béthouart was the French Divisional Commander at Casablanca at the time of the invasion of Morocco. Having fought at Narvik, he was very anti-German and was one of the few French leaders ready to accept Giraud as Supreme French Commander.

DIARY   *17th December, 1942*

Eden reads out a statement about the persecution of the Jews, and to our shame and astonishment a Labour Member[1] (having been deeply moved by a speech by Jimmy Rothschild) suggests that we should all stand up as a tribute. The Speaker says, 'Such an action must be spontaneous', so everybody gets up including the Speaker and the reporters. It is rather moving in a way.

H.N. TO B.N. & N.N.   *20th December, 1942*
Sissinghurst

Montgomery has assured us that he has 'cut Rommel's panzer Divisions in two'. It would seem that there was no truth in this. There is a certain anxiety in London regarding the boastfulness of Montgomery's communiqués. Nor do people enjoy the hunting terms which he is apt to use. People who admire him point out that Nelson and Baden-Powell were equally immodest and self-advertising.

The military arrived at Sissinghurst. It consisted of the Headquarters of a tank Brigade on exercise, heralded by a young officer of the name of Rubinstein. Recalling how but three days before I had stood in tribute to the martyred Jews of Poland, I was most polite to Captain Rubinstein. His parents, it appeared, live in Leicester. He told us that his Brigadier, plus five officers plus cook plus batmen, would appear by tea-time and wanted to stay the night. We showed him the brew-house, the oast-houses, Nigel's room, Ben's room and the loft beyond. He said that it would do nicely, and departed to inform his Headquarters what a pleasant little welcome was being prepared.

It was at that moment that Mummy remembered the onions stored on the floor of the loft. They number between two and three thousand. She said that the Army always stole onions and that we must remove them at any cost before they arrived. I said that we were only having a Brigadier and his officers, and that (a) they would probably not want to steal more than three onions each, and (b) we should not miss them much if they did. She said that you could never tell with officers nowadays, so many of them were promoted from the ranks. So we got three sacks and two shovels and all afternoon till darkness came we carried the sacks across to the Priest's House and spread them on the floor of Pat's room. We had scarcely finished with the last onion when the Brigadier appeared. He was a nice well-behaved man and looked so little like an onion-stealer that Mummy at once asked him to dinner.

[1] W. S. Cluse, M.P. for South Islington since 1935.

H.N. TO B.N. & N.N. *22nd December, 1942*
Sissinghurst

I went to lunch with General de Gaulle at the Ritz. It was a very formal luncheon. The General sat in the centre of the table having on his right the Secretary of State for Air[1] and on his left the Permanent Under-Secretary of State of Foreign Affairs.[2] Opposite sat his Commissary for external relations, M. Pleven, having on his right the Member for West Leicester and on his left Sir Walter Layton, proprietor of the *News Chronicle*. The interstices were filled by Admiral Valin, Gaston Palewski and the A.D.C.s. Now Palewski is one of the most conversational men I know, being able to converse with equal facility on Wedgwood dessert services and who was Albertine. But in the presence of de Gaulle a great hush falls on *la France Combattante*. Pleven spoke to me in whispers. They were disquieting whispers, since I had been under the impression that our own copybook was spotless in so far as Darlan was concerned. When I suggested this, he gave a whispered snort. '*Et Cunungham* (*sic*, whispered), *votre Amiral— lui—vous devriez savoir mieux que moi.*' I said I knew nothing. '*Il a signé un. . . .*' His voice at this last word dropped below the level of a whisper, and became an unidentifiable sigh. '*Un quoi?*' I asked. '*Papier*', he whispered. All of which confirms my impression that war is too serious a business to be dealt with by Generals, and still less so by Admirals.

DIARY *26th December, 1942*

A cold slate-grey day. I write an article on Parliament in 1942. I weed the lime-border in the afternoon. Viti is at work on her poem *The Garden*. She is finding it very difficult, and alternates between depression and elation.

Darlan has been assassinated by a Frenchman with an Italian mother.[3] Giraud says he hopes de Gaulle will join him.

---

[1] Sir Archibald Sinclair.   [2] Sir Orme Sargent.
[3] On the afternoon of 24th December Darlan was shot down at the door to his office in Algiers by a young man of twenty named Bonnier de la Chapelle, who was connected with the plot to bring the Comte de Paris to Algiers as head of a provisional administration in opposition to Vichy. The assassin was tried by court-martial on Giraud's orders and executed on 26th December.

DIARY   *31st December, 1942*

Our present worry is (a) the U-boat campaign. It is very serious indeed. We can lose the war by this; (b) the badness of our Army. The cream of our officers and men have been drained off by the R.A.F. and the Commandos. What remains is pretty poor. With good troops we ought to have brought off the dash to Tunis. As it is. . . .

I go down to the House to fire-watch. I sit in the map-room feeling pretty glum. I hear Big Ben strike out the old year. There are distant shouts of *Auld Lang Syne*, sung with an American accent. Then the snoring in my dormitory resumes its sway.

1943

Showing American doughboys round the House – Attlee's unimpressiveness – René Massigli – 'I despair of de Gaulle' – Churchill on the Casablanca Conference – debate on the Beveridge Report – Red Army Week in Leicester – the new Speaker – will H.N. go to the House of Lords? – Mark Bonham Carter taken prisoner – Churchill on the Tunisian campaign – Lord Vansittart – the Tunisian victory – Eden on his visit to the United States – meeting with Field-Marshal Wavell – Montgomery and Alexander – Pierre Viénot on de Gaulle – Lloyd George in old age – H.N.'s temporary loss of self-confidence – breakfast with Baldwin – Mussolini's resignation – Russian victories – a row on the B.B.C. Board – Italy makes peace – landings at Salerno – disappointment about German recovery in Italy – Churchill reports to Parliament – Colonel Knox – fear that Russia may make a separate peace – H.N.'s visit to Sweden – invitation to visit Australia – release of Mosley from prison – bombing of Italian cities – V.S-W. on not becoming a Roman Catholic – General de Lattre de Tassigny – Churchill ill with pneumonia at Carthage – farewell to Long Barn – Ben and Nigel meet in Jerusalem

'I should like to feel that this is the year of victory, but I don't'[1]

The main events of the first three months of the year were the meeting of Roosevelt and Churchill at Casablanca (12th–25th January), the surrender of the German 6th Army at Stalingrad (31st January), the capture of Tripoli by the 8th Army (23rd January) and its link-up with the 1st Army in Tunisia (7th April).

The Casablanca conference adopted Churchill's strategic plan to complete the conquest of North Africa by the spring, invade Sicily, bring pressure on Turkey to enter the war on the Allied side, prepare for landings in north-west Europe later in 1943, defeat the U-boats and step up the strategic bombing of Germany. Politically its results were the Allies' demand for the 'unconditional surrender' of their enemies, and the shot-gun marriage between Giraud and de Gaulle, which left the political relations between them unresolved. As regards Japan, it was decided that the defeat of Germany and Italy should have priority, but a limited operation would be undertaken by the British to open up the Burma road to China. The Americans meanwhile completed the conquest of Guadalcanal on 9th February.

Stalin had been invited to Casablanca, but pleaded that he could not leave Moscow at such a critical moment. General Paulus (promoted Field-Marshal by Hitler the previous day) surrendered with the 91,000 survivors of his army at Stalingrad, having lost another 200,000 in the fighting and the bitter cold. Throughout the winter the Russians maintained their counter-offensive and regained nearly all the ground they had lost in the summer of 1942. On 14th February Rostov-on-Don fell, and on the 16th Kharkov, which was temporarily recaptured by the Germans in March. German pressure on Moscow and Leningrad was also eased. Stalin continued to urge the Allies to open a Second Front in France, but it was already beginning to appear doubtful whether a full-scale operation could be mounted in 1943. If Turkey had entered the war, Russia would have benefited immediately by the opening of a new supply-route through the Black Sea and the bombing of the Rumanian oil-fields. Churchill met President Inönü of Turkey on 30th January at Adana on the Syrian border, but the only result of the meeting was the

[1] Typed by H.N. on 1st January.

supply of some British military equipment to Turkey and the promise of troops should Turkey be attacked by Germany.

Churchill made his way home by Cyprus, Cairo, Tripoli and Algiers. At Tripoli he met Montgomery a few days after its capture, and at Algiers, Harold Macmillan (who had been sent out as the British Resident Representative) and Generals Eisenhower and Alexander. Eisenhower was in overall command of the North African theatre, but active operations were carried out by Alexander (his Deputy Commander) on land, by Cunningham at sea and by Tedder in the air. Large forces on each side now faced each other in Tunisia. The 1st Army (under General Anderson) had failed to reach the coast at any point along its 200-mile front and was hard pressed to maintain its own positions once Rommel had pooled his forces with Von Arnim's in Tunisia to launch a series of attacks before the 8th Army could join the 1st. The most serious of these came at the Kasserine Pass on 17th February. The situation was saved by Montgomery's rapid advance from Tripoli. He outflanked the Mareth Line in southern Tunisia on 28th March, and ten days later joined forces with Anderson for the final assault on the Axis armies in the north.

In the House of Commons the main events were Churchill's report on 11th February about the Casablanca Conference and his subsequent tour of the Middle East, the death of Speaker Fitzroy on 3rd March, and the great debate on the Beveridge Report on 16th–18th February, which resulted in a vote by almost all Labour Members not in office for a stronger affirmation of the principles of the Report than the Government were then prepared to concede. In Churchill's vast history of the war there is no mention of this debate and only a brief reference (in an Appendix) to the Report itself. But at the time Churchill was ill with pneumonia, from which he quickly and fully recovered.

In these months V. Sackville-West, having temporarily put aside her long poem 'The Garden', began work on 'The Eagle and the Dove', a joint study of the two Saints Teresa, of Avila and Lisieux, published by Michael Joseph in October. Ben was with the 9th Army in the Lebanon, and Nigel took part in many of the operations of the 1st Army in Tunisia, now as Intelligence Officer of the 1st Guards Brigade in the 6th Armoured Division.

DIARY   7th January, 1943

Have a long talk with Archie Clark Kerr.[1] He says that he is not satisfied that he is a good man for the Moscow post. He says he is a

[1] Later Lord Inverchapel. British Ambassador in the U.S.S.R., 1942–46.

good mixer and gets on well with the orientals. But in Moscow there is no chance of mixing at all: he is followed by five detectives wherever he moves, and is not allowed to know anyone outside. No Russian dares come to the Embassy. It would be intolerable were it not for the delight of occasional visits to Stalin.

H.N. TO B.N. & N.N.   *7th January, 1943*
Sissinghurst

I had an appointment to conduct some American doughboys round the Palace of Westminster. In they slouched, chewing gum, conscious of their inferiority in training, equipment, breeding, culture, experience and history, determined in no circumstances to be either interested or impressed. In the Chamber we bumped into another party, of Dominion heroes this time, being shown round by no less a person than the Lord Chancellor of England. I have never cared for John Simon, but I must confess that on this occasion he displayed energy and even charm. Embarrassing he was, to be true. For having stood at the Prime Minister's place and lifted the dust-cloths from the box and table, he asked me to go opposite to show them the relations between the Government and the Opposition benches. 'Thank you, my dear Harold. Now, ladies and gentlemen, assume for the moment that I am the Prime Minister and that Mr Nicolson is the Leader of the Opposition.' Fifty blank faces, their jaws working at the gum, turned with languid interest in my direction. 'Now Harold . . .' But I was firm. 'No', I said, 'I am no good at amateur theatricals.' So we went into the House of Lords[1] and Simon sat on the Woolsack and showed them how a Lord Chancellor behaves. 'The Amendment standing in the name of the Noble Marquess . . .' Jaws chewed unflinchingly in silence. 'Now', he said briskly, 'come to my room, boys—or should I call you doughboys?—and I will show you the Great Seal.' Through the corridors they slouched apathetically, expecting to be shown a large wet animal such as they had seen so often at the Aquarium in San Francisco. But not at all. All they were shown were two cylinders of steel with a pattern inside. And then a man fetched the mace for them to see. 'I must now ask you, my friends, to leave me to my labours. Even a Lord Chancellor sometimes has work to do. Harold, perhaps you will conduct our friends to the exit?' Harold did. We slouched along to Central Hall. To my surprise and pleasure one of the dough-

[1] The House of Lords were sitting in the Robing Room while the House of Commons occupied the Chamber of the House of Lords.

boys suddenly ceased chewing, flung his wad of Wrigley into his cheek with a deft movement of his tongue, and said, 'Say, Sur, who was that guy?'

DIARY   *19th January, 1943*

Lloyd George enters the House and receives a warm welcome on his recent eightieth birthday.[1] Eden, fairly wobbling with charm and grace, congratulates him. He replies in a few very halting phrases. He is very old.

We have a short Secret Session. We are told why it is that Attlee will make the Government statement on the progress of the war.[2] We resume in public and Attlee begins his statement. Had he announced the fall of Bizerta, it would still have been unimpressive. He is like a snipe pretending to be an eagle. He is exactly like Lloyd George's imitation of him.[3]

DIARY   *23rd January, 1943*

On the 1 o'clock news we hear that our troops entered Tripoli at dawn today, having pursued Rommel for 1,400 miles. Lord Haw Haw[4] at 10.30 says, 'May I quote the picturesque, if slightly vulgar, phrase used by General Montgomery? He said his object was "to put Rommel in the bag". In fact his aim was not to take Tripoli, but to take Rommel. He has failed.'

H.N. TO V.S-W.   *28th January, 1943*
                                                       4 King's Bench Walk, E.C.4

I do not think that de Gaulle and Giraud have come together. I think they have been pushed together. René Pleven, de Gaulle's Foreign Minister, said to me, 'From all who were at Casablanca I receive the same account. De Gaulle proved himself in everything a better man than Giraud.' Poor French people, they seem to have lost everything but their competitive instinct and their jealousy. I doubt whether we shall ever be able to build them up. They have been so dishonoured.

---

[1] David Lloyd George was born in Manchester on 17th January, 1863. He died in 1945, having been created Earl Lloyd George of Dwyfor a month before.
[2] Because Churchill had left for Casablanca on 12th January.
[3] See vol. 1 of these diaries, p. 269.   [4] See above, p. 55, note 1.

DIARY   *29th January, 1943*

Dine with Bob Boothby, Jimmy Rothschild, Kingsley Martin, Aneurin Bevan and Archie Clark Kerr. Archie thinks that the Chinese will be democratic enough when peace comes. He has a passionate admiration for Chiang Kai-Shek. He thinks that Stalin may make a separate peace if we do not help him. By help he means diverting German divisions. It is not correct to say that he has a bee in his bonnet about invading Western Europe. He might be just as pleased if we attacked elsewhere, provided that we lost men and killed Germans. If we do nothing he may make terms with Hitler. He thinks the Russian spirit is due (in this order) to (a) obedience; (b) indoctrinated patriotism; (c) fear of the Ogpu; (d) a feeling that the farms and the factories belong to them and not to someone else. He says that when he gets back he will try to induce Stalin to allow him to get to know a few Russians.

Kingsley and Aneurin start a hare by saying that Ll.G. was a finer man than Churchill. Churchill is 'adolescent', which is suitable in times of emotional strain. Ll.G. is the wise statesman. I say that Ll.G., if he had not been so gaga, would have been our Pétain. They agree to this, but still say he is a great man.

We discuss the position of Stafford Cripps and agree that he has lost all influence in the House. But we make the reservation that no man can have influence in the House without a Party behind him. We also agree that the main quality demanded of a politician is not that he should be gifted or honest or wise, but 'formidable'. But to be formidable implies the capacity to bring votes into the lobby. A very agreeable dinner.

DIARY   *2nd February, 1943*

In the midnight news we hear that the last of the Germans at Stalingrad, including Field Marshal Paulus, have surrendered.

DIARY   *4th February, 1943*

Massigli dines. He tells me in great detail of his escape.[1] He had, after his dismissal from the Ankara Embassy, returned to France. He had seen Pétain, who had quite clearly indicated to him that his attitude

[1] René Massigli was Political Director of the French Ministry of Foreign Affairs, 1937–38, and Ambassador to Turkey, 1939–40. In 1943 he became de Gaulle's Commissioner for Foreign Affairs in North Africa, and French Ambassador in London, 1944–55.

and policy was one of *attentisme*.[1] He had also seen much of Weygand whom he found pro-British but anti-de Gaulle. In November last a man had come to see him and told him that de Gaulle wanted him to come to London. He was to disguise himself. He was to walk along a certain street in Lyons (incidentally, a street of ill-fame). From that moment on he became 'a registered parcel'. He was edged towards the Riviera. An aeroplane was to come to pick him up. They listened to code-messages through the B.B.C. '*René salue Victorine et la prie d'avoir tout courage.*' That meant forty-eight hours later. The underground service (which consisted of *gros industriels* and peasants) was marvellous. Night after night he stood there under the stars with his little trunk, waiting for a 'plane. At last it could be heard zooming above. They flashed their torches. It passed over. Again it came and again they flashed. For the second time it disappeared. The third time it began to circle and eventually landed. Massigli climbed in. They landed at Bristol.

Massigli is a godsend. He is the one Frenchman (a) of authority; (b) commanding absolute confidence here; (c) who has known Vichy and the state of mind in France; (d) who has definitely joined de Gaulle. The latter evidently wants him to become Commissary of Foreign Affairs in place of Pleven. He has no special prejudice against the men of Vichy, only against the Laval lot. But he is convinced that in Metropolitan France de Gaulle is the great symbol. What is he to do? I tell him that Carlton Gardens is a *panier de crabes*. I urge him to wait until he is quite recovered before deciding. I beg him that when he does decide, he will insist upon his appointment being conditional upon some joint communiqué. This should state that 'in view of his desire to do all that he can to foster unity among Frenchmen . . .' He rather agrees with this.

I see quite clearly that he has come, not to join de Gaulle, but to join Winston Churchill—and they are two very different things.

DIARY   *5th February, 1943*

Charles Peake[2] tells me one thing about de Gaulle which terrifies me. He had complimented his difficult and tricky General upon the performance of Leclerc.[3] 'Ah yes', said de Gaulle, 'he is a younger man.

[1] Waiting to see what happened.

[2] British Representative to the Free French National Committee, 1942–44.

[3] General Leclerc (originally de Hauteclocque) who had led the Free French forces from Chad to join Montgomery at Tripoli.

My Generals will all be like that. You will see.' This shows that he really imagines that he will one day become Dictator of France. I despair of de Gaulle. Charles told me that Catroux[1] said that the Mareth Line was not any good.[2] He had given his own map of it to Montgomery.

H.N. TO B.N. & N.N.   *9th February, 1943*
                                                            Sissinghurst

I took Monsieur Pierre Bloch to the House of Commons. He was a *député* in the French Chamber and agreed that with us there is '*plus de calme*'. Winston came in for the first time since his return from Africa and received a resounding cheer. He answered a few simple questions, and M. Bloch was enormously impressed. '*Alors c'est le Président du Conseil lui-même qui répond aux interpellations?*' '*Mais toujours*', I answered untruthfully. In the smoking-room afterwards Winston got us to gather round him and told us stories about his visit. He was looking amazingly well and almost brown. What seems to have impressed him most was the reception given him by the Italian population in Tripoli. 'They cheered me', he said, 'and clapped their hands like this', and at that he stuck his cigar into his mouth and clapped his hands, saying 'Eeveever', which I suppose was intended to represent *Evviva*.

DIARY   *11th February, 1943*

The Prime Minister is given a good reception when he rises at 12.7. He has a slight cold, looks less well than he did on arrival, but is in tearing spirits. He begins by saying that the United Nations are now warrior nations, 'walking in fear of the Lord, very heavily armed, and with an increasingly clear view of their salvation'. This Cromwellian utterance produces cheers and laughter. Some are not quite clear whether he is parodying a Covenanter, and others believe that he is speaking with deep religious conviction. On he goes to discuss the U-boat campaign, putting it in the very forefront of his whole speech. He speaks of 'very serious depredations'. He admits that this wastage of ships, cargoes and crews constitutes a 'repulsive and sombre panorama'. He concludes this section of his speech by saying that the

---

[1] General Georges Catroux, Governor of Algeria, 1943-44.
[2] A system of fortifications built by the French before the war to guard the approaches from Libya into southern Tunisia.

enemy by their U-boat campaign cannot avert, but may delay, their doom.

He then passes to Casablanca and explains what was meant by the 'unconditional surrender' clause. This does not mean that 'we shall stain our arms by any cruel treatment of whole populations'. But it does mean that we shall exact justice 'upon the wicked and the guilty'. Till then he has kept his hands to his breast in that characteristic gesture, as if patting his breast-pocket to see whether he has forgotten his letter-case. When he gets to this stage he drops his hands and makes a sweeping dismissive gesture with flat palms, as if smoothing out a tea-cloth. 'No vestige of the Fascist or Nazi power, no vestige of the Japanese war-plotting machine . . .' He smooths and sweeps them all away.

He passes to the Adana meeting.[1] He described how he 'descended' (and here he indicates by a fall of his arms and a bend of his knees that the descent had been ponderous) upon the Turkish airfield, and how he then observed 'out of the snow-capped Taurus Mountains there crawled like an enamel caterpillar the Presidential train'. He goes further than I had expected in dealing with Turkey. While begging us not to read a word more into the communiqué than actually exists there, he made it quite clear that we were equipping Turkey as an ally whom we expected to become belligerent. Then he goes on to Cairo and Tripoli. He pays a tribute to the Desert Army, saying that never has he seen spit and polish brought to such perfection, 'as if they had just left Wellington Barracks'.[2] He slurs over the political situation in North Africa and then announces the new commands. Eisenhower to be C.-in-C.; Alexander to be Deputy C.-in-C., with Montgomery and Anderson under him; Tedder to command the Air Force; Cunningham the Fleet.

About the military situation in Tunisia he says little. He admits that the Germans have some 250,000 troops in the Tunisian tip. But he says that their presence there indicates the 'master touch', the touch which led to Stalingrad.

[1] With President Inönü at Adana, in southern Turkey. See introductory note, p. 273.
[2] In describing this speech in his letter to his sons, H.N. added: 'At the mention of Wellington Barracks, there was a movement of restlessness among the Labour benches. Winston noted it immediately. "Never", he added quickly, "have I seen so smart an army since I reviewed the Guard of Honour which greeted me at the Moscow airport." The Socialists laughed loud at this sally. They love him deeply.'

DIARY   *16th February, 1943*

First day's debate on the Beveridge Report. Greenwood opens, urging immediate legislation. [Sir John] Anderson makes a clever speech approving in principle, urging that the thing must be done by stages, and offering some immediate action. He refuses, however, to appoint a Minister of Social Security.

DIARY   *17th February, 1943*

To the House early. The temperature has risen since a Labour Party meeting early this morning at which they threw over Greenwood's motion. Had the Government decided to reaffirm the promises indicated by Anderson yesterday, then all might have been well. But they put up Kingsley Wood to make a clever speech, and all the doubts which were stilled yesterday are now more virulent than ever. In the afternoon Quintin Hogg[1] makes a 'young Tory' speech which has considerable effect. He says that when destitution exists, the possession of private property is a humiliation rather than an opportunity. There is wide general excitement. In the smoking-room, Harvie Watt,[2] Winston's P.P.S., is 'sounding opinion'. He asks Labour Members whether they will agree not to vote against the Government if they are given the immediate appointment of a Minister of Social Security. The more moderate say that they will do this. Aneurin Bevan, however, is adamant. Bellenger[3] says that the Labour Party would really prefer the Tories to run the war provided that Labour runs the peace. He would like the Government to be defeated tomorrow, for Winston to form another Government without the Labour Members, and for Labour to act as the official Opposition pledged to support the Government in all matters directly affecting the war effort. I tell Harvie Watt that the Government ought to have realised the depth of feeling; that they ought to have said, 'This we cannot do, but that we can.' To accept the Report in principle, and then qualify that acceptance by all manner of dodges, merely creates suspicion. There is a great deal of loose thinking about the Beveridge Report. The Government would have scored if they had pointed out that 30 per cent of it was dependent upon imponderables, and that they would accept the remaining 70 per cent. In fact Kingsley Wood is too adroit to deal with an emotional

[1] Conservative M.P. for Oxford City since 1938. He was then aged 35.
[2] Conservative M.P. for Richmond since 1937. He was Parliamentary Private Secretary to Winston Churchill from July 1941 to July 1945.
[3] F. J. Bellenger, Labour M.P. for Bassetlaw. Secretary-of-State for War, 1946–47.

situation like this. I fear they may drag out Winston tomorrow to crack the whip of National Unity. I hope he can keep clear of this. If only he had refused to head the Conservative Party!

DIARY   *18th February, 1943*

The Labour Party have met in the morning, and have insisted upon voting in favour of their own revised amendment against the wishes and advice of their leaders. James Griffiths[1] opens the debate. He takes the line, 'I speak the mind of the people.' He sneers at the words 'export trade' as if it were 'vested interests'. 'Our people', he says, 'pay for the export trade in lack of food.' Herbert Morrison winds up. He admits that a vote of the Labour Party against the Government 'will raise constitutional and Parliamentary issues of a serious order'. He makes a fine clear speech. Had it been made on the first or second day, there would not have been any Division at all. The Labour Party listen in silence and in unspoken sympathy.

Then we have the Division. 338 to 121. This means that if one deducts the Cabinet Ministers, Parliamentary Secretaries and P.P.S.s, practically all the Labour Party have voted against.[2] They may now ask their Ministers to retire from the Government. A major political crisis would then arise.

I met Beveridge in the lobby, looking like the witch of Endor. I said, 'Well, are you enjoying this?' He said, 'I am having the fun of my life.' 'Upsetting Governments and wrecking constitutions?' He said, 'My two previous reports led to the fall of two Ministers.[3] This one may bring down a Government.' He is a vain man.

H.N. TO B.N. & N.N.   *20th February, 1943*
                                                       Sissinghurst

It was 'Red Army Week' in Leicester. It began with a luncheon at which I sat between an Air Marshal and the Soviet Air Attaché, a neat young man with a blue chin and insufficient English. He said to me, 'It is strange, not?—and pleasing for us—that our two air forces should be called R.A.F.' 'How's that?' I asked. 'Well, you have Royal Air Force and we have Red Air Force, no?' ' No!' I said, being, as you know, always infuriated by *le charme slav*. 'No. The Russian for red is *krassnoe*.' 'That is so', he answered with a smile of utter grace; 'we

---

[1] Labour M.P. for Llanelly since 1936. Minister of National Insurance, 1945–50.
[2] All but two. It was the only serious Labour revolt in the entire war.
[3] On the Coal Industry, 1925, and Unemployment Insurance, 1936.

call our Air Force *Krassnoe Podrasdelenie Sokol*, or, as you say, R.A.F.'
I do not care for falsity in any form. I do not care for Russians. I
loathe amateur theatricals. I detest music. And there, on that lovely
spring day, I had to march in a procession and then stand at a saluting
point, while the A.R.P. Wardens, the A.T.S., the W.A.A.F. and so on
marched past, eyes right, while the Air Attaché saluted hard and long.
Then, with a roll of drums and a fanfare of trumpets, we streamed into
the de Montfort Hall. The workers of Leicester lined our passage with
applause. I was horrified to see how pale and ill they all looked. Then
we sang a hymn and the Leicester choir rose in their hundreds to sing
about Alexander Nevsky and the drums rolled again, and everybody
behaved with the utmost foolishness.

Noel Coward was staying at the Grand Hotel, having a new play
tried out at the Leicester theatre. I entered his sitting-room as he was
having his bath. A valet was opening endless scent bottles and folding
clothes. There was a large apparatus in the corner, in front of which
Noel, clad only in a triangulo, seated himself with an expression of
intense desire and submitted himself to five minutes of infra-red,
talking gaily all the while. So patriotic he was, so light-hearted, and
so comfortable and well-served. He is a nice, nice man.

DIARY   *21st February, 1943*

I am worried, deeply worried, by the news from Tunisia. The
Americans have taken a severe knock at Gafsa and have been driven
back on the hills. The Germans then capture the Kasserine Pass and
drive on to Tebessa. The Guards are hurriedly sent down to Sbiba,
which they hold. But all the German strength will be concentrated
on them, and it looks as if the 1st Army may be defeated before the
8th arrive. I sleep badly.

DIARY   *22nd February, 1943*

Dine with our Monday Evening Club, which is a group of British
and Americans. I have to address them afterwards. I say that a difficult
diplomatic situation may arise between us, Russia and the U.S.A. The
Russians will demand a gigantic reward which may entail the suppression of the independence of ten smaller powers. America's mis-
sionary spirit will resent this, and her isolationist spirit will not allow
her to help us resist it. Anti-British opinion will concentrate on the
theme that America had again been ensnared by British propaganda,
and that so far from making the world safe for democracy, we have

made it safe for Jo Stalin. It would have been better to take Germany's side. T. S. Eliot,[1] who is there, thinks that the only cure is a great international federation into which the smaller powers can merge without thinking too much about their independence. Ed Murrow refers to my 'soul-satisfying pessimism', but agrees with what I say. Dick Law is neutral.

H.N. TO B.N. & N.N.   *9th March, 1943*
                                                        Sissinghurst

I came up for the election of the new Speaker.[2] It was clear that the only possible candidate was Clifton Brown.[3] The Serjeant at Arms, with the mace at his shoulder, stalked into the House as the clock struck 11, and laid the mace under the table. The Senior Clerk thereupon rose and darted out an arm and accusing finger at Anthony Eden. The latter informed us that His Majesty had been pleased to signify his assent to our electing a new Speaker. Clifton Brown meanwhile was sitting all careless on a back-bench, dressed in a very neat morning coat. So his name was proposed and seconded, and when the proposer and seconder advanced towards him, he made defensive gestures, indicative of reluctance. Firmly they grasped him by the arm and propelled him, resisting slightly, to the Chair. He stood there, looking very small and thin, and said a few words of thanks. He then tucked his tails under his arms and sat down. Since then he has appeared in his gown and wig. For all these years I have been accustomed to see that wig, that throne, framing the Carolean features of Fitzroy; saturnine he was, and sallow, and tall. Clifton Brown is pink and gay and white. The effect is strange. It is like seeing the fireman's nephew, on holiday from Wolverhampton, putting on his uncle's helmet.

DIARY   *12th March, 1943*

I dine at Pratts with Osbert Lancaster and Charles Peake. Charles tells me about the latest de Gaulle row. De Gaulle had decided to go to Syria and Charles had been instructed to say No. '*Alors*', he had said, '*je suis prisonnier.*' He retired to Hampstead. Winston had telephoned Charles saying, 'I hold you responsible that the Monster of Hampstead does not escape.' Charles had wanted to hint that he was being kept

[1] He was born in St Louis, U.S.A., in 1888.
[2] The previous Speaker, Captain E. A. Fitzroy, had died in office on 3rd March.
[3] Douglas Clifton Brown, later Lord Ruffside. He remained Speaker until October 1951.

for the invasion of France, but had been told that this would not happen till 1944. Winston was enraged with de Gaulle, since he had at first refused to come to Casablanca. Roosevelt had said, 'Your cock won't come on to the field.' This had hurt Winston's vanity. Poor Charles!

H.N. TO B.N. & N.N.   *18th March, 1943*
                                                        Sissinghurst

We had a debate on the reform of the Foreign Service. The main idea is to fuse the Diplomatic with the Consular and Commercial Services. I have been in favour of it for thirty years. But the debate went wrong as usual. The women Members felt that their rights were being trampled on, and staged a full-dress attack on the exclusion of women from the Service. Nancy Astor, as the senior woman Member, insisted on voicing their complaint. She has one of those minds that work from association to association, and therefore spreads sideways with extreme rapidity. Further and further did she diverge from the point while Mrs Tate beside her kept on saying, 'Get back to the point, Nancy. You were talking about the 1934 Committee.' 'Well, I come from Virginia', said Lady Astor, 'and that reminds me, when I was in Washington. . . .' I was annoyed by this, as I knew that I was to be called after her. It was like playing squash with a dish of scrambled eggs. Anyhow I made my speech and it went well enough. Lady Astor had said that women had never been given any chance to show their capacity in foreign politics. I said that they might not have been *given* chances, but from the days of Helen of Argos to the days of the Noble Lady the Member for the Sutton Division of Plymouth they had *taken* chances, and that the results had been disastrous. 'You mean mistresses', shouted Lady Astor. I said No, I was thinking of women's virtues and not their frailties. Intuition and sympathy were the two main feminine virtues, and each of these was of little value in diplomacy.

H.N. TO B.N. & N.N.   *28th March, 1943*
                                                        Sissinghurst

I had a talk with de Gaulle which I cannot repeat for security reasons.[1] I suggested to him that it was a good thing that de Bergeret[2] had been dismissed. I suggested that it would not be a very good thing if he

[1] He did not give de Gaulle's replies in his diary, nor in his letter to V.S-W.
[2] Member of the Committee of National Liberation in Algiers.

285

delayed too long his overt reconciliation with Giraud. And, by the way, I see that Bergeret's successor is 'M. Maurice Couve de Murville'. He is stated in *The Times* to be a very young man. Can it be the tutor who came to Long Barn?[1] I remember trying to teach him to repeat the sonnet 'When in disgrace with fortune and men's eyes'.

The general impression in the House is that the Labour Party will sooner or later insist upon their leaders leaving the Cabinet and thus breaking up the Coalition. They will not do so if things go badly, and even if they do, they will pledge themselves to support Winston in the conduct of the war. But they feel that they must retain their liberty to fight bye-elections and to form a Government of their own if the electorate return them to power. People do not think that this will happen immediately, but they expect it to happen within the next four months. This will give the Young Tory group which is gathering round Quintin Hogg, Hinchingbrooke[2] and Hugh Molson a great opportunity. As usual the Tory Party will be saved by its young men.

DIARY   *30th March, 1943*

Winston after Questions announces that Freyberg's swing towards El Hamma has succeeded and that we have got the Mareth Line plus Gabes.[3] The House cheers loudly, but Winston shakes his head at them. 'I should not close,' he adds, wagging his fat cheeks in denial, 'without uttering a warning against underrating the task which lies before the Allied Armies and Air Forces in Tunisia. The country is very difficult and abounds in defensive positions.' Ivor Thomas gets a laugh by asking, 'Is the Rt. Hon. Gentleman aware that if General Montgomery were in the German Army, he would still be a sergeant?'[4]

I go to the Lords to hear their debate on the reform of the Foreign

---

[1] M. de Murville, who became French Foreign Minister in 1958, had been engaged by H.N. as French tutor to Ben and Nigel during the summer holidays of 1928, when he was aged 21.

[2] Viscount Hinchingbrooke, who succeeded his father as Lord Sandwich in 1962 and renounced his peerage to become Victor Montagu, had been Conservative M.P. for South Dorset since 1941, and was Chairman of the Tory Reform Committee, 1943–44.

[3] The Mareth Line had been outflanked by the New Zealand Division's wide sweep through the desert, and the whole Mareth defences were in Montgomery's hands by 28th March.

[4] This referred to the Socialist quip, 'If Rommel had served in the British Army, he would still be a sergeant.'

Service. I stand there lolling over the barrier and Beaverbrook comes up and nudges me. 'Like to come in here, Harold? You could, you know. Come along!' I do not want to get a peerage. But I should like to succeed to one, were it not that this would mean a further holocaust among my nephews.[1]

Lunch at the Beefsteak. Duff startles me by breaking into a lovely rendering of the last lines of *The Land*.[2] 'What a poem!' he says.

I go back to the Lords. Bobbety Cranborne makes a splendid speech in reply. His father[3] sits next to him, listening through his telephone apparatus. What a family these Cecils are! And what amuses me is to think that Bobbety, who is a master of every Parliamentary art, broke down completely in his maiden speech. I feel a little ashamed at comparing the quality of the House of Lords debate with our own on the same subject.

Violet [Bonham Carter] rings up. She is in agony. A telegram has arrived saying that Mark is missing.[4]

---

[1] H.N. was the third son of the first Baron Carnock. His father died in 1928. His eldest brother, Frederick, succeeded to the title and died unmarried in 1952. His second brother, Eric, then succeeded, and had two sons, Peter and David. Peter was killed in action in 1942, and David Nicolson is now (1967) heir to the Carnock barony.

[2] V.S-W.'s long pastoral poem, which had been awarded the Hawthornden Prize in 1927, ends as follows:

> Then thought I, Virgil, how from Mantua reft,
> Shy as a peasant in the courts of Rome,
> Thou took'st the waxen tablets in thy hand,
> And out of anger cut calm tales of home.

The poem was based upon Virgil's *Georgics*, and she wrote the second part of it while she was staying with H.N. in Persia in 1926.

[3] The 4th Marquess of Salisbury, who had held several Government offices and was Leader of the House of Lords, 1925–29. He died in 1947 at the age of 85. His son, Lord Cranborne, later the 5th Marquess, was called to the House of Lords in 1941 as Lord Cecil, and was Leader of the House, 1942–45 and 1951–57.

[4] Mark Bonham Carter, Lady Violet's elder son, was then aged 21. He was serving as a subaltern in the 6th Battalion, Grenadier Guards, which attacked an outpost of the Mareth Line during the night 16–17th March. His company reached its objective, but was surrounded by the Germans, who took him prisoner. Later in the year he escaped from a German prison-camp in Italy, and returned safely to London in October 1943.

3rd April, 1943
Sissinghurst

We have been following the Tunisian battle with unceasing interest. It is not merely that Nigel is there. I should rather have fought that campaign than any other short of Waterloo. It seems to me strategically and tactically an almost perfect operation of war. The popularity of Rommel in this country is second only to that of Montgomery. Alexander is respected and admired: but Monty is the chap for the people. You can imagine how this irritates me. But Alexander is the darling of the Cabinet. They think him wonderful.

Poor Violet, she is in a dreadful state. She says to herself, 'On that day, at that hour, we were here drinking coffee and listening to the wireless.' She imagines agonising things. Moreover she thinks that if Mark had been with the 3rd Battalion, he would have been among people whom he really knew and liked. He would have shared that gaiety of which Virginia Cowles[1] has so lavishly informed London. He would have been the happy warrior. As it is, he arrived with a draft, was surrounded by strange faces, and did not, it seems, have that sense of adventure and companionship which must be the only solace of war. She told me this in the little waiting-room where we hang our hats at the B.B.C. She spoke so calmly, and then she broke down. Now, when silly people cry, I am merely irritated. But to see a strong person, and one whom I so deeply admire, break down and sob, is to me a real anguish. It goes round and round in my head.

9th April, 1943
Sissinghurst

I was visited by an elderly but earnest American at King's Bench Walk. His function, it seems, is strategic research, and I gather that this means that he travels throughout the country reporting on British morale and the attitude of the ordinary Englishman to the United States. Not, I should imagine, a very enlivening enquiry. Anyhow he sat down and asked me for my reactions. I said that such prejudice as existed (and, really, there is not much) should be divided into an upper and a lower level. He was thrilled by this, since it suggested graphs and pseudo-scientific diagrams. The upper level were afraid that

[1] The American author and journalist, who married Aidan Crawley, M.P., in 1945. She had visited the 1st Guards Brigade at Thala and Sbiba, and had broadcast on her return to London a glowing account of what she had seen.

America would insist on imposing its idealism upon Europe, and would then withdraw into a self-righteous shell. The lower level did not care for American boasting, much disliked their being richer than our men, and thought that all their Hemingway he-men were soft, hating cold, shuddering in the slightest draught, and starting to limp if asked to walk more than two miles. Oh my God! he wrote all this down in a really horrible pocket-book bound in crocodile-skin.

After the junction of the 8th and 1st Armies in southern Tunisia, it was hoped that together they might succeed in separating the Afrika Korps from Von Arnim's army in the north by breaking through the mountain barrier at Fondouk and capturing the port of Sousse. The attempt was made on 9th April, but although Kairouan fell on the 11th and Sousse next day, the Germans had escaped and formed a tight line at Enfidaville which was extended in a wide loop to the north coast, covering Tunis and Bizerta. The Germans continued to reinforce their armies by air all through April, losing heavily to the R.A.F., and made several spoiling attacks against the Americans on the Allies' left flank. The Enfidaville position was too strong to pierce, and in great secrecy three Divisions of the 8th Army were transferred to the 1st Army's front south of Medjez-el-Bab. Here on 6th May they attacked in great strength on a narrow front, and broke through. Within 36 hours Tunis fell to the British and Bizerta to the Americans. The 6th Armoured Division, of which the 1st Guards Brigade formed a part, then swung east and south, breaking through the defile of Hamman Lif on the 9th, and took the Afrika Korps north of Enfidaville in the rear. All was over by 12th May. 250,000 prisoners were taken: only 650 men of the Axis armies escaped. Von Arnim was captured, but Rommel himself had been invalided back to Germany in mid-March. It was a tremendous victory and the vindication of Churchill's whole strategy. He received the news at Washington, for which he had sailed in the 'Queen Mary' on 4th May.

H.N. TO B.N. & N.N.   *13th April, 1943*
                                                       Sissinghurst

I lunched with Raymond [Mortimer] and Palewski, de Gaulle's Chef du Cabinet. A great deal of my time is spent trying to pour oil on these troubled waters. All might have been well had de Gaulle been an ordinary General or even an ordinary man. He is not. He is an extraordinary man. He is an eagle with bad habits. Winston, who is a house-trained eagle, does not see claw to claw with him. In theory the difference between the two G's is that Giraud wants to constitute a Council from the existing pro-consuls[1] and then surrender his authority to some French body the moment France is liberated. De Gaulle wishes to create something more representative by making a Council out of the existing Deputies, the elements of resistance, the underground people and the Algerian *Conseils Généraux*. But this is not the real difference. The real difference is (a) personal—who will be top dog?; and (b) ideological. Giraud is thinking in terms of 1920. De Gaulle realises that France is in a revolutionary mood and that no authority will have any prestige which is based on the old gang. Giraud won't see this. And when de Gaulle suggests it to him, he replies, '*Mais, excusez-moi, mon Général, je connais la France d'aujourdhui mieux que vous.*' Which simply is not true. What did he know of the French Underground in his villa at Cap d'Antibes?

DIARY   *14th April, 1943*

I go to the Aeolian Hall for the poetry reading organised by Osbert and Edith Sitwell for the benefit of the Free French. The Queen arrives accompanied by the two Princesses. The poets file in—Masefield,[2] T. S. Eliot, Gordon Bottomley, Arthur Waley, Edmund Blunden and Vita. Masefield pays a tribute to Laurence Binyon,[3] and then the readings start. I cannot hear most of them as I am in the gallery and they are muffled by a lectern which Osbert found in the Caledonian Market. I am impressed by Eliot's reading from *The Waste Land* and rather moved by the Poet Laureate. Then there is an interval during which the poets are received by the Queen in an anteroom. Then the second series begins, and Viti reads her piece. She stands there looking magnificent and modest, and recites *The Land* quite perfectly. I hear a low murmur of delight passing through the audience. She was by far the best of the lot and I am so proud of her. She is as serene as a swan.

DIARY   *15th April, 1943*

When I enter the Chairman's room at the B.B.C., the old boy is all gay. 'Good news', he says. 'Lady Violet's son is a prisoner.' It seems that last night the monitoring people picked up a message from the

[1] Peyrouton, Governor General of Algeria; Noguès, Governor General of Morocco; and Boisson, Governor General of French West Africa.
[2] John Masefield, Poet Laureate since 1930.
[3] He had originally been included in the programme, but died on 10th March.

Vatican: 'Lieutenant Mark Bonham Carter.' They had got on to Bongie,[1] as Violet was at Clovelly. What joy for them.

DIARY   *20th April, 1943*

In the smoking-room I talk to Duff[Cooper] about the poetry reading. Suddenly I see a look of embarrassment in his eye, and find that Winston has come to sit next to us. As usual he is very gay. He has a small glass of port. I ask him about the German wireless reports on the Katyn massacres.[2] He grins grimly. 'The less said about that the better.' I tell him that Nigel expected the Americans to catch the Germans on the flank at Fondouk. 'Tell him', he says, 'from me, that it is now going to be scrunch and punch.' He says that the transport 'planes which we have shot down in such numbers were on their way back to Sicily from Tunis having landed Von Arnim's reinforcements. 'I only pray', he says, 'that they were not carrying our prisoners.' The thought of Mark flashes through my mind. I ask him what is the present position of the Bey of Tunis. He says, with one of his most delighted grins, 'He is in a most unfortunate position: a position of great humiliation: he is at the mercy of the Germans: he will have to call himself *Obey* in future.'

DIARY   *22nd April, 1943*

I have a long talk with Brendan [Bracken]. He says that the battle in Tunisia is reaching its start, and will be the most terrific battle ever seen. We are already ahead of our programme. The 1st Army is in action, and doing well. He cannot tell me the date that Montgomery has fixed for his entry into Tunis, but if I knew it I would be amazed.[3] 'Monty has always made rash predictions, and has always carried them out.' He says that we have an overwhelming fleet ready; that our concentration of aircraft under Tedder is such as the world has never seen; and that we shall prevent any real evacuation and crush them to pieces. He says that Eisenhower is much mortified by the poor part played by the U.S. armies and that Alexander has cheered

1 Sir Maurice Bonham Carter.
2 On 13th April the German wireless had charged the Soviets with the murder of 14,500 Polish prisoners of war at Katyn, Poland, captured during the German–Russian invasion of Poland in 1939. The Germans claimed to have found the bodies buried in mass graves. The Russians counter-claimed that the Germans had murdered these men. The Poles broke off diplomatic relations with the Soviet Government.
3 7th May, the date on which Tunis actually fell.

him up by saying that our own 8th Army was no good at first. He is worried by the American Press, which is now boosting the British, a thing that he regards with suspicion. He had been seeing the new incendiary bomb which is Harris's[1] pet. It is a devil. He had also seen photographs of Cologne and Essen. At the former place we hit the shelter in front of the Cathedral with one of our largest bombs and blew it to pieces. At the latter place there is not a roof standing.

Dine with Jim Lees-Milne at Brooks. It has retained all its old atmosphere. The Travellers, on the other hand, has become a battered caravanserai, in which the scum of the lower London clubs are served inadequately by scared Lithuanian waitresses.

V.S-W. TO H.N.   *22nd April, 1943*
                                                        Sissinghurst

Darling, I have been reading your book[2] instead of writing my own.[3] You *do* write well. I know this, because reading even a page of yours instantly fills me with the desire to write myself—it is an uplift instead of a dejection—and we have always agreed that this is the true test. Whenever I open a page of yours, it never fails. It is not only that you are a good stylist, but that you have your unmistakable voice. I am so proud of you.

DIARY   *2nd May, 1943*

The news from Tunisia is none too good. We have had heavy casualties and the Germans have regained most of the ground we had taken. But the really big push, I suppose, has not begun yet.

H.N. TO B.N. & N.N.   *4th May, 1943*
                                                        Sissinghurst

I went down to dine and sleep with the Vansittarts[4] at Denham. Van and I walked about the garden discussing foreign affairs. There he is— having reached the summit of his profession, having twice refused the Embassy at Paris, loaded with stars and ribbons, a peer, married to a lovely wife, owning a beautiful Queen Anne mansion replete with

---

[1] Marshal of the Royal Air Force Sir A. T. Harris, Commander-in-Chief, Bomber Command, 1942–45.
[2] *The Desire to Please*, published in May by Constable.
[3] *The Eagle and the Dove*.
[4] Sir Robert Vansittart had been created Baron Vansittart in 1941, when he retired as Chief Diplomatic Adviser to the Foreign Secretary.

tapestry and pictures, conscious that he is still a leading figure in public life—and yet still mumbling about Chamberlain's betrayal of him and the ill-luck that has dogged his footsteps. I like Van, and have always liked him. But it is conceited to feel that such honours as have been showered upon him bear no relation to his true merit. He gave me a marvellous dinner: trout, lamb, fruit and a bottle of Pomeroy '98. I slept in an enormous four-poster bed in an enormous room, and my feet, when I crossed the carpet, made a long trail of footsteps in the pile.

H.N. TO B.N. & N.N.   *8th May, 1943*
                                                              Sissinghurst

I came down here yesterday, and we listened to the 9 pm. news. All we knew up till then was that the Americans were near Ferryville and that the 1st Army had entered Massicault. You can picture our surprise, therefore, when the announcer said that the Americans were in the outskirts of Bizerta and the 1st Army in the outskirts of Tunis. I went to bed shortly after, hugging myself with pleasure at the thought that the 1st Army had got there first. But I foresaw heavy fighting, and was worried about the probable destruction of Tunis. Lapped in these pleasant and anxious thoughts, I drifted off to sleep. I was suddenly awakened five minutes after midnight by Mummy standing at the door. She had been listening to the midnight news. 'Tunis', she said, not without a touch of drama, 'and Bizerta are ours.'[1] That is how the news came to Sissinghurst. A gale blowing outside and my open windows straining at their catches; my door opened against the light on my staircase; and Mummy standing there in her pyjamas enunciating these great truths.

I look out of my window as I write this and see the four yew trees twirling in the gale. 'Units of the 1st Army have entered the suburbs of Tunis.' The words swing in my mind. How drab in comparison are the events of my week here in England.

I dined last Monday with Rob Bernays. He says that the mistake I make in the House is not to be formidable. 'But, my dear Rob, I was not designed by nature to be formidable.' 'Well, take it from me, unless you become formidable, you will be overlooked.' 'But nobody

---

[1] The Derbyshire Yeomanry, the reconnaissance regiment of the 6th Armoured Division, reached the centre of Tunis at 4 p.m. on Friday, 7th May, thirty-six hours after the opening of the final offensive. In the same hour the Americans entered Bizerta.

can become formidable when he has been unformidable for 55 years.' 'You take it from me, Harold ...' So I suppose that something has got to be done.

DIARY   9th May, 1943

The German troops between Bizerta and Tunis, having been driven to the marshes at the mouth of the Medjerda, are surrendering. We have got 20,000 prisoners so far, including three Divisional Generals with their staffs. The rest of the enemy is fleeing into Cap Bon. What a weekend this has been!

DIARY   10th May, 1943

Lunch with Pierre Viénot[1] at Boulestin. He has been here only ten days, having been twice imprisoned by Vichy. He says that between Giraud and de Gaulle there is no real choice: Giraud is not a name at all in France; de Gaulle is more than a name, he is a legend. What did the Tunisians cry to our troops? '*Ou sont les Gaullistes?*' I say that if that be really the case, then de Gaulle can afford to be generous. What we have against him is his *mesquinerie*.[2] For instance, people here understood why de Gaulle refused to make terms with the Boissons, the Peyroutons and the Noguès.[3] But we did not understand his haggling over whether he met Giraud at Algiers or Biskra. He had taken his stand on a little point of procedure which was unworthy of him. I begged Viénot to ask de Gaulle, when he finally left, to write in his own hand a warm and grateful letter to Winston. A touch of well-timed sentimentality might soften Winston's heart.

He had seen Reynaud in prison. He said that he was as gay as a game-cock. Léon Blum is not in such good spirits. Herriot is a sick man. Mandel is fine. Pétain had sent a high General to him to enquire whether he had any complaints of his treatment. '*Monsieur*', replied Mandel, '*vous êtes au service de l'ennemi. Je vous prie de vous taire.*'

Dine at our Monday Evening Club. The guests are Anthony Eden and Harold Butler,[4] and on the American side, Winant. I have a talk with Anthony before we sit down. He says that Giraud is the vainest man alive and is convinced that he captured Tunis single-handed.

[1] He was soon to become de Gaulle's Diplomatic Representative with the British Government.
[2] 'Meanness.'   [3] See p. 290, note 1.
[4] Former Director of the International Labour Office, and Minister at H.M. Embassy, Washington, 1942–46.

He talks to us about his visit to the States.[1] He says that the danger is that the American Army will be too large. How could we ever transport such vast quantities of men? He had visited some of Kaiser's ship-yards.[2] The problem of housing the workmen is difficult indeed. They 'paste together' these ships at a tremendous rate. He said that he had seen landing-barges set off across the Atlantic under the charge of midshipmen. They took six weeks to arrive, but they arrived. He says that the Americans are very suspicious of Russia and that we must always remember that their hatred of Japan takes the form of love of China. He was astonished (and Butler confirmed this) to observe that the Indian question had completely died out in America. Nobody asked him any questions about India at all. He said that the State Department are not really backing de Gaulle. The only difference in our French policy is whether, when a de Gaulle–Giraud Government is established, we should recognise it as the Government of France. We wish to do so: the Americans do not.[3] He told us that Cordell Hull[4] had said to him, 'I do not pretend that if you and we are agreed, all European problems will be settled automatically. But I do contend that if we disagree, no problems will be settled at all.'

Go on to Pratts, where I meet Harold Balfour,[5] just back from Tunisia. He does not think that the Germans will hold out long on the Cap Bon peninsula. They are done. Dunkirk is avenged.

H.N. TO B.N. & N.N.   *11th May, 1943*
Sissinghurst

We had a short Secret Session[6] and then Attlee, as Deputy Prime Minister, made a statement about the Tunisian position. I cannot convey to you the absurdity of that small man. As someone remarked afterwards, 'It is difficult to make a defeat sound like a victory: but to

---

[1] Anthony Eden had been in Washington for nearly three weeks from 12th March.

[2] Henry J. Kaiser, the American industrialist, was the manager of seven ship-yards on the west coast of the United States.

[3] Anthony Eden later wrote of this controversy: 'It seemed to me that Roosevelt wanted to hold the strings of France's future in his own hands so that he could decide that country's fate. I did not like this and preferred a French civil authority to work with the Allied forces from an early stage.' Lord Avon. *The Reckoning* (Cassell, 1965), p. 372.

[4] Secretary of State of the United States, 1933–44.

[5] Later Lord Balfour of Inchrye. Conservative M.P. for the Isle of Thanet, 1929–45, and Parliamentary Under-Secretary of State for Air, 1938–44.

[6] To announce that Churchill had sailed for the United States on 4th May.

make such a victory sound like a defeat is a masterpiece in human ingenuity.' Attlee stood there like a little snipe pecking at a wooden cage. The House likes and respects him, but had he gone on five minutes more, we should burst into a *fou rire*. And what was so strange was that he did not give us the latest news. Already the word was circulating that the 6th Armoured Division had cut through Hammam Lif.[1] Already we knew they were at Grombalia, and even on the outskirts of Hammamet. But Attlee just pecked and pecked as if nothing had happened.

DIARY   *12th May, 1943*

I meet Viénot and Massigli at the Club. The latter says that people in this country have no conception of the effect on German opinion of the Tunis disaster. Their propaganda—in that it led them to expect a stand in the Tunis–Bizerta triangle, and later on at Cap Bon—has been very unwise. It will come as a thunderbolt to an opinion wholly unprepared.

I return and switch on the midnight news. 'The long African campaign is over. General von Arnim has been captured. The total of our prisoners now numbers 150,000.'[2]

The summer months saw the fall of Mussolini and the capitulation of Italy. For some time past the Italian people had become increasingly critical of the régime, following the loss of the entire Italian Empire in Africa and the undisguised contempt shown by Germany towards Italy. Mussolini himself was sick and defeatist. Not even Hitler could rally his flagging spirits at their meeting at Feltre on 19th July. Mussolini returned to Rome to face a constitutional crisis. On 24th July the Fascist Grand Council, led by Grandi and Ciano, voted to replace him in office by a National Government under the supreme authority of the King, and on the next day Mussolini was arrested and detained on the island of Ponza and later in the Abruzzi. A provisional Government was set up under Badoglio, who publicly declared that 'the war continues' but secretly opened negotiations with the Allies.

After the capture of Pantellaria on 11th June, a large Anglo-American

[1] The Division had forced the defile of Hammam Lif, and captured the Bey of Tunis in the town, by dusk on 9th May. At that moment, 11 a.m. on 11th May, they were entering Hammamet, thus completing the sealing-off of the base of the Cap Bon peninsula.

[2] When they had all been counted, the total was nearer a quarter of a million.

*army invaded Sicily on 10th July. The entire island was in Allied hands
by 17th August. On the 31st the Badoglio Government accepted terms
of unconditional surrender, and the Armistice was signed at Syracuse on
3rd September, the very day on which the 8th Army leapt the Messina
straits to land in the toe of Italy at Reggio. But the Armistice was not
publicly announced until the 8th, at the moment when other Allied invasion forces were approaching Taranto and the Salerno beaches. In a
few hours the Germans occupied the whole country by force. The
Badoglio Government escaped from Rome and sought the protection of
the Allies at Brindisi, and the larger part of the Italian Fleet managed to
reach Malta. But Churchill's hope that the Allies might immediately
occupy Italy as far as the Pisa–Ancona line, or even the line of the Po,
was disappointed. They were obliged to fight their way up the peninsula
against increasing German resistance. Even the great majority of our
prisoners were removed from Italian to German camps before they could
be liberated.*

*Many of these events had been controlled by Churchill and Roosevelt
from Quebec, where they met on 17th July. Churchill did not return to
England until 20th September. At the Quebec Conference, detailed
decisions were made to launch Operation Overlord, the invasion of
Normandy, in the early summer of 1944, and firmer plans were laid for
the reconquest of south-east Asia, of which Mountbatten was made
Supreme Allied Commander.*

*Almost the only point of friction between the Americans and British
concerned the continuing rivalry between de Gaulle and Giraud in North
Africa. The British were committed to the support of de Gaulle, but
Cordell Hull, the American Secretary of State, influenced his President to
withhold full recognition of the French Committee of National Liberation
in Algiers, on which both de Gaulle and Giraud sat in uneasy partnership.
Churchill was determined that the issue should not cause a breach between
the western Allies, and a compromise was reached at Quebec which gave
the Committee semi-official recognition on a day-to-day basis, without
implying that its authority would automatically extend to Metropolitan
France once it was liberated. The struggle for power between the two
French Generals continued under this pretence of unanimity, but de
Gaulle gradually won the upper hand because his name was already the
symbol of national resistance in France itself, where Giraud's meant
little or nothing. Harold Nicolson was deeply involved in this dispute at
the London end, having great respect and qualified admiration for de
Gaulle, and seeing much of his supporters and his detractors in Britain.*

The war which won the war was meanwhile being waged in Russia. Within two months, July and August, any German hopes of recovery were shattered in the three great battles of Kursk, Orel and Kharkov. By September the German armies were in full retreat along the whole central and southern fronts. Stalin waged this crucial battle almost in isolation. He had not been invited to Quebec; he was deeply disappointed by the postponement of 'Overlord' from 1943 to 1944; and Allied convoys to Russia were temporarily suspended.

DIARY   *17th May, 1943*

Dine with Sibyl [Colefax] at Lord North Street. The Devonshires, Camroses, Rothermeres, Desmond Morton and D'Arcy Osborne were there. Morton[1] told me that Monsignor Spellman (Archbishop of New York) has cast a spell over Churchill. Spellman had told him exactly what he intended to say to De Valera. Churchill replied, 'I would not say that, Monsignor; you will give the poor man a fit.' 'Far be it from me', answered the Archbishop 'to cause the death of any man, but if Almighty God should wish that De Valera should lose his life on hearing the truth, I shall say many Masses for his soul.' D'Arcy Osborne[2] does not share this enthusiasm for Spellman, who is much affected by the desire to please and apparently gave the Vatican the impression that he was bitterly anti-British. We discuss the future of Italy. Osborne is convinced that there will be a great and universal desire to get out of the war, coupled with the realisation that Italy in her present condition must lose her Empire and will only exchange one form of occupation for another. The latest idea is that we should give Libya to the Maltese.

DIARY   *28th May, 1943*

I speak in Leicester on 'When will the war end?' I say that it all depends on what happens during the next few weeks in Russia and on the Second Front. If we succeed, or at least deny the Germans success, then indeed it may end this year. But if the Germans knock out Russia, it may not end till 1945. In any case, we shall then be left with Japan, and it will be hard indeed to keep the British public interested in a Japanese war.

---

[1] Personal Assistant to the Prime Minister, 1940–46.
[2] Sir D'Arcy Osborne, British Minister to the Holy See, 1936–47.

DIARY   *1st June, 1943*

Go to Chips'[1] house to meet Field-Marshal Wavell.[2] A stocky man
with one blind eye. I am reminded of the day when I was waiting in
the ante-room of the Quai d'Orsay and there entered a square little
man clasping an enormous portfolio. I thought, 'That must be a
sergeant in the Ordnance Department come with statistics for his chief.'
I then thought, 'What a remarkable face for a sergeant!' I then
thought, 'My God, it's Foch!' Wavell was rather restless and embarrassed. He talked to me about his book on Allenby in which he
corrects or contradicts a statement I made in *Curzon*. I say I do not
mind. What worries him, I think, is that Chips has also invited some
of the wives of his staff. They arrive rather dim and defiant, and call
him 'General Archie'. Chips has also asked M.P.s and Lady Willing-
don and Leonard Woolley.[3] They do not fuse very well. That is what
makes Wavell anxious and ill at ease.

DIARY   *2nd June, 1943*

I find a message from Bobbety Cranborne asking me to come and see
him in the Lords. I do so. He has had qualms about my diary, thinks
that he is depriving the world of a new Greville, has spoken to Anthony
Eden (who had said, 'Tell him to go ahead'), and was in fact anxious for
me to reconsider my decision not to publish.[4]

DIARY   *8th June, 1943*

Winston makes a statement about his visits to Washington and Tunis.[5]
It is not a dramatic speech but is effective for what he leaves out. There
is understatement of our victory rather than jubilation. He is extremely
cautious and moderate. But in a way I think the House liked it better
even than his most triumphant oratory. It was so eminently strong,
powerful, sincere and confident. He ended by paying a tribute to the
House itself. He had a great reception.

In the smoking-room afterwards he was in splendid form. He had
been much amused by a story of an American chaplain, who, when a

[1] Henry Channon, Conservative M.P. for Southend since 1935.
[2] Wavell was then Commander-in-Chief, India, but his appointment as Viceroy was
to be announced on 19th June. He took up his appointment in October.
[3] Sir Leonard Woolley, the archaeologist and excavator of Ur.
[4] See p. 182. H.N., in spite of this encouragement, did not proceed with the idea of
publishing his 1939 Diary, thinking it premature and liable to give offence.
[5] Churchill had been in Washington from 11th to 26th May, and thence went to
Algiers and Tunis.

German major complained of the lack of organisation in the prisoners' cages, replied, 'It is no good talking to me. I came out here to bury you guys.'

H.N. TO B.N. & N.N.   *9th June, 1943*
                                                        Sissinghurst

At the Beefsteak I sat next to Osbert Sitwell. He told me that he had been a subaltern with General Alexander and liked him well. They used to go to London dances together and walk back in the dawn discussing life and battle. Years later he had met him again on a Channel steamer and had said to him, 'Alex, between ourselves, you are really a very clever man, aren't you?' Their relations had not been disturbed by this remark, and continued intimate for many years. A few days ago Osbert was leaving a shop in Curzon Street when he felt a tap on his shoulder. 'Hullo, Osbert!' said a voice. Osbert turned to find himself confronted by Scipio Africanus. In the interval, their relative proportions had changed. Osbert, being sensitive to this, completely lost his head. He blushed, he babbled, he showed utter and unrestrained embarrassment. He could see in Scipio's eye a look that meant, 'My God, are all my old friends going to behave in this way?' Osbert, still blushing and babbling, broke away, cursing himself for his ineptitude at having failed to cope with what was an unusual, but still not an insurmountable, social occasion. So he went into Berry Bros., and to rectify his ungainliness, sent Scipio a magnum of champagne.

Back I went to the House (having enjoyed this story, since it is a good illustration of shifting values) where I received a deputation of tomato-growers. In they trooped in their country clothes. I took them to a Committee Room and managed to gather together a few other M.P.s. Their spokesman addressed us on the injustice being imposed on tomato-growers by the Ministry of Food. I took notes. I said a few vague and hopeful things, and one of them presented me with a huge tomato. I do not in any circumstances like carrying objects in my hand, even when these objects are small and hard and dry. I roamed the lobbies miserably holding the thing in my palm as if it were an orb of majesty instead of a huge and squashy vegetable. Then I darted into the kitchen and laid it firmly on the table. 'Thank you, sir', said one of the cooks, as if it were customary for M.P.s to appear suddenly like Pomona and deposit upon their tables the teeming riches of the soil.

I had that evening to go to a *conversazione* given by the Authors' Society. As it had taken me some time to dispose of my tomato, I arrived late and H. G. Wells was already talking nonsense in front of a microphone and a plate of biscuits. Gilbert Murray also spoke. Thereafter I mingled with my fellow authors. There was Rose Macaulay and G. M. Trevelyan and Elizabeth Bowen and Lady Astor and Lindsay Drummond[1] and Arthur Koestler.[2] The latter talked to me about Richard Hillary.[3] He is editing some book about him or a collection of correspondence. This is always a guilty spot in me. I do not like heroes. I feel mean about all this, but I do not like the T. E. Lawrence brood. Koestler is intelligent on the subject. He thinks that Hillary would have become a great writer. He says that he was marred first by his amazing good looks, secondly, after his skin-graft, by his horrifying ugliness. But surely, surely, the man was a cad at heart, even as T.E.L. was a cad at heart. The literary temperament is only tolerable so long as it remains cowardly. Once it becomes courageous it is an unpleasant thing to meet.

DIARY   *12th June, 1943*

Begin on my Introduction to the new edition of *Peacemaking*.[4]

Pantellaria was occupied yesterday morning, after a month's plastering from sea and sky.[5] De Gaulle has started a new row with the local Generals, this time on Army organisation.

DIARY   *21st June, 1943*

I go to see Pierre Viénot at Carlton Gardens. He is to be made the Ambassador of the National Committee in London. I found him deeply depressed. The negotiations between Giraud and de Gaulle at Algiers had almost resulted in an agreement. Giraud had made several concessions, the result of which would have been to enable de Gaulle to create a new French Army, highly technical, and led by young and

[1] The publisher.
[2] Author of *Darkness at Noon* (1940), *Arrival and Departure* (1943), *The Yogi and the Commissar* (1945), etc.
[3] The Battle of Britain pilot and author of *The Last Enemy*. He was terribly burned when shot down during the Battle, and his face was re-made by plastic surgery. He was killed in an air accident in January 1943.
[4] First published by Constable in 1933. Revised edition, with new Introduction, 1943.
[5] The Italian fortified island between Tunisia and Sicily. It was subjected to constant naval and air bombardment after the fall of Tunis, and surrendered to a small British force on 11th June. Over 11,000 prisoners were taken with negligible losses to the Allies.

ardent men. But at the last moment Eisenhower, in his capacity as C.-in-C., summoned the two Generals and insisted that Giraud should be in supreme command. The latter had then withdrawn all the concessions which he had previously made. The effect of this upon the Fighting French will be disastrous. He hoped that de Gaulle would take it reasonably and would not go off to Brazzaville in disgust. He showed me in confidence a telegram sent to de Gaulle by the four leaders of the Resistance movement who happen to be in London at the moment. They begged him to remain in North Africa and to wait in patience for the day when his cause would triumph.

Viénot takes a gloomy view. He knows how difficult de Gaulle is and what political blunders he often makes. But he says that nonetheless de Gaulle is the only man whose legend is strong enough to rally the whole French people. The idea of getting back to the old France represented by Giraud and his friends is pure fantasy. By their intervention the Americans have faced France with civil war.

H.N. TO B.N. & N.N.   *23rd June, 1943*
                                                          Sissinghurst

We had a coal debate at which Gwilym Lloyd George made a heavy impressive speech. His old father sat opposite, smiling in affectionate pride. In the lobby afterwards I bumped into the old man. 'Well,' I said, 'what did you think of Gwilym?' 'He lacks my fire', the old man answered. 'You see, Nicolson, he is not a Welshman. He is a Scandinavian. You have only to look at him to see that he is pure Scandinavian. His mother is directly descended from the Vikings.' It amused him saying that, and for an instant the old charm and vigour reappeared, but then once again there fell on his face that mask of extreme and inarticulate old age. He is now a yellow old man with a mane of dead-white hair, and uncertain movements of his feet and hands.

DIARY   *28th June, 1943*

People are becoming impatient with this long lull.[1] They know that the bombing of the Rhineland and Westphalia is a major operation of war and is doing great damage to the German war potential and morale. But we do not know where the blow is to fall and I stretch out my

[1] The Tunisian campaign ended on 12th May. The attack on Sicily began on 10th July. In the interval, apart from the capture of Pantellaria and neighbouring islands, there was no military activity in the Mediterranean.

hands (*caelo supinas manus*) to catch the first fat drops of the approaching storm. *Peut-être pas pour nous, mais cessera l'orage.*[1]

DIARY   *30th June, 1943*

Dine with the Belgian Ambassador. Sit next to the Prime Minister, Hubert Pierlot. He says that unless we feed Belgium soon, there will be starvation. Walk back with Moley Sargent.[2] He tells me that the F.O. are enraged with events in North Africa and our complete surrender to the Americans. The whole thing was not merely wrong; it was unnecessary. I see Osbert Lancaster afterwards. He tells me that Winston with his own hand wrote the directive instructing the Press to spread the idea that de Gaulle was not a friend of this country.

DIARY   *5th July, 1943*

Lunch with Viénot. Spaak, the Belgian Foreign Minister, is there. He tells me that Sikorski[3] and Victor Cazalet were killed last night in an aeroplane accident off Gibraltar. Sikorski's loss is a major blow. He was the only man who could control the fierce resentment of the Poles against Russia, and force them to bury their internecine strife. He is one of those rare people whom one can describe as irreplaceable.

Viénot is still very bitter about American intervention in Algiers. I think that someone has told him of Winston's famous remark to de Gaulle: '*Si vous m'opposerez, je vous liquiderai.*' It is a pity that so much personal vanity and rancour should have come into this business. There is the vanity of Cordell Hull, the rancour of Winston.

H.N. TO B.N. & N.N.   *14th July, 1943*
                                                              Sissinghurst

I dined at Pratts, meeting great puffs of optimism from the several Service swells there present. They are delighted at the collapse of the German offensive in Russia.[4] They are delighted at the present im-

---

[1] Louis Aragon. From *Le crève-coeur*, a volume of Resistance poems published in London during the war.
[2] Sir Orme Sargent, Permanent Under-Secretary of State for Foreign Affairs, 1946–49.
[3] General W. Sikorski, Prime Minister of the Polish Government and Commander-in-Chief of the Polish Army since 1939. Victor Cazalet had been political liaison officer to Sikorski since 1940.
[4] On 5th July Hitler had opened his offensive to regain Kursk. It was his last great offensive of the Russian campaign. The Russians were prepared for it, and it ended in a decisive defeat for the Germans.

provement in the Battle of the Atlantic. They are overjoyed by the bombing of Germany. But above all they are jubilant at the success of our Sicilian landings. I am not so optimistic. I do not believe that even if Italy collapses, we shall bring Germany down before October 1944.

H.N. TO V.S-W.   *14th July, 1943*
4 King's Bench Walk, E.C.4

An odd thing happened to me yesterday. I am puzzled by it. I went down to the House for the Colonial Debate and felt that I should say something about African education.[1] But somehow I felt that I could not do it. It was not nervousness, but a great wave of defeatism. 'What does it matter what I say?' I know that it may be due to liver or nerves or something. But I have never before lost confidence in myself to that extent. I must pull myself together, as otherwise I shall drop out of things. I do feel it strange that a person of my experience is so much ignored nowadays. I suppose that the fact that I got into the Government (and in a post where I *ought* to have made good) and was thereafter discarded, has created the impression that I am a dud. This must often happen to people. But what I mind is that it has damaged my self-confidence and that I have not got the guts to assert myself in face of a reputation for failure. This induces in me moods of depression which themselves increase my diffidence. I am furious with myself for not having spoken yesterday. I don't want to drift into being an old buffer.

V.S-W. TO H.N.   *15th July, 1943*
Sissinghurst

I am so glad that you have written as you have, because for some time I have been suspecting that something of the sort was going on in your head. I don't think you should attribute too much importance to your suddenly getting cold feet over speaking about African education. It is not a true loss of confidence, but a mere stage-fright. Your nerves were probably right in telling you not to speak, when your reason told you that you should. No, I don't worry about such temporary lapses, but I do worry about your tendency for dispersal. I feel that there is a tide in the affairs of men when they should go in for a little stock-taking and decide upon a definite line. You are now floating

[1] In 1937 H.N. had been a member of a Government Commission sent out under the chairmanship of Lord De la Warr to enquire into native education in East Africa.

on that tide, but instead of bobbing like a cork on different waves, I feel that it is time that you made an invasion, landing on some definite beach. It seems to me that your mind was never more vigorous or more capable of canalisation, but that you are allowing it to run into many little rills, each of them clear and useful, but in the aggregate detracting from the power of a main stream. Let me tabulate your activities in two separate categories:

(1) *Marginal Comment*.[1] Altogether admirable, a great success, well worthwhile; no question about that.

B.B.C. Financially essential; very useful, if only the position of the Governors can be reformed.

Free French. Yes, Important. You are specially well qualified.

Your own books. You know what I feel about these. One of your strongest suits, which, with curious modesty, you do not esteem nearly highly enough.

House of Commons. Well, obviously you must keep that on.

(2) *Endless Committees and odd speeches and odd articles*, mostly undertaken because you cannot say No. This is dispersal, and disapproved of by me. The energy and time you sacrifice to them could be better employed. To give you a concrete example, I was appalled when you said that you were going to write a book on the Colonies.[2]

To be constructive, I should like to see you scrap as much of (2) as possible, and devote yourself to *one* thing in their place. Personally I should like you to take up the rebuilding and planning of England, both urban and rural. I think you have very special gifts in this direction, but I believe that you have the idea that it is not sufficiently 'public life'. But do remember that the war will not go on for ever, and that the design of England will.

DIARY   *19th July, 1943*

We have our Monday Night Club for British and Americans. We dine in a private room at the Ritz. Our guest is Wavell, clad in civilian clothes. He tells us that when in command in Egypt, he was terrified by the consequences of the French collapse in 1940. 'I had',

[1] H.N.'s weekly articles for the *Spectator*.
[2] The Ministry of Information had asked him to do this. H.N. submitted a synopsis, but the Ministry turned it down as too independent an approach to the subject, and encouraged him to write the book for publication by non-official publishers. But he gave up the idea with some relief.

he said, 'been dreading bad news for three days. I went out to play golf at Gezira. When I had just done the 16th hole, my Intelligence Officer appeared in a great state with a telegram informing me of the capitulation of Bordeaux. I decided to finish the game. I am proud to think that I did the 17th in four and the 18th in three.' He then talked about the Indian Army, explaining how in the old days we took the cream, but now the quality of the troops is not as high as formerly and the problem of finding British officers, or trusting Indian officers, is very great. He said that the greatest problem of India was an economic one. They were increasing at the rate of ten millions a year and God knows what would happen to them in future. He gave us in a few chosen phrases (70,000 villages whose only communication with the outer world is a bullock track), and without mentioning Congress at all, the impression that it was a mere pimple on the surface of Indian life. He then spoke of the war with Japan. He spoke of the psychological difficulty of maintaining a fighting spirit in this country or in India once Germany is beaten. Secondly, the physical problem—the climate, the fact that modern equipment and power are not effective in jungle warfare, the obstinate heroism of the Japanese. The fact that we could not open communication with China—the Burma road (even if we regained it) would take a year to reconstruct. Conversely, if the Japanese ever lost the oil and rubber, they would be done. Already they were very short of shipping. What it all boiled down to was, unless Russia came in against Japan, it would take us many years and great energies to clear the Japanese out.

He was calm, solid, determined, powerful. My admiration for him was very much increased.

DIARY   *21st July, 1943*

I have breakfast at the Dorchester with Lord Baldwin.[1] We sit at opposite ends of a tiny table, with a kipper in front of each of us. He is lame and slightly deaf, but I see no diminution either in his curiosity or his memory. He talks of Kipling, and is trying to find out whether he ever refused the laureateship. Salisbury offered it to him; so did Asquith; did MacDonald also? He then talks of Ramsay and describes his last visit to him when he left in the funereal boat.[2] Ramsay was

---

[1] Lord Baldwin who as Stanley Baldwin, was Prime Minister in 1923-24, 1924-29 and 1935-37, was then aged 75. He died in 1947.

[2] Ramsay MacDonald died at sea in November 1937 on a holiday voyage to South America.

talking of all the books he meant to write and all the journeys he hoped to make. Baldwin knew all the time that he was a shattered man. He talks of human ambition and endeavour, and says that in his long life he has found always that in the end men and women are as good as one thinks them.

He then passes on to Winston. The latter had asked him to luncheon and given him three hours, telling him about all that was happening. 'I went out into Downing Street', said Baldwin, 'a happy man. Of course it was partly because an old buffer like me enjoys feeling that he is still not quite out of things. But it was also pure patriotic joy that my country at such a time should have found such a leader. The furnace of the war has smelted out all base metals from him.' He lives in a sort of pool or ambient water of forgiveness. He said that the only man he could never forgive was Beaverbrook.

I did not notice much change in him. His nose has got squarer and more bulbous, and now he really looks like what Low made him look like years ago. His face is still that strange colour, as if lightly dusted by ginger-powder.

Bob Boothby asked the Prime Minister his question, who admitted that he wrote the hand-out about de Gaulle,[1] but said that he could only give his explanation in Secret Session. I have a drink with Stokes[2] and Aneurin Bevan. Much to my horror I therefore find myself surrounded by the anti-Winston group. I can see James Stuart[3] looking at us with angered contempt. He supposes that I have joined that gang. I am reminded of Baldwin's words of advice, 'You will find in politics that you are much exposed to the attribution of false motive. Never complain and never explain.'

DIARY   *22nd July, 1943*

Dine with Sibyl [Colefax]. She had managed to get hold of the Wavells, and had chosen a careful party. The Duchess of Devonshire, T. S. Eliot, Oliver Lyttelton, Stephen Spender. She had also invited Dicky Mountbatten and Edwina, but they were summoned to dine at the Palace. The Wavells arrive late. Oliver makes the party go with imitations of Woolton, Kingsley Wood and the C.I.G.S. He is a wonderful mimic. Sibyl, to stimulate conversation, says, 'Who is the

[1] See above, under 30th June, 1943.
[2] Labour M.P. for Ipswich since 1938. He had been a persistent critic of the Government's policy on tank-production.
[3] Government Chief Whip, 1941-45.

dullest celebrity that you have ever known?' We take up this gambit, but it is clear that Wavell is wounded by it. Upstairs afterwards, he half picks up a book and then lays it down again. Sibyl becomes restless.

Stephen Spender talks about the proletariat with whom he is in constant contact in the fire-service. He says that 'liberty' means nothing to them. All they hate is class privilege. If he tries to tell them about Russia, pointing out that labour is conscripted there and forced to go where it is wanted, they say he is 'talking fascist'. They worship the very thought of Stalin. Russia is their only religion. Yet they refused to volunteer for a parade on Red Army Day. 'What's the good? It won't help the Soviets and it will wear out our shoe-leather.' The wireless is always on and is never turned off except when something serious is played.

T. S. Eliot is in a charming mood, and we walk together to the Westminster Underground. I do not think that poor Sibyl felt her dinner to be a success, as Wavell was so clearly bored.

DIARY   25th July, 1943

I had written my diary and gone to bed. Scarcely had I laid my head on the pillow when the door opened and there stood Viti dressed in her brown overcoat and an old Etonian sweater of Ben's. I was horrified, thinking for a moment that she had delirium and was wandering in her mania. 'Go back to bed at once', I said. But she said, 'Mussolini has resigned.'

She had been listening to the wireless, when suddenly the programme was interrupted at 11.4. A voice said, 'We interrupt this programme to say that the Rome wireless has announced the resignation of Mussolini.' I get up and come round with her to the Priest's House.[1] I telephone to Violet [Bonham Carter], who had herself heard the news. For her it means Mark's release. We then listen to the midnight news. The King has taken command of the Armies and Badoglio is in supreme power. They do not play *Giovinezza*, nor does the decree bear the date Anno XXI.

DIARY   27th July, 1943

To the House. Winston when he enters is given a great reception. He makes a measured speech to the effect that it would pay us to make

[1] One of the outlying cottages in the garden at Sissinghurst, where the dining-room was situated. V.S-W., who then had 'flu, was sleeping in the bedroom above.

peace with Badoglio since we do not want internal disturbance in Italy, nor to carry on our shoulders something that should carry itself. He deprecates attacks in the Press or in Parliament against the King of Italy. His only unfortunate phrase is, 'Let Italy stew in her own juice.' Apart from the vulgarity of this, it is untranslatable into Italian. I tell our B.B.C. people to be careful not to use words which could be twisted to mean, 'Italy must boil in her own oil.' I suggest, '*L'Italia farà il suo proprio minestrone.*'

DIARY   *29th July, 1943*

I gather that the War Office view is that the Germans are running terribly short of men. They can only just hold the fronts they are holding at present, and if they lose the Divisions now in Crete, Sardinia and Italy, they will be in a bad way. In fact, in such a bad way that their only hope now is to make a separate peace with Russia. They can offer Russia Poland and the Balkans. They can even offer her the Dardanelles. On the other hand, Russian public opinion would not stand for a separate peace, and German propaganda has spent so much energy on preaching the anti-Bolshevik front, that even for them it would be difficult suddenly to reverse their policy. Meanwhile Hungary and Bulgaria are showing signs of dislocation. Franco in Spain is obviously uneasy. The whole world is in suspense, and conjecture whirls round and round.

DIARY   *2nd August, 1943*

We go to the village fête at Sissinghurst. All the village children dress up and there is one little boy who impersonates Montgomery riding on a tank. There are many side-shows. One of them is a dart contest, in which people are invited to throw darts at large cartoons of Hitler, Tojo and Mussolini. Captain Reed is in charge of the Mussolini target and does no business at all. Hitler and Tojo attract great crowds, but people do not want to throw darts at Mussolini as they say he is 'down and out'. Really the English are an amazing race.

The 9 o'clock news tells us that Montgomery has begun the offensive against Catania. There is a message recorded by Montgomery which is really not too bad. He says something Montgomeryish about Mussolini having been knocked off his perch, but he is very generous about the Americans, which pleases me. We then listen to a really brilliant feature by Stephen Potter about how to talk to children.

DIARY   *9th August, 1943*

The Russians have scored an enormous victory at Bielgorod and are threatening Kharkov and Briansk. We are advancing slowly but surely on Messina. Meanwhile it looks as if the Germans had surrounded the Badoglio Government in Rome and were forcing them to continue the war. Churchill, it appears, is visiting Stalin.[1] A most necessary visit.

DIARY   *13th August, 1943*

Lunch with Norman Angell[2] who has returned after three years in the United States. He says that the Americans are deeply anglophobe, since we are the only respectable scapegoats that they can find. It is not respectable to put the blame on the Jews as Hitler did; so that anglophobia is their brand of anti-semitism. Another cause is the constant oversimplification by Americans of moral issues. 'Imperialism' is evil; so they must condemn British imperialism as sin. They never think (a) about their own imperialism; (b) that they would never have existed without British imperialism. If we had not beaten the Armada, if we had not turned the French out of Canada, if we had not protected the New World from the Holy Alliance—then the United States could never have expanded. I ask him about the terrible lack of realism among the Americans, amounting to an ignorance of truth. He says their greatest danger is their 'economic illiteracy'. They really believe that they can maintain world trade and a high tariff policy. He agrees with me that America (having run out of the frontier and limitless opportunity) will be faced with the rise of an internal proletariat, composed partly of their Negro population and partly of the non-Anglo-Saxon immigrants. Already, he says, in left-wing circles, it is a disability to possess an Anglo-Saxon name.

He has little hope of Anglo-American relations improving on a basis of liking. He thinks that the only hope is to explain and demonstrate our community of interest. I say that the difficulty is that whereas for us Anglo-American cooperation means security, for them it suggests danger. He admits this, but thinks that when the German war is over and the Japanese war continues, it will be we, not they, who will have to make the offer. Then they will see the importance of our imperialist

[1] No: he was on his way across the Atlantic to meet Roosevelt at Quebec.
[2] Sir Norman Angell, who passed his youth in America, ranching, prospecting and working as a journalist, was the author of the world-famous book *The Great Illusion* (1910). He was awarded the Nobel Peace Prize in 1933.

outposts and will realise fully what India means. He does not think that the Indian Congress will have many American sympathisers once India becomes an American base.

H.N. TO B.N. & N.N.   *19th August, 1943*
                                                        Sissinghurst

You may soon hear that Violet [Bonham Carter] and I have resigned from the Board of B.B.C. Governors. The issue is this. We have for a year been fussing about the quality of our programmes, and have always been assured that once they got the right man, they would appoint him Deputy Director-General with the sole job of devoting himself to the improvement of intellectual standards. I had suggested John Maud of Birkbeck College for the post, and he was interviewed and generally approved. We agreed however that other candidates should also be interviewed. The second candidate to appear before us was a man called Haley,[1] Editor of the *Manchester Evening News*, which is a paper of the same quality as the London *Evening News*. He was a clever man, but not at all suited to the cultural job which we had in mind. But to my horror the Chairman of the Board informed us that he had already obtained Brendan Bracken's consent to his appointment, and that he had got Haley to agree to take it. Violet and I said that we did not agree with the appointment. Nor did we agree that it was fair to face us with a decision without consulting us beforehand. We insisted on a vote being taken and Violet and I were outvoted by a majority of five to two. The question therefore arises whether Violet and I should resign, (a) on the principle that Haley was unsuitable; (b) on the procedure of forcing a man down our throats. I have written to the Chairman saying that 'I must consider my position.'

[1] This was the first time that H.N. had ever met or heard of (Sir) William Haley. His formal education had been at Victoria College, Jersey, and he had since read very widely. His remarkable career began in 1922 as a reporter on the *Manchester Evening News*, of which he became Managing Editor in 1930. In the same year he became a Director of the *Manchester Guardian*, and in 1939 a Director of the Press Association and Reuters. He was Editor-in-Chief at the B.B.C., 1943–44, Director-General of the B.B.C., 1944–52, and became Editor of *The Times* in 1952. Lady Violet Bonham Carter had no objection to his appointment on the grounds of his qualifications, of which she knew little at the time. Her objection was to the method by which he was appointed, and she made this quite clear to Mr Haley soon after the meeting described above. On being shown this passage in 1966 (when she had become Lady Asquith), Lady Violet wrote: 'He became, and still is, a very close and dear friend of mine. He was *far and away* the best Director-General whom we had at the B.B.C. during my spell as Governor.'

DIARY   *25th August, 1943*

I discuss my B.B.C. difficulty with Vita. She is as wise as usual. We amuse ourselves by drawing up a general knowledge paper, which could be used as a test for any candidate, to see whether he was suitable to supervise our programme output. If he were unable to answer satisfactorily 17 out of the 20 names suggested, then he could be regarded as unfitted. The question is: 'What do you know of the following: Jeremy Bentham, John Stuart Mill, Leslie Stephen, Debussy, Faraday, Cézanne, Manley Hopkins, Paxton, Lucretius, Inigo Jones, Emily Dickinson, le Corbusier, Ibsen, John Donne, Talleyrand, Capability Brown, William Morris, Alexander Hamilton, General Boulanger, Locke?'

DIARY   *26th August, 1943*

B.B.C. Board. The luncheon takes place in an atmosphere of rather chill cordiality. We then adjourn to the Board Room, and having taken the ordinary business, we start on the question of Haley's appointment. We begin by saying that the question of principle has now to some extent been decided since Haley has accepted the job. We therefore decide to discuss the procedure.

Violet begins by saying that at our penultimate meeting she had definitely asked the Chairman whether we were going to discuss Maud's appointment or whether he had any other candidates in mind. The Chairman had evaded her question. It was now clear, however, that on that date he had already discussed the appointment of Haley, not only with Foot,[1] but also with Bracken. Was it right that the Chairman should discuss with others a problem on which he knew that Violet held very definite views, while refusing even to mention to Violet the name which he had in mind?

I then said that I was not clear how far the Chairman had consulted other members of the Board. Had he consulted Millis[2]? Yes, he had. Had he consulted Mann? Yes, he had, and Mann, as a professional journalist, would rightly have been consulted about the candidature of a fellow-journalist. Had he consulted Mallon? At this stage the Chairman exclaimed, 'I refuse to be cross-examined!' I replied, 'But, Mr Chairman, upon these points turns what for me may be a very grave decision, namely whether I can continue as a member of the Board. I cannot continue if I feel that other members have been given

[1] Director-General of the B.B.C., 1943–44.
[2] C. H. G. Millis, Company Director. Vice-Chairman of the B.B.C. Board, 1937–46.

due warning of Haley's candidature, while the matter has been concealed from Lady Violet and myself.' Mallon then intervened to say that the Chairman had mentioned the matter to him, but only incidentally, and Fraser added that he had never been consulted and felt that the Chairman was right in not consulting him. I commented on this by saying that the Chairman was obviously aware that Fraser would in any case be opposed to the appointment of a man of general education. The argument then centred on whether you could define 'general education'. Mann produced a letter from Ivor Brown assuring him that Haley was more 'widely and deeply read' than he was himself. This made a considerable effect on the Board, and the angry waters were stilled by the Chairman saying that he had never intended to go behind the backs of any member of the Board, and if I had derived that impression, he wished to apologise to me.

Thus I felt that we could no longer threaten resignation. We go away rather shattered by this meeting and with our nerves and personal relations somewhat strained.

H.N. TO LADY VIOLET BONHAM CARTER   *28th August, 1943*
4 King's Bench Walk, E.C.4

On my long journey to Edinburgh yesterday, I thought over the sad episode of the Haley controversy. I remain convinced that the Chairman deliberately excluded you and me from prior consultation, hoping that our objections would be overruled 'by the general feeling of the Board'. It has left me with grave doubts as to the present relations between the several members of the Board on the one hand, and between the Board and the Executive on the other.

Throughout my life (at Balliol, in diplomacy, in literature and even in politics) I have been dealing with people who, if they did not share my opinions, did share, or at least understand, my values. We may have differed as to the relative values of such virtues as truth, beauty, tolerance, fairness, generosity, courage, faithfulness and taste. But the assumption has always been that these were desirable virtues possessing a certain absolute validity. We took it for granted that to these ethical values certain intellectual values should be added—intelligence, wit, humour, knowledge—and the importance of these great things formed the 'language' in which we discoursed. They were even more than that. They were the accepted currency with which we interchanged ideas. Suddenly I have found myself faced with a group of people who not only do not understand, but actually do not know, these weights and measures. It is as if for such current phrases of measurement as '2½ feet', 'forty-two minutes', 'eleven stone', '4/-', one used Siamese expressions indicating *yens* or *tickals* or whatever it may be. I feel in dealing with these men the same gap in communication as I do when I hear people talking about batting averages or football pools or racing form. I believe that they are honestly quite unaware of the standards which to us seem the axioms of life.

Thus even when we have reached agreement on some point, we have not really reached agreement. It is as if, having agreed with someone to meet him at the Travellers Club at 7.30, he supposed that one had fixed a meeting at Lyons Corner House at 11.45. I do not accuse them of dishonesty; only an honest lack of comprehension.

It is the absence of any sense of corporate function which renders the Board so contemptible a body. We are about to enter an age when all the old values will be called into question and many of the most precious of them discarded, not because they lack validity, but merely because they are old. We cannot hope that the Press as a whole will swim against the tide of vulgarization which will sweep in from the west. Only the B.B.C. can teach the public to think correctly, to feel nobly, to enjoy themselves intelligently, to have some conception of what is meant by the good life. Our responsibility is tremendous. I do not want to shirk that responsibility. And yet in seeking to convey it to my colleagues, I have to introduce words and concepts of which they have no understanding at all. They remain completely unaware of what we mean when we talk of the B.B.C.'s unerring instinct for the second-rate.

DIARY   *31st August, 1943*

Down to Sissinghurst at last. My train is late owing to hop-pickers, and I find the station-master at Staplehurst excited by a report in the *Daily Express* that Italy has already sued for peace.[1]

DIARY   *3rd September, 1943*

This morning at 4 am. we crossed the Straits of Messina and landed at Reggio di Calabria. At the same time we bombed Bolzano, Trento

[1] This report was correct. That morning, General Castellano, the emissary of the Badoglio Government, accepted in principle the Allies' terms for the Italian surrender. It was agreed, however, that it should not be announced until the Allies had landed in Italy to protect their Government against the Germans.

and (alas!) Bologna. Aircraft droned overhead all morning on their way to France.

DIARY   *7th September, 1943*

In Calabria we are still advancing against little opposition. But, as the Germans point out on their wireless, we are only using about a quarter of our available troops and the main leap will be elsewhere.

DIARY   *8th September, 1943*

I go to our Greek Committee, which sits under the chairmanship of Irene Ravensdale.[1] The Greek Ambassador[2] had telephoned to say that he would be rather late as he had been sent for by Anthony Eden. He arrives about 6.30 pm. with his eyes shining like two stars. He takes me into the corridor. 'It's all over,' he says. 'The Italians have surrendered unconditionally. Eden has just told me.' 'Is it to be published?' I ask. 'Not till they are certain that Badoglio will broadcast to his people telling them to oppose the Germans.'

I go off to the Reform to dine with Wilson Harris and there I find the place agog. They have had the news on the tape. The Armistice was actually signed in Sicily on 3rd September. It is amazing news. Wilson Harris has to dash off and rewrite his leading article. Raymond [Mortimer], who is also there, runs away to help Kingsley Martin recast his. Apparently Kingsley had written an attack on Winston for his 'unconditional surrender' demand, saying that but for this, Italy would be out of the war by now.

What a day for the Germans! Stalino has fallen; they have lost nearly all the Donetz basin; and on top of it comes this dastardly stab in the back from Italy.

DIARY   *9th September, 1943*

There is complete confusion in Italy. The Germans have occupied Genoa and Verona. We have landed at Amalfi[3] and met with some German opposition. The Germans have told the Croats to take over

---

[1] Baroness Ravensdale, eldest daughter of Lord Curzon, was a Baroness in her own right and was also created a Life Peeress in 1958.
[2] Thanassis Aghnides. H.N. had a very special link with him. When he first met Aghnides in 1911, he was a junior clerk in a solicitor's office in Constantinople and gave H.N. Turkish lessons at 5/- an hour. H.N. later recommended him to Venizelos, and he rose rapidly in the Greek diplomatic service to become Ambassador in London in 1942.
[3] At Salerno.

Dalmatia and have established an anonymous Fascist Government 'acting in Mussolini's name'. We are anxious about the fate of our prisoners in northern Italy. The Italian Fleet has responded to our invitation to go to Sicily.[1]

It may amuse me to read later what the situation seems to me to be, six days after the signature of the Armistice. I imagine that the Germans will occupy the Franco-Italian frontier, disarm all Italian troops in that area, remove our prisoners, and dig themselves in. I imagine that we shall land at Leghorn or somewhere, and try to separate the German divisions in north Italy from those in the centre. I imagine that we shall very shortly occupy Corsica, Sardinia and the Dodecanese. We may be in Taranto already and Brindisi. We shall then take the Ionian islands and command the Adriatic. Our problem will be whether to start a major campaign in Italy to drive the Germans out, or to attack the Balkans instead.

Meanwhile I have a feeling that we are on the verge of an invasion of northern France. An 'exercise' on an enormous scale was carried out in the Channel yesterday and today. We did not meet much opposition. The Germans have some 300,000 troops in Italy. But with the Russian front in danger, they cannot really spare enough men to hold all these fronts. If they cut their losses, they can hold out for long in the inner fortress. But if they try to hold everything at the same time, their man-power will be seriously strained.

H.N. TO B.N. & N.N.   *11th September, 1943*
Sissinghurst

I came down here yesterday morning. The 1 o'clock news was disturbing. Gunfire had been heard that morning on the outskirts of Rome. By the evening we knew the worst. The Germans had seized the capital, Italian armies were surrendering to them everywhere, and Badoglio had fled. I was terribly disappointed, since all the information I had was that we did not expect them to make a stand south of the Apennines, and that Perugia, Siena, Assisi and Florence would not be in the area of operations. Moreover, my heart went out to Violet, who must have felt certain that Mark would be released. I was deeply upset, and for once in my life did not sleep.

But today the news is better. At least the Italian fleet has surrendered and we have taken Salerno. I listened to Hitler's speech. He was in a strange mood. He gabbled through his stuff at a tremendous rate and

[1] In fact, to Malta, where it arrived on 10th September.

was difficult to understand. The sunset waned while I was listening, and a little owl came and sat on the tree outside. I felt that Pallas Athene herself had come to stand beside me in my distress.

All my love to you both during these tremendous days.

The battle of Salerno hung in the balance for several days. The Germans were able to build up their forces against the beach-head faster than the Allies could within it. The situation was saved by fierce counter-attack and close Naval support, and by the arrival on the battlefield of the 8th Army advancing from Calabria. Naples fell on 1st October. The Allies pressed on across the River Volturno during November to reach the main German line, which ran through Cassino, and remained halted there for the rest of the winter, with the southern 300 miles of the Italian boot firmly in their hands. Corsica was occupied by the Free French and Sardinia by the Italians. The Badoglio Government declared war on Germany on 13th October, and was awarded 'co-belligerent' status, one remove short of full alliance. Mussolini had by that time been rescued from his internment in the Abruzzi, and was carried off by German parachutists to set up a shadowy Fascist régime in northern Italy.

The only military failure was in the Dodecanese and neighbouring Aegean islands. It had been hoped that the Italian troops in Rhodes and Crete would overwhelm the small German garrisons, but they yielded before the British could come to their aid, and the Americans were reluctant to divert forces to these side-shows in the Eastern Mediterranean. In consequence, the small British forces landed in Cos, Leros and Samos were captured or evacuated. The incident led to one of the few serious recriminations between Churchill and the Americans. The latter concentrated their attention on the forthcoming invasion of northern France, to the detriment of the strategic possibilities opened up by the Italian change of sides.

The Second Front in France was the main subject of the first meeting of the Big Three (Roosevelt, Churchill and Stalin) at Tehran between 27th November and 1st December. The meeting had been preceded by a Foreign Ministers' Conference in Moscow in late October, and by Churchill's talks with Roosevelt and Chiang Kai-shek in Cairo in mid-November. At Tehran the main decisions were to pursue the Germans up the length of Italy as far as the Pisa–Rimini line, and only then to decide whether to turn north-east towards Vienna or westwards into southern France; to launch an Allied force across the English Channel in May 1944, combined with landings in the French Riviera; to support the Balkan partisans, who were tying down as many German Divisions as the Allied Armies in Italy; to give eastern Poland to Russia and part of eastern Germany to Poland; for Russia to declare war on Japan as soon as Hitler was defeated; and to maintain pressure on Turkey to enter the war. To implement this last decision, Churchill and Roosevelt met President Inönü in Cairo on 4th December, but they made little progress. Churchill then flew on to Tunis, where he fell ill with pneumonia for the second time in 1943. He recovered quickly and at the end of the year went for two weeks' convalescence to Marrakesh.

Harold Nicolson flew to Sweden on 18th October to lecture on behalf of the Ministry of Information. On his return on 4th November, he was soon asked to undertake another lecture tour, to Australia. He accepted from a sense of duty, but, greatly to his relief, the visit was cancelled. The year ended with the huge popular success of V. Sackville-West's new book, 'The Eagle and the Dove', which was published on 8th November. Ben, who had been conducting courses in air-photograph interpretation in Syria, Cyprus and Cairo, met his brother Nigel, who was sent from North Africa to a gas course at Gaza, in Jerusalem on 27th December.

DIARY   *12th September, 1943*

I am depressed by the Italian news. The Germans (unless we do something very dramatic shortly) will prove to the world that they are still able to use terrific and immediate force, and that we linger and delay. We creep along the toe of Italy while they swoop down on two-thirds of the country, disarm 400,000 Italians and resume control of the situation. It will end as an increase rather than a diminution of their prestige. Our hope is, of course, that they will over-strain themselves and think more of prestige than of strategic wisdom. I daresay that with the capture of Brindisi we have gained a great deal. I daresay that the surrender of so large a proportion of the Italian Fleet is an immense advantage. But for the moment, and for those who do not argue carefully, German might has been demonstrated as terrific and our weaknesses as still apparent. Pray to God that they will not turn us out of Salerno, where the fighting is very heavy.

The Armistice terms and the story of the negotiations are published. They show that the Italians opened negotiations almost immediately after 25th July. We therefore had plenty of warning. The Germans profited by this: we did not.

318

H.N. TO B.N. & N.N.   *13th September, 1943*
                                                         Sissinghurst

We learn that a body of German paratroops and S.S. men have rescued Mussolini. This is highly irritating, not because the Duce and his duodenal ulcers will be of much effective value in future, but because the incident completely discredits Victor Emmanuel and Badoglio, gives a tremendous fillip to German morale, and will act as a douche of very cold water to all the Badoglios in Central and Eastern Europe. Moreover, since it is one of the most dramatic events in history, it will much increase German prestige, giving to them that meed of admiration which is the only emotion (other than fear and hatred) which they can hope to arouse. It creates, in the form of one of the best of all news-stories, the impression of extreme competence on the one side, and extreme incompetence on the other. In thinking over all these elements in the event, I became more than irritated. I became depressed.

DIARY   *14th September, 1943*

The news is bad. True it is that we have taken Bari and Salamaua.[1] But at Salerno we are in a difficult position. We were apparently surprised by a Panzer Division at Eboli and driven back to our beaches. The Germans can pound us there. According to German Press messages we are sending transports to take our men off. We are also landing reinforcements further south. It looks as if we are heading for another Dunkirk and grave humiliation. So far the whole thing has turned to Germany's advantage and not to ours. But there is of course more to come.

DIARY   *15th September, 1943*

I have recovered from my shattering disappointment over the Italian misfortunes. I had, I suppose, felt underneath that the surrender of Italy really meant the shortening of the war. I was angry and mortified that the Germans could exploit the situation so rapidly whereas we seemed to have lost every trick. But after four days of real distress, my old easy confidence has returned. I imagine that my feelings were typical of the mass of the people, although the ordinary citizen probably does not realise to the same extent as I do what a fillip the release of Mussolini will have given to German opinion. They will again feel themselves to be invincible.

[1] In New Guinea. It was captured from the Japanese by the Americans and Australians on 13th September.

As Robin [Maugham] and I this evening walked from Pratts to the Green Park Underground, the siren went off. Nobody paid the slightest attention. It is a strange psychological fact that the sound of the siren gives one a sense almost of pleasure. 'There's that familiar sound again.' Now why should this be so? Is it that we feel that no serious raids are likely and that we enjoy being reminded of past dangers in present tranquillity? Or is it only a feeling, 'Well, they can come here if they like, but we are more powerful than they are'? If and when raids begin again in earnest, then we shall have feelings of dread and fear.

DIARY   *17th September, 1943*

The Salerno news is better. The 5th Army has counter-attacked and the 8th Army is approaching from the south. In fact, some correspondents from the latter were able to motor straight through. The Germans have made the mistake of letting their people imagine that another Gallipoli was impending. In the evening we hear that patrols of the 8th Army have established contact with the 5th.

H.N. TO B.N. & N.N.   *21st September, 1943*

The House met again today. The Speaker startled us by announcing the death of Kingsley Wood.[1] On getting out of bed this morning, he fell down stone dead. After the first moment of surprise, the House buzzed with prognostications regarding his successor. It was still buzzing slightly when Winston came in, beaming genially with a 'Here I am again' look,[2] and was loudly cheered. A few minutes later he rose to make his speech on the progress of the war. The speech was divided into two parts and lasted two hours, broken by a luncheon interval. He began, as always, in a dull, stuffy manner, reciting dates and chronology, reading slowly from the typescript on the box. But as he progressed, he began to enliven his discourse with the familiar quips and gestures. His most characteristic gesture is strange indeed. You know the movement that a man makes when he taps his trouser pockets to see whether he has got his latch-key? Well, Winston pats both trouser pockets and then passes his hands up and down from groin

[1] Sir Kingsley Wood had been Chancellor of the Exchequer since May 1940. He was succeeded by Sir John Anderson.

[2] Churchill had just arrived back from the Quebec Conference with Roosevelt and subsequent talks at Washington. He had been away from England for six weeks.

to tummy. It is very strange. You will have read or heard the main lines of the speech, and I shall comment only on those aspects of it which cannot be conveyed by the wireless or the printed word. It was obvious that he was in some logical difficulty over the implicit anomaly that we had asked for 'unconditional surrender' whereas the Italians had asked in effect to be allowed in on our side. He dealt with this sturdily and stubbornly but in a somewhat laboured way. And when he got through the argument, he leant across to the Opposition and said in a conversational tone, 'That all right?' They grinned back affectionately. When he came to discussing the escape of Mussolini, he took off his glasses, stepped back from the box, and put on an expression of rather perplexed amusement. By his manner, rather than by what he said, he was able to convey to the House that this escape was no more than an irritating and (if one looked at it in the right way) an entertaining episode.

At the end of the first act, and before we adjourned for luncheon, he did an amusing thing. He referred to Italy and expressed pleasure that the Italian people, 'rescued from their state of servitude', could now take 'their rightful place among the democracies of the world'. 'The satellite States', he continued, 'suborned and overawed . . .' and then he raised his arm as if about to deliver the most terrific thunderbolt from his rich armoury of rhetoric, but he dropped his arm suddenly and took off his spectacles, '. . . may perhaps be allowed to work their passage home', he concluded, grinning. It is in this that one finds his mastery of the House. It is the combination of great flights of oratory with sudden swoops into the intimate and conversational. Of all his devices it is the one that never fails.

I dashed off to the Beefsteak with Duff Cooper and Eddy Winterton and we swallowed a sausage each. We returned to find Winston again at the box, also having enjoyed his luncheon. He went on to talk about Sardinia and Corsica, and paid a neat tribute to the French, which was greeted with only one 'Hear, hear!'—my own. He made a wide sweeping gesture such as a reaper makes or a man throwing at base-ball. 'We feel the power', he said: 'We feel the power', he repeated, swinging his arm round in the air, 'of the encircling arm of a great world movement.' 'A great world movement,' he repeated chal-lengingly—and then again that drop into the conversational and the intimate, 'and I am certainly going to do nothing to hamper that.' He ended by a catalogue of our power by air and sea and land. He sat down, leaving the House stunned by the magnitude of his performance.

Old Pethick-Lawrence,[1] his head shaking apoplectically, rose to reply from the Labour benches. Lloyd George walked out towards the bar of the House. Winston rose in his seat, scurried along to catch him, calling out over his shoulder to Lawrence, 'It's all right, I'm coming back.' He stood for a moment at the bar talking to Lloyd George. It was strange to see those two fathers of victory standing there together. The eyes of the House were upon them. The pink rows of faces were turned not towards poor Pethick-Lawrence, but towards the two famous men at the bar. Then Winston scurried back to his seat and the House resumed its accustomed boredom. The rest of that day, the debate was colourless. Everybody wanted to read Winston's speech all through before making any comment.

I went off and dined with my friend Tilea[2] and his Polish associates. They want us, of course, to induce Turkey to let us through the Straits and then to land at Constanza and seize Ploesti. Russia would never allow us to do that. Whatever Second Front is opened, they want it to be as far as possible from Russia's present line of battle and future sphere of influence.

The next day, the debate was resumed. Winston came down early and answered a string of Parliamentary questions as humbly as if he had been the youngest of Under-Secretaries. This again is a thing that endears him to the House. He might so easily have asked Attlee to answer for him, or put on a casual or condescending manner. But he answered all the questions and supplementaries dutifully, carefully, subserviently. Members know that when he proclaims himself the 'Servant of the House', he really means it. In doing so he maintains and elevates the whole standard of our public life.

But the debate itself was a feeble affair. Aneurin Bevan tried to pretend that if from the outset we had made terms, not with the King and Badoglio, but with the workers' leaders in Milan and Turin, we could have seized the whole Italian peninsula. But the suggestion impressed nobody, since it was exposed to the crushing answer, 'Do you seriously believe that the Fleet or the Generals commanding in Sardinia would have obeyed orders from strike-leaders in Northern Italy?' Moreover, the early days of the battle of Salerno had convinced the House that these amphibious operations are not as simple as they

[1] F. W. Pethick-Lawrence, formerly Financial Secretary to the Treasury, 1929–31, was to become Secretary of State for India, 1945–47. He was then aged 71.

[2] V. V. Tilea, previously Rumanian Minister in London, and founder of the Free Rumanian Movement during the war.

seem. One cannot, in Winston's words, 'just throw troops ashore'. The operations in Sardinia, Corsica and Dalmatia had suggested that our General Staff had not been quite so sleepy as some supposed. The general feeling of the House was that, although we had not scored in Italy the immense gains which the optimists had at first hoped for, we had in fact acquired by skill and tenacity many valuable assets. In the end the Government were left in a position far firmer than before.

In the intervals of all this, I lunched with Camrose to meet Colonel Knox, the Secretary of the Navy at Washington. A large florid amiable man, with a friendly eye and a tongue which is too large for his mouth and keeps on coming out like that of a llama. He spoke at length about the danger that when we had beaten Germany we might in this country be unwilling to continue the war against Japan. If we backed out, then all future cooperation between America and ourselves was gone for ever. We told him that there would naturally be some demand for general demobilisation over here; that some of the workers might say that we were carrying on a war for the profit of Wall Street and the Malay planters; but that it would not be necessary for us to send great masses of troops to the Pacific. There would always be enough airmen, sailors and regular officers prepared to go. Eventually our man-power would come from the Chinese and the Indian Army. We did not think that he need be afraid that we would let the United States down.

He talked to us about the new rocket bomb which the Germans are using, and about the sudden revival of the U-boat campaign. He was in no sense gloomy about them. But we must face the fact that our recent run of uninterrupted successes cannot last for ever.

I dined with Raymond [Mortimer], and went on to sit with him in the *New Statesman* offices, as it was his night for fire-watching. Poor Raymond is suffering from the familiar and historic disillusion which affects all Girondists who discover that 'the people' are not as attractive as they seemed when they were oppressed. He cannot share Kingsley Martin's view that whatever Holy Russia does or may do is unalterably right, and that whatever our own Government does or may do is unquestionably wrong. Raymond's Socialism, as mine, is due rather to dislike of the capitalist and sympathy for the proletarian, than to any profound and burning convictions of right or wrong. He finds that the masses do not care for truth in the way that we care for it; that they are apt to identify the virtues of loyalty, tolerance and honesty as bourgeois inhibitions, and that for them the things of the mind are reactionary and slightly out of date. 'I see what you mean', I said. 'You mean that Kingsley's friends regard Siena as a class privilege?' 'Hm, hm, hm', he nodded sadly, sitting over the gas fire. Raymond is one of those people who have improved enormously during the war. He is brave and calm and wise.

I hear that a Labour man[1] of small experience is to act as Under-Secretary at the Foreign Office. I quite see that they must put a Labour man there, and I have long resigned myself to the fact that I can never again hope to enter the Government. But I do think that they might have given the job to Philip Noel-Baker who has devoted his whole life to the study of Foreign Affairs. I feel rather sick about this. Moreover I have got to go to Sweden for a fortnight. I shall not enjoy the journey. But I admit that it will be fascinating to see Europe, after all these years, from another window.

DIARY   24th September, 1943

The Germans have evacuated Smolensk. I have a dreadful feeling that they have agreed with the Russians to evacuate up to the Curzon Line in Poland, and that when they have reached this, they will make a separate peace with Russia. I dread this from the marrow of my bones.

DIARY   7th October, 1943

It is my night for fire-watching in the House. I go up to the Victoria Tower platform and remain there rather cold for three hours. I hear Big Ben chime 9 and 10 and 11. The guns spit and fire all round us, the river lies milkily in the misty moon, the searchlights sweep and cluster, and suddenly converge to a cone, and there high above our heads is a little white gadfly which is a German bomber. Our own night-fighters, dropping identification flares, go up to meet it. Another cone towards the east catches another little gadfly driving along in a different direction. The guns boom and crackle, the rockets soar, and we hear two bombs whistling down from the stars in the direction of Lewisham. There is a lull, and then it all begins again. Finally, at 11.45, we retire to rest. The deep drone of our own bombers going out to Germany throbs through the night.

[1] George Hall (later Viscount Hall). He began work as a miner at the age of 12, and was first elected to Parliament in 1922. He had already held office as Civil Lord to the Admiralty, 1929–31, and Parliamentary Under-Secretary of State to the Colonial Office, 1940–42. He became Secretary of State for the Colonies, 1945–46 and First Lord of the Admiralty, 1946–51.

H.N. TO B.N. & N.N.   *7th November, 1943*

It is almost a month since I last wrote to you. During the interval I have been in Sweden. I left on 9th October and returned on 4th November.

I flew from Leuchars near Dundee in a Mosquito. I donned a huge quilted suit like that of a Mandarin. On top of that I put a sort of gaberdine which fastened all round me with a zip. Then came the Mae West,[1] in the pocket of which there was a small whistle and a little flash-lamp. 'If we are ditched, Mr Nicolson, do not waste energy shouting. Merely blow the whistle and flash the lamp.' I was not encouraged by the picture of myself blowing a lonely whistle in the middle of the North Sea. Then came the parachute harness and I was trussed and hooked up and tied down. I was then led (since I could scarcely walk, having become a tight parcel and no longer a mobile man) towards the aeroplane. I had to go on all fours beneath it and then rise up into a little hole. I was connected with the intercom and oxygen tubes and shown how to adjust the oxygen supply when told to by the pilot. Slowly the bomb doors closed below me. I was completely alone in a little box feeling like a hazel-nut in its shell. The engine started. There was a bump or two. And we were off.

By some mischance my intercom became unscrewed from the start. I did not dare to touch any of the tubes or gadgets around me, fearing that I might release myself through the bomb doors. I had a little reading-lamp and read *Elizabeth and Essex*[2] which I had bought in Dundee. I just guessed at the amount of oxygen I should need. When, as I calculated, we were over the middle of the North Sea and five miles up above the world, I turned out the little reading-lamp and communed with myself. 'This', I thought, 'is the moment for deep philosophic reflections.' But none came. So I turned on the light again and went on reading. After about two hours from the start, I was aware of a slight movement which indicated that we were over land. Having adjusted my parachute in case I released myself, I began very gingerly to finger the tubes and gadgets which surrounded me. Yes, the switch of the intercom had got detached. I adjusted it and said, 'Hullo!' 'Thank God, Mr Nicolson', came the pilot's voice. 'I thought you had passed out.' A few minutes later I heard his voice again. 'I can now see the lights of Stockholm.' Within a trice there came a few muffled bumps, the engine stopped, the bomb doors opened slowly revealing below me a square of cement identical with the square I

[1] An inflatable life-jacket.   [2] By Lytton Strachey (1928).

had said goodbye to at Leuchars 2½ hours before. I undid my various umbilical cords and let myself down upon the soil of Sweden. Down on all fours I went to creep under the machine and then straightened myself to observe a blaze of countless arc-lights. I took off my flying-helmet and was greeted by an English voice. 'My name is Leadbetter. I come from the Legation. I hope you had a pleasant journey.'

The next few days were a tremendous rush and I shall not attempt to narrate them in detail. I spent the first four of them in my lovely room at the Grand Hotel, and then moved to the Legation. During the day the white ferry boats puffed and glittered in the autumn sun. At night, from the five windows of my room, I could see lights of every colour dancing on the waters. It was most agreeable. Strange voices would ring me up. 'Is that Mr Nicolson, so? I am a true friend of your country. I wish to speak with you.' To all such enquiries (which I knew to be Finnish or Rumanian or Hungarian) I replied, 'All appointments must be made through the Press Attaché at the Legation.' I wanted to feel that I had had no communication with any enemy agents. But that did not prevent some forty journalists coming in the whole time with their bloody flashlights.

Then there were banquets and luncheons and receptions. A huge supper given by the Anglo-Swedish Society for some 300 people. A dinner by the P.E.N. Club, a dinner by the Swedish Chamber of Commerce, a dinner by the Swedish B.B.C., a luncheon by the British colony. Then there were lectures of all sorts. At first I could not understand the fuss that was made of me. I thought they must imagine that I was far more important than I really am. But I think that it was merely that they hate the Germans and like welcoming Englishmen. Moreover, they were flattered that an elderly M.P. should trouble to undertake so hazardous a journey on their behalf. Anyhow, my first week passed in an orgy of schnapps, smoked eel, lobsters, elk, reindeer, cakes, Swedish punch and compliments.

I lunched with the Crown Prince. I wrote my name at the Palace. I went to the Riksdag. And all the time the telephone never ceased. When I transferred myself to the Legation and the amazing hospitality of Victor Mallet[1] and his delightful wife, all these telephone calls suddenly stopped.

I went down to Goteborg, where there were more banquets and speeches. I drove on a lovely autumn afternoon from Goteborg and Hälsingborg, from where across the water I could see the towers of

[1] Sir Victor Mallet, British Minister at Stockholm, 1940–45.

Elsinore and the coast of occupied Europe. The Swedes have no petrol and run their cars on gas generated from charcoal. Huge paper bags like hop-pockets are massed on top of the car. Every thirty miles the car stops and the chauffeur rakes out the dead ashes. At Hälsingborg, in the intervals of more speeches, I went to see the refugee camp. Since Hitler established his New Order in Denmark, some eight thousand refugees have slipped across the Sund, which is no wider than from Ryde to Portsmouth. There they all were with their babies and their bundles, looking exactly like caricatures in *Der Stürmer*. When I entered the room briskly with the Mayor and Chief of Police, the sentries leapt to attention. I saw a spasm of real panic pass over the faces of the refugees. They thought for a second that the Gestapo had arrived. So I shouted something out in English and they all relaxed immediately and grinned at each other. I was delighted to see that one word of English can change expressions of terror into expressions of delight. They crowded round me. Among them were some Danish officers who had also escaped. 'Can you take us to England', they said; 'we wish to fight those devils', pointing to where the hills of Denmark glimmered in the sun. They seemed lost, stranded and bemused.

But you will want to know my impressions of Sweden. In the last war the Swedes were pro-German, and in the early stages of this war they felt sure that Germany would win and that it was best to be on the safe side. All this has changed since Alamein and Stalingrad. The German behaviour in Denmark and Norway has filled them with loathing. They are almost unanimously on our side. Two instances: in the bookshops one can only see English books—not a German book is on show. The propaganda shops in the main street, where British and German news is displayed, offer a curious contrast. Ours is gay and has a little crowd round it. In front of the German shop three policemen parade, since the windows are always being broken.

The Swedes of course fear the Russians, and are anxious lest we shall be too late to share the Russian victories in Europe. I must have met some twenty different types of Swedes who have been in Germany lately. They were all unanimous in saying that collapse is very close. 'The whole thing', they said, 'is like a rotten pear, only kept together by its rind.' When I said to them, 'But we don't believe in an early collapse. It will only be in July next that we shall be able to strike with our full force', they merely smiled. 'We know', they said, 'the true state of Germany and the real despair that has seized the German people. You don't.' The corruption among the Nazis and the S.S. is something terrible. The whole feeling is one of utter disillusionment and defeatism. 'Who can save us?' is what they all cry. I have come back immensely optimistic and cheered. You cannot conceive how high our prestige is.

The great news here is that Mark [Bonham Carter] has escaped, and walked through the German lines. I hope to see him next week.

H.N. TO V.S-W.   9th November, 1943
                                                                    4 King's Bench Walk, E.C.4

I had a visit from *The Times* correspondent in Algiers. He says that Giraud is really very stupid, and that if left to himself de Gaulle would sweep the board. But the Americans do not like de Gaulle, as they feel that he is too independent, whereas they imagine that Giraud will open all North Africa to American capital and exploitation. Thus they seem determined not to allow de Gaulle to get too far. The French realise that this is not our fault and blame the Americans, but if we continue to allow the Americans to do all they want, they will start blaming us. The fact is that the United States are the only really Tory power in the world. We are far more advanced. I despair sometimes about the Americans. They have no keel and veer with every wind. They will pass in a puff from thinking that we are ruled by robber-barons to the idea that we are riddled with Communism.

DIARY   10th November, 1943

We finish the B.B.C. Board early, and I walk away with Violet [Bonham Carter]. She tells me details of Mark's escape. When the Germans arrived at Modena, they divided the prisoners into eleven categories. Mark foresaw that they would move them in numerical order and got himself into the eleventh category, which would be the last. He thought at first of hiding in a sewer, but it was really physically impossible. Then a man who had tunnelled a hole under the floor of his hut said, 'You can have my hole. I cannot manage to remain there more than two hours at a time.' So Mark, with a Major in the Grenadiers, climbed down into the hole and remained there for 36 hours. The lack of air was agonizing, and he felt his heart would burst. They were stung by mosquitoes, and Mark said, 'If a mosquito can live in this, so can I.' After two days in the hole, they thought it might be safe to come up. The camp was basking in sunlight and not a soul was to be seen. They climbed the wall and jumped over. Some little Italian boys rushed at them whispering, '*Tedeschi! Tedeschi!*', and surely enough the prison wall was being patrolled by German sentries. They mingled with the children and walked very slowly away. Mark had dyed his khaki trousers by pouring ink on them. They then started on their month's trek, keeping to the hills and avoiding bridges and roads. They begged food from the peasants and were always given it. The only map they had was one torn from Trevelyan's book on Garibaldi. As they came nearer to the front, the peasants would tell them where the Germans were. On one occasion they were about to knock on the door of a cottage when they saw a field-telephone wire in the grass. They knew it was a German post. As they got closer to the line, they descended to the valleys foreseeing that the German gun-positions would be on the hills. On they went, getting nearer and nearer. The Germans whom they met took them for peasants. Then suddenly one afternoon they emerged from a wood straight upon an English gun-crew. They shouted in English. 'By God, I thought you blighters were Jerries!' said the corporal. 'Then why', said Mark, his officer status returning to him, 'then why the hell did you not fire at us?'

H.N. TO B.N. & N.N.   *10th November, 1943*
                                                          Sissinghurst

I went down to the House where I had a Leicester deputation about the relief of famine in Europe. The old Peace Pledge Union people have concentrated on the slogan 'Feed the starving men and women of Europe'. This is a great pity, since there is really something to be said for relaxing the blockade in so far as Greece and Belgium are concerned. The advocacy of these people compromises what is an excellent cause. I was very cold with them and pointed out all the difficulties. But I promised to speak the next day when the matter came up on the Adjournment. I did speak. I made the best House of Commons speech that I have made since my Italian speech.[1] The House filled up and I was warmly cheered. But of course the whole thing was spoiled by the pacifists coming in and backing me. *Non tali auxilio*, but there it is. I think I did a little good, and we got promises out of the Government that they would send more food, and of a different quality, to Greece.

---

[1] On 22nd February, 1938. See vol. I, p. 325.

18th November, 1943

All the newspapers I see are furious at the surrender of Leros.[1] What happened, I suppose, is that we counted too readily on the Italian garrison capturing Rhodes and that our schemes for the occupation of the other Italian islands were based upon having the Rhodes aerodromes. Once we lost these, we lost fighter-cover and should have got out of Leros and Cos as soon as possible. This surrender of 3,500 British and 5,000 Italian troops will give the Germans just the fillip they want, and will have a deplorable effect in the Balkans and Turkey. There will be severe criticism all round.

Altogether the war is passing through a bad phase. We have been held up in Italy 'by the weather', which is rather a lame excuse considering what the Russians are doing.

I go to see Mark Bonham Carter. He looks such a school-boy still, in spite of his experiences. But there is about his face something leonine and strong which I much admire.

19th November, 1943

I go to the Dominions Office to see Bobbety Cranborne and Paul Evans by appointment. They said they wanted to see me urgently. I had a suspicion what it was. My suspicion was correct. For, after a long desultory conversation about my visit to Sweden, Bobbety says, 'Would you undertake another trip?' 'Where to?' I ask. 'Australia.' At first I say No, pointing out that I am a civilian of the old liberal school and this may not go down. 'You need have no feelings of inferiority', says Bobbety, 'with the Australians about not fighting. But seriously', he adds, 'I want you to go.' 'Well, if it's like that', I say, 'I have only one answer. But Vita will never forgive you.'

I lunch with Raymond [Mortimer]. I ask him, as my dearest friend, whether I should be cowardly in not defending Tom Mosley if he is attacked in the House.[2] He says that I should leave it to Morrison to defend his action, and that I should be quixotic to rush into the breach over Mosley. I loathe feeling that I funk moral obligations. But he says, 'My dear Harold, nobody thinks you disloyal or cowardly.

[1] See the introductory note to this section, p. 317.

[2] Sir Oswald Mosley and his wife had been imprisoned under Regulation 18b since 1940. Herbert Morrison, the Home Secretary, now proposed to release them on two grounds: first, that Sir Oswald's health had deteriorated in confinement; and secondly, that the grave national emergency which had made his imprisonment necessary had now passed, and it was contrary to the spirit of British law to keep men in detention without fair trial.

Keep your powder for better causes.' But there is something in me (my enemies call it lack of judgement) which forces me to espouse hopeless causes.

I walk back feeling miserable about Australia. If the Government think I am any good, why do they not give me a real job instead of these potty little lecture tours?

DIARY   *23rd November, 1943*

When I get to the House I find a procession of workers with banners protesting against the release of Mosley. Herbert Morrison makes a statement which I find admirable. He takes full responsibility for the release and says that he is not going to allow a man to die in detention. The House is really with him, and if there had been a vote, he would have won hands down. But the *Daily Worker* has been stoking up the Communists and there are demonstrations all over London.

I go to the Beefsteak with Rob [Bernays]. I tell him about Australia. He says (a) that I am mad to absent myself from Parliament at this moment; (b) that I shall be a ghastly failure in Australia. They will see in me all that they most dislike about the British.

DIARY   *1st December, 1943*

I had a talk with Archie Sinclair[1] today about the bombing of Italian cities. I said, for instance, that if they wanted to bomb the marshalling-yards at Pisa, they ought to pause for a moment and consider whether the destruction of a few trains was worth the destruction of the Baptistry. He said that Tedder was under Eisenhower's orders, and that if the Generals knew that a concentration of materials was taking place at Pisa they must bomb regardless of all artistic treasures. But the Americans did have a list of works-of-art and historic buildings and in normal circumstances they did seek to avoid them. He was quite reasonable about it.

The news is published that Winston, Roosevelt and Chiang Kai-shek have met in Cairo. They go on, I suppose, to Tiflis[2] to meet Stalin. It will increase the prestige and self-esteem of that dictator to bring two elderly men all the way to the Caucasus. But in such matters Roosevelt and Churchill are great enough to be able to afford a little flattery.

[1] Sir Archibald Sinclair, Secretary of State for Air, 1940–45.
[2] Actually, Tehran.

H.N. TO B.N. & N.N. *3rd December, 1943*
Sissinghurst

A workers' deputation from Leicester factories came to see me about Mosley. They were not in any way hostile or impolite. But I could see that anything I might say in defence of Morrison was 'propaganda' and untrue. I feel that it is most dangerous that the working-classes should have lost all confidence in their leaders. They will believe anything 'against the Government' and nothing which its defenders can assert. One has the sad impression that the 'sound common sense' of the British working man is a mere legend. Hitherto they have been apathetic and have left politics to their own leaders. They are now becoming extremely conscious of politics and very subject to Marxist slogans.

I don't think I have a chance of keeping my seat in the next Election. Nobody in a constituency where the majority are working-class will keep his seat. I still have to stand, of course, but it will be an unpleasant ordeal and the end will be defeat. I am lucky to have had the seat for nine years and to have sat in one of the most important Parliaments that there has ever been. But, as I said, I have no chance of remaining the Member for West Leicester.

V.S-W. TO H.N. *7th December, 1943*

You know, Hadji, it disconcerts me so much having someone to stay that I am not at all nice at first, and then I adjust myself and it gets all right. I know that I was horrid and aloof to Gwen[1] on Monday, but had recovered by Tuesday and could get at the real Gwen whom I know and can talk to. And then this morning she goes away and I find little coffee-cups[2] which twist my heart, and all my irritation goes and I wish I could have it all over again and be nicer. You are never like that. You never seem to get knocked off your perch as I do. Only your perch is consistently more mobile.

H.N. TO V.S-W. *8th December, 1943*
4 King's Bench Walk, E.C.4

Of course you get knocked off your perch. You see, a person who sleeps every night in the middle of Dartmoor is liable, if given a bedroom overlooking St Pancras station, to sleep badly. Similarly a person

[1] Lady St Levan, H.N.'s sister.
[2] The half-empty coffee-cup which one finds on returning to the house after saying goodbye to a much-loved guest: hence any reminder of this sort.

who has lived all his life overlooking St Pancras station (*vous n'imaginez pas comme ça gazouille*) would lie awake all night on Dartmoor unable to sleep for the silence. But there is something worse than that about it. If I am knocked off my perch I clamber back only a trifle out of breath. But you are not used to being off your perch, and you don't know how to get back on it. You flounder about like a parrot who has drunk a glass of brandy.

I went to the House all afternoon. We had a reception for the Chinese mission. They grinned and bowed under the arc-lights. Then that foul man John Simon made a speech. How dare he?—since he is the main betrayer of China. We walked out. Nancy Astor (who has guts about these things) walked out snorting loudly. She thinks you are going to become a candlestick.[1] I assured her this was not true. She dreads it nonetheless. I said I did not believe in God at all. She gasped like a fish. But you know, tiresome as she is, there is something in her. A flame somewhere.

V.S-W. TO H.N.   *10th December, 1943*
                                                              Sissinghurst

No, I shall never become a candlestick. But I do not see how you cannot believe in God at all. Call him 'Thing' if you like and if the word 'God' puts you off because of all its connotations. But I do not see how you can get out of the idea of a Creator and inventor. I mean ... well, I should have to write another book to explain what I mean. You see there must be *some* explanation, some solution; and that is God. It seems to me so simple, stated like that: what muddled it, are the decorations which man has added to meet his own needs, fears, desires and longings for comfort and reassurance.

DIARY   *10th December, 1943*

I lunch at the Ritz with General de Lattre de Tassigny.[2] He is a vital and amusing man. A little vain. He is apt to repeat too often that he commanded an Army Corps, that he had many decorations, that he was wounded seven times and that he had eight *citations*. But he is a fine fellow nonetheless, and a worthy pupil of what he calls '*la maison*

---

[1] A Roman Catholic. This widespread rumour was based upon V.S-W.'s recently published book, *The Eagle and the Dove*, which had shown great sympathy towards the two Saints Teresa, of Avila and Lisieux.

[2] One of the two ablest commanders (General Juin was the other) of the Free French military forces.

Foch-Weygand'. He had lived near Clemenceau at the end of the old boy's life and would visit him every morning. Clemenceau had warned him against Smuts, whom he called *'le saboteur du Traité de Versailles'*. De Lattre told me that when he had escaped, having been imprisoned by Pétain, the latter sent him a message to express his congratulations and 'solicitude'. 'Tell the Marshal', he had replied, 'that there is only one thing he can do to redeem his treachery. That is to die very quickly.' Anyhow, he is now off to Algiers to command an Army Corps of seven divisions. He says that the only thing which will save France and restore her love for her Army is that these divisions should fight hard and well. He is a curious man, somewhat excitable, rather vain.

DIARY   *16th December, 1943*

Dine with Gladwyn and my god-son Miles [Jebb] at the Travellers. Gladwyn was just back from Tehran where he had attended the Conference. He said that when Stalin handed the Sword of Stalingrad[1] to Voroshilov, he took it the wrong way up and the thing slipped out of its scabbard. He said that Stalin was not grey but green in colour. Very short. Like Lord Baldwin.

H.N. TO B.N. & N.N.   *17th December, 1943*

I arrived late at the House to find them all with blank faces. Attlee had just given the news that Winston was down with pneumonia.[2] People were horrified. I went on to the B.B.C. and Violet telephoned at once to Downing Street. They had no other news than that given on the wireless. But I gather that he is now past the crisis, although they were very worried indeed for the first few hours. Apparently he had a cold and a touch of fever when he left Cairo. But Gladwyn, who was with him in Tehran, said he had never seen him in such good form. Clemmie [Churchill] has flown out there to be with him.

---

[1] This sword, specially forged and suitably inscribed, was the gift of King George VI to the City of Stalingrad as a token of the British people's admiration for the defenders of the city. It was taken out to Tehran by Churchill and presented to Stalin by him. Churchill says in his Memoirs: 'I handed the splendid weapon to Marshal Stalin. He raised it in a most impressive gesture to his lips and kissed the scabbard. He then passed it to Voroshilov, who dropped it.' *Closing the Ring*, p. 321.
[2] Pneumonia was diagnosed when Churchill reached Tunis on 11th December.

DIARY   *18th December, 1943*

Walk in the orchards with James [Pope-Hennessy]. He reads my diary. He finds it unbelievable that a man who in ordinary life is gay and amusing should become so pompous and dull when he comes to write his diary. 'But it's all about politics!' he says in indignation.

H.N. TO B.N. & N.N.   *20th December, 1943*
                                                          Sissinghurst

I went to see Viénot[1] in his huge study at Carlton Gardens, very much Monsieur l'Ambassadeur, and sitting in the seat where once de Gaulle plotted and raged. Viénot is worried about this very problem. He regrets that he is unable to establish human relations with Anthony Eden. '*Il s'esquive derrière son charme.*' How true that is! Anthony has managed to create out of affability a smoke-screen more impenetrable than any cloud of sullenness. Anyhow Viénot was delighted with my speech[2] and showed me telegrams from Algiers expressing the same opinion. '*Il est bien quand on nous appuie. Il est encore mieux quand on le fait avec tant d'intelligence.*' So I was pleased.

I went that evening to one of Sibyl Colefax's Ordinaries.[3] Everybody loathes them, and one feels a sort of community of dislike binding together what would otherwise be a most uncongenial company. Sibyl knows in a way that people hate these ghastly functions. She adopts a mood of will-power. She manages us firmly as if we had all come to the Dorchester to give a blood-transfusion. No nonsense and no delay. 'You sit there . . .'

DIARY   *26th December, 1943*

We go over to Long Barn.[4] I walk sadly in the damp fog thinking of all the happy days of youth passed among those poplars and meadows. Fifteen years was Long Barn my dear home, and now it is to be sold to a film magnate called Soskin. It is looking very pretty. Viti and I

[1] He had become the French Ambassador to Britain when the French National Committee was established in Algiers in May 1943.
[2] In the House of Commons on 15th December, in the debate on British policy towards France.
[3] Lady Colefax was giving dinner-parties, called her 'Ordinaries', for about thirty people each week at the Dorchester. The guests paid for their meals.
[4] The small fourteenth-century house near Sevenoaks, where H.N. and V.S-W. had lived from 1915 to 1930, when they bought Sissinghurst. During the war it was used as a home for displaced children.

rather sadly measure furniture to see what we shall take to Sissinghurst. Afterwards the refugee children sing carols for us.

I feel depressed by the war and the coming revolution and the loss of my past life and values. Even Europe, which I knew and loved so well, has ceased to be important. *Les Scythes ont conquis le monde.*

DIARY   *30th December, 1943*

Bobbety Cranborne tells me that after full investigation they find that they cannot send me out to Australia except by sea, and cannot guarantee that they can get me back by air. This means that my condition that I should be back by April cannot be fulfilled. Therefore he thinks that I had better chuck the whole Australian idea. I had been amused to find that I did not know in myself (such were the conflicts of interest and distaste) whether I really wanted to go or not. But when he indicated No, I felt a rush of relief and delight. So I never wanted to go at all. Or was it that my rush of delight was simply relief about Vita's anxiety? I don't know. All I know is that I felt a definite pleasure thrill and not a disappointment sink. I come home immediately and telephone to V. She is delighted.

H.N. TO B.N. & N.N.   *31st December, 1943*
                                                            Sissinghurst

There have been two world-shaking events this week. The first was the arrival today of a telegram from Jerusalem signed by both of you. It gave us intense pleasure to feel that you would see the New Year in together at King David's royal hotel, and listen to the bells of Bethlehem ringing out the old. The second event of importance is that I have definitely managed to evade my Australian expedition.

I dined yesterday at the Travellers and sat next to a friend of mine and yours called James Langley, who, as you know, has a most dreadful stammer. An elderly gentleman came in just as we had begun and took the table on my other side. James told me that he had had a letter from Nigel. He added that Nigel had had himself photographed in order to please Mummy and me. But when the photograph was developed it was too awful to send. 'He told me', James continued', that it made him look so beastly —m—m—m—m—m—m—m—m—m.' The man on the other side finished his soup and started on some hashed chicken. 'So beastly', persisted James, 'm—m—m—m—m—m—m— m—m.' The man finished his chicken and was given (as I saw out of my left eye) some cold Christmas pudding. 'So beastly m—m—m—

m—m—m—m—m—m—m.' 'Untidy?' I suggested, wishing to help. James shook his head firmly in the negative and began again. 'So beastly —m—m—m—m—m—m—m—m—m.' 'Fat?' I tried, not wishing to be hard on Nigel, but hoping somehow to bring this umming to an end. James again indicated dissent. The gentleman beside me finished his Christmas pudding, and said he thought he would like to try an apple. 'So beastly m—m—m—m—m—m—m—m—MMMMM—STOUT', he ejaculated at last. The old gentleman by then had paid his bill and left.

1944

Greece – H.N.'s speech on the subject – Churchill's imitation of his reception of Sforza – the Rundstedt offensive in the Ardennes – H.N. on V.S-W.'s poetry – Ben's accident in Italy

'Perhaps the beginning of the end'[1]

During his illness at Tunis and his convalescence at Marrakesh, Churchill was planning the Allied assault on Anzio, south of Rome. The landing took place on 22nd January. Its object was to force the withdrawal of the German armies from their winter-line at Cassino by cutting their communications, and, if possible, to seize Rome itself by a coup-de-main. The landing took the Germans by surprise. One British and one American Division were put ashore at Anzio almost without casualties, and the way to Rome was wide open. But the American Corps Commander, who had fought at Salerno, was primarily concerned to build up his strength in the beach-head to resist the inevitable counter-attack and lost his opportunity to press on quickly to the Alban Hills. The Germans reacted with far greater speed by bringing divisions down from northern Italy and France in order to confine, and then crush, the beach-head, while they held their positions at Cassino. They launched two major attacks, on 3rd and 16th February, and each was held with difficulty by the Allied superiority in gunfire and air-attack. By 1st March the German effort was spent, but instead of breaking the deadlock on the Italian front, Anzio became a beleaguered fortress which was not relieved until the Cassino front collapsed in May.

The Italian operations naturally claimed the attention of the House of Commons more than any other. At the same time, the progress of the war now raised more acutely the political problems of territories about to be liberated. There was the problem of Greece, precipitated by the conflict between E.D.E.S. and the Communist-inspired E.L.A.S., and the mutiny, quelled by the British in April, of military and naval forces in Cairo and Alexandria. There was the problem of Poland, whose pre-war frontiers were crossed by the Russians at the beginning of January, and the other Eastern European countries over which the Soviet Government already claimed political control in defiance of the principles laid down by the Atlantic Charter. There was the problem of Yugoslavia, where the Partisans were fighting simultaneously the Germans and the Royalist forces of Mihailović, and had come to dominate both to such an extent that Churchill decided in February to switch all his support to

[1] Typed by H.N. on 1st January.

341

Tito. And there was the continuing problem of de Gaulle, whose National Committee in Algiers claimed against strong American opposition to become the Government of France once France was liberated.

With all these difficulties, political more than military, Harold Nicolson was much concerned. He was living for most of the time in London, now the target of renewed German air-attacks in retaliation for the severe bombing of Germany by the Americans in daylight and the R.A.F. at night. Apart from the House of Commons and his weekly 'Marginal Comment' for the 'Spectator', his main occupation was as a Governor of the B.B.C. He also wrote during the first two months of 1944 a pamphlet on 'The Last Peace and the Next' for the Army Bureau of Current Affairs, while V. Sackville-West wrote for the Ministry of Agriculture an account of the Women's Land Army.[1] Both their sons were still overseas: Ben organising photo-interpretation courses near Cairo, and Nigel with the 1st Guards Brigade in the mountainous bridgehead across the River Garigliano and, after 7th April, in the ruins of Cassino.

DIARY   *5th January, 1944*

Lunch at the Beefsteak. Gerry [Wellington][2] is there. He tells me of his experiences in Sicily. He simply loathed the sight of corpses. He saw people who had had all their clothes burnt off. The stench was awful. On entering Syracuse he was sent for by Montgomery. 'I must have the streets cleared within the hour of all masonry and débris.' Gerry went down to the shelters where the population were hiding and turned them all on to work. Montgomery was pleased, and gave him a cigarette-lighter as a present. Later, at a place called Lentini, Montgomery's A.D.C. appeared at Gerry's office. He was embarrassed at having to put to Gerry the request which Montgomery told him to make. In driving through, Monty had seen a cage of canaries outside a house. Could Gerry get them for him? So off Gerry went with the A.D.C. and they found the house and brought back the canaries. 'You see', said the A.D.C., 'the General says that these little birds keep him in a good temper.' This makes me ill. Never has there been such a careful creation of a legend. Montgomery today is the second most popular figure in England.

[1] *The Women's Land Army.* Michael Joseph. 1944.
[2] The Duke of Wellington (Gerald Wellesley), one of H.N.'s oldest friends. He had been a Lieutenant-Colonel in Allied Military Government until he succeeded his nephew as 7th Duke in September 1943.

I ask him about looting. He says that all soldiers loot, but that they generally have no idea of values and do not want to possess or carry things they do not need. For instance, they will always steal a mandoline if they can find one. What is far worse is the American passion for souvenir-hunting. The American dough-boy is better educated than his British opposite number, in the sense that he has heard about Girgenti[1] and Archimedes, and will chip off fragments of the columns to send home. There seems to be no limit to their mailing facilities. They even tore things off a house at Brontë, because it had something to do with Nelson.

DIARY   *6th January, 1944*

The *Evening Standard* carries a most pernicious cartoon by Low. It represents some highly idealised Cossacks crossing the Polish border to be met by a gentleman in a frock-coat carrying under his arm pieces of paper bearing the words 'Curzon Line' and so on. They say to him, 'Are you on our side or on theirs?' and he answers, 'On mine.' This is a distortion of the whole principle of the Atlantic Charter and an assumption that no small country has in future any right to exist. Considering that we entered the war to protect Poland's independence, it is heart-rending that such irresponsible conceptions should be printed in London. It is curious to note how these Colonials like Beaverbrook, Smuts and Low are able to influence British opinion by airing their anti-European prejudices. There is a definite tendency growing up to regard 'Europe' as something old-fashioned and therefore reactionary. There is no realisation of the fact that if Europe were abolished, we should ourselves almost immediately decline to the status of a third-rate power. Low and Beaverbrook would rather like that, since they think it would increase the prestige of Australia and Canada.

DIARY   *7th January, 1944*

Go down home. A lovely day. Begin notes for my A.B.C.A. article.[2] In the evening we hear a talk about the new aeroplane which runs on compressed air.[3] I do not understand a word of it. The inventor says a few very modest words at the end.

---

[1] Agrigentum (the modern Girgenti) in Sicily, where there are several Doric temples in a wonderful state of preservation.
[2] On 'The Last Peace and the Next' for the Army Bureau of Current Affairs.
[3] The jet engine, developed by (Sir) Frank Whittle, was just coming into production.

H.N. TO B.N. & N.N.   *11th January, 1944*
                                                       Sissinghurst

I had to go to the Foreign Office as one of a deputation to see Anthony
Eden. It was a fine deputation. Lords Horder, Perth and Lytton from
the Lords, and Eleanor Rathbone, Quintin Hogg and myself from the
Commons. Poor Anthony had been seeing the Polish Prime Minister
three times that day seeking to persuade him to return to the Tass
communiqué a reply which would be less provocative than they felt.[1]
But in spite of this he received us with great cordiality and for one
hour we discussed what could be done to rescue a few more Jews from
Germany. I sat there gazing round at that ugly and once familiar
room. The room in which I had seen Edward Grey pacing the carpet,
gnawing at his under-lip; the room in which I had stood by Curzon
while he munched hot toast and raspberry jam; the room in which I
had seen Ramsay MacDonald actually twisting in agony over the
Dodecanese question; the room in which we had first discussed with
Austen Chamberlain the basis of Locarno. It is true, of course, that
Anthony is apt to hide behind his own charm. One goes away thinking
how reasonable, how agreeable and how helpful he has been, and then
discovers that in fact he has promised nothing at all.

H.N. TO B.N. & N.N.   *18th January, 1944*
                                                       Sissinghurst

This was an exciting day. The House met again after the Christmas
Recess and I went down there early. I happened to have been told
that Winston had arrived home that morning,[2] but the rest of the
House were wholly unaware of that fact. We were dawdling through
Questions and I was idly glancing at my Order Paper when I saw (*saw*
is the word) a gasp of astonishment pass over the faces of the Labour
Party opposite. Suddenly they jumped to their feet and started
shouting, waving their papers in the air. We also jumped up and the
whole House broke into cheer after cheer while Winston, very pink,
rather shy, beaming with mischief, crept along the front bench and
flung himself into his accustomed seat. He was flushed with pleasure
and emotion, and hardly had he sat down when two large tears began

---

[1] The communiqué hinted broadly that Russia expected to annex the eastern provinces
of Poland and to have a say in the appointment of Ministers to the future Government of Poland.
[2] From Marrakesh, where he had been convalescing since 27th December.

to trickle down his cheeks. He mopped at them clumsily with a huge white handkerchief.

A few minutes later he got up to answer questions. Most men would have been unable, on such an occasion, not to throw a flash of drama into their replies. But Winston answered them as if he were the youngest Under-Secretary, putting on his glasses, turning over his papers, responding tactfully to supplementaries, and taking the whole thing as conscientiously as could be. I should like to say that he seemed completely restored to health. But he looked pale when the first flush of pleasure had subsided, and his voice was not quite so vigorous as it had been.

In the smoking-room afterwards he told us how, when flying from Carthage to Marrakesh, he had indicated to the pilot that they seemed to be flying very low and might bump into the Atlas. 'That's just it', said the pilot, 'but I have orders not to take you above 6,000 feet.' 'Nonsense', said Winston, 'I give you different orders. Go up to 11,000 feet immediately.' And this had done him no harm. Tommy Lascelles[1] told me that when that morning Winston had been to see the King, he (Tommy) had met him at the Palace door. Tommy asked after his health. 'I'm quite all right', said Winston, 'quite all right. Only I'm a little groggy still on my pins.' 'Would you like the lift?' asked Tommy. 'Lift?' said Winston—and ran up the stairs two at a time. When he reached the top, he turned round to Tommy and cocked a snook.

I dined with Sibyl [Colefax]. Archie Clark Kerr was there on his way (via New York) from Tehran to Moscow. I had found people in the House very worried about recent Russian behaviour. They had been distressed by the truly brutal way in which the Russians had treated the overtures of the Polish Government. They had been even more distressed by the publication in *Pravda* of a rumour that we had been holding secret conversations with Joachim von Ribbentrop. What did this mean? Archie was consoling. He laughed at the idea that Russia was preparing some sort of get-away. 'Nobody could think that who has been in Russia. Certainly nobody could think that who has been in Tehran.' But he was puzzled nonetheless by the *Pravda* incident. He thought that it was probably nothing more than a piece of oriental mischief. He says that the Russians want very much to be admitted as a civilised member of the Concert of Europe. 'They want to belong to the Club.' Well, I hope all that is true. But Archie

[1] Sir Alan Lascelles, Private Secretary to the King, 1943–52.

is not the type of diplomatist (like my father and Nevile Henderson) who refuses to believe anything bad about the country to which they are accredited. Had he thought there was any danger, he would have said so, and his attitude cheered me considerably.

DIARY   27th January, 1944

It looks as if we had had something of a check at the Nettuno bridge-head.[1] The Americans have lost ground. There is some criticism of the fact that having boasted about taking the enemy by surprise, we did not exploit our advantage better. I am assured however that all is going according to plan.

DIARY   29th January, 1944

Our wireless has gone wrong, and when (during a raid) Viti and I start fiddling with it, there is a swish in the air and then two explosions which shake the cottage. We open the door and see a white incandescent light outside which shortly turns to red. We go out into the rose garden and see a great blaze of fire at what seems to be the Hammer Brook bridge. As we watch, the fire-engine with its bells clanging dashes along the road. Mrs Staples[2] comes to tell us that it was a German bomber which crashed in flames, only missing the tower by a few yards. There is no doubt that this part of Kent is much exposed and I am worried about my darling Viti.

DIARY   31st January, 1944

Muray[3] comes to see me. He is working with the Pioneer Corps at Buxton. He says that most of the men who come back from the front state openly that once Germany is beaten, they will refuse to do any more. They are not revolutionary but believe that they have been fighting for 'a better Britain' and identify that with the Beveridge Report. They are interested only in what may affect their own future position. They are slightly sceptical about Russia, and disconcerted by

---

[1] Nettuno and Anzio are coastal resorts side by side. The Germans called it the Nettuno beach-head; the Allies came to call it after Anzio. The landings had taken place on 22nd January, and the deepest exploitation had been no more than ten miles from the coast.

[2] The cook at Sissinghurst. The bomber crashed at Three Chimneys, $1\frac{1}{2}$ miles away, but it released a bomb which fell in a field just beyond the garden. The German crew were all captured next day by the local Home Guard.

[3] An anglicised Austrian friend, who had been working in the British Political Intelligence Division of the Foreign Office.

the *Pravda* statement, which none of them believe. They do not for one moment think that Russia is the workers' paradise, but they do believe that Russia is the place where the working-man governs and does well. The efficiency of Russia has had far more effect on them than any Marxist idealism.

Dine with Stuart Preston[1] at Boulestin. He says that his fellow-Americans compare everything in Britain to the Frigidaires and other conveniences of Des Moines, and that they have no conception at all of the interest of Europe. He says that our men may be just as stupid, but they are at least modest and believe that there may be some things that they do not know. To the Americans (both officers and privates) the suggestion that they do not know about a thing implies that the thing is feudal or bad.

DIARY   *7th February, 1944*

I fear that Winston has become an electoral liability now rather than an asset.[2] This makes me sick with human nature. Once the open sea is reached, we forget how we clung to the pilot in the storm. Poor Winston, who is so sensitive although so pugnacious, will feel all this. In the station lavatory at Blackheath last week I found scrawled up, 'Winston Churchill is a bastard.' I pointed it out to the Wing Commander who was with me. 'Yes', he said, 'the tide has turned. We find it everywhere.' 'But how foul', I said. 'How bloody foul!' 'Well, you see, if I may say so, the men hate politicians.' Winston a politician! Good God!

DIARY   *8th February, 1944*

People are worried about the Anzio beach-head. (*O diva gratum quae regis Antium.*) We have made a mess of this, and a 'British military commentator' in Washington has admitted our 'disappointment'. Everybody at once assumes that this is preparing us for a Gallipoli. Blame is put on different people. We say the Americans run away the moment a shot is fired. The Americans will say that it is the fault of Alexander. Alexander's friends will say it is the fault of Mark Clark.[3] And the War Cabinet will allow it to be supposed that it is the fault of

[1] A young American art-historian who was serving in the U.S. Army in Britain.
[2] The Government had lost recent bye-elections to the Common Wealth Party.
[3] The American C.-in-C. of the 5th Army, under whose command the Anzio operation fell. The Corps Commander on the spot was Lt.-Gen. J. P. Lucas.

Jumbo Wilson,[1] who is being called in official circles 'the wizard of Cos'.

DIARY   *10th February, 1944*

I lunch with Camrose at the *Daily Telegraph*. The other guests are Lord Ashfield[2] and Sir Alan Brooke, the C.I.G.S. When the latter enters the room, Camrose begins cheerily with, 'Well, what about the bridgehead?' The C.I.G.S. is obviously annoyed, mutters, 'It is difficult to judge such matters at this distance', and pours himself a sulky glass of sherry. But when we get into the next room and sit down and have some claret, things brighten up, and a slow flush spreads over the handsome face of the C.I.G.S. He begins by describing how he first noticed that Winston was on the verge of a great illness. It was at Cairo. He had a fly-swat in his hand and was more interested in swatting flies than in listening to his military advisors. Then they had great difficulty in preventing him leaving for Italy and were almost relieved when he developed fever.

Brooke himself had gone over to Italy. He says that the terrain defies description. It is like the North-West Frontier; a single destroyed culvert can hold up an army for a day. He then went on to talk about the Germans. He says they are fighting magnificently. 'Marvellous it is, perfectly marvellous. But their strategy must be being dictated by Hitler, as it is all wrong. When one is on the wave of victory one can successfully violate all the established rules of war. But when one starts to decline, one cannot violate them without disaster.' Thus Hitler, in insisting on holding on at Nikopol[3] and establishing a front so far down the leg of Italy, was setting himself a formidable task. The Russian offensives indicate that he is short of immediate mobile reserves. The fact that he has had to reinforce Italy from the Balkans and Southern France indicates that he has not many reserves in Germany itself. He cannot hope to run four fronts—Russia, the Balkans, Italy and France. He may hope that during the wet period between 15th April and 1st June he can transfer troops from Russia to the West—and he certainly has good transport facilities for a shuttle in the east-west direction, but not in the north-south direction—but he

[1] General Sir Henry Maitland Wilson, the British Supreme Allied Commander in the Mediterranean. Alexander was C.-in-C. of the whole Italian campaign. Thus Alexander was subordinate to Wilson and senior to Clark.
[2] Chairman of the London Passenger Transport Board, 1933–47.
[3] On the lower Dnieper.

cannot carry on like this for many months. It does not yet look as if the Germans are short of material. Our hopes that they would run out of oil have been disappointed. The morale of their troops is still admirable and only a slight change can be seen in the quality of the prisoners captured. There is slight evidence that some senior officers are practising the 'gentleman' stunt in order to affect British sentimentality. Von Thoma[1] is very outspoken and tells us exactly what influence Hitler really has. For instance, the Italians were opposed to the advance on Alamein, but Rommel insisted; but when Rommel got there, he saw he was in a bad way and decided to come home to receive his Marshal's baton while there was still time. He then asked Hitler to transfer him to some other front. Hitler refused and said, 'Go back and take Cairo'. Rommel had not the courage to say, 'But, mein Führer, I'm afraid I can't.'

As we leave, Brooke pauses before the huge map of the Pacific. How are we going to attack? Through Burma? Through Singapore? Via New Guinea? Or via Formosa? How? How? He swings his finger across these four alternatives but gives us no answer.

DIARY   16th February, 1944

I have supper with Rothermere. A discussion starts about whether we should sacrifice lives in order to spare works-of-art. I say that we should realise that works-of-art are irreplaceable, whereas no lives are irreplaceable. If the war could really be shortened by destroying Perugia, then I might agree to do so. But I am not satisfied that the strategic value of fighting up through Italy justifies the enormous loss to civilization which it entails.[2] Ronald Storrs[3] and Sibyl Colefax hedge hard until they see that the majority agree with me. Esmond Rothermere is very good about it.

We then discuss who should be Prime Minister if Winston were killed. We all agree on Eden for the moment. The majority agree on Herbert Morrison after that.

[1] General Ritter von Thoma, the actual commander of the Afrika Korps under Rommel's overall command, gave himself up to the British during the closing stages of the battle of Alamein. He called Hitler's order to stand fast, 'a piece of unparalleled madness. I cannot go along with this any longer.'

[2] H.N. developed this argument in a 'Marginal Comment' a few weeks later, stating that he would rather his son were killed at Cassino than that the Monastery should be destroyed. He did not then know that his son was at Cassino.

[3] Governor of Cyprus, 1926–32, and author of Orientations.

V.S-W. TO H.N.   16th February, 1944
                                                                    Sissinghurst

Darling, Knole has been bombed. All the windows on the front of the house and in the Green Court and Stone Court, and on the garden side (including a window in the chapel), are broken. A special sort of bomb fell just in front of the wicket—no, not just in front, but slightly to the left. Eddy[1] rang me up to tell me. Then I rang up Uncle Charlie[2] who says he had written me a long letter about it today, which I suppose I shall get tomorrow. I mind frightfully, frightfully, frightfully. I always persuade myself that I have finally torn Knole out of my heart,[3] and then the moment anything touches it, every nerve is alive again. I cannot bear to think of Knole wounded, and I not there to look after it and be wounded with it. Those filthy Germans! Let us level every town in Germany to the ground! I shan't care. Oh Hadji, I wish you were here. I feel hurt and heart-sick.

H.N. TO B.N. & N.N.   21st February, 1944
                                                                    Sissinghurst

I dined with Stuart Preston at my Club. It was bitterly cold, since all the windows had been smashed and the curtains failed completely to keep out the north-east wind. We hurried over our dinner and crouched over the fire downstairs. Stuart said to me, 'Harold, do you mind criticism of your books?' I said, 'Well, it depends.' He said, 'What I mean is, does it make you unhappy to read a general review of your literary work which is unfavourable?' 'Out with it', I said, scenting something disobliging. Then very gingerly he pulled from his pocket an article from the New Yorker.[4] I felt I did not care a hoot what might be said about me in any article in the New Yorker, but being polite I did not tell Stuart so. But when I glanced at the signature and saw it was by Edmund Wilson,[5] I felt differently. I knew that I should care very much indeed what Edmund Wilson said.

[1] Edward Sackville West, V.S-W.'s first cousin, who became Lord Sackville in 1962. He was a distinguished writer and musical critic.
[2] Lord Sackville, Edward Sackville West's father and V.S-W.'s uncle.
[3] Although she loved Knole deeply, and had been born and brought up there, she only once returned to the house between 1928 and 1960. Her reasons were complex, but one was that she could not inherit Knole although she was her father's only child.
[4] The issue of 1st January, 1944.
[5] The leading American critic, and author of To the Finland Station etc.

It was supposed to be a review of *The Desire to Please*, but was in fact a review of most of my work, and it was entitled 'Through the Embassy window'. The general theme was that in spite of my literary talent, I had been unable to write a good book, with the exception of *Some People*, owing to the fact that between me and life there intervened a sheet of glass. That sheet of glass consisted of my aristocratic prejudices and puritan upbringing. Thus I had been deeply shocked by Byron, Verlaine and Swinburne; I had failed to understand the deep social movements of my time; and my diplomatic studies are 'schoolboy stories in which England is always St George'.

It seems absurd to me that any man of Wilson's great intelligence should regard me as 'well-brushed and well-bred' or suspect that I could ever be shocked by the depravity of men of genius. I believe that he has got the *symptoms* wrong, but I have a nasty feeling that he has got the *illness* right. There is something (is it a hatred of emotion, or merely a lack of muscles in the mind?) which renders most of my writing superficial. I am sorry about this, since I must have written ten million words in my day and it is sad that they should be so valueless. But when I read the article a third time, my irritation disappeared. I felt glad that Wilson should have devoted an article to books which he had clearly read carefully, and his nice remarks about *Some People* made up for all his classing of the rest as 'unsatisfactory'. But if in truth I have gone through life regarded by the respectable as a Bohemian and by the Bohemians as conventional, there must be something very very wrong.

V.S-W. TO H.N.   *23rd February, 1944*
                                             Sissinghurst

As I read the *New Yorker* article (getting more and more indignant), I thought, 'This man, although he is saying some exceedingly foolish things, is a man of intelligence who also writes very well.' Then I looked for a signature and found 'Edmund Wilson'. It is of course absurd to say that you are shocked by Byron or Swinburne, and where he goes wrong over criticising you for so obviously belonging to a definite class, by birth, education, experience and consequent outlook, is that he ought to have stated it as a fact and not as an adverse criticism. He is falling into a common error of critics, which is to demand that a writer shall be something he is not. It is no good expecting a gentle person of sensibility and culture to care for the rough-and-tumble. I think that both your merits and your shortcomings as a writer proceed from things in your own character. I think, for instance, that your almost morbid dislike of emotion is at the root of much of what E. Wilson is trying to say; only he has not got the clue to the puzzle.

DIARY   *22nd February, 1944*

I go down to the House early. It is packed. Winston gets up soon after noon. He is looking well again, but he has a slight cough. He is not of course as vigorous or as pugnacious as in 1940. But he has no need to be. He is right to take the more sober tone of the elder states-man.

He begins quite abruptly with the words, 'This is not a time for sorrow or rejoicing. It is a time for preparation, effort and resolve'. He goes on to state our own contribution to the war-effort. He discloses that we have lost 38,300 pilots and aircrew and over 10,000 machines since the beginning of the war. He forecasts reprisals by the Germans which have hitherto been 'modest', but which will increase. He refers to the secret weapon.[1] In describing how our air superiority is gradually asserting itself, he ends with the words, 'There is a strange, stern justice in the long . . .' and then he sways his hands below the level of his waist '. . . long swing of events.' He admits that the Anzio landing has proved a disappointment and was not carried out according to plan. He then refers to the new commands. The names of Eisenhower and Alexander are warmly greeted; at the mention of Montgomery there is one isolated 'Hear! Hear!'.

He then passes to the political side and speaks of Badoglio and Tito. About Italy we shall take 'a new view' once we have got Rome. He devotes a long and brilliant passage to Marshal Tito and 'a young friend of mine, an Oxford don, Lieutenant-Colonel Deakin, D.S.O.'[2] He refers to King Peter and says that our principle is 'to keep good faith with those who have kept good faith with us'. He then refers to the squabbles among the Greek guerrilla leaders, and says that they do not represent the mass of the Greek people, who are longing only for the hour of liberation. 'They shall not wait in vain.' He then goes on to our relations with Russia. 'None of the ground made good at Moscow and Tehran has been lost.' He said that Stalin had personally

[1] The German pilotless 'plane, the V.1, and their rocket missile, the V.2.
[2] F. W. D. Deakin, a Fellow of Wadham College, Oxford, who had helped Churchill for five years before the war with his literary work, and was sent by him to lead the first British Military Mission to Tito in May 1943.

assured him that what he wanted was 'a strong, integral, independent Poland as one of the leading Powers of Europe'. He says that he agrees that it is 'reasonable and just' that Russia should have the Curzon Line and that Poland should obtain 'compensation at the expense of Germany both in the north and in the west'. In this connection he defines what he means by unconditional surrender. The Atlantic Charter does not apply to Germany; we are not to be bound to Germany by any pact or obligation; we shall have a free hand, but that does not mean that we shall behave barbarously or against our conscience. He makes a passing reference to internal dissensions [in the House of Commons] and to those 'little folk who frolic alongside the juggernaut of war to see what fun or notoriety they can extract from the proceedings'.

DIARY   1st March, 1944

I pick up Viti and go to Buckingham Palace for a tea-party. It takes place in the hall. The company is divided into two groups each side of the Propylaea, and the King and Queen stand in the middle. There are many foreign diplomatists whom they greet. I am taken to talk to the Princesses. Princess Elizabeth is a clear, nice girl. I talk to her about the Grenadiers.[1]

I dine with James [Pope-Hennessy] at Rules and we go on to Pratts. James cannot understand how it comes that I am so interested in politics. Pratts is a political kitchen. During the raid last Wednesday there was a committee meeting on. Suddenly there was a crash, all the lights went out, and the building rocked. Then the lights went on again. 'Well, gentlemen', said Eddy Devonshire, 'I am not quite clear whether we elected that fellow or not.'

It is sad on my return to see so many people sleeping on the tube platforms. It is more disgraceful than ever to see the Americans with the East End Jewish girls, shouting among those unhappy and re-cumbent forms. I hate it.

DIARY   2nd March, 1944

We have a long B.B.C. meeting. It begins with a private meeting between Foot[2] and ourselves. He makes a statement about our rela-

---

[1] Princess Elizabeth, who was then nearly 18, had been appointed Colonel of the Grenadier Guards in February 1942.
[2] R. W. Foot, Director-General of the B.B.C. since 1943, and in 1942, Joint Director-General with Sir Cecil Graves. He was succeeded later in 1944 by (Sir) William Haley and became Chairman of the Mining Association of Great Britain.

tions. It is a confused statement. He begins by saying that there is nothing personal about his attitude, and that he regards us as friends. He had imagined that with strong management the relations between the Board and the Executive would improve. He had been disappointed. He had been specially disturbed by the paper I had written after Christmas which showed a complete divergence of view between himself and the Board as to the proper functions of the Governors. He based his case on paragraph 16 of the Ullswater Report. He also quoted the minute of his appointment which said that the running of the B.B.C. should be the 'joint concern' of himself and the Editor-in-Chief.[1] He claims that the committee formed of the Chairman, Haley and himself was only meant to decide disputes between himself and Haley. It was his sole right to decide what went before the Board and what did not. The D.G. must be the 'master' and given full confidence. We did not give him that confidence: he instanced our lunching alone without his being present.

He was nervous, looked ill and made his points badly. But he agreed to withdraw his resignation.[2] I cannot reconcile his contention that we are 'aloof' and 'remote' with his contention that we interfere. I point out to him that the B.B.C. is not like the Gas, Light and Coke Company[3]; it has a wide national responsibility; the Board is not composed of uniform people, but of deliberately disparate people; and the House would never for one moment consider handing over 'absolute mastery' to a man whom they have not chosen and whose actions cannot be scrutinised. We ask him to give instances of 'interference'. He says that we asked that the Archbishop of York on his return from Russia should do a Sunday postscript. This was such a trivial instance that it left us aghast.

H.N. TO B.N. & N.N.   *5th March, 1944*
Sissinghurst

Jan Masaryk,[4] whom I saw this week, told me three strange stories.

When Konrad Henlein[5] came to see him at the Czechoslovak Legation in London, he appeared accompanied by an S.S. tough, and

---

[1] (Sir) William Haley.

[2] He had handed in his resignation on 28th February, on the grounds that the Board interfered too much with his authority.

[3] Foot had been General Manager of the Gas, Light and Coke Company, 1929–42.

[4] Czechoslovak Minister to Great Britain, 1925–38; Czech Minister of Foreign Affairs since 1940.

[5] Leader of the Sudeten German Party in Czechoslovakia before the war.

when Jan appeared surprised at his presence, he said, 'My friend here accompanies me wherever I go.' Jan opened the door into his drawing-room and whistled for his Aberdeen terrier. The dog arrived wagging its tail. 'My friend here', he said to Henlein, 'accompanies me wherever I go.' Henlein was amused. The Gestapo man was not amused at all.

He told me that between Godesberg and Munich he had been to see Neville Chamberlain at Downing Street. Chamberlain was in a highly irritable mood and kept on saying, 'Do not interrupt me!' Jan said, 'Mr Chamberlain, I fear I am not a professional diplomatist. I was never meant to be one. After the last war I was offered £50,000 a year to become President of the Skoda works.' Chamberlain's eyes glinted at such commercial magnificence. 'And why on earth didn't you take it?' 'I felt, you know, that Masaryk's son ought not to make instruments of war but instruments of peace, and that is why I became a diplomatist.' Chamberlain was much impressed by this and treated him more politely thereafter.

The third story made my blood run cold. After Munich, Perry Brownlow[1] gave Chamberlain a cigarette-case on which was engraved a map of Europe with three sapphires marking Berchtesgaden, Godesberg and Munich. When Jan, having resigned his post, came to say goodbye, he was taken up so see Mrs Chamberlain. The atmosphere was slightly strained and in order to ease it, Mrs Chamberlain said, 'Oh, Mr Masaryk, I *must* show you the lovely cigarette-case which Lord Brownlow has just given Neville!' The cigarette-case was produced. 'I call that', said Jan, 'the ugliest cigarette-case ever owned by a British Prime Minister.' 'What on earth makes you say that?' asked Mrs Chamberlain.

DIARY   *10th March, 1944*

The miners' strike continues and is creating much ill feeling. Public opinion at the moment is not good. They are exhausted by five years of war, and do not stand things as well as they used to. The recent raids have created far more fear than the great blitz of 1940–41. People dread another winter of war. But let us hope that the Second Front when it comes will again galvanize our energies.

[1] Lord Brownlow, Personal Lord-in-Waiting to King Edward VIII, 1936, and Parliamentary Private Secretary to Lord Beaverbrook, 1940.

DIARY   *14th March, 1944*

The Russians have startled everybody by recognising the Badoglio Government and accrediting an Ambassador to it. There is an amusing side to this, since all our left-wing newspapers have been accusing Churchill of his reactionary tendencies towards the Badoglio Government, and now Holy Russia has gone much further than we ever dreamt of going. But it is a grave perturbation of the Tehran front. It will give the Italians the impression that the war is now over and that they can expect to be treated as an allied rather than a conquered nation.

In the House Winston makes a statement about Eire. He is looking his most sturdy and pugnacious, and glowers terribly during the process.

H.N. TO B.N. & N.N.   *19th March, 1944*
                                                                  Sissinghurst

I went up to Leicester for my annual general meeting. They are annoyed with me for having said that Montecassino was more important than Nigel's life or mine.[1] Moreover, I had to tell them what I should do if there were a General Election. I said that National Labour is over; that I would not go either Conservative or Labour; and that if they wanted to choose another candidate, they must let me know in time; otherwise I should stand as Independent with their support.[2] So if they refuse to support me, I shall not fight the seat but stand somewhere else. They receive my words well and kindly. I do not know what they will decide. Then I came down here, a mere wreck of a man to find a wreck of a woman.[3]

DIARY   *27th March, 1944*

People seem to think that Winston's broadcast last night was that of a worn and petulant old man. I am sickened by the absence of gratitude towards him. The fact is that the country is terribly war-weary, and the ill-success of Anzio and Cassino is for them a sad augury of what will happen when the Second Front begins. The upper classes feel that all this sacrifice and suffering will only mean that the proletariat will

[1] See p. 349, footnote 2.
[2] In fact he stood at West Leicester in June 1945 as the National Candidate, in support of Winston Churchill.
[3] Both H.N. and V.S-W. had 'flu.

deprive them of all their comforts and influence, and then proceed to render this country and Empire a third-class State.

DIARY   *28th March, 1944*

I lunch with Negrin[1] in his flat off Sloane Square. I find there Vernon Bartlett, Philip Noel-Baker, the new Russian Ambassador to the Allied Governments, and Viénot. The Russian Ambassador cannot speak one word of any known tongue and is accompanied by an interpreter who grins horribly. Viénot is pleased by the way in which the British Press have taken up the French cause. He seems to imagine that this is due to my influence, but it is not. As always with Negrin, we have a marvellous lunch—salmon and stuffed eggs, plover, a chocolate cream. I like Negrin enormously. He is a fine wise man.

H.N. TO B.N. & N.N.   *2nd April, 1944*
                                               Sissinghurst

It has been a bloody week, ruined by the idiocy of the House of Commons. It all began with Thelma Cazalet.[2] She had put down an amendment to Clause 82 of the Education Bill, proposing that equal pay be given to men and women teachers. Rab Butler[3] pointed out (a) that the principle of equal pay could not be established in a minor clause to an Education Bill; (b) that, in any case, teachers' pay was settled under the Burnham scheme, and the women teachers were themselves against it. Everybody imagined that Thelma would withdraw her amendment, and most people went off to dinner. But Quintin Hogg and the young Tories butted in to say that they would support Thelma and the women. Nobody imagined for one moment that they would press it to a vote, but when the Division came at 8 pm. on Tuesday, the Government were defeated by one vote. Rab Butler became very indignant and the House broke up in a state of great embarrassment. I went to Pratts where I met some of the rebels. They were very ashamed of themselves. Hinchingbrooke said it was a good thing anyway. Rob Bernays said he had voted for the amendment because he did not like this system of employing cheap female labour. Bill Mabane said it was a disgrace for supporters of the

[1] Dr Juan Negrin, the former Republican Prime Minister of Spain, who went into exile after Franco's victory.
[2] Conservative M.P. for East Islington, 1931–45. She became Parliamentary Secretary to the Ministry of Education in May 1945.
[3] Minister of Education, 1941–45.

Government to vote against it when it was likely that the Government might be defeated.

Next day when we met, Winston was obdurate. He said that he couldn't let the matter pass; that the clause must be deleted from the Bill by a vote on the next day; that it would be a Vote of Confidence; and that that was that. Everybody was ruffled and annoyed. The only person who really enjoyed it was Winston himself. He grinned all over. A man came up to him in the smoking-room and said that he thought it exaggerated to make them all swallow their vote, and could some other means not be devised whereby confidence could be reaffirmed? 'No', said Winston. 'Not at all. I am not going to tumble round my cage like a wounded canary. You knocked me off my perch. You have now got to put me back on my perch. Otherwise I won't sing.'

So next day, Wednesday, we all trooped down and were then dismissed for the afternoon like naughty schoolboys. And on Thursday we met again to record a vote of confidence by 425 to 23. Thelma had to withdraw her vote. Quintin Hogg had to apologise. Winston grinned boyishly. It was all most foolish.

Now, I mind that sort of thing. The technicalities of the vote and counter-vote are not understood by the public, and the general impression left is that the Mother of Parliaments got a brain-storm and fell downstairs with her skirts over her head. I wish that Winston had slurred over the matter and postponed his vote of confidence for another occasion. The absurd finale is that the National Union of Teachers put up their man to say that they had never wanted the amendment.

Meanwhile all manner of rumours are going around about Anthony Eden. It is said that Beaverbrook (who, as you know, has a mesmeric influence on Winston) is jealous of Eden and wishes to get him out of the Foreign Office. It was rumoured, even, that Alec Cadogan is to be made Foreign Secretary and that Beaverbrook will thus be able to control foreign policy from behind. All this is nonsense. The true story is that Anthony cannot possibly run both the leadership of the House and the F.O. at the same time. The work is far too great for one man. Therefore he must give up one or the other. Of course he would prefer to keep the F.O., but there is a difficulty. While it would be fairly easy to get Cranborne[1] to take the F.O. with Dick Law as

[1] Lord Cranborne had been called to the House of Lords in his father's barony of Cecil in 1941. He was Secretary of State for Dominion Affairs, 1943–45.

spokesman in the House of Commons, it is absolutely impossible to find another Leader of the House who could replace Anthony. He is the only person who can do it. Attlee has not got the personal influence. Anderson would enrage the Labour people. Herbert Morrison would not be agreeable to the Tories. So Anthony is obliged to retain the leadership (which he does admirably) and may have to give up the F.O.[1] I am of course very sorry about this. I merely tell you the whole story (which I can assure you is correct) as some strange rumours may reach the Venafran fields[2] or the City of On.[3]

DIARY   *6th April, 1944*

Go to see Viénot. He tells me that he had had a long conversation with Eden, who seemed to agree with the point of view of the French National Committee.[4] He had then seen Winston, who was reserved and repeated all his old grievances against de Gaulle, from Casablanca to Syria. He had said, '*Je cherche la France que j'aime.*' Viénot had replied, 'But the France you love is there—in the maquis, in Algiers, in Italy'. Winston nodded sadly and said, 'But President Roosevelt is unwell. The formula he devised was not devised hastily. It was worked out after very careful consideration. It would be difficult to persuade him to alter it, especially after Pucheu's murder.'[5] Viénot had assured him that Pucheu would not be a precedent. 'I hope not', said Winston. 'When I was in Algiers I was invited to luncheon by Giraud to meet Flandin and Peyrouton. It would be distressing if they were killed.' '*C'était une erreur*', replied Viénot, leaving it unclear whether it was Giraud or Winston who had committed the mistake. He said that the P.M. had been polite but 'terribly lethargic'. I am afraid his last illness has really pulled him down.

DIARY   *19th April, 1944*

I lunch at the Beefsteak. Gerry Wellington, Tommy Lascelles, Clive Bell, John Maud, Gladwyn Jebb. The latter is deep in discussions with Stettinius. He says that he prefers 'broad views' to details. He

---

[1] He retained both offices until the end of the war in Europe.

[2] *Tendens Venafranos in agros. Horace.* Venafro was near Cassino.

[3] The old name for Heliopolis outside Cairo, where Ben was still stationed.

[4] The dispute was about the exercise of civilian authority by de Gaulle in France once it was liberated. Roosevelt still tended to believe that the French people might rally round Pétain. Eden's own conviction was that 'the majority of French opinion was overwhelmingly behind de Gaulle'. *The Reckoning*, p. 447.

[5] The former Vichy Minister of the Interior whom de Gaulle had executed.

says that he fears the Americans do not realise that there will be no such thing as a German Government when the collapse comes. We shall have to occupy the country for five years. He himself and the Foreign Office are not in favour of the partition of Germany. Yet that is bound to come owing to the zones of occupation and relief. He seems to be pretty pessimistic about the whole thing.

On 20th April Harold Nicolson flew to Algiers on a speaking tour of North-West Africa organised by the Ministry of Information and the Foreign Office. After a few days in Algiers, he flew to Tunis, returned to Algiers, and thence motored through Morocco via Oran, Fez and Casablanca to Marrakesh. He flew back to England from Casablanca on 10th May.

The political situation in North Africa was that de Gaulle was now established as sole President of the Committee of National Liberation, having recently obliged Giraud to resign his joint-Presidency of the Committee and his command of the French armed forces. Since the previous November, the French Consultative Assembly, representing not only the Free French but the various Resistance movements within metropolitan France, including the Communists, had been meeting in Algiers, and had agreed that the Committee of National Liberation 'represented France at war' and that de Gaulle's Government 'was that of the Republic'. On 15th May they went a stage further. The Assembly decreed that the Committee should be 'the provisional Government of the Republic' when France was liberated. On the strength of these decisions de Gaulle claimed that the civilian authority in liberated France should pass to him, pending national elections to be held as soon as liberation was complete.

This claim was challenged by Roosevelt and Eisenhower (now designated Commander-in-Chief of the Allied invasion force), but was well understood by Duff Cooper, the British Ambassador in Algiers, and by Anthony Eden. Churchill's attitude to de Gaulle was still luke-warm, owing to his personal antipathy to the French leader and his fear of opening a breach between Britain and the United States. So de Gaulle found himself excluded from the inner councils of the Allies. He had not been invited to Tehran. He was not consulted on the terms of the Italian armistice, although his own troops liberated Corsica. He was not told the date or objectives of D Day until shortly before the invasion took place. There was still uncertainty whether his political officers would be permitted to accompany the invasion forces. And on 21st April, the

*day on which Harold Nicolson reached Algiers and dined with de Gaulle,
the British Government forbade him to exchange coded telegrams with
Viénot, his Ambassador in London, on grounds of security.*

DIARY   *21st April, 1944*
                                            Gibraltar–Algiers

After breakfast we climb back aboard the 'plane. They keep the
black-out on the windows until we have left Gibraltar harbour, and
then remove the muslin slides. I gaze down. There, far below me, is
the mass of Gibraltar, straggling out into a blue Mediterranean like a
small white and grey lizard. Beyond are the Sierra Nevada, the wide
lands of Spain, and on the other side the houses of Ceuta and the great
mass of the Djebel Musa. A little torpedo-boat below looks like a
minnow making a huge wake across the calm blue sea. The sun at my
elbow is hot. I feel well and glucosed and triumphant. At 12.45 we
land at Maison Blanche, the airport of Algiers. I am taken to the
Embassy. Duff Cooper greets me warmly. Virginia Cowles is also
staying here.

Duff and I and Eric Duncannon (who is acting as secretary) go to
dine with de Gaulle. It is getting dark, and as we enter the villa the
white turbans of the Guard of Honour twinkle under the trees. Duff
salutes gravely. We are received at the door by de Gaulle's A.D.C.
The house is in the Moorish style, but is brilliantly lit by what is
evidently an elaborate electric-light system just installed. We go in.
De Gaulle greets me with what for him is almost warmth. Then I am
greeted by André Gide,[1] looking old and ill but as gay as a *perroquet*.
Then Massigli[2] and Bonnet[3] and Gaston Palewski.[4] We go into
dinner. Caviar-eggs and sole and meringues. A good white wine.
Very simple.

Massigli is enraged by the ban on diplomatic correspondence.[5] He
points out that it is all right for the other Allies, as they have their
Governments in London. But how can he possibly communicate with
Viénot? I have a long talk with de Gaulle. He is bitter about things,
especially the ban. I say, '*Vous avez le droit d'être furieux: vous n'avez pas
le droit d'être blessé.*' He grunts. We go off early and drag Virginia

[1] The French author, awarded the Nobel Prize in 1947. He was then aged 74.
[2] René Massigli, Commissioner for Foreign Affairs in the French National Committee.
[3] Henri Bonnet, Commissioner for Information in the National Committee.
[4] Du Gaulle's Chef de Cabinet.
[5] See introductory note above.

Cowles out of her bed to have a drink with us. Duff is very gay and very friendly. I go to bed happy—not knowing whether today is yesterday or tomorrow.

DIARY   *23rd April, 1944*
                                                                               Algiers

I get up early and go down to the Colisée to give my lecture at 10 am. The theatre is packed. Most of the National Committee are there, and I espy old André Gide grinning in a stall. The lecture is given under the auspices of the *Association France—Grande Bretagne—Etats Unis.* Bonnet is in the chair. The stage on which we sit alone is not well arranged as I have nothing on which to arrange my notes except a low table. This makes me nervous and uncomfortable, but I soon get over it and at the end I am much applauded. '*Les applaudissements prolongés*', writes the *Alger Républicain, 'd'un public chaleureux s'élévèrent en hommage et en remerciement.*' After it is all over the Commissaires crowd on to the stage to congratulate me. I return to the Embassy.

Duff takes me and Virginia Cowles out to luncheon at Tipaza, some 25 miles along the coast. On our way there, and without Duff having said anything about it, we stop suddenly on the high road near a group of trees. A young British officer joins the car. He is gay and very Oxford; neat white hands with freckles; freckles all over his nose. I notice with surprise that he wears the badges of a Colonel. I notice also that he has the ribbon of the D.S.O. I listen to his gay and modest prattle—about Winston and Clemmie and Randolph, about the Partisans and Tito—and suddenly I realise that it is Bill Deakin, Winston's 'young friend' who was parachuted on to Tito's army six months ago.[1] He is the T. E. Lawrence of this war. But what a difference! Just boyish, frank, gay, chatterboxy and amazingly modest and natural. I take an immense liking to him.

Tipaza is lovely. An old Roman town in a bay enclosed by a huge grim mountain with flowers everywhere (a lovely pink Morning Glory, mesembryanthemum everywhere, borage, a silver-grey wormwood in huge masses, marigolds). There are the ruins of the forum and of villas built right down to the rocks on which the sea beats. The sun has come out and the Mediterranean puts on the 'shore-sea green and the deep-sea blue', but across the distance is a band of deep purples, a great stretch of wine-dark sea. It is warm. We lunch

[1] See p. 352, note 2. He was then aged 30.

at the inn and walk about afterwards. We drive back along the coast. The sea catches the sunset tinge.

I dine late with Massigli. Henri Frénay[1] is there. He is head of the Resistance movement and holds the post here of Commissioner of Prisoners and Refugees. A young man and fair with a clean chin, but strong and male. The others are all Resistance people, most unlikely types: an obvious member of the *Comité des Forges*, an evident schoolmaster, a trades union leader. But they are gay and positive and heroic. I enjoy the conversation very much indeed.

They begin by talking about anti-British propaganda in France: the long delay in the Second Front, the inability to provide arms, the muddle about contacts and liaison—all this has discouraged the Resistance. They object bitterly to the bombardment of France. They contend that we only succeed in killing civilians, and that they themselves can carry out sabotage with far greater effect and less loss of life. When we shoot up a railway engine, we kill the driver and do not damage the engine at all; when they blow up an engine, they give the driver warning and he escapes. The Germans exploit this skilfully. They printed millions of copies of Smuts' speech[2] and left them in the Metro for people to pick up. They also printed Winston's speech under banner headlines, 'Mr Churchill reviews the future of Europe and does not even mention the name of France'.

They tell me about the early beginnings. Frénay started *Combat* on a typewriter doing twelve carbon copies. It now has a *tirage* of 300,000. He says the Resistance movement is representative of all classes and all interests. They have no definite programme for the future, since to draw up such a programme would be to split them. But they are all conscious of some unexpressed purpose which will save France. 'France today is pregnant, not exactly with revolution, but with a new ethic.' They are not, he assures me, going to be chauvinist. On the contrary, they are internationalists. They see the difference between the Nation and the State. Let us proclaim *'les droits des Nations'* and see that each nation has its own rights; but above that, let the State be a federal, an international, State, looking after the economic interests of all its members.

One thing they say which is important to remember. The German

[1] Frénay was the publisher of *Combat*, the journal of one of the two leading groups in the French resistance. He was in Algiers as a member both of de Gaulle's Committee of National Liberation and of the Consultative Assembly.
[2] Smuts had declared publicly that France would never be a great power again.

occupation has on the surface been absolutely correct. The German officers and soldiers behave with considerable tact. It is the Gestapo which commits the atrocities. Will we be equally correct? There will be no Gestapo, of course, but our troops and the Americans may not behave individually as carefully as the Germans behave. This is a danger.

I come back and find Duff still up and have a drink with him. He says I fidgeted too much during my speech. Although I have had today all manner of congratulations, it is this one criticism which sticks in my mind. So I go to bed feeling less successful than I did this afternoon.

DIARY   *24th April, 1944*
                                                                    Algiers

Duff and I drive to General Catroux's villa for lunch. He is Governor General of Algeria and also a member of the National Committee. At the entrance to the villa there is a guard of *spahis* and the usual polite A.D.C.s to welcome us. We are taken into a high cool room across a really lovely patio. Catroux is most courteous. The ribbons on his tunic extend to four rows interrupted by many rosettes like the buttons on my wireless set. Duff and I had been somewhat apprehensive of this luncheon, since the Vichy wireless had announced this morning that Catroux's family had been arrested and would be held as hostages for any further Pucheu incidents.[1] But Catroux shows no signs of any anxiety or distress.

There are other generals and officers there, and M. Gérard Jouve,[2] who is head of de Gaulle's News Agency. We go into luncheon, which is served by Annamite waiters,[3] very soft and quiet, presided over by a Negro butler in full uniform. I sit on Catroux's right, and Duff is given the place opposite. Catroux complains in a gentle way about the lack of discipline among the American troops. There are many 'incidents'. Our people, it seems, are better behaved. '*Vos Tommies aiment les enfants et les animaux. Ça nous touche.*' I do my usual stunt of sticking up for the Yanks. But it is evident that the French here really hate them, and dread their ignorant and amateurish interference in French affairs.

We have coffee on an enormous and very beautiful terrace looking out over the Mediterranean and the town. Catroux had read, curiously

[1] See p. 359, note 5.
[2] Among other duties, he controlled the main Free French radio station at Brazzaville.
[3] From Annam, in French Indo-China.

enough, my article about Horatian associations with the Italian campaign. Did I know that the Chevalier Bayard[1] had won his spurs at a crossing of the Garigliano? No, I had never heard of that. He takes us round the garden where there are many kinds of mimosa (now over), and great seas of marigold and roses. He remarks quite casually, '*J'ai entendu à la radio ce matin que Vichy a arrêté ma famille. Ça doit être mon frère et mes neveux.*' He did not seem to mind terribly. His son is here and is going to the Embassy at Rio.

I go down to the University to lecture on 'Proust and England'. It was a lecture which I gave in Paris in 1936 when it proved a great success. But I can feel at once that they do not like it here. They do not like my making fun of their insularity, and they do not really care about Proust. I read and deliver it easily, and they do not miss a word. But I have that sense of a certain restlessness which means that it is not being a success.

DIARY   *25th April, 1944*
Algiers

I come back to the Embassy to find two of the Resistance waiting for me—Duroc and Berthin. The latter was Number Two in the movement after Frénay. On demobilisation he had started a transport company in Marseilles, beginning with a *charrette* which he pushed from and to the station. It became an immediate success, and after a few weeks he had an office and thirty-nine people under him. He had met Frénay by chance. The latter told him that they were creating a Resistance movement—would he join? He said he would. Frénay was the first to think of making the thing a real organisation and not merely an instrument of propaganda. He instructed Berthin to produce six *copains* by the next week. They had no money at all. Berthin would get into conversation with people in the park and draw them on the subject of the war. If they were favourable to our cause, he would say, 'How much do you want the British to win?' 'I want it above everything.' 'How much would you give to help?' 'I would give all I possess.' 'One hundred francs, please.' And he always got it. Frénay was the inspiration of the whole thing. His faith could move mountains. They started in August 1940, and by August 1943 their organisation was spread all through France and perfectly disciplined. He gave up his transport company and went to Lyons where he worked

[1] Le Seigneur Pierre de Bayard (1473-1524), the most famous of the French medieval knights, '*Le chevalier sans peur et sans reproche*'.

with Madame Albrecht. She was denounced, and the Germans cut off her head with an axe. Their first paper was called *Les Petites Ailes*. Later it was fused with *Liberté* and *Vérité* (two independent underground papers) and became *Combat*. He was betrayed by a friend. He was arrested by Vichy and released. He was then seized by the Gestapo—his leg was broken—but he managed to crawl into the street and be arrested by a gendarme. Then he had to escape.

We are joined by Douglas Fairbanks[1] and Diana [Cooper], who listen entranced. There is no doubt that all that is most courageous and disinterested in France resides in the Resistance. Frénay is a god to them. Now these two people, sitting on Moorish leather footstools beside me, are going back. I look into their eyes and remember them. Will they be tortured also? A friend of theirs was flayed alive because he would not confess. They pulled the skin off his shoulders, tugging till it went down to the breast. He kept on fainting and they revived him with injections. When they had pulled off the skin as far as the navel, he no longer responded to the injection and they then shot him in the head. All this was done in front of another member of the Resistance in order to frighten him into betraying his comrades. This man escaped afterwards and told the story. They all now carry cyanide of potassium with them.

I dine with Duff at the villa of de Lattre de Tassigny some miles from the town. It is a beautiful villa high up above a wide valley with mountains beyond. De Lattre, besides being in command of *Armée 'B'*, has a school at his villa for training young men. There was the usual fuss of Guards of Honour and A.D.C.s, and we are taken up into the little pine-wood behind the house where his school is camped. There were 160 young Frenchmen just escaped, and being fed up, disciplined and toughened. Some of them play basket-ball in the evening sun and others stand around watching under the pine-trees. They are all completely naked except for shorts. Thereafter there is a march-past and the lowering of the flag at sunset. Duff takes the salute. I admit that it is all rather moving.

We then go and dine. De Lattre tells us the story of how he resisted the German advance into the unoccupied zone. His plans were disclosed at the last moment, and he was accused of making a *putsch* against Giraud. The troops were surrounded and told that he had been shot. They surrendered. Finally he was taken to the *préfecture* under

[1] The film-actor. He was Vice-President of the Franco-British War Relief Committee, and was then serving in the U.S. Navy.

guard and embraced by the Mayor who thereafter, with tears in his eyes, arrested him. He had just heard that his wife and little son had escaped from France and were at Gibraltar. He raised his glass to 'Notre doux allié'. Eve Curie[1] is acting as one of the A.D.C.s and I glanced towards her. Such a look she gave me. Restrained but lovely. But, as always, no French junior officer will speak in the presence of his senior officer, and the conversation was entirely confined to Duff, myself and the General.

DIARY   *26th April, 1944*
                                                                 Algiers

I go to see Harold Macmillan,[2] who arrived today from Naples. His private secretary, John Wyndham, had already telephoned to say 'Would I dine?' I was tired and had another early start tomorrow, and I therefore said that I should dine quietly at the Embassy but would come and see Harold before dinner. So I went there and Harold greeted me with outstretched arms as if I had been his oldest and most intimate friend, which I cannot claim to be. 'Are you positive', he said, 'that you cannot dine tonight?' 'I'm afraid I have another early start, and would rather dine quietly at home.' 'I am so sorry', he said. 'I have a quiet dinner also. Only General Alexander and Smuts.' Now, I could not say, 'In that case I should love to dine.' I merely persisted in my refusal.

He showed me his reports on Giraud and de Gaulle. They are brilliantly written—but really *brilliantly* written—in the style of Macaulay. He told me that Giraud had every card in his hands and threw them away one by one. Giraud's only fault was lack of strength, and his successive abandonment of his friends destroyed even his moral authority. His brain is nil. Of de Gaulle Harold wrote that he was conscious always that a Sieur de Gaulle had been one of Jeanne d'Arc's knights. This gave him that visionary and ecstatic attitude.

DIARY   *27th April, 1944*
                                                                 Tunis

I am called at 6.30 and drive to Maison Blanche airport. As usual we are kept waiting for hours. Malcolm Muggeridge, who is a Major in the Intelligence Corps, comes to talk to me. An agreeable and intelligent man with a passionate admiration for *The Land*. Then we get off.

[1] Daughter and biographer of Madame Marie Curie, the scientist.
[2] He was then Minister of State at A.F.H.Q., Mediterranean Command.

We fly high and it is somewhat cold. Suddenly I see below me the Medjerda valley and I try to pick out Medjez-el-Bab. There are few signs of the fighting from the air, but I see here and there the zig-zag of a trench and the empty roofs of destroyed farms. We get to Tunis about 2 pm. and are met by the representatives of the Resident General and the Consul.

Tunis is a larger and gayer town than I had imagined. The French quarter is exactly like Cannes. There is a Cathedral with twin towers surmounted, to my astonishment, by the Croix de Lorraine.[1] The streets are crowded and the shops as empty as those of Algiers.

I dine with the Resident General, General Mast. A neat, stocky, clean-shaven little General, very correct. We have a marvellous dinner. Afterwards I give my lecture on 'The Last Peace Treaty and the Next'. The theatre is amazingly packed. I have a great reception. At the end there is the sort of applause which goes on and on. I mentioned Nigel, saying that I had come in the steps of my son who almost exactly a year ago had also visited Tunis in a different capacity. That aroused a storm of applause.

DIARY   *28th April, 1944*
                                                              Tunis

I made them take me to Hammam Lif.[2] We went down to the beach. 'It was through these waves', my guide said, 'that the Sixth Div. passed.' 'You mean the Sixth Armoured Division?' There are rows of tiny Peacehaven villas along the beach. I noticed the names of the Villa Ninna and the Villa Mathilde. At the end of this line, two of the villas jutted out into the beach itself. 'They had to go round those two —that's why they went through the sea.' A drainpipe, broken and crushed in two, is all that remains of their passage. But I was able to my delight to reconstruct that amazing moonlit scene.

DIARY   *1st May, 1944*
                                                          Algiers — Oran

We start from Algiers at 7.30 am. Our objective is Rélizane near Oran where I was to lunch and address the 1st Division *Blindée* of the French Army. We had arranged to be there by 12.30. But as we were skimming along the road at 11, there was a sudden sigh and our tyre

---

[1] It was flown as the symbol not of de Gaulle, but of the Archbishop of Carthage.
[2] Where the 6th Armoured Division broke through the last German defence line on 9th May, 1943.

Rabbits. October 1. 1944.

I must not tell, how dear you are to me.
It is unknown, a secret from myself
Who should know best. I would not if I could
Expose the meaning of such mystery.

I loved you then, when love was Spring, and May ..
Eternity is here and now, I thought ;
The pure and perfect moment briefly caught
As in your arms, but still a child, I lay.

Loved you when summer deepened into June
And those fair, wild, ideal dreams of youth
Were true yet dangerous and half unreal
As when Endymion kissed the matchless moon.

But now when autumn yellows all the leaves
And thirty seasons mellow our long love,
How rooted, how secure, how strong, how rich,
How full the (harvest of our garnered sheaves!
(barns that ~~fields~~ holds)

Manuscript of a poem, 'Rabbits', by Vita Sackville-West
addressed to Harold Nicolson, October 1st, 1944

Harold Nicolson with Colonel de Lagatinerie of the Free French Forces in London

Harold Nicolson in Morocco,
May 1944

went flat. We had no spare wheel and nothing to mend it with. Eventually an American lorry came along. We thumbed them. They stopped, and jumped off and with many jokes mended the tyre for us. They also gave us their rations. Nothing could have been more obliging nor more gay than they were. But all this made us two hours late. Instead of arriving at 12.30 we arrived at 2.40. General de Vigier, who commands the Division, had made elaborate preparations. A banquet had been prepared in a tent erected over a swimming pool. And for my address a site had been prepared among the pine-trees. We were given a hurried and delicious lunch, and then walked to the place where I was to speak. It was at the side of the pine-wood, and some 800 officers and men had been drawn up in a semicircle. They were backed by eight tanks forming an *estrade*, and on each side was a huge flag-staff with the French and British flags. I thanked God that all these preparations had not been made wholly in vain.

I spoke to them without notes for some 45 minutes and they listened with extreme attention. Afterwards they crowded round me and asked questions. Did I really think France would be treated as an equal after the war? and so on. It was pathetic and deeply moving to see those young clean faces and to note their anxiety. I spoke to them at length again, and the General was delighted for me to do so. Then I was introduced to all the officers (including one of Giraud's sons) and we were given a drink before leaving. Of all the speeches I have ever made, that is the one which I shall never forget.[1]

DIARY   *3rd May, 1944*
                                                    Taza (Morocco)–Fez

We leave Taza at 9. There is a sirocco blowing, and it is very hot indeed. I am feeling happy in the heat and I sing my Turkish song as we bowl along. We leave the desert country and enter rolling downs rich in wheat and vines. There are flowers by the roadside and I stop to examine them. Great sheets of marigold, loosestrife and bugloss. A member of the pea family. Some pink mallows. But most beautiful of all, three varieties of Morning Glory—a pink one, a pale-blue one, and a dark-blue one with a white calyx. From time to time we sail past huge fields of *Linum* in flower. As we top the edge of a col we see Fez spread below us.

I am taken to see General Suffren who commands the garrison. A

---

[1] The 1st French Armoured Division took part in the landings in the South of France in August.

lovely Moorish house with guards and A.D.C.s, and two fountains bubbling violently over blue tiles. I then give my lecture in a cinema. The place is packed from floor to ceiling. They applaud loudly.

We then go to the Palais Jamai. It is as lovely as ever. I trip down the high garden-staircase to visit my poplars.[1] I thought they were as white as silver birches. But not at all. They are grey and gnarled. I tell them about my sponge-bag, but I do not do it well as I have forgotten the French for sponge-bag. But they understand quite well, and rustle with pride and pleasure at the fate of their progeny.

DIARY

10th–11th May, 1944
Casablanca–London

The 'plane is huge, larger in width and height than an underground train. We have the usual aluminium bench and nothing else. We fly over Casablanca and I say goodbye to Africa. There is a marvellous sunset over the Atlantic, a great Egyptian sea of red to the west, and a splutter of cirrus clouds which turn the colour of strawberry mash. Then the portholes are closed and we drive on into the night. I lie down on the floor, using my satchel as a pillow. I manage to sleep a bit. It gets colder and colder. I see a glow of dawn. People begin to get up. I rise also, and at that moment there is a sudden bump. We have arrived at St Mawgan in Cornwall. It is 4.30 am. We are taken in the bus to the station at Newquay and thrust into the London train. The country is amazing. Hawthorn and bluebells and cows deep in buttercups. I get home at 5.50 pm. I ring up Viti at once. It is heaven to be back again.

On 11th May, the day on which Harold Nicolson returned to London from North Africa, General Alexander opened his offensive on the Italian front. Fifteen Allied Divisions were concentrated on the twelve-mile stretch between Cassino and the sea. By the 18th the breach was made and Cassino captured. The German reserve-line was overrun a few days later. On the 23rd the six Divisions in the Anzio beach-head broke out eastwards and linked up next day with the Americans advancing along the coast. The Germans escaped the trap, but poured back through central Italy, leaving Rome to be captured almost without a fight on 4th June. The advance then accelerated. Perugia fell on 20th June and Arezzo

---

[1] During a journey to Morocco in 1934, H.N. had taken cuttings from these poplars, brought them home in his sponge-bag and planted them in the garden at Sissinghurst. They are now (1967) sixty feet high, and are still known as 'the Fez poplars'.

on 16th July. The Arno was reached at Florence by the end of the month.

Two days after the capture of Rome, the Italian operations were eclipsed by the Allied landings in Normandy. Five infantry Divisions and three airborne Divisions landed at dawn on 6th June, after the invasion had been postponed by one day owing to bad weather. The Germans had guessed neither the place nor the day. Except on one American beach, the coastal defences were soon overwhelmed, but the advance inland was slow. 250,000 men were ashore by the evening of 7th June, but Cherbourg was not captured till 26th June, and Caen, the main objective on the British front, did not fall till 10th July. By the middle of the month there were thirty Allied Divisions in the beach-head and Montgomery made preparations for the major offensive which was launched on 18th July.

On the night of 12th June the first pilotless planes (the V.1), carrying a ton of explosives, were launched by the Germans on London from bases in north-west France. In the first week of the bombardment they caused 10,000 casualties, but by the end of July only one 'doodle-bug' in seven was penetrating the fighter, anti-aircraft and balloon-barrage screens. In all, 8,000 were launched before the Allied Armies overran the bases in late August. Sissinghurst lay directly beneath the line of flight of very many of them, and the diary records in great detail the impact of these new weapons on civilian morale.

On 20th June the Russians began their major summer offensive in the centre of their front, and the two hundred German divisions were soon in full retreat into Poland and Rumania.

Harold Nicolson made a major speech in the House of Commons on 24th May criticising the Allied attitude towards General de Gaulle. At the end of May he left London for a lecture tour of the Fleet at Scapa Flow, delivering twenty-two lectures in seven days to ships and shore-establishments. The news of the capture of Rome reached him in the Orkneys, and of the D Day landings when he returned to London on the morning of 6th June.

DIARY   *18th May, 1944*

To the House. People do not, as I expected, say, 'Hullo, Harold, have you had 'flu? I haven't seen you for some days.' They say, 'Well, what was your impression of Africa?' All of which shows that the *Spectator* is widely read. We have a Secret Session about the hours of sitting. As it was not concerned with an essential war matter, I may as well say what happened. The Tories want to revert to our old hours, more or less, and sit from 2 pm. till 9. The Labour people, who have wives cooking supper for them at Wimbledon and Wembley, wish to keep to our present hours. Behind it all there is a difference of principle as well as a difference of convenience. The Labour people tend to regard Parliament as a whole-time job and like to live in the House; the Tories regard it as a half-time job and like the mornings free for other work. In fact the Tories are right, and the old system did diminish the professionalism of politicians and lead to a more worldly attitude, a more liberal attitude. Anyhow, the Tory case is put by Quintin Hogg who is so tactless, so long and so insensitive to the social differences involved, that he puts the whole House against him and does himself harm.

H.N. TO V.S-W.   *23rd May, 1944*
                                                 House of Commons

I called in at Pratts where I had a port with Eddy Devonshire. He told me that at Eastbourne on Sunday (he has a large mansion there) the chaplain to the local forces had invited the vicar to preach the sermon. 'Very few of you young men', he began, 'will be alive to see the harvest. A curtain of fire and steel awaits you over there', waving his arm towards the Marine Parade. 'But I can tell you this: six months from now you will be in paradise.' Alarm and despondency spread through the assembled forces. 'Even the iron discipline of the Guards', said Eddy, 'was seen to be severely shaken.'

H.N. TO B.N. & N.N.   *24th May, 1944*
                                                    Sissinghurst

In the morning I had something of a shock. It was the first day of the Foreign Affairs debate, and Winston was known to be opening at 12 noon. That meant that he would finish at 1.30 when everybody would pour out to luncheon. Now the usual practice is that the Prime Minister is followed by the Leader of the Opposition. But Greenwood (and I do not blame him at all) refused to do it. 'As head of the Labour Party', he said, 'I refuse to get up when everybody is leaving.' So the Speaker telephoned to me. 'Would I help him? Would I be a sport? Would I hold the breach?' Well that was hell, but what could I say?

I went to the House feeling rather hollow inside. Winston spoke for exactly one hour and a half. He went round the map of Europe and with amazing frankness told us of our relations with each of the Powers he named. To our surprise he went miles out of his way to shower roses and lilies upon Franco. To our regret he spoke of France, correctly, but in a cold, cold voice. He was as lucid as ever. There were here and there some of the old striking phrases. His humour and charm were unabated. But his voice was not thunderous and three times Members called out to him, 'Speak up!' Then finally he sat down, and, as foreseen, 300 Members left for luncheon.

I bobbed up and my name was called. The first three minutes was a confusion of moving figures, and then the crowd cleared and I was left with about 100 Members on the benches. Winston sat there to my left, cocking his head forward, popping eyes up at me, as if to say, 'What is the fellow going to say, poor chap?' But I managed all right and reproved him for his ill-treatment of small Powers and the snubs he gave to France.[1] That was the theme set for criticism, and thereafter members of all Parties echoed my remarks. The French, of course, were delighted. Well, I bear many crosses, and the *Croix de la Libération* is not the least desirable.

I dashed out to luncheon after my speech and found a table next to Shinwell. Now Shinwell sits on the front Opposition bench and is the most redoubtable of Winston's critics. Beside him sits Lord Winterton. The House of Commons joke is that they sit there looking like arsenic and old lace. But Shinwell had interrupted the P.M. at one moment, and Winston grinned across at him and said, 'The Hon. Member has often been a vigilant and severe critic of His Majesty's Government, but as a real Opposition figure he has failed, because he can never conceal his satisfaction when we win—as we sometimes do.' Loud cheers. Shinwell was touched and pleased. 'There is a grace about Churchill', he said to me at luncheon. 'One cannot get away from that.'

I dined with Maud Russell, Sammy Hood and Phil Nichols.[2] Sibyl [Colefax] was there. 'Why', she said to me, 'do you miss no occasion to attack de Gaulle?' I wished to spare her the dreadful revelation

[1] H.N. said in the course of his speech: 'It seems to me and many Frenchmen that the United States Government, with His Majesty's Government in their train, instead of helping the French and welcoming them, lose no opportunity of administering any snub which ingenuity can devise and ill-manners perpetrate. I hope that the Foreign Secretary will go further than the negative and even ungracious statement made on this subject by the Prime Minister. It is most unwise, most weak and most ill-informed of the United States Government to refuse to accord any special recognition to the National Committee or provisional Government. I am convinced that this is a grave error of policy.'

[2] Sir Philip Nichols, British Ambassador to the Czechoslovak Republic, 1942–47.

that she had got it all wrong. 'Oh', I said, 'he has many qualities.' 'But my dear Sibyl', Sammy exploded, 'you cannot have read a word of Harold's speeches. For three years he has been defending and praising de Gaulle in season and out of season.' 'Yes', said Phil, 'and you should have heard him this afternoon.' Poor Sibyl—out of date by three hours, a great friend misunderstood, humiliated and proved ignorant in front of people who might (nay, who certainly would) repeat the incident. She fiddled and faddled, confused and angry, with her bread.

DIARY   *27th May, 1944*

A hot train down and very crowded. But a beautiful evening and Sissinghurst looking wonderful. The ceanothus is such as I have never seen anywhere else. Viti and I are anxious and excited about the Italian news. We are within shelling distance of Valmontone which cuts the main escape-route from the Liri Valley. It looks as if Kesselring may have to face a major disaster. These days are full of deep suspense. And all day and night the aeroplanes roar above us.

DIARY   *31st May, 1944*
                                                                           Scapa Flow

I am taken after breakfast to H.M.S. *Dunluce Castle*. She was an old Union Castle liner, and is very dolled up, or rather, dolled down. She is now a depot ship. I lecture to her. Then I am fetched by the smartest of all pinnaces and taken to the Fleet Flagship, the *Duke of York*, where I lunch. Then off I go to the *Bermuda*, a cruiser, and lecture again. Then I am taken ashore and driven to the Admiral's private house, which was built by rich people with a passion for William Morris, but charming in its way. The Admiral is Sir Henry Harwood, of River Plate and *Graf Spee* fame. He is a gay sea-dog.

DIARY   *5th June, 1944*
                                                                           Scapa Flow

I come down to breakfast and find Colonel Simpson there. He looked up at me and said in his Caithness accent, 'Heard the news? We entered Rome at 11 pm. last night.' Well, I never.

DIARY   *6th June, 1944*
                                                                           London

I can now say (having passed through the censorship ban) that at Hatston aerodrome [Orkneys] yesterday, about an hour before I left, a tremor passed through the ward-room. 'Panic stations order',[1] was the word passed round. A sense of imminence affected the whole place.

I typed this diary in my sleeper [from Edinburgh] and then went to bed. I did not sleep well as I was cold. The train arrived at 7.35 and I drove straight to K.B.W.,[2] missing the 8 am. news owing to a sudden short-circuit of the light. This was at once put right. I then turned on the 9 am. news in the General Forces Programme, and heard to my excitement the following announcement: 'The German Overseas News has just put out the following flash: "Early this morning, the expected Anglo-American invasion began when airborne forces were landed in the Seine estuary." ' I then wait till a later flash which says, 'The combined landing operations comprised the whole area between Havre and Cherbourg, the main centre of attack being the Caen area.' Then Miss Niggeman comes and I dictate accumulated letters hard.

I go down to the House, arriving there about ten to twelve. When I enter the Chamber, I find a buzz of conversation going on. Questions had ended unexpectedly early and people were just sitting there chatting, waiting for Winston. It was an unusual scene. He entered the Chamber at three minutes to twelve. He looked as white as a sheet. The House noticed this at once, and we feared that he was about to announce some terrible disaster. He is called immediately, and places two separate fids of typescript on the table. He begins with the first, which is about Rome. Alexander gets a really tremendous cheer. He ends with the words, 'This great and timely operation', stressing the word 'timely' with a rise of the voice and that familiar bending of the two knees. He then picks up his other fid of notes and begins, 'I have also to announce to the House that during the night and early hours of this morning, the first of a series of landings in force upon the Continent of Europe has taken place. . . .' The House listens in hushed awe. He speaks for only seven minutes and then Greenwood follows with a few words. We then pass to the Colonial Office Estimates in Committee of Supply.

I lunch at the Beefsteak and then go down to Sissinghurst. There is an elaborate B.B.C. news programme and Howard Marshall gives a good account of the landings on the coast. The general impression is that the ferrying across the Channel was marvellously successful; that the beach obstacles were not as severe as foreseen and that the Germans

[1] This is what H.N. typed. He probably meant 'Action stations'.
[2] King's Bench Walk, H.N.'s chambers in the Temple.

were not as numerous; that we have played the first trick better than could have been hoped. But people know very well that the hard test is still to come and that no jubiliation of any kind can be permitted for several days.

During the night aeroplanes roar over the house carrying lights. They never stop. Neither Viti nor Mrs Staples nor Jo sleep a wink.

DIARY   7th June, 1944

Tilea comes to see me. He also feels that anything may happen if we manage to establish a good beach-head. But until we can get a real harbour, there is little chance of our being able to accumulate an offensive force.[1] It is sufficient to pray to God that we can accumulate a defensive force.

Dine at the Beefsteak. Bruce Lockhart[2] is there. He tells me that there was terrible difficulty again between de Gaulle and Winston. De Gaulle insisted upon being allowed to land troops in France. Winston wrote him a letter saying, 'The aeroplane which I placed at your disposal will be ready to take you back to Algiers tomorrow.' Anthony [Eden] prevented this being sent. Then there was a row about de Gaulle's broadcast. The Americans refused to drop leaflets in his name over France. In the end all these difficulties were surmounted, but only when Anthony had been dragged from his bed at 4 am.[3]

[1] H.N. did not then know of the two artificial harbours (Mulberries) which were being assembled on the invasion coast.
[2] Sir Robert Bruce Lockhart, H.N.'s former colleague on the *Evening Standard*, who was then Director-General of the Political Warfare Executive at the Foreign Office.
[3] This account of events is not confirmed by the Memoirs of Churchill, Eden, de Gaulle and Duff Cooper. There was no dispute about the use of Free French forces in France: their commando, air and naval forces were already engaged, and Leclerc's Division was awaiting embarkation. The dispute was about the civilian control of liberated French territory. The Americans intended to set up a military administration under their own control, which would govern France until elections could be held throughout the country to ascertain the people's will. De Gaulle claimed that his Committee of National Liberation was already the *de facto* Government of France. The British, with the exception of Churchill, backed de Gaulle, but Churchill told de Gaulle on 4th June that 'each time I have to choose between you and Roosevelt, I shall always choose Roosevelt'. In Eisenhower's broadcast to the French people on D Day, not a word was said about de Gaulle: the French people were told to carry out the orders of the Allied invasion force. The Americans also issued French currency notes without asking de Gaulle first. Only Duff Cooper mentions Churchill's threatening message: 'He dictated a letter to de Gaulle, which was fortunately not despatched, ordering him to return to Algiers immediately.' (*Old Men Forget*, p. 331.)

The weather is really terrible. A slow black cloud with rain hangs over the town. This means that our great air-superiority is rendered ineffective. But it is not windy, which is something.

Lunch at the Beefsteak. They are all worried. It is indeed alarming to see that thin line on the map and to know that Rommel is massing his divisions for a thunderous assault.[1] We do not seem to be going on very quickly, and we have little hope of holding Bayeux.

I dine with Viénot to meet de Gaulle. The other guests are Dejean,[2] Archie Sinclair, Dick Law and Palewski. Viénot wants me to convince de Gaulle that he must send for his Government and change a diplomatic conversation into Government action. De Gaulle is looking ill and tired, but is in a most agreeable mood. I ask him about the war. He says it is going well. He says that we have been able to land so many troops and so much material that we are now in a firm position. I ask whether it is true that we cannot land heavy tanks unless we have a major harbour. He says that for tactical operations no heavy tanks are necessary, provided that we have sufficient anti-tank guns. We are, he says, tactically on the offensive and strategically on the defensive.[3] I say that I am a fool about military matters, but that I trust his opinion: what is it? He says, 'Ça va très bien—au delà de nos espérances. C'est la dernière année de la guerre. La guerre sera finie avant Noël.'

Then Archie Sinclair arrives. He says it is going 'quite well'. He underlines 'quite'. De Gaulle says, 'But you are thinking only of the air: these clouds have interrupted your action.' Archie admits this.

We then dine. Afterwards I have another talk with de Gaulle. He is all tied up by his immediate difficulties. He is worried by Eisenhower's proclamation and about the bank-notes which the Americans have prepared for issue in France. 'C'est de la fausse monnaie.' I tell him that he ought to profit by this occasion to bring his Government, or some of it, to London. He says that London does not count,

[1] Rommel was in command of the French coast from the Dutch border to the Loire, under the overall command of von Rundstedt. The main German reserves were moved up to the Caen area, but suffered terribly from Allied air-attacks before they could be brought into action. The Normandy beach-head was never in danger of being overwhelmed like the beach-heads at Salerno and Anzio.

[2] Maurice Dejean, now de Gaulle's Ambassador to the exiled Allied Governments in London.

[3] *Sic* in the diary, but de Gaulle must certainly have put it the other way round.

and that he will not *'faire la navette entre Londres et Washington'*. I say that he is thinking of his dignity, and that if I were Charles de Gaulle, I should not worry about my dignity. I beg him to *faire le grand geste*. He is amused, and more human than I have ever seen him. But he looks ill, like all of them. Dick Law approves of what I say. I know that Anthony is with him. I urge de Gaulle to press the situation at this moment. He says he has heaps of time. He wags his finger at me: 'You will admit one day that I was right.' So he will return to Algiers, having accomplished nothing and being more anti-American than ever. I go away rather sad.

H.N. TO B.N. & N.N.   *11th June, 1944*
Sissinghurst

You will want to know the general atmosphere during invasion week. First, at Sissinghurst. It is literally dominated by aeroplanes. All night they howl and rage above us. It is like sleeping in the Piccadilly Underground—trains roar past at different levels and going in different directions all the night. Then in daytime there is also much activity: great fleets of bombers floating slowly above us in the empyrean, their drone being a throb all round us and not a definite noise coming from a definite object. And then the fighters at a lower level swishing along at enormous speeds. So far that is all that Sissinghurst has seen of the invasion. Otherwise the trains run the same, the papers come the same, everything is the same. We listen intently to the wireless at all hours.

In London it is different. There are people who ring up under the illusion (a) that I have inside knowledge, and (b) that if I had it, I should repeat it over the telephone. There is a continual crowd around the ticker-tape in the House of Commons corridor. There are all sorts of rumours buzzing through the smoking-room. And there is the hourly expectation that Winston may make another statement. Apart from this, and the fact that the newspapers are snapped up the moment they appear on the streets, there is nothing much to notice. People are relieved that it has begun. They scan the weather a little more acutely than usual, and notice the direction of the wind. But on the whole we are all amazingly calm.

I have the impression that both we and the Germans are waiting to see what the other does next. They hesitate to move their main armies until they see where we are going to land next; we hesitate to make further disembarkations until we see how they move their main armies.[1] Meanwhile we have got thirty miles of coast, on an average four to ten miles deep. Few people imagine that we can yet claim to have established an impregnable foothold. There is the abiding knowledge that the real struggle is before us, and may be very terrible indeed. From all fronts comes the cry, 'Where is the Luftwaffe?' I watch the weather, watch which way the cowls of the oast-house are turning, watch how violently the Fez poplars are being agitated, scrutinize the glass—all in a state of some apprehension. Meanwhile the little Norman towns which Nigel and James [Pope-Hennessy] toured in their youth are exposed to fierce destruction.

DIARY   *12th June, 1944*

National Labour meeting. Malcolm MacDonald is there. He says he will insist on either resigning his post in Canada or resigning his seat.[2] The P.M. says that if Malcolm's appointment is raised in the House, he will make it a vote of confidence. That would be a grave error. Malcolm thinks from conversations with friends in both Parties that the Election will take place on party lines some four or five months after the Armistice. He believes that when the Election is over, there is a chance of the Coalition being reformed. What everybody wants to avoid is a competition in promises. Anyhow, we all agree to do nothing until the Election comes.

The Americans have taken Carentan and are pushing on towards St Lô. We and the Canadians are having a tough time of it on the Caen canal. Winston went over to visit the beach-head yesterday accompanied by Smuts and Alan Brooke. How incredible that he should take Smuts of all men with him and not de Gaulle! I was right in referring to 'every snub which ingenuity can devise and ill-manners perpetrate'.[3]

DIARY   *14th June, 1944*

There have been mysterious rocket-planes falling in Kent. The thing is very hush at the moment.[4]

[1] The Germans retained nineteen Divisions in the Pas de Calais area until late July, in expectation of a second Allied landing. There was also a widespread belief in England that Normandy was not to be the only point of attack.
[2] The criticism was of Ministers like Harold Macmillan, Duff Cooper and Malcolm MacDonald retaining their seats while they were serving abroad.
[3] See p. 373, note 1.
[4] On 13th June four pilotless aircraft (V.1s) crossed the coast, and one fell at Bethnal Green, killing six people. The others caused no casualties.

DIARY   *16th June, 1944*

Morrison announces that the 'planes which came over last night were 'pilotless 'planes'. There are three or four more alerts during the morning.

I go home. Viti has been kept up and rendered sleepless by the robot 'planes. They come over after we have gone to bed. I can see them clearly, since they are illuminated like little launches at a regatta. They fly slowly and low,[1] and it is a mystery how any of them get through at all. They make a terrific noise like an express train with a curious hidden undertone. In a week or so we shall have learnt how to deal with them. The Germans, of course, have boosted the thing immeasurably and tried to raise the spirits of their people by claiming that this secret weapon can really destroy London. In fact Goebbels says that London is 'paralysed'. This is absurd. There was not a sign of anything yesterday and the traffic continued just as usual.

DIARY   *18th June, 1944*

A fine day at last with less wind. The bombers stream over, totally disregarding the secret weapons which scream across Kent underneath them. I do my article on Normandy and Proust, and also write to the boys.

It is reported that the Americans have cut the Cotentin peninsula. We are also holding on well at Caen. Meanwhile in Italy Alexander has done wonderfully. He is already at Piombino and approaching Perugia.[2] The French have taken Elba. Everything is going very well.

DIARY   *19th June, 1944*

The German propaganda is still making a great deal of its secret weapon. They are putting out stories of panic, of the evacuation of London, of vast explosions, of a pall hanging over the city which prevents the Luftwaffe from taking photographs. I see no signs of all this. My train arrives on time, there are buses running as usual, and I can see no difference in the streets. One of the robot 'planes fell near the Law Courts and smashed many windows. Another fell in Tottenham Court Road, and another yesterday fell on the Guards Chapel while there

[1] They flew at 3,000 feet at 400 m.p.h.
[2] Nigel was the first Allied soldier to enter Perugia after its evacuation by the Germans on 20th June.

was a service on, killing Lord Edward Hay, Ivan Cobbold and many others.

DIARY   *20th June, 1944*

I saw Victor Cunard[1] this evening. He told me that Winston made a row about Badoglio's resignation. How did the Italians dare to change their Government without his consent? He almost insisted that the Bonomi Government should not be recognised. Stalin was well prepared to agree to this, but fortunately Roosevelt refused. Now this will get out in America and Winston will be much blamed over here. I fear that he is losing such judgement as he ever had in foreign affairs and is unhappily authoritarian. I wish he could die now quite suddenly. I dread any clouds coming over that superb sunset.

DIARY   *21st June, 1944*

Bevin opens the debate on the Government White Paper on unemployment very sturdily, very mildly, very acutely. It is a good debate and reaches a high level. I am glad to observe that nobody tries to make party capital out of it.

I have a talk with Florence Horsbrugh.[2] She says that there is no doubt that Hitler's secret weapon, unless we can control it soon, will make heavy inroads on our nerves. People are unable to sleep, and the continuity of the bombardment is very trying. What is more distressing is that other, and perhaps more serious, secret weapons are about to be launched. I fear we are in for a bad two months.

Dine with Herbert Morgan[3] at Claridges to meet Munnings,[4] the new President of the Royal Academy. I sit between Lamb, the Secretary of the R.A., and Professor Bodkin of Birmingham. Munnings is like something out of Jorrocks. Everybody makes speeches which are simply terrible. Munnings himself keeps on saying, 'Whatever the highbrows may think. . . ', and others refer to him as 'so sane, so robust, so English'.

---

[1] Formerly *The Times* correspondent in Rome. He settled in Venice for most of his life, except the war-years, when he broadcast on the B.B.C.'s Italian service.
[2] Parliamentary Secretary, Ministry of Health, 1939–45.
[3] Sir Herbert Morgan, the industrialist.
[4] Sir Alfred Munnings. He was P.R.A. from 1944 to 1949.

DIARY   *26th June, 1944*
The doodle-bug attack became so serious last night that Viti and I
waited up in my room for the midnight news. There was nothing
new. We are kept awake during the night by the rocket-bombs
howling overhead, and we hear as many as twelve explosions. It
gets better after 2 am. and we get a little sleep.

H.N. TO B.N. & N.N.   *27th June, 1944*
                                                                    Sissinghurst
Viénot told me the story of de Gaulle's visit to Bayeux.[1] On landing,
they went straight to see Montgomery and spent an hour with him
while he explained the situation. (De Gaulle was delighted by this,
as his professional side, his Ecole de Guerre side, was aroused. He is
amazed by the capacity which we and the Americans have shown, and
his optimism on his return was unbounded). On leaving Montgomery
they got into two jeeps and drove in the direction of Bayeux. They
then realised that they had so far not seen a single citizen of France.
They determined to stop the first Frenchman whom they saw and
engage him in conversation. Two kilometres on this side of Bayeux
they saw coming towards them two gendarmes on bicycles. General
Koenig hailed them: '*Hé, les gendarmes!*' Seeing two senior French
officers, they got off their bicycles. Viénot then realised that no Frenchman in France would recognise de Gaulle, since they had never seen
his portrait. He remarked on this to the General, who thereupon introduced himself. '*Le Général de Gaulle*', he said stiffly. Not '*Je suis le
Général . . .*' but just giving his name like a German introducing himself
at a *Bierabend*. The gendarmes were completely taken aback. They
dropped their jaws and almost dropped their bicycles. Then they
sprang to attention and saluted as they had never saluted before. The
General said to them, 'Where are you off to?' They answered that
they were going to a village near the beach-head. 'Turn round', said
the General, 'and go back to Bayeux. Tell the people I am coming.
We will wait here for five minutes in order to give you time.' So
they turned round and bicycled back furiously. While they were
waiting, Viénot said to de Gaulle, 'Now you have really committed an
act of a dictator. You have instructed two French gendarmes to
disobey an order.' 'And they obeyed me', said de Gaulle, purring to
himself.
    They went to the *sous-préfecture*. The *sous-préfet*, a man called
[1] On 14th June.

Rochat, had been secretary to Pucheu and was, as such, suspect. The door was opened by Madame Rochat who nearly dropped dead when she was told it was de Gaulle. She showed them to her husband's study. Evidently he had just heard that they were coming. He was standing with his back to them on a stool taking down Pétain's portrait from above the fireplace. 'Descendez, monsieur', said de Gaulle. That was all. It is not true that he was sacked immediately.[1]

H.N. TO B.N. & N.N.   *28th June, 1944*
Sissinghurst

Up on the Victoria Tower I stood on guard with Hinchingbrooke gazing out towards the Surrey hills. It was a comparatively quiet night, and I managed to get some sleep upon my pallet. But there was a lovely effect towards 4.30 am. when something like light began to creep over the sleeping city, and the great mass of Westminster Abbey below me grew out of the darkness. Hinch and I discussed politics. The Tory Reformers (Hinchingbrooke, Quintin Hogg, Peter Thorney-croft, etc.) want me to join their group. I do not see how I could do so without also joining the Tory party. That I refuse to do. I know it seems a foolish prejudice, but I cannot forgive a Party which ought to stand for the defence of Empire and the honour of this country, approving as they did the surrender of Munich. I do not say that this surrender was not necessary; it may have been. But what I do say is that the Tory Party, instead of realising that it was the greatest diplomatic defeat in our history, deliberately backed Chamberlain's statement that it was 'peace with honour'. That I cannot forgive. I am not by nature a Tory, nor am I really by nature a Socialist; I am an Asquithian Liberal, and were I a free man (and not tied as I am by personal loyalties and obligations to the Leicester Conservatives), I should stand as a Liberal. As it is, I shall fight West Leicester (and it will be a hopeless fight) as an Independent.

H.N. TO V.S-W.   *29th June, 1944*
4 King's Bench Walk, E.C.4

I gather that people regard the puny little battle now being fought by Montgomery round the Odon and the Orne as one of supreme

---

[1] De Gaulle's own account in his War Memoirs (vol. ii, p. 234) does not mention the gendarme incident, but says: 'At the *sous-préfecture*, in the waiting-room where the Marshal's portrait was still hanging an hour before, Rochat put himself under my orders pending his relief.'

importance. It seems that if he can get his armour on the open ground south of Caen, anything may happen. There is a spirit of excited optimism at Montgomery's Headquarters. I was told this by a man who lunched with Montgomery on Tuesday. He also told me that Montgomery had just received a telegram from Alexander saying, 'Hang on. Hope to be with you shortly.' That was a good joke on Alexander's part, but Montgomery was not at all pleased.

DIARY   *4th July, 1944*

Lunch at the Beefsteak. Evelyn Waugh[1] is there. He is off tomorrow to visit Tito in the company of Randolph Churchill.[2] He is as pleased as a boy. I like him very much in spite of his quarrelsome nature. Laurence Olivier is there as a new member. Also Mottistone.[3] He tells me that the C.-in-C. Portsmouth, who went over to Normandy, told him that when he actually saw the fleets of transports and warships operating without interference from the enemy, he knew that the war was won utterly.

DIARY   *5th July, 1944*

I go to 108 Eaton Square to listen to an address by Louis Marin.[4] On my way there, a doodle-bug comes over our bus and we all crouch down to avoid the shattering of the window-glass. People are very calm, and when it passes, they just go on reading their newspapers.

Louis Marin had been announced as talking about the Resistance movement, but the old boy merely talked about the German menace and how we should have another war unless we gave France the Rhine frontier. He points out (which is true) that it is not only the young S.S. and S.A. men who are the danger; the German children, boys and girls, have all been indoctrinated. He saw them when they were evacuated to France. They were little beasts who jeered at the French. They are the fathers and mothers of the future Germany. When he reaches his peroration, a doodle-bug comes right over the house in the last stages of its course; it coughs and misses fire, which means that its petrol is running out. As we are sitting in a drawing-

[1] The novelist. He was then writing *Brideshead Revisited*.
[2] Randolph Churchill had already been dropped by parachute on Tito's headquarters as his father's emissary.
[3] The first Lord Mottistone, who was Secretary of State for War in 1914.
[4] The former French *député*, recently arrived from France to support de Gaulle.

room with huge plate-glass windows, this is rather alarming. But only a few people rise in their places, and old Marin continues without a pause. When Sibyl [Colefax] and I come out a few minutes later, there is a cloud of dust in the air which stings the eyes and grates the throat; so it must have been pretty near.

I dine with Jim Thomas[1] in his flat. The other guests are young George Mercer Nairne[2] who had been with Leclerc in the Fezzan, and Anthony Eden, who is in tremendous form.

Anthony begins by telling me about his bitter battles on behalf of de Gaulle. The Prime Minister had invited de Gaulle to come over here for the big battle of France. On 4th June, Winston and he had gone down in a special train to near Portsmouth. De Gaulle and his own party came there by car and Anthony went to meet them. Then they lunched in the train and Winston produced champagne and drank to the health of France. Roosevelt had said that de Gaulle was not to be told the plan of operations, but Winston ignored that, told him everything, took him across to see Eisenhower and forced the latter to show him the maps. Not one word of thanks from de Gaulle. Winston, feeling rather hurt, said, 'I thought it only fitting that you should be present with us today.' 'I see', said de Gaulle glumly; 'I was invited as a symbol.' Viénot and Béthouart were in despair. Anthony was almost beside himself, feeling that Winston was deeply moved emotionally by the thought of the occasion, and that de Gaulle's ungraciousness would make him dislike the man all the more. Finally Winston asked de Gaulle to dine with him. 'Thank you, I should prefer to dine alone with my staff.' 'I feel chilled', said Winston to Anthony.[3]

Anthony went on to say that his great difficulty throughout has been that Winston is half an American and that he regards Roosevelt almost with religious awe. Anthony does not share these feelings. He regards Roosevelt as an astute politician and a man of great personal vanity and obstinacy. Thus, over this de Gaulle business, Winston and Anthony have had terrible rows. One night, or rather at 2 am. one morning, Winston was really insulting, accusing Anthony of having

[1] J. P. L. Thomas, Conservative M.P. for Hereford since 1931 and Financial Secretary to the Admiralty, 1943–45. He was a close friend of Anthony Eden.
[2] The 8th Marquess of Lansdowne, then aged 31. He was then serving as a Major with the Free French forces, and was to become Private Secretary to Duff Cooper when the latter was appointed H.M. Ambassador in Paris later in 1944.
[3] See p. 376, note 3.

set on the Press and Parliament to hound him, and even suggesting that he was trying to force Winston to resign. Anthony left him still fulminating. Next morning, the telephone: 'Anthony, I am going down to see Ike; can you come with me?' So Anthony went round to the garden-gate at Downing Street where Winston's great limousine was standing. Winston appeared. They got in, and Winston lowered the arm at the back of the seat which turns the two places into two arm-chairs. 'I hope', he said as he lowered the arm, 'that this is the only thing that will ever separate us.'

He tells us about the extraordinary meeting which he and Winston held at Tours just before the collapse of France.[1] It was a tiny château and packed with staff officers and Ministers with only one telephone. That single telephone convinced them more than anything that the end was near. Paul Reynaud was there, and Weygand and Pétain, and (curiously enough) de Gaulle.[2] Weygand in a calm voice explained the position. 'I have no reserves', he said. 'If my present line is pierced, *c'est la fin.*' Reynaud intervened to say sharply, 'That would be a political decision.' Weygand bowed and said, 'Certainly.' 'Well', said Winston, 'it is for you to decide. I release you from the obligations of our alliance. You are free to conclude a separate armistice. All I ask is that your Fleet should go to North Africa. And I can assure you that we shall go on fighting. *Nous combattrons.*' Pétain smiled a feline, senile smile. '*Mais comment?*' he asked. '*On les coulera sur la mer, et ceux qui mettront le pied en Angleterre, on les frappera sur la tête.*' Pétain smiled pityingly. Weygand and Reynaud did not smile. They looked at Winston with a wild surmise.

He told us about Tehran. Winston had had a late and rather boisterous last night in Cairo, and when they arrived at the aerodrome early next morning, he had lost his voice. 'I feel very ill', he whispered to Anthony. They then got into the 'plane and Anthony picked up his Trollope. Winston, not being able to talk, was absolutely miserable.

[1] H.N. cannot be reporting Anthony Eden correctly, for three separate events are confused in the account which follows. There was the meeting on 11–12th June 1940, between Churchill, Eden and the French leaders at the Château de Muguet, Briare, near Orléans, at which Churchill used his famous phrase, *On les frapper sur la tête.* On the 13th June there was a further meeting at Tours, when Eden was not present, at which Churchill said that he could not agree to the French making a separate peace. On the 16th the British gave their consent to this through their Ambassador at Bordeaux, provided that the French Fleet was not allowed to fall into German hands. Pétain sued for an Armistice on the 17th.
[2] He had just been appointed Under-Secretary for National Defence.

Aching with self-pity, he drummed on the table. Then he called his servant. 'I am feeling very ill indeed: I have lost my voice.' 'Would you wish me to fetch you a cough-lozenge, Prime Minister?' 'No, you bloody fool, a whisky-and-soda, of course.'

The drinking at Stalin's table was perfectly awful. Timoshenko got dead drunk. Stalin was a little ashamed. 'Do your generals drink as much?' he asked Winston. 'No. But then it may be because they are not such good generals.' Stalin was delighted by this.[1]

Anthony says he cannot understand why the Germans have brought so many troops to the West. I say that it is because they do not believe that the Russians will go outside what they consider to be their own borders. 'But even the Germans can't think that', he says. 'They must know more or less that whole zones of occupation were settled in Tehran.' He also thinks the war will be over soon. 'Luckily', he said, 'we have now reached full agreement regarding the Armistice terms. They are ready to be delivered at any moment.'

He then talks about home politics. Young Mercer Nairne wants to enter politics but hesitates to be a Conservative: 'I don't want to be an Archie Southby.' Anthony becomes excited. 'But you do not imagine', he says, 'that I shall ever consent to lead a party of Southbys and Waterhouses? I will do no such thing. I will not represent the moneyed interests. There are young men who think differently from the old men; young men who see clearer than we do the prospects of a new Toryism. It is them whom I wish to lead.'

He takes me back in his grand car with his detective. I have never known him so friendly or so frank. A most enjoyable evening.

DIARY   *6th July, 1944*

Winston makes his statement about the flying-bomb. I had feared that he might dismiss the thing as a mere nuisance and thus offend the many people who are really frightened of it. But he took the opposite line and, if anything, exaggerated its danger. This was most effective and the House felt generally that there was nothing more to be said.

---

[1] Here, too, there is a confusion of dates. Churchill does not mention this incident at Tehran. But Eden (in *The Reckoning*, p. 302) says that Timoshenko drank too much at a Kremlin dinner in 1941. 'Stalin . . . said quietly to me, "Do your Generals often get drunk?" To which I replied, I hope diplomatically, "They don't often get the chance." ' Lord Avon (in 1966) confirms that this was the occasion referred to.

H.N. TO B.N. & N.N.

9th July, 1944
Sissinghurst

I sit here typing at the window in my study, looking out on my pretty garden with the four yew trees, and wondering whether this time next year you will both be here. I think it most likely and probable. I do not share the optimism of many of my friends (even of those who are very much in the know) that the war will be over before the autumn. I feel that the Nazis still retain control of the whole country and that there is little possibility of revolt. The dismissal of Rundstedt,[1] the frequent 'accidents' which are occurring to other Generals of the old Army, indicate that Himmler and the rest are very well aware that a military *putsch* might occur at any moment and that all dangerous elements must be eliminated. I also have a theory that recent Nazi atrocities (the murder of our air-officers at Görlitz, the V.1, the truly horrible massacres of the Jews in Hungary) are all designed to implicate the Services and the whole German people in the Nazi crimes. The Nazi leaders see that the only form of resolution which will soon be left to the German people is the resolution of despair. They are therefore trying deliberately to increase hopelessness by increasing complicity in crime. They are burning every boat so that nobody can get away. Up to a certain point this stratagem may succeed; the final resistance may be desperate. I foresee therefore that when the military situation is hopeless, there will follow a further 'desperation' stage which may last for two months more.

I should imagine that, if only we can have a spell of settled weather, the next week will be the most decisive of the whole year. The Russians are already at Vilna; Nigel may be facing the Gothic Line[2]; and anything on earth may happen in Normandy.

I dined with James [Pope-Hennessy]. Philip Toynbee was there, distinguished and polite. I can't make out why I ever disliked him. We are joined by Cyril Connolly. He admits to being frightened by the V.1s. I said that he ought to think of his dear ones at the front who are in far greater danger than he is. 'That wouldn't work with me at all, Harold. In the first place, I have no dear ones at the front. And in the second place, I have observed that with me perfect fear casteth out love.'

[1] He was replaced as C.-in-C. West by von Kluge on 1st July, but was reinstated two months later.
[2] The German fortified line in the Northern Apennines between Pisa and Rimini, which the Germans held throughout the winter. Nigel was then at Arezzo.

DIARY   *15th July, 1944*

I notice a certain uneasiness about Normandy. A week ago people were saying, 'Give us a week of fine weather and we shall cut through them like butter.' Now they are saying that Montgomery missed his opportunity and that the Germans have succeeded in sealing off our beach-head.

Montgomery's tactics were misunderstood by Harold Nicolson and most other civilians. His purpose was to draw as many as possible of the German reserves, particularly their armour, to the left flank of the beach-head, where the British were fighting just beyond Caen, in order to weaken the forces opposing the Americans on the right flank, where Montgomery intended to make his major break-through. Thus the new British offensive which was launched on 18th July met very heavy resistance, and its lack of progress aroused corresponding criticism in London. But a week later General Patton was able to cut through the thinner part of the German line to capture Avranches. The whole German front then crumpled rapidly. Brittany was overrun in early August by a single American Corps, and a huge German force was trapped in the Falaise pocket between the British in the north and the Americans swinging up from the south-west. The jaws closed on 20th August, and although many Germans escaped, eight of their divisions were annihilated. The Allies raced for the Seine, taking Paris in their stride on 25th August, and were in Brussels by 3rd September.

On 15th August eleven Allied divisions landed in the south of France. Churchill had strongly opposed the opening of this new front, originally conceived at Tehran, on the grounds that the troops could be better employed to break through the Gothic Line in Italy, debouch into the Po valley, and thence advance north-east in the direction of Vienna. Roosevelt would not agree, arguing that the southern French ports would relieve his supply problems and open up a route for a new Army to deploy on Eisenhower's right flank. Marseilles and Toulon were soon captured, and the Army advanced up the valley of the Rhône to make contact with the northern Armies near Dijon on 11th September. By that time almost the whole of France was liberated, just three months after the original landing in Normandy. The attempt on Hitler's life on 20th July, and the subsequent execution of many of his leading Generals, including Rommel, showed that the end was near. Most people expected it before Christmas.

On the Eastern front the Russians flooded into Finland, Poland and the Balkans. Encouraged by Russian broadcasts, the Poles in Warsaw rose on 1st August, when the Russian armies were less than a score of miles away, hoping to hand over their city to the advancing Russians in the same way as the French Resistance had delivered Paris intact into the hands of the Western Allies. But the Russians halted on the far side of the Vistula. In spite of Churchill's urgent appeals to Stalin, the Russians stood by while the Poles were massacred. They held out for sixty days, but Stalin made little effort to conceal his satisfaction that the Poles in Warsaw, who looked to the West for political support in the coming struggle over Poland's post-war status, should be utterly destroyed. The event, of which Harold Nicolson became fully aware only during its closing stages, was to leave an indelible mark on Europe's relations with the Soviets.

Harold Nicolson's attention was naturally focused on the dramatic campaigns in France and Italy. In August, during the Parliamentary recess, he began to write his history of the Congress of Vienna.

DIARY   *19th July, 1944*

I go to Pratts with Charles Peake. He is now working at Shaef.[1] He tells me that we have now got a thousand tanks and over a million men in Normandy. The battle there is not really as successful as Montgomery pretends. It had been intended to take Falaise on the first day and we are no further than Cagny. Shaef criticises Montgomery for being over-cautious and they regret that he told his commanders 'to take no risks'. They are also irritated by his informing the Press yesterday that it was 'a good day' and that he is 'satisfied'. They do not regard it as a good day and are not satisfied. Winston is going to go over to Normandy for four days today and so is Eisenhower. It may still be, however, that the crossing of the Orne means a great victory in a day or two.

Meanwhile the Poles have captured Ancona, and the Americans Leghorn.

---

[1] Supreme Headquarters, Allied Expeditionary Force. This was Eisenhower's Headquarters in London. He did not permanently cross over to France until 1st September, when Shaef was moved to Versailles. Meanwhile Montgomery was in direct command of all the Allied troops, including the Americans, in Normandy.

21st July, 1944

Hitler broadcast to Germany at 1 am. this morning that a bomb had been placed in his room by Colonel Graf von Stauffenberg, and that although one of his staff had been killed and others injured, he himself was unhurt.[1] He adds, 'What fate would have been in store for Germany had this attempt on my life succeeded, is too horrible to think of.'

I lunch at the Greek Embassy. The guests are the two Ministers Vassiliades and Cartalis, plus Dixon of the F.O.[2] and Anthony Eden. The latter tells us that he has no more news of the German military revolt. He has the impression that it is far more serious and widespread than the Hitler broadcast (which was hysterical, curiously timed and inconsequent) might suggest. The Swiss Minister had received a telegram to say that something like civil war was proceeding in Germany. It is evident that Himmler has been given full powers and that the S.S. and S.A. are patrolling the streets of Berlin. Unfortunately the rebels failed to seize any wireless station, and all the news we get is from the Nazis.

Anthony says that if they are to suppress the revolt (as they assuredly will), they must either kill all the Officer Corps or kill some of the suspected leaders. Fromm, who is in command of the troops in Germany, is suspected of being the centre of the movement.[3] Beck has already committed suicide or been killed.[4] The effect on German opinion and in the Army will be tremendous. Hitler may claim that this is 'an ambitious clique anxious to seize power', but the people will know that it represents a desperate attempt by the Generals to rescue the Armies from the impossible strategic position in which Hitler's intuition has placed them.

[1] The account which follows shows that the news which had already reached London was fairly full and accurate. Von Stauffenberg placed his time-bomb in a despatch-case beside the table in Hitler's map-room. It went off at 12.42 pm. on the 20th. Three officers in the room were killed, and several others injured. Hitler's legs were burned, his right arm temporarily paralysed and his ear-drums pierced. Stauffenberg escaped to Berlin, where he was seized and executed that same night.

[2] Sir Pierson Dixon, Principal Private Secretary to Anthony Eden.

[3] General Fromm was, in fact, most reluctant to join the conspirators when he heard that Hitler was still alive, and was arrested by them for a few hours. He was then rescued and ordered Stauffenberg's immediate execution. But he himself was executed for complicity in the plot in March 1945.

[4] General Beck, the senior military conspirator, tried twice to kill himself that evening, and was finally despatched by a sergeant on Fromm's orders.

I go to Leicester to address the 1936 Club. I stay the night with Bertie Jarvis, and as usual I am touched by the charm of their house and the trouble Soph[1] takes to make me comfortable. They are each of them among the most delightful people that I know.

DIARY   24th July, 1944

At 4.45 this morning I am suddenly awakened by the sound of a flying bomb zooming over my head. I do not wake up with any start, but quite calmly and completely. As I hear it (a few seconds only), it cuts out and I know that it is about to descend. I bury my head in my pillow and then comes quite a small crash and no sense of blast through the room. But a second later I hear things falling and splintering in my sitting-room and I get up to look. The shutters have been thrown open and the iron bars smashed out. Only one pane is broken. My lovely apothecary pot with lilies in it is also destroyed. I put on a great-coat and go out into the court. There are points of torches everywhere and the wardens running about to see if anyone is hurt. They tell me it has fallen in Essex Street. I notice a thick soup-like haze in the air and all today my eyes have been red and smarting. I go back to bed and sleep.

DIARY   25th July, 1944

I listen to a talk about the situation given by Jan Masaryk in a Committee Room of the House. He is extremely informative and witty. He says that Czechoslovakia will become a neighbour of Russia and must get on to good terms with her. This will entail some switch of home policy in the direction of State Socialism and the nationalisation of mines and forests. But at the same time Czechoslovakia does not wish to lose contact with Mother Europe. They want their old frontiers back, but might be willing to cede some enclaves like Asch and Eger. They will expel most of the nasty Germans, but are quite prepared to keep the nice ones provided that they become good Czech citizens. They will not have any minority treaties again. Czechoslovakia must become a national State.

---

[1] Mrs Jarvis. W. B. Jarvis was Chairman of the West Leicester Conservative Association.

H.N. TO B.N. & N.N.   *30th July, 1944*
                                                        Sissinghurst

I gave a lecture at an American mess and found them intelligent and appreciative. They all agree that British and American troops *always* get on badly when they just glower at each other in the streets, and *always* get on well when they have a joint job to do. Their cooperation in Normandy has apparently been quite splendid. People are enormously cheered. It is very much due to Eisenhower's personal tact and charm. The criticism of Montgomery continues and it is especially ferocious in the Air Ministry—I cannot explain why. But the recent turn which his offensive has taken and the capture of Avranches by the Americans may still the disquiet.

DIARY   *5th August, 1944*

I walk up and down the lime-walk considering what book I should write. I do not feel in tune for a sequel to *In Search of the Past*,[1] since it all seems so meaningless in face of current events. I think vaguely that I might do a book on the Vienna Congress. When I get to breakfast, I find a letter from Curtis Brown[2] saying that Doubleday Doran[3] want a book on Metternich and would I do it? I am not anxious to do this, since it is too vast a subject and anyhow Algernon Cecil has done it so well.[4] But the receipt of this letter confirms me in my decision to write about that period and I am happy starting at once on a new notebook.

The 9 pm. news is astonishing. Not only have the Americans got as far as Châteaubriand in their drive to Nantes, but they have actually sent tanks into Brest. The Germans have abandoned Laval (the town, not the person), and it looks as if they are in a bad way indeed. They say that the Guards have entered the southern bit of Florence. The Russians are driving on to Cracow. An amazing bag of news.

H.N. TO B.N. & N.N.   *13th August, 1944*
                                                        Sissinghurst

Each of you in your letters shows anxiety about the V.1s. I have not mentioned the thing much because I do not wish to be indiscreet, and because it is absurd to dramatise what is a perfectly secondary and useless form of attack. The anxiety it causes to individuals is limited in

[1] The general title given to his two books *Helen's Tower* and *The Desire to Please.*
[2] His literary agents.   [3] The American publishers.   [4] Published in 1933.

space and time. In space, because one gets to know the line it is taking and nine times out of ten it is not on one's own line. In time, because the actual moment of personal danger is only a few seconds. You see, by day you can trace the things (and often see the things) owing to the distinctive noise that it makes—when near, it sets up a vibration that shakes the whole room. One can see its little black body hurtling along with something flapping behind it which looks like gauze being blown out from an electric fan, but which is really the exhaust. At night this exhaust flames like a meteor, and one can follow the thing as it hurtles through the sky like a falling star, like a moving beacon, tense, deliberate, unswerving, vindictive, horribly purposeful. But truly it does not in any sense dislocate or even disturb our lives. If I were a German I should be enraged that so much fuel, so much ingenuity, so much labour, so many false hopes, should have been centred upon an infernal machine which can have no decisive influence at all. Of course it has a serious nuisance-value; so have wasps. But even as they harvest the oats and barley regardless of wasps, so also, as the doodle-bugs hum and throb over southern England, do the farm-carts lumber up the lane and only rarely does a land-girl shade her eyes to watch their passage above the Weald. Before long we shall have turned the Germans out of the sites from which they launch their wicked toys.

The delight of being alone for a few days, of seeing the sun upon the garden, of listening to the victorious news, of knowing that Florence is safe—all this is a foretaste of the coming calm of peace.

DIARY   *15th August, 1944*

I turn on the 1 o'clock news and hear a bald announcement that we have landed in the South of France between Nice and Marseilles. The announcement is followed by the *Marseillaise*. There is great excitement.

DIARY   *23rd August, 1944*

I am working on my notes for *The Congress of Vienna* and have just reached the point where the Allies enter Paris. I look up and see that it is already 1 pm. and I dash up to Viti's bedroom to listen to the news. It takes some time before the current gets through, and so I come into the middle of the first sentence: '... fifty thousand armed men with the assistance of many thousands of the unarmed population. By noon yesterday all the official buildings were in the hands of the Resistance.

Paris is free.'[1] I am so excited that I scarcely notice that we have also taken Grenoble.

Viti rushes across to share the excitement. Mrs Staples[2] says, 'How glad I am that they did it themselves', which is characteristic of our deep spirit of generosity. All of us have a glass of gin and toast the future of France.

DIARY   *25th August, 1944*

I go round to see Duchesne[3] at Bush House. He had been ill from excitement yesterday. He showed me sheets of transcripts which had just come in from the monitoring people, taken from a very weak station operating from Paris. It gave a complete record of the morning's events. Appeals from several *arrondissements*: 'We are running out of ammunition; we are being heavily attacked; please send reinforcements at once.' These gloomy messages accumulated under the time-headings, and then, in the same ticker-tape type, came the news, *'La Division Leclerc approche'*; *'Le Général Leclerc est arrivé à l'Hôtel de Ville'*; *'Le carillon de Notre Dame proclame la délivrance'*. Then an officer saying he is going back to fetch de Gaulle. Poor, dear Duchesne. He is not looking well; he seems very excited; but his great joy is that 'at least in appearance' Paris has been liberated by the Parisians themselves.

H.N. TO B.N. & N.N.   *27th August, 1944*
                                                          Sissinghurst

Mummy hates ladders. She has an idea that I ought to fix the bottom of the ladder in a crack of the pavement so that it will not slip outwards. She has an idea that if the ladder rests slantwise so that my full weight as I climb up is thrown upon the lime-trees, either the ladder or the lime-tree will break. She has an idea that greater safety would be secured if the ladder stood somehow on its end so that the weight of my body would fall upon the rungs and not upon the trees. I pointed out to her gently that in such a posture the ladder might leave the limes and fall backwards. 'You don't understand', she said: 'I can't

---

[1] The news was slightly premature. On the 23rd the Germans were still holding strong-points in Paris, but the Resistance had gained possession of most of the streets. On the 24th Leclerc's Division penetrated the outer suburbs, but it was not till the 25th that the city was fully liberated.

[2] The Nicolsons' cook, who remained with them from 1926 to 1967.

[3] The war-time pseudonym of Michel St Denis, the actor and producer, who was head of the B.B.C.'s French Section, 1940–44.

explain, but it is as simple as hydraulics.' The latter branch of science is not one of the departments of knowledge on which your mother is really authoritative or even sane. But I did not say so. I merely said that a ladder which stands on its toes is apt to fall backwards, a very dangerous thing to do. She said that I was a physical imbecile. And I confess that when I had finished with the lime-walk, it looked as if a giraffe had strayed into the garden and taken large munches out of the trees.

Then this evening the bee-man came. He looks like the Apostle James-the-Less and he puts on a big black veil and talks through it about the mystery of the Pyramids and the lost tribe of Israel. Little Jo[1] joined me as I watched him dowsing the bees. 'Why does he wear that funny hat, Mr Nicolson?' 'So that the bees won't sting his eyes, Jo.' 'But why should the bees sting his eyes, Mr Nicolson?' 'Because they might be angry when he opens their hive.' 'But why should they be angry when he opens their hive?' 'Because they know that he means to take their honey away from them.' 'But how do they know that he means to take their honey away from them?' 'The bee,' I answered, 'although you would not call it an intelligent insect, is a creature of amazing instinct.' 'But why do you call it an intelligent instinct, Mr Nicolson? And why doesn't Mrs Nicolson come?' I explained that she was allergic to bees. 'Allergic', she muttered to herself in the intoxicating way that children have when they find a new and lovely word.

DIARY   *28th August, 1944*

I have a talk with Massigli. He says that Leclerc's columns only arrived just in time to prevent the Commune from being declared in Paris. He evidently fears, as I fear, social revolution in France. It is not that I have any apprehension regarding French Communism, which will not be an aggressive or a proselytising thing. But it may mean civil war, and that would be regarded in this country as proof that the French are really impossible. The high repute they have won would be sacrificed. Evidently the French wish to diminish the importance of the 'disturbances' during de Gaulle's entry into Paris.[2] I notice that *The Times* this morning scarcely mentions it, and it is

[1] Josephine Hayter, Mrs Staples' daughter by her second marriage. She was then aged 6.

[2] Shots had been fired as de Gaulle entered Notre Dame, and during the service inside, but it was never established who had fired them. De Gaulle was unharmed.

significant that *France* merely inserts a paragraph on the back page headed 'An incident'. Massigli leaves for Paris tomorrow.

DIARY   *30th August, 1944*

Vernon Bartlett[1] has broken the silence about the Russian behaviour in Warsaw. Having encouraged the Polish partisans to rise against the Germans, they have done nothing to help them. Even when we offered to drop supplies, the Russians would not allow our aeroplanes to land in Russian territory. It looks as if they wanted the Germans to wipe out the Polish resistance movement, so that no decent Poles will be left when they get there. It is a tragedy that such immense power should be in the hands of people so ruthless and unreliable.

H.N. TO B.N. & N.N.   *31st August, 1944*
                                                                  Sissinghurst

At the Beefsteak at luncheon there was Hugh Seely,[2] A. P. Herbert and Freddy Birkenhead.[3] Hugh tells me that the Americans are now not at all keen on our helping them in the Far East. 'Never', we say to them, 'will England let you down. You helped us out in 1941. We will help you out against Japan.' They don't like that at all. They feel quite rightly that they can knock Japan out unaided. And Madame Chiang Kai-shek has convinced them that such things as Hong Kong and Singapore stink in the nostrils of every Chinaman. So neither Russia nor ourselves will be really wanted.

Alan Herbert had been staying with Montgomery at his H.Q. in Normandy. He is an old family friend. He said that Montgomery simply loathes the destruction of French towns. 'Come', he said to him, 'and I shall show you what liberation means.' He took him to Caen and Troarn. Yet, in fact, in this most destructive of all wars, most of the French and Italian cities will emerge unscathed.

Freddy Birkenhead is going out to join Randolph and had a bedside audience with Winston. Randolph's marriage is going wonky[4] and Winston is terribly distressed. The old boy is tremendously domestic and adores his family.

---

[1] Publicist and broadcaster. M.P. for Bridgwater, 1938-50.
[2] Lord Sherwood, Parliamentary Under-Secretary of State for Air, 1941-45.
[3] The 2nd Earl of Birkenhead.
[4] Randolph Churchill's marriage to Pamela Digby was dissolved in 1946.

DIARY   *4th September, 1944*

An amazing day for news. At 1 o'clock I hear that the British 2nd
Army has occupied Brussels. Hostilities between Finland and Russia
have ceased. Then at 9.30 pm. we turn on the French news and hear
that our troops have crossed the Dutch border.[1] Since D Day we have
taken 300,000 German prisoners in France alone. The German Army
appears to be in utter confusion. In the south Lyons is free. We have
penetrated deep into the Gothic Line. It is almost impossible to follow
this sequence of triumphs, and to remember what happened yesterday
or today, and what will happen to morrow.

We have had no doodle-bugs for three days and I am almost beginning to feel that by some miracle Sissinghurst has escaped destruction
in this war.

DIARY   *6th September, 1944*

Viti and I go up to the top of the tower to see if we can catch any
flashes in the clouds from the battle at Calais. We see nothing beyond
a corona of search-lights all round us, and a red light signalling Morse
from the North Downs. Below us the oast-houses throb and roar
as they dry the hops.

DIARY   *8th September, 1944*

At lunch the Belgian Ambassador tells me that Antwerp is undamaged.
His Government left for Brussels this morning.

It is an odd feeling that we are released from the flying bomb. One
realises that one was much more frightened of it than one confessed.
I observe that when I hear menacing sounds, such as the rumble in
the oast-houses or the throb of some heavy engine, I am conscious of a
tremor of relief when I suppose there was a repressed tremor of fear
before.

I take the 3.15 home. I find the proofs of my book *Friday Mornings*.
These are reprints of my articles in the *Spectator*. I wish now that I had
never agreed to republish them. They use up paper which might have
gone to some young writer publishing a new book.

It is evident that there is a pause in our advance. The Germans are
beginning to recover from the shock and are resisting quite well on the
Albert Canal, the Meuse and the Moselle. Meanwhile our armies are
regrouping for the second round, the battle of Germany.

[1] This news was premature. The border was not crossed until 10th September.

The Allied advance slowed down gradually. Although Antwerp had been captured almost undamaged, the approaches to it along the Scheldt were still in German hands, and the enemy clung tenaciously to the Channel ports, all of which except Cherbourg had been by-passed by the summer campaign. They fell one by one, but the hardest fight was for the island of Walcheren in the Scheldt estuary, which was not captured by the Canadians until 3rd November. Convoys were then able to sail direct to Antwerp. To break the deadlock along the Meuse and lower Rhine, Montgomery landed three parachute Divisions (two American and one British) on 17th September at Grave, Nijmegen and Arnhem, and launched the British 2nd Army on a narrow front to link up with them. The first two parachute Divisions were successfully relieved, but the Germans blocked the road from Nijmegen to Arnhem and the survivors of the British force in Arnhem were withdrawn on 25th September. On the remainder of the Western front the Allied advance was held up by supply difficulties, the worsening weather and stiffening German resistance. Strasbourg was captured by the Free French, and Aachen, the first town in Germany, by the Americans on 21st October.

Churchill left England on two major journeys during these autumn months, the first to meet Roosevelt at Quebec in September, and the second to confer with Stalin at Moscow in October. The Quebec conference was mainly concerned with operations in the Far East where Churchill was 'determined to regain our rightful possessions, and not to have them handed back to us at the peace-table'. His offer of the British Fleet for operations against the Japanese under American command was immediately accepted by Roosevelt against the wishes of his naval staff, but the major battle of Leyte Gulf (20–26th October) was won solely by United States Forces. Roosevelt was not present at the Moscow conference because he was engaged in the Presidential Election campaign, from which he emerged successfully for a fourth term on 7th November. In his absence Churchill and Stalin were not able to conclude much business. Although they agreed that Britain should have a major influence in Greece so long as the war lasted, and Russia in Rumania, they were unable to reach any agreement over Poland.

In France de Gaulle consolidated his position against the Communists of the Resistance. Harold Nicolson's speech in the House of Commons on 29th September was greatly praised as a contribution to improved Anglo-American-French relations. De Gaulle's Government was at last recognised by the three major Allies on 23rd October, and Churchill

received an ovation in Paris when on 10–12th November he paid his
first visit to the city after its liberation.

DIARY   *12th September, 1944*

There was a loud explosion in London at dawn. It is the V.2.[1] It
began on Friday, when a shell descended on Orpington.

H.N. TO B.N. & N.N.   *17th September, 1944*
                                                    Sissinghurst

The reports about the Gothic Line fighting are not very encouraging.[2]
But the fact remains that Alexander's mixed armies have contained,
retained and beaten some of the best German Divisions which might
otherwise have manned the Siegfried Line. It is of course distressing,
when one has fought from Medjez to the Arno, to feel that the *coup de
grâce* may be given by other armies on other fields. But to hold down
one huge paw of the wounded beast while others get at its throat is
something more than a mere contribution to victory. I am glad that
Nigel has been in the Italian rather than in the French campaign. It is
so much less bedint,[3] *si j'ose m'exprimer ainsi.*

It looks today as if Aachen will fall at any moment. Then once we
have really pierced the Siegfried Line and paused for a little laundry-
work,[4] we shall advance on Cologne and Coblenz. Will German
opinion stand invasion of their country on two fronts? I think they
are too disciplined and lethargic to do anything else. Many of the
more civilian troops will surrender in droves. But S.S. and S.A.
guerrillas will remain in isolated groups, and there will be no security
and no complete peace for many a day. That is my forecast.

---

[1] This was the German long-range rocket, fired from Holland, which carried a ton
of explosives and reached a height of fifty miles before dropping without warning
on London 200 miles away. It caused less anxiety and fewer casualties than the
V.1, but the British never found an answer to it other than by bombing the
launching pads. About 1,300 were fired on London between September and March.
[2] The Gothic Line in the Northern Apennines had already been penetrated in several
places, particularly on the Adriatic front, but further advance was very slow.
[3] 'Bedint', in Sackville language, was derived from the German *bedienen*, 'to serve'.
Hence originally it meant 'servant'. Later, as an epithet, it came to mean 'lower or
middle-class', 'second-rate', 'vulgar'.
[4] A reference to the song popular in the British Army in the early months of 1940:
    'We're going to hang out our washing on the Siegfried Line,
    Have you any dirty washing, mother dear?'

DIARY   *17th September, 1944*

At 1 o'clock we hear that we have landed a huge airborne army in Holland behind the German Lines. It is the largest force ever sent by air.

DIARY   *19th September, 1944*

The evening news tells us that the 2nd Army has made a dash for Eindhoven to within a few miles of Nijmegen. That brings them almost to the Waal. It represents an advance of thirty miles in five hours. It is hard to believe.

DIARY   *21st September, 1944*

Go and see Miss Macleod at the Ministry of Information. She says that they want to start an important information service in Paris combining Press, radio and British Council. We must have someone there 'whom the French trust absolutely'. Would I take on the job? I say that it would mean resigning my seat in Parliament, since I do not approve of Members residing out of the country. It would also mean my resigning from the B.B.C. since I do not approve of absentee Governors. And would I be any good? Have I the drive or toughness? Do I get on well enough with journalists? And apart from that, the French might imagine that I had been sent to keep an eye on Duff.[1] He himself might not like it. Anyhow, I promise to think it over, but my answer will be 'No'. I was amused at the thought that after twenty years in diplomacy I should be invited back in the capacity of a Press Attaché. The 1 o'clock news tells us that we have captured the Nijmegen bridge intact. A marvellous achievement.

DIARY   *24th September, 1944*

The report is that our patrols have joined up with 'some' of our parachute troops at Arnhem. The situation is critical, since if we win this battle we shall have won the battle of Germany.

DIARY   *27th September, 1944*

To the Beefsteak where I meet Alba.[2] He speaks with great enthusiasm of *The Eagle and the Dove* and says he looks forward to taking Vita to see St Teresa's convent. Rob Bernays joins me. He says, 'I hope what I've heard is not true?' 'What have you heard?' 'That you are

[1] Duff Cooper had been British Ambassador in Paris since 13th September.
[2] The Duke of Alba, the Spanish Ambassador in London, 1939–45.

thinking of going to the Lords.' Now if he had had that from Oliver Stanley or someone like that, I should be quite prepared to believe that this was a sounding from on high. But I suspect that it was one of Sibyl Colefax's little plans. Anyhow I said, 'I should love to go to the Lords, but I see little prospect of it.' He said, 'But you never realise that you are a national figure . . .' pause '. . . of the s-s-s-s-s-second d-d-d-d-d-degree.'

The midnight news tells us that 2,000 of our Airborne Division have managed to rejoin our troops on the southern bank [of the Rhine]. That means that this particular landing failed, and that we have not succeeded in turning the German right flank. This is a sad pity.

DIARY   *28th September, 1944*

I go to the House to hear Winston. On my way there, I consider how, were I in his place, I would treat the Arnhem surrender. On the one hand, it was necessary to represent it as an episode of relative unimportance in proportion to the wide sweep of war. On the other hand, it was necessary not to suggest to anxious parents that it had all been no more than an incident. Winston solved this difficulty with mastery. He spoke of the men of the 1st Parachute Division with great emotion: ' "Not in vain" is the boast of those who returned to us. "Not in vain" is the epitaph of those who fell.' He then passes on to the war as a whole. He tells us that since the Battle of Normandy we have taken nearly half-a-million prisoners, and thereby he puts the thing implicitly in its right proportion. He is in fine form at the start, finding his words easily, thumping upon the box. But after three-quarters-of-an-hour his voice gets husky and his delivery hesitant. We adjourn for an hour for lunch, and when Winston resumes, he has not entirely recovered his first brio. He lags a bit, and appears to be tired and bored.

The debate dawdles on, and in the late evening I hear Quintin Hogg make a speech about Poland and Russia which is not merely extremely sensible, but quite admirably delivered. It is far the best that I have heard him, or indeed any back-bencher, make.

H.N. TO B.N. & N.N.   *29th September, 1944*
                                                                                   Sissinghurst

I sat in the House all day listening to the continuation of the debate. I made a short speech of twenty minutes calling Anthony Eden's attention to certain discrepancies in the P.M.'s statement and asking for an assurance that the French Provisional Government would be recognised shortly, and that France would be admitted as 'an equal and potent partner in the discussions on the future of Europe'. In his reply Anthony took particular care to give these assurances, and I felt that I had, for once, been able to do some good. In fact, from the practical point of view of eliciting assurances, it was the most successful speech I have ever made.

DUFF COOPER TO H.N.   *3rd October, 1944*
                                                    British Embassy, Paris

Paris is almost as delightful as ever, and becoming steadily more delightful as things settle down. We must arrange for you to pay us a visit as soon as possible. We were able to start working in the Embassy at once and hope to be living there fairly shortly.

My difficulties have been increased by the P.M.'s references to France in his last speech, and Anthony's answer to your question, although it cleared up the ambiguity, did not make matters much better from the French point of view, for they cannot see what on earth it has to do with us whether they have a large Consultative Assembly or a small one; and they ask bitterly what we should say if de Gaulle, in a public speech, were to express the view that it was about time we had a General Election. I am afraid that the quarrel between Winston and 'Le Grand Charles' will never be made up, and the President,[1] who although being more disingenuous can conceal his feelings in public, will continue to nurse a grudge against de Gaulle for having succeeded in spite of him. These personal misunderstandings are really very unhappy, because they may spoil the wonderful opportunity that exists of forming a firm and lasting friendship between the two countries. Never have the English been so popular in France as they are today, and the most popular of all of them is the Prime Minister, who would get a delirious welcome if he came here. But he could only come here as a friend of de Gaulle, and they would have to be seen together. One drive down the Champs Elysées would be quite enough. The general public have not the slightest idea that they are anything but the firmest of friends. But he cannot come until we have recognised their Government, and the longer we put off doing so now, the more foolish we appear, and the less thanks we shall get, when we eventually do so. In fact, I am afraid we shall get no

[1] President Roosevelt.

thanks at all even now. The people just cannot understand why we treat the Government of France so coldly and the Government of Italy so warmly.

Communications and transport are at the bottom of every difficulty that exists here at the moment. There is plenty of food and plenty of everything in France, but it is almost impossible to move it from one place to another. The official price of an egg in Paris is 20 francs, and twenty kilometres outside Paris it is 2 francs 50. There are elements of potential disorder in the south, owing to the large numbers of armed men who are not properly under control, and owing to the activities of the Communists. It is very difficult to get news from there, but such as we do get is, on the whole, reassuring, and I for one do not believe for a moment in a Communist revolution.

V.S-W. TO H.N.   *4th October, 1944*
                                                                  Sissinghurst

I went to my Biddenden institute,[1] which I found seething with indignation over Warsaw.[2] They had been listening to the 6 o'clock news. Very shrewd and shrewish they were, and I thought what good sense the English usually display when put to the test. In the course of business the Chairman had to announce that there was going to be a 'day' for Mrs Churchill's Aid to Russia Fund, at which there was just one hoot of derision from the whole audience.

DIARY   *4th October, 1944*

I find that people in the House are really horrified at the collapse of the Resistance in Warsaw, and think that Russia has behaved abominably. Moreover, the idea is gaining ground that Russia is seeking to establish herself in the Balkans and has given up all idea of fighting the Germans in East Prussia. Anthony [Eden] does not share this pessimism. But nonetheless distrust of the Russians is universal, and by no means confined to people of the right or middle wings.

Dine with Tilea. He does a 'told-you-so' about Russia. He does not wish to return to Rumania. He asks me about the marvellous secret weapon which we shall have ready in six months and which will change the face of the war.[3] Armed with this weapon we could afford to

---

[1] The Women's Institute at a village four miles from Sissinghurst.
[2] See Introductory Note, p. 390.
[3] This is the first reference in the Diary to the atomic bomb, but H.N. cannot now (1967) remember whether he knew what Tilea was talking about.

go to war with Russia. I discourage him from such fantasies, which are worthy of Goebbels.

I lunched with Massigli[1] to meet Paul Claudel.[2] The other guests (arranged by me) were Desmond [MacCarthy], Raymond [Mortimer], Clive [Bell] and Charles Morgan. In addition there was Anthony Eden, not arranged by me, but arranged by Massigli. We lunched at the Savoy. Claudel is not an attractive man, being senile and leery and a trifle mean. He told me that it was true that the *Figaro* had been suppressed for publishing a little quatrain of his on the subject of his grand-daughter. She had been born '*le jour même de la victoire de Tel-el-Alamein*'. They had christened her Victoire, and Claudel had written this little poem to her, beginning, '*Petit poisson dodu . . .*' and saying in effect, 'How right you were, my dear, to choose such a lovely name.' At which the *Figaro* was suppressed. Claudel was glad to tell this story, since he also wrote a long panegyric to Pétain which (although he may not know it) is circulating in London. But he was *not* a nice man, and he spoke in a bad way about Gide, saying that his exposure of his own vices reminded him of the monkeys on Monkey Hill, *faisant des obscénités avec une triste dignité*, and he was disagreeable about everyone else.

Anthony said across the table that my speech on Friday had been the best I had made. They all heard! Vanity is a foolish thing, but agreeable to the mouth like a warm sweet pudding with raspberry sauce. I was so pleased!

At 5 pm. Attlee rose to make a statement. He announced that he was glad to inform the House that Winston and Anthony had arrived safe and sound in Moscow. Now, such a statement, a year ago, would have provoked a burst of cheering from all benches and especially from the Labour benches. But there was a hush and a mutter instead. I thought at first that this was due to the fact that Holy Russia is momentarily in disgrace for her conduct of the Warsaw business. But it wasn't that. It was merely that people are worried about Winston's health.

---

[1] French Ambassador in London since September 1944.
[2] The French poet and diplomatist. He was then aged 76.

Why should it always be he who dashes about from one corner of the earth to the other? 'He oughtn't to do it', murmured the Socialists. 'Poor old boy, he really oughtn't to do it.' It is difficult to conceive the personal affection which Winston enjoys among all Members of the House.

I dined with Ed Murrow to meet Shirer,[1] who had just arrived back from Washington. He was interesting about the Election prospects.[2] He said that if there was a large vote, Roosevelt would get in; but if the vote was small, then Dewey would have a chance. For this reason the Republicans were not stoking up Election fever by wild speeches; their moderation, he said, was a careful political calculation and not due to nobler motives. He did not seem to think that Roosevelt's chances would be much affected by the battle-front. Of course, if, before 7th November, there were some enormous victory in Germany, then people might think that all was over and that they might now risk trying Dewey. But on the whole he felt that the war was quite honestly being detached from the issue. He said that Roosevelt's bitterest opponents had never suggested that he was telling Eisenhower to postpone the decisive operations until after the Election. 'Even our politicians', he said, 'are not quite as darned mean as to suggest that.'

DIARY   16th October, 1944

Aachen is now surrounded; we are advancing on Walcheren; we have landed regular troops at the Piraeus.[3]

H.N. TO B.N. & N.N.   19th October, 1944
                                                              Sissinghurst

I went to St Paul's for the service to commemorate the liberation of Athens. It was a service conducted jointly by the Church of England and the Greek Orthodox. For the Church of England there was the Bishop of London arrayed in a terrific cope, surrounded by the Dean and Chapter in purple and gold and accompanied by an orderly dressed in scarlet who carried his crozier. For the Orthodox Church

---

[1] William L. Shirer, American author and journalist. His *Berlin Diary* had been published in 1941.
[2] Roosevelt's Republican opponent in the Presidential Election was Governor Thomas E. Dewey, whom he defeated by 3½ million votes.
[3] On 12th October the Germans withdrew from Athens and a British force occupied the capital during the next few days to save the country from civil war.

there was my little friend the Archbishop of Thyateira, whom I know so well as a member of my Greek Relief Committee. On these occasions, when we meet under the chairmanship of Irene Ravensdale, it is a small round mousy prelate who sits there saying, 'Yes, Madame German: no, Madame German.' But in St Paul's I was faced by the semblance of God the Father in all his majesty. Arrayed in gold, surmounted by a huge black head-dress, grasping a crozier in the shape of those walking-sticks we bought at Olympia, he sailed along majestically, his chin thrust out in vigour, the great amethyst cross on his bosom catching countless reflections from the lights, and his train carried by an elderly gentleman in a frayed white dressing-gown and pince-nez, who did not look like a Byzantine deacon or archimandrite, but like a shipping-clerk from Nauplia.

There we all were—the King of Greece, the Duchess of Kent, the Ambassadors and Generals and the Greek choir from Bayswater who were hidden behind a screen. The Bishop of London said, 'Brethren, we are met today to return thanks to God . . .' and so on, all in a very Church of England voice. Then we knelt down and were told to give thanks unto the Lord our God, to which we replied in a general murmur, 'It is meet and right so to do.' I was becoming bored at this stage, and was startled from my day-dream by a loud ululation which echoed through the dome and sent the pigeons outside scurrying in panic. My little Archbishop of Thyateira had reached the microphone and let forth a loud Greek cry. A second time he yelled aloud through the microphone, and then from behind the screen the Greek Choir began intoning *Kyrie eleison! Kyrie eleison!* to which the British choir responded, 'Lord, have mercy upon us', after which the Bishop of London took off his cope, handed it to his orderly, climbed the pulpit arrayed in lawn sleeves and delivered an address which was so inadequate as to be almost unbearable.

As I walked out, I felt my arm gripped from behind. It was the Lord Chancellor. 'You and I, my dear Harold, could have devised that a trifle better, I think. A passage from Simonides, perhaps, or even a few words from the funeral oration?' God, what a toad and a worm Simon is!

I lectured that night to a course of officers being trained for work on the Control Commission for Germany. I dined afterwards in their mess. They turned on the 9 o'clock news. The Brigadier was called out to the telephone, and when he came back he said, 'Well, was there any news?' 'No, sir', replied the Colonel, 'nothing of serious importance.' 'Steady on', I said, forgetting my manners, 'we were told that we had between us captured Belgrade, Aachen and Dubrovnik. The Americans have landed in the Philippines. And a detailed communiqué has been issued after the Moscow Conference.' 'Really now?' said the Brigadier.

I know that I should not have intervened, and I know that my remark was tactless. But I was so astounded by their ignorance or indifference that I forgot myself. This is not the first time that I have observed with distress that officers on special courses (who are presumably chosen because they are more intelligent than the rest) take no interest at all in the war as a whole and have no conception of what is important and what is not. I believe this to be at the root of what foreigners take to be our lack of intelligence. It is not that we are more stupid than other people; but since we are not trained to be actively intelligent, as we are trained to take physical exercise, the ordinary Englishman seems to imagine that intellectual activity must be confined to working hours.

H.N. TO B.N. & N.N.   *23rd October, 1944*
                                        Sissinghurst

It was the anniversary of Alamein, and we had on the wireless a message from Montgomery. He introduced few sporting images, but he did end with Kipling's *If.* My distaste for that General passes all reasonable definition. It is childish to be deterred from admiration by a few quirks of language and intonation which recall the least pleasant among the masters at a private school. He must be a *grand stratège*—that I am prepared to believe. But he remains distasteful. But then none of us would at the time have cared for Nelson. I had all my feathers smoothed down by hearing that the three Governments have at long last recognised de Gaulle's Government. So that is settled after months of fuss and estrangement.

H.N. TO B.N. & N.N.   *27th October, 1944*
                                        Sissinghurst

Winston made a statement about the Moscow Conference. He did it with the utmost ingenuity, calm and skill. In fact he is quite himself again. A few months ago he seemed ill and tired and he did not find his words as easily as usual. But today he was superb. Cherubic, pink, solid and vociferous. After he had made his speech he came into the smoking-room. He went to the bar. 'Collins', he said to the barman,

'I should like a whisky-and-soda—single.' He sat down in an arm-chair. He then struggled out of his arm-chair and walked again to the bar. 'Collins', he said, 'delete the word "single" and insert the word "double".' Then, grinning at us like a schoolboy, he resumed his seat.

DIARY   *28th October, 1944*

Gladwyn Jebb was at the Beefsteak, back from Dumbarton Oaks.[1] He says that the Russians absolutely refuse to allow Geneva to be the seat of the future League since they think the Swiss behaved badly to them.

DIARY   *31st October, 1944*

Winston makes his statement about the prolongation of Parliament and the General Election. He says that it is unlikely that the war with Germany will end before Easter or even early summer. As soon as we can announce that all organised resistance in Germany has ceased, the Labour and Liberal Ministers will leave the Cabinet. He does not, however, wish to hold a General Election at the moment of jubilation, and feels it wiser to wait for a short period to allow public opinion to quieten down. This is as much to say that he does not wish the Conservative Party to cash in on his own war popularity. He indicates that after the break-up of the Coalition the Conservative Party will have to carry on as a Caretaker Government while the Election is being prepared. He also indicates that when the Election takes place (probably in October next), the war with Japan will still be going on and likely to last for another 18 months. The assumption is, therefore, that the Coalition will reform after the General Election. I have never admired Winston's moral attitude more than I did this morning.

H.N. TO B.N. & N.N.   *2nd November, 1944*
                                                                  Sissinghurst

B.B.C. Board. Winston, who is childish about such things, is tiresome about our use of the name 'Aachen'. He told Brendan Bracken to tell us that we should use the name 'Aix-la-Chapelle'. We pointed out (a) that the public would think it was a French town, whereas we want to emphasise that it is a German town; (b) that in any case the communiqués and Shaef, as well as the newspapers, always referred to the place as 'Aachen', and if the B.B.C. were to take a different line, much

---

[1] This conference, which met at Dumbarton Oaks, Washington, between 21st August and 7th October, drew up draft proposals which served as a basis for the United Nations Charter.

confusion would result. But that did not satisfy Winston. So incensed was he that he asked Violet [Bonham Carter] to lunch and gave her a tremendous talking-to. He said that the B.B.C. were 'affected' in their pronunciation of foreign place-names. We said 'Breyda' instead of 'Breeda' (the Dutch pronunciation is, I believe, 'Breddaaa'), and 'Catarnia' instead of 'Cataynia', and so on. Anyhow he issued a ukase that in future it must be Aix-la-Chapelle.[1] How can it be that so busy a man fusses so much about a detail like this? Anyhow, he is so wise and good and so generous in most things that we are only too glad to give him pleasure in such small ways.

H.N. TO B.N. & N.N.   *7th November, 1944*
                                                              Sissinghurst

I went to a lunch given by 'The Thirty' for Massigli. I found on arrival that the Thirty were four hundred and we had a huge banquet at Claridges. I proposed Massigli's health and he replied in terms which embarrassed me very much. He spoke in English, a language the relative values of whose terms he does not appreciate. He called me 'this famous friend of France'. I know that what he meant was *fameux* in the sense of 'stout', but I absolutely loathe being called famous when I am nothing of the sort. Poor Massigli, he suffers from an obstruction of the palate which must be similar to that from which Demosthenes suffered. The difference is that Demosthenes removed the pebbles before he addressed any very large audience, but Massigli keeps them in a bunch in his mouth.

At the House we have in Committee Room 12 the plans, elevations and models of the new Chamber which Sir Giles Gilbert Scott is to erect for us in place of that destroyed by the Luftwaffe on the night of 10th May, 1941. The point about these designs is that they provide for one storey above the Chamber and two storeys below it. In the former will be housed the many scattered offices of the Clerks of the House. In the latter are conference rooms, Ministers' rooms and, above all, typists' and interviewing rooms which will be most useful. The Chamber itself is to be very much the same, only far brighter and lighter than the old one. I do not suppose that I shall ever sit in it myself, but Nigel may.

---

[1] Nevertheless, throughout his War Memoirs, Churchill refers to it as 'Aachen'.

8th November, 1944
                                                        Sissinghurst

Tommy Lascelles told me that Jasper Ridley[1] was much worried by
the decline of Balliol. It no longer attracts the best type of Fellow. All
this has been made serious by the departure first of Humphrey Sumner[2]
and secondly of Roger Mynors.[3] Jasper feels that the only way of
rescuing the College is to appoint a new Master with energy and
worldly wisdom. He had asked Tommy whether I would possibly
consider the job, but even if I wanted it (which I do not), I do not
possess the necessary academic distinction. I am told that Field-Marshal
Montgomery let it be known that he also would like to become the
Head of some College in one of the older Universities. My informant
suspected that Montgomery had merely thrown out the remark in
order to elicit the unanimous protest, 'But you will be needed for far
greater work than that!' No such protest followed.

I dined with Robin Maugham[4] at the Garrick to meet his great
American friend, Marshall Dill, who is in the U.S. Navy. They started
discussing happiness, and the relation to happiness of the pleasures of
the flesh. Poor Robin, who has a piece of shrapnel in his head, said
that he regretted now that he had been such a Puritan when he was
young:

> *'Combien je regrette*
> *La jambe dodue ...'*

Dill did not agree with him. He said that it was a matter of deep
satisfaction to look back upon a virginal youth. They asked me for
my opinion. I said I was too old to have any. *Sie haben alles hinter
sich, und sind (Gott lob!) recht tugendlich.* But I did not say this. I said
that one was inclined to identify as wicked those special temptations
which one did not oneself find tempting, and as virtuous those particular
merits which came easily to one. It was not a temptation to me to be
cruel or dishonest, and I therefore regarded kindness and honesty as
the supreme virtues. I did not regard as real vices those acts of self-
indulgence by which I happened to be tempted. This made them both
very thoughtful, and we went out into the black night to have some

---

[1] Chairman of Coutts & Co, a Fellow of Eton College, and Chairman of the Trustees
of the Tate Gallery.

[2] Tutor in Modern History at Balliol, 1925–44, and soon to be appointed Warden of
All Souls. He had been tutor to both Ben and Nigel.

[3] Classical Tutor at Balliol, 1927–44, when he became Professor of Latin at Cambridge.

[4] The author and playwright, who succeeded his father as 2nd Viscount Maugham in
1958. He had been wounded in the fighting in the Western Desert.

beer with a friend of Robin (a Mrs Williamson) who had a nice house, with a smell of cedar-wood and tapestries of great merit on the walls.

DIARY   *10th November, 1944*

I lunch with Sibyl [Colefax]. Hamilton Fish Armstrong[1] tells me that Roosevelt's hesitation about de Gaulle was perfectly sincere and due to a combination of circumstances. He loves France and has a sentimental feeling for her. He never believed that a French Marshal could really be bad, and he thus sent Leahy[2] to be with Pétain and to hold his hand. Leahy and Murphy[3] between them persuaded him that Vichy really meant well, and that de Gaulle was a military rebel. Then when Leahy returned, the President wanted a man of some military standing as coordinator between Marshall and King. Leahy was old enough to gain their respect and not an active officer who might arouse their jealousy. He thus found himself again in the President's intimacy, and his pro-Vichy attitude again became effective. Then de Gaulle behaved rudely and trickily, and this added to the President's hesitations.

DIARY   *14th November, 1944*

Anthony Eden makes a statement regarding his visit to Paris. Winston only gets back later in the day, having been to visit the Vosges front in a dreadful snow-storm. I have a talk with Anthony in the Lobby afterwards. He tells me that when they drove up to the Arc de Triomphe, the crowd did not recognise Winston in his Air Force uniform, and that it was only when he came back and they saw him walking with de Gaulle that they realised who he was. I asked him whether de Gaulle was better as a host than as a guest, and he replied, 'Yes, I *think* he was, but anyhow he was a very stiff host.' He added that not for one moment did Winston stop crying, and that he could have filled buckets by the time he received the Freedom of Paris. He said that they really yelled for Churchill in a way that he has never heard any crowd yell before.

---

[1] Editor of *Foreign Affairs* since 1928.
[2] Admiral William D. Leahy, U.S. Ambassador to Vichy, 1940–42, and then Chief of Staff to the President.
[3] Robert D. Murphy, the President's personal representative in North Africa and Italy.

H.N. TO B.N. & N.N.   *29th November, 1944*
                                                             Sissinghurst

By the time I reached the Chamber, Winston was about to rise. When he came back from his Italian visit, we had all been horrified by his apparent exhaustion. But Moscow did him good, and the snow-drifts of the Vosges did him even more good. He is, or seems, as fit as he ever was, even in his best days. It is incredible that he should be seventy, all but a day. He made a lovely speech. He spoke of tradition as the flywheel of the State. He spoke of the need of youth—'Youth, youth, youth, and renovation, energy, boundless energy'—and as he said these words, he bent his knees and pounded the air like a pugilist—'and of controversy, health-giving controversy'. 'I am not afraid of it in this country', he said, and then he took off his glasses and grinned round at the Conservative benches. 'We are a decent lot', he said, beaming upon them. Then he swung round and leant forward over the box right into the faces of the Labour people: 'All of us', he added, 'the whole nation.' It read so mildly in the newspapers next morning. Yet in fact it was a perfect illustration of the Parliamentary art.

DIARY   *1st December, 1944*

Up to Leicester. I discuss future prospects with Bertie Jarvis. I say that if many members of his Conservative Association would prefer to fight the seat with a young Conservative, I shall retire gracefully. He says that there would be no chance of any Tory winning the seat, while I have a chance of holding it.

DIARY   *2nd December, 1944*

The Greek Ambassador[1] is terribly frightened lest Bulgaria should join the Yugoslav Federation, and that profiting by the added strength and virtue thus acquired, the Federation with Russian backing would demand, not Kavalla merely, but Salonika. He tells me that the Russians really did behave with incredible treachery about the Bulgarian Armistice. We had been begging the Soviets for months to declare war on Bulgaria, but they had consistently refused. When Bulgaria collapsed and applied to us for an Armistice, we informed Russia and then flew the Bulgarian Armistice delegates to Cairo. We then telegraphed to Moscow the terms which we meant to impose and they replied approving them. A few hours later Russia invaded Bulgaria, told us that as she was now in occupation of Sofia, the

[1] Thanassis Aghnides.

413

Armistice negotiations must be conducted solely by the Soviets, and insisted that the Cairo negotiations be at once suspended. This was about the stiffest practice yet seen, and at Moscow Winston made it quite clear to Uncle Jo that such conduct, if persisted in, would break up the Alliance. Uncle Jo expressed deep penitence and has in fact behaved well since then.

Aghnides told me that Eden's visit practically saved Greece.[1] The inflation created by German methods would have led to riots and revolution, and Eden's rapid understanding of the situation and his firm action in sending David Waley[2] to Athens has just saved the position in time.

In December the Allies were suddenly faced by two critical situations, one in Greece and the other on the Western Front.

Britain was committed to support Papandreou's provisional Government in Athens, and had landed troops to lessen the risk of civil war when the Germans withdrew. The Communist E.A.M., with its military wing E.L.A.S., had nominally joined Papandreou's Cabinet, but when a decree was passed ordering E.L.A.S. to disarm, the Communists refused, and on 3rd December civil war broke out in Athens. Churchill ordered the British troops to take strong action to restore order, and for this he was heavily criticised in the United States and in the House of Commons. It was alleged that he was interfering in the processes of democracy in an allied and liberated State. Churchill replied that it was a 'swindle democracy', and that E.L.A.S. were nothing more than rebels and mutineers who wished to seize power by force. Meanwhile the British troops were proving too weak to pacify the capital, and were surrounded in the centre of Athens, without proper communications to Piraeus and the airport.

Harold Macmillan and the British Ambassador, supported by Eden, pressed for the establishment of a Regency under Archbishop Damaskinos, pending full elections once the crisis had passed. The King of Greece, then in London, refused this temporary compromise, and Churchill supported him. On Christmas Eve the crisis, both political and military, had grown so acute that Churchill determined to fly immediately to

---

[1] Eden visited Athens at the end of October, and had a great personal welcome from the Greeks. He took immediate action to save the country's economy from collapse.

[2] Sir David Waley, an Under-Secretary at the Treasury, flew out to Athens on Eden's suggestion to advise Papandreou's Government on finance.

Athens with Eden. They succeeded in bringing Damaskinos together with representatives of E.A.M., and it was agreed on 27th December that E.A.M. would accept the Archbishop's Regency. On their return to London, the British Ministers also gained the consent of King George II of the Hellenes to this arrangement. By mid-January British troops were in control of all Attica and a truce was signed between E.A.M. and the Archbishop–Regent.

The later stages of the Greek crisis coincided with Rundstedt's offensive through the Ardennes. By mid-December the Allies stood all along the German frontier from Switzerland to the lower Rhine, with the exception of a pocket on the west bank of the river round Colmar. At Aachen they had penetrated the Siegfried defences, and entered Germany itself. They were preparing for two major offensives, one striking hard eastwards from Aachen and the other from Alsace in the south. At this moment, on 16th December, Rundstedt launched his attack with twenty-four Divisions on a part of the line held by a single U.S. Corps. They penetrated the American defences to a maximum depth of sixty miles and reached within four miles of the Meuse. Their objective was Antwerp, but the attack was contained by counter-attacks from north and south of the salient, and by the dogged American defence of the chief road-junction at Bastogne. By the end of December, the German effort was spent, and they began to withdraw to their start-line under overwhelming air-attack.

On 21st December Harold Nicolson received the news that his elder son, Ben, had been injured in a road-accident in Southern Italy. His injuries were serious enough to keep him in hospital for several months and necessitate his eventual return to England. This was the only casualty that his immediate family suffered during the whole war.

DIARY   *3rd December, 1944*

There has been a bad E.A.M. riot in Athens, and the police have fired on the mob in Constitution Square. The B.B.C. reporter describes it in a way that will turn British sympathy away from Papandreou and towards E.A.M. That is unfortunate.

DIARY   *5th December, 1944*

The news from Athens is very bad, and something very like civil war has broken out. I go to see Anthony Eden with Ivor Thomas and Strabolgi and Perth. We ask him whether he would like us to form an Anglo-Italian Committee. He says he is all in favour of having a Committee, but we should not make too much of a splash. He says that the essential problem in Italy, as elsewhere, is one of shipping. Although the submarine sinkings have dropped to negligible proportions, the calls on shipping entailed in the extended Pacific front are simply enormous. If we had 300 ships devoted to feeding occupied Europe, most of our difficulties and troubles would be at an end.

I can see that Anthony is in rather an unhappy mood about Greece and Belgium, to say nothing of Italy. Stettinius in America has started his career as Secretary of State by repudiating British policy completely, and by saying that the United States will never interfere in the internal affairs of other countries.[1] This will not ease the situation in either Athens or Rome.

DIARY   *7th December, 1944*

We have a lunch with Carandini[2] at the House. He makes an admirable little speech and one of great modesty and distinction. In private conversation he says that the difficulty is that the real Government of Italy is the Allied Control Commission and that the Ministers cannot do anything without their permission. He says that Harold Macmillan has been absolutely admirable and that all Italians are very grateful to him. When he is asked whether the Trades Union leaders in northern Italy will be able to prevent their movement from being collared by the Communists, he says he is very hopeful of that. They are strong and well-organised, and Communism has never been a really dangerous element in Italian life.

H.N. TO B.N. & N.N.   *8th December, 1944*
                                                                Sissinghurst

This was the day of the Greek debate. Winston was in one of his boyish moods, and allowed himself to be interrupted all the time. In fact, he seemed to me to be in rather higher spirits than the occasion warranted. I don't think he quite caught the mood of the House, which at its best was one of distressed perplexity, and at its worst one of sheer red fury. The debate became heated, and when I was at last

[1] Edward R. Stettinius had said: 'Since Italy is an area of combined responsibility, we have reaffirmed to both the British and Italian Governments that we expect the Italians to work out their problems of government along democratic lines without influence from outside. This policy would apply to an even more pronounced degree with regard to Governments of the United Nations in their liberated territories.' The last was a clear reference to Greece.
[2] The newly appointed Italian Ambassador to London.

called, I tried, not without success, to throw oil upon the waters.[1] But everything in the end was redeemed by Anthony making by far the best speech that I have ever heard him make. He just narrated the facts. There is no doubt that E.A.M. have broken all their pledges and had staged a *coup d'état* to take place the day before they were to lay down their arms. The Labour people did not know what to do, and although some voted for the Government and some against, there were many who abstained.[2]

In the smoking-room afterwards Winston came across to congratulate me on my speech. 'I was not in the House at the time', he said, 'but I am assured on all sides that it was most helpful. I am most obliged to you.' 'At one point', I said, 'I went rather far, I fear. I called Sforza "an elderly peacock".' 'You did not go too far', he answered. 'That is exactly what he is. When he came to see me on his way through London, he wasted ten minutes in explaining to me how far older the Sforza family was than the House of Savoy. I was obliged to interrupt the man. I was obliged to say to him, "Count Sforza, these dynastic personalities have little to do with the prosecution of the war".' 'Since then', continued Winston, 'he has behaved with the utmost lack of faith.[3] When I saw him the other day at Naples, I was rude to him. I was very rude. I will show you exactly how rude. Now you be Sforza queuing up with the other Ministers and I shall be me.' Then followed a dumb-crambo in which Winston, all genial and smiles, bowed and grinned and grasped the hand of the man who came in front of Sforza. Then it came to my turn, in my unwanted role as Sforza's impersonator. Winston drew himself up with an expression of extreme disgust and gave me a hand like the fin of a dead penguin. I do not know how my colleagues in the smoking-room interpreted this strange scene.

---

[1] In the course of his speech H.N. said: 'I never thought I should live to hear my old friend Papandreou called a Fascist and a reactionary. Still less did I ever dream of such an elderly peacock as Count Sforza being described as a proletarian martyr. . . . It has been suggested in this debate that in some queer way, we have intervened in Greece on behalf of the Royalists and against the Republicans. It is nothing like that. It has been stated quite openly that in regard to the Monarchy, there is to be a plebiscite. Until that takes place, the issue does not therefore arise.'

[2] The Vote of Confidence was carried by 279 to 30.

[3] Count Sforza, an anti-Fascist exile in America, had given Churchill the impression that he would support the Badoglio Government. On arrival back in Italy, however, he turned anti-Badoglio and anti-monarchist.

H.N. TO B.N. & N.N.   *13th December, 1944*
                                                              Sissinghurst

I lunched today with a man called O'Neill who writes for the *Spectator* under the name *Strategicus*.[1] I asked him which of all the campaigns in this war was to his mind the most brilliant. 'Without question', he said, 'Alexander's campaign in Italy. It may be that the battle of Hammam Lif was the most brilliant feat of arms ever performed by a British army'—I was delighted by this—'and it may be that the battle of Avranches represents the most signal defeat ever inflicted upon the German Army. But the Italian campaign stands by itself: it is a work of art.' I forebore to suggest that other campaigns would seem to the public to have been more rapid and decisive. I pressed him to explain why. 'Because there you had two of the best Generals in the world, Kesselring and Alexander, facing each other. Because there you had comparative equality of forces, since even if we had more men and more equipment, the Germans possessed vast advantages of terrain and communications. And Alexander won.'

DIARY   *15th December, 1944*

The Greek situation is easing. I gather that our people are not in any serious military danger, since E.L.A.S. do not really want to attack our troops. And there is a hope that Harold Macmillan will arrange for Damaskinos to be Regent, and that under him some Government will be formed.

DIARY   *18th December, 1944*

I have a meeting of the Management Committee of National Labour. We discuss the eternal question of our name. Shall we go on with it? In favour of doing so is (1) once you have a name, it is a mistake to change it, even if it is a bad name; (2) some of us may have been elected on the grounds that the inclusion of the word 'Labour' in our title gives us a working-class vote; (3) Winston is anxious to have his Government as broad as possible. The replies to this are: (1) the name is a lie, and insulting to the Labour Party; we have no right to use their name, still less to profit by it; (2) the fact that the Tories want us to keep the name for their own purposes is an argument against rather than in favour. In fact, we do not know what to do.

[1] H. C. O'Neill, previously Assistant Editor of *The Observer*. It was generally agreed that his weekly military commentary in the *Spectator* was the best in all British journalism.

Lunch at the Beefsteak. Tommy Lascelles tells me something that excites me much. No more and no less than that Vita's name has been 'mentioned' for the O.M. I do not think he would have said this to me had it not been 'mentioned' seriously. If she gets it, she will be overjoyed: the first woman since Florence Nightingale. But I shall say nothing to her, since if it does not go to her, she will be disappointed, and so far the idea has never entered her dear head.[1]

Rundstedt has staged a startling offensive in the Malmédy sector. It seems that it started three days ago and that he has penetrated our lines by as much as twenty miles. The optimists say that this is the last suicide fling: the pessimists say that there is nothing to stop him getting to Paris or at least to Liége. But what most people seem to think is that it has the comparatively limited objective of forcing us to leave the sacred soil of the Fatherland. It may be that they will succeed, and then we shall have a peace-offer.

I meet Cyril Joad at the Wildenstein Gallery. He says he likes being famous. He says he likes being recognised in public and hearing people whispering. Now I loathe that sort of thing beyond words, and it is for that reason that I do all I can to keep my picture out of the papers. Yet when I said that I hated it, I could see that Cyril thought I was being insincere. Yet God knows it is absolutely true, and that I should *loathe* being recognised in public places.

H.N. TO B.N. & N.N.   *19th December, 1944*
                                                              Sissinghurst

People are pretty glum about the Rundstedt offensive. 'Is it serious?' I whispered to Anthony Eden. 'Yes', he answered, 'it's bad, very bad indeed.' But people have now begun to perk up a bit. The sun shines in a cloudless sky after all this fog, the glass is high, and the bombers and fighters have been streaming over Sissinghurst in the direction of Belgium like flock after flock of geese. Slow and intent they fly— very low over the tower, out across the sea, and down eventually upon Rundstedt's spearheads and formations. It has created a gloom such as I have not seen for months. And as we are a sporting folk, it has also aroused some admiration for von Rundstedt's skill and enterprise. Our usual resilience is now reasserting itself.

---

[1] Nothing more was heard of this proposal, but V.S-W. became a Companion of Honour in 1948.

V.S-W. TO H.N. *19th December, 1944*
Sissinghurst

I went down to have a look at the lake, and to see if it was doing any-thing wild. It wasn't. I went out of a sense of duty towards it. I have lost all pleasure in the lake, and indeed in the woods, since soldiers came and invaded them and robbed them of all the privacy I so loved. You didn't understand when I minded the tanks cutting up the wild flowers. It was a thing of beauty, now tarnished for ever—one of the few things I had preserved against this horrible new world. I wish I could sort out my ideas about this new world. I feel one ought to be able to adapt oneself, and not struggle to go back to, and live in, an obsolete tradition.

All this makes me very unhappy. And my back worries me too.[1] I don't mind it hurting, but the weakness it brings to my limbs worries me. You see, I used to be so strong; but now I daren't make a rash movement, and I'm frightened of falling down. I feel that I and the lake and the wood are all damaged and spoilt for ever. Our lost youth, in fact. If only I thought I could write good poetry, I should not mind anything. That is what I care most about—that and your safety. I live in constant terror of your having an accident. I could not bear that. *Tam cari capitis.* . . . You are my anchor in all my tumultuous seas.

H.N. TO V.S-W. *21st December, 1944*
4 King's Bench Walk, E.C.4

I do so understand your unhappiness at the moment. I think that everyone in these dark autumn days is truly unhappy. Partly war-weariness, partly sadness at things not going right, and partly actual malnutrition. But I also know that yours is a deeper unhappiness. You do not ask much from life, but you do desire passionately privacy and the respect of your independence and quiet. The tanks in the wood were a real symbol; the boat being sunk by carelessness or actual malevolence is another symbol.[2] The world for people like you and me is becoming a grim place. Then, of course, added to this is your arthritis which makes everything seem dim through a cloud of pain.

But there is one thing that I do not agree about, namely your poetry. I do not think that you have ever written better than you are writing

---

[1] Fifteen years earlier she had torn a muscle in her back. It had ceased to give her trouble, but now the weakness and slight continuous pain returned, and were never to leave her again.

[2] The rowing-boat on the lake at Sissinghurst had been found smashed.

now. Even if you never wrote another line of poetry, your fame as a poet is anchored in *The Land*. Scarcely a day passes in which someone does not mention that poem to me. At the Club on Tuesday, Tommy Lascelles said to me, 'I suppose *The Land* is about the only truly classic poem written in our times.' But I believe *The Garden*[1] will be as good, and certainly the cradle poem[2] is among the finest that you have ever written.

Oh, my sweet, sweet Viti, how it hurts me that you should be unhappy. When people behave meanly or badly, I think of you—so serene and lovely—and it all seems to smooth itself out. As I said to Duff [Cooper] the other day, when he said that he thought the Government had treated me rather shabbily, 'Well, you see, someone who has had my happiness in life has no right to feel bitter about anything.' 'You mean Vita', he said. He understands.

H.N. TO B.N. & N.N.   *20th December, 1944*
                                                                 Sissinghurst

We had a second and quite unnecessary debate on Greece. I am amazed at the way in which Anthony Eden keeps his temper. His father, as you may know, was one of the most violent-tempered men in the world, and when Anthony was an undergraduate, he used to have bouts of rage. He has completely mastered this now, and can display a patience which is truly laudable. But he is tired, tired, tired, after a long month of incessant House of Commons debate, great public worry, and nerve-wracking Cabinet meetings. He took me to have a drink. He wanted sympathy. I gave him both. I said, 'Anthony, you are like a man in a lighthouse who sees the gnats and the mosquitoes and the moths circling round the light, but we at a distance see it beaming across the waters, untroubled and undimmed.' He seemed to like that. He has a real liking for Stalin. He says that Stalin has never broken his word once given. He tells me other things which are not for the typewritten word.[3]

---

[1] V.S-W. had resumed writing this second long poem, after temporarily laying it aside until she had finished *The Eagle and the Dove*. *The Garden* was published in 1946.

[2] A Christmas poem just published in *The Times Literary Supplement*.

[3] In his diary H.N. added: 'It had all gone well with Stalin [at Moscow] from the start. "And what about the Balkans?" Eden had asked at the first meeting. "Well," replied Stalin, "I am interested in the Black Sea countries and you are interested in the Mediterranean countries. You look after Greece."'

DIARY   *21st December, 1944*

I am writing this diary when the telephone rings. A young man called Captain Haycock, who was in photographic interpretation with Ben, says that he has heard that Ben was knocked down by a lorry on 15th December and injured his head. He is in hospital and they think he will be there for four weeks.

DIARY   *22nd December, 1944*

The thought of Ben in pain and suffering all alone in Italy is something that brings a stab to my heart like an exposed nerve.

The news of Rundstedt's offensive is slightly better this evening. He appears to have got forty miles inside the American lines but has been halted on the flanks. Eisenhower has issued an Order of the Day to his troops saying that we must turn this defeat into a victory. The news from Athens is very bad, I fear. All peace negotiations have broken down and the fighting is increasing in severity.

DIARY   *26th December, 1944*

The 1 o'clock news tells us that Winston and Anthony have descended together upon Athens, summoned a meeting of E.L.A.S. under the chairmanship of Archbishop Damaskinos, and propose to remain until a settlement is reached. It will make a great effect that Winston at the age of 70 should fly out on Christmas Day to Athens.

DIARY   *28th December, 1944*

It is the coldest Christmas we have had for 54 years. But it is clear and bright and the bombers stream over on their way to Belgium. I spend the whole day reading Hardy's *Dynasts* since it covers my period.[1] I cannot understand why it should enjoy such a reputation. It seems to me to be mere prose turned into a jingle.

The news is better. Winston has left Athens, having been shot at by a sniper and used the expression 'Cheek!' In the Ardennes and Belgium we seem to have held Rundstedt some seven miles from the Meuse and to have relieved Bastogne. The Germans are beginning to blame 'the unprecedently fine weather' for their failure to achieve a complete break-through.

[1] Of *The Congress of Vienna*.

DIARY   *29th December, 1944*

I start writing my book on the Vienna Peace Congress.[1]

DIARY   *30th December, 1944*

It really does look as if the Rundstedt offensive has been snapped. The King of Greece has agreed to appoint Damaskinos Regent. Good work for Anthony and Winston.

DIARY   *31st December, 1944*

The end of 1944. A wonderful year marked by the most successful military operation we have ever undertaken. But a year in which internal dissension and distrust have much increased. A year saddened towards its end by Viti's arthritis, which I fear will become a permanent ffliction. And by Ben's accident.

---

[1] This means that he started work on his actual manuscript. His research was finished.

1945

---

*Death of Robert Bernays – V.S-W. on hating democracy –
E. M. Forster disillusioned with the left – the Yalta Con-
ference – Churchill's trust in Stalin – H.N.'s speech on
Yalta – he visits Paris – P. J. Grigg – Ben returns home in
plaster – crossing of the Rhine – the final offensive in Italy –
death of Lloyd George – death of Franklin Roosevelt – The
United Nations Charter – Churchill's speech to the Press
Gallery – American and Russian forces meet on the Elbe –
Mussolini's death – Hitler's suicide in Berlin – Germany
surrenders in Italy and northern Europe – V.E. Day in
London – misgivings about Russian intentions – conditions
in France and Germany – H.N.'s last speeches in the
Commons – H.N. on his parliamentary career – the General
Election – H.N. campaigns in Leicester – disappointment in
Churchill as a Party leader – Polling Day – the count at
Leicester – H.N. loses his seat – Churchill's tribute to him*

'A year, I trust, of victory'[1]

At the beginning of the end of the war, political disillusionment clouded military triumph. The Russians began to impose their Socialist system upon areas of Eastern Europe which they rapidly overran, and the Western Allies, making slower military progress and conscious that Russia had been the chief agent in destroying Hitlerism, were in no position to prevent it. Their attempts at Yalta to secure free elections for Poland, in return for a readjustment of the Polish eastern boundary in favour of Russia, met with failure.

In early January the German Army was already compressed within the boundaries of Germany, with the exception of northern Holland, Scandinavia, northern Italy, and parts of Hungary and Poland. Rumania and Bulgaria were already under Soviet control. Budapest, which had been surrounded since December, fell to the Russian armies in March. Warsaw was captured on 17th January, and at the end of the month Russian troops moved across the German frontier to seize East Prussia and penetrate deeply into the industrial zone of Upper Silesia. On the western front, the Allies succeeded in clearing the west bank of the Rhine during February and early March. Cologne was captured on 7th March, and on the same day the Americans seized a bridge-head over the Rhine at Remagen.

The last conference to be held between Roosevelt, Stalin and Churchill took place at Yalta in the Crimea between the 3rd and 11th February. Their minor business included the settlement of the voting procedures on the Security Council of the proposed United Nations Organisation; a decision on the zones of occupation of Germany; and a secret agreement on the terms of Russia's entry into the war against Japan once Germany was defeated. But their most important discussion concerned Poland, and it raised the whole principle of Soviet postwar relations with the West. It had already been agreed at Tehran that the Poles would lose their eastern provinces to Russia (the Curzon line) in exchange for new territories in the west taken from Germany (the Oder–Neisse line). But hitherto there had been no agreement about the future Government of Poland itself. Stalin hoped to control the country through the Communist

[1] Typed by H.N. on 1st January.

427

Lublin Committee. Roosevelt and Churchill declared that the Poles must be given the opportunity to choose their own Government, and that meanwhile a new provisional Government should be formed from members of the Lublin Committee, from the Polish Underground, and from the exiled Polish Government in London. A declaration was published in these terms pledging Stalin to the principle of a 'strong, free, independent and democratic Poland'.

After Churchill's return from Yalta via Athens and Cairo, the House of Commons debated the agreement on 27th February. Many Members considered that Poland, in spite of the safeguards, was merely exchanging one conqueror for another, and twenty-five of them, mainly from the Conservative right, voted against it. Harold Nicolson was among those who argued, with considerable misgivings, that Stalin could be trusted to keep his word. In this they were mistaken, for it soon became clear that Stalin had no intention of reforming the Polish Provisional Government in accordance with the Yalta decisions. By raising trivial objections to the names submitted to the Allied Commission in Moscow, he played for time until the Lublin Committee should have established itself firmly in control. Western observers were forbidden to enter Poland to discover the true feelings of the people, and a large number of anti-Communist Poles were deported to Siberia. In the early part of March the Russians also set up the puppet-Government in Rumania. Thus the betrayal of Yalta dominated the closing stages of the war as it did the opening years of peace.

Harold Nicolson continued to write 'The Congress of Vienna' in the intervals of his Parliamentary work and a triumphant visit to Paris, and he began to select with V. Sackville-West passages of poetry and prose for inclusion in their joint anthology 'Another World than This'. Their elder son Ben, the upper part of his body now encased in plaster because two dorsal vertebrae had been broken by his accident, was invalided back to England in the middle of March. Nigel was still with the 8th Army in the northern Apennines.

DIARY   *1st January, 1945*

Viti and I hear in the New Year crouching over the fire in the dining-room. As the strains of *God Save the King* still reverberate from the wireless, the telephone rings and it is Mrs Drummond[1] wishing us a Happy New Year. I turn on Berlin, the *Deutschlandsender*, and then

[1] Katherine Drummond, wife of General Laurence Drummond, close friends and neighbours of the Nicolsons.

Hamburg, and we get Hitler's horrible but quite unmistakable voice. The reception is not good, and he gabbles off his piece so fast that I may have missed something. But it seemed to consist entirely of reflections on Germany's fate if she loses her moral staunchness, on the fate of the satellites who have dropped out, on the strength of the *Führung*, on the need for unanimity, on the *sein oder nicht sein* theme. Then we go to bed: Mrs Drummond and Hitler within a few minutes of each other—indeed a curious effect.

H.N. TO B.N. & N.N.   *6th January, 1945*
                                                          Sissinghurst

The whole of this week I have been at home writing, writing, writing. I have done three chapters of *The Congress of Vienna*, and I have thus effected a penetration. Whether there is any value in the book is quite another matter. So far as I know, there does not exist in any simple form a narrative of the events from 1812 onwards. Most of the books are too technical, too detailed or too partial to be of much value to the ordinary reader. And the subject is one which by next Christmas should be of interest and usefulness. In any case it has been immense fun to do.

H.N. TO B.N. & N.N.   *18th January, 1945*
                                                          Sissinghurst

Winston opened the two-day debate on Greece and the general war situation. He started by telling us that he had a bad cold in the head—and in fact he was pink about the nostrils and somewhat hoarse—but he spoke for two hours with immense vivacity, persuasiveness and humour. He made a terrific attack on *The Times*, which was greeted with cheers such as I have not heard since that unhappy Munich morning.

He had a good reference to 'unconditional surrender'. Without actually repudiating that regrettable phrase, he made it clear that it signified only 'total victory', *la victoire intégrale*. He rebuffed all assertions that it was our intention to exterminate or trample on the German people. 'Not at all', he said—and then he took off his glasses and turned aside to face the Speaker. He struck his breast like an orang-outang. 'We remain bound', he shouted, 'by our customs and our own nature.' Very effective.

I dined that night at the Carlton Grill with Desmond Shawe-Taylor.[1] He had invited to meet me Captain Nigel Clive who had just returned from Athens. He was at Oxford with Nigel: a handsome

[1] The music critic.

boy he was, gay and nonchalant. A tough veteran arrived, decorations on his chest, a parachute upon his shoulder. Still handsome he was, making graceful gestures with shapely hands, and with the light behind him he still seemed boyish and comely. But when he faced the light one could see the lines forming from nostril to chin, one could see wrinkles taking shape on his forehead, one could see (as one does at that uncertain age) both what he had been like at eighteen and what he would be like at fifty. He is no fool at all, and he told me exactly as I like about his experiences in Greece. He had been dropped in Epirus as liaison officer with the E.D.E.S. He told me that David Wallace[1] had arrived as representative of the Ambassador and in a mainly political capacity. But David was so afraid of being thought a civilian that he had insisted on accompanying E.D.E.S. on one of their patrols against E.L.A.S. He exposed himself recklessly and was shot. God, what a waste!

Anyhow, Nigel Clive said that neither side would really fight the Germans. Unfortunately, when Italy collapsed, the Pinerolo Division surrendered to E.L.A.S. with all their equipment. This gave the latter an advantage over E.D.E.S. Our people managed to patch up a truce between them, but so little did they trust each other that they would not move a man against the Germans for fear of being stabbed in the back by their own side. It is not, I fear, a very philhellene story. But Clive was not deterred by it at all. He likes the Greeks. He is convinced that we were right to intervene in Athens and thinks that we shall earn the undying gratitude of the Hellenic people. He is a nice man and I took to him very warmly.

I took them on to Pratts. Eddy Devonshire was there. He told me an extraordinary story about Charles I. As you probably know, King Charles refused to bow his head to a subject and insisted on being executed face-upwards. The executioner was embarrassed by this unwonted position and botched his first shot, cutting off the King's chin and beard. They fell upon the scaffold and were picked up and treasured by the Captain of the pikemen who surrounded it. From generation to generation did this grisly piece of bone and skin and beard descend to the family of the Captain of the pikemen, until a few years ago the then holder of the relic felt qualms about it and sent it to King George in a box with a letter of explanation. The King for

---

[1] One of the most gifted men of his generation, and a contemporary of Ben at Oxford. He was killed in a skirmish with Germans (not E.L.A.S.) near Paramythia, Epirus, where he is buried.

his part was also embarrassed. Being a conscientious man, he consulted that old ass the Archbishop of Canterbury, who told him that the missing bit must of course be returned to King Charles' chin. So one night they went down to the vault, had the lead coffin opened, and replaced the missing bit. The body was perfectly preserved—with the head put on neatly—but as they gazed upon it, it melted into ashes. Being among his ancestors, King George took a look round. There was an enormous coffin of lead which had burst open, and from it protruded a huge shoulder-blade. It was like the bone of a mammoth. It was the shoulder of Henry VIII.[1]

DIARY   *25th January, 1945*

I chuck my B.B.C. Board since we have a debate on the reconstruction of the Chamber of the House of Commons. Winston makes a short speech recommending the report. There is an amendment saying that we ought to have thrown the thing open to competition. In theory I agree that it is unimaginative and feeble to make a 1945 copy of an 1834 copy of an assumed Gothic original. But I do not see what the alternative is. It would be even more incongruous if we adopted Charles II or Regency. Therefore the only alternative is modern. And modern, admirable though it is for hospitals etc. is no good as yet for domestic interiors. I make a speech on the subject.

DIARY   *26th January, 1945*

I buy a copy of the *Evening Standard* and read that Rob Bernays is missing in a 'plane over Italy.[2] This knocks me silly. I go to the House

[1] This story is reproduced as an historical curiosity, but it cannot be true. Although H.N. starts by saying, 'As you probably know, King Charles . . . insisted on being executed face-upwards', all contemporary evidence shows that he was executed face-downwards. The block was exceptionally low, about 10 inches high, and the King lay on the scaffold with his head upon it. It is recorded that he took great care that his hair should not impede the falling axe, and that the head was severed at a single blow. Moreover, to face the executioner would have been taken as an honour to him, not a dishonour as the story implies. Miss C. V. Wedgwood, to whom I am indebted for these facts, suggests that the legend arose later when people told tales about heroes facing firing squads with their eyes uncovered. It is true, however, that a vertebra was removed from the King's coffin in the vaults of St George's Chapel, Windsor, when it was opened in 1813, and this was restored to the coffin by the Prince of Wales (later Edward VII) in 1888. The Duke of Devonshire's story may be based upon this incident.

[2] Robert Bernays, H.N.'s most intimate friend in the House of Commons, had been a member of a Parliamentary delegation visiting troops in Italy. He had spent a

where I find gloom and apprehension. I gather from Anthony [Eden] that there is mighty little hope. I feel crushed by this. All my best House of Commons friends are now dead—Rob, Ronnie Cartland, Jack Macnamara.

(H.N. TO B.N. & N.N., same date). I dined with John Sparrow as I wanted consoling. He is fussed about his future. He would like to be Warden of All Souls, but it seems that the Fellows do not think him old enough or young enough or something. Anyhow he realises that he would not be elected. So he is now tempted to apply for the Librarianship of the Bodleian. I said that this was not the moment to make such a decision. Without realising it, he was probably overtired and overworked, and that through the cold of London the firelight playing on the books acquired a disproportionate beauty. But to be Librarian at the Bodleian meant much more than firelight on books. It meant dining at Worcester high-table on Sunday off cold pork; it meant walking in the Parks with the sub-Librarian; it meant a little house in North Oxford, and a bicycle. Wouldn't it be better just to go back to the Chancery Bar, to hunt books in the Charing Cross Road, to stand for Parliament, to become Solicitor, or even Attorney-General, or even Lord Chancellor Hawke or Sparrow Hawke if he liked? He could always end up in North Oxford if the worst came to the worst.[1]

V.S-W. TO H.N.   *7th February, 1945*
                                                          Sissinghurst

There is an agitation on foot to get a bus-service between Biddenden and Cranbrook. This is horrid for us, as it will mean the buses skirting our wood, but it would be nice for the inhabitants of Biddenden and Three Chimneys who are entirely cut off from the world—the world in this case being Cranbrook. We cannot resist it; so we had better cooperate. Why people have this passion for moving about passes my understanding, but there it is. What a world! It is like drawing up one's own death-warrant, and it is all on a par with the tanks coming into our wood.

---

night with Nigel's Brigade in the front line. Two days later he flew in a light 'plane from Rome to Brindisi, and continued to Athens. The 'plane was never heard of again. It is presumed that it crashed in the Adriatic.

[1] John Sparrow did return to the Bar in 1946, but he became Warden of All Souls in 1952.

My Manifesto: I hate democracy. I hate *la populace.* I wish education had never been introduced. I don't like tyranny, but I like an intelligent oligarchy. I wish *la populace* had never been encouraged to emerge from its rightful place. I should like to see them as well fed and well housed as T.T. cows, but no more articulate than that. (It's rather what most men feel about most women!)

Oh, *à propos* of that, I've been absolutely enraged by a book about Knole, in which Eddy [Sackville West] is described as 'author and musician', and I am described as 'the wife of the Hon. Harold Nicolson C.M.G.'. I don't grudge Eddy being described as an author and musician, but I do resent being dismissed merely as somebody's wife with no existence of my own, especially in connection with Knole and my name. I am very, very cross about this. You know I am not a feminist, but there are limits.

H.N. TO V.S-W.   *7th February, 1945*
                                          4 King's Bench Walk, E.C.4

There has been another 'plane accident. This time it occurred to one of the machines bringing the F.O. and War Cabinet staff to the Three Power Conference.[1] They lost their way and crashed near Lampedusa. About a third of them were rescued, but two-thirds were drowned. I was terrified at first that Gladwyn [Jebb] was among them, but apparently he was in the other 'plane. But Peter Loxley (Cadogan's Private Secretary and one of the lights of the F.O.) is known to be dead and several others. Moreover all the papers and maps are now at the bottom of the Mediterranean and it will cast a gloom over the Conference. It will do more than that. It will raise a stink in the House about War Transport. They say, of course, that in ordinary circumstances no airmen would have taken the risk of flying in such weather, and that it was only the urgency of the thing that forced them to act dangerously. But all the same, if we cannot secure the safety of these key people, then nobody will travel after the war by British airlines. Already it is said that people prefer American pilots.

---

[1] The Yalta Conference. Flying out to join Churchill and Eden at Malta, the pilot had failed to find the island in the mist, and the 'plane came down in the sea and fifteen of the passengers and crew were drowned.

H.N. TO B.N. & N.N.   *12th February, 1945*
                                                                    Sissinghurst

I went to the London Library Committee, where I took the chair. Morgan Forster[1] was there. I took him to the Travellers. He was upset about Greece. Until now he has felt that to take the 'left' point of view was the right point of view. 'In Spain', he said, 'there was no doubt at all which side was in the right and which was in the wrong. But this Greek thing disturbs me. I hate tyranny as much as I hate anarchy.' I tried to talk to him about Liberal principles. The dictatorship of the proletariat is just as evil a thing as the dictatorship of monarchs or party bosses, and nobody could contend that it was a very civilised thing to murder 1,400 Trades Union leaders in cold blood. He put his hands to his face. He was really in distress.

DIARY   *15th February, 1945*

I attend a Committee meeting in the House about Polish deportees. There are three escaped Poles there who tell us their stories. 1,230,000 Poles have been deported and only 9 per cent of them have got away afterwards. One really lovely woman tells us how her father, a bank-manager, herself and her mother were put in cattle-trucks and sent off to Kazan where they were made to work on the land and live with the Kalmuks. Her father disappeared. Another man tells us that he was in prison for eight months in Moscow on no charge. Hynd[2] asks them what suspicion they had against them. The woman answers that she was a member of a Catholic society called 'The Daughters of the Virgin Mary', and that they kept on bothering her to find out what political basis there was to this society. The other woman says she had travelled and learnt languages. They said to her, 'But you cannot expect us to believe that anyone travels for anything but a political motive?' All this is convincing and profoundly disturbing.

V.S-W. TO H.N.   *15th February, 1945*
                                                                    Sissinghurst

Winston is home. How nice. Now I feel safe again. This letter is scribbled in the middle of writing poetry. If only you were in your brown room among the flowers, it would be perfect. Now I am going back to my poem.[3] I'm writing about sowing annuals in March. I

[1] E. M. Forster, the novelist.
[2] J. B. Hynd, the Labour M.P. for Attercliffe (Sheffield) since 1944.
[3] *The Garden.*

don't think my poem is much good, but it keeps me good and happy, and one must justify one's existence somehow. Wouldn't it be awful if one were a person who just existed, getting through one day after the other, all filled up with idiotic little preoccupations that had no importance at all? I mean washing up and cleaning the front door-step and gossiping about one's neighbours?

DIARY   21st February, 1945

Gladwyn [Jebb] says that at Yalta he and the minor staff were put in a sort of Convalescent Home which was crawling with bugs, and that Lord Moran[1] came down with disinfectants in the hope of saving them from typhus. He says that President Roosevelt was an utterly changed man since he had last seen him. Not only did he look twenty years older, but he was scarcely able to speak. He reminded him of Ramsay MacDonald in the last year of his life. Gladwyn naturally defends the decision of the Conference, but disclaims all responsibility for what happened later in Cairo. It looks as if Winston had repudiated all our pledges both to the French and to the Jews.[2]

To the House. I have a talk with Oliver Stanley. He says that the news published in the United States to the effect that Palestine, Iraq and the Levant Republics are to be placed under the joint trusteeship of Russia, the U.S.A. and ourselves is untrue. 'Or rather', he says, 'I have not been told a word about it, which is only just possible if it is true.' Considering that he is S. of S. for the Colonies, it seems odd that he should not have been told.

DIARY   26th February, 1945

I dine with Guy Burgess, who shows me the telegrams exchanged with Moscow. It is clear that the Ambassadors' Commission is not to be a farce in the least.[3] They insist on Mikolajczyk[4] being included in the Provisional Government. Archie [Clark Kerr] seems to be handling the thing well.

Archie Southby says that his lot (the diehard Tories) will oppose the

---

[1] Winston Churchill's doctor, previously Sir Charles Wilson.

[2] Churchill spent two days in Cairo with Roosevelt after their return from Yalta, but no business of importance was conducted there. The rumours mentioned in these two paragraphs of the Diary were unfounded.

[3] The Commission consisted of Molotov and the British and American Ambassadors in Moscow. Its purpose was to settle the composition of the new Polish Provisional Government.

[4] The former Prime Minister of the exiled Polish Government in London.

[Yalta] settlement 'as a matter of principle'. Hinchingbrooke says that he will support it as a matter of world policy.

DIARY   *27th February, 1945*

The House is more crowded that I have ever seen it. M. Bidault[1] is in the gallery grinning down on us. Winston opens punctually at 12. He talks about France. 'The first principle of British policy in Western Europe', he says, 'is a strong France and a strong French Army.' He then goes on to talk about the San Francisco Conference[2] and the general problems of the control of Germany. He then talks about Poland. He makes an extremely good case for arguing that Poland in her new frontiers will enjoy an independent and prosperous existence. But in his closing words before luncheon he rather destroys all this by saying that we will offer British citizenship to those Polish soldiers who are too frightened to return. In the afternoon he concentrates mainly upon the improved arrangements for Italy and his recent visit to Greece. Incidentally he pays a tremendous tribute to Anthony Eden, which is well, but not rapturously received by the House.

Greenwood makes a conventional speech and Dunglass[3] an excellent one, bitterly attacking the Polish settlement. Meanwhile the extreme Tories under Petherick[4] and Southby rush about getting signatures for an amendment expressing regret at the Polish provisions.[5]

Buck De la Warr is there and I take him out for a drink. We are joined by Winston who for once in his life does not seem to be in the least bit of a hurry. 'Collins', he says, 'you will give me a large brandy. I deserve it.' He then shakes himself contentedly and begins talking.

---

[1] De Gaulle's Minister of Foreign Affairs.
[2] This conference, which drafted the United Nations Charter, opened on 25th April.
[3] Lord Dunglass, later Lord Home, and (when Prime Minister) Sir Alec Douglas-Home. He had been Member for South Lanark since 1931, but held no office during the war years.
[4] Maurice Petherick, Conservative M.P. for Penryn and Falmouth.
[5] As this amendment raised the central issue of this very important debate, it is worth reproducing in full: 'Remembering that Great Britain took up arms in a war of which the immediate cause was the defence of Poland against German aggression and in which the overriding motive was the prevention of the domination by a strong nation of its weaker neighbours, regrets the decision to transfer to another power the territory of an ally contrary to treaty and to Article 2 of the Atlantic Charter, and furthermore regrets the failure to ensure to those nations which have been liberated from German oppression the full right to choose their own Government free from the influence of any other power.'

He is really very sensible. He says he does not see what else we could possibly do. 'Not only are the Russians very powerful, but they are on the spot; even the massed majesty of the British Empire would not avail to turn them off that spot.' Moreover, it seemed to him a mistake to assume that the Russians are going to behave badly. Ever since he had been in close relations with Stalin, the latter had kept his word with the utmost loyalty. During the three weeks of the Greek crisis, for instance, a single article in *Pravda* would have tipped the whole balance, but Stalin kept an obstinate silence which was of immense value to us. At the mention of Greece his whole face lit up. He put his hand on my arm. 'I have had great moments in my life', he said, 'but never such a moment as when faced with that half-million crowd in Constitution Square.[1] You will understand that.' I ask him whether he thinks it would be indiscreet of me to say that the test of the Crimean resolution will be whether or not Mikolajczyk and Romer[2] are invited to Moscow. He thinks for a moment and then says, 'Yes, that would be a good thing. I could not say that, but you can'. As he goes, he says with his funny schoolboy grin, 'I hope in your speech tomorrow you will not attack me very bitterly. I count you among my firmest friends'.

Winston is as amused as I am that the warmongers of the Munich period have now become the appeasers, while the appeasers have become the warmongers. He seemed in wonderful form during his speech, but he confessed afterwards that he felt 'tired all through'.

H.N. TO V.S-W. *28th February, 1945*
4 King's Bench Walk, E.C.4

I telephoned to you this evening to say that I had made my speech. I was fussed about it as I know that people are rather influenced by what I say about this sort of thing, since they believe that I really know about foreign affairs and really speak from my conscience. But I was not quite clear where my conscience was. Emotionally I feel for the Poles very deeply. As you know, I think the Russians imperialistic and unscrupulous. But on the other hand, I really do believe that Winston and Anthony did save Poland from a fate far more terrible than might otherwise have been hers. I was absolutely sure in my own inner heart and mind that the Yalta decisions were not expedient only, but ulti-

---

[1] In Athens on 14th February.
[2] The ex-Prime Minister and Foreign Minister of the exiled Polish Government in London.

mately to the benefit of the Poles and mankind. So I supported those decisions with complete ease of mind and conscience.[1]

I was called late in the debate on purpose, and for this reason my speech will not *read* very well since it was replying to all manner of cross-currents which had been ebbing and flowing. Moreover, my throat was very hoarse (too many cigarettes) and I spoke inaudibly. But apart from that, it was, I think, the most effective speech I have made. There was a very full House and the galleries were crammed. Afterwards in the smoking-room Winston took his glass up from where he was sitting and crossed the room to sit beside me. *Ça c'était une manifestation.* He said, 'Harold, you made a powerful speech. A most powerful speech. You swung votes. I thank you. I congratulate you. I give you'—and here he made a sort of offering gesture—'my congratulations. I only wish that I could also have given you one of my throat lozenges. Excellent they are. That horrible man, Lord Moran, who bullies the life out of me, prescribed them.'

Darling, you don't think I am being boastful, do you? It is simply that when one is successful, one feels warm inside, and you are the only person in the world to whom I can say these things without seeming silly or caring even if I do seem silly. I hate not sharing with you all my (perhaps babyish) triumphs, even as I share my more foolish defeats and worries. But not a word to anybody else. This is our own secret.

H.N. TO V.S-W.
1st March, 1945
4 King's Bench Walk, E.C.4

I had such a funny experience this evening. You know how I have always said that the moment when I knew the last war was over was when my opposite number at the War Office telephoned one morning in October 1918 to say that three Bulgarian emissaries were crossing the line to ask for an armistice. One of the names was obscure. Could I help them? It began Lia . . ., but the rest of the name was indecipherable. I said 'Liaptcheff'. Then he rang off. I had scribbled down the

[1] In the course of his speech H.N. said: 'I regard what was done at Yalta as without question the most important political agreement that we have gained in this war. . . . What is written in the Yalta communiqué could not be more precise, definite and absolutely compulsory; no written words could better express the obligation to see that the independence, freedom and integrity of Poland are preserved. What we are discussing is therefore whether we can trust Russia. . . . To say, "Oh, but you cannot trust Marshal Stalin", when he has demonstrated by his actions ever since the war that he is about the most reliable man in Europe, is to say something which I think is a little pessimistic.'

three letters LIA on my blotter and stared at them. 'That is the end', I said to myself. Then I went in to see Crowe.[1] 'The war is over', I said. And told him the message.

Now something like this happened tonight. I met Anthony [Eden] in the corridor and he asked me to come and have a drink. As we edged our way through the smoking-room, we passed the *Evening News* spread out on the back of an armchair. It bore the headlines, 'Tanks massing for Cologne'. Anthony tapped them with the back of his fingers and said, 'I think, Harold, that it is very nearly over.' 'What do you mean?' I said. 'The war', he replied.

He was so nice to me about my speech. He is unlike Winston. The latter was overjoyed by the vote tonight[2] and behaved like a schoolboy. Anthony was quite different. He said to me, 'My God, what a mess Europe is in! What a mess!'

H.N. TO B.N. & N.N.   *11th March, 1945*
                                                          Sissinghurst

On 2nd March, after the debate, I went to Paris. As I stepped ashore from the steamer at Dieppe, I bent down and touched the soil of France with a sacerdotal gesture. '*Monsieur a laissé tomber quelque chose?*' asked my porter. '*Non*', I replied, '*j'ai retrouvé quelque chose.*' I told this story to Jean Marin next day, and he relayed it on the *Radio-diffusion Française*. I am not quite sure that I was pleased by this.

The train got to Paris at 5 o'clock in the morning. I drove through the empty, sleeping streets to the British Embassy. I was shown to my room. I had a bath. I read my letters. I was brought a gorgeous breakfast. Duff [Cooper] came in to see me. Diana [Cooper] summoned me to her room, where I found her being manicured in the bed of Pauline Borghese.[3] And then I went out into the streets of Paris. It is to all intents and purposes completely intact. The fact that there is little traffic in the streets enables one to see the great sweep of her avenues and perspectives. I have never seen her looking more beautiful. And a warm spring sun broke upon it all, bringing warmth to frozen limbs and aged hearts.

You must picture me in the Embassy—that lovely house with its

---

[1] Sir Eyre Crowe (1864–1925), Assistant Under-Secretary of State for Foreign Affairs, 1912–20, and Permanent Under-Secretary, 1920–25.
[2] The Amendment was defeated by 396 votes to 25.
[3] The British Embassy in Paris was originally the house of Pauline Borghese, Napoleon's sister.

silk walls and attentive attachés. You must picture official dinners and luncheons and a good deal of fuss. A reception for me at the *Radio-diffusion Française*, when all the staff were brought up to be introduced; a dinner given by the Minister of Education; a dinner given by the *Société des Gens de Lettres*; a luncheon given by Paul Valéry—dear old man, as gay and amusing as a young chicken; a luncheon given by André Siegfried;[1] and several small dinners at the Embassy.

I gave two lectures. The first, on 'What the British think of the French', was at the *Théâtre des Ambassadeurs*, and was a *succès d'estime*. No, I think it was more than that. Anyhow, Duff, who is not lavish of praise, was very pleased indeed. All the toffs were there—Bidault, General Koenig[2] and so on. The second was at the *École des Sciences Politiques*, where there were all my old friends of diplomatic days plus 1,000 students in the galleries and corridors. My God, what a reception they gave me! I mean, not clapping merely, but bravos and hands waving and that sort of thing. I must say, the French are really full of gratitude and admiration for us. Very remarkable it was.

After it all, when I got back to the Embassy, there was Jean Cocteau waiting for me, looking like an aged cockatoo. He came up to my room while I washed. He described how he had felt that he owed it to his art not to join Aragon and others in open resistance. He explained how the *milices* had beaten him up and nearly knocked out his eye. Somehow it was not very dignified or encouraging. So we went downstairs and dined with Diana, Lord Rothschild, Noel Coward and Mr Attlee. Rather an odd dinner-party to my mind. And thereafter we went on to the Sadler's Wells ballet, which was none too bad.

H.N. TO N.N.[3]
13th March, 1945
Sissinghurst

Today P. J. Grigg introduced the Army Estimates. He did not seek in any way to indulge in rhetoric. He simply read a long narrative and allowed the narrative to speak for itself. This was a wise decision. The story he had to tell was so tremendous, the effort and organisation which it represented so formidable, the success achieved so gigantic,

---

[1] The writer and professor. He had been a member of the French Academy since 1944.

[2] Appointed by de Gaulle Military Governor of Paris.

[3] Ben was now on his way back from Italy, so H.N.'s remaining letters were addressed to Nigel alone.

that not one extra word was needed to drive home the effect. The House was sympathetic and impressed. They have got over their dislike of P. J. Grigg, who at first annoyed them by the ill-concealed contempt with which he regarded them. But since then they have come to see that he is a very hard-working and most efficient man. The actual perfection of the Army's organisation has at last convinced them that he is an excellent Secretary of State for War. So he was warmly received.

He is a funny man. He was so delighted when it was all over that he became almost human. He bounced up to me in the Lobby and said, 'Now tell me, how did it go?' I told him that it had gone very well. 'Tell me this', he added. 'Why is it that whenever I mention the name of Montgomery, there is always a cold hush?' I said it was because the left-wing people imagine that Montgomery is a political General. I have no idea what grounds there are for this suspicion. The right-wing people, on the other hand, have the impression, curious though this may seem to you, that he lacks modesty. They seem to imagine that he seeks by self-advertisement to endear himself to the great public and that some of his expressions like 'good hunting' or 'hit them for six' are popular expressions, and as such not to be esteemed. P.J. said that he knew that this extraordinary theory was current in some circles. 'It is', he said, 'due to Montgomery's very personal technique. But the fact remains that he is the greatest General that this country has produced since Wellington.'

Everybody is pleased and excited by the present strategic position. The Americans seem to have exploited with skill and daring the bit of luck given them by the capture of the Remagen bridge. Above all, Patton's three-pronged drive into the Palatinate would seem to put the German forces in the Saar in a very awkward position. We have had too many disappointments to be unduly optimistic. But I do derive the impression that when the great heave comes (and it will come before long), we may find that a final collapse is really achieved. Then comes the question whether, if we capture Hanover, Hamburg, and Spandau and join up with the Russians in the northern plains, the Nazis will retire to their Alpine redoubt[1] and seek to prolong the struggle from such portions of Czechoslovakia, Austria, Bavaria and

[1] The German 'National Redoubt' in the Alpine fastness of southern Bavaria and western Austria was a propaganda invention of Goebbels. It never existed, but the legend deceived Eisenhower's Headquarters sufficiently to affect the strategy of the closing stages of the war.

Venetia as they can retain. The general idea is that they will seek in some such way to stage a Götterdämmerung. They wish at any cost to prolong their own invincible legend. But there are others (who know a great deal) who do not share this idea, and who believe that once we debouch on the plains there will come a series of large-scale and progressive capitulations. All of which boils down to the fact that the war may last till Christmas, but it may end by June. Nobody can tell.

H.N. TO N.N.   *18th March, 1945*

I have finished chapter VI of my book.[1] It will, I think, contain some fifteen chapters and be very long and dull. I do not think that for-gotten diplomatic controversies make very good reading to anybody. They happen to amuse and interest me, but I do not imagine that many readers will really care whether Genoa was or was not allotted to Piedmont or why Lord William Bentinck was so cross. People will feel that there is no *purpose* in my book. It is not a work of historical research. I publish nothing that has not been published already. I have no specially new interpretation of the facts. And, therefore, why write all over again what has been done so well by Temperley and Webster? I don't know the answer to this question. All I know is that I have derived immense interest and pleasure from reading up my material and that however boring the book may be to others, it has been delightful to myself. Which is a good enough justification in any case.

H.N. TO N.N.   *24th March, 1945*
                                                               Sissinghurst

I sent you an airgraph describing the arrival at Staplehurst of your broken brother. Since then, he has been to Delhez and had his moustache clipped and his hair reduced to some sort of order.[2] He no longer resembles a veteran of the Old Guard after the retreat from Moscow; he resembles a cornet in the Polish Lancers serving under Soult in Spain. But the awful thing is that he does not realise that the plaster with which his face is surrounded has become stained by war. Thin and enormous he stalks through the streets of London, arousing pity and terror. He is indifferent to this. The only thing he seems to

[1] *The Congress of Vienna.*
[2] Ben arrived home on 19th March. He was encased in plaster from the waist up, and it covered his chin and the back of his head. He was in no pain.

mind is when people imagine that he has been wounded in some heroic action. Patiently he murmurs, 'No, I was hit by a lorry and broke a bone in my back. It is nothing really.'

Osbert Lancaster was at the Beefsteak at luncheon. He has flown over from Athens for a few hours' consultation.[1] He is not terribly optimistic about the future internal situation in Greece, although he says that Archbishop Damaskinos is a shrewd and powerful man. He told me that after Winston had finished his speech in Constitution Square, the crowd waited hushed by their own gratitude and enthusiasm. Dusk descended and then darkness, and then the evening star. There were 30,000 people still in the square. Winston was getting into his car. And then suddenly the Acropolis leapt out floodlit from the shadows. The crowd gave a deep religious gasp. They are short of electricity, and could only keep the floodlights on for four minutes. But the drama of the scene was well worth it.

On 23rd March General Montgomery began to force a crossing of the Rhine on each side of Wesel, and the Americans broke out of their two bridge-heads at Remagen and south of Mainz. Both the northern and the southern offensives developed very rapidly. Frankfurt was captured on 29th March, and the Ruhr, with its 325,000 defenders, was encircled on 2nd April. The Germans were incapable of putting up further organised resistance except in isolated pockets, particularly on the approaches to the northern ports which were the main British objectives. In the centre, the Americans pressed eastwards through the disintegrating German divisions. On 19th April they crossed the Czechoslovak border, and on the 25th met the Russians at Torgau on the Elbe. The German Army was cut in half.

Churchill was anxious that the Anglo-Americans should occupy as much territory as possible in Central Europe, including, if possible, Berlin and Prague, as he was appalled by the Russians' political ambitions which they now barely troubled to conceal. A puppet Government was set up by the Soviets in Vienna soon after its fall on 13th April; and Stalin concluded a treaty with the Communist Government in Warsaw in continued violation of the Yalta agreement. Roosevelt, in his declining days, did not view Russian designs with quite the same degree of anxiety, and when he died on 12th April, he was succeeded by his Vice-President, Harry Truman, who had hitherto been kept so much in the background that Churchill had never even met him. The initiative in the field there-

[1] He was attached to the British Embassy in Athens, 1944–46.

fore largely rested with Eisenhower, to whom the political considerations naturally meant less than the military. He halted his armies on the Elbe and just within the Czech borders. It was left to the Russians to capture Berlin and Prague, but Montgomery succeeded in sealing off the base of the Danish promontory by his capture of Lübeck ahead of the Russians.

The Allied armies in Italy had joined in on 9th April. Alexander launched an offensive against the numerically superior and most cohesive army left to the German High Command, and broke through on the Adriatic flank to pin a large number of German Divisions against the Po. The river was crossed on 23rd April and the whole of northern Italy was quickly overrun. Venice, previously captured by Italian partisans, was occupied on 29th April by the New Zealanders, and the 8th Army entered southern Austria on V.E. Day.

The German army in Italy, though the last to be attacked in this final offensive, was the first to surrender. A total capitulation was signed at Caserta on 29th April and came into force on 2nd May. In Germany itself, soundings had been made by Himmler for a general capitulation in the west to the Western Allies alone, but his offer was rejected. On 4th May, at Luneberg Heath, Montgomery accepted the surrender of all German forces facing him in north-west Germany, Holland and Denmark. In the early morning of 7th May the remaining German armies surrendered at Eisenhower's Headquarters at Rheims to representatives of the three main Allies and France. Germany was now under the nominal leadership of Admiral Doenitz. Both dictators were dead. Hitler had committed suicide in Berlin on 30th April. Mussolini had been shot by Italian partisans two days earlier.

DIARY   *25th March, 1945*

An amazingly early spring. I work at chapter VII [of *The Congress of Vienna*]. The Rhine push goes well. We are across on a front of thirty miles. Winston went over himself and had 'a cruise on the Rhine'. Meanwhile Patton has broken through in the Oppenheim area and taken Darmstadt. We are also advancing from Remagen. The Russians are pushing on to Vienna. The thing appears to be reaching its climax.

H.N. TO N.N.   *27th March, 1945*
                                                         Sissinghurst

I lunched with Negrin. He evidently anticipates that with the collapse of Hitler, Franco cannot last many days. He well knows that Spain is sick of troubles and wants only the rule of law and the prospects of a peaceful private life. He therefore hopes to be able to establish a shadow Government capable of taking over the moment Franco disappears. Such a Government would proclaim a political amnesty, discourage all disorder, forbid reprisals, and proceed to hold General Elections. With this in mind he hopes to go before long to Mexico and there gather together all the members of the old Cortes and a sort of Conservative Assembly on the Algiers lines.[1]

I like Negrin. He is both firm and agreeable. He seems to be a wise man and not fanatical in the least. I wish him well. He was particularly shocked by the Argentine declaring war on Germany just in order to be admitted to the San Francisco Conference. Even more disgusted was he by the Press campaign which Franco is launching against Japan. It seems disgusting to him (as it does to me) that that beastly Caudillo should imagine that by abusing one of our enemies he can obliterate the fact that he sought in the dark days to help the other two. 'This is unworthy', said Negrin, 'of the dignity of a most dignified country.'

DIARY   *28th March, 1945*

Lunch at the Beefsteak. Rothermere there. He says the news is just as good as is possible. I go to the House and find the Lobbies still bubbling. We have funeral orations for Lloyd George.[2] I meet Winston in the smoking-room and ask him whether the news is as good as it seems. 'We have nothing in front of us', he says. But owing to the blackout on troop movements we do not know where they have got to, and there are fantastic reports flying around, such as that Patton has got to Nuremberg[3] and is approaching the Czech frontier. What we all dread is that the Führer will gather all his followers and S.S. and S.A. into the Bavarian highlands and surround them with all our prisoners-of-war. He will then say, 'Come on and do your damndest.'

I am elected Chairman of the Anglo-French Interparliamentary Committee.

[1] Juan Negrin resigned as Spanish Prime Minister in exile in the hope of uniting all the émigrés, and died in Mexico in 1956.
[2] David Lloyd George died on 26th March.
[3] Nuremberg was not in fact captured until 16th April.

H.N. TO N.N. *1st April, 1945*
Sissinghurst

My perplexity regarding the nature of German strategy has been much increased during the last ten days. It is curious to reflect that night after night one indulges in conjectures and toys with place-names, knowing little of what is really happening, and yet conscious that day by day the thing is drawing to its close. Even so, in 1814, most people had read of Laon and St Dizier and Montereau, only to wake up one morning and hear that Paris had been captured by the Allies and that Napoleon had abdicated in favour of his son.

Ben and I came down here by the afternoon train. Like a wounded camel Ben stalked down the platform at Charing Cross. The train was crowded with people leaving for their Easter holidays. We found a carriage in which all the corner-seats were occupied, but in which two middle seats were vacant. Ben, with a wince of suffering nobly borne, lowered himself into the seat opposite me. Beside him was a Major-General covered in decorations. He gazed at Ben in a comradely way, as one soldier to another. Observing the pangs of agony which from time to time would pass over Ben's face, he addressed him politely. 'Let us exchange places,' he said. 'I feel you might be more comfortable in a corner-seat.' 'I am sure I should,' said Ben contentedly, and took his place. Not a word about thank-you or 'Sir' or anything like that. Just a stricken warrior relapsing with relief into the comfortable seat vacated by an unstricken warrior. Ben closed his eyes for a moment, indicating gratitude and a momentary release from pain. The train started and at Tonbridge we got out. It was a disgraceful proceeding, since in fact Ben suffers nothing at all except an occasional itch.

DIARY *10th April, 1945*

Winston is heckled about the recent outbursts by Bevin and Brendan Bracken, and is asked whether this means the break-up of the Coalition. He replies with amazing good humour, and the whole House rocks with laughter. In no other Assembly in the world could so delicate a matter have been passed off as a joke. Our tolerance and decency are beyond praise.

DIARY *11th April, 1945*

Dine with Vincent Massey[1] at the Dorchester. Winant is there and the Camroses. I ask Winant about my idea of having in London a duplicate

[1] High Commissioner for Canada in London, 1935–46.

Mount Vernon as a memorial to America's war-effort.[1] He seemed to like the idea. Bobbety Cranborne is there. He seems to think that once we have joined up with the Russians, smashed the German eastern armies and taken Munich, we can rightly proclaim that the war 'in' Germany, but not 'with' Germany, is over. He thinks that this will happen in a very short time, especially now that the U.S. 9th Army have reached the Elbe.

H.N. TO V.S-W.   *13th April, 1945*
                                        4 King's Bench Walk, E.C.4

I woke up to hear on the wireless the awful news about Roosevelt.[2] It is really a disaster. I feel deeply for Winston, and this afternoon it was evident from his manner that it was a real body-blow. Under that bloody American Constitution they must now put up with the Vice-President who was actually chosen because he was a colourless and harmless man. He may, as Coolidge did,[3] turn out to be a person of character. But I have not yet heard any man say one good word in his favour. And when one thinks of the problems ahead, it is a misery that this happened.

Shanks,[4] with whom I had a long talk today and whom I like, told me that as he gets older, he finds rhymes come less easily to him. Is that the case with you? He also says that he cannot now remember whether a line is one of his own lines or something which he has read years ago.

V.S-W. TO H.N.   *14th April, 1945*
                                               Sissinghurst

No, I don't find that rhymes come less easily. On the contrary, an appalling virtuosity seems to have descended on me, like a juggler who can spin twenty plates at a time if he wants to. My fear is that facility may damage quality. I feel I have immense control, and can say anything I like, however complicated and difficult. But I also feel that flatness has come with increasing competence.

As to remembering whether a line is by me or by someone else, you

---

[1] His idea was to erect in Hyde Park a duplicate of George Washington's house as a setting for American exhibitions. It came to nothing.

[2] Franklin Roosevelt died at Warm Springs, Georgia, on 12th April at the age of 63.

[3] Calvin Coolidge became President on Harding's death in 1923. Harry S. Truman, Roosevelt's successor, had been elected Vice-President in 1944 as a compromise candidate.

[4] Edward Shanks, the poet, was then 52, the same age as V.S-W.

know very well that I never could. The first shock of this realisation came when I very laboriously hammered out a line, choosing every word most carefully, and arrived at:

'Men are but children of a larger growth'.[1]

Since then I have been cautious.

H.N. TO N.N.   *15th April, 1945*
Greenfields, Marazion, Cornwall[2]

Gwen [St Levan] is settling down to taking things humorously and without ostentation, and the Mount is gay and very beautiful. The garden is lovely, and although Gwen cannot master the difference between annuals and shrubs, and although (panting with excitement) she plants things upside down, the result is amazing. The fact that one always looks down from upper parapets upon the flowers and sees them against the background of a deep-blue sea, adds to their colours and their shape. Then Jessica[3] is in one of the cottages by the harbour; and John is on leave and Piers on leave and Giles on vacation.[4] All this is a cheering sight.

Ben has had to go into hospital again at Tunbridge Wells. Until the middle of May he may be stuck there in the firm grasp of a Swedish masseuse and with batteries attached to his torso. After which he may get his discharge and plunge with Anthony Blunt into cataloguing the Royal Collection.[5] I find him completely unchanged. He is a most agreeable companion and I feel completely at ease with him. He might never have left. He was always a silent person except when he talked. But he is a good listener, and never lends an ear to one's more vapid remarks. He is stimulating by his very fastidiousness. Underneath there is real kindness of heart, which I regard as one of the most agreeable of all human virtues.

---

[1] 'Men are but children of a larger growth;
Our appetites as apt to change as theirs,
And full as craving too, and full as vain.'
Dryden. *Alexander's Feast.*
[2] H.N. was visiting his mother, Lady Carnock, who was living with her eldest son, the 2nd Lord Carnock, in a house opposite St Michael's Mount, which now belonged to Lord St Levan, H.N.'s brother-in-law.
[3] Jessica Koppel, the elder daughter of Lord and Lady St Levan.
[4] John, Piers and Giles St Aubyn, the three sons of Lord and Lady St Levan.
[5] Ben had already resumed his pre-war job as Deputy Surveyor of the King's Pictures. (Sir) Anthony Blunt was Surveyor.

H.N. TO N.N.   *17th April, 1945*
                                                         Sissinghurst

We were all assembled to hear Winston make his funeral oration on
Roosevelt, but before he started an absurd incident occurred. A young
man of the name of McIntyre had been elected as Scottish Nationalist
for Motherwell.[1] He refused to be introduced by any sponsors, since
he does not recognise the Mother of Parliaments and wishes to advertise
himself. He advanced to the Bar without sponsors and the Speaker
told him that he could not take his oath, as that was contrary to Standing
Orders. At which many Members rose offering to sponsor the cub
and put an end to the shaming incident, but he refused. He was therefore told to go away and think it over, which he did, shrugging vain
shoulders. Next day he thought better of it and accepted sponsors;
but even then, as he reached the box, he said, 'I do this under protest',
which was not liked at all. He is going to be a sad nuisance and pose as a
martyr.

Then, thus delayed and with the early inspiration gone, Winston
rose and spoke about Roosevelt. I did not think him very good—
nothing like as good as when he made the funeral oration on Neville
Chamberlain, which was truly Periclean. Which all shows that when
one really does mind deeply about a thing, it is more difficult to write
or speak about it than when one is just faintly moved by pity or terror.

Then we had a debate about San Francisco and Yalta. I said that the
Dumbarton Oaks plan was about as perfect a machine as could be
devised, but that Yalta meant that we should never be able to use the
machine against anybody other than Germany and Japan.[2] *Quis
custodiet ipsos custodes?* In fact the Government had rather a poor time
of it since all the speeches were critical.

H.N. TO N.N.   *22nd April, 1945*
                                                         Sissinghurst

The Italian offensive seems to be developing splendidly.[3] I pray at odd
moments that you will not be killed. The first cuckoo of the year

[1] R. D. McIntyre was Assistant Medical Officer of Health for the County of Stirling,
and Secretary of the Scottish National Party. He remained an M.P. for only three
months, April–July, 1945.

[2] This was H.N.'s last major speech in the House of Commons. He criticised the
veto as a fatal flaw in the United Nations Charter.

[3] The 6th Armoured Division, in which Nigel was serving, reached the southern
bank of the Po on this day, and three days later his own Battalion, the 3rd Battalion
Grenadier Guards, was the first British unit to cross the river.

H.N.D.   449   2F

provokes a silent prayer, as also the first asparagus and the first green peas. It is curious and strange that a man who believes himself as rational as I believe myself to be, should succumb to such pagan, and indeed barbaric, rites. In any case, I have been able this week to indulge to the full my gift of prayer, since by a curious combination of circumstances it has been an almost wholly ecclesiastical week spent in the company of bishops and archbishops and all the company of heaven.[1]

We drove through the orchards and vineyards[2] of Kent to Canterbury. It was the most perfect spring day that I have ever known. There was the Cathedral almost undamaged and looking so proud of itself. We went first to the Bishop of Dover's house where there was a large luncheon *al fresco* on the lawn with all manner of Generals, Chaplains General, Admirals, Air Marshals, Sheriffs and Lord Lieutenants. We had lovely seats in the main choir and we sat there for two hours watching the enthronement of 'the Most Reverend Father in God, Geoffrey Lord Archbishop of Canterbury'. It was a fine sight, and the B.B.C. orchestra was there to supplement the Cathedral choir, and the trumpets were sounded and everything was very stately and calm. We had seen that morning in the newspapers photographs of Buchenwald and of the bundles of corpses stacked together for removal. The contrast was very marked. I took the special train up to London in the company of Dorothy Thompson and her new Czech husband.[3] We all dined together with Walter Elliot.

H.N. TO N.N.   *23rd April, 1945*
                                                      Sissinghurst

A man from the War Memorials Advisory Committee came to see me, wanting advice on publicity. Their aim is to prevent silly people putting up silly memorials in our pretty little villages. I wrote to Camrose, and by Jove! the next day there was a long and appropriate article in the *Daily Telegraph*.

Then off I went to the House for a Press luncheon. Winston was to make the main speech and Nancy Astor the secondary speech. Winston

[1] In addition to the enthronement of Dr Fisher as Archbishop of Canterbury on 19th April, H.N. also attended a memorial service for Robert Bernays on the 20th in Bristol Cathedral, and was godfather at the christening of his son, Robert Edward John Bernays, then two months old, after the service.

[2] A reference to V.S-W.'s poems *Orchard and Vineyard* (The Bodley Head, 1921).

[3] Dorothy Thompson, the American journalist and author, had married Maxim Kopf in 1943. She was divorced from Sinclair Lewis in 1942.

was very good, but warned the Press against shouting that V Day was on the verge of reality. 'How can we possibly rejoice when our men are still losing their lives in Holland, in Norway maybe, in Italy still, and certainly in Burma?' At the same time let us not feel that our lack of boasting is losing us prestige. 'Honour will come to us: we need not go out and seek it.'

Then Nancy got up. For once she had got some notes in her hand, but each note suggested an idea and each idea some other idea, and then that reminded her of a story her nurse had once told her in Virginia and how little, now she came to think of it, the British Press knew about Virginia although Sir Walter Raleigh had colonised it and how odd that Raleigh was less known in England than in the United States although we knew all about Philip Sidney not the V.C. of course[1] such a nice young man and the best type of Conservative although she herself was not a Conservative really although her husband was and nor was Winston really since he had been a Liberal once and oh yes she must tell them about Winston she had asked him why he was so cold to her when she first entered the House and he had said because I feel you have come into my bathroom and I have only a sponge with which to defend myself not that she had not forgiven Winston we had all forgiven Winston but it was really the merchant navy which had done the great deeds where should we be without the merchant navy now in Plymouth. . .

At this stage Waldorf,[2] who was sitting beside her, gave a slight tug to her dress. 'Now, where was I?' she said looking at her notes. 'Oh yes . . .' and then she started again. This was perhaps the last speech she would make in the House of Commons and she had a favour to ask Winston, would he please make her a peer, as she would wake up the House of Lords as she had woken up the House of Commons, and Philip Lothian always used to say. . . At which came another tug from Waldorf, so strong that Nancy sat down suddenly with an expression of pained surprise. I suppose her rambling is amusing, but it rather saddens me, as I like her, and I wish that she would not make quite such an idiot of herself in public.

DIARY   *27th April, 1945*

I dine at the Grand Hotel[3] and listen to the news afterwards. It is pretty startling. The American and Russian forces linked up on

[1] Lord de L'Isle and Dudley, who won the V.C. at Anzio.
[2] The 2nd Viscount Astor, whom Lady Astor had married in 1906.   [3] In Leicester.

Wednesday afternoon [25th April] at Torgau on the Elbe. Messages are relayed from Winston, Truman and Stalin. It is odd to hear the latter's voice echoing through the lounge of the Grand Hotel. The Russians have completely encircled Berlin and taken Spandau and Potsdam. They are in the Tiergarten. The Germans insist that Hitler and Goebbels are still in the capital, and it may in fact be true that they wish to commit their final act of suicide in Berlin.[1] Thus the capture of Berlin means the end. There is a general rising of the Italian partisans, who have taken over Milan, Genoa and, it seems, Turin. There is even a rumour that Mussolini, 'yellow with rage', has been captured by them.[2] Meanwhile the 8th Army are beyond Verona and have cut the German armies in two. They have before them the Adige and Venice.

H.N. TO N.N.   *29th April, 1945*
                                                                  Sissinghurst

You can imagine what an exhilarating week this has been. The surrounding of Berlin; the link-up with the Russian armies; the overtures made through Bernadotte by Himmler;[3] the reported capture and execution of Mussolini; the alleged death of Goering;[4] the stroke which, it is said, has laid Hitler low. It must be comparable to the crop of news which suddenly burst upon Europe in March and April 1814, which nobody quite believed at the time, but which in the end led to the capitulation of Fontainebleau.

How I wish you had been with us as well as out there! The maddening thing is that the map I have for my little pin-flags stops short at Innsbruck. It would be far more fun for me to stick the Union Jack into Vicenza, Padua and Venice than to stick the hammer-and-sickle into Rathenow or Koenigswusterhausen. We follow your campaign with intense interest. Alexander has the knack of gaining his victories

---

[1] Both did.

[2] Mussolini and his mistress, Clara Petacci, were captured by Italian partisans while trying to escape from Como into Switzerland on 26th April, and were executed on the 28th. Their bodies were taken to Milan and strung upside down from the girders of a petrol-filling station.

[3] Late on 24th April Count Bernadotte, head of the Swedish Red Cross, informed the British that he was authorised by Himmler to propose a German capitulation on the whole Western front. The reply was that the surrender should be unconditional and simultaneous to the three major Powers.

[4] Goering was alive, and was later taken prisoner by the Americans in a Tirolean village.

at the very moment when more dramatic victories are being won elsewhere. The glamour of Rome was dimmed by the excitement of D Day. The glory of the present really miraculous campaign is shadowed by the searchlights over Berlin and the rumours of capitulation. But I am aware how strange it must be for you to watch the laughter of Lake Benacus[1] and to find yourself at Padua, by the waters of the Brenta, or finally on the edge of those lagoons. But supposing— just for the sake of argument—that you have not been killed and do get this letter, you must surely agree with me that not to every man is it given to witness Hammam Lif, Cassino and the forcing of the Po and the Adige. As a slice of experience, you will admit that it is pretty full of plums.

H.N. TO N.N.   *1st May, 1945*
Sissinghurst

Winston was asked whether he had any statement to make regarding the war situation. He replied, 'Yes, it is definitely more satisfactory than it was this time five years ago.' Generally, he is good at making this sort of joke. But he was feeling ill or something—his manner was languid and his face puckered and creased—and it did not go down well. There was a perfunctory laugh, and then a feeling that we wished he hadn't said it.

It had snowed hard during the night and the coloured lilac looked strange under the puffs of snow. It was like seeing Lady Cunard covered in salt or flour after a visit to a salt-mine or a miller's shop. I had chattering teeth. But I was warmed by the news. Mussolini had been caught and murdered, and we had really dreadful photographs of his corpse and that of his mistress hanging upside down and side by side. They looked like turkeys hanging outside a poulterer's: the slim legs of the mistress and the huge stomach of Mussolini could both be detected. It was a most unpleasant picture and caused a grave reaction in his favour. It was terribly ignominious—*Sejanus ducitur unco*—but Mrs Groves[2] said that he deserved it thoroughly, 'a married man like that driving about in a car with his mistress'.

I dined at Pratts. Lionel Berry was there (the son of Lord Kemsley) who told us that the German wireless had been putting out *Achtungs* about an *ernste wichtige Meldung*, and playing dirges in between. So

[1] The Roman name for Lake Garda. The reference is to Tennyson's 'The Lydian laughter of the Garda lake below'.
[2] H.N.'s housekeeper at King's Bench Walk.

we tried and failed to get the German wireless stations with the horrible little set which is all that Pratts can produce. Having failed to do this, we asked Lionel to go upstairs to telephone to one of his numerous newspapers, and he came running down again (it was 10.40) to say that Hitler was dead and Doenitz had been appointed as his successor.[1] Then Ben and I returned to King's Bench Walk and listened to the German midnight news. It was all too true. '*Unser Führer, Adolf Hitler, ist . . .*'—and then a long digression about heroism and the ruins of Berlin—'*. . . gefallen.*' So that was Mussolini and Hitler within two days. Not a bad bag as bags go.

DIARY   2nd May, 1945

I dine with Mrs George Keppel at the Ritz. The party consists of Violet Trefusis, the Belgian Ambassador, the Portuguese Ambassador, the Andersons, Lady Moncrieffe and Robin McDouall. I lean across to Cartier de Marchienne[2] and say, 'Well, Mr Ambassador, I saw you in the House this afternoon, expecting a statement by the Prime Minister which never came.' 'But it came tonight', said Ava Anderson. 'What came?' And then she told me that Churchill had come in at 7.30 and told the House that all the German and Italian forces in Italy and the Tirol had surrendered unconditionally to Alexander. I get John Anderson to repeat it carefully. I feel quite ecstatic. It is almost incredible.

There is still much uncertainty about Hitler. Some think that he is not dead at all but has gone underground. Others think that he has had a stroke and died a week ago. Others say that he and Goebbels committed suicide. It will be many months, if ever, before we learn the truth.

---

[1] At 3.30 pm. on Monday, 30th April, ten days after Hitler's fifty-sixth birthday, and twelve years and three months after he had become Chancellor of Germany, he shot himself in the bunker of the Chancellery in Berlin. Eva Braun, whom he had married only a few days previously, took poison. Their two bodies were burned in the courtyard outside, which was already under Russian shell-fire. Before his death Hitler drew up a will appointing Admiral Doenitz (who was then at Ploen in Schleswig) as his successor in place of Goering, who had forfeited the Führer's confidence by assuming prematurely that Hitler was no longer capable of exercising command.

[2] The Belgian Ambassador in London from 1927 until his death in 1946.

H.N. TO N.N.   3rd May, 1945

People are distressed by the Russians, who appear to be behaving with the most arrogant duplicity. There are, moreover, terrible stories seeping through about their treatment of our prisoners. It seems that the men who had preserved their wrist-watches through five years of captivity had them stolen from them by their Russian liberators, and they were not allowed out of their prison barracks in which they had been confined. All of which will not make for blood-brotherliness with the U.S.S.R. But what are we to do? We simply must practise appeasement. And there is this comfort in it. In appeasing Hitler we knew that we were appeasing an advancing tide, and that he would consolidate every position gained. But I do not think that the Russians are an advancing tide. I think that, as in 1814, they will gradually recede. I pray to God that I am right in thinking this, because, if I am wrong, then the Balance of Power is permanently dislocated.

DIARY   4th May, 1945

While we are having dinner, Pat [Staples][1] comes across to say that the B.B.C. have issued a flash news that the Germans in Holland and Norway have surrendered to Montgomery. 'Are you sure about Norway?' I ask suspiciously. She hesitates. At 9 we have the news, and it is clear that only north-west Germany, Holland and Denmark have surrendered. But this is good enough.

DIARY   5th May, 1945

At San Francisco Molotov has informed Eden that the Polish emissaries whom they had invited from Warsaw to discuss matters have been arrested for activities harmful to the Red Army. Eden has replied deploring this, and stating that in these circumstances all further conversations regarding Poland must be interrupted. Stettinius has followed suit. This means that Russia has flagrantly violated the Yalta agreements and that it is no longer possible to maintain even the fiction of her good faith. The prospects are gloomy. In Vienna, in Trieste, to say nothing of the Balkans, she is behaving as if she were our enemy and not our ally. I am convinced that our only policy is to swallow everything and to hope that time will bring improvement. But all this will cast a gloom over our victory celebrations.

[1] The elder daughter of the cook at Sissinghurst.

7th May, 1945

At 3 comes the news that an hour ago Schwerin von Krosigk[1] had spoken on the wireless from Flensburg.[2] He has said that Germany was obliged to surrender unconditionally, crushed by the overwhelming might of her enemies. Ben and I dash to tell Vita who is in the courtyard. The three of us climb the turret stairs, tie the flag to the ropes, and hoist it in the soft south-west breeze. It looks very proud and gay after five years of confinement.

I decide to go up to London. The news of Schwerin's broadcast has apparently spread. In Staplehurst we see a handful of children fluttering little flags. When I get to London there are flags everywhere. At Cannon Street I see the B.B.C.'s Chief Engineer, Noel Ashbridge, escaping exhausted from London. He says that everything is completely tied up, that we cannot get Moscow to agree to a time for a simultaneous announcement and that everything is to be postponed until tomorrow.

I dine at Pratts, which is empty and dull. Coming back, I find a few instances of celebration. A Jewess in a paper cap is strolling down St James's Street turning a rattle. A few drunken soldiers.

H.N. TO N.N. *8th May, 1945*
Sissinghurst

The normality continued in the morning. I attended a meeting of the *Institut Français* and lunched at the Beefsteak. By that time things began to liven up. There was some cheering in the streets and crowds in Leicester Square. But when I had finished my luncheon, I found a very different scene. The whole of Trafalgar Square and Whitehall was packed with people. Somebody had made a corner in rosettes, flags, streamers, paper whisks and, above all, paper caps. The latter were horrible, being of the comic variety. I also regret to say that I observed three Guardsmen in full uniform wearing such hats: they were *not* Grenadiers; they belonged to the Coldstream. And through this cheerful, but not exuberant, crowd I pushed my way to the House of Commons. The last few yards were very difficult, as the crowd was packed against the railings. I tore my trousers in trying to squeeze past a stranded car. But at length the police saw me and backed a horse

---

[1] He had been Minister of Finance continuously since his appointment by von Papen in 1932, and was Foreign Minister in the Doenitz Government.

[2] The town on the Danish border where Doenitz had set up his rump Government.

into the crowd, making a gap through which, amid cheers, I was squirted into Palace Yard. There I paused to recover myself, and seeing that it was approaching the hour of 3 pm., I decided to remain there and hear Winston's broadcast which was to be relayed through loud-speakers. As Big Ben struck three, there was an extraordinary hush over the assembled multitude, and then came Winston's voice. He was short and effective, merely announcing that unconditional sur-render had been signed, and naming the signatories. (When it came to Jodl, he said 'Jodel'[1].) 'The evil-doers', he intoned, 'now lie prostrate before us.' The crowd gasped at this phrase. 'Advance Britannia!' he shouted at the end, and there followed the Last Post and *God Save the King* which we all sang very loud indeed. And then cheer upon cheer.

I dashed back into the House and into the Chamber. After the roar and heat outside, it was like suddenly entering an Oxford quadrangle on Eights Week night. Cool and hushed the Chamber was, with P. J. Grigg answering questions as if nothing unusual were impending. The clock reached 3.15, which is the moment when Questions auto-matically close. We knew that it would take Winston some time to get to the House from Downing Street in such a crowd. We therefore made conversation by asking supplementary questions until 3.23. Then a slight stir was observed behind the Speaker's chair, and Winston, looking coy and cheerful, came in. The House rose as a man, and yelled and yelled and waved their Order Papers. He responded, not with a bow exactly, but with an odd shy jerk of the head and with a wide grin. Then he started to read to us the statement that he had just made on the wireless. When he had finished reading, he put his manuscript aside and with wide gestures thanked and blessed the House for all its noble support of him throughout these years.

Then he proposed that 'this House do now attend at the Church of St Margaret's, Westminster, to give humble and reverend thanks to Almighty God for our deliverance from the threat of German domina-tion'. The motion was carried, and the Serjeant at Arms put the mace on his shoulder and, following the Speaker, we all strode out. Through the Central Lobby we streamed, through St Stephen's Chapel, and out into the sunshine of Parliament Square. We entered St. Margaret's by the West door which was furthest away from us, and that meant a long sinuous procession through a lane kept open for us through the crowd. I had expected some jeers or tittering, since politicians are not

[1] The Chief of Hitler's Operational Staff of the Wehrmacht.

popular and in the mass they seem absurd. But not at all. Cheers were what we received, and adulation. The service itself was very short and simple, and beautifully sung. Then the Chaplain to the Speaker read in a loud voice the names of those who had laid down their lives: 'Ronald Cartland; Hubert Duggan; Victor Cazalet; John Macnamara; Robert Bernays'—only the names of my particular friends registered on my consciousness. I was moved. The tears came into my eyes. Furtively I wiped them away. 'Men are so emotional', sniffed Nancy Astor, who was sitting next to me. Damn her.

Then back we streamed into the House and adjourned for the day. Winston made a dash for the smoking-room. When he was passing through Central Hall the crowd there broke into loud clapping. He hesitated and then hurried on. A little boy dashed out: 'Please, sir, may I have your autograph?' Winston took a long time getting out his glasses and wiping them. Then he ruffled the little boy's hair and gave him back his beastly little album. 'That will remind you of a glorious day', he said, and the crowd clapped louder than before. In the smoking-room Kenneth Pickthorn produced a bottle of champagne and we clinked glasses.

Then came an anti-climax. I was taken out in a police-car to beyond Kensington to lecture to a Police course. They were very intelligent for bobbies, and I quite enjoyed it. And then, with great difficulty because the streets were blocked, I was taken back by the police-car to the Travellers where I dined with Robin McDowall and a nice naval friend of his called Wyndham Goodden. We had champagne and then went downstairs to the inner room to listen to the King's wireless address.

I went on to a party at Chips Channon's. Why did I go to that party? I should have been much happier seeing all the flood-lighting and the crowds outside Buckingham Palace. But I went and I loathed it. There in his room, copied from the Amalienburg, under the lights of many candles, were gathered the Nurembergers and the Munichois celebrating *our* victory over *their* friend Herr von Ribbentrop. I left early and in haste, leaving my coat behind me. A voice hailed me in Belgrave Square. It was Charles, seventh Marquess of Londonderry,[1]

---

[1] Lord Londonderry was Secretary of State for Air, 1931–35. He was severely attacked in England by Labour and pacifist circles for opposing the abolition of bombing aircraft by international agreement. He met the Nazi leaders in 1936 and 1937. Ribbentrop came to stay with him. He died in February 1949, as the result of a gliding accident in 1947.

Hitler's friend. As we walked towards his mansion in Park Lane, he explained to me how he had warned the Government about Hitler; how they would not listen to him; how, but for him, we should not have had the Spitfires and 'all this', waving a thin arm at the glow above a floodlit Buckingham Palace, at the sound of cheering in the park, and at the cone of searchlights which joined each other like a maypole above our heads.

Enraged by this, I left him in Park Lane and walked back through the happy but quite sober crowds to Trafalgar Square. The National Gallery was alive with every stone outlined in flood-lighting, and down there was Big Ben with a grin upon his illumined face. The statue of Nelson was picked out by a searchlight, and there was the smell of distant bonfires in the air. I walked to the Temple and beyond. Looking down Fleet Street one saw the best sight of all—the dome of St Paul's rather dim-lit, and then above it a concentration of searchlights upon the huge golden cross. So I went to bed.

That was my victory day.

As soon as the war with Germany was over, the thoughts of Parliament turned towards the General Election. In the previous October, Churchill had suggested that an Election should be held within a month or two of the defeat of Germany. Now he changed his mind. He considered that the Coalition should remain together until after the defeat of Japan, and that the death of Roosevelt and the disquieting attitude of Russia since Yalta made a unified British Government all the more essential. The Labour Party took a different view. The present Parliament, they argued, was already ten years old, and the urgency of certain social reforms was already in dispute between the Parties. On 23rd May Churchill therefore announced that Parliament would be dissolved on 15th June and that Polling Day would be on 5th July. In the interval, he formed his 'Caretaker Government', composed of Conservatives and Independents only.

As Harold Nicolson records, the Japanese war aroused little interest in Britain. The fall of Rangoon to General Slim's 14th British Army on 2nd May had not even been mentioned in his Diary, nor was the fierce fighting by the Americans for Okinawa in April, May and June. Apart from the mounting Party battle at home, attention was focused on the behaviour of the Communists in Europe and of France in the Middle East. The most critical situation developed at Trieste and in southern Austria, which Tito's victorious partisans claimed as their own, although the British 8th Army were in occupation of both. A war with Yugoslavia was narrowly averted by the tact and firmness of the British troops on the spot. Eastern Europe and the Balkans (apart from Greece) were already under Soviet control, but the governments of Poland and Austria were still disputed between the Russians and the Western Allies. Churchill was for taking a firmer line than Truman, who suspected that Britain wished to back right-wing or monarchist parties without considering sufficiently what the true wishes of the peoples might be. He began to see himself more as an arbiter or mediator between Russia and Britain than as Britain's ally against a new menace. At one moment he proposed that he should hold private talks with Stalin before Churchill joined them for the Potsdam Conference, and in spite of Churchill's reiterated arguments for a stand-still of the Allied Armies on the line reached in Germany when the fighting stopped, Truman decided to withdraw to the agreed Anglo-American occupation zones of Germany further west, and the British had no choice but to conform.

Harold Nicolson foresaw that he would lose his seat in West Leicester at the General Election, although the local Conservatives had decided to back him to the full. He hoped to be appointed Chairman of the British Council if he were defeated. Meanwhile, during this uneasy period between the end of the German war and the opening of the Election campaign, he spent more time than usual at Sissinghurst, writing 'The Congress of Vienna' and editing with V. Sackville-West 'Another World than This'. In his letters to his son a more reflective and sadder note replaces the exuberance of his letters during the final stages of the war. The Diary is scrappy in comparison.

DIARY   *13th May, 1945*

In the evening Winston gives a 40-minute wireless talk. It is full of stuff, but does not contain any oratorical fireworks. It is notable for an envenomed attack on De Valera, and for a strong hint to Russia that we shall not tolerate police States and totalitarian systems. The latter statement was very bold indeed. He says that if the country wants to get rid of him and turn him out to grass, he will go with a good grace, but he warns them that there are many further difficulties ahead. This will lead his opponents to say that he is making party propaganda.

DIARY   *15th May, 1945*

Peter Tennant[1] comes to see me from Paris. He tells me that the French are almost unbearably sensitive and difficult. They refuse to release sufficient men from the forces to get the economic machine working again, since they desire at all costs to maintain their position as a military power. They will not even detach men to run convoys of motor lorries. We had, for instance, lent them 100 lorries to secure the provisioning of Lille, but these lorries fell into disrepair almost at once because they were not properly serviced. The only way in which they can get convoys to work is to allow them to work for the Black Market, the high proceeds of which offer an inducement to the men to keep their vehicles in order. He also says that de Gaulle is losing all hold on the popular imagination, and is much blamed for not taking a stronger line regarding internal reconstruction. On a recent visit to Lille, for instance, he brushed aside their requests for repair material and delivered to them a long lecture on Indo-China.

H.N. TO N.N.   *16th May, 1945*
                                                         Sissinghurst

Richard Rumbold[2] came to see me, having just returned from Germany, where he had gone as correspondent for (I regret to say) the *News of the World*. He was intelligent about it all. He said that the expression 'a world in dissolution' had possessed no meaning for him until he had seen the Germany of today. The destruction is inconceivable; the desolation complete; the despair unutterable. The Germans were completely shattered and numbed; their only apparent reaction was a passionate desire to be conciliatory to us, and an almost panic fear of being handed over to the Russians. Now this will have a strange effect upon our troops. I shall be interested to discover how far the mood of hatred induced by Buchenwald will be succeeded by a mood of pity. One of the odd and confusing things is that those of our prisoners who happened to be in a good camp with a Commandant of the old school return with the assurance that 'Gerry was not too bad on the whole'. Whereas others who fell into S.S. or Gestapo hands cannot speak too bitterly of the cruelties and humiliations to which they were exposed.

---

[1] Then a member of H.M. Foreign Service. Information Counsellor at the British Embassy in Paris (the post which H.N. himself had been offere)d from 1945 to 1950. In 1952 he became Overseas Director of the F.B.I.

[2] Author of *My Father's Son* etc. He was a very close friend of H.N.

Thus public opinion here will have two entirely different accounts and I foresee much bewilderment.

DIARY   *16th May, 1945*

The newspapers, I regret to say, are starting an agitation against war-criminals. The fact that our military authorities are obliged to employ ex-Nazi civil servants as administrators tempts them to suggest that we are 'trying to get in with the old Nazi gang'. Memories of Badoglio and Darlan are revived. This is dishonest and inconvenient propaganda. It has been encouraged by the interviews which journalists were allowed to have with Goering and by a photograph of Kesselring lunching luxuriously with American Generals in some Berchtesgaden hotel. Eisenhower has rightly stopped this form of fraternisation. But meanwhile there is a growing agitation to bring these criminals to trial. I foresee an unpleasant period during which a few guilty men will be shot and many comparatively innocent men handed over to the Russians. It is not by such means that we can re-educate Germany or restore sanity to a nerve-shattered world. We are the only Power which possesses sufficient moral authority, prestige and good sense to impose reason upon all this witch-hunting.

H.N. TO N.N.   *17th May, 1945*
                                                            Sissinghurst

The King and Queen attended a ceremony in the Royal Gallery. It was almost wholly domestic. The Lord Chancellor made a short speech; the Speaker made a short speech; the King read a long speech. He has a really beautiful voice and it is to be regretted that his stammer makes it almost intolerably painful to listen to him. It is as if one read a fine piece of prose written on a typewriter the keys of which stick from time to time and mar the beauty of the whole. It makes him stress the wrong word. 'My Lords and Members ... *of* the House of Commons.' Then they walked down the aisle which separated the Lords from the Commons; very slowly they walked, bowing to right and left. The Queen has a truly miraculous faculty of making each individual feel that it is him whom she has greeted and to him that was devoted that lovely smile. She has a true genius for her job. But we listened in silence to the King's speech: a silence which seemed un-grateful for all the excellent work that he has done. But Winston, with his sense of occasion, rose at the end and waved his top hat aloft and called for three cheers. All our pent-up energies responded with three yells such as I should have thought impossible to emanate from so many elderly throats.

I spoke shortly on two themes this week in the House of Commons. Once to complain about the categories for family allowances. I talked about you and Ben. I thought it nice to say something about each of you in the House of Commons. My remarks about you were greeted with low but sympathetic cheers. On the second occasion I rose in defence of the Civil Service. It is rare that I address the House on any subject other than Foreign Affairs.

H.N. TO N.N.
18th May, 1945
Sissinghurst

I went down to my dear old school to address a discussion group. It is always a strange experience for me to revisit Wellington and to smell again those pine-trees which cast such a blight across my early youth. I am haunted by the picture of myself at thirteen, bored and sensitive, wandering about idly and not knowing one little bit what life is about. If only I could have foreseen in those days the forty years of happiness and work that lay ahead of me! Lack of any self-assertiveness has always been my main disability, and I believe that it was born (or perhaps only intensified) in the grim methodical discipline of Wellington College. Everything is much freer now and more enlightened. The boys seemed to me extraordinarily alert. I came back next morning glad to leave the beastly place and glad to have been there once again.

H.N. TO N.N.
20th May, 1945
Sissinghurst

What will be worrying and puzzling you will be the Russian situation.[1] I do not view it as gloomily as some people do. In the first place, the Russians do not behave like Europeans even in the best of circumstances and at their most sober. Actions, which if performed by Europeans, would suggest the most dangerous purposes and intentions, do not with Russians convey the same sinister implications. They are just bad manners. Moreover, the Russians are actually drunk with victory, and when a Russian gets drunk, he behaves in a manner which even —— would regard as extreme. Nor is this all. Every Russian has been brought up in the determinist and materialist concept

[1] Nigel was then in Southern Austria, where Tito's partisans were causing great trouble.

of history. It is with him a fundamental article of faith that man is an economic animal only, that in the conflict between capitalism and communism there can be no middle way at all, and that therefore sooner or later there must be a battle between the Eastern and Western worlds. He thus interprets our every action as being dictated solely by the inevitability of such a conflict. If, for instance, we hesitate to massacre every German officer who has surrendered to us, the Russian suspects, not that we are showing ordinary humanity, but that we are preparing a nice little German General Staff to help in the future war. This explains their acute suspicion. Russia at the same time is terribly exhausted and burningly anxious to return home and repair the losses and ravages to which she has been exposed. She is thus not only drunk with victory but pressed for time. She wants to get as much as she can while the going is good. When you add to these facts the consideration that the Soviet Marshals have got a little out of hand and that Stalin has not the absolute control which so many of us imagine, then you get a further explanation of their provocative conduct.

People say to me, 'But why, when you cursed us for wishing to appease Hitler, do you advocate the appeasement of Stalin?' I reply, 'For several reasons. First, because the Nazi system was more evil than the Soviet system. Secondly, because whereas Hitler used every surrender on our part as a stepping-off place for further aggression, there does exist a line beyond which Stalin will not go. To put it on a purely material basis, Stalin requires desperately from America the machine-tools and agricultural implements without which he cannot get his country going again. He cannot therefore go too far in alienating United States opinion. If we are firm and patient, the tide of Russian aggressiveness will sooner or later recede.'

I am sure this is the reasonable attitude to adopt. Yet I confess that we shall have many dangerous and humiliating episodes to face. You will yourself have come right against it in Carinthia and Venezia Giulia.

H.N. TO N.N.   27th May, 1945
                                                              Sissinghurst

The House has been enjoying the Whitsun Recess and I have been at a comparatively loose end. I was able to complete the two most difficult and dullest chapters of *The Congress of Vienna*. The delicious calm which I experienced in the process was broken by the political crisis. Winston resigned,[1] and then my constituency and National Labour got busy. I am frankly dreading the General Election. I dislike the falsity, the noise, the misrepresentation, the exhaustion and the strain of the whole thing. I am bad at posing as a demagogue. I dislike being abused and heckled. I have not the combative instincts which lead some people actually to enjoy the conflict. And, above all, I have no prospect of success. In normal times, if things were quiet, I might possibly reap some reward from the long and conscientious work I have put in at Leicester. But times are not normal. People feel, in a vague and muddled way, that all the sacrifices to which they have been exposed and their separation (*l'absence—le moins clément de tous les maux'*)— from family life during four or five years, are all the fault of 'them'— namely the authority or the Government. By a totally illogical process of reasoning, they believe that 'they' mean the upper classes, or the Conservatives, and that in some manner all that went well during these five years was due to Bevin and Morrison, and all that went ill was due to Churchill. Class feeling and class resentment are very strong. I should be surprised, therefore, if there were not a marked swing to the left. I am not sure that I think that this would be a bad thing. I mean, the difficulties of demobilisation, the problem of inducing people to go to the Far East, are all so pressing and complicated that they will entail the utmost confidence between the government and the governed if disturbances are not to occur. In any case, even a slight swing to the left will sweep away my 87 majority.

I shall earn all your sympathy when the day comes that I cease to be a Member of Parliament. I have loved my ten years at Westminster, and have found there that combination of genial surroundings with useful activity which is the basis of all human happiness. If I learn on 26th July that my political career is over (perhaps for ever), I shall accept it with philosophic resignation and devote such years as may remain to me[2] to serious literary work. I have a domestic retreat of the utmost felicity and a second string to my bow. My God! what right have I of all men to complain?

I was, as I think I told you, rather dreading to be asked to join Winston's Caretaker Government. It would have meant a severe financial sacrifice (giving up the B.B.C. and the *Spectator*), and it would have done me harm in the constituency[3] and extinguished the

---

[1] But he was immediately invited by the King to form his Caretaker Government.
[2] H.N. was then 58.
[3] This remark may seem surprising, considering that H.N. was supported by all

little match-light chance I may still have of being re-elected. But such is the perversity of human nature, that when I heard the list of minor appointments yesterday, I was disappointed and hurt at not having been asked. I did not want to go to the party but I should like to have been invited. It is indeed strange that Winston should have filled up all his minor appointments entirely from the Conservative ranks, and that not one single post should have been given to the Liberal Nationals or to ourselves. But being amused at myself, I was amused at finding, quite unexpectedly, that I was annoyed at not having been offered something that I did not want. And being amused, the feeling of hurt —and, truly, it was no more than the brush of a nettle-leaf against the forearm—passed by me in a smile.

So that is the end of a week uneventful in occurrences, but moving in emotions. Everybody, whether at Klagenfurt or in London, is feeling flat and cross after the V.E. celebrations. The Japanese war arouses no interest at all, but only a nauseated distaste. We must expect human nature, after having risen to such heights of feeling and resolution, to deteriorate into petty meanness and rancour. But all this will pass.

Darling Niggs,[1] whatever disasters may happen to you, there is always a sure haven for you in the love that Mummy and I bear towards you, and although neither of us will ever intrude upon your private life, you know that all your pleasures are our delight and all your pains our sorrow. It is something even in the worst thunderstorm, even when the rain pours down in sheets, to know that outside the monsoon there is always one spot on earth where you will always be loved and cherished, and where your interests and adventures are welcomed and shared.

DIARY   *31st May, 1945*

National Labour meeting. We consider the resignation of Lord Elton and Malcolm MacDonald's refusal to fight Ross and Cromarty. We are thus only standing in four constituencies. We decide to dissolve ourselves and to become 'The National Campaign Committee'.

---

the Conservatives in his constituency. But he believed that many non-Conservatives also supported him because he was not too closely associated with the Conservative clique.

[1] The family name for Nigel.

DIARY   *3rd June, 1945*

Spend the whole day, except for an interval of weeding, in writing my Election Address. I hate it. I loathe the falsity and artificiality of such things.

H.N. TO N.N.[1]   *4th June, 1945*
                                                                   Sissinghurst

My attitude towards my constituents in West Leicester has been that of a kindly doctor. I go and see them. I write them letters. I try to help them in their unhappiness and bewilderment, but always with the quiet, comforting (and, I dare say, slightly superior) manner of the doctor visiting his patients. Now I have to enter whole wards of patients, clapping my hands together and being hearty and comradely. Well, I just won't do it. I know that I am a good Member and that my family doctor attitude is not only sincere but authentic in me. Any other attitude is not authentic: it is sham, histrionic and fatuous.

I had the idea (it was a bad idea) that it would be better to have my Election photograph taken by a Leicester supporter rather than by a Bond Street beauty specialist. It was only when I was in the train that I remembered that I was to be photographed that day, and I had put on my dark butcher-blue shirt. It is a shirt which I like, but it is not a shirt which an elderly Parliamentary candidate should choose. When I got to the photographer, he opened his eyes and dropped his mouth. 'But you can't be photographed in that shirt, Mr Nicolson. Not for the Election, you can't. It makes you look like a Fascist, it does truly. You look like Lord Haw Haw or Sir Oswald Mosley.' That was very awkward, coming from a photographer and a supporter. I suggested that with his technical skill he might perhaps lighten the shirt in the proof and make it look less totalitarian. 'Not on your life I couldn't, Mr Nicolson.' Now, the photograph was required immediately for posters and so on, and it takes time to have a block made. I asked him to lend me some clothing-coupons, being prepared to run out and buy a white shirt in the High Street. No, he wouldn't do that. So I asked him to lend me his collar. He seemed hesitant about this. I thought at first that it was lack of generosity or the team spirit. But it was shame. In desperation I insisted. I tucked the edge of my own deep-blue shirt

---

[1] This was the last of the 130 three-thousand-word letters which H.N. had written to his sons since October 1942. Nigel was about to come home from Austria, as he had been invited by his Regiment to write the official war-history of the Grenadier Guards.

inside my neck and inserted outside the drab, striped, white thing which he held out to me, all warm. It was too tight to fix on to my collar button, and I had to keep it on by pulling my tie tight. Having donned the shirt of Nessus, I sat down on the stool and put on an expression suggesting hope, love and charity, combined with deep experience and alert intelligence. Combined also, I fear, with a lurking anxiety lest the photographer's collar might suddenly detach itself from its moorings and float in the air.[1]

DIARY   5th June, 1945

I write to Bill Mabane[2] suggesting that my name might be considered as Chairman of the British Council. I make a condition that the administrative side should be in the hands of a highly competent permanent official. My idea is that it should be run more or less on B.B.C. lines, with a Board and a Chairman directing policy, and a Director General running the show.

I dine with the Kenneth Clarks in Hampstead. They have repaired the library, and the house is really most beautiful. The other guests are Stephen Spender, the Carandinis[3] and Eddy Sackville West. We listen to Attlee's speech on the wireless. I fear he scored off Winston. He says that 'the voice was the voice of Churchill, but the mind the mind of Beaverbrook'. He also derides Winston's gloomy suggestion that the Socialists will establish a Gestapo and rob the poor of all their savings.

DIARY   13th June, 1945

I have a talk with Mabane about San Francisco, from where he has just returned. He defends the veto arrangements on the familiar lines that if you come up against a Great Power you are done for anyway. I say that, as a result, the new Charter can only be used, so far as I can see, against Franco's Spain which everybody dislikes. But if the Bulgarians attack Greece and seize Salonika, the Security Council can do nothing about it except to say, 'How very regrettable.' We are joined by Oliver Stanley, who says that the Trusteeship Chapter is quite unworkable. Bill is distressed by this. He tells us that the outstanding figure at the Conference was Bobbety Cranborne, who won

[1] The resulting photograph by Fisher & Potter, Leicester, is reproduced opposite.
[2] Minister of State in the new Caretaker Government.
[3] The Italian Ambassador in London and his wife.

A photograph of Harold Nicolson taken for the 1945 election.
See pages 467–8

Harold Nicolson in 1945

golden opinions all round. Our own delegation was streets better than anybody else's.

I do not think that anybody of any Party has any clear idea of how the Election will run. The Labour people seem to think that the Tories will come back with a majority of between 50 and 150. The Tories feel that the Forces will all vote for Labour, and that there may be a land-slide towards the left. They say that the *Daily Mirror* is responsible for this, having pandered to the men in the ranks and given them a general distrust of authority. The Jewish capacity for destruction is really illimitable.[1] Although I loathe anti-semitism, I do dislike Jews.

DIARY   15th June, 1945

To the House at 11. We have prayers, and then just sit chatting till 11.20 when Black Rod knocks on the door. We all crowd into the House of Lords, but the entrance is too narrow to see anything and we stand and chatter outside. We then stroll back to the House. Finally the Speaker returns without the mace. He sits down at the Clerks' table and we file past him and shake hands. I go to the smoking-room where I have a final drink with Jim Thomas and Florence Horsbrugh. I then sadly leave the building. The police are very affectionate. My special friend who calls me taxis bids me a fond farewell: 'Good luck, sir, and by God, you will need all of it in Leicester!' I shake his hand and leave the House, perhaps for ever. How happy I have been there these ten years!

I then take the train for Leicester.

For several years Harold Nicolson had wondered under what banner he should fight the General Election when it came. He had been elected in 1935 as National Labour. He refused to call himself 'Conservative', because he did not feel Conservative, but equally he would form no part of an alliance ranged against Churchill. The National Labour Party, which had for long been almost meaningless as a separate political group, virtually dissolved at the outset of the Election campaign, when its nominal leader, Malcolm MacDonald, declined to return home from Canada to contest his own seat. So Harold Nicolson was left without a Party, though the Leicester Conservatives had generously agreed to put their whole organisation at his disposal. In the end, his Election literature bore the legend: 'Support Churchill and vote for Harold Nicolson, the National Candidate'. This imprecise label did not particularly worry the

[1] H.N. had the idea that the Board of the *Daily Mirror* was mainly composed of Jews.

electors. Those who backed him did so out of admiration for his personal qualities and record, or because of his avowed link with Churchill. Those who voted against him did so in spite of their recognition that he had been a good Member, both in the constituency and in Parliament, and most now admitted that he had been right to oppose Chamberlain in the years before the war.

Harold Nicolson fought the Election conscientiously, but acknowledged to himself that he was doomed to fail. V. Sackville-West paid her first visit to Leicester during the campaign, reversing her 1935 decision to have nothing to do with it. So when he lost his seat, there was nothing with which he needed to reproach himself or others, either during his ten-year occupation of the seat or during the campaign itself. The overwhelming victory of the Labour Party was due to reasons which have been well summed up by A. J. P. Taylor:[1]

'The Conservatives relied chiefly on the glory of Churchill's name, and he, egged on by Beaverbrook, zestfully turned against Labour the talent for political vituperation which he had previously reserved for Hitler. His greatest card was to discover in Professor Harold Laski, then Chairman of the Labour Party, the sinister head of a future British Gestapo. This card proved ineffective. The electors cheered Churchill and voted against him. They displayed no interest in foreign affairs or imperial might. They were not stirred by any cry to Hang the Kaiser or to extract reparations from Germany. They cared only for their own future: first housing, and then full employment and social security. Here Labour offered a convincing programme. The Conservatives, though offering much the same programme, managed to give the impression that they did not believe in it. Folk memory counted for much. Many electors remembered the unemployment of the 'thirties. Some remembered how they had been cheated, or supposed that they had been cheated, after the General Election of 1918. Lloyd George brought ruin to Churchill from the grave.'

That admiration and gratitude towards Churchill could coexist with reluctance to re-elect him as peacetime Prime Minister was cogently argued by Raymond Mortimer in his letter to Harold Nicolson of 10th July and even by V. Sackville-West in hers of 30th June.

---

[1] A. J. P. Taylor. *English History 1914–1945*, p. 596. (Oxford, 1965.)

DIARY

16th June, 1945
Leicester

Go through the Speaker's Notes[1] and read up about housing. In the evening we go to the Working Men's Club in Newfoundpool. The officers seem rather embarrassed at my going and I hate it. I feel so false in such surroundings.

H.N. TO V.S-W.

19th June, 1945
Leicester

The campaign opened yesterday. The first meeting was inauspicious. It was in a slum quarter and the Communists were there. They listened quite politely, but then the questions began. 'I wish to ask the Candidate why on 12th April 1938 he voted against the proposal of the Labour Party?' I say naturally, 'What was that proposal about?' 'Oh, I see that you have forgotten it.' Then it turns out that it was something to do with a Catering Bill. But I was rather amused when they said that I had no right to support Churchill since I had slavishly supported Chamberlain. I must say that this led to some protests among the audience. One man got up and said that they didn't want a chap who talks to them about Czechoslovakia rather than the wages of the poor. I was able to reply to this that if they had listened to me about Czechoslovakia the war might have been prevented. All this is saddening because it shows such a complete distortion of the facts and such utter ignorance of motive and realities. One ought to grow another skin and not mind. But I am one of those people who are depressed by ignorance.

The second meeting went better and there was much applause. The Labour people are embarrassed by Laski having told Attlee that he must keep his mouth shut if he went to the Berlin conference.[2] It was a bad blunder.

---

[1] Issued by Conservative Central Office. This is an example of how H.N. had the benefit of the Conservative organisation, although not a Conservative.

[2] Churchill had invited Attlee, as Leader of the Opposition, to accompany him to Potsdam for the conference with Stalin and Truman. When this invitation was made public, Laski commented that if Attlee went to Potsdam, 'it should be as an observer only'. Churchill then wrote to Attlee suggesting that this was derogatory to him, and Attlee agreed to come as a full participant.

V.S-W. TO H.N. *22nd June, 1945*
Sissinghurst

You know I have an admiration for Winston amounting to idolatory, so I am dreadfully distressed by the badness of his broadcast Election speeches. What has gone wrong with him? They are confused, woolly, unconstructive and so wordy that it is impossible to pick out any concrete impression from them. If I were a wobbler, they would tip me over to the other side. Archie Sinclair and Stafford Cripps were both infinitely better. I mind about this.

Quite a lot of people have been to see the garden, which always pleases me. How much I prefer strangers to my friends. But, oh my love, it is *you* I want.

H.N. TO V.S-W. *22nd June, 1945*
Leicester

One of my meetings this evening was dominated by an intoxicated workman who kept on yelling, 'You're a liar, you are!' That meant that I had to raise my voice. But what was worse was a sort of Madame de Krüdener[1] and Lady Macbeth all in one who waved her arms aloft and uttered incantations. One of her incantations was that I was a bloated land-owner who lived in a castle and ground his tenants for rent. No good at all my saying that Sissinghurst wasn't a castle but only the remains of a ruined manor-house; that it didn't belong to me but to you; and that Ozzy Beale,[2] was not, so far as I was aware, being ground into the earth. But I didn't at all like Sissinghurst, that shrine of quiet and loveliness, being dragged into this squalid controversy. It was like seeing a piece of Tudor embroidery in the mud.

DIARY *26th June, 1945*
Leicester

Janner[3] got a rough meeting last night. One of my supporters asked him whether he was giving his sincere opinion or not when he wrote that Labour was not to be trusted. He was quoting from Janner's

[1] The Russian mystic (1764–1824) who had a great influence on Czar Alexander I.
[2] A. O. R. Beale, the tenant-farmer at Sissinghurst, who was one of the most highly respected farmers in Kent.
[3] (Sir) Barnett Janner, H.N.'s Labour opponent. He was a solicitor, and became President of the Board of Deputies of British Jews. He had been Prospective Labour Candidate in West Leicester for many years, and defeated first H.N., and then, in the 1950 Election, Nigel, to remain M.P. for North West Leicester until the present day (1967).

Election Address when he stood as a Liberal Candidate many years ago in Whitechapel. Now I knew that Moore[1] had unearthed this document, and I had said that it must not be used against him. It is always easy to dig out some statement like that, and such methods savour of mean gambits.

Vita arrived looking so lovely and graceful and gentle. We go off to a women's meeting and she makes a little speech. The women are enraptured.

The United Nations Charter is signed at San Francisco.

DIARY   *28th June, 1945*
Leicester

It is very difficult to decide how the Election is going. Since the first days, I have not been exposed to any severe heckling. The Labour people seem to be concentrating on Waterhouse[2] and Lyons.[3] I regard my own comparative immunity as somewhat ominous. Is it that the Labour people regard West Leicester as a certainty? Or is it that they are holding their fire and will seek to wipe me out in the last three days? I do not know. Accounts vary. Some say that I am doing very well; others say that Janner is making great headway. I fear, however, that the final result will be determined by the unseen voter, the man and woman who do not even know the names of the candidates but who just vote Labour blind.

V.S-W. TO H.N.   *30th June, 1945*
Sissinghurst

What I don't understand is why you don't hold meetings in the factories. The factory manager would induce his people to attend. Of course I see that there are solid Labour votes, but there must also be wobbly votes. I was a Liberal yesterday, having listened to Sir William Beveridge, but I am Labour today having listened to Morrison. As Winston is speaking tonight, I expect to be a Conservative again by tomorrow.

Seriously, if I wasn't a Conservative, I shouldn't be one, if you see what I mean. I am afraid that I think the argument 'Churchill won the war' is a bad argument. There seems to me to be little connection

---

[1] H.N.'s Election Agent.

[2] Captain Charles Waterhouse, M.P., and now Conservative Candidate, for South Leicester. He lost his seat at this Election, but regained it in 1950.

[3] A. M. Lyons, M.P., and Conservative Candidate for East Leicester. He also lost his seat at this Election.

between the two things. It is as though we said 'Sissinghurst is lovely and romantic, therefore it will make a good work-house.' I don't think that Winston has the temperament to deal with the immediate difficulties at home. I don't believe that you think so either.

H.N. TO V.S-W.   *3rd July, 1945*
                                                                        Leicester

I do agree with you so much about Winston. I thought his Saturday broadcast very good, but my eye may have been put out by a fortnight's electioneering. But everybody at an Election seems to behave below their own level. I refuse to do so. In fact when one of my workers said something mean on the loud-speaker van and it was repeated to me, I went out of my way to apologise for it in public. The Labour people do not heckle me, but they send agents around whispering things against me. They say that I voted three times against old age pensions, which is untrue. They say that I am in favour of raising the school-leaving age, which is true. I suppose my people do the same, more or less, although I have told them not to. All of which makes electioneering a torture. But I do feel this: (a) that it is possible for someone to fight an Election with clean hands; and (b) that if people like me say 'we will not soil our hands with politics', then our whole political life will be left to the professional politicians with a resulting decline in standards. I am quite convinced of this.

I had a good meeting last night in one of our poorest quarters. You could have heard a pin drop. But I well know that this is no indication of how they will vote. They listen to me because I interest them. They are prepared to admit that I am a decent bloke. But a friend told me that his newspaper-seller said to him, 'Mr Nicolson is far the best candidate in the whole city. We all know that. But he hasn't a chance of getting in—not a chance.' Anyhow it will not be a dishonourable defeat.

DIARY   *5th July, 1945*
                                                                        Leicester

Polling Day. A beautiful hot day and a cloudless sky. I go round the Committee Rooms, and again in the evening. I hear the Town Hall clock strike nine and know that the Election is over. At about 9.30 we drive to Treroose[1] and cross the market square where we see

[1] The house in Leicester belonging to Sophie and Bertie Jarvis, the Chairman of the West Leicester Conservative Association.

policemen carrying away the boxes in which the votes will be stored until 26th July. Soph feels that things have gone well. Bertie is more pessimistic.

RAYMOND MORTIMER TO H.N. *10th July, 1945*
The New Statesman and Nation

I think that Churchill more than anyone else was responsible for the squalid lies in these elections. He started the rot with his talk of Mr Attlee's Gestapo. But I dare say that these Hogarthian spatterings are inseparable from our parliamentary system. The gloomy result is to make sensitive people keep out of politics. It is particularly tough on you to be saddled with all the sins of Margesson, but again Churchill chose to go to Walthamstow with Margesson, the man who did most to keep him out of power. It is infinitely regrettable that you did not all join the Liberals in Munich days. If you get in—as I pray you will—you will find yourself again in a minority on your own side, unwilling to vote against your leaders, but horrified by their policy—particularly on housing.

I would certainly rather have Eden than Bevan at the Foreign Office. Churchill, on the other hand, I should like to see retire to write his memoirs, which would be incomparably interesting. I don't think he is any longer needed for the war. I think him quite the wrong man for directing the reconstruction of England. Our debt to him is probably greater than to any other politician in our history, but I could not feel on that account any obligation to vote for him. And I bitterly resent the notion he put forward that his is a 'national' Government in any sense that the alternative governments would not be.

I say all this to explain why and how I differ from you. But this does not mean that I do not simply *long* for you to be elected. I think no back-bencher has done better work than you. I feel more optimistic than you are about your chances.[1]

The votes cast at the General Election were sealed for three weeks, to allow time for the Service votes to be collected from many parts of the world and added to the pile. All were counted on 26th July. Harold Nicolson, with his reunited family (Nigel had returned from Austria on the 17th), attended the count at Leicester. He lost his seat by 7,215 votes.

[1] On receiving this letter, H.N. wrote to V.S-W.: 'I enclose a nice letter from Raymond. A very nice and really wise letter. I agree with much of what he says.'

Labour had a majority of 180 seats in the new Parliament, and Churchill handed over power to Attlee that same evening.

In the interval between the casting and the counting of the votes, while Harold Nicolson continued to write 'The Congress of Vienna', an even more significant Conference opened at Potsdam. It was attended by Churchill, Stalin and Truman. Attlee was invited as Churchill's possible successor, but not de Gaulle. Little progress was made. The Polish western frontier had been advanced de facto to the Western Neisse line, and Stalin would not now hear of a withdrawal to the Oder–Eastern Neisse line provisionally agreed in principle at Yalta. This subject occupied the leading place on the Agenda, but another was the occasion for a few brief words exchanged in private between Truman and Stalin. On 24th July the American President informed him that a bomb of devastating power had just been successfully exploded in the Mexican desert, and would shortly be used against Japan. It did not appear that Stalin took in the significance of this information.

H.N. TO V.S–W.   *12th July, 1945*
4 King's Bench Walk, E.C.4

I lunched with the French Ambassador and had a long talk with him. As you know, he is on the European Council which decides matters of common interest to the Big Four. They had been working for weeks on the Zones of Occupation in Austria and had at last reached agreement. They assembled to sign the protocol. A map, prepared by the F.O., was attached to it. It was an old War Office map, and it was entitled: 'Austria. Now in Nazi occupation'. The Russian Ambassador refused to sign any document which bore the word 'Nazi'. It was pointed out to him that the word, as it occurred in this context, had no significance at all and that to reprint the map would mean three days delay. He said, 'No, the U.S.S.R. could not approve of that word appearing.' They were in despair. Then Sammy Hood, who was acting as Secretary, rose in his majesty with a pair of scissors and neatly cut out the offending word. The Russians then signed. 'A country', said Massigli to me, 'whose Ambassadors behave with such childishness, can never become a great Power.'

DIARY   *17th July, 1945*

A lovely, indeed a perfect, Sissinghurst day. I work hard at chapter XII and finish it. I bathe. I eat peaches, and weed. After tea I am writing the passage about the German Confederation when at 5.55 the telephone tinkles beside me. It is Nigel speaking from London. He had flown today from Naples. I rush out and get Vita and she telephones to him again. I go on with the German Confederation and finish it.

Listen in the evening to Benjamin Britten's *Peter Grimes*. It is a lovely night. The Potsdam Conference opened today. There has been a heavy naval action off Japan. And Niggs is home.

DIARY   24th July, 1945

William Jowitt[1] is at the Beefsteak. He says he has no idea at all how the Election has gone. Some people feel that there has been a wide swing to the left and that a Labour Government will be returned. Others imagine that Winston will be back with a fifty-seats majority.

I leave about 10.30 and am astonished to find a completely different London. For years I have crept out of the Club with my torch, seeking and peering for the little step on the threshold. Tonight I emerged into a London coruscating with lights like Stockholm. My old way along the Embankment from the Temple Station, which I have traversed such countless times, feeling my way between the surface shelters and the trees, was lit up by a thousand arc-lights. All these were turned up on 15th July when double-summer-time ended. I had not realised what a transfiguration had been achieved. Meanwhile all the sticky stuff has been removed from the windows of the buses and undergrounds,[2] and we shall no longer remember how we used to peep out through a little diamond slit in the texture to read the names of the stations as they flashed by. One forgets these things at once.

DIARY   25th July, 1945

The four of us go up to Leicester. We are met by Bertie [Jarvis]. He had spent the day going through the Service votes and fusing them with the ordinary votes. Although the voting-papers were turned face downwards, it was possible in many cases to see through, and Bertie predicts a huge swing to the left—which means that I have lost the seat. He is pretty glum. He takes us to the Grand Hotel.

[1] Sir William Jowitt, who was soon to be appointed Lord Chancellor in Attlee's Government.
[2] For the protection of passengers from flying glass if the windows were broken by bomb-blast.

DIARY   *26th July, 1945. Dies irae, dies illa*

We breakfast, and then I pay the bill. In the hall an old gentleman in uniform mutters to me, 'Bad luck: you are out—well out'. I do not know who he is, but I imagine that he must be some assistant to the Returning Officer.

It is thus with a heavy heart that I go to the de Montfort Hall. All the tables are set out and the counting has begun. I watch the piles being collected and it is evident that I am badly beaten. To my surprise, Kirby[1] seems to have got a huge amount of votes. It is a sad business seeing the Janner–Janner–Janner piles increasing. I have a talk with him, and his wife and daughter. Monty Lyons is there, walking nervously about, and Charles Waterhouse. The latter is most uneasy although his people do their best to reassure him. While I am talking to him, Lyons' Agent comes up to him and says, 'You are in, sir, by a few hundred.' He looks relieved. My own workers are sad but resigned as the counting continues.

At 11.15 the piles have been passed up to the platform and the Mayor, Alderman Minto, knocks on the rostrum and there is a sudden hush. He begins with the East. Lyons has lost by 13,232. He then takes another sheet of paper and announces Leicester West. I am standing in the body of the hall, and Viti is sitting at one of the tables at my right. He reads out: 'Janner, 20,563; Nicolson, 13,348; Kirby, 4,639'. There is slight cheering. Janner and I then go on to the platform. He compliments me on the 'decency and distinction' with which I have conducted my campaign. I second in a few words, saying that there is no bitterness in my sadness, since I was indeed fortunate to have represented West Leicester, on so slight a majority, for ten years in the most historic of Parliaments. There is applause at this, in which Janner's supporters join. I then come off the platform and am greeted by my disheartened supporters and also by many of the Labour people who say, 'I only wish it had not been you.'

I rejoin Viti and Bertie and Soph and the boys. We go out. It is raining, and there is no crowd at all. We drive to Treroose. We have drinks. We listen to the 12 o'clock news. The Tories have already lost 45 seats, including Amery, Harold Macmillan and Brendan Bracken. We go on talking and listen again at 1. The land-slide gathers impetus. At 2 there is a further land-slide. We take the train to London, which we reach at 6. On our arrival at K.B.W. we are greeted by Elvira Niggeman.[2] Churchill is out and Attlee has a clear

[1] H.N.'s Liberal opponent, J. A. Kirby.   [2] H.N.'s secretary.

majority! Nobody foresaw this at all. We drive down home. We get there just in time for the 9 pm. news. Winston has been to Buckingham Palace to hand in his resignation. Attlee followed at 7.30 and was entrusted with forming a new Government.

I go to bed with two aspirins, a rare performance for me. I feel as if I had been run over by a tram, but mainly owing to the physical exhaustion and nervous strain. It is like what Nigel said about the German surrenders in North Africa—when they surrendered singly they were miserable and crushed, but when the mass-surrenders came, they were almost elated. But I am not elated. I think, on the whole, that it is a good thing for the country that we should have a Government backed by a strong majority in the House. I had never expected to win myself. But I feel sad at closing what has been a very happy chapter in my life, and at bidding farewell to Leicester and my beloved House of Commons. Bertie [Jarvis] has got a plan under which Nigel would stand in my place in West Leicester.

So that was the end of a most imperfect day.

DIARY   1st August, 1945

Robin Maugham rings me up. He had been round to No. 10 on 26th July. Winston was in magnificent form and took his defeat with humour. He confessed that it was distressing after all these years to abandon the reins of power. Someone said, 'But at least, sir, while you held the reins, you managed to win the race.' 'Yes', said Winston, 'I won the race—and now they have warned me off the turf.'

Somebody mentioned that I had lost the seat at West Leicester. Robin remembered the actual words which Winston used and memorised them. 'The House', he said, 'will be a sadder place without him'—then he paused, and added, 'and smaller.' This pleases me more than anything.

INDEX

Index

483